STUDIES IN THE PSYCHOLOGICAL FOUNDATIONS OF EXCEPTIONALITY

EAN K. DISSINGER & CAROLE R. ARNOLD

STUDIES
IN THE PSYCHOLOGICAL
FOUNDATIONS
OF EXCEPTIONALITY

STUDIES IN THE PSYCHOLOGICAL FOUNDATIONS OF EXCEPTIONALITY

Edited by

JEAN K. DISSINGER
Iowa State University

CAROLE R. ARNOLD
Iowa State University

BROOKS/COLE PUBLISHING COMPANY
MONTEREY, CALIFORNIA
A Division of Wadsworth Publishing Company, Inc.

This book is dedicated to our students.

ISBN: 0-8185-0137-5
L.C. Catalog Card No.: 74-15191
Printed in the United States of America

10 9 8 7 6 5 4 3 2 1

PREFACE

This anthology is designed for use in undergraduate courses in psychology, education, and child development in which the study of exceptionality is emphasized. Students using this book are assumed to be acquiring (or to have previously acquired) a knowledge of the basic characteristics of exceptional persons through one of several basic textbooks on exceptionality. The articles in this book can also serve as a basis for generating critical class discussion on research methodology in advanced undergraduate and introductory graduate courses in exceptionality.

The foremost objective of this book is to supplement the standard textbooks that are widely used in introductory courses on exceptionality. Each chapter corresponds to an area of study generally included in a survey course on exceptionality. The author of a textbook can provide excellent summaries of research but is seldom able to provide detailed information on the methods used in the conduct of individual studies. Hence, a secondary objective of this book is to introduce the reader to the research process as one means of acquiring knowledge about exceptionality. An introductory chapter on the fundamentals of research methodology has been provided to help the student understand the research methods commonly used in the behavioral and social sciences. Also, it is hoped that the student, as a potential consumer of research, can learn to recognize the merit as well as some of the limitations of the research reports in this book.

Readability, significance, and recency were used as criteria in selecting the articles included in this book. Approximately 100 students enrolled in the editors' classes on the psychology of exceptional children participated in field testing the selections for readability. The students were primarily juniors and seniors enrolled in either the College of Education or the College of Sciences and Humanities at Iowa State University. The articles represent a variety of educational and psychological journals and reflect the recent trend toward the longitudinal study of exceptional groups as well as the trend toward the study of multiply exceptional persons.

We gratefully acknowledge the cooperation received from the authors and publishers in granting permission to reprint the articles that appear in this anthology. Gratitude is further extended to John F. Feldhusen of Purdue University, H. Carl Haywood of George Peabody College for Teachers, James M. Sawrey of California State University, San Jose, Charles W. Telford of California State University, San Jose, and E. Paul Torrance of The University of Georgia for the helpful guidance provided by their reviews and to Charles T. Hendrix of Brooks/Cole Publishing Company for his valuable editorial assistance. Special thanks are conveyed to Linda Porath and Marilyn Anderson for their competent clerical assistance.

Jean K. Dissinger
Carole R. Arnold

CONTENTS

1
ORIENTATION

INTRODUCTION TO
THE STUDENT

The psychology of exceptionality is that facet of differential psychology encompassing the study of atypical individuals and groups. This definition is consistent with Telford and Sawrey's (1972) thesis that the problems studied through research on exceptionality are the problems associated with individual differences among people in general.

The readings in this book illustrate the building blocks that collectively form the foundations of empirical knowledge on exceptionality. Since the social sciences are generally rather primitively developed, it should not be surprising to learn that the literature on exceptionality shares this characteristic. The incomplete status of the existing body of knowledge on exceptionality can be as challenging to the research scholar as it is dismaying to the educational practitioner. In no other area of the behavioral and social sciences are the issues more salient and the need for their resolution more in demand by parents and teachers than in the psychology of exceptionality. One purpose of this book is to help the student acquire the background necessary for understanding research on exceptionality, thus enabling him to obtain new information as it becomes available through published reports. The student is encouraged to examine the references appearing throughout this anthology in order to identify journals that can become important sources of future knowledge about exceptionality.

The student who acquires an understanding of the way knowledge is accumulated through research and who simultaneously develops a zest for seeking new knowledge is apt to find that he has adopted the criti-cal-thinking skills used by the scientist. Furthermore, the student who develops the ability to selectively apply knowledge gained through the reading of research reports to the resolution of practical problems can be regarded as relatively more professional than his fellow students. Yet, the astute learner will recognize that studying the available research is only one of several ways of seeking information relevant to the solution of a specific problem. Other sources include tradition, authority, personal experience, philosophy, and situationally specific determinants.

It is anticipated that the reader who becomes a teacher, school psychologist, counselor, research scholar, or informed layman can and will apply his skill as a "consumer of research" in various ways. The future teacher in search of effective methods and materials might ask some pertinent questions: What evidence supports the effectiveness of these learning materials or teaching methods? How were the outcomes measured? What were the characteristics (age, sex, IQ, educational history) of the children on whom the methods or techniques were tested? By seeking answers to these questions, the teacher is collecting information that can contribute to an "educated" guess regarding the appropriateness of materials or methods for use with a particular child or class. Similarly, the school psychologist, the special educator, or the informed parent might ask: What does this test score represent? How valid and reliable was the measuring instrument used to obtain the score? Or, general concern for the outcome of an educational program might be reflected by asking: Is this educational program being evaluated? If not, why?

CHAPTER ONE

TOWARD AN UNDERSTANDING OF RESEARCH ON EXCEPTIONALITY

This chapter will help the potential consumer of research acquire at least an intuitive level of understanding of the research process. The student who aspires to develop a relatively more formal concept of research than is afforded by the present text or who intends to plan and conduct a research project will need to gain sophistication in research methodology and statistical analysis from other sources. However, the information presented in this chapter can assist the student toward an understanding and an appreciation of research.

RESEARCH GOALS

Research workers are currently collecting and reporting scientific evidence that can contribute to the foundations of knowledge on exceptionality. However, before introducing the reader to the research strategies that are used frequently in the study of exceptionality, it seems appropriate to examine the scientific purposes underlying research. What major goals do behavioral and social scientists try to achieve? Or, alternatively, what are the reasons for conducting research? In general:

The aim of research in science is to discover facts and bring them into mutually explanatory relations with one another. This undertaking is primarily an intellectual task. Its immediate purpose is to understand the world [Freeman, 1942, p. 39].

Research—a systematic process of investigation—is a tool used by the scientist as he searches for the answers to questions. Such answers may be abstract or general, as is often the case in basic research, or they may be concrete and specific, as is often the case in applied research (Turney & Robb, 1971). Basic research is conducted primarily for the acquisition of fundamental knowledge and is most likely to be of immediate interest to the research scholar. The problems studied through basic research are frequently undertaken to bring theoretical structure into line with experimental results or to suggest new lines of theoretical development. On the

other hand, applied research is directed toward the resolution of practical problems and is conducted primarily for consumption by the practitioner or the layman. The designation of a particular research project as either basic or applied is somewhat arbitrary. Borderline cases exist, and a single program of investigation may cross the dividing line as the work progresses (Cronbach & Suppes, 1969). The study of practical problems may lead to the investigation of more general or more abstract problems, and scientific generalizations realized from basic research may explain or illuminate the results of practical inquiry (Freeman, 1942).

The state of knowledge in a given area may partially determine the goals of research. Explanations of an increasing generality become possible as the work in an area progresses. The role of research in man's search for explanations has been described by Van Dalen and Meyer (1966) as follows:

The essential purpose of research is to go beyond mere description of phenomena and provide an explanation for them. A scientist is not completely satisfied with naming, classifying or describing phenomena. . . . Going behind casually observed factors to search for some underlying pattern that explains them is his objective. After discovering a possible relationship between antecedent factors and the particular event or condition, he frames a verifiable generalization that explains how the variables involved in the situation behave. Explanation—not mere description—is the product of his effort. . . .

Formulating generalizations—conceptual schemes—that explain phenomena is a major goal of science. A generalization which explains a limited body of phenomena is useful, but the objective of science is to develop ever more far-reaching conceptual schemes. Hypotheses, theories, and laws are generalizations of gradually increasing generality. Since the generalization that offers the most comprehensive explanation is of the greatest value, a law is of greater importance than a theory or hypothesis. . . .

Science aims at the progressive unification of its generalizations. The ultimate goal of science is to seek laws of the highest generality—laws of the utmost comprehensiveness [pp. 41–42].[1]

[1]From *Understanding Educational Research: An Introduction*, by D. B. Van Dalen & W. J. Meyer, McGraw-Hill, 1966. This and all other quotes from the same source are reprinted by permission.

Further goals of research include the prediction and control of naturally occurring events.

An explanation that does not increase man's power over nature is useful, but it is not as valuable as one that enables him to predict events. A scientist, therefore, is not satisfied merely with formulating generalizations that explain phenomena; he also wants to make predictions concerning the way a generalization will operate in new situations. His objective is to take known data and accepted generalizations and from them to predict some future event or hitherto unobserved phenomena. . . .

Scientists strive to attain such a thorough understanding of the laws of nature that they are able not only to predict but to control an increasing range of events. "Control" refers to the process of manipulating certain of the essential conditions that determine an event so as to make the event happen or prevent it from occurring [Van Dalen & Meyer, 1966, pp. 42–43].

STAGES IN THE RESEARCH PROCESS

There is a world of difference between the published research report and the process of arriving at that report (Scott & Wertheimer, 1962). For the purposes of logical description, the research report is organized into five or six steps: Problem (or Introduction), Method, Results, Discussion, Conclusions, and/or Summary. In practice, however, the steps in research overlap considerably and may not emerge in exact logical order. The way in which the steps are managed in a particular study depends on the nature of the problem as well as on the skill and imagination of the investigator (Barnes, 1964).

The Research Problem and Research Hypotheses. Perhaps the most difficult in a series of decisions that must be made by the investigator is that of narrowing or defining precisely the problem to be studied. Every question one may seek to answer cannot be formulated into a researchable problem. Research problems must be phrased so that experimentation and observation in the real world can be used to yield the objective data needed to investigate the problem (Barnes, 1964).

The research problem begins to materialize as the investigator reflects on the nature of phenomena as they are known to exist or could conceivably exist in the real world. The problem may be revised several times as the investigator gains additional insight into its nature—perhaps by searching the literature in the field related to the problem, by conducting a pilot study, or by using models to refine his thinking (Van Dalen & Meyer, 1966). The problem statement appearing in the final report may be expressed either in question or statement form. For example:

Statement form: The present investigation was concerned with providing and evaluating a highly cognitively structured preschool experience for very young disadvantaged Mexican-American children. (See the Plant and Southern article in Chapter Six of this book.)

Question form: Can the naturally formed black-white concept attitudes of Caucasian preschool children be weakened by laboratory reinforcement procedures? Will any modifications in the black-white concept attitude be found to persist during a period of approximately two weeks? (See the Williams and Edwards article in Chapter Six of this book.)

Closely associated with the precise statement of the problem is the formulation of one or more research hypotheses. The research hypothesis suggests a provisional or possible explanation of the relationships that the research worker is trying to understand (Van Dalen & Meyer, 1966). The hypothesis is justified on either logical or empirical grounds. Logical justification requires the development of arguments based on concepts or theories related to the hypothesis, whereas empirical justification requires reference to other research (Tuckman, 1972). The research hypothesis is typically expressed in "if-then" form: if test conditions of kind *C* are realized, then an event of kind *E* will occur (Hempel, 1966). However, other forms of assertion are acceptable as long as the hypothesis contains a prediction that if certain conditions are provided, certain results can be associated with those conditions (Barnes, 1964). Examples of research hypotheses and the problems with which they correspond follow.

Example 1

Problem. The present investigation was designed to examine the possibility that cerebral-palsied children with normal auditory acuity may be so satiated with auditory stimuli that this stimulation or their reaction to it may be interfering with their intellectual, cognitive, and perceptual functioning.

Research hypothesis. There will be a positive change in the performance of normally hearing cerebral-palsied children on selected tasks of memory, attention, learning, and perceptual abilities under conditions of reduced auditory input. (See the Fassler article in Chapter Four of this book.)

Example 2

Problem. The current study was a limited empirical exploration of the possibility of increasing in preschool children the capacity for verbal symbolization, or verbal intelligence, by encouraging meaningful verbal interaction between very young children and their mothers.

Research hypothesis. The hypothesis for the experiment was that the verbal intelligence of the Experimental Group would rise after this exposure as compared with that of the Control Group. (See the Levenstein and Sunley article in Chapter Six of this book.)

Operations. The research hypothesis is a particularly useful way of expressing the problem because it indicates the kind of solution needed (Barnes, 1964; Van Dalen & Meyer, 1966). However, the research hypothesis must be translated from the conceptual level to an operational level for the purposes of investigation. In other words, the phenomena being dealt with in the research hypothesis must be defined in an observable way. For some concepts this is a straightforward matter; that is, anyone would be expected to agree that the chosen operation is appropriate (Scott & Wertheimer, 1962). However:

Things are not this clear-cut for most psychological concepts. At best, a commonly accepted operation may be found which, though somewhat arbitrary, at least identifies the concept precisely for other researchers. Other concepts are defined so poorly that no single operation for them can be universally accepted [Scott & Wertheimer, 1962, p. 60].[2]

It should be apparent that the operational definitions used in some areas of exceptionality are far more objective than those used in other areas. For example, the instruments used to measure visual acuity and auditory loss are far more precise than those used to assess emotional disturbance, social deviancy, and learning disabilities. Whenever clinical appraisal serves as the criterion for identifying exceptional children, there exists the possibility that another clinician or group of experts would fail to confirm the original diagnosis. Confirmation across clinicians and other groups of observers can be attained only when the behavior serving as the basis for classification is described explicitly. The following bases for judging the adequacy of an operation have been presented by Scott and Wertheimer (1962).

The critical issue in assessing the adequacy of an operation is its validity: Do the operations really yield the desired information? How adequate is the "fit" between the concept and the measure of it? In devising the operational form of a hypothesis, the aim is to make the measures as objective and replicable as possible, as reliable as possible, without sacrificing their fit with the concepts they are intended to represent [p. 37].

Two general kinds of operational definitions, the measured and experimental operational definitions, are needed to specify completely the procedures used in research on exceptionality. A measured operational def-

inition describes the way a concept has been measured (Kerlinger, 1966). Data might be collected by administering tests, by observing behavior directly (for example, defining social interaction as the frequency of looking at or touching another child), or by establishing the existence of a precondition (for example, defining cultural disadvantage in terms of income level or housing conditions). Scientists refer to the concepts of the behaviors and traits they study as variables. Narrowing down to the operational definitions always involves decisions about which particular values on the variables need to be studied (Scott & Wertheimer, 1962). A value on a variable may be a score, a rank, or a category, depending on the kind of measuring scale used.

A nominal measuring scale allows one to categorize by type, for example, type of teaching method or remedial program. Ordinal scales place entities in a clearly defined rank order, but the distances between the intervals on the scale are unknown and not necessarily equal (Van Dalen & Meyer, 1966). Asking teachers to rank their pupils on classroom achievement would yield ordinal data; that is, one knows that the student ranked first is perceived by the teacher as having achieved more than the student ranked second, and so on. However, one cannot infer that the distance between the students ranked first and second is equal to the distance between the students ranked second and third, and so forth. The problem of equal distance between the values on a scale can be solved in part by using an interval scale. An interval scale permits the research worker to say that the distance between scores *A* and *B* is equal to the distance between scores *B* and *C* (Van Dalen & Meyer, 1966).[3] Standardized tests of intelligence and achievement yield interval data. The investigator's insight into the hypothesized relationships among the variables guides his choice of measuring scale. Although the ordinal data yielded by teacher rank may be precise enough for investigating one problem, interval data may be needed to study another. Furthermore, the range of values on the variables that can best detect the hypothesized relationship varies in light of the problem.

An experimental operational definition spells out clearly the details (operations) of the investigator's manipulations of a variable (Kerlinger, 1966). For example, in reporting a study on the effects of reinforcement on social interaction, the researcher would describe exactly when and how subjects were reinforced for socially acceptable behavior. The manipulation of variables is considered further in the next section.

[2]From *Introduction to Psychological Research*, by W. A. Scott & M. Wertheimer. © 1962 by John Wiley & Sons, Inc. This and all other quotes from the same source are reprinted by permission.

[3]Zero levels of psychological concepts are generally not defined; hence, one cannot infer that *A* with a score of 10 is twice as good as *B* with a score of 5. To satisfy this requirement, one must employ a ratio scale, which offers an absolute zero as a consistent starting point for measurement (Van Dalen & Meyer, 1966).

RESEARCH STRATEGIES

Research strategies differ primarily in the degree of active control exercised by the investigator over the variables (Scott & Wertheimer, 1962). In general, the amount of control needed depends on the kind of relationship one wishes to demonstrate. Ordinarily, the investigator wishes to determine (1) whether the manipulation of an antecedent or independent variable influences another variable (the dependent variable) or (2) whether two or more variables tend to occur, or not to occur, together (Scott & Wertheimer, 1962). Of the research strategies to be presented in this section, the experimental method is used to investigate the effects of one variable on another, whereas the correlational method is used to study concomitant variation. An additional strategy, the ex post facto method, is used primarily to search for possible antecedent variables.

An understanding of research strategies and hence the conclusions of published reports in which these strategies are used depends in part on one's ability to classify variables. Tuckman (1972) defined five kinds of variables and illustrated their use as follows:[4]

The independent variable. The independent variable, which is a stimulus variable or input, operates either within a person or within his environment to affect his behavior. It is *that factor which is measured, manipulated, or selected by the experimenter to determine its relationship to an observed phenomenon.* If an experimenter studying the relationship between two variables, X and Y, asks himself, "What will happen to Y if I make X greater or smaller?" he is thinking of variable X as his independent variable. It is the variable that he will manipulate or change to cause a change in some other variable. He considers it independent because he is interested only in how it affects another variable, not in what affects it. He regards it as an antecedent condition, a condition required preceding a particular consequence.

The dependent variable. The dependent variable is a response variable or output. It is an observed aspect of the behavior of an organism that has been stimulated. The dependent variable is *that factor which is observed and measured to determine the effect of the independent variable,* i.e., that factor that appears, disappears, or varies as the experimenter introduces, removes, or varies the independent variable. . . It is considered dependent because its value depends upon the value of the independent variable. It represents the consequence of a change in the person or situation studied.

. . . In many experiments, the independent variable is *discrete* (i.e., categorical) and takes the form of the presence versus the absence of a particular treatment or approach being studied or a comparison between different approaches. In other experiments, the independent variable may be *continuous,* and the experimenter's observations of it may be stated in numerical terms indicating its degree. When two continu-

ous variables are compared, as in correlation studies, deciding which variable to call independent and which dependent is sometimes rather arbitrary. In fact, in such cases the variables are often not labeled as independent or dependent since there is no real distinction.

Independent variables may be called *factors* and their variations may be called *levels.* In a study of the effect of music instruction on ability to concentrate, experimental treatment (music instruction) versus no experimental treatment (no music instruction) represents a single independent variable or factor with two levels. The amount of music instruction is the factor. The first level is some degree of music instruction; the second level is no degree of music instruction. . . .

Some examples of independent and dependent variables

Hypothesis . . . Under intangible reinforcement conditions, middle-class children will learn significantly better than lower-class children.

Independent variable: middle class versus lower class
Dependent variable: ease or speed of learning
Hypothesis . . . Perceptions of the characteristics of the "good" or effective teacher are in part determined by the perceiver's attitudes toward education.

Independent variable: perceiver's attitude toward education
Dependent variable: perceptions of the characteristics of the "good" or effective teacher

The moderator variable. The term moderator variable describes a special type of independent variable, a secondary independent variable selected for study to determine if it affects the relationship between the primary independent variable and the dependent variables. The moderator variable is defined as *that factor which is measured, manipulated, or selected by the experimenter to discover whether it modifies the relationship of the independent variable to an observed phenomenon.* The word moderator simply acknowledges the reason that this secondary independent variable has been singled out for study. If the experimenter is interested in studying the effect of independent variable X on dependent variable Y but suspects that the nature of the relationship between X and Y is altered by the level of a third factor Z, then Z can be in the analysis as a moderator variable.

An example of the moderator variable

Hypothesis . . . Male experimenters get more effective performances from both male and female subjects than female experimenters, but they are singularly most effective with male subjects.

Independent variable: the sex of the experimenter
Moderator variable: the sex of the subject
Dependent variable: effectiveness of performance of subjects

Control variables. All of the variables in a situation (situational variables) cannot be studied at the same time; some must be neutralized to guarantee that they will not have a differential or moderating effect on the relationship between the independent variable and the dependent variable. These variables whose effects must be neutralized or controlled are called control variables. They are defined as *those factors which are controlled by the experimenter to cancel out or neutralize any effect they might otherwise have on the observed*

[4]Extracted from *Conducting Educational Research,* by Bruce W. Tuckman, copyright 1972 by Harcourt Brace Jovanovich, Inc. Reprinted by permission.

phenomenon. While the effects of control variables are neutralized, the effects of moderator variables are studied. . . .

An example of a control variable

Hypothesis . . . Under tangible reinforcement conditions, middle-class children will learn significantly better than lower-class children.

Control variable: reinforcement conditions

Intervening variables. All of the variables described thus far—independent, dependent, moderator, and control—are concrete. Each independent, moderator, and control variable can be manipulated by the experimenter, and each variation can be observed by him as it affects the dependent variable. An intervening variable is *that factor which theoretically affects the observed phenomenon but cannot be seen, measured, or manipulated; its effect must be inferred from the effects of the independent and moderator variables on the observed phenomenon.*

In writing about their experiments, researchers do not always identify their intervening variables, and are even less likely to label them as such. It would be helpful if they did.

An example of an intervening variable

Hypothesis . . . As task interest increases, measured task performance increases.

Independent variable: task interest
Intervening variable: learning
Dependent variable: task performance

The researcher must operationalize his variables in order to study them and conceptualize his variables in order to generalize from them. Researchers often use the labels independent, dependent, moderator, and control to describe operational statements of their variables. The intervening variable, however, always refers to a conceptual variable—that which is being affected by the independent, moderator, and control variables, and, in turn, affects the dependent variable (pp. 36–46).

CORRELATIONAL METHODS

Correlational research constitutes an important segment of research on exceptionality. Social scientists frequently use correlational techniques in exploratory research—that is, to investigate a large number of relationships in order to generate hypotheses for directing further study. In addition, correlational methods are used to study the reliability and validity of measuring instruments and, in this regard, are indispensable in research on exceptionality.

In general, correlational techniques are used to determine the co- or joint-relationship found between or among variables (Neale & Liebert, 1973). Variables may be closely related, moderately related, or virtually unrelated. Furthermore, the direction of existing relationships may be either positive (an increase in one variable tends to be associated with an increase in another variable) or negative (an increase in one variable tends to be associated with a decrease in another variable). The correlation coefficient encountered most frequently in

research on exceptionality is the Pearson product-moment correlation coefficient, *r.* The statistic *r,* which is calculated when the variables have been measured on an interval scale, provides an estimate of the linear (straight-line) relationship between two variables. Other types of correlation coefficients are used when the data are nominal or ordinal, and when a curvilinear relationship[5] is hypothesized.

Correlation coefficients range in size from zero to 1.00, and the direction of the relationship may be either positive or negative. A value of zero indicates that the variables are unrelated, whereas a value of plus or minus 1.00 indicates that the variables are related perfectly. However, perfect correlation coefficients are observed rarely in the social sciences. Social phenomena tend to be highly complex, and the methods used to study them are virtually always subject to many unwanted influences. Sources of variability affecting the measurement of any given phenomenon include variation in the administration and scoring of the measuring instrument, in the testing or laboratory situation, and within the individual. Even if near-perfect control were achieved over the foregoing sources of variability, other factors would influence the magnitude and stability of the correlation coefficient. In general, the greater the time lapse between the measurement of any two variables, the lower the correlation observed (Cronbach, 1970). Likewise, any restriction that narrows the range of values on one or both of the variables decreases the magnitude of the correlation coefficient. Too, correlations vary when computed on different samples, particularly if the size of the sample is small. As a general rule, the larger the sample the more stable the correlation, if the sample is random (Cronbach, 1970).

Correlation coefficients found in research reports vary between 0.00 and 1.00 when the relationship between the variables is positive and between 0.00 and −1.00 when the relationship is negative. A rough guide for interpreting[6] the degree of relationship reflected by the correlation coefficient has been provided by Turney and Robb (1971, p. 100):

.80 to 1.00   Very high correlation
.60 to .79   High correlation
.40 to .59   Moderate correlation
.20 to .39   Slight correlation
.10 to .19   Very slight correlation

The direction, positive or negative, of the correla-

---

[5]If the two variables are plotted against one another on a graph, the trend of the plotted points can best be represented by a curved line rather than by a straight line. For example, as one variable increases the other may first increase and then decrease.

[6]Interpretation assumes that the correlation coefficient is significant statistically (see the section on statistical inference in this chapter).

tion coefficient has no effect on the strength of the relationship. A positive $r = .70$, for example, denotes the same degree of association as a negative $r = -.70$. Furthermore, it is incorrect to interpret a high correlation as showing that one variable "causes" another (Cronbach, 1970). Some possible explanations for a high observed correlation between variables (for example, variables *A* and *B*) include the following:

A may cause or influence the size of *B, B* may cause *A,* or both *A* and *B* may be influenced by some common factor or factors. The correlation between vocabulary and reading may be taken as an example. Does good vocabulary cause one to be a good reader? Possibly. Or does the ability to read well cause one to acquire a good vocabulary? An equally likely explanation. But to some extent both scores result from high intelligence, a home in which books and serious conversation abound, and superior teaching in the elementary schools. A theoretical understanding of the processes involved, or data from controlled experiments, permits us to draw conclusions about causes that underlie a correlation. Without such information, the only safe conclusion is that correlated measures are influenced by a common factor (Cronbach, 1970, p. 133).[7]

Further, it should be noted that logic rather than statistical method determines whether a meaningful independent-dependent relationship exists (McNemar, 1962). The researcher who is interested in analyzing variation and its possible sources will prefer the interpretation of the correlation coefficient that follows.

Correlation and Prediction

Although one cannot infer causality from a high correlation coefficient, the coefficient does indicate a strong association between the variables being correlated. Hence, the relationship can be used for the purpose of predicting one variable from another. Because the observed relationship is imperfect, the researcher asks: What proportion (or percentage) of the total variance in the *Y* scores, the dependent variable, can be attributed to *X,* the independent variable? What proportion (or percentage) of the variance in the dependent variable cannot be accounted for by *X*? In short, the researcher is interested in explaining the variation in one characteristic or trait in terms of variation in another characteristic or trait.

The investigator proceeds on the assumption that the total variation in the *Y* scores is attributable to one of two sources: (1) the part that can be predicted from *X* or (2) the part that cannot be predicted from *X*. From this assumption, it can be shown that the square of the correlation coefficient, r^2, yields the proportion of *Y*

[7]From *Essentials of Psychological Testing, Third Edition,* by L. Cronbach, Harper & Row, 1970, p. 133. Reprinted by permission.

variance that can be attributed to variation in *X* (and that $1.00 - r^2$ yields the proportion of *Y* variance due to sources other than *X*). By shifting decimals, one can interpret r^2 as the percentage of variation in *Y* that can be explained by *X* (McNemar, 1962). Assume, for example, that a correlation of .70 has been observed between scores on an intelligence test and a reading achievement test. The correlation coefficient, .70, can be interpreted by saying that 49 percent of the total variance in reading achievement can be accounted for by differences in intelligence; however, 51 percent must be attributed to sources other than intelligence. As a general rule, one should multiply the correlation coefficient by itself to determine the proportion of variance in one variable that can be attributed to another. The squared correlation coefficient, r^2, is called the coefficient of determination.

Reliability

Any given score on a test, task, rating scale, or behavioral checklist is only one of many that might have been measured. Data could have been collected at a different hour on a different day, the measuring scale could have been administered and scored by a different person, and so on. The research worker is concerned, therefore, about the reliability or replicability of a set of scores. The reliability coefficient estimates the proportion of the total variation in a set of scores that can be attributed to "true" variance (or true scores) rather than to uncontrolled sources of variation. Thus, the reliability coefficient is also a coefficient of determination (Kerlinger, 1966). It tells the degree to which a given set of scores is free from unwanted, extraneous influences.

Several methods can be used to estimate reliability. The test-retest method involves retesting a sample of subjects on the same test (or on an equivalent form of the original test) after a brief lapse in time. If the first and second administrations yield approximately the same ranking of individuals, then the measuring instrument is considered reliable or stable (Kerlinger, 1966). Other approaches to reliability are based on the internal consistency of the test items rather than on the stability of the test scores. Such estimates are based on the average correlation among items within a test (internal consistency) and the number of items on the test (Nunnally, 1967). Coefficient alpha and KR_{20} (a formula developed by Kuder and Richardson) are estimates of internal consistency encountered frequently in research on exceptionality. Other estimates of reliability are obtained by subdividing a test and scoring each half separately. One might, for example, derive two scores for each person by counting the number of odd-numbered and even-numbered items answered correctly on the test. The correlation coefficient calculated between the two sets of scores and corrected for length[8] yields an estimate of reliability.

The size of the reliability coefficient needed is contingent on the use to be made of the test scores. Some authors recommend that only tests with reliability coefficients above .90 be used for discriminating among individuals—that is, for individual placement. This ideal is attained rarely in practice and many reliability coefficients are reported in the .80's and even below (Guilford, 1965). The question of an acceptable level for a reliability coefficient warrants a discussion of greater depth than is appropriate here. However, to the extent that the measuring instruments used in research lack reliability, important relationships that can contribute to knowledge about exceptional persons may be obscured by measurement error.

Validity

Experts on measurement agree that validity is the single most important characteristic of measuring instruments (Karmel, 1970). Validity is the degree to which a measuring instrument reflects the concept it is intended to represent. Since measuring instruments are used for a variety of purposes, different methods of investigation are needed for assessing their validity. An instrument considered valid for its intended purpose may be invalid if used for a different purpose. A test designed and validated for the assessment of reading achievement, for example, may be invalid if used to diagnose learning disabilities. Studies of test validation usually take one or some combination of the following forms.

Content validity. Content validity is established by determining whether test items are representative of the content the instrument is designed to measure (Borg & Gall, 1971). Ordinarily, questionnaire items and information obtained through personal interviews are justified by the extent to which the items on the scale reflect the stated purpose of the instrument. Content validity is particularly useful in achievement testing where the judgment of the test developer—often the teacher—is used to determine whether the test measures the kind of information covered in a given course or curriculum. Caution must be exercised in interpreting the scores of children in special education classes on measuring instruments that were designed and standardized for children attending regular classes. Unless

one assumes that the programs conducted in special education classes (say, for hearing-impaired, emotionally disturbed, or retarded children) and regular classrooms are highly similar in content, it makes little sense to expect the same achievement test to validly assess the outcomes of both.

Criterion-related validity. Criterion-related validity involves the use of test scores (the independent or predictor variable) to predict some performance external to the test (the criterion or dependent variable). The correlation coefficient observed between the predictor and criterion variables is called the validity coefficient. Criterion-related validity can be assessed by administering the predictor and criterion instruments either concurrently or after a lapse in time varying from several weeks to several years. When the criterion is administered after a lapse in time, an estimate of predictive validity is obtained. Research on the relationship between creativity test scores earned in high school and creative performance in adulthood exemplifies this technique. Whenever predictor and criterion scores are measured at about the same time, an estimate of concurrent rather than predictive validity is obtained. For example, one might ask whether creativity test scores earned in high school correlate with indicators of creative achievement, with peer ratings of creative behavior, or with some other concurrently administered criterion.

The single greatest difficulty in predictive validation is the problem of identifying, operationally defining, and accurately measuring the criterion. Frequently, the criterion against which one wishes to validate a test is difficult to define behaviorally. Unless both the predictor and criterion instruments are valid and reliable, the relationship between the independent and dependent variables cannot be demonstrated. Whether a validity coefficient is high enough to warrant prediction from the test depends on such practical considerations as the urgency of improved prediction (Cronbach, 1970). In general, the magnitude of the correlation coefficient needed for validity is somewhat lower than that required for reliability. In studies of predictive validity, the time interval separating the measurement of the predictor and criterion variables allows a number of uncontrolled variables to influence the criterion, thus reducing the size of the correlation coefficient. Although far from perfect, it is unusual for a validity coefficient to rise above .60 (Cronbach, 1970).

Construct validity. Construct validity is determined by investigating the psychological qualities, traits, or factors measured by a test (Downie & Heath, 1965). A construct is a concept that has been deliberately invented or adopted for a special scientific purpose (Kerlinger, 1966). For example:

---

[8]When the test is scored on an odd-even basis, the length of the original test is cut in half. Since the reliability of a test is related directly to the length of the test, the correlation coefficient obtained by correlating half-test scores is corrected for length by using the Spearman-Brown prophecy formula (Downie & Heath, 1965).

Intelligence is a concept, an abstraction from the observation of presumably intelligent and nonintelligent behaviors. But as a scientific construct, "intelligence" means both more and less than it may mean as a concept. It means that scientists consciously and systematically use it in two ways. One, it enters into theoretical schemes and is related in various ways to other constructs. We may say, for example, that *school achievement* is in part a function of *intelligence* and *motivation*. Two, "intelligence" is so defined and specified that it can be observed and measured. We can make observations of the intelligence of children by administering X intelligence test to them, or we can ask teachers to tell us the relative degrees of intelligence in their pupils [Kerlinger, 1966, p. 32].[9]

When the expert in measurement inquires about construct validity, he investigates the psychological properties that can explain the variance of the test (Kerlinger, 1966). Test developers frequently apply factor-analytic techniques to demonstrate that the traits being studied can be reduced to factors.

For example, mental ability has been reduced to factors that have been called verbal, numerical, spatial, and memory. A test that correlates significantly with such factors as these would be said to have factorial validity, a type of construct validity [Downie & Heath, 1965, p. 223].

Criterion-related validity, too, can be used as a means of assessing construct validity. Construct validity is differentiated from other forms of test validation primarily because of its emphasis on defining the theoretical constructs underlying the test (Kerlinger, 1966). The investigator interested in construct validity is not content with "looking at" the relationships among variables; instead, he wishes to understand the constructs underlying those relationships.

EXPERIMENTAL METHODS

Experimental methodology can be used most effectively when an area of study has been sufficiently well-defined to permit the identification of (1) the hypotheses that need to be tested and (2) the potentially biasing variables that need to be controlled (Mouly, 1970). Hence, experimental techniques are frequently used to follow up the correlational investigations discussed in the previous section.

An experiment is designed to examine the tenability of a research hypothesis. The research hypothesis suggests that an antecedent or independent variable is related to one or more dependent variables. The relationship between the variables is investigated by manipulating the independent variable and observing the effects of this manipulation on the dependent variable. The

dependent variable may increase, decrease, or remain unchanged as the independent variable is manipulated. If all of the extraneous variables that could possibly affect the relationship between the independent and dependent variables are controlled, then the investigator can conclude that variation in the independent variable accounts for any significant change occurring in the dependent variable. Thus, the task of the researcher is to design an experiment that allows him to attribute change in the dependent variable to variation in the independent variable rather than to some other influential, but extraneous, variable. Experiments that allow such inference possess internal validity (Campbell & Stanley, 1963). For illustrative purposes, consider the following single group pretest-posttest design that lacks internal validity.

The Single-Group Pretest-Posttest Design
The *Experimental Group* receives:

Pre-experimental ⟶ Exposure to the ⟶ Post-experimental
observation on the   independent   observation on the
dependent variable   variable   dependent variable

Assume, for example, that pretest and posttest scores have been obtained on a reading achievement test, the dependent variable, and that an experimental reading program, the independent variable, has been administered. Further, assume that the experimental treatment (the reading program) consisted of 30-minute training sessions administered daily over a two-month interval to randomly selected first-grade children. An internally valid design would permit one to assume that any significant pretest-posttest increment in reading achievement could be attributed to the experimental reading program. However, such an inference cannot be drawn unequivocally from the single-group design presented above. One cannot discredit the possibility that an increase in the dependent variable resulted from practice on the pretest, from maturation in the children over the two-month treatment interval, or from extra-experimental practice on reading skills. In other words, even though the researcher may be able to conclude that change occurred over the course of the experiment, he is unable to specify the source of variation accounting for the observed change. An experiment is regarded as internally valid only when the effect observed on the dependent variable can be unequivocally attributed to the independent variable (Neale & Liebert, 1973).

One of the most popular internally valid or true experimental designs is highly similar to the single-group design just presented. The independent variable is manipulated by assigning subjects to conditions that represent two levels of the independent variable (experimental and control) rather than one level (experimental). The experimental and control conditions differ

[9]From *Foundations of Behavioral Research*, by F. Kerlinger. © 1966 by Holt, Rinehart and Winston, Inc. Reprinted by permission.

only in the administration of the treatment of interest. The treatment (the experimental reading program, in this case) is introduced in the experimental condition and withheld in the control condition, as follows:

Pretest-Posttest Design with One Experimental Group and One Control Group

The *Experimental Group* receives:

Pre-experimental observation on the ⟶ Exposure to the treatment ⟶ Post-experimental observation on the
dependent variable   of interest   dependent variable

The *Control Group* receives:

Pre-experimental observation on the ⟶ No treatment ⟶ Post-experimental observation on the
dependent variable   dependent variable

One assumes that any influential, but extraneous, variables affect the posttest scores of the experimental and control groups in the same way. Thus, any significant posttest differences observed between the experimental and control groups can be attributed to the treatment of interest rather than to uncontrolled sources of variation. One must, of course, be able to rule out the possibility that the groups differed on the dependent variable at the outset of the experiment. Control over pre-existing intersubject differences is another essential feature of experimental methodology (Scott & Wertheimer, 1962).

Ordinarily, the experimenter relies on the random selection and assignment of subjects to conditions to balance out any initial differences between them. The research worker interested in obtaining two comparable groups from a pool of first-grade children would: (1) select the subjects at random—that is, so that each person has an equal chance of being chosen,[10] (2) randomly assign half of the children to group one and the other half to group two by a process equivalent to tossing a coin for each person, and (3) randomly determine which group would be labeled experimental and which group would be labeled control—again by a process such as tossing a coin. To the extent that the initial pool of children varied in age, sex, intelligence, socioeconomic status, and other characteristics, these differences would be expected to balance out between the experimental and control groups (Kerlinger, 1966). However, differences between groups tend to balance out only if group size is approximately 100, and many experimenters using small groups prefer to match subjects on variables known to influence the dependent variable.

Sources of variation affecting internal validity: A summary.   In general, anything that affects the controls of an experiment becomes a problem of internal validity

---

10Ordinarily, the research worker uses a Table of Random Numbers to select subjects and assign them to groups.

(Kerlinger, 1966). The sources of variation that affect internal validity were described by Campbell and Stanley (1963) and are summarized in Table 1.

Table 1. Sources of variation affecting internal validity (based on Campbell and Stanley, 1963).

History: change-inducing events that occur in addition to the experimenter's treatment (for example, regular classroom instruction, parental support in the home).
Maturation: biological and psychological processes that vary with the passage of time.
Testing: improvement on the posttest that may be due to practice on the pretest.
Instrumentation: change in the test examiner's use of the measuring instrument. (For example, observers may become more skillful.)
Statistical regression: tendency of pupils who score extremely low (or high) on a pretest to shift toward the average of the total group on the posttest (perhaps due to poor luck on the initial test, change in motivation, and so on).
Group selection bias: subjects pre-assigned rather than randomly assigned to groups (for example, use of intact classrooms, use of institutionalized subjects).
Experimental mortality: loss of subjects over the course of the experiment (for example, subjects drop out or are withdrawn because a remedial program is unsuitable for them; subjects refuse to participate at the time of follow-up).
Interaction of selection and other variables: positive treatment effect possibly due to a combination of selection and experience in test-taking, selection and statistical regression, selection and maturation, and selection and history.

THE EX POST FACTO METHOD

For ethical reasons, the researcher is not always free to select, control, and manipulate the independent variable in order to study its effects on the dependent variable. The investigator is not free, for example, to manipulate variables hypothesized to contribute to emotional disturbance, delinquency, mental retardation, or learning disabilities. Consequently, groups displaying these characteristics must be studied through the ex post facto method. The researcher locates subjects who possess the characteristic of interest and then searches for possible antecedent conditions that may have contributed to the development of that phenomenon. "Ex post facto" is a Latin term, which is translated literally as "from what is done afterward."

In its simplest form, the ex post facto method involves the comparative study of an "exceptional" versus a "contrast" group on one or more dependent variables. Thus, the independent variable consists of two levels: (1) an "exceptional" group of subjects, in whom the characteristic of interest is present (for example, a delinquent or creative group), and (2) a "contrast" group of subjects, in whom the characteristic of interest is either absent (for example, a nondelinquent group) or present to a different degree (for example, a low-creative group). Frequently, the research worker studies only those subject groups with extreme scores (high versus low) on the independent variable in order to maximize initial differences between the groups. The rationale underlying the extreme-groups strategy is that:

... if *X* and *Y* [the variables being studied] are actually related [linearly], then a wide or well-chosen difference in *X* should be more likely to produce a large measured difference in *Y*, hence making the relations of *Y* and *X* more "visible" than if a smaller or an ill-chosen difference were used [Scott & Wertheimer, 1962, p 39].

Restrictions may be placed on the range of the variables either intentionally (for example, through the selection of extreme groups) or inadvertently (for example, through the use of homogeneous intact groups). The basis used for selecting and assigning subjects to groups must be kept in mind whenever one wishes to (1) determine the population of persons to whom the conclusions of a research report can be generalized or (2) compare the results of published research reports. If the behavior classified as gifted by one researcher is considered normal by another, then discrepancies in the conclusions may be a function of the different cutoff values used. The problem of generalizing beyond the conditions used in a research study is discussed in the next section.

The major limitation of the ex post facto method is its "after the fact" nature. The investigator must start with observed effects and then attempt to discover the antecedents of those effects. In studying delinquency, for example, one might argue that any differences found between delinquent and nondelinquent groups developed after, rather than before, delinquent acts were committed. Such arguments plague research outcomes whenever the ex post facto method is used. However, despite the difficulties encountered in achieving internal validity, the ex post facto method is definitely superior to the single-group pretest-posttest design in reducing the equivocality of experimental outcomes (Campbell & Stanley, 1963).

EXTERNAL VALIDITY

In general, questioning the external validity of an experiment is tantamount to asking: Can the relationships observed in this study be generalized beyond the specific conditions reported? Or, alternatively: To what persons, ecological settings, and experimental and measurement variables can these conclusions be generalized (Van Dalen & Meyer, 1966)?

Generalizing is the process of drawing inferences about a population[11] from data collected on a sample

of that population. Because of the importance of external validity in research on exceptionality, sampling, ecological, and variable representativeness are examined in the following paragraphs. (The work of Kerlinger, 1966, on which this discussion is based, is gratefully acknowledged.)

Sampling representativeness. The research worker is interested in generalizing the relationships observed in a given study to a larger group of persons called the population. Hence, the question here is: To what persons can the conclusions be generalized? Will the relationship observed hold for all children or for all children of a certain age? Or must the conclusions be restricted to the subjects who participated in the study? The investigator interested in generalizing research outcomes to a heterogeneous population of children is obligated to select a sample of subjects who represent that population. On the other hand, the researcher can limit the population to any well-defined group—for example, to young children from lower-class families with both parents living in the home.

Ecological representativeness. Ecological generalizability becomes a problem in research on exceptionality whenever an experiment is carried out in a single institution or school. Questions with respect to ecological generality pertain to the social setting in which the experiment was conducted. For example, can the relationship observed in nongraded elementary schools be generalized to graded elementary schools? Can the conclusions based on observation in a laboratory setting be generalized to a classroom setting? Unless these questions can be answered in the affirmative, the study may be open to question with respect to ecological generalizability.

Variable representativeness. When a researcher works with social and psychological constructs, he assumes that his variables are constant (Kerlinger, 1966). Yet questions about variable representativeness can be and should be asked. Is the "delinquency" observed in the inner city the same "delinquency" found in rural areas? Are the "behavioral problems" observed in one classroom the same "behavioral problems" found in another classroom? Is the "creative expression" observed in the preschooler the same "creative expression" found in the adult? Trait constancy is frequently assumed in research on exceptionality in the absence of empirical verification. Lack of variable representativeness can markedly limit the generality of observed relationships.

Research scientists designing studies on exceptionality are sometimes faced with a "trade off" between internal and external validity. Despite the importance of external validity, internal validity is given preference when it appears that one may interfere with the other.

[11]Population is a statistical concept arbitrarily defined by naming the unique characteristics of the persons, objects, or reactions being studied; it rarely encompasses the population of a nation, city, or geographical area as we commonly define the term (Guilford, 1965).

The researcher is first concerned with demonstrating a relationship and then concerned with its generality. Campbell and Stanley (1963) reported several major threats to external validity:

1. *The interaction of pre-experimental activities and the independent variable.* Experimental outcomes may not generalize to persons who have not experienced a specific pre-experimental condition if that experience sensitizes them to the criterion (for example, if taking a pretest tells the subjects what to learn during the experiment).

2. *The interaction of selection and the independent variable.* Results may generalize only to schools or institutions similar to those cooperating in the original study (for example, low socioeconomic-status district, nongraded school).

3. *Experimental setting.* The effects may not be replicable in the absence of formal experimental procedures (for example, an educational program carried out in the public schools by university personnel may be ineffective when conducted by local classroom teachers).

4. *Multiple-treatment interference.* When several different treatments are presented to the subjects, there exists no sound basis for generalizing to possible situations in which only one of those levels is either continually present or presented only once.

STATISTICAL INFERENCE

The research scientist is interested in generalizing from the sample on which data were collected to some larger universe known as the population. The degree to which inferences from samples to populations are appropriate and the degree of error that can be expected when such inferences are made depends on the outcome of the statistical analysis of the data as well as on the procedures used in collecting the data. If all the members of a population were included in a study, there would be no need for inferential statistics. The entire population would have been measured and the results would apply to the universe of interest. However, since it is usually neither possible nor desirable to measure all members of a population, researchers select random samples from the population of interest. The statistics derived from such samples are used to estimate the values that would have been obtained if the entire population had been measured (Van Dalen & Meyer, 1966).

One purpose of introducing statistical analysis is to determine whether the relationship observed between the variables supports the research hypothesis. The test of the research hypothesis is indirect rather than direct; the research hypothesis is considered tenable only if the "null" hypothesis, the hypothesis of no differences or

no relationship in the population, is rejected. Consider the following example.

Research hypothesis: Creativity and intelligence are positively related.

Null hypothesis: There is no relationship between creativity and intelligence.

Although the null hypothesis may not be stated explicitly in published research reports, it can be inferred directly from the research hypothesis. The decision to reject the null hypothesis is determined on the basis of probability. It is rejected when there exists a low probability or slim chance of obtaining the sample value being tested given that the variables are unrelated in the population. In other words, the null hypothesis is rejected when it appears to be false in light of the data observed. When the null hypothesis is rejected, its alternative, the research hypothesis, receives support as one possible explanation for the data. By rejecting the null hypothesis, the research worker is supporting but not proving the research hypothesis. Statistical inferences are based on the probability of the occurrence of phenomena and never on absolute fact. Decisions regarding the rejection of null hypotheses are always made with some margin of error. The question of how much error can be tolerated is determined by the level of significance set up in advance by the investigator. Ordinarily, research workers consider a sample value "significant" and reject the null hypothesis when the probability of rejecting the null hypothesis erroneously is very low—only five times in 100 samples. This level of significance is symbolized $p < .05$. On the other hand, when investigators report that the outcome of a statistical test is "not significant," they are indicating that the null hypothesis cannot be rejected. In other words, given the size of the sample studied, the value observed could reasonably have occurred through sampling error. However, failure to reject the null hypothesis does not imply that it is true. The researcher might have rejected the null hypothesis if more precise measuring instruments or different research methods had been used.

The concept of significance applies to correlational analyses as well as to average (mean) differences between conditions in experimental and ex post facto designs. The magnitude of the sample values needed for significance varies in part with the number of subjects studied. A discussion of factors affecting statistical significance is beyond the scope of the present chapter; however, the reader should keep in mind that a reasonably large, representative sample is generally preferable to a small, unrepresentative sample. For statistical purposes, the division between large and small samples is in the range of 25 to 30 (Guilford, 1965).

ACHIEVING EXPERIMENTAL CONTROL

As discussed previously, the research worker has little control over the selection of subjects who fall into exceptional groups when ex post facto methods are used. The subjects are assigned to an exceptional group because they have a history of emotional disturbance, a physical handicap, a delinquent record, and so on. The exceptional and contrast groups, then, are not selected at random from the same population, and the success of the study may depend on the investigator's skill in selecting groups that are homogeneous with respect to certain critical variables (Borg & Gall, 1971). This procedure consists of "matching" subjects in the contrast group with those in the exceptional group on one or more variables that are either known or believed to correlate with the dependent variable. The matching technique eliminates any differences that might be observed between the groups as a consequence of the variables on which the subjects were equated or matched. In other words, by matching on a variable, the experimenter has eliminated any chance of its emerging as a possible source of exceptional versus contrast group differences. Yet, even with the matching procedure, it is virtually impossible to carry out research that meets the standards of controlled, experimental methodology (Underwood, 1957).[12]

The use of analysis of covariance, a statistical tool, is another means of equating groups for initial subject differences. The analysis of covariance allows one to eliminate the effects of one or more influential variables (the covariates) from the dependent variable. Stated another way, the effects of the independent variable on the dependent variable can be assessed independently of the effects of the covariates, which are measured prior to the experiment and removed statistically from the criterion scores. For example, the investigator who is studying the effects of an experimental reading program on the dependent variable, reading achievement, may be forced to use subjects from intact classrooms in forming the experimental and control groups. Further, he may wish to eliminate initial experimental versus control-group differences (initial classroom differences, in this case) in intelligence from the criterion scores on reading achievement. The analysis of covariance allows one to test the differences between experimental versus control classrooms for that part of the variation in reading achievement that is independent of intelligence, the covariate. The covariate could,

of course, have been used as a moderator variable by stratifying subjects on intelligence (perhaps by dividing them into high, middle, and low IQ groups). Experimental designs encompassing two or more independent variables permit the investigator to look for interaction effects—that is, the relationship between the dependent variable and two or more independent variables. For example, in studying the effects of intelligence (high IQ, middle IQ, and low IQ) and treatment (experimental reading program and control program) on reading achievement, one might observe that the experimental program was superior to the control program only for children with low intelligence. Analysis of variance and multiple-regression techniques are used frequently in analyzing the effects of two or more independent variables on the dependent variable.

Balancing is another technique used in controlling the effects of variables (Turney & Robb, 1971). Balancing does not eliminate the effects of an extraneous variable, but it does ensure that the effects are distributed equally across the conditions being studied. For example, in studying experimental versus control training programs, one might rotate the training schedule so that each group of subjects receives training at the same hour on different days of the week. Conceivably, subjects may experience extra-experimental activities that can influence learning at certain hours of the day on certain days of the week. Thus, a consistent bias that might be introduced by time of day or day of week can be controlled through balancing.

Finally, it is important that relationships observed in research on exceptionality be studied through replication. If the effects observed in the original study can be reproduced on a different sample of subjects drawn from the same population, then one's faith in those effects can be markedly increased.

PRACTICAL APPLICATIONS

The application of research outcomes to the solution of practical problems is a complex and challenging task. First and foremost, the person who wishes to apply generalizations based on research to specific problem settings must be familiar with the professional literature in the area of concern. The reading of selected articles, as afforded by this book, can contribute to the development of one's talent as a consumer of research but in no way ensures the acquisition of the depth of knowledge necessary for decision-making in applied situations. Thus, the knowledge gleaned from research should be synthesized with other sources of information about exceptional persons for application in particular settings. One of the most relevant questions to be asked

---

[12]The advanced student is referred to Campbell and Stanley (1963) and Underwood (1957) for a discussion of the problems encountered in using the matching technique.

by the practitioner concerns external validity; that is, are these research outcomes likely to generalize to this particular applied setting? The aspiring teacher and school psychologist should recognize the large gap between replicating research and applying research. In the former, the original conditions are either maintained or varied systematically, whereas in the latter many variables are changed simultaneously.

The student who acquires skill in using knowledge gained through reading educational and psychological journals will discover many interesting relationships as well as many inconsistencies as he reviews the research on exceptionality. One should keep in mind that the acquisition of knowledge is an ongoing process and therefore be alert to new developments as they appear in the journals.

2
GIFTEDNESS AND MENTAL RETARDATION

CHAPTER TWO

CREATIVE AND INTELLECTUAL GIFTEDNESS

Beginning in 1965, the bulk of research on gifted children shifted from the study of children with high intelligence to the study of the creative process (Frierson, 1969). Since that time, the issue of whether creative and intellectual giftedness represent the same or separate facets of intelligence has generated a great deal of controversy. Arasteh (1968) reported a distinction among several aspects of giftedness: intelligence, musical ability, creative writing, and social leadership. If the construct of giftedness is differentiated further by research workers, a better title for this area of exceptionality might be "talent."

One of the foremost questions in the search for giftedness, or talent, concerns the validity of the instruments used to assess that talent. The construct validity of intelligence and creativity tests has not been as clearly demonstrated as is often inferred. By and large, tests of intelligence (IQ) have been validated against other measures of IQ and academic achievement. This practice has yielded uniformity across tests rather than evidence of construct validity. Research indicating that intelligence tests tap the behavioral correlates deemed "intelligent" in children and adults is much less extensive than one might expect (McClelland, 1973). Similarly, strong evidence of construct validity has not characterized the measurement of creativity.

The criterion-related behavior against which creativity tests should be validated has been difficult to identify because of the controversy concerning the definition of creativity. If creativity is regarded as a mental process rather than the invention or creation of a product, then the criteria for measuring performance must vary accordingly. The articles by Torrance and by Kogan and Pankove represent pioneering efforts in the longitudinal study of creativity and provide information on the predictive validity of the measuring instruments used.

The complex nature of the relationship between creativity and intelligence can be inferred from both the Kogan and Pankove and Frierson articles. Kogan and Pankove cite (and indirectly generate) evidence suggesting that the correlation between creativity and intelligence is determined in part by variables in test administration (for example, whether game- or test-like instructions are given to subjects). In addition, the results of Frierson's study suggest that socioeconomic level may affect the relationship between creativity and intelligence.

Various theorists have suggested that home and school factors may be instrumental in fostering or hindering the development of creative and intellectual giftedness. Hence, the environmental correlates of intellectually gifted and creative behavior have been studied to seek antecedent variables that may contribute to the development of talent. Both Domino and Bishop provide descriptive information on the characteristics of adults whose influence may promote the development of talent. Domino studied the maternal correlates of sons' creativity, and Bishop attempted to identify some of the traits that characterize successful teachers of the gifted. Further, Granzin and Granzin, reporting that peer awareness of traits characterizing giftedness is present by the time children reach the fourth grade, used peer nominations as a technique for screening intellectually gifted children.

In summary, research affords a wealth of information on the descriptive traits of intellectually gifted or creative groups. However, the bulk of these data yields inconclusive evidence on the nature and development of giftedness. As concluded by Kogan and Pankove, talented accomplishments appear to be a complex function of creativity, intelligence, motivational disposition, and social setting.

PREDICTIVE VALIDITY OF THE TORRANCE TESTS OF CREATIVE THINKING

E. Paul Torrance

Abstract. Seven- and twelve-year follow-up studies were conducted to determine whether scores earned on creativity tests during the high school years would predict creative behavior in adult life. Significant, moderately high correlations between tests of creative potential and measures of creative achievement were reported. Findings tended to support the predictive validity of the Torrance tests of creativity in the "advantaged" sample studied.

The major long-range prediction study of the *Torrance Tests of Creative Thinking* was initiated in September, 1959. At that time, the total enrollment of the University of Minnesota High School (grades 7-12) were administered the *Torrance Tests of Creative Thinking*. A majority of the subjects were sons and daughters of professional and business people. At this time, however, the enrollment also included a large block of students from a less affluent neighborhood lacking a school building. The mean intelligence quotient of the total group of students as assessed by the Lorge-Thorndike test was 118, and the mean percentile rank of the *Iowa Tests of Educational Development* was 84 on national norms.

The test battery consisted of the following tasks: Ask Questions, Guess Causes, Guess Consequences, Product Improvement, Unusual Use of an Improved Product, Unusual Use of a Common Object, and Circles. The creativity tests were scored in 1959 according to the scoring guides then in use for the following variables: fluency (number of relevant responses), flexibility (variety of categories of responses), inventive level (following the criteria of the United States Patent Office), elaboration (amount of detail used to describe how ideas would be executed). In 1961, all tests were rescored for originality according to a guide developed at that time. The interscorer reliability of each of the scorers in all cases was in excess of .90 for all variables.

Near the end of the senior year, the subjects were administered a five-item peer nominations questionnaire. Subjects were asked to make three nominations on the basis of each of the following criteria:

1. Who in your class comes up with the most ideas?
2. Who have the most original or unusual ideas?
3. If the situation changed or if a solution to a problem wouldn't work, who in your class would be the first ones to find a new way of meeting the problem?
4. Who in your class does the most inventing and developing of new ideas, gadgets, and the like?

Abridged with permission from *Journal of Creative Behavior,* 1972, **6**(4), published by the Creative Education Foundation, Buffalo, New York.

5. Who in your class are best at thinking of all the details involved in working out a new idea and thinking of all of the consequences?

The first follow-up of this study was with the class of 1960 and was executed in 1966, using a questionnaire designed by Erickson (1966) and Torrance (1969ab). The instrument requested information concerning the subject's marital status, number of children, occupation, spouse's occupation, highest level of education attained, undergraduate and graduate colleges attended, honors, employment experiences, post-high school creative achievements, a description of most creative achievement, and a statement of aspirations.

Even though many of the 44 subjects who had returned their questionnaires were still in graduate school or military service in 1966 when Erickson analyzed the data, a considerable amount of creative activity was reported. Erickson obtained an index of creative achievement by adding the number of achievements reported in all categories. The following product-moments of correlation were obtained between this index and the measures of creative thinking derived from the tests administered in 1959:

Fluency   .27 (Significant at .05 level)
Flexibility   .24 (Significant between .05 and .10)
Originality .17 (Not significant)
Elaboration .16 (Not significant)

Tetrachoric correlations successfully predicted participation in the following activities at better than the .05 level; subscribed to professional magazine or journal; learned new language; wrote a poem, story, song, or play; wrote a book (unpublished); changed religious affiliation, handled in-service education for co-workers; suggested modifications in job situation that were adopted; received research grant for original proposal; had scientific paper published; elected or appointed to a student office; gave a public music recital; performed on radio or television; developed an original experimental design.

Torrance (1969ab) later reanalyzed the data using responses received by 46 of the original 69 subjects and revising the creative achievement index by eliminating items regarded as not necessarily creative achievements. The items eliminated included: subscribed to professional magazine or journal, learned new language, gave a public speech, took up a new hobby, changed religious affiliation, elected or appointed to a student office, joined professional club or organization. The major achievements included in the new index are as follows:

Poems, stories, songs written
Poems, stories, songs published
Books written
Books published
Radio and television scripts or performances
Original research designs developed
Philosophy of life changed
In-service training for co-workers created
Original changes in work situation suggested

Research grants received
Scientific papers published in professional journal
Business enterprises initiated
Patentable devices invented
Literary awards or prizes received for creative writing, musical composition, art, etc.

An index of quality of creative achievement was obtained by having five judges (all advanced students of creativity) rate on a 10-point scale the originality of the most creative achievements. An index of quantity of creative behavior was obtained by assigning a weight of one for each achievement attained once or twice and a weight of two for each achievement attained three or more times, and then adding the weights. The five judges also rated the degree of originality necessary to realize each subject's vocational aspiration. Reasonably high agreement among the judges was obtained, as indicated by the mean interscorer reliability coefficient of .65 for highest creative achievement and .69 for creativeness of aspirations.

Using the three new indexes of creative achievement, Torrance (1969ab) obtained the results shown in Table 1. It will

TABLE 1 Product-moment coefficients of correlation between creativity predictors established in 1959 and criterion variables established in 1966.

	Criterion Variables		
Predictors	*Creat. Qual.*	*Creat. Quan.*	*Creat. Motiv.*
Intelligence Test	.37*	.22	.32
High School Achievement	.20	.09	.15
Peer Nominations on Creative Criteria	.13	.13	.18
Fluency (TTCT)	.39*	.44*	.34
Flexibility (TTCT)	.48*	.44*	.46*
Originality (TTCT)	.43*	.40*	.42*
Elaboration (TTCT)	.32	.37*	.25

* Coefficient of correlation is significant at the .01 level

be noted that only one of the nine coefficients of correlation for the non-creativity variables is statistically significant at the .01 level, while nine of the 12 coefficients of correlation for the creativity predictors reach this level of significance. If we lower the level of significance to the .05 level, two of the coefficients of correlation for the non-creativity predictors and 11 for the creativity predictors are significant. Flexibility and Originality appear to be the best predictors with Fluency, Elaboration, Intelligence, High School Achievement, and Peer Nominations following in that order.

By combining the Fluency, Flexibility, Originality, and Elaboration scores through stepwise regression, multiple correlation coefficients of .50 (with Highest Creative Achievement), .46 (with Quantity of Creative Achievements), and .51 (with Creativeness of Aspirations) were obtained.

Procedure. A 12-year follow-up of the 1959 University (Minnesota) High School population (N = 392) was conducted in 1971. At the time the data reported here were analyzed, completed questionnaires had been obtained from 117 of the women and 119 of the men. The questionnaire was similar to the one used in 1966 and requested information concerning marital status, number of children, occupation, spouse's occupation, highest level of education attained, undergraduate colleges and graduate school attended, honors, employment experiences, post-high school creative achievements and activities, descriptions of three most creative post-high school achievements, and a statement of aspirations. Generally, subjects supplied rather complete data, rich in information about what has been happening to these young people who were now between the ages of 25 and 31.

A measure of quantity of creative achievements was obtained by adding the number of creative achievements checked and/or listed by each subject. The checklist consisted of those items used by Torrance in his analysis of the 1966 data. The measure of quality of highest creative achievements was based on the ratings of five expert judges (mature researchers and doctoral candidates with concentrations on creative studies) of the descriptions of the three most creative achievements reported by each subject. The judges were instructed to rate these data on a 10-point scale in terms of the level of creativeness reflected by the achievements described. The measure of creativeness of aspirations was based on similar ratings of the statements of each subject concerning what he would most like to do in the future, assuming the necessary talent, training, and opportunity. The mean reliability coefficient of the five judges was .91.

Results. Combining the scores on the creativity test battery to predict the combined creativity criteria, a canonical correlation of .51 was obtained for the full sample. A canonical correlation of .59 was obtained for men alone, and one of .46 for women alone. While the predictive validity of the tests is significant at better than the 1 per cent level for both men and women, the finding gives some credence to the belief that the creative achievements of women are less predictable than those of men.

Table 2 provides more detailed information concerning the predictive validity of the specific creativity variables along with the coefficients of correlation of the criteria of creative achievement and Lorge-Thorndike I.Q. It will be noted that all of the coeffcients of correlation involving the creativity variables as predictors are significant at better than the 1 per cent level of confidence. In general, however, those of the women are a shade lower than those for the men. This trend is accentuated for intelligence quotient as a predictor of creative achievement, especially for quantity of creative achieve-

TABLE 2   Correlation of selected creativity variable and intelligence quotient with adult creativity criteria for males and females.

Predictors	Males (N = 119)			Females (N = 117)		
	Quantity	Quality	Aspir.	Quantity	Quality	Aspir.
Fluency	.31*	.29*	.27*	.28*	.33*	.27*
Flexibility	.32*	.31*	.27*	.25*	.32*	.23*
Inventive level	.42*	.43*	.42*	.28*	.41*	.32*
Elaboration	.27*	.34*	.37*	.27*	.35*	.29*
Originality	.41*	.45*	.45*	.37*	.40*	.30*
I. Q.	.24*	.40*	.37*	.06	.29*	.18**

*Significant at the .01 level

**Significant at the .05 level

ment. The creativity measures are consistently better predictors of the women's adult creative achievement than is the measure of intelligence....

Conclusion

Although the subjects of this 12-year predictive validity study were fairly advantaged and most of them had ample opportunities and freedom to develop their creative abilities, the results do indicate that creativity tests administered during the high school years *can* predict real-life adult creative achievements. It is doubtful that such favorable results would be found for a population severely limited in opportunity and/or freedom. The subjects of this study now range in age from 25 to 31 years, and we do not know whether these results will continue to hold up at the end of another 12 years. An examination of the clues provided by the detailed responses of the subjects, however, suggests that the creative achievement differences between the more creative and and less creative subjects are likely to widen as time elapses.

No attempt has been made yet to determine whether creativity tests administered to elementary school children will predict adult creative achievements. Such studies were initiated in 1958 and 1959, and follow-up is planned for 1975. There will also be further follow-ups of the high-school study described here.

REFERENCES

BENTLEY, J. C. Creativity and academic achievement. *Journal of Educational Research,* 1966 59, 269-272.

BURKHART, R. C. & BERNHEIM, G. *Object question test manual.* University Park, PA: Department of Art Education Research, Pennsylvania State University, 1963, (Mimeographed).

CROPLEY, A. J. Some Canadian creativity research. *Journal of Research and Development in Education,* 1971, 4(3), 113-115.

ERICKSON, G. The predictive validity of a battery of creative thinking tests and peer nominations among University of Minnesota high school seniors seven years later. Master's research paper, University of Minnesota, 1966.

FLANDERS, N. A. Interaction analysis in the classroom: a manual for observers. Ann Arbor, MI: University of Michigan, 1960, (Mimeographed).

HANSEN, E. A comparison of the teaching behavior of creative and less creative basic business teachers. Doctoral dissertation, University of Minnesota, 1967. (University Microfilms Order No. 67-14, 614; *Dissertation Abstracts 28:* 06A/2136).

LEHMAN, R. A. A study of the effects of creativity and intelligence on pupils' questions in science. Research paper, Nova University, Ft. Lauderdale, FL, 1969.

MacDONALD, J. B. & RATHS, J. D. Should we group by creative abilities? *Elementary School Journal*, 1964, *65*, 137-142.

McPHERSON, J. H. A proposal for establishing ultimate critera for measuring creative output. In C. W. Taylor & F. Barron (eds.), *Scientific creativity: its recognition and development.* NYC: Wiley, 1964, 24-29.

STROM, R. D. & LARIMORE, D. *Predicting teacher success: the inner city.* Columbus, OH: College of Education, Ohio State University, 1970.

TORRANCE, E. P. *Guiding creative talent.* Englewood Cliffs, NJ: Prentice, 1962.

TORRANCE, E. P. *Education and the creative potential.* Minneapolis: University of Minnesota Press, 1963.

TORRANCE, E. P. *Torrance tests of creative thinking: Norms-technical manual.* (research edition) Princeton, NJ: Personnel Press, 1966.

TORRANCE, E. P. Prediction of adult creative achievement among high school seniors. *Gifted Child Quarterly*, 1969(a), *13*, 71-81.

TORRANCE, E. P. Will creatively gifted high school seniors behave creatively seven years later? *TAG Gifted Children Newsletter*, 1969(b), *12(1)*, 24-31.

TORRANCE, E. P. & HANSEN, E. The question-asking behavior of highly creative basic business teachers identified by a paper-and-pencil test. *Psychological Reports*, 1965, *17*, 815-818.

TORRANCE, E. P., TAN, C. A. & ALLMAN, T. Verbal originality and teacher behavior: a predictive validity study. *Journal of Teacher Education*, 1970, *21*, 335-341.

WEISBERG, P. S. & SPRINGER, K. J. Environmental factors in creative function. *Archives of General Psychiatry*, 1961, *5*, 554-564.

WITT, G. The life enrichment activity program: a continuing program for creative, disadvantaged children. *Journal of Research and Development in Education*, 1971, *4(3)*, 14-22.

WODTKE, K. H. A study of the reliability and validity of creativity tests at the elementary school level. Doctoral dissertation, University of Utah, 1963. (University Microfilms Order No. 64-3148; *Dissertation Abstracts* 24: 4091).

YAMAMOTO, K. Creative writing and school environment. *School and Society*, 1963, *91*, 307-308.

CREATIVE ABILITY OVER A FIVE-YEAR SPAN

Nathan Kogan
Ethel Pankove

Fifth-grade middle-class children whose levels of associative creativity had been assessed with the Wallach-Kogan tasks were retested on identical and similar tasks 5 years later in the tenth grade. In the smaller of 2 school systems employed in the research, tenth-grade creativity data were obtained by an individual examiner; in the larger system, group administration was employed. Substantial stability in ideational productivity and uniqueness scores over a 5-year period was observed for males in the setting of group administration and for females in the context of individual testing. Creativity and IQ, which were unrelated at fifth-grade level, remained unrelated for females at tenth grade but became positively correlated for males. Multiple regression analysis indicated that fifth- and tenth-grade creativity and fifth-grade IQ accounted for approximately half of the variance in extracurricular activities in the smaller school system. Predictability was considerably poorer in the larger school system. A possible interpretation of the differential predictability across school systems is offered.

In *Modes of Thinking in Young Children,* Wallach and Kogan (1965) demonstrated the essential independence of traditional intelligence measures from indices of associative creativity when the latter are assessed in a gamelike, nonevaluative context. Since the publication of that volume, a number of partial replications have appeared (e.g., Cropley & Maslany 1969; Pankove & Kogan 1968; Wallach & Wing 1969; Ward 1968), all supporting the original Wallach-Kogan conclusions concerning the creativity-intelligence distinction. It should be noted that the Wallach-Kogan research was based on a sample of American fifth-graders—children approximately 10–11 years of age. The partial replications cited above have extended the age generalizability of the observed creativity-intelligence distinction both downward and upward in age. The effects appear to be quite similar in nature from kindergarten through university levels. Furthermore, the effects seem to be generalizable across differences in social class (Ward, Kogan, & Pankove 1972).

All of the foregoing research has been cross-sectional. The present investigation represents a first attempt to examine the long-term longitudinal stability of associative creativity when assessed with the Wallach-

Kogan tasks.[1] A subsample of the fifth-grade children studied by Pankove and Kogan (1968) was reexamined 5 years later in the tenth grade. Explored, in addition, were the relative independence of creativity and intelligence over the 5-year period, and the predictive power of fifth- and tenth-grade creativity measures in relation to talented accomplishments outside of the classroom context. The latter issue is more ideally suited to students in their final year of secondary school, for tenth-graders have had only a limited opportunity to manifest such accomplishments. Nevertheless, a preliminary look at the issue appeared worthwhile at the present time. The authors intend to obtain data on the talented accomplishments of these same students during their last year of secondary school.

METHOD

The Pankove-Kogan (1968) investigation was based on a sample of middle-class fifth-grade children in two separate school systems. Of a subtotal of 46 children (25 males and 21 females) in school system *A,* 29 (16 males and 13 females) were available for study in the tenth grade. For school system *B,* 116 children (59 males and 57 females) were examined in the fifth grade, and of that number, 72 (38 males and 34 females) were still enrolled in the system 5 years later. Across both school systems, 62.5% of the original fifth-grade sample was included in the study. A comparison of these *S*s with those who moved out of the two school systems between fifth and tenth grade indicated that the two subsamples were highly similar on the fifth-grade creativity and IQ measures.

Because of limitations of time, and given the high reliability of the Wallach and Kogan tasks, only four of the original eight items in each task were given in the tenth grade. The items in two of these tasks were verbal (uses and similarities); the items in the other two

This study was supported by the National Institute of Child Health and Human Development, under research grant 1 P01 HD01762 to the Educational Testing Service.
Abridged from *Child Development,* 1972, **43,** 427–442. © 1972 by the Society for Research in Child Development, Inc. Reprinted by permission.

[1] Longitudinal studies of the predictive validity of creativity assessment have appeared based on the Torrance tests (Torrance 1969; Torrance, Tan, & Allman 1970) and on a combination of the Guilford and Torrance tests (Cropley 1972). The serious methodological shortcomings of the foregoing tests have been thoroughly documented by Wallach (1970).

tasks were figural (patterns and lines). It should be further noted that only one verbal and one figural procedure—uses and patterns, respectively—had been administered at the fifth-grade level. Hence, it was possible to examine stability over the 5-year period for tasks taken previously and tasks encountered for the first time. Tasks were scored for ideational productivity (the total number of responses) and uniqueness (responses occurring but once in the sample). Responses deemed inappropriate or bizarre (approximately 2% of the total) were excluded from the foregoing scores. Scoring was carried out by a judge highly experienced with the Wallach-Kogan tasks through participation in prior research projects. Accordingly, interjudge reliability was not considered in the present work. Such reliability has been amply demonstrated in previously published research.

At the fifth-grade level, the procedure described in the Wallach and Kogan (1965) volume was employed. The instruments were described as educational games and administered without time limits by an encouraging, nonevaluative examiner. This type of testing context could not be maintained at the tenth-grade level. Fifteen-year-old adolescents are prone to suspect an outside examiner who claims that his purpose is to try out various educational games. In school system *A*, where an individual administration was employed, *S*s were informed that the present work was a continuation of the study in which they had participated 5 years previously. A male and female examiner were used for male and female *S*s, respectively. The examiner's purpose, as communicated to the *S*s, concerned stability and change in thinking processes over time. The *S*s were told that the current study had no connection with their official school work, and scheduling was arranged so that all *S*s had sufficient time to complete the tasks. Comparable instructions were employed for school system *B*, but males and females were examined separately in groups. Booklets were prepared containing one task item per page, with adequate space provided for *S*s to write their responses.

Information on intelligence levels was available in the school records for both fifth- and tenth-grade classes. These were based on the California Test of Mental Maturity and the Differential Aptitude Test, respectively. The biographical inventory devised by Wallach and Wing (1969) was administered for the purpose of assessing extracurricular activities and accomplishments in the areas of leadership, art, social service, literature, dramatic arts, music, and science. A subject's score consisted of a simple count of all of the activities and accomplishments checked. Differentiated scores for the separate areas did not appear to be warranted at the tenth-grade level.

RESULTS AND DISCUSSION

Intercorrelations between and within creativity tasks at fifth- and tenth-grade levels were calculated separately for males and females. Consistent with previously published research, between-task correlations for ideational productivity scores at both fifth and tenth grade were almost uniformly significant and substantial. Correlations were of approximately equal magnitude in males and females, the coefficients ranging from .39 to .93 with a median r of .67. For uniqueness, intertask generality was less strong; coefficients ranged from $-.14$ to .85, with a median r of .38. The difference in the degree of intertask generality between ideational productivity and uniqueness partially reflects the lower intratask reliabilities customarily obtained for the latter measures. Also congruent with prior studies is the evidence for strong within-task relationships between productivity and uniqueness. These coefficients ranged from .46 to .97 with a median r of .72.

The consistency of performance across a 5-year period concerned us next. For males in school system *B* (group administration of creativity tasks), correlations for productivity of .52 ($p < .01$) and .39 ($p < .01$) were obtained for uses and patterns, respectively. The corresponding correlations for uniqueness were .38 ($p < .01$) and .42 ($p < .01$). These results offer strong evidence for the long-term stability of a dimension of creative ability in males from childhood into adolescence. It should be further noted that the significant correlations were not confined to pairings of the same task. Thus, correlations for productivity between fifth-grade uses and patterns, on the one hand, and tenth-grade similarities and lines, on the other, ranged from .31 to .51, all significant at the .05 level and beyond. A comparable analysis for uniqueness, however, showed a decline in the magnitude of the correlations. These ranged from .18 to .28—all in the positive direction, though three of the four r's were nonsignificant. It should be noted, however, that composite fifth- and tenth-grade uniqueness scores (obtained by summing standard scores across individual tasks) were substantially correlated (r's of .49 and .47, $p < .01$).

Results for males in school system *A*, where creativity tasks were administered individually, were less consistent. The correlation coefficients across fifth- and tenth-grade measures for the matched productivity and uniqueness composites were nonsignificant—.10 and .39, respectively. Furthermore, most of the other correlations between fifth- and tenth-grade creativity measures fell short of statistical significance. Thus, it would appear that a face-to-face encounter between a male examiner and an adolescent male *S* yielded a type of performance that departed considerably from performance 5 years prior. The two school systems employed in the research were quite similar in socioeconomic composition of the student body, and hence the differences observed in males in the two systems cannot be attributed to that source. It should be noted in this connection that the overall productivity level of male tenth-graders in the individual-administration condition declined to a near-significant extent from the prior fifth-grade level, whereas a comparable comparison for all other subgroups indicated no change or moderate to substantial increases in productivity (table 1). A performance decline of the kind obtained is unusual across the age span studied for a cognitive dimension, and this again points to the presence of some inhibitory interpersonal influence for the individual testing context where adolescent males are concerned.

For females, a different correlational pattern emerged. In the case of school system *B*, where the tasks were group administered, neither productivity nor uniqueness scores demonstrated long-term stability. Between-grade correlation coefficients were .07 and .19 for the matched composite productivity and uniqueness indices, respectively, and not a single between-grade creativity correlation achieved statistical significance. For school system *A*, on the other hand, the foregoing composites were not significantly correlated (*r*'s of .13 and .35), but considerable stability was observed between fifth grade tasks and those tasks (similarities and lines) administered for the first time in the tenth grade.

To sum up the data on stability of creativity scores over a 5-year period, it appears that the sex of *S* and the testing context acted as moderator variables. Boys showed higher consistency when the assessment at adolescence took place in an impersonal mass testing; girls manifested more consistency when the assessment at adolescence was carried out by a nonevaluative female examiner. For adolescent boys, in other words, the interpersonal component in a face-to-face assessment may have been debilitating. Under such conditions, a more purely cognitive dimension may have been tapped in the group administration, thereby contributing to cognitive stability over time. For adolescent girls, on the other hand, the impersonality of a group setting may have had negative consequences. Consistency in ideational productivity and uniqueness for girls over time may demand a direct personal contact with an encouraging nonevaluative examiner. It might be worth noting in this connection that correlations between fifth-grade general anxiety level and productivity in girls, which were significantly positive at fifth-grade level ($r = .37$, $p < .05$, for the composite of uses and patterns) became significantly negative in the tenth grade when creativity

was assessed via group testing ($r = -.38$, $p < .05$, for the same composite).[2] For girls responding to the creativity tasks in the individual administration, the correlations with anxiety remained positive.

Results reported in table 1 clearly show the absence of any consistent increase or decrease in productivity and/or uniqueness over the 5-year period under study. The differential effect on males and females of the individual testing context at tenth grade has already been pointed out. Males appeared to be considerably more inhibited in their output by the male examiner than were females by the female examiner. In the case of school system *B*, where the creativity tasks were administered in groups, productivity on the verbal uses task showed considerably more gain than productivity on the figural patterns task.

These findings are consistent with other bodies of cross-sectional data suggesting that creativity tasks containing verbal stimulus material yield larger age discrepancies than do tasks of the same character using figural stimulus material. For example, the mean productivity difference between the Wallach and Kogan (1965) middle-class fifth-graders and the Wallach and Wing (1969) college freshmen favored the latter sample, but the discrepancy was considerably larger for verbal than figural items. Also of interest is evidence indicating that the black disadvantaged fifth-graders studied by Ward, Kogan, and Pankove (1972) were less productive than their middle-class age counterparts on verbal items but somewhat more productive on figural items. It is possible that a task such as alternate uses favors the richer experiential repertoires of older and middle-class subjects, whereas figural tasks have more to do with the organization and accessibility of repertoires. Alternatively, the differences may reflect the way in which experience is encoded—increasingly semantic for older and middle-class subjects, more iconic for younger and lower-class subjects. These inferences are conjectural, of course, and need to be tested in experiments explicitly directed to the issue of verbal-figural differences.

In respect to creativity-IQ correlations, . . . these were generally negligible (but sometimes moderately negative) for females at the fifth- and tenth-grade levels. Ideational productivity and uniqueness in girls were not positively associated with traditional measures of aptitude or ability, a finding consistent with most of the accumulated evidence concerning the Wallach-Kogan tasks (see Kogan 1971). For males, on the other hand, correlations between fifth-grade measures of creativity

[2]A 20-item general-anxiety scale adapted from Sarason, Davidson, Lighthall, Waite, and Ruebush (1960) and a 19-item test-anxiety scale constructed by the same authors were administered. The latter yielded differences in the same direction as general anxiety, but less strong.

Table 1. Mean changes in productivity and uniqueness from fifth to tenth grade.

| | School System A | | | | | | School System B | | | | | |
| | Males (N = 16) | | | Females (N = 13) | | | Males (N = 38) | | | Females (N = 34) | | |
	$\overline{D}$	$SE_{\overline{D}}$	t	$\overline{D}$	$SE_{\overline{D}}$	t	$\overline{D}$	$SE_{\overline{D}}$	t	$\overline{D}$	$SE_{\overline{D}}$	t
Productivity:												
Uses	−3.94	2.22	1.77*	3.46	3.11	1.11	2.00	1.21	1.66	5.62	1.67	3.37**
Patterns	−4.00	2.27	1.76*	5.77	3.48	1.66	−0.18	1.46	0.13	−0.18	1.34	0.13
Uniqueness:												
Uses	−1.38	0.74	1.86*	−1.08	0.72	1.50	−0.08	0.35	0.23	0.15	0.40	0.37
Patterns	−1.38	0.96	1.43	3.62	1.86	1.94*	0.37	0.60	0.61	0.09	0.48	0.18

Note. Negative mean differences reflect declines in productivity and uniqueness.
* $p < .10$.
** $p < .01$.

and IQ, which were nonsignificant at the fifth-grade level, turned statistically significant and positive at the tenth-grade level. This contrasting pattern of findings for males and females does not readily lend itself to interpretation. Possibly, open-ended tasks of divergent thinking are more likely to engage personality and motivational factors in girls, whereas boys' performance is under stricter cognitive control. Recall the significant anxiety-creativity correlations in girls reported earlier. No such correlations were obtained in the male sample.

The final set of findings concerns activities and accomplishments outside of the classroom context. Do fifth- and tenth-grade indices of creative and intellective abilities predict these "real-world" performances? To answer this question, multiple regression analysis was employed (table 2). The predictor variables consisted of fifth-grade productivity, uniqueness, and IQ, the three corresponding tenth-grade measures, and sex. The seven variables were entered into the prediction equation in the order indicated. Since the present research was aimed at long-term prediction, it seemed reasonable to see how much variance could be accounted for by the fifth-grade variables before the tenth-grade variables were considered.

For school system A, fifth-grade ideational productivity and IQ contributed significantly to the multiple R, whose value for fifth-grade predictors alone was .57 ($p < .01$). When tenth-grade productivity was added to the fifth-grade data, the multiple R increased to .70 ($p < .01$). Other variables—tenth-grade uniqueness and IQ, and sex—contributed little more to the overall prediction. In sum, a combination of fifth- and tenth-grade productivity, plus fifth-grade IQ, accounted for approximately 50% of the variance in the criterion in school system A. In the case of concurrent prediction, tenth-grade predictors alone when entered first into the regression equation yielded a multiple R of .60.

Fifth-grade creativity and IQ made essentially non-overlapping contributions to the variance in extracurricular activities. Part correlation coefficients between the activities index, on the one hand, and productivity and uniqueness, on the other (with IQ taken out of the latter variables), were .41 and .40, respectively. The corresponding part correlations between the activities index and IQ (with productivity and uniqueness taken out of the latter variable) were .43 and .48, respectively. All of the foregoing part correlations were significant beyond the .05 level. At tenth-grade level, in contrast with the fifth-grade data, only the creativity variables accounted for a significant portion of the variance in the activities index. These part correlations (with IQ held constant) were .56 and .57 for productivity and uniqueness, respectively, both significant at the .01 level. With productivity and uniqueness held constant, the part correlations between IQ and the activities index were .17 and .20, respectively (McNemar 1962, pp. 167–168).

For school system B, predictability of the criterion behavior was low. The multiple R, exclusive of sex of subject, was .20. With sex included it was .27. Somewhat better predictability was obtained when the regression analyses were carried out separately for the two sexes. The multiple R's were .41 and .40 for males and females, respectively. Neither of these R's achieved statistical significance, however.

These school system differences are not easily explainable. It is possible that the differential size of the two school systems is a contributing factor. Where a school class is smaller, and this is indeed the case for school system A, the opportunity for extracurricular activity at the tenth-grade level is correspondingly greater. Mean number of activities and accomplishments were, in fact, significantly greater in school system A than in school system B—$t(99) = 1.71$, $p < .05$, a finding

Table 2. Multiple regression analysis for prediction of tenth-grade activities and accomplishments.

Predictors	School System A			School System B		
	df	R^2	F	df	R^2	F
Productivity—fifth grade	27	.134	4.16*	70	.001	0.06
Uniqueness—fifth grade	26	.138	0.14	69	.001	0.00
IQ—fifth grade	25	.330	7.13**	68	.003	0.13
Productivity—tenth grade	24	.496	7.89***	67	.015	0.84
Uniqueness—tenth grade	23	.507	0.51	66	.015	0.00
IQ—tenth grade	22	.508	0.04	65	.042	1.82
Sex	21	.515	0.30	64	.071	2.00

*$p < .10$.
**$p < .05$.
***$p < .01$.

that is consistent with the observations of Barker and Gump (1964) in their study of large and small high schools. Of course, the likelihood of involvement in extracurricular activities should increase with passage to higher grades, and it is quite possible that the differences between the two school systems will have vanished by the end of the twelfth grade. A reassessment of the students at that time will inform us whether this conjecture is correct.

If the foregoing conjecture concerning the inhibitory effect of the larger school system has any basis in fact, we should find that the poor predictability observed for school system *B* particularly distinguishes those students who are motivationally inhibited in some way. It is even possible that the removal of those subjects will result in higher levels of predictability in the remaining subjects. As a possible index to such motivational inhibition, test anxiety scores can be used. Test anxiety has been linked to fear of failure by Atkinson (1957), and shown to be associated with extreme caution or risk taking. In the present context, we should expect that extracurricular activities pursued by test-anxious subjects would have more to do with coping with fear of failure than with the cognitive dispositions tapped by creativity tasks. Accordingly, test anxiety might function as a moderator variable, enhancing relationships between ideational productivity and extracurricular activities for those low on the moderator, and diminishing such relationships for those high on the moderator.

Support for the foregoing hypothesis was found in moderator analyses carried out in school system *B*, where no overall relations between creativity and outside activities were observed. When the 34 girls of the sample were divided at the median into subsamples low ($N = 19$) and high ($N = 15$) on test anxiety, the resulting correlations between tenth-grade ideational productivity and out-of-school activities were significantly higher for the low-anxious than for the high-anxious

females. For the tenth-grade productivity composite across the four tasks, the correlations with extracurricular activities were .46 ($p < .05$) and .04 for the low and high test-anxious girls, respectively. This difference, given the small subsample sizes, fell short of statistical significance, however ($z = 1.24$). For the tenth-grade creativity composite based exclusively on the uses and patterns task, on the other hand, the resultant correlations were .61 ($p < .01$) and .04 for the low and high test-anxious girls, respectively, and the difference between these coefficients was significant at the .05 level ($z = 1.77$).

Comparable effects were obtained in the same school system when the male sample was divided at the median into low ($N = 21$) and high ($N = 17$) test-anxious subjects. Here, in puzzling contrast with the females, the fifth-grade rather than the tenth-grade creativity data showed differential predictive effects. Correlations for low test-anxious males between fifth-grade ideational productivity and uniqueness composites, on the one hand, and extracurricular activities, on the other, were .39 and .42, respectively, both significant at the .05 level. The equivalent correlation coefficients in the high test-anxious males were −.19 and −.27, respectively, neither significant and both in a direction opposite to expectations. The foregoing correlations also differed significantly (z's of 1.72 and 2.02, respectively, $p < .05$).

In sum, in the larger school system, validation of creative ability measures against out-of-classroom criteria of activity and accomplishment was obtained where anxiety (fear of failure) was not present as a disruptive element. Where the school system was rather large and extracurricular activities were assessed early in the student's school career, only those students who were not debilitated by anxiety showed reasonable consistency between performance on cognitive tasks and relevant "real-world" behavior.

CONCLUSIONS

In our view, the findings offered by the present study, though intricate and complex, are nevertheless encouraging. For the first time, evidence has been adduced pointing to the fact of long-term stability of creativity measures, at least when assessed under specified conditions. Also offered for the first time is evidence suggesting that performance on creativity tasks administered at age 10 or 11 will in certain cases be predictive of activities and accomplishments outside the classroom at age 15 or 16. Both of the foregoing assertions had to be qualified, of course, because of the evidence for failures of consistency and predictability.

A great advantage in the longitudinal study of creativity is the fact that a common set of tasks can be employed almost without modification from the nursery school to the university graduate school. The price one pays for this great convenience, however, is the considerable susceptibility of performance to variations in the testing context. Further, those variations, in turn, appear to interact with the sex and motivational characteristics of the subject. It has been shown that the testing context—whether gamelike or testlike—can affect the magnitude of the correlation between creativity and IQ indices (e.g., Boersma & O'Bryan 1968; Kogan & Morgan 1969). That we were unable to achieve a total separation of these domains of thinking in the present investigation suggests less than perfect success in eliminating an evaluative component from the testing procedures. One must also allow for the possibility of less than perfect independence between the creativity and intelligence domains, particularly where males are concerned. Finally, where talented accomplishments are at issue, it may be most productive to view these as a combined function of creativity, intelligence, motivational dispositions, and the social setting.

As an initial foray into the complexities of longitudinal investigation of creative ability as assessed by the Wallach-Kogan procedures, the present study makes no claims to definitiveness. Additional longitudinal work over the present age span as well as at younger and older age levels will be necessary before any conclusive generalizations can be put forth concerning the long-term stability and predictive power of an associative creativity dimension.

REFERENCES

Atkinson, J. W. Motivational determinants of risk-taking behavior. *Psychological Review*, 1957, **64**, 359–372.

Barker, R. G., & Gump, P. V. *Big school, small school.* Stanford, Calif.: Stanford University Press, 1964.

Boersma, F. J., & O'Bryan, K. An investigation of the relationship between creativity and intelligence under two conditions of testing. *Journal of Personality*, 1968, **36**, 341–348.

Cropley, A. J. A five-year longitudinal study of the validity of creativity tests. *Developmental Psychology*, 1972, **6**, 119–124.

Cropley, A. J., & Maslany, G. W. Reliability and factorial validity of the Wallach-Kogan creativity tests. *British Journal of Psychology*, 1969, **60**, 395–398.

Kogan, N. A clarification of Cropley and Maslany's analysis of the Wallach-Kogan creativity tests. *British Journal of Psychology*, 1971, **62**, 113–117.

Kogan, N., & Morgan, F. T. Task and motivational influences on the assessment of creative and intellective ability in children. *Genetic Psychology Monographs*, 1969, **80**, 91–127.

McNemar, Q. *Psychological statistics.* (3d ed.) New York: Wiley, 1962.

Pankove, E., & Kogan, N. Creative ability and risk taking in elementary school children. *Journal of Personality*, 1968, **36**, 420–439.

Sarason, S. B., Davidson, K. S., Lighthall, F. F., Waite, R. R., & Ruebush, B. K. *Anxiety in elementary school children.* New York: Wiley, 1960.

Torrance, E. P. Prediction of adult creative achievement among high school seniors. *Gifted Child Quarterly*, 1969, **13**, 223–229.

Torrance, E. P., Tan, C. A., & Allman, T. Verbal originality and teacher behavior: a predictive validity study. *Journal of Teacher Education*, 1970, **21**, 335–341.

Wallach, M. A. Creativity. In P. H. Mussen (Ed.), *Carmichael's manual of child psychology.* Vol. **1**. New York: Wiley, 1970. Pp. 1273–1365.

Wallach, M. A., & Kogan, N. *Modes of thinking in young children.* New York: Holt, Rinehart & Winston, 1965.

Wallach, M. A., & Wing, C. W., Jr. *The talented student: a validation of creativity-intelligence distinction.* New York: Holt, Rinehart & Winston, 1969.

Ward, W. C. Creativity in young children. *Child Development*, 1968, **38**, 737–754.

Ward, W. C., Kogan, N., & Pankove, E. Incentive effects in children's creativity. *Child Development*, 1972, **43**.

MATERNAL PERSONALITY CORRELATES OF SONS' CREATIVITY

George Domino

California Psychological Inventory scores of 33 mothers of creative high school males, as identified by both teachers' nominations and test scores, were compared with scores of a control group. Mothers of creative Ss exhibit greater self-assurance, initiative, and interpersonal competence; they prefer change and unstructured demands; they are more insightful about others, more tolerant, and value autonomy and independent endeavor. They are, however, less sociable, less conscientious, less dependable, less inhibited, less concerned about creating a favorable impression, and less nurturant and obliging towards others.

Numerous studies have focused on creativity but relatively little is known about what specific parental aspects may be related to filial creativity. The research literature suggests that the home climate of highly creative persons is significantly divergent from that of less creative in several aspects, and it seems reasonable to assume that parental personality characteristics influence a child's creative development.

Weisberg and Springer (1961), in a study comparing psychiatric interview ratings of parents with children's scores on Torrance's tests of creativity, reported that the parents of highly creative children exhibited greater expressiveness with lesser dominance, and were more indifferent towards their children's regressive tendencies. These investigators characterized the emerging family pattern as involving somewhat distant interactions, little clinging to each other for support, little stress on conformity to parental values, mediocre sexual adjustment, paternal exercise of authority, and maternal ambivalence.

MacKinnon (1962, 1965) was able to identify a number of differentiating parental characteristics from the retrospective reports of his creative architects. For example, the parents were seen as exhibiting an extraordinary respect for the child and confidence in his ability to do what was appropriate, while often there was a lack of intense closeness between parent and child.

Dreyer and Wells (1966) studied the instrumental-expressive orientation, role tension, and degree of autonomy-granting of parents of more and less creative children. Parents of more creative children showed greater intrafamilial variance in their rankings of 10 domestic values, and greater role tension reflecting more individual divergence and expression of feeling.

The present report represents one facet of a research project designed to explore parental factors related to filial creativity. This paper will report on maternal personality correlates of sons' creativity. The focus on mothers reflects the assumption that, at least in the American culture, mothers are likely to have more opportunities than fathers to influence their children's psychological growth.

METHOD

Teachers in nine New York State high schools were asked to nominate students who had produced some observable evidence of creativity. These schools are located in primarily middle- to upper-class suburban areas. The specific directions, modified from Schaefer (1967), and reflecting MacKinnon's (1962) definition of creativity, were:

We are interested in identifying creative students. Please nominate any students you know that you consider as creative. For our purposes, creativity is a process characterized by: 1) originality, novelty, or freshness of approach; 2) adaptiveness to reality in that it must solve a problem, achieve a goal, in general be a reality oriented response; and 3) the original insight or approach must be developed or elaborated. In order to be nominated then, a student must have actually produced a specific product that can be regarded as both novel (fresh, unusual, imaginative) and of genuine merit or value. The original product might be a drawing, poster, poem, display, composition, invention, experimental design, special project, etc. In identifying creative students, please remember that the novelty and merit of individual products may bear little or no relation to the intelligence of a student, or to whether he is an intellectual, hard-worker, beatnik, or troublemaker. Try not to let any personal feelings influence your evaluation of a student's creativity.

A total of 114 male students were nominated, 37 for artistic activities, 62 for scientific activities, and 15 for both types of activities.

The Remote Associates Test (Mednick & Mednick, 1967) and the Alternate Uses test (Wilson, Christen-

From *Journal of Consulting and Clinical Psychology,* 1969, **33,** 180–183. Copyright 1969 by the American Psychological Association. Reprinted by permission.

sen, Merrifield, & Guilford, 1960) were administered to those 114 male nominees. To be retained in the creative group, it was arbitrarily decided that a nominee must obtain a raw score of 15 or above on the Remote Associates Test (14 represents the lowest 50th percentile for college students reported by Mednick & Mednick, 1967), and a score of 26 or above on the Alternate Uses test (equivalent to the 54th percentile of college freshmen norms).

Both the teachers' nominations and the stringent test norms were deliberately used in order to identify Ss who could be justifiably called creative. A total of 38 students met the test criteria. Of these 38 Ss, 12 had been nominated for artistic activities, 17 for scientific, and 9 for both. A chi-square analysis of type of activity versus test criteria yielded a nonsignificant value, indicating that use of the Remote Associates Test and the Alternate Uses test did not discriminate against either the artistic or scientific nominees.

A control group of 38 Ss matched on sex, educational level, grade-point average, and geographical residence, was formed by using school records to identify possible matches, eliminating those nominated as creative or scoring above the cutoff points on the creativity tests. Table 1 gives means and standard deviations of the creativity tests for both control and creative Ss.

Mothers of Ss were then invited to participate in a study of "the influence of the family on children's abilities" by completing the California Psychological Inventory (Gough, 1964a); 33 mothers of creative Ss and 31 mothers of noncreative Ss were tested. These women can be characterized as upper middle class, median age 39, all high school graduates with slightly over one-fourth holding college degrees.

The CPI was used since it has been well validated on large samples of normal Ss and has been used in various studies of creativity (e.g., Helson, 1967; MacKinnon, 1962a, 1962b, 1965). Analyses of mean differences for each of the 18 CPI scales were carried out by means of t tests.

TABLE 1

MEANS AND STANDARD DEVIATIONS OF CREATIVITY TESTS

Ss	Remote Associates Test		Alternate Uses	
	$\bar{X}$	SD	$\bar{X}$	SD
Creative	19.2	3.6	29.2	1.9
Control	12.4	2.7	21.5	2.0

Note.—For Creative, $N = 38$; for Control, $N = 38$.

RESULTS

Twelve mean differences reached statistical significance, 11 at the .01 level and one at the .05 level. The data are presented in Table 2.

Mothers of creative Ss scored significantly higher on Dominance (Do), Capacity for Status (Cs), Tolerance (To), Achievement via Independence (Ai), Psychological-Mind-edness (Py), and Flexibility (Fx); they scored significantly lower on Sociability (Sy), Responsibility (Re), Socialization (So), Self-Control (Sc), Good Impression (Gi), and Femininity (Fe).

DISCUSSION

Although the CPI profiles for both groups are above average as compared to the general population, the results clearly indicate that mothers of creative Ss differ significantly from mothers of noncreative Ss on several dimensions of personality. Mothers of creative Ss exhibit greater self-assurance and initiative (Do) and interpersonal competence (Cs); they prefer change and unstructured demands (Fx); they are more insightful about others (Py), but at the same time more tolerant (To), and they value autonomy and independent endeavor (Ai). They are, however, less sociable (Sy), exhibit less responsibility (Re) and social probity (So), are less inhibited (Sc), less concerned about creating a favorable impression (Gi), and less nurturant and obliging toward others (Fe).

The general picture generated by this CPI mean profile is that of a highly independent and capable woman perceptive in her interpersonal relationships but little disposed to worry about the impression she creates. She can adapt to change and variety, and in fact is restive when faced with rules and constraints. She is free in her expression of impulse, but perhaps not always dependable.

These themes emerging from the CPI profile have in many cases been previously reported as characteristic of creative persons (cf. Barron, 1965; Gough, 1964b; MacKinnon, 1963).

One theme relates to interpersonal endeavor. These women have the assurance, the versatility and ascendancy necessary to achieve a position of high community visibility. Yet they do not. Of the 33 mothers of creative Ss, only four were actively involved in some community activity, as opposed to 17 of the 31 mothers of noncreative Ss ($\chi^2 = 15.17$, $p < .01$). They are also moderately indifferent to social demands: of the six CPI scales addressed to various aspects of socialization and control, they score significantly lower on four (Re, So, Sc, Gi). These results are consonant with those of Dreyer and Wells (1966) who found that the mothers of creative children were much less concerned with a place in the community and more concerned with everyday interests. MacKinnon (1961) reported that his creative archi-

TABLE 2

CPI Scores of Mothers of Creative and Noncreative Adolescents

CPI Scale	Creative		Noncreative		t
	$\bar{X}$	SD	$\bar{X}$	SD	
Dominance (Do)	30.2	5.2	26.1	4.9	3.25**
Capacity for Status (Cs)	23.8	3.1	19.2	3.3	5.74**
Sociability (Sy)	22.7	4.7	26.9	4.6	3.61**
Social Presence (Sp)	35.4	5.3	35.2	5.2	0.07
Self-Acceptance (Sa)	22.9	3.7	22.6	2.9	0.36
Well-Being (Wb)	38.8	3.6	39.5	4.4	0.69
Responsibility (Re)	29.1	4.5	34.6	3.9	5.48**
Socialization (So)	35.6	5.1	42.1	4.6	5.36**
Self-Control (Sc)	27.5	7.2	35.5	6.1	4.81**
Tolerance (To)	27.3	4.3	24.1	3.9	3.12**
Good Impression (Gi)	16.6	5.5	20.3	6.1	2.54*
Communality (Cm)	24.5	1.8	25.1	1.3	1.53
Achievement via Conformance (Ac)	29.3	4.2	29.4	3.7	0.10
Achievement via Independence (Ai)	24.3	3.8	21.1	2.9	3.80**
Intellectual Efficiency (Ie)	44.8	5.2	42.9	4.1	1.62
Psychological-Mindedness (Py)	15.8	2.9	12.6	2.4	4.82**
Flexibility (Fx)	14.9	3.6	11.3	3.3	4.17**
Femininity (Fe)	22.4	3.5	24.8	3.7	2.66**

Note.—For Creative; $N = 33$; for Noncreative, $N = 31$.
* $p < .05$.
** $p < .01$.

tects revealed less desire to be included in group activities than any other group studied by him and his coworkers. Yet, when these architects chose to participate they did so with consummate skill.

A second theme concerns interpersonal closeness. These mothers are perceptive individuals, alert to the needs of others, informal, tolerant, and observant (To, Py, Fx). Yet, these socially desirable characteristics are counterweighted by a degree of indifference and detachment (Gi, Sy). These results are consonant with the recollections of MacKinnon's achitects who reported a lack of intense closeness with their parents. They also agree with the findings of Getzels and Jackson (1962) that mothers of more creative children were less observant of failings in their children than were mothers of less creative.

A third theme reflects impulse expression, as shown primarily by the lower mean on the Sc scale, but also supported by lower means on So and Re. Barron (1957) has seen this factor as indicating the potentiality of the pleasure principle occasionally to become ascendant over the reality principle. One might speculate that this reduction of self-control allows the person to regress in the service of the ego, and that mothers of creative children are themselves more creative than their peers.

A fourth theme concerns initiative. These women exhibit certain personality characteristics which in our culture tend to be labeled as more masculine. This can be seen in the significantly higher means on the Do and Ai scales, as well as by the lower mean on the Fe scale. Helson (1967) has reported that a masculine component is an important factor in the syndrome underlying creativity in women.

A final theme has to do with independence. Independence in thought and action as a characteristic of creative persons has been reported by several investigators. Dreyer and Wells (1966) reported that the mothers of high creative children stressed emotional security, leading to greater confidence and independence in their offspring. MacKinnon (1961) found that creativity in architects correlated highly with self-assertive independence. The present CPI findings are consonant in revealing these mothers to be more independent, autonomous, and self-reliant.

It is interesting to note a possible (but superficial) discordance in these themes: high social poise with little affiliation; interpersonal insight with indifference; achievement drive and masculine initiative with biological femininity. Thus there is a balance between contrasting dynamic forces, in which positive and negative characteristics are both allowed expression. Jung's concept of the transcendent function which accomplishes the successful integration of opposites is relevant here.

The findings presented here indicate quite clearly that mothers of creative adolescents possess personality characteristics not only significantly different from those of mothers of noncreative adolescents, but quite similar to those observed among creative adults. Although there is no direct evidence, it is reasonable to postulate that the mothers of creative *S*s are themselves more creative than the general population, and that both their personality characteristics and their creativity are evocative of greater creativity in their children.

REFERENCES

BARRON, F. Originality in relation to personality and intellect. *Journal of Personality,* 1957, 25, 730–742.

BARRON, F. The psychology of creativity. In, *New directions in psychology: II.* New York: Holt, Rinehart & Winston, 1965.

DREYER, A., & WELLS, M. Parental values, parental control, and creativity in young children. *Journal of Marriage and the Family,* 1966, 28, 83–88.

GETZELS, J., & JACKSON, P. *Creativity and intelligence.* New York: Wiley, 1962.

GOUGH, H. G. *California Psychological Inventory manual.* (Rev. ed.) Palo Alto, Calif.: Consulting Psychologists Press, 1964. (a)

GOUGH, H. G. Identifying the creative man. *Journal of Value Engineering,* 1964, 2, 5–12. (b)

HELSON, R. Personality characteristics and developmental history of creative college women. *Genetic Psychology Monographs,* 1967, 76, 205–256.

MACKINNON, D. W. The personality correlates of creativity: A study of American architects. In Gerhard S. Nielsen (Ed.), *Proceedings of the XIV International Congress of Applied Psychology, Copenhagen, 1961.* Vol. 2. Copenhagen: Munksgaard, 1962. (a)

MACKINNON, D. W. The nature and nurture of creative talent. *American Psychologist,* 1962, 17, 484–495. (b)

MACKINNON, D. W. Creativity and images of the self. In R. W. White (Ed.), *The study of lives.* New York: Atherton, 1963.

MACKINNON, D. W. Personality and the realization of creative potential. *American Psychologist,* 1965, 20, 273–281.

MEDNICK, S. A., & MEDNICK, M. T. *Examiner's manual for the Remote Associates Test.* Boston: Houghton Mifflin, 1967.

SCHAEFER, C. E. Biographical inventory correlates of scientific and artistic creativity in adolescents. Unpublished doctoral dissertation, Fordham University, 1967.

WEISBERG, P. S., & SPRINGER, K. J. Environmental factors in creative function. *Archives of General Psychiatry,* 1961, 5, 554–564.

WILSON, R. C., CHRISTENSEN, P. R., MERRIFIELD, P. R., & GUILFORD, J. P. *Alternate uses: Manual.* Beverly Hills, Calif.: Sheridan Supply, 1960.

PEER GROUP CHOICE AS A DEVICE FOR SCREENING INTELLECTUALLY GIFTED CHILDREN

Kent L. Granzin
Wilma J. Granzin

Abstract. Sociometric techniques were investigated as a means of identifying fourth-grade gifted children. Eighty-eight pupils in three homogeneously grouped classrooms distinguished between 15 traits characteristic of gifted children and 15 traits descriptive of children in general. After a one-month interval, subjects listed the names of their classmates who were perceived to possess each of the 15 traits of gifted children. Significant Spearman rank-order correlation coefficients were found between frequency of peer nomination and teacher rank of giftedness. Results tentatively suggested that peer nomination can serve as a useful device for screening gifted children.

While standardized, objective psycho-educational tests and observations by teachers currently provide acceptable means for screening intellectually gifted children in the schools, there is an ever-present need for new methods to aid this task. This need for new screening devices is particularly acute where the cost of administering individual intelligence tests makes their use for accurate identification impractical.

Reprinted with permission of the authors and publisher from *Gifted Child Quarterly,* 1969, **13,** 189–194.

Sociometric techniques have been successfully used in singling out children gifted in terms of their competency in social interactions (Gold, 1965). In particular, the "Guess Who" technique has been suggested for screening children in terms of their non-intellectual alilities (Jarecky, 1959). This paper reports results of a preliminary study to determine the value of using sociometric methods as a device for screening intellectually gifted children. The study sought to determine: (1) whether fourth-grade children are able to recognize characteristics of the gifted child; and (2) whether these pupils, both gifted and non-gifted, can associate these traits with those of their peers who possess them.

A priori, it seems children must be able to distinguish traits of intellectual giftedness if they are to recognize their peers who possess them. Therefore, it was first hypothesized that fourth-grade pupils are able to discriminate traits of giftedness from traits applying to all children. It would further seem this ability to discriminate depends on the child's intellect. A second hypothesis investigated was that gifted children are better able to distinguish characteristics of giftedness than are non-gifted children. Given that pupils do recognize gifted traits, the question remains whether they can perceive them in their peers. Therefore, a third hypothesis was that rankings of their peers by both gifted and non-gifted children agree with rankings by another acceptable standard.

PROCEDURES

The instruments were administered to fourth-grade students in a single public elementary school in Urbana, Illinois during April and May, 1967. These children came from families having a relatively high socio-economic status, and had a median group-IQ score of 121. Regular classroom assignment came from dividing the pupils into three rooms on the basis of their intellectual potential, as judged by teacher observation and group-IQ scores. Thus, Room A was the "gifted" room and contained those pupils adjudged to have the greatest potential, while Room B was the "middle" group, and Room C had "low" students.

The first instrument consisted of thirty randomly-ordered characteristics descriptive of grade-school children. Fifteen characteristics pertained primarily to gifted children and fifteen represented children in general; i.e., furnished control traits. Traits of gifted children were such as: "Learns quickly and easily;" "Thinks clearly and reasons things out;" and "Reads books that are above his grade level." These traits were culled from several writings presenting them as characteristic of gifted children (Kough and DeHaan, 1955; Hildreth, 1966; Laycock, 1957). Control traits were such as: "Has good manners;" "Shows kindness toward others;" and "Behaves well in class." These traits were selected from a list of almost 500 phrases suggested by fifth-and sixth-graders as having general applicability. After the listing of each trait, a five-choice Likert scale gave subjects these alternatives for indicating whether the trait represented giftedness: Strongly agree, Agree, Undecided, Disagree, and Strongly Disagree.

This instrument was administered to the three groups of students, one room at a time. One of the authors read the subjects a short introduction to the nature of the questions, and stimulated a ten-minute discussion to ensure the children understood the basic concepts involved. The subjects then indicated on the instrument whether they believed each of the thirty traits fitted only gifted children. Choices were scored from +2 for Strongly agree through +1, 0, -1, to -2 for Strongly disagree. For each pupil, total score for the fifteen control traits was subtracted from total score for the fifteen gifted, maintaining algebraic signs. Thus, the control traits served to "normalize" the pupil's score and allow for conservatism or liberality in judgment.

Individual scores for all 88 subjects using this instrument were rank-ordered, and the Wilcoxen Matched-Pairs, Signed-Ranks Test (Siegel, 1956) was applied to test whether pupils were significantly able to distinguish between gifted and control traits. Then scores were separated into those for subjects having group-IQ scores of 120 or higher and those below 120. Hereafter, the former are referred to as "gifted," the latter as "non-gifted." The Mann-Whitney U Test (Siegel, 1956) was used to determine whether the "gifted" and "non-gifted" groups differed in ability to perceive traits pertaining only to gifted children.

The second instrument, administered a month later, featured the same fifteen gifted traits, each followed by five blanks where subjects could write names of their peers. The subjects were told to list as many as five of their classmates whom they felt best represented the given trait. They were assured that listing less than five—or none at all—was perfectly acceptable. During administration subjects were instructed to concentrate on the meaning of each individual trait and the children it related to; thus, no mention was made of the concept of giftedness. While 88 subjects (including fourth-graders in a combination third and fourth grade room) took the first instrument, to avoid confusion produced by identification with third-grade peers only the 77 pupils in Rooms A, B, and C took the second instrument. No recall effect suggesting interaction between the two instruments was noticed.

The number of times a pupil's name was mentioned by classroom peers was recorded, with no distinction among traits with which it was associated. The resulting data consisted of total times each individual pupil was mentioned. (Totals for those absent were discarded to avoid introducing bias due to those who were "out of sight, out of mind.") For each of the three rooms, pupils were ranked on the basis of: (1) teacher judgment; (2) group-IQ score; (3) number of times mentioned by gifted classroom peers; and (4) number of mentions by all classroom peers. Spearman Rank Correlation Coefficients for each room were computed to indicate degree of agreement between rankings by teachers and rankings by group-IQ scores— to ensure the former provided a (quasi-) standard. Then agreement of both gifted peers' mentions and all peers' mentions with the standard was similarly checked.

RESULTS

Table 1 presents extreme and central scores on the first instrument for the 88 subjects who indicated whether the traits were general for all children or characteristic primarily of the gifted. Scores are broken down also for those scoring 120 or above on the group-IQ test and those scoring lower. Scores of 11 elementary teachers who also took the test are furnished for comparison purposes. Null hypothesis that all pupils were unable to distinguish gifted from general traits was rejected at a significance better than .001, and the alternative that they could distinguish was accepted. In addition, the null hypothesis that gifted pupils were unable to more readily recognize traits of giftedness than their non-gifted peers was rejected at significance better than .005 (one-tailed test). Its alternative that they could more easily recognize them was also accepted.

TABLE 1

Extreme and Central Scores on Trait Recognition

Subjects	Number	Low	Median	High
All pupils	88	-11	+12	+42
Gifted	47	-8	+14	+42
Non-Gifted	41	-11	+7	+35
Teachers	11	+16	+29	+48

Table 2 presents a breakdown of the 3685 times pupils in the three classrooms were mentioned by a peer as possessing one of the fifteen gifted traits. Increasing numbers of per-pupil "mentions" with decreasing ability of those mentioned (that is, Room A had lowest average mentions per trait per pupil, while Room C had highest) suggests subjects' perception of those possessing gifted traits is a relative matter.

TABLE 2

Breakdown of Times Pupils Mentioned by Rooms, Pupils, and Traits

Type of Breakdown	Room A (27)*	Room B (26)	Room C (24)
Total Mentions per Room	1232	1252	1201
Average Mentions per Pupil	45.7	48.2	50.4
Average Mentions per Trait per Pupil	3.0	3.2	3.4

Number of pupils in the room is shown in parenthesis.

Table 3 indicates the distribution of the number of times each pupil was mentioned by all peers in his classroom. These figures reinforce the above suggestion that pupils name those most able among their peers, regardless of whether they qualify in an absolute sense.

TABLE 3

Extreme and Central Numbers of Mentions by All Classroom Peers

Rank of Pupil	Room A	Room B	Room C
High Pupil	206(7.9)*	126(5.6)	149(6.5)
Median Pupil	41(1.6)	41(1.6))	45(2.0)
Low Pupil	10(0.4)	11(0.4)	17(0.7)

Figures in parenthesis give the average number of mentions per peer.

Table 4 presents results of analysis of the data summarized in Tables 2 and 3. This analysis compared these peer rankings, and those from group-IQ scores, with teacher rankings. Table 4 gives Spearman Rank Correlation Coefficients (rs) for these comparisons. Since correlations by themselves have little meaning, the null hypothesis that rs differed from 0 only by chance was tested. On all counts the null hypothesis was rejected, resulting in acceptance of the alternative that the underlying standards used to measure giftedness for each pair of methods were related. That is, underlying rationale for ranking of, say, gifted peers is similar enough to the teacher's to give significant correlation. Results of this test of significance are shown below RS in the table.

TABLE 4

Spearman Correlation Coefficients and Levels of Significance for Teacher Rankings Vs. Three Other Ranking Methods

Ranking Method	Room A	Room B	Room C
Group-IQ Scores	.50	.47	.83
	p .01	p .01	p .01
By Gifted Peers	.41 (25)*	.59 (15)	.46 (2)
	p .05	p .01	p .05
By All Peers	.40 (27)	.49 (26)	.63 (24)
	p .05	p .01	p .01

Number of pupils scoring their peers is shown in parenthesis.

Rankings by group-IQ scores, by gifted peers, and by all peers correlate significantly with the quasi-standard, rankings by classroom teacher. Both IQ and rankings by all peers are generally more significant than rankings by gifted peers. While this finding is surprising in view of the results obtained by scores on trait recognition, the difference is not clear-cut.

DISCUSSION

Results support all three hypotheses concerning ability of fourth-grade children to recognize traits of gifted children and to further recognize those of their peers who possess them, at least in a relative sense. In addition, while data showed that fourth-graders in general can distinguish general traits from those of giftedness, those possessing these gifted traits themselves perform better than their non-gifted peers in this test of recognition. Had the first hypothesis not been confirmed, it would have been pointless to continue investigation into pupils' ability to apply their recognition ability to the task of distinguishing those of their peers possessing traits of giftedness.

While teacher's ranking of students' ability does not furnish an unequivocal standard for comparison, it does provide a point of reference. Rankings by group-IQ scores correlated highly with the quasi-standard, supporting the latter's usefulness for comparison purposes. Confirmation of the third hypothesis was provided by significant correlations between this standard and rankings of classroom peers by both gifted and all pupils. One other limitation worthy of note is the arbitrary division of pupils into gifted and non-gifted groups on the basis of IQ score of 120. There is, however, no reason to believe that any other such yardstick would have provided results different from those presented here.

Although the children participating formed a small sample which is unrepresentative of the intellectual ability and socio-economic background of fourth-graders across the nation, it appears children at this school level understand the concept of giftedness. Further, these children are able to indicate the *relative* order of intellectual ability of their peers. To provide indication of giftedness in the *absolute* sense, if indeed fourth-graders are capable of providing it, an instrument different from that used in this study must be administered. In addition, usefullness of this sociometric method can be expected to differ with grade level. Informal investigation of ratings by third-graders suggests that children below the fourth-grade level may have difficulty in accurately perceiving the gifted among their peers.

Finally, while the method presented in this report seems to hold promise for further development into a *screening* device for recognizing children who may be gifted, *identification* must ultimately be left to more sophisticated tools, such as the individual Stanford-Binet Scale, whenever their administration is feasible.

SUMMARY

Fourth-graders were asked to distinguish between fifteen traits pertaining primarily to gifted children and fifteen traits pertaining to children in general. They were later asked to name those of their peers possessing the fifteen gifted traits. Analysis of results showed both gifted and non-gifted pupils able to distinguish traits of giftedness, although the former group performed significantly better. Peer-group choice of gifted pupils agreed significantly with teacher rankings, although no superior performance by gifted pupils themselves was noted on this task. These results suggest the value of peer-group choice as an additional method for screening potentially gifted children.

REFERENCES

Gold, Milton J. *Education of the Intellectually Gifted*. Columbus, Ohio: Charles E. Merrill Books, 1965.

Hildreth, Gertrude H. *Introduction to the Gifted*. New York: McGraw-Hill, 1966.

Jarecky, Roy K. "Identification of the Socially Gifted." *Exceptional Children,* 1959, *26*, 415-419.

Kough, Jack, and Robert F. DeHaan. *Teacher's Guidance Handbook. Vol. I: Identifying Children with Special Needs*. Elementary School Edition. Chicago: Science Research Associates, 1955.

Laycock, Samuel. *Gifted Children*. Toronto: Capp-Clark, 1957.

Namy, Elmer. "Intellectual and Academic Characteristics of Fourth Grade Gifted and Pseudogifted Students." *Exceptional Children,* 1967, *34*, 15-18.

Siegel, Sidney. *Nonparametric Statistics for the Behavioral Sciences*. New York: McGraw-Hill, 1956.

SUCCESSFUL TEACHERS OF THE GIFTED

William E. Bishop

Abstract: The purpose of this study was to analyze selected characteristics of high school teachers who were identified as successful by intellectually gifted high achieving students, and to discover what differentiated these teachers from teachers not so identified. More specifically, the study was concerned with personal and social traits and behaviors, professional attitudes and educational viewpoints, and classroom behavior patterns of effective teachers of gifted high school students.

WHILE it is widely recognized that the success of any special educational program depends largely on the teacher, very little research attention has been given to the special qualities which may be desirable for teachers of gifted and talented students. If it is true that learning emphases and teacher roles vary in relation to the characteristics of the students taught, it is important to gain increased understanding of the traits and behaviors which characterize successful teachers of the gifted.

The basic research question of this study was: What characterizes high school teachers who are identified as successful by intellectually gifted, high achieving students and what differentiates these teachers from teachers not so identified? More specifically, the investigation attempted to discover answers to the following questions:

1. What are the personal and social traits and behaviors which characterize high school teachers who are identified as successful by intellectually gifted, high achieving students?
2. What professional attitudes and educational viewpoints characterize these teachers?
3. What are the patterns of classroom behavior of teachers who are judged effective by gifted students? How do they perceive their teaching role and how do they assess their effectiveness in this regard?

It is believed that the identification and description of teachers who are successful in working with gifted students will provide reliable information as a basis for increased understanding of the desirable qualities for teachers of the gifted. The identified teachers may provide a model or prototype insofar as the traits and behaviors investigated by this study are concerned. The description and analysis of their characteristics might provide useful clues for those who are concerned with the preservice education and the inservice placement of teachers for gifted students. It might also provide guidance to teachers who are faced with the challenge, whether in regular or special classes, of adequately providing for the special educational needs of intellectually superior students.

Background of Study

The study was an outgrowth of the First Annual Governor's Honors Program for gifted and talented high school students in Georgia. Of the 186 high school seniors from 65 different school systems who participated in an academic area of the program, 181 completed questionnaires wherein they listed their high school teachers for academic subjects prior to their participation in the Governor's Honors Program. Each student indicated the teacher who, in his judgment, best represented each of twelve descriptive statements on the questionnaire relative to teacher traits and/or behavior. He selected and discussed the teacher who was, in general, the best and most successful teacher for him—the one who had made the greatest difference in his educational career.

Study Groups. From the lists of teachers submitted by the students, three groups were selected for study. One group included 109 teachers selected by one or more gifted students as his "most successful" high school teacher. Another group included 97 teachers who were selected at random from a list of over 500 teachers who had formerly taught students in the First Governor's Honors Program, but who had not been selected by any of these students as his "most successful" teacher. The group of

From *Exceptional Children,* 1968, **34,** 317–325. Reprinted by permission of The Council for Exceptional Children.

109 identified teachers was called the identified group; the group of 97 "nonselected" teachers was called the validity sample.

The third group included 30 teachers in the identified group who were selected for intensive study, including a personal interview. This group, called the interview sample, was a stratified random sample of the total number of identified teachers. It included 30 teachers from 29 different schools of varying sizes in all sections of Georgia.

Sources of Data. Every teacher in the study completed a copy of the Teacher Characteristics Schedule (Ryans, 1960). The schedule (TCS) is a 176 item inventory which purports to estimate teachers' classroom behaviors, attitudes, educational viewpoints, verbal ability, and emotional adjustment from their responses to multiple choice items relating to preferences, judgments, activities, personal background, etc. The items have been empirically validated and are known to be correlated with more direct criterion data reflecting teacher traits and behaviors. The following teacher traits and behaviors are estimated by the TCS scales (Ryans, 1960):

warm, understanding, friendly versus aloof, egocentric, restricted teacher classroom behavior

responsible, businesslike, systematic versus evading, unplanned, slipshod classroom behavior

stimulating, imaginative versus dull, routine teacher classroom behavior

favorable versus unfavorable opinions of pupils

favorable versus unfavorable opinions of democratic classroom procedures

favorable versus unfavorable opinions of administrative and other school personnel

learning centered ("traditional" or "directive") versus child-centered ("permissive" or "indirective") educational viewpoints

superior verbal understanding (comprehension) versus poor verbal understanding

emotional stability (adjustment) versus instability [p. 388].

A response analysis of the TCS items provided additional data relative to the personal and professional status of teachers in the different study groups. Questionnaires were completed by the students who selected the teachers for this study. These questionnaires provided extensive data relative to the identified teachers.

In addition to information obtained from the TCS and the student questionnaires, data on the interview sample were collected from the following sources: (a) personal interview with each teacher, (b) Wechsler Adult Intelligence Scale (verbal section), (c) Edwards Personal Preference Schedule, and (d) college transcripts.

In the personal interview, each teacher was asked to respond to a series of open ended questions relating to role perception, professional aspirations, attitudes toward gifted students, and related issues. As part of the interview, an assessment was made of the teacher's general intellectual ability through the administration of the verbal section of the Wechsler Adult Intelligence Scale. Written permission was obtained from each teacher to review copies of his college transcripts on file in the Division of Certification at the State Department of Education. Copies of the Teacher Characteristics Schedule and the Edwards Personal Preference Schedule (EPPS) were left with each teacher to complete and return.

Each of the sources listed above provided data relative to important teacher characteristics. One major phase of the study was concerned with a description and comparison of teachers included in the identified group and the validity sample. Other aspects of the study were confined to a description and analysis of characteristics of those teachers in the interview sample, as revealed by the more extensive study procedures employed with this group.

Discussion

Major study findings are presented within the framework of the specific questions listed in the statement of the problem. The first question was stated as follows: What are the unique personal and social traits and behaviors which characterize high school teachers who are identified as successful by intellectually gifted, high achieving students?

It has been proposed that "teachers of the gifted should be deviant with respect to those qualities common to the gifted group [Ward, 1961, p. 115]." Several findings of this study lent empirical support to the validity of this proposal. One of the areas where this was best demonstrated was the intellectual level and interests of the identified teachers.

Intelligence Level of Identified Teachers. Several findings suggested the intellectual superiority of teachers identified as successful by gifted high school students. The most cogent was the mean score earned on the Wechsler Adult Intelligence Scale (WAIS), which was given to teachers in the interview sample. Their mean score of 128 on the WAIS placed them 1.87 standard deviations above the mean, or in the upper 3 percent relative to the general adult population. While giftedness is generally conceded to be a broader concept than can be represented by a single IQ, it is recognized that those who score in the upper 3 percent on an individually administered test of intelligence evidence mental superiority.

Additional evidence of the superior mental ability of the identified teachers was revealed by their mean score on the scale of the TCS, which is purported to estimate the respondent's verbal ability (comprehension). The mean score of teachers in the identified group was significantly higher than the mean score of teachers in the validity sample on this TCS dimension.

Teacher Interests and Activities. Several significant differences between the identified group and the validity sample were revealed in the intellectual nature of the personal interests and activities they pursued. These data suggested a total life pattern of the identified teachers dissimilar to other teachers. This was perhaps best demonstrated by their literary interests. A significantly higher percent of the identified group than the validity sample followed what they called a literary hobby. This was evidenced in several ways. A significantly higher percent belonged to a book purchasing club. A significantly larger number frequently read collections of poems, essays, stories, etc. The same was true relative to the reading of biographies. A larger proportion of the identified group indicated that they frequently read fiction, read book reviews in newspapers or magazines, and preferred *Harper's* magazine to *Saturday Evening Post, Popular Mechanics,* or *Redbook.*

Teachers in the identified group also indicated a higher level of cultural interest and involvement. A significantly higher proportion stated that they attended concerts, exhibits, and the like when the opportunities were available. A higher percent had visited an art gallery or museum within the past year and a significantly greater number had bought some painting or art work within the past year.

The desire for intellectual growth was cited as a reason for choosing teaching as a career by a significantly greater number of the identified teachers. Continued evidence of this desire was reflected in the higher incidence of teachers in the identified group who had taken a college course within the past two years..

Achievement Level of Teachers. It has been suggested that gifted students have much to gain from teachers who manifest high intelligence and characteristics positively correlated with superior intellect (Ward, 1962). High achievement tends to be positively correlated with high intelligence. Several data obtained in this study indicated that the identified teachers were characterized by a high achievement level.

A strong need to achieve on the part of the successful teachers was reflected in their mean score on the achievement scale of the Edwards Personal Preference Schedule (Edwards, 1959). Edwards defines achievement as "the need to do one's best, to be successful, to accomplish tasks requiring skill and effort . . . to do a difficult job well . . . to be able to do things better than others [Edwards, 1959, p. 11]." In six of seven comparisons with normative data and with teachers in other study groups (Merrill, 1960; Guba, et al., 1959; Jackson and Guba, 1957), the interview sample showed a higher mean score on achievement. In three comparisons the mean score on achievement was significantly higher.

Evidence of high achievement was also reflected in the past scholastic performance of teachers in the interview sample. These teachers earned a mean grade point average at the undergraduate level of 2.95 in professional education courses and 3.14 in courses in their major teaching area, based on a 4.00 system. At the graduate level, they earned a mean grade point average of 3.30 in professional education courses and 3.48 in the teaching area preparation. Over 70 percent of the teachers in the identified group indicated that they were "good" or "outstanding" students while in college.

Less direct data relative to the identified teachers' high achievement level were provided by other findings of this study. Ninety-three percent of the identified teachers indicated that they chose teaching as a career because they enjoyed past satisfactory experience in school work. A significantly greater number of teachers in the identified group were advised by former teachers that they would be good teachers.

While the teacher advisor may have had numerous and varied reasons for his advice, it seems unlikely that the suggestion would have been proposed to a low achiever.

Student descriptions of the selected teachers included repeated testimony to the achievement level of the teachers. A thorough command of their subject matter and a patent desire to increase their own knowledge and understanding were frequently noted by the students. The following excerpts from students' statements about different teachers are representative:

> Her own desire for more knowledge has inspired most of her students and awakened in us a longing to reach out and to learn.
>
> Her vast knowledge and interest in a variety of subjects influenced me to desire learning for the sake of becoming a well-rounded, intelligent person rather than merely for the sake of making high grades.
>
> Through her enthusiasm for her subject and for innumerable other topics, she instills in her classroom an atmosphere of intoxicating discovery.

Other Personal Traits and Behaviors. Several other traits and behaviors of teachers were considered in this study. On several variables there were no significant differences between teachers identified as successful by gifted students and teachers not so identified. These included such variables as sex, marital status, type of undergraduate institution attended, highest degree held, course work preparation, and extent of association with professional organizations.

Two personal variables on which teachers in the two groups did differ were age and length of teaching experience. These differences were not great, however, and could not be tested for statistical significance. The median age of teachers in the identified group was in the 40 to 44 age range; the median age of teachers in the validity sample was 45 to 49. The median length of teaching experience for the two groups was from 10 to 14 years and 15 to 19 years, respectively.

The use of student evaluations as a research procedure in studies on teaching effectiveness has been widely criticized. Morsh and Wilder (1965) contend that students will choose a teacher who is "young, genial, and entertaining, while the serious, more experienced individual . . . is rarely popular [p. 61]." This criticism of student evaluations for research purposes does not seem justified, relative to the present study. Less than 2 percent of the selected teachers were in the 20 to 24 age range, while more than 8 percent were in the 60 or over category. Fewer than 3 percent of these teachers had less than three years' teaching experience and nearly 30 percent had 20 or more years' experience. It is true, however, that the students preferred teachers who were slightly younger and less experienced than their teaching colleagues.

Professional Attitudes and Educational Viewpoints

The second question posed in the statement of the problem was: What professional attitudes and educational viewpoints characterize these teachers (those identified as successful by gifted students)? Data relative to this question were collected from several sources and are discussed in this section.

Two of the teacher characteristics estimated by the TCS relate to professional attitude and philosophy. One purports to estimate favorable versus unfavorable attitudes toward pupils, and the other indicates learning centered "traditional" versus student centered "permissive" educational viewpoints. TCS results for the identified group on these two scales indicated that these teachers had more student centered educational viewpoints and more favorable attitudes toward students than teachers in the validity sample. The difference was statistically significant on both dimensions.

The results of the EPPS administration lent additional support to the conclusion that identified teachers were characterized by sensitivity to others, which was probably reflected in a student centered approach to teaching. Mean scores on five EPPS variables were especially suggestive of this attitude.

The EPPS variable on which the interview sample scored most consistently and significantly higher than comparison groups (Merrill, 1960; Guba, Jackson, and Bidwell, 1959; Jackson and Guba, 1957) was Intraception. Edwards defines Intraception as follows:

> To analyze one's motives and feelings, to observe others, to understand how others feel about problems, to put one's self in another's place, to judge people by why they do things rather than by what they do, to analyze the behavior of others, to analyze the motives of others, to predict how others will act [Edwards, 1959, p. 11].

An EPPS variable on which both male and female teachers in this study scored lower than all comparison groups was Autonomy. In five cases the difference was statistically significant. Autonomy has been defined by Guba, Jackson, and Bidwell (1959) as the need "to act without regard to the opinion of others [p. 3]." An EPPS variable on which female teachers in the study scored significantly lower than the three groups with whom they were compared was Exhibition, which has been defined by Guba and his associates as the need "to talk cleverly for the sake of impressing others, to be the center of attention [Guba, et al., p. 3]."

Male teachers in the interview sample scored significantly lower than three of four groups with whom they were compared on two EPPS variables, Succorance and Aggression. Succorance reflects a self centered interest in the need "to gain encouragement and sympathy from others when one is depressed or hurt [Guba, et al., p. 3]." Aggression has been defined as "the need to show anger and criticize others openly [Guba, et al., p. 4]."

This profile of EPPS results suggests that the teachers in this study were not overly concerned with themselves. They seemed to be sensitive to the feelings and needs of others, e.g., their students.

The teachers' favorable attitudes toward students also were manifested specifically in relation to gifted students. All teachers in the study were asked to indicate what type of class they would prefer to teach. A significantly higher percentage (.01 level) of the identified group than the validity sample stated that they would prefer to teach a class of exceptionally bright students rather than a class of average students, a class of slow and retarded students, or a class of children of widely varying ability. Nearly three-fourths of the identified group stated this preference. Not one of them stated that he would prefer to teach a class of slow or retarded students. A significantly higher percentage of the teachers in the validity sample than in the identified group indicated that they would prefer to teach a class of average children. Favorable attitudes toward gifted students were further evidenced in the teacher interviews with the interview sample. Every teacher in the sample expressed his support for special educational attention to the gifted, though the specific proposals for meeting the need varied widely. Most preferred special grouping by ability, achievement, and/or interest.

Teacher Classroom Behavior

The third specific question listed in the statement of the problem was stated as follows: What are the patterns of classroom behavior of teachers who are judged effective by gifted students? How do these teachers perceive their teaching role and responsibility and how do they assess their success in this regard? Conclusions based on study findings relative to this question are presented below.

Three of the dimensions estimated by the TCS relate to teacher classroom behavior. On two of those three variables, the identified teachers differed significantly from the teachers not so identified. The identified group scored significantly higher on the scale which provides an estimate of the respondent's responsible, businesslike, systematic versus evading, unplanned, slipshod classroom behavior. They also scored significantly higher than the validity sample on the scale which purports to measure the teacher's stimulating, imaginative versus dull, routine teacher classroom behavior.

It was previously noted that teachers in the identified group also scored significantly higher on the TCS variables which reflect favorable attitudes toward students and student centered educational viewpoints.

The estimates of teacher classroom behaviors of the identified teachers indicated by TCS results are supported by other findings of this study. Testimony of the identified teachers' stimulating and imaginative classroom behavior was provided by the student questionnaire responses. The most frequent reason the students mentioned for having selected the teachers for the study was the teacher's stimulating, motivational, and inspirational qualities. Typical student comments in this regard follow:

Mrs. E., more than anyone else, made me realize how much I had to learn. Only when I saw this did my real education begin.

She presented new horizons rather than new barriers. . . . Above all, she set an example—an example of excellence.

Mrs. S. encouraged me to aspire to seemingly unattainable heights, some of which I have already reached.

Mr. D. showed me that my opinion *is* of value, and explained the importance of individual thinking.

Mr. T. makes a student do a great deal of thinking for himself.

Her dedication to teaching has made a lasting impression on me. It is because of Mrs. P. and her work that I have chosen teaching as a career.

Mr. H. was one of the few teachers I've had who provoked me and my classmates to think clearly and speak factually. He encouraged us to evaluate, analyze and understand whatever we heard and read.

She stimulates the willing and the unwilling to accomplish on their own. Her continued interest encourages the faltering and spurs the worker to seek higher goals.

The second most frequently mentioned reason given for selecting a teacher was the teacher's success in initiating or increasing the student's interest in a particular subject area. The following excerpts from student comments are typical:

Before Miss B. gave literature meaning, I was too science-oriented, but now I have learned to appreciate other things.

He took science, which previously had been only vaguely interesting to me, and made it come to life and greatly increased my desire to become an engineer.

Under her, I first began to truly read poetry, and this is one experience I now treasure.

He encouraged and guided my interest in his subject by leading me to discover and experience it for myself.

She taught me to love a subject which I had hated and thought I simply didn't have the ability to learn.

The third reason most often mentioned by the students for selecting a teacher was related to teaching methodology—the ability of the teacher to present his subject in a meaningful way and/or to communicate it effectively to his students.

When you're working with Miss L., it's as though you are the only two people in the room—a two-man team with a captain who won't holler "enough" until his team-mate understands all.

Miss M.'s imaginative and enthusiastic presentation of world history made interesting a subject that usually bores me to tears.

She "supervised our education" rather than "force fed" us.

He was a neat teacher who did not treat a possibly dull subject in a dull manner.

Additional evidence in this regard is provided by the teachers' self descriptions. Teachers were asked to indicate characteristics which they felt were most descriptive of themselves. A significantly higher proportion of the identified group than the validity sample stated that enthusiasm was a strong trait in their own make-up.

Student comments also lent support to the findings that the identified teachers had favorable attitudes toward and interest in their students. The teacher's personal interest in his students was the fifth most frequently given reason stated by students for selecting a teacher. The spirit of student statements in this regard is expressed in the following excerpts:

She honestly cares whether or not her students learn the material and is genuinely interested in her students as people and not merely as names to be associated with grades.

Mr. W. was my only teacher who was willing to go above and beyond his duty to encourage independent study. He was never too busy to stop his own work during his spare time to discuss important topics with me or to suggest new things to do to broaden my interests.

She was interested in me and had confidence in me so I couldn't let her down. I became a different student because of her loyal interest in my welfare.

Further evidence of the identified teachers' permissive (student centered) educational viewpoints was provided by their own expressions of opinion. A significantly smaller proportion of those in the identified group than in the validity sample stated that they believed attentiveness of students to be a more important indication of a good class than willingness of students to try and to volunteer, preparedness of students, or courtesy of students. A larger proportion of the identified teachers indicated that willingness of the students to try and to volunteer was a better indication of a good class than the other three factors mentioned above. The greater emphasis of the identified group on student activity and participation, rather than on student attentiveness (which implies a passive student response), indicates a more student centered philosophy. More of the identified group than the validity sample indicated their belief that a severe and aloof manner is a more important failing in a teacher than an inability to maintain a systematic, orderly approach or an inadequate mastery of subject.

It should not be concluded from this and related findings reported above that the identified teachers deemphasized the importance of subject matter. The majority of the identified teachers indicated their belief that inadequate mastery of subject matter is a more important teacher failing than inability to maintain a systematic and orderly approach or a severe and aloof manner. A larger proportion of the identified group than the validity sample also stated that they believe it is more important for a teacher to extend subject matter knowledge rather than to keep up to date on educational theories or to take part in community activities.

Several other study findings indicated that teachers who are judged successful by gifted students emphasize the importance of subject matter. The students often cited the teacher's interest in and command of his particular discipline as their major reason for choosing him as their most effective teacher. The teacher's success in transmitting this interest in a particular subject to the students was also noted by many students.

Role Perception. Interviews with the teachers in the interview sample provided data relative to the teachers' classroom behavior as they perceived it. These data provided additional support to the major conclusions suggested above.

The majority of teachers interviewed stated that they believe their major role is one of motivating students to want to study, learn, and think independently. They frequently noted their responsibility to instill an interest in and appreciation for their particular subject as well as for learning in general. Very few, however, saw their major role as imparting a specific body of knowledge. They emphasized the importance of demonstrating a personal interest in each student.

Their descriptions of personal incidents which they felt represented effective and ineffective classroom behavior reflected this philosophical position. Effectiveness was usually defined in terms of methodological and/or motivational success experiences, and ineffectiveness was represented by lack of success in these areas.

Conclusions

The conclusions which are suggested by the major study findings can be summarized as follows:

1. Teachers who were judged effective by intellectually gifted, high achieving students did not differ with respect to teachers not so identified, relative to such variables as sex, marital status, type of undergraduate institution attended, highest degree held, course work preparation, and extent of association with professional organizations.

2. Successful teachers of gifted students tended to be mature, experienced teachers.
3. Teachers who were successful with mentally superior students were mentally superior themselves. They stood in the upper 3 percent, relative to the general adult population, and significantly higher than their teaching colleagues.
4. The effective teachers tended to pursue avocational interests which were "intellectual" in nature. They had a significantly greater interest than their teaching colleagues in literature and the arts, and in the cultural life of their community.
5. The identified teachers were characterized by high achievement needs—they attempted to do their best and to succeed. This was reflected in past scholastic achievement as well as present teaching success.
6. A significantly greater number of the identified teachers decided to become teachers because of a desire for intellectual growth and because each was advised by a teacher that he would be a good teacher.
7. Effective teachers had more favorable attitudes toward students than other teachers. They took personal interest in their students and were sensitive to the students' motives and behaviors; they attempted to see things from the students' point of view and to understand how the students felt.
8. Effective teachers tended to be more student centered in their teaching approach. They encouraged students to participate in class activities and they took students' opinions into consideration.
9. Effective teachers were more systematic, orderly, and businesslike in their classroom approach.
10. Teachers who were effective with gifted students were more stimulating and imaginative in the classroom than their teaching colleagues. They were well grounded in and enthusiastic about their particular subject and about teaching. They defined their success in terms of how well they motivated their students to want to study, to learn, and to think independently. They were able to instill interest in and appreciation for their subject in their students.
11. Teachers identified as effective by gifted students supported special educational provisions for gifted students. A significantly greater percent of them preferred

to teach a class of exceptionally bright students than did their fellow teachers.

In summary, these conclusions indicated that there are unique personal and social traits, professional attitudes, educational viewpoints, and classroom behavior patterns which characterize successful high school teachers of intellectually gifted, high achieving students.

Implications

The major findings of this study and the conclusions proposed above suggest several implications for educational planning and programing. It behooves those who have the responsibility for the preservice education, placement, and/or guidance of teachers to base their policies and decisions on the most reliable information available.

Assuming that the identified teachers in this study can serve as a prototype, the conclusions listed above suggest factors which might guide the decision making processes of those charged with the important responsibilities of educating, selecting, and guiding teachers of gifted high school students. More specifically, the implications this study suggested follow:

1. School administrators should give careful consideration to the proper selection and placement of teachers for gifted students. Teachers placed with special classes of bright students should possess those qualities which are common to the gifted group. They should also have a special interest in working with these students. The findings of this study indicate that a large percentage of teachers who are successful with these students state a definite preference for teaching students of exceptional ability.

   A recent report of the National Commission on Teacher Education and Professional Standards (National Education Association, 1965) notes that misassignment ranks fifth among the twelve most important factors which educators cite as limiting the quality of education. One of the violations mentioned in the report is the teachers' failure to understand particular groups of students. The majority of misassignments is reported in grades ten through twelve.

   Teachers are sometimes assigned to classes of gifted students on the basis of seniority. Another common practice is to assign high school teachers to several different types of classes (i.e., slow, average, gifted) on the pretext that such an assignment adds variety to a teacher's work schedule and effects a form of "distributive justice." Both of these practices undoubtedly result in misassignment of teachers for gifted students. While gifted students may continue to learn "in spite of" and not "because of" the teacher, the results of this study indicate that there are special qualities which characterize teachers who are successful with these students. Attempts should be made to identify those teachers who will provide the optimum educational experience for students of exceptional ability and then make assignments on this basis.

2. The special qualities and interests which characterize teachers who are successful with gifted students suggest the need for identifying preservice as well as inservice teachers to work with these students. The problem of attracting able young people into the teaching profession has received considerable attention in recent years. The report of the Commission on Teacher Education and Professional Standards (National Education Association, 1965) calls this the number one problem limiting the quality of education today.

   If teacher education institutions were to develop special courses or programs at the undergraduate and graduate levels which would specifically prepare able young people to teach gifted high school students, more superior college students might be attracted to the teaching profession.

3. Special preparatory programs for teaching gifted students should result in special certification in this area. The unique nature and needs of gifted students call for the recognition of educational personnel who possess those personal qualities and professional competencies which will guarantee that gifted students receive the optimum educational experience which they deserve and which the democratic ideal demands.

References

Edwards, A. L. *Edwards Personal Preference Schedule manual.* New York: Psychological Corporation, 1959.

Guba, E. G., Jackson, P. W., and Bidwell, C. E. Occupational choice and the teaching career. *Educational Research Bulletin,* 1959, **38**, 1-12, 27.

Jackson, P. W., and Guba, E. G. The need structure of inservice teachers and occupational analysis. *School Review*, 1957, **65**, 176-192.

Merrill, R. M. Comparison of education students, successful scientists, and educational administrators on the Edwards Personal Preference Scale. *Journal of Educational Research*, 1960, **54**, 38-40.

Morsh, J. E., and Wilder, E. W. *Identifying the effective instructor: a review of quantitative studies, 1900-1952.* San Antonio, Texas: Air Force Personnel and Training Research Center, 1955.

National Education Association, National Commission on Teacher Education and Professional Standards. *The assignment and misassignment of American teachers: a summary of the complete report.* Washington: The Commission, 1965.

Ryans, D. G. *Characteristics of teachers: their description, comparison and appraisal.* Washington: American Council on Education, 1960.

Ward, V. *Educating the gifted: an axiomatic approach.* Columbus, Ohio: Charles E. Merrill, 1961.

UPPER AND LOWER STATUS GIFTED CHILDREN: A STUDY OF DIFFERENCES

Edward C. Frierson

Abstract. Groups of gifted and average elementary-school children from upper- and lower-status backgrounds were compared on measures of height, weight, personality traits, interests, activities, and creative thinking. Group differences between upper- and lower-status gifted children were found to be associated with differences in socioeconomic background. Group differences between gifted and average children regardless of socioeconomic background were also disclosed. The findings emphasize the importance of controlling for socioeconomic status in studies where gifted and nongifted children are compared.

The educator who is willing to provide for both gifted children and for disadvantaged children is relieved to find that the literature is consistent in describing these groups. There is general agreement that gifted children as a group are taller, heavier, and healthier than the average. They have more interests, show more selectivity in reading, have higher aspirations, more independence and drive than do average children. Gifted children are more creative, perseverent, emotionally stable, and have better attitudes toward school and learning than do average children. Gifted children mature earlier, achieve better in school and adjust to social situations better than average children. The gifted children thus described, however, are from predominantly upper and middle socioeconomic backgrounds.

Profiles derived from studies of children from low socioeconomic backgrounds present a direct contrast in stereotypes when compared with the profiles derived from studies of the gifted child. The achievements, attitudes, drives, learning styles, adjustment, verbal facility, aspirations, and physical status of the lower class child are different from the upper and middle class child. That they are also different from the characteristics of the gifted child is implicit. The health status of the lower class child is inferior to that of middle and upper class children as is his language development and school achievement. The lower class child is marked by absence of long range aspiration, reduced motivation, slower problem solving abilities, and other traits generally antithetic to the traits of the gifted child.

There is a greater difference in the development of conscience between the gifted and the average in the upper middle class than between the gifted and the average in the lower class (Boehm, 1952). Changes in IQ reflect social class (Oppel, Rider, and Weiner, 1963). The

From *Exceptional Children*, 1965, **32**, 83-90. Reprinted by permission of The Council for Exceptional Children.

upper class background is associated with rising IQ's; the lower class background with declining IQ's. The importance of knowing more about the number and characteristics of the gifted from lower social strata is emphasized by the fact that the greatest absolute number of bright children is to be found at lower levels in the socioeconomic scale (Fleming, 1943).

The Interaction of Class Status and Giftedness

When samples of gifted children are drawn largely from upper socioeconomic groups, characteristics attributed to the sample may be correlates of giftedness or socioeconomic status or both. Terman reported "only one man (father) gave his occupation as 'laborer' which is 0.2 percent of our fathers as compared with 15.0 percent of the general population classified as laborers in the census report" (Terman, 1925, p. 63). According to a five grade classification, the gifted group in Terman's study included the following percentages: Professional, 31.4 percent; Semiprofessional, 50.0 percent; Skilled Labor, 11.8 percent; Semiskilled Labor, 6.6 percent; and Common Labor, .13 percent.

The neighborhood environment represented in Terman's study was rated on a five level scale. For the gifted sample, the average rating was "superior," and the average home index was "very superior." These conditions being true, the question asked by many today is that which Bonsall and Stefflre (1955) raised:

> Is it possible that Terman in *Genetic Studies of Genius* in describing the multiple superiority of the gifted child, is simply describing children from the upper socio-economic levels? If this is so, many of our assumptions about the "differences" of the gifted which call for special educational approaches and methods will need to be reconsidered (p. 165).

What effect does cultural deprivation have upon the gifted child and the development of talent? Burt (1961) argues that the environment is less a determinant of recognized giftedness than is heredity. He cited the wide range of variation among children raised similarly and the after-histories of high ability persons whose environments were impediments. Carroll (1940) even suggests that low socioeconomic status helps to develop ability: "Probably no one would, if he could, consciously assign gifted children to an early life of poverty, but it is, nevertheless, a fact that many

children born on a low socio-economic level owe their later eminence to that fact" (p. 37). The Carroll point of view is anecdotally supported, but the more widely accepted thesis, based upon research evidence, is that low status obscures ability and prevents the full development of much human potential.

Design of the Present Study

The present study was conducted with four groups of elementary school children in Cleveland, Ohio. To facilitate identification, the four groups were labeled as follows:

I. Upper Socioeconomic Status—Gifted ($N=88$)
II. Lower Socioeconomic Status—Gifted ($N=56$)
III. Upper Socioeconomic Status—Average ($N=86$)
IV. Lower Socioeconomic Status—Average ($N=55$)

It is appropriate to note that the study was conducted (a) in a school system where identification of gifted children begins in the primary grades, (b) in a large urban center where all socioeconomic levels are well represented, and (c) in schools having special classes for gifted students which are not geographically delimited. In addition, all classes for gifted children are comparable in size, objectives, and procedures. The teachers are uniformly selected according to highest standards and the conduct of the special class program is under the same central supervision. Regardless of status, the in-classroom experience of the gifted children in this study has been essentially the same.

Groups were matched on the basis of sex, age, ethnic background, grade, and school experience with differences between any two groups being socioeconomic background or mental ability differences. The mean IQ of the upper status gifted group was 133.2; the upper status average group, 102.9; the lower status gifted group, 132.1; and the lower status average group, 96.8.

Data were collected by means of the Institute for Personality and Ability Testing Children's Personality Questionnaire (the CPQ), The Minnesota Tests of Creative Thinking, and the Northwestern University-United States Office of Education Interest Inventory Record (abridged). In addition, height, weight, and selected home information were included for each subject. Standardized procedures, developed with a pilot group, were employed throughout the periods of data collection.

Definition of Terms

This research was designed to examine certain generalizations which have been accepted about gifted children and to increase the understanding of the gifted child from upper and lower socioeconomic backgrounds. Following are definitions of several terms as they were operationally accepted in this study.

Gifted child. A child who scored not lower than IQ 125 on the Stanford-Binet Intelligence Scale was referred to as "gifted." (Children were first screened with Kuhlman-Anderson Intelligence Test.)

Socioeconomic background. The expression, "socioeconomic background," was used to represent a social area containing persons having the same level of living, the same way of life, and the same ethnic background (Shevky and Bell, 1955).

Upper socioeconomic status. The expression, "upper socioeconomic status," identified those individuals who lived in an area which included 1960 census tracts having a Shevky-Bell Social Rank Index which fell within the upper three deciles in a ranking of all census tracts in the Cleveland, Ohio metropolitan area (Uyeki, 1963).

Lower socioeconomic status. The expression, "lower socioeconomic status," identified those individuals who lived in an area which included 1960 census tracts which had a Shevky-Bell Social Rank Index that fell within the lower three deciles in a ranking of all census tracts in the Cleveland, Ohio metropolitan area.

Average child. An average child was one who scored between 85 and 115 on the Kuhlman-Anderson Intelligence Test.

Results

An analysis of the data was made to test the null hypothesis that there were no significant differences between gifted children from upper and lower socioeconomic backgrounds on the selected measures of characteristic traits. Gifted children and average children from the same socioeconomic backgrounds were also compared to determine the extent to which differences between gifted and nongifted children were associated with social class.

Differences in Physical Characteristics. The heights and weights of gifted children from upper and lower socioeconomic backgrounds were compared with five standards. These standards included the Baldwin-Wood height and weight tables which Terman used in his comparative study of gifted children, the Stuart-Meredith tables which provide percentile norms, a compilation table based upon 12 major height-weight research studies in the United States, a study conducted in metropolitan Cleveland, and a midwest regional study of height and weight.

Substantial differences between the heights and weights of the gifted and all standards were noted. However, differences between the present research groups and more recent standards were much smaller than differences found between the present research groups and older standards. Two theses were confirmed: (a) general population norms for height and weight increased from 1923-1954, and (b) a noticeable difference in mean height and weight generally occurred when regional samples were compared with broad representative samples or compiled national standards.

Analysis of variance of height and weight among the upper and lower status gifted and average groups yielded no significant differences. The *t* values indicated that there was less difference between the upper and lower status gifted groups in height than between lower status gifted and average groups. The reverse was true for weight. Both height and weight differences among the groups could have occurred on the basis of sampling error alone.

The conclusion must be made that generalizations concerning the physical superiority of gifted children, when based upon regional samples compared with national standards or interregional norms, are likely to be biased although not necessarily in favor of the regional sample. Differences between gifted and average children were not significant at the .05 level when drawn from the same regional population. Therefore, the null hypothesis that no significant differences existed between the height and weight characteristics of gifted children from upper and lower socioeconomic backgrounds was accepted.

Differences in Interests and Activities. An Interest-Activity Inventory Record was completed by each subject. The items on the inventory were designed to elicit the following information:

1. Play and other activities preferences.
2. Television, radio, and movies interests and habits.
3. Reading interests and activities.
4. Vocational and educational interests and aspirations.

Five of the 37 items were found to differentiate between upper and lower socioeconomic gifted groups at the .05 level of significance using the t test and the standard error of the difference between two uncorrelated percentages. Additional items yielded t values at the .10 level of significance. The upper status gifted group differed from the lower status gifted group in the following ways:

1. The upper status gifted had a greater desire to read during nonschool hours than did the lower status gifted.
2. The upper status gifted read more educational type magazines at home than did the lower status gifted.
3. The upper status gifted knew that their parents wanted them to go to college.
4. The lower status gifted indicated a greater preference for adventure-hero type comics than did the upper status gifted.
5. The lower status gifted earned lower grades in science than the upper status gifted.
6. The lower status gifted did not like school so well as the upper status gifted.
7. The lower status gifted preferred competitive team sports to a greater extent than did the upper status gifted.

The Interest Inventory Record contained 13 items which differentiated the lower status gifted and average groups at the .05 level of significance. One additional item returned proportions of affirmative responses at the .10 level of significance.

The lower status gifted group, according to responses, differed from the lower status average group in the following ways:

1. The lower status gifted were more likely to play musical instruments than the lower status average.
2. The lower status gifted aspired to higher status occupations than the lower status average.
3. The lower status gifted read the news section of the daily paper more than the lower status average.

4. The lower status gifted made up more games to play than did the lower status average.
5. The lower status gifted preferred competitive team sports as their favorite type game to a greater extent than the lower status average.
6. The lower status gifted read "classic" or "true" comic books more often than the lower status average.
7. The lower status gifted earned their highest grades in reading.
8. The lower status average children disliked reading.
9. The lower status average children preferred cowboy and Indian stories.
10. The lower status average children were not as likely to read the newspaper as were the lower status gifted.
11. The lower status average children showed a greater preference for commercial games than did the lower status gifted.
12. The lower status average children's favorite activity was "just play."
13. More of the lower status average children did not read comics or magazines at all.
14. The lower status average children received their highest grades in spelling (not necessarily higher grades than the gifted).

Differences between the gifted and the average groups were greater in number than differences between the gifted groups from upper and lower socioeconomic backgrounds. The total effect of the differences noted may be less or greater when qualitative criteria are employed or when the long range effects of the differences are evaluated. The level of aspiration possessed by a ten year old may have far more importance than the degree to which he chooses to read cowboy and Indian stories. Lack of parental encouragement for higher education for the lower status gifted student may ultimately deprive our society of unique ability, the consequences of which are different from those resulting from a poor reader's lack of interest in comic books.

Irrespective of the subsequent value research will place on each characteristic presented, rejection of the null hypothesis is justified.

Differences in Personality Traits. A personality questionnaire (the CPQ) was administered to all subjects. Scores were derived for 14 personality factors which have their theoretical bases in the psychological and psychiatric literature (Cattell, 1957). Mean raw scores were obtained for boys and girls separately.

Responses, which had been corrected for sex and age, (Porter and Cattell, 1960) were then combined to give means for each personality trait representing the four groups in the study. Using only Form A of the CPQ reduced the possible range of variability tending to "squeeze" all group means closer together. The authors of the test advise users to be aware of this tendency in making interpretations.

None of the group means deviated sufficiently from the population mean to be classified other than normal. Certain means attract attention because of the direction of deviation indicated. For example, the lower status average group was somewhat lower than all other groups on Factor G (Super Ego Weakness versus Super Ego Strength). A low G score, or low Super Ego Strength, proves to be associated with lying, stealing, temper tantrums, and defiance of law and order. Means on Factor G would support the contention that the development of Super Ego in lower status gifted children is more like that of upper status children at the upper elementary school age.

The upper status groups (gifted and average) had group means which were higher than the lower status groups on two factors—Factor G and Factor Q_3. This indicates that upper class children, regardless of mental ability, have more Super Ego Strength (Factor G), are more conscientious, attentive to rules and people, more consistently ordered, and more persevering. Higher Factor G means that upper status children are more self-controlled, are more ambitious to do well, considerate of others and better able to control emotions.

The lower status groups ranked higher than the upper status groups on Factors D, N, and Q_4. This suggests that the lower status children are more excitable (Factor D), demanding, attention getting, overactive, self-assertive, undependable, and possessed of more nervous symptoms. In addition, they are more shrewd (Factor N), realistic in thinking, cool, and aloof. Higher Q_4 scores are associated with higher Ergic Tension, a tendency to be tense, worried, and frustrated.

The lower status gifted group had the highest mean score on two factors. Factor F, Surgency, is characterized by talkative, cheerful, happy go lucky traits. These children are usually more expressive, frank, quick, and alert. The low status gifted were also highest on Fac-

tor J, Coasthemia. This factor marks children who prefer to do things on their own, who tend to be intellectually individualistic, have strong private views, and tend to forget if treated unfairly.

The upper status gifted group was highest on one factor. This factor, called tenderminded (Factor I, Premsia), is characterized by demanding, impatient, subjective behavior. They are dependent, sometimes affected, and have an imaginative inner life, an interest in dramatics, travel, and literature typically.

Cattell's method for computing the personality pattern similarity coefficient (r_p) between the profile of a given student and the profile of a given occupational group was used to calculate the personality similarity coefficient between each of the sample groups (Cattell, 1957). The differences were slight; consequently, the similarity was great among all groups.

A slightly greater degree of similarity was found between upper and lower status gifted children than there was between lower status gifted and average children. Since the differences were not significant according to the specification criterion (.05 level), the null hypothesis that no difference in personality patterns exists among all groups was not rejected. Nonetheless, affirming that gifted children of lower socioeconomic backgrounds are somewhat more likely to have a personality pattern similar to upper status average children than they are to have a personality pattern similar to lower status average children is an important disclosure. Such a finding demonstrates that high ability may be a relatively stronger determinant of personality than is socioeconomic background particularly when "gifted" (very high general intelligence) characterizes the individual's intellectual endowment.

Differences in Creative Thinking Ability. The performances of subjects on both measures of intelligence and measures of creativity are influenced by sociocultural factors. Therefore, some indication of the differences between the top 20 percent IQ children from upper and lower socioeconomic backgrounds on measures of creative thinking were sought in the present study.

First, the hypothesis was tested that there is no difference between the creativity test performance of the upper status (top 20 percent IQ) group and the lower status (top 20 percent IQ) group. The mean IQ of the upper status (top 20 percent) group was 149.1. The mean

IQ of the lower status (top 20 percent) group was 145.7. Table 1 presents the findings, which led to the rejection of the null hypothesis.

TABLE 1

t Scores Derived from Analysis of Creativity Test Performance of Upper and Lower Status Gifted Children

Creativity Test	MN Upper Status	MN Lower Status	t Values (df = 24)	Level of Significance
Fluency	77.7	63.0	1.78	.10
Flexibility	40.7	35.2	1.08	NS
Adequacy	25.3	20.7	1.31	NS
Originality	109.5	75.9	3.00	.01
Elaboration	58.1	46.6	2.09	.05
Total	311.9	241.6	2.31	.05

The difference in performance on the measurement of originality was significant at the .01 level. The groups differed significantly at the .05 level on the measurement of elaboration. One other measure, fluency, produced a substantial difference. This difference was not significant at the .05 level, however.

The mean total creativity score for the two groups was also significantly different leading to rejection of the null hypothesis. The upper status top 20 percent gifted group outperformed the lower status group on every submeasure, raising the possibility of the existence of socioeconomic bias in the test stimuli.

The correlation between IQ and creativity test subscores was determined for each group. It was found that there was a higher correlation between IQ and each of the subtests among the lower status sample than among the upper status sample. One subscore, adequacy, was found to produce a coefficient of correlation which could only occur five times in one hundred trials from sampling fluctuations alone if the population r were actually zero.

The differences between coefficients of correlations derived from the upper and lower status top 20 percent IQ groups were tested for significance by means of the z conversion and t test of critical ratio technique. It was expected that the very small sample size would tend to discount all but extremely large differences. The results of this test of significance applied to differences in obtained r's revealed that none of the differences were significant at the .05 level.

Incorporating the factors of age and IQ, the following regression equation was solved:

$$\overline{X}_1 = b_{12.3}x_2 + b_{13.2}x_3$$

where $\overline{X}_1$ = creativity score (the criterion)

X_2 = age in months

X_3 = IQ

Calculation of Beta coefficients, or Beta weights, enables one to determine the relative weight each independent variable contributes to the criterion independently of other factors.

For the upper status group $Beta_{12.3} = -.14$ and $Beta_{13.2} = .13$. Multiple R in terms of Beta coefficients was calculated in order to determine the proportion of variance of the criterion measure (creativity) attributable to the joint action of the variables of age and IQ.

In the upper status, high IQ sample $R^2_{1(23)}$ was found to be .03; accordingly, only three percent of whatever makes upper status, high 20 percent IQ children differ in creativity can be attributed to differences in age and general intelligence. The remaining 97 percent of the variance in creativity within this group must be attributed to factors not measured in our research.

$R^2_{1(23)}$ for the lower status, high 20 percent IQ sample was found to be .34. Thus, 34 percent of the variability in creativity can be attributed to differences in age and intelligence. The remaining 66 percent of the variance in this group's creativity must be attributed to factors not measured in this study. The data further revealed that the independent contribution of age to the variance in creativity was 24 percent and the contribution of general intelligence was only 10 percent.

Small multiple R's and small samples yield results to be interpreted with caution. Neither R obtained was significant when the group R had been corrected for "inflation." The lower limit of the .95 confidence interval was negative and the population R could well be zero in both cases. It can only be concluded that there would be no correlation between earned and predicted scores on creativity tests using the regression coefficients obtained from these samples.

Summary

Samples of gifted and average children from upper and lower socioeconomic backgrounds were compared on measures of personality, interests, activities, creativity, height, and weight. An attempt was made to determine in which traits gifted children from lower socioeconomic backgrounds differed from gifted children from upper socioeconomic backgrounds. When differences were not significant, an effort was made to determine the relative affinity of the four groups (i.e., Would low status gifted children appear to be more like upper status gifted children or more like lower status average children?).

Greater differences were found between the gifted groups in the present study and national standards than between the gifted and norm groups drawn from the same region. Height and weight differences between the gifted children from upper and lower socioeconomic backgrounds were not significant at the .05 level when samples were drawn from the same population. Although height and weight data indicated that the gifted were superior to the nongifted regardless of status, the null hypothesis that no significant differences exist among the groups in height and weight was accepted.

Interest and activity data revealed several group differences. The upper status gifted children read more and "better" magazines and books than did the lower status gifted. The upper status gifted group was aware that their parents aspired for them to go to college. Many of the lower status gifted were not conscious of such parental support. The lower status gifted did not like school so well nor did they achieve so well in certain subjects as the upper status gifted. The lower status gifted group preferred competitive sports more than the upper status gifted group.

Many interests and activities differentiated the lower status gifted children from lower status average children. There were 13 items whose proportionate response was significantly different (.05 level) for the two lower status groups, while five items produced significant differences between the two gifted groups.

Group means were derived for 14 personality traits. Differences in group means for each factor were tested for significance. None of the separate factor differences was significant at the .05 level. Therefore, the null hypothesis of no difference in separate factors among the research groups was accepted.

Personality profile similarity coefficients were calculated to analyze group differences. It was found that the personality patterns of upper status gifted children and lower status gifted children were slightly more similar than were the personality patterns of lower status gifted children and lower status average children.

On measures of creativity, the upper status gifted group was superior to the lower status gifted group. The correlation between IQ and creativity was higher for the lower status gifted group. In addition, it was determined that a substantial group difference existed in the amount of variability in creativity test performance attributable to the influence of age and IQ. It was suggested that some untested factors which contribute to the variability in creativity among gifted children are socioeconomically oriented.

The data clearly indicate that several differences between groups of gifted children are associated with differences in the socioeconomic background of the children. It is equally clear from the data that many differences between gifted children and average children exist regardless of the socioeconomic backgrounds of the children.

References

Boehm, Leonore. The development of conscience: a comparison of American children of different mental and socio-economic levels. *Child Development*, 1952, **33**, 575-590.

Bonsall, Marcella R., and Stefflre, B. The temperament of gifted children. *California Journal of Educational Research*, 1955, **6**(4), 162-165.

Burt, C. The gifted child. *British Journal of Statistics Psychology*, 1961, **14**, 123-139.

Carroll, H. A. *Genius in the making.* New York: McGraw Hill Book Company, 1940.

Cattell, R. B. *Personality and motivation structure and measurement.* New York: World Book Company, 1957.

Fleming, C. M. Socio-economic level and test performance. *British Journal of Educational Psychology*, 1943, **12**(11), 74-82.

Hathaway, Millicent L. *Heights and weights of children and youth in the United States.* US Department of Agriculture, Agricultural Research Service, Institute of Home Economics. Home Economics Research Report No. 2. Washington, D.C.: Superintendent of Documents, US Government Printing Office, 1957.

Meredith, H. V. Relation between socio-economic status and body size in boys 7 to 10 years of age. *American Journal of Diseases of Children*, 1951, **82**, 702-709.

Oppel, W., Rider, B. U., and Weiner, G. Some correlates of I.Q. changes in children. *Child Development*, 1963, **34**, 61-67.

Porter, R. B., and Cattell, R. B. *Handbook for the IPAT Children's Personality Questionnaire (the CPQ)*. Champaign, Illinois: Institute for Personality and Ability Testing, 1960.

Shevky, E., and Bell, W. *Social area analysis*. California: Stanford University Press, 1955.

Terman, L. M. *Genetic studies of genius*. Volume 1. *Mental and physical traits of a thousand gifted children*. California: Stanford University Press, 1925.

Uyeki, E. S. Shevky-Bell indexes for the 1900 census tracts in the Cleveland metropolitan statistical area. Unpublished manuscript. Case Institute of Technology, Department of Humanities and Social Studies, 1963.

CHAPTER THREE

MENTAL RETARDATION

Relative to research in other areas of exceptionality, the literature on mental retardation is voluminous. Not only are more studies being conducted in this area, but the work being completed is exemplary in several respects. Foremost among the positive aspects of research on mental retardation is the consistent use of a common operational definition in the selection of research subjects. The classification system in use was first adopted in 1919 and has been revised periodically by committees of the American Association of Mental Deficiency (AAMD). For instance, the 1973 revision eliminates the category of "borderline" in psychometric intelligence. Noteworthy features of the AAMD classificatory system include (1) the use of dual medical-behavioral classifications, (2) a provision for operational definition, (3) an emphasis on current functioning, and (4) a limitation to conditions that first appeared during the developmental period (Warren, 1973). The adoption of similar constraints on subject characteristics would markedly enhance communication among researchers and practitioners in other areas of exceptionality.

The field of mental retardation has further been advanced through theory. Several theoretical approaches toward mental retardation have been of heuristic value in directing the goals of and methods used by the research scientist. The necessity of selecting research methods that are instrumental in answering specific research questions has been emphasized by Haywood (1970) and Heal (1970) in a recent symposium on research strategy. The basic versus applied approach toward the study of mental retardation is illustrated in the articles by Kershner and by Wiesen, Hartley, Richardson, and Roske. Kershner tested the relationship between family stress and institutionalization of retarded children, and Wiesen and his colleagues investigated the practical application of behavior-modification techniques.

Perhaps the greatest impetus for research on mental retardation has come from practical and societal concerns. Practitioners are in constant search of effective techniques for educating and rehabilitating retarded persons. The strategies of special education and the issues surrounding placement of mildly retarded children in special-education classes are discussed by Hammons. The effects of integration versus segregation in classroom placement of the educable mentally retarded are examined more closely by Goodman, Gottlieb, and Harrison.

EDUCATING THE MILDLY RETARDED: A REVIEW

Gary W. Hammons

Abstract: A review of articles and comments emanating from Dunn's (1968) criticisms of the education of the mildly retarded is presented to analyze some of the facets of the current controversy. Many writings prior and subsequent to Dunn's are cited to show a growing disenchantment with the current course of special education and the lack of viable alternatives currently available. The review is concluded with an emphasis on change rather than reaction and on the desire that inappropriate practices be altered rather than abolished as advocated by some writers.

A NUMBER of recent writings in special education, this one included, have begun with a reference to Dunn's (1968) article, "Special Education for the Mildly Retarded—Is Much of It Justifiable?" Yet, in spite of the multitude of citations, this work was only symptomatic of a growing disenchantment with emerging practices of special education. For example, the original efficacy studies of Bennet and Pertsch during the 1930's were undoubtedly initiated as a result of concern for the aca-

From *Exceptional Children*, 1972, **38**, 565–570. Reprinted by permission of The Council for Exceptional Children.

demic progress of educable mentally retarded children (Reynolds, 1971). In addition to comments concerning the numerous efficacy studies, the professional literature in the past decade contains several comments similar to Dunn's. For example, Blatt (1960) pointed out that no supportable advantages of special classes for this population have been established, and Johnson (1962) said:

It is indeed paradoxical that mentally handicapped children having teachers especially trained, having more money (per capital) spent on their education and being enrolled in classes with fewer children and a program designed to provide for their unique needs, should be accomplishing the objectives of their education at a lower level than similar mentally handicapped children who have not had these advantages and have been forced to remain in the regular grades [p. 207].

Connor (1964) expressed concern for the problem of ". . . the practice of placing children in a special class because they cannot be handled in the regular program regardless of their being able to learn in the special setting available [p. 207]." Others, Fisher (1967), Reger, Schroeder, and Uschold (1968), have questioned the appropriateness of using medically derived criteria for grouping handicapped children rather than criteria reflecting their educational and social needs. Prior to publication of Dunn's article, Schwartz (1968) pondered the growing stress on the establishment of special classes to the exclusion of specialized education. He further noted that for secondary level special classes, adaptation has been overlooked in favor of using IQ scores as a placement criterion. A substantial body of research shows (a) serious doubt of the efficacy of special classes, (b) clearly deleterious effects of labeling a child as mentally retarded, and (c) the fact that friends, parents, and work associates of this group do not think of them as retarded.

Focal Point

The reception Dunn's article met represented the culmination of dissatisfaction with current practices more than the response to the contentions he advanced. However, the quantity and variety of reactions have probably surprised even Dunn himself. These reactions have generally taken three forms: (a) support and elabo-

ration of Dunn's contentions, (b) further inquiry into the efficacy studies, and (c) discussion of problems of categorization.

Those writers who have supported Dunn generally reiterate the position that, because of lack of evidence to the contrary, special classes should be abolished for all but the profoundly handicapped. Lilly (1970), for example, said that ". . . traditional special education services as represented by self-contained special classes should be discontinued immediately for all but the severely impaired . . . [p. 43]." Christoplos and Renz (1969) questioned the justification for special classes for all populations served by the schools, and Johnson (1969) reiterated their point and typified the position of several writers that special classes were initially created to serve a relieving function for regular education and to reduce classroom disruption by exceptional children. Johnson and others (Franks, 1971; Lilly, 1970; Simches, 1970) further contended that these classes are now used by the schools to perpetuate racism.

Efficacy Revisited

Dunn's article also appears to have stimulated renewed interest in the efficacy studies: their design and implications. Often cited as most comprehensive and yet inconclusive, the Illinois study of Goldstein, Moss, and Jordan (1965) has been prefaced by Kirk and analyzed by Guskin and Spicker (1968). Kirk indicated that, even with the excellent methodology of this study, nothing conclusive was established and researchers should concentrate instead on processes by which the retarded develop mentally, socially, and academically. Guskin and Spicker countered:

If we are to agree with Kirk that what we need to study are learning and developmental processes rather than administrative arrangements, the same argument could have been just as legitimately made before carrying out the study. If we demand evidence for the effectiveness of special class arrangements, this study may be the best we have so far, but it is far from decisive [pp. 239-240].

Lilly (1970) attempted to relegate the efficacy studies to obscurity, stating:

To avoid exhaustive argument with regard to research design and confounding variables in these efficacy studies, let us accept the statement that they are inconclusive to date. It must be added, however, that in the true spirit of research they will be inconclusive forever [pp. 43-44].

However, Nelson and Schmidt (1971) analyzed several facets of the issue not considered elsewhere. They concluded:

If there is any sustaining value in the position of those who challenge or uphold the effectiveness of the special class, it must be the systematic examination of the statements which are used to reject or justify special classes. To challenge on any other basis leads to trivial conclusions [p. 384].

Categorization

In addition to renewed interest in the efficacy studies, a related concern appears to be with the problems manifested in categorization of exceptional children. This apparently stems from considerations of the stigma of special classes. Blatt (1971) related that, in spite of long overdue progressive developments, ". . . children continue to be labeled and stigmatized . . . some to be placed in segregated programs while others to be excluded or exempted from public schools [p. 3]." Hurley (1971) echoed, "There are many issues in education today but the 'Hottest' by far is the issue of labeling children and its corollary, the elimination of traditional categories of special education [p. 9]."

Some teacher training institutions are responding to this pressure by redesigning their instructional sequences to deal more with exceptional children on a noncategorical basis, under the justification that most of the techniques demonstrated are applicable to all handicapping conditions. However, some writers (Reynolds & Balow, 1971; Lucas, 1971; Guskin & Spicker, 1968) have suggested that when terminology is used to describe programs and teachers rather than children, communication and programing are thereby improved.

Alternative Proposal

Many of Dunn's contentions have been extensively expanded by later writers. These include:

1. Labeling and categories do more harm than good.
2. The efficacy studies do not support continued existence of special classes.

3. General education has improved its ability to cope with a greater range of individual differences.
4. The existence of special classes protects regular education from facing its failures.

While Dunn suggested several alternatives to special classes, many of his fellow critics have supported only resource room or consultant intervention. Lilly (1971) proposed returning special class teachers and students to regular classes and providing instructional specialists to assist them with their educational problems. He also suggested a three part program that would eliminate failure completely, both on the part of the student and the regular class teacher. This model, which stresses the training of teachers to handle problems rather than to refer them to others, would provide personnel to aid the classroom teacher in coping with exceptional situations. Christoplos and Renz (1969) proposed that many of the same arguments advanced for elimination of special classes for the slow learner also are valid for all other exceptional categories and therefore that total integration of all handicapped students into regular classes should be considered. Hurley (1971), commenting on the issues of special classes and categorization, said, "Since we recognize that we deal with failures of the educational system, we cannot decategorize unless we get involved in the whole system and not just special education [p. 5]."

Not Carefully Read

Recently, however, Johnson (1971) and Lucas (1971) have pointed out that the critics of special classes who credit Dunn's writing (1968) as their inspiration have not read this article well. They pointed out that his position, while not popular at the time, was limited in terms of population affected and that the alternatives he proposed were much more encompassing than only resource room concepts. Both Johnson and Lucas apparently have read the article well; they emphasize that Dunn was concerned primarily with the borderline or mildly retarded and that *some* classes for this population are inappropriate. Johnson and Lucas take exception to the contention of Dunn and others that the existence of special classes provides shelter for regular education from its failure to teach this low group effectively. In fact, several writers have recently exposed inequities in regular education's ability to provide for this population at all. Hurley (1969) stressed that educators have not only been remiss in intervening but have virtually guaranteed repetition of the cycle by this generation's children. Stein (1971) affirmed the contention: "The average child in eighty-five per cent of the Black and Puerto Rican schools is functionally illiterate after eight years of schooling in the richest city in the world [p. 158]." Thus, Dunn's premise that regular education has greatly improved its ability to deal with a wide range of individual differences may not be supportable.

The general conclusion of those who have examined Dunn's contentions carefully, and not necessarily agreed with him, has been that the situation is far more complex than appearances indicate. It has not yet been demonstrated that any one method or strategy is either superior or without redeeming value in educating exceptional children. Furthermore, the general feeling that evidence is not sufficient to indicate any definite stance is well stated by Engel (1969) :

> In this case it is fallacious to argue for the abolishment of special classes on the basis of the research evidence; the classes exist, the groupings are in effect, but after that we still have to construct new teaching methods before we have anything to assess [p. 382].

While the reasons advanced by critics appear credible and convincing in isolation, they may have a serious flaw in their logic. Frequent justification for replacing special classes with resource teachers or consultants is that the efficacy studies show special classes to be deficient, yet virtually no significant studies are available showing the alternate model to be efficacious. While this might be excused or justified on the grounds that such programs have not existed long enough for proper evaluation and that there is a need to explore this programing experimentally, it is pretentious to expect regular educators to accept or even tolerate consultation from special educators. Smith (1971) succinctly pointed out that special educators traditionally have argued that the best way to handle underachievers is to place them in special classes. Now that this does not seem to be effective, the proposal that special educa-

tors serve instead as consultants is like saying, "We were unable to teach them anything, so you get them back. However, we retain the right to tell you how to do it." The possibility of regular education accepting such a strategy would seem remote.

Furthermore, resource room, consultant, or crisis teacher programs have several serious flaws in their functional design. In striving to justify their existence, teachers in these positions tend to extend their services into all areas of instruction. While this may be sound educationally, it has the net effect of diluting or reducing aid to the populations the concept was devised to serve. Additionally, the tendency of school districts to abandon traditional special classes completely in favor of resource rooms increases the threat of total abolishment of special education. As the financial crisis in education worsens and programs are curtailed, resource room programs are more susceptible to budget cuts than traditional classes, since their demise would not result in educationally difficult students being returned to the regular classroom.

Early Intervention

Most writers, with the possible exception of Reynolds (1971), have ignored Dunn's limitation of attention to only young children, that is, ". . . the emphasis of the article is on children, in that no attempt is made to suggest an adequate high school environment of adolescents still functioning as slow learners [Reynolds, 1971, p. 6]." In addition, the tendency to react as if a crisis exists and to make an immediate unilateral shift or return in educational programming for the slow learner could well create a crisis. The hazard, as Dunn recognized, is in conceptualizing the situation about a single point in time and making decisions and provisions which are, in effect, only short range responses to a long range problem. As Reynolds (1971) observed, education should consider foremost what each child will be like as a result of the education he receives or should receive and then should consider the most appropriate strategies presently available.

A growing response has been prefaced with concern and agreement in principle, but it requires more realistic and timely strategies than simple abolishment. Johnson and Balow (1971), Reynolds (1971), Lucas (1971), and MacMillan (1971), among others, have reiterated Kirk's contention that the real concern should not be what kind of administrative arrangement best handles slow learners but what is best for them educationally and what system of grouping is best to accomplish this. Johnson further argued that whether this population is considered retarded tomorrow is highly dependent on what is done for them educationally today.

Many writers, in addressing themselves to the question of justification of separate classes for the slow learner, regardless of their point of view, have stressed that the current introspection has been beneficial to special and regular education. Miller and Schoenfelder (1969) expressed this view:

> It is quite right and proper that special education not be considered sacrosanct, and that special educators be forced to consider their basic assumptions, premises, and philosophical foundations. Professions seem to take a long, hard look at themselves in this sense only when under critical onslaught. No field which is expanding as rapidly as is special education should be allowed to so grow without having a strong philosophical and theoretical foundation [p. 397].

Stephens (1967) emphasized that the current status of special education is part of an evolutionary process: ". . . whatever its other virtues, the school has been a survival device which some societies evolved, or borrowed, or stumbled upon, or otherwise acquired during the remote past [p. 37]."

Crossroads

If, indeed, the current controversy is part of an evolutionary process, special education must now be at a crossroads of conflicting courses of action. The transition it undergoes will be highly dependent on forthcoming strategies of special education leadership. To continue current self flagellation and recrimination without adequate provisions for shifting to a more viable position is to risk abolishment of all special education. While this might be more in keeping with the professed goals of some writers (Christoplos & Renz, 1969; Lilly, 1970), it could cause irreparable damage to many programs not involved in the controversy. Thus, professionals must reckon with the forces of change, channeling them into courses of action beneficial to the improvement of education for all handicapped populations.

The present controversy concerning special classes might better be viewed as an opportunity to explore needed changes than as evidence that special education is in the throes of a survival crisis. Increased concern with long range solutions, coupled with more systematic application of research and implementation, would allow for orderly transition. Furthermore, that a major shift in programing is required may not be obvious to all concerned (Nelson & Schmidt, 1971). Thus, special education professionals must seek more empirical evidence of the most appropriate course of action, while continuing to maintain and improve the current level of service to the handicapped. Valletutti (1969) has summarized the situation appropriately:

> Segregation or integration is not the critical issue. The values and attitudes of teachers and their effects on the pupil's self-perception and performances are the key questions. Segregation without a program is just as destructive as integration without understanding. Returning to an educational system which ignores the promise and possibility of the special class would disregard the imperatives of educational history, which have mandated an alternative to wide range heterogeneity [p. 407-408].

References

Blatt, B. Some persistently recurring assumptions concerning the mentally subnormal. *Training School Bulletin*, 1960, **57**, 48-59.

Blatt, B. Public policy and the education of children with special needs. *Proceedings of the Conference on the Categorical/Non-Categorical Issue in Special Education*. Columbia: Special Education Department, University of Missouri, 1971. Pp. 49-62.

Christoplos, F., & Renz, P. A critical examination of special education programs. *Journal of Special Education*, 1969, **3**, 371-379.

Connor, F. P. Excellence in special education. *Exceptional Children*, 1964, **30**, 206-209.

Dunn, L. M. Special education for the mildly retarded—Is much of it justifiable? *Exceptional Children*, 1968, **35**, 5-22.

Engel, M. The tin drum revisited. *Journal of Special Education*, 1969, **3**, 380-382.

Fisher, H. K. What is special education? *Special Education in Canada*, 1967, **41**, 9-16.

Franks, D. J. Ethnic and social status characteristics of children in EMR and LD classes. *Exceptional Children*, 1971, **37**, 537-538.

Goldstein, H., Moss, J. W., & Jordon, L. J. The efficacy of special class training on the development of mentally retarded children. Cooperative Research Project 619. Washington, D.C.: HEW, Office of Education, 1965.

Guskin, S. L., & Spicker, H. H. Educational research in mental retardation. In N. Ellis

(Ed.), *International review of research in mental retardation.* Vol. 3. New York: Academic Press, 1968. Pp. 217-278.

Hurley, O. L. A categorical/non-categorical issue: Implications for teacher trainers. *Proceedings of the Missouri Conference on the Categorical/Non-Categorical Issue in Special Education.* Columbia: Special Education Department, University of Missouri, 1971. Pp. 39-40.

Hurley, R. *Poverty and mental retardation—A causal relationship.* New York: Random House, 1969.

Johnson, G. O. Special education for the mentally retarded—A paradox. *Exceptional Children,* 1962, **29,** 62-69.

Johnson, J. L. Special education and the inner city: A challenge of the future or another means for cooling the mark out? *Journal of Special Education,* 1969, **3,** 241-251.

Johnson, G. O. Why special education for the mentally retarded: A rebuttal of criticisms. In *Exceptional Children Conference Papers: Trends and Issues in Special Education.* Papers presented at the 49th Annual Convention of The Council for Exceptional Children, Miami Beach, April, 1971. Pp. 127-134.

Lilly, M. S. Special education: A teapot in a tempest. *Exceptional Children,* 1970, **37,** 43-49.

Lilly, M. S. A training based model for special education. *Exceptional Children,* 1971, **37,** 745-749.

Lucas, C. J. The use and abuse of educational categories. *Proceedings of the Conference on the Categorical/Non-Categorical Issue in Special Education.* Columbia: Special Education Department, University of Missouri, 1971. Pp. 14-22.

MacMillan, D. L. Issues. In R. L. Jones (Chm.), Special education for the mildly retarded—

How justifiable? Symposium presented at the International Conference of The Council for Exceptional Children, Miami Beach, April, 1971.

Miller, J. G., & Schoenfelder, D. S. A rational look at special class placement. *Journal of Special Education,* 1969, **3,** 397-403.

Nelson, C. C., & Schmidt, L. J. The question of the efficacy of special classes. *Exceptional Children,* 1971, **37,** 381-384.

Reger, A., Schroeder, W., & Uschold, D. *Special education: Children with learning problems.* New York: Oxford University Press, 1968.

Reynolds, M. C. What is special education? In R. L. Jones (Chm.), Special education for the mildly retarded—How justifiable? Symposium presented at the International Conference of The Council for Exceptional Children, Miami Beach, April, 1971.

Reynolds, M. C., & Balow, B. Categories and variables in special education. *Proceedings of the Conference on the Categorical/Non-Categorical Issue in Special Education.* Columbia: Special Education Department, University of Missouri, 1971. Pp. 82-96.

Schwartz, R. H. Toward a meaningful education for the retarded adolescent. *Mental Retardation,* 1968, **6** (2), 34-35.

Simches, R. F. The inside outsiders. *Exceptional Children,* 1970, **37,** 5-15.

Smith, J. O. Personal communication. University of Washington, Seattle, 1971.

Stein, A. Strategies for failure. *Harvard Educational Review,* 1971, **41** (2), 158-204.

Stephens, J. M. *The process of schooling, a psychological examination.* New York: Holt, Rinehart, & Winston, 1967.

Valletutti, P. Integration vs. segregation: A useless dialectic. *Journal of Special Education,* 1969, **3,** 405-408.

SOCIAL ACCEPTANCE OF EMRS INTEGRATED INTO A NONGRADED ELEMENTARY SCHOOL

Hollace Goodman
Jay Gottlieb
Robert H. Harrison

20 intermediate unit and 16 primary unit nonEMR children equally divided between the sexes were administered sociometric questionnaires to determine their social acceptance of 3 groups of children: nonEMR children, EMR children who were integrated into the academic routine of a nongraded school, and EMR children who remained segregated in the nongraded school's only self-contained class. The results indicated that both integrated and segregated EMR subjects are rejected significantly more often than nonEMR subjects, that younger subjects are more accepting of others than older subjects, that male subjects express more overt rejection than females, and that integrated EMR children are rejected significantly more often than segregated ones by male subjects but not by females.

An unresolved issue in the field of special education is the determination of the most effective model to edu-

cate mildly mentally retarded (EMR) children. Educational models range from the segregated special class to the fully integrated—no special treatment—setting, with various compromises in between. A partial integration setting where academic segregation is combined with non-academic integration is an example of such

This research was supported pursuant to grant No. OEG—0—8—080506—4597 (607) from the U. S. Office of Education.

Reprinted with permission of the authors and publisher from the *American Journal of Mental Deficiency,* 1972, **76,** 412-417.

compromise. The assessment of the social acceptability of EMR persons to their normal peers has frequently been employed as one of several criteria to evaluate the effectiveness of educational models for the retarded individual.

The literature on the social acceptability of EMR children in different educational placements has been plagued by numerous methodological approaches and diversified findings as noted by Cegelka and Tyler (1970). Some of the methodological questions which have contributed to this state of affairs are: (a) Who are the judges—the EMR subjects' retarded peers, their nonretarded peers, or their teachers? (b) With whom are the EMR subjects being compared—with nonretarded or EMR persons, in the same or different classes? (c) What are the criteria of acceptability—degree of liking, degree of rejection, or degree of indifference? Other variables such as the presence of physical stigmata in EMR children, and the age and sex of the judges and those being judged have further complicated the issue. Irrespective of the methodological considerations raised, no single educational model has been found to be clearly superior for fostering positive social attitudes and relations between EMR children and their regular class peers. As a result, various models are being initiated on an experimental basis in an effort to fill this void.

The present study evaluated one of these experimental models, the nongraded elementary school. In this type of school which is concerned with vertical rather than horizontal organization (Goodlad & Rehage, 1962), all children, including EMR children, are integrated into a variety of flexible groupings depending on the child's competence in different subject matter areas. Thus, a 9-year-old child may be reading first-grade level materials, but working on mathematical concepts usually presented in fourth grade. Each child's strengths and weaknesses are reflected in the educational plan the teachers determine for him. In the nongraded school in which this study was conducted, many children are scheduled for tutorial work in remedial reading and speech, and some for psychotherapy. Thus, the children maintain more complex individualized instructional schedules than is customary in the graded classroom model.

In this suburban school, with a total student body of approximately 140 children, the integration experiment has been functioning for 4 years. The number of integrated EMR children has never exceeded ten during any one year. In addition, eight EMR children, CA 11 to 13 years, are in a segregated special class housed in the school building.

It was hypothesized that the nongraded school should enhance the social acceptability of EMR children since there is no stigmatizing effect of being in a special class for part of the day, as there is in the partial integra-

tion model. The EMR children are in a home room with their age mates enabling nonretarded children to interact maximally with them. Since exposure has been found to relate to favorable attitudes (Jaffe, 1966), the social status of EMR individuals was expected to be reflected accordingly. In addition, although the teachers know the identity of the integrated EMR children, presumably the children do not. The availability of in-class remedial work for all children accustoms them to the fact that any of their peers could require "special" help. As all children have access to individual remedial help, such circumstances may minimize the stigma attached to inadequate academic performance, even in this suburban middle-class school.

An aspect of the issue of finding suitable educational models is to determine the most propitious time to implement them. Is integration into a nongraded school best for the EMR child during his first few school years, or is it advisable to wait until the fourth or fifth grades before integrating him? Will the younger EMR child be more favorably received by his peers than the older EMR child? Although one study did not find the age of the evaluator to be a significant differential determinant of attitudes toward special-class retarded children (Gottlieb, 1969), there was a tendency for second and third-grade nonEMR children to express more tolerant attitudes than fourth through seventh graders. Gottlieb's data appear to support the view that the early integration of EMR individuals would be to their advantage.

In this investigation, the social acceptance of EMR children was examined in relation to the sex of the rater. This variable was included for consideration because previous research has resulted in conflicting findings. Clark (1964) reported that average IQ females are more tolerant of EMR individuals than average IQ males. Gottlieb (1971) did not find this sex difference among Norwegian children. Jaffe (1966) observed that girls express more favorable attitudes when measured by an adjective check list but that there were no significant differences as a function of sex when the semantic differential was employed to measure attitudes.

This study, then, investigated the social acceptance of EMR children who were integrated into a nongraded school as it might relate to the age of their placement and the gender of the nonEMR judge.

METHOD

SUBJECTS

Twenty male and 20 female average IQ children equally divided between the primary (first, second, and third grades) and intermediate (fourth, fifth, and sixth) units of a suburban elementary school comprised the initial sample of this investigation. Subjects were randomly sampled from among the school's population of 123 nonEMR children. Of this latter group of children, 54 were in the primary unit and 69 in the intermediate unit. Subjects ranged in age from approximately 6 to 12 years.

INSTRUMENTS

The Peer Acceptance Scale, an experimental sociometric instrument, was used to obtain social status scores. The instrument booklet contained five pages of seven rows per page. Each row consisted of three sets of stick figures. From left to right on the booklet page, these figures represented: (*a*) two children playing ball together, (*b*) two children at a blackboard, and (*c*) two children with their backs toward each other. These figures were respectively labelled "friend," "alright," and "wouldn't like."

PROCEDURES

During individual testing sessions, each subject was read a list containing the names of children in his unit (primary or intermediate) by one of two experimenters. Each subject in the primary unit was presented a list containing the names of six EMR children (4 boys, 2 girls) interspersed among the names of 29 nonEMR children. The six EMR children were integrated into the primary unit. Four such lists of 35 names were randomly generated in order to include as many nonEMR children as was possible. However, in each list, the names of the same six EMR children appeared. Similar procedures were employed for generating four lists of names for intermediate unit children. Three of the four lists contained 39 names while the fourth contained 37. Included among these were the names of four integrated (1 boy, 3 girls) and eight segregated (5 boys, 3 girls) EMR children. The segregated children were enrolled in the school's only self-contained classroom.

The experimenter read a list of names to each subject and asked him if he knew or ever had heard of each child on the list. The list was then read a second time but now included only those names with whom the subject indicated he was familiar. Two primary level male subjects and one primary level female were discarded from any subsequent analysis of their data since they didn't know any of the EMR children. Data on an additional primary level female who indicated that she knew only one of the EMR children was also discarded in order to obtain proportional cell frequencies.

Each subject was asked to state how he felt about each name by circling the appropriate stick figure: "friend," "alright," or "wouldn't like."

Responses to the *categories* (friend, alright, wouldn't like) and *groups* (average IQ, EMR) were tabulated separately for the factor of *sex* of rater and *unit* (primary, intermediate). Scores were computed as the proportion of children selected within a category relative to the total number of children within a group whom the subject indicated he knew or had heard of. For example, if a subject stated that he knew five EMR children and he then selected two of the five as friends, his score in the "friend" category for the EMR group was .40. Similarly, if he knew 20 nonEMR children and "wouldn't like" five of them, his score in this category for the nonEMR group was .25.

RESULTS

Analyses of variance were computed separately for each of the three categories. Within each analysis, the sex of the rater and the unit were treated as the between subjects effects, while the group factor (average IQ, EMR) was considered as the within subjects effect (Lindquist, 1953).

An analysis of the "friend" category revealed two significant main effects. EMR children were chosen as friends less often than nonretarded children ($F = 14.88$, $1/32$ *df*, $p < .01$), and primary unit subjects selected more peers (irrespective of IQ status) as friends than did intermediate subjects ($F = 7.59$, $1/32$ *df*, $p < .01$). The same general response pattern emerged for the "wouldn't like" category. EMR children were not liked significantly more often than nonretarded children ($F = 4.88$, $1/32$ *df*, $p < .05$), while intermediate unit subjects were more rejecting than primary ones ($F = 9.13$, $1/32$ *df*, $p < .01$).

A significant Sex X Group interaction appeared on the "alright" category ($F = 6.77$, $1/32$ *df*, $p < .05$). Additional analysis of this interaction revealed that non-EMR boys and girls accept their average IQ peers as being alright equally often, but that girls accept EMR children as being alright significantly more so than boys ($t = 5.37$, 32 *df*, $p < .01$). A summary of the means appears in Table 1.

Further consideration of the above data indicated the need to examine the three categories simultaneously. It is entirely possible that the findings for the "wouldn't like" category are simply a restatement of the results for the "friend" category, rather than being independent of them. Therefore, a trend analysis of the difference in proportions between nonretarded and EMR subjects across categories was undertaken. These analyses are presented in Table 2 and indicate two significant findings. The significant linear categories main effect and the absence of a significant quadratic main effect in-

Table 1. Means of the sociometric choices by groups for EMR and nonretarded children.

	Sociometric choice		
Group[a]	Friend	Alright	Wouldn't like
Intermediate boys			
EMR	.117	.242	.642
Nonretarded	.194	.440	.367
Intermediate girls			
EMR	.100	.517	.383
Nonretarded	.281	.387	.332
Primary boys			
EMR	.275	.475	.250
Nonretarded	.344	.416	.239
Primary girls			
EMR	.229	.625	.146
Nonretarded	.371	.491	.138

[a] Each EMR and Nonretarded subgroup refer to the experimenter's classification of the children being rated by the four main groups.

dicate that the three categories form an approximately linear continuum so that the nonretarded subjects are chosen more than EMR subjects as "friends" and less than EMR subjects as "wouldn't like." They are chosen approximately equally often as "alright."

The significant quadratic Category X Sex interaction ($F = 4.34$, 1/32 *df*, $p < .05$) indicates that girls tolerate, rather than accept or reject, EMR children more than boys do.

Although the previous analyses were confined to a comparison of regular grade children and integrated EMR children, an equally compelling question concerns the social acceptance of these two groups in relation to the segregated EMR group. Are EMR children in self-contained classrooms accepted to the same degree as their integrated and nonretarded peers?

The revelant data to examine this question were analyzed in two-way analysis of variance designs. In these analyses, intermediate unit boys versus girls comprised the between factor while the three groups (nonretarded, integrated EMR, segregated EMR) constituted the within factor. Separate analyses were computed for each of the three categories.

Two significant findings emerged for the "friend" category, a Sex X Group interaction ($F = 4.14$, 2/36 *df*, $p < .05$) and a group main effect ($F = 7.57$, 2/36 *df*, $p < .01$). The significant interaction indicated that male raters do not differentiate among the three groups in the proportion of "friend" choices they assign, but female judges favor the nonretarded children over both the integrated EMR children ($t = 4.29$, 18 *df*, $p < .001$) and the segregated ones ($t = 5.48$, 18 *df*, $p < .001$). The female raters did not significantly differ in their degree of liking for EMR children as a function of the latters' group status.

Comparable findings appeared for the "wouldn't like" category. Here, too, a significant Sex X Group interaction ($F = 4.16$, 2/36 *df*, $p < .05$) and a significant main effect for groups ($F = 4.41$, 2/36 *df*, $p < .05$) were obtained. Tests for simple effects of the interaction revealed that girls did not single out any one of the groups for prominent rejection, but boys reject the integrated EMR children more than the segregated ones ($t = 2.56$, 18 *df*, $p < .05$). Integrated EMR children are also rejected more than nonretarded children ($t = 3.40$, 18 *df*, $p < .01$) by male raters.

A significant Sex X Group interaction emerged for the "alright" category ($F = 4.00$, 2/36 *df*, $p < .05$). Further analysis of this finding indicated that girls do not differentiate the three groups on this category. Boys, however, view nonretarded children as being more "alright" than integrated EMR children ($t = 2.71$, 18 *df*, $p < .02$). No significant differences were obtained in the male judges' expressed perceptions of the two EMR groups, nor did these raters significantly differentiate between nonretarded and segregated EMR children on this category.

DISCUSSION

The main findings of this study were as follows: (a) NonEMR children accept EMR children less often and reject them more often than they do other nonEMR children. (b) Young nonEMR children are more accepting of other children than older nonEMR children. (c) Sex differences in patterns of rejection are apparent.

Table 2. Trend analysis for differences in proportions for sociometric choices for nonretarded and EMR children.

Source	Degrees of freedom	Mean square	F
Within subjects	72		
Trials			
Linear	1	.818	20.45**
Quadratic	1	.107	1.18
Trials X Unit			
Linear	1	.139	3.48
Quadratic	1	.080	
Trial X Sex			
Linear	1	.005	
Quadratic	1	.395	4.34*
Trials X Unit X Sex			
Linear	1	.040	1.00
Quadratic	1	.138	1.52
Error			
Linear	32	.040	
Quadratic	32	.091	

*$p < .05$.
**$p < .01$.

Girls express their rejection by not selecting EMR children as friends while boys are prone to use the "wouldn't like" category to express their rejection. (*d*) Integrated EMR children are rejected significantly more often than segregated EMR children by male raters but not by females.

Although the generalizability of our data is seriously constrained by the small sample size, nevertheless, our findings are consistent with other reports (e.g., Johnson & Kirk, 1950) that EMR individuals are rejected more often and accepted less often than nonretarded individuals. Thus, even in an educational environment in which every attempt is made to integrate the EMR children, they still are not socially accepted by nonEMR children as well as their nonretarded peers. Possibly, our data confirm Johnson's (1950) finding that EMR persons are rejected primarily as a result of their behavioral problems rather than for their academic limitations. Unfortunately, the present data do not allow us to examine this issue with greater rigor.

There are, however, other possible explanations for the greater rejection of EMR children. The first of these is the fact that all the EMR children in the study samples were bussed in from other neighborhoods. The remaining children in the school were all community residents. Thus, it is possible that the EMR children were labelled as being different not on the basis of school-designated class placement, but rather because they lived in a different neighborhood and did not have the opportunity to cultivate friendships with nonEMR children during after-school hours. A second possible explanation for the EMR children's less favorable acceptance than their nonEMR peers concerns the visibility of the supportive educational services offered the retarded children. The integrated EMR child's academic routine includes regularly scheduled sessions with the remedial tutor. NonEMR children, on the other hand, visit the tutor on a sporadic basis as a need arises. Consequently, the possibility exists that there is a stronger association between the integrated EMR children and the utilization of specialized remedial services than for the nonretarded children's need for these supports.

The fact that primary unit children are more accepting and less rejecting of their peers offers partial support for Gottlieb's (1969) findings that second- and third-grade Norwegian children tend to be more positively disposed to special class children than fourth through seventh graders. However, the present data extend this finding to include all children. That is, younger children are more tolerant of their peers, whether nonretarded or EMR, than older children. This may result from the fact that older children attend to more subtle features of their environment (Hemmendinger, 1960) than younger children. As such, older children may have a more clearly defined conception of those aspects of their peers that displease them.

The present data indicated that girls are more likely than boys to tolerate EMR children. This would appear to be consistent with the view that girls, by virtue of their prescribed sex roles, have a need to be nurturant (Mischel, 1970). Since girls did not view their peers as "friends" significantly more than boys, a more plausible interpretation would be that girls have a need to avoid an appearance of non-nurturance. The fact that girls and boys are equally likely to rate average IQ children as "alright" but that girls rate EMR children "alright" more than boys do may also be explained by the possibility that it is not socially desirable to actively reject certain children who are "different." Since girls, more than boys, have been found to exhibit behaviors which are socially desirable (Crowne & Marlowe, 1964), they (girls) may be prone to tolerate EMR children so as to maintain the aura of presenting a socially acceptable facade.

With regard to the issue of the relative acceptance of integrated versus segregated EMR children, the data for the intermediate unit did not indicate that an integrated educational placement is conducive to greater social acceptance of the EMR child. On the contrary, male raters rejected integrated EMR children significantly more often than segregated ones. As there was no segregated EMR class for comparison at the primary level, at present the issue regarding the interaction between age of placement and educational model as it affects social acceptance remains unresolved.

It is of interest to speculate on the possible reasons for the greater rejection of integrated EMR children. It may be that regardless of intellectual level, the labelling of certain children as retarded may affect the expectations that nonEMR children maintain for them. In other words, nonEMR individuals may accept more readily deviant behaviors when the behaviors are manifested by children who are clearly defined as being deviant. Integrated EMR children, on the other hand, who are not labelled as retarded may be expected to conform to the behavioral standards of nonEMR children. The failure of the integrated EMR children to adhere to these standards may result in their social rejection. In short, nonEMR children may shift their criteria for acceptable behaviors in other children when they are labelled retarded. The same behaviors which lead to rejection when exhibited by nonEMR children may not result in social rejection when manifested by children who are classified as retarded.

These findings raise many questions regarding the effects of social contact upon intergroup relations. What other variables interact with social contact to influence social acceptance? What is the relationship between amount of contact and degree of acceptance? Is voluntary social contact essential for the development of favorable attitudes or may social contact between nonretarded and EMR children be imposed? Perhaps various activities designed to improve the retarded child's social status, such as those described by Chennault (1967) and Rucker and Vincenzo (1970), may be a necessary addition to an integration program.

Although in this study a nongraded educational model did not result in improved acceptance of EMR children, other variables encompassing social adjustment remain to be examined. Included among these are the self-concept, attitudes toward school, and classroom behaviors of EMR children. These issues are presently being studied by the investigators.

REFERENCES

Cegelka, W. J., & Tyler, J. L. The efficacy of special class placement for the mentally retarded in proper perspective. *The Training School Bulletin*, 1970, **67**, 33–68.

Chennault, M. Improving the social acceptance of unpopular educable mentally retarded pupils in special classes. *American Journal of Mental Deficiency*, 1967, **72**, 455–458.

Clark, E. T. Children's perceptions of educable mentally retarded children. *American Journal of Mental Deficiency*, 1964, **68**, 602–611.

Crowne, D., & Marlowe, D. *The approval motive: Studies in evaluative dependence.* New York: Wiley, 1964.

Goodlad, J. I., & Rehage, K. Unscrambling the vocabulary of school organization. *National Education Association Journal*, 1962, **51**, 34–36.

Gottlieb, J. Attitudes toward retarded children: Effects of evaluator's psychological adjustment and age. *Scandinavian Journal of Educational Research*, 1969, **13**, 170–182.

Gottlieb, J. Attitudes of Norwegian children toward the retarded in relation to sex and situational context. *American Journal of Mental Deficiency*, 1971, **75**, 635–639.

Hemmendinger, L. Developmental theory and the Rorschach method. In M. A. Rickers-Ovsiankina (Ed.), *Rorschach psychology.* New York: Wiley, 1960.

Jaffe, J. Attitudes of adolescents toward the mentally retarded. *American Journal of Mental Deficiency*, 1966, **70**, 907–912.

Johnson, G. O. Social position of mentally handicapped children in regular grades. *American Journal of Mental Deficiency*, 1950, **55**, 60–89.

Johnson, G. O., & Kirk, S. A. Are mentally handicapped children segregated in the regular grades? *Exceptional Children*, 1950, **55**, 60–89.

Lindquist, E. F. *Design and analysis of experiments in psychology and education.* Boston: Houghton Mifflin Company, 1953.

Mischel, W. *Sex-typing and socialization.* In P. H. Mussen (Ed.), *Manual of child psychology.* New York: Wiley, 1970.

Rucker, C. N., & Vincenzo, F. M. Maintaining social acceptance gains made by mentally retarded children. *Exceptional Children*, 1970, **36**, 679–680.

INTELLECTUAL AND SOCIAL DEVELOPMENT IN RELATION TO FAMILY FUNCTIONING: A LONGITUDINAL COMPARISON OF HOME VS. INSTITUTIONAL EFFECTS

John R. Kershner

42 mentally retarded children were tested before entering an institution and 1 year later on measures of SQ (Vineland) and IQ (Stanford-Binet) and their families pre- and postinterviewed to assess the adequacy of family functioning. Comparisons were made with 27 community-based families and their children who were of similar CA and IQ. Family functioning, SQ, and IQ/SQ discrepancy were found to be related to family decisions to seek long-term residential placement. Community families and children showed decreases over the year on all measures taken, whereas institutional families tended to improve in functioning. In the community group, significant positive correlation was found between IQ decrement and family pre-posttest losses. In the institution group, significant negative correlation was found between low initial SQ and family increments in functioning. Results point up the important reciprocal relations existing between the retarded child and his family.

During recent years, it has become apparent that mental retardation is a psychosocial as well as a biological phenomenon. Consequently, there has been a broadening of perspective away from singular consideration of the mentally retarded child in isolation from his social context and toward a purview of the reciprocal relations existing between the retarded child and his family (Cummings, Bayley, & Rie, 1966; Downey, 1963; Fackler, 1968; Farber, 1968; Fowle, 1968; Hansen & Hill, 1964; Hess & Handle, 1967; Mercer, 1966; Peck & Stephens, 1960; Schaffer, 1964; Stone, 1967; Stone

The study was assisted under Grant No. 60 of the Ontario Mental Health Foundation as part of a larger project, Retardation, Family Adequacy and Institutionalization, that was conducted in metropolitan Toronto, Ontario, Canada.

Reprinted with permission of the author and publisher from the *American Journal of Mental Deficiency*, 1970, **75**, 276–284.

& Parnicky, 1966; Thurston, 1960; Tizard & Grad, 1961).

The theoretical formulation of the present study posits the family as a cardinal unit of psychological function involving a complex interplay of family, child, and community variables. The presence of a mentally retarded child is viewed as a source of family stress; institutionalization is one of the family's means of coping with the stressful situation. The purpose of the study is to investigate the influence of child and family factors on the decision to seek institutional placement, and the comparative effects of long-term residential vs. home care on selected child and family factors.

There is a paucity of data bearing on mentally retarded children's social development as it relates to the adequacy of family functioning and intelligence whereas IQ per se as an important factor leading to placement in a residential institution has been the focus of numerous studies. Social quotient (SQ) has generally been reported higher than IQ among retarded populations (Barclay, 1969). However, Pringle (1951) presented evidence indicating that if the tendency of retarded children toward relative acceleration in social competence is reversed (IQ higher than SQ), problem behaviors occurred and the children tended to come from psychologically unfavorable homes. It would appear that the socio-emotional functioning of families, the social adequacy of mentally retarded family members, and the relationship of the retarded child's SQ to his IQ might be interrelated factors that are implicated in the decision to seek institutional placement.

A recent analysis of the effects of institutions (Sarason & Doris, 1969) pointed up the difficulties in making valid inferences from the comparative studies that have been presented in the research literature. Institutionalization has been reported as having a deleterious effect on intellectual and social functioning (Centerwall & Centerwall, 1960) and as exerting a stabilizing influence on IQ (Alper & Horne, 1959), as well as resulting in gains in performance IQ scores over time (Rosen, Stallings, Floor, & Nowakiwska, 1968). However, as pointed up by King and Raynes (1968), little systematic work has been done on identifying variables that may be common to home and institutional environments or in determining the reciprocal relations that may exist among these factors and the longitudinal, social, and intellectual development of retarded children.

In a study that considered family influence, Clarke and Clarke (1954) found that children coming from poor homes showed an increase in IQ following institutionalization, with no such increase observed in children coming from relatively good homes. Clarke and Clarke concluded that the depressing effect of the pre-institutional home environment was the salient factor in the

children's subsequent intellectual growth. In further support of an interrelationship of child and family factors, Barclay and Goulet (1965) found that SQ increases in noninstitutionalized retarded children were more complexly related to family and environmental factors than the IQ advances observed which were largely a function of chronological age (CA).

Following from the theoretical formulation of the present investigation which predicts more stress in families who have reached the decision to admit their retarded children, improvements in the child's and family's functioning would be anticipated subsequent to institutionalization. On the other hand, families who seek counsel but whose retarded child continues to live in the community might be expected to show decrements on measures of family and child functioning over time.

METHOD

The overall plan was to obtain a sample of children who were to be institutionalized in a long-term residence for the mentally retarded and a comparable sample of retarded children for whom institutional placement had not been requested. Information on the children's intellectual and social development as well as the level of functioning of their families was obtained through direct testing of the children and through parental interviews. This constituted the preadmission (Year 1) phase of the investigation.

The postadmission (Year 2) phase consisted of collecting similar data with the exception of SQ scores in the institution sample, after the institution sample had been living in the institution for one year.

SUBJECTS

The subjects were 69 mentally retarded children. The institution sample of 42 retarded children was selected from a larger group that consisted of all admissions (116) to a provincial institution for the retarded from metropolitan Toronto over a 13-month period. The community sample of 27 retarded children was selected from 38 children seen at an outpatient retardation clinic in metropolitan Toronto over the same time interval. The experimental samples represent those children from the 116 institution-based cases and 38 community-based cases on whom all relevant pre- and postadmission data were collected. The groups were of similar ethnic origin (all Caucasian) and matched by CA and mental age (MA). Analysis of IQ and CA between groups indicated that there were no statistically significant differences on intelligence or age at preadmission. The sex ratio within groups differed, with the institution sample having 25

Table 1. Means (standard deviations in parentheses) of IQ and CA at year 1 for institution and community samples.

Analyses	Institution	Community	t
IQ	38.12 (21.49)	43.33 (20.09)	.815
CA (months)	115.21 (47.85)	111.47 (48.88)	.32

Note.—df=67.

boys and 17 girls and the community sample having 22 boys and 5 girls. The number of girls in the community sample was too small to submit to analysis, but within-group analyses between girls and boys in the institution sample on IQ, SQ, IQ/SQ discrepancy at preadmission, and IQ change indicated that there were no differential reactions on any of the measures due to the sex of the children.

PROCEDURE

In the institution sample, the institution notified the family of the date of pending admission, informed the family about the investigation, and solicited the parents' cooperation. In the community sample, the outpatient clinic acquainted the family with the investigation. In both samples, if the family was prepared to cooperate, permission was obtained and dates set for testing the child's IQ, SQ, and for the family interviews.

Intellectual status data were obtained by administration of the Stanford-Binet, Form L, or the Cattell Infant Intelligence Scale (CIIS) which represents a downward extension of the Stanford-Binet, Form L. The same research psychologist attached to the outpatient clinic performed the pre- and postadmission IQ test administrations.

The institution families at preadmission and the community families at pre- and postadmission were asked to complete a Vineland Social Maturity Scale rating (Doll, 1953) on their retarded child.

The data on family functioning were obtained by a social worker attached to the outpatient clinic who held two 2-hour personal interviews with the parents. The measuring instrument of family functioning was an adaptation of the St. Paul Family Functioning Scale (Geismar & Ayres, 1960). The scale approaches family functioning by considering the varied roles that the members play in their family life activities and attempts to compare the adequacy of their role performance with that of a similar normative family. As used by Geismar, and others recently, the technique employed consisted of creating a family protocol from interview data and using this as a basis for ratings on the major categories of family functioning (home and household practices, economic practices, social activities, health and health practices, care and training of children, family relationships and family unity, individual behavior and adjustment). In adapting the scale for use in the present study, the upper limit of scoring each item was expanded from 7 to 10 points to allow for greater sensitivity at the more adequate levels of functioning. In addition, the retarded child's scores were isolated to enable evaluation of family functioning with or without the presence of the retarded child. The adapted scale yields an overall family functioning score ranging from 1 to 10 that represents the average of the seven major areas.

Geismar's original procedures were followed in the collection of data. Lengthy interview protocols were prepared and each was scored by four "naive" raters according to standardized instructions. The raters were not supplied any information regarding the research design or purpose. The modal value of the four raters' scores was then selected as the appropriate score. Previous studies supported the reliability of the original scale (Brown, 1968; Crane, 1967; Geismar & Ayres, 1960; Geismar & La Sorte, 1964; Wallace & Smith, 1965). Evidence now in preparation has been collected on the reliability and validity of the adapted family functioning scale indicating that it was a useful instrument for the purposes of the investigation.

Table 2. Means (standard deviations in parentheses) of IQ, SQ, IQ change, and IQ/SQ discrepancy for institution sample.

Analyses	Institution		t
	Male (N = 25)	Female (N = 17)	
SQ	38.50 (18.56)	37.40 (20.30)	.18
IQ	39.60 (21.59)	35.80 (21.84)	.55
IQ change	3.50 (4.69)	3.20 (2.23)	1.2
IQ/SQ discrepancy (absolute difference between IQ and SQ scores)	7.50 (7.31)	8.90 (6.24)	.65

Note.—df=41.

RESULTS

The following is divided into two subsections. The first, Factors Related to Decision to Institutionalize, is an analysis of SQ, SQ/IQ discrepancy, and family functioning as factors possibly related to institutionalization as well as an analysis of initial SQ and family functioning change over the 1-year period of the project. The second subsection, Comparative Consequences of Institution vs. Community, is an assessment of pre-posttest changes in IQ, SQ, and family functioning in relation to the home and institution environment.

FACTORS RELATED TO DECISION TO INSTITUTIONALIZE

1. Social maturity as reflected by SQ is predicted to be a significant consideration in the decision to institutionalize or not to institutionalize mentally retarded children. Therefore, the SQs of the community sample are predicted to be greater than the institution sample at preadmission. Similarly, the family functioning of the families who seek institutionalization is predicted to be lower than families who have not decided to place their retarded children in an institution.

The SQs of the community children and the family functioning of the community families were found to be significantly greater than the institution sample at preadmission, supporting the predictions that SQ and family functioning as reflected by the instruments used in the present study are important factors in the decision to admit mentally retarded children to an institution or keep them at home.

2. It is hypothesized that the institution sample in comparison to the community sample shows a greater frequency of children with IQs higher than SQs. The SQs of the community children were almost without exception greater than their IQs, whereas the IQ/SQ discrepancy varied in both directions in the institution sample. This finding supports the position that a reversal in the IQ/SQ relationship is an important factor associated with the decision to institutionalize, in addition to possibly denoting a stressful family environment. A chi-square analysis of the frequency of reversals between males (11 reversals out of 25 males) and females

(5 reversals out of 17 females) yielded a chi-square of .8, $p = .40$, indicating that the finding was not influenced by sex differences between groups.

3. Removal of the mentally retarded child from the family is predicted to result in improvement in the level of family functioning as reflected by pre-posttest change in family functioning scores, whereas the continued presence of the retarded child in the home is predicted to result in decrements in family functioning scores. In addition, attesting to the depressing effect that the retarded child's degree of social maturity has upon family functioning, in the institution sample the greatest gains in family functioning are predicted in those families who have children with relatively lower SQ scores. In the community sample, it is predicted that the greatest decrements in family functioning are found in families whose retarded children are relatively lower in SQ.

As predicted, it is apparent that community family functioning tended to decline over the year, whereas the institution family functioning tended to improve. The frequency of families who manifested improvement differed significantly between groups, indicating that the frequency of family functioning score increments among the institution sample was greater than in the community sample. In the institution sample, the initial SQs of the children were significantly negatively correlated with family functioning gain scores (transformed to an unidimensional gain score by the addition of a constant), supporting the prediction that the degree of social maturity of the retarded child is a factor that can have a depressing effect upon the family. The initial SQ scores of the community children showed a non-significant negative correlation with family functioning pre-posttest decrease (transformed to an unidimensional loss score by the addition of a constant). Thus, contrary to the prediction in the community sample, children with lowest SQs were not related to those community families who showed the greatest family functioning pre-posttest losses.

COMPARATIVE CONSEQUENCES OF INSTITUTION VS. COMMUNITY

1. It is predicted that the institution sample families and the community sample families change significantly

Table 3. Means (standard deviations in parentheses) of institution and community samples at year 1 on SQ and family functioning.

Item	Institution	Community	t
SQ	38.07 (19.02)	50.52 (22.11)	2.49*
Family functioning	4.71 (1.65)	6.33 (.94)	5.11*

Note.—$df = 67$.
* $p < .05$.

Table 4. Patterns of SQ in relation to IQ for institution and community samples, year 1.

Item	Institution			Community		
	N	%	IQ/SQ Mean difference	N	%	IQ/SQ Mean difference
SQ higher	24	57.1	7.04	22	81.5	10.77
No difference	2	4.8		3	11.1	
SQ Lower	16	38.1	10.68	2	7.4	8.00
Total	42			27		

in family functioning over the course of the project and that the direction of change favors the institutional sample.

As predicted, the institution sample exhibited a significant pre-postadmission gain in family functioning and the community sample showed a significant pre-postadmission loss in family functioning. In addition, an analysis of covariance on family functioning Year 1-Year 2 gain scores between groups using the preadmission family functioning scores as a covariate to compensate for initial sample differences revealed that the magnitude of the change between samples was statistically significant. The resulting F ratio was 11.64, $p < .05$.

2. The continued presence of the retarded child in an increasingly stressful family situation is predicted to result in pre-posttest losses in IQ and SQ among the community children. In the institution sample, separation from a comparatively stressful family situation is predicted to result in an increase in intellectual functioning.

As predicted, the children in the community sample manifested a significant loss in IQ from Year 1 to Year 2. The prediction that the community children would decrease in SQ was not supported, which is consistent with the nonsignificant relationship found between initial SQ and family functioning loss in the community sample. The finding that the institution children's IQ scores decreased significantly from Year 1 to Year 2 is the opposite of that predicted. Separation from a comparatively stressful family situation did not result in an increase in intellectual functioning. However, it should be understood that the prediction was made sole-

ly on the basis of information about the family and that the institutional setting was considered as a neutral environment. A description of institution parameters was beyond the scope of the study but would need to be examined in detail before a meaningful interpretation of the results could be attempted.

3. It is predicted on the basis of indications gleaned from the literature (Koch, Share, Webb, & Graliker, 1963; Shotwell & Shipe, 1964; Sternlicht & Siegel, 1968; Rosen et al., 1968) that IQ change over time is partially explained by the children's age or initial IQ variations (see Table 6).

After conversion of the IQ change scores to unidirectional loss scores by the addition of a constant, no relationship was found in either community or institution sample between age or initial IQ and the general IQ decrement found in each sample.

4. A significant correlation between initial family functioning and IQ change in the institution sample is predicted. Children who are removed from homes which are relatively more unfavorable are expected to exhibit relatively greater improvements or relatively smaller decrements in IQ. Similarly, in the community sample, a significant correlation between initial family functioning and IQ change is predicted (see Table 6).

Contrary to the prediction, the general IQ decrement found in both groups was not related to the initial functioning of the families.

5. It is predicted that in both community and institution samples there are significant correlations between family functioning change and IQ change over the year of the study (see Table 6).

In the community sample, following conversion of

Table 5. Patterns of family functioning change from year 1 to year 2 for institution and community samples.

Years 1-2 change (raw scores)	Institution		Community	
	N	%	N	%
Family functioning increase	23	54.8	6	2.2
No difference	12	28.6	8	29.6
Family functioning decrease	7	16.6	13	48.2

Table 6. Product-moment correlations between initial and change IQ, SQ, CA, and family functioning scores for institution and community samples.

Groups	Institution (N = 42)	Community (N = 27)	Combined sample (N = 69)
Initial SQ and family functioning, years 1–2 change	−.37*	−.29	
Initial family functioning and IQ change	+.25	−.08	
Family functioning change and IQ change	+.04	+.41*	
Initial CA and IQ, years 1–2 change			+.09
Initial IQ and IQ change			+.05

* $p = <.05$.

family functioning change and IQ change to unidirectional loss scores, the findings revealed a significant positive correlation which supports the prediction. The degree to which the community families decreased in family functioning over the year showed a strong relationship to the loss in IQ shown by their children. In the institution sample, following conversion of family functioning change to unidirectional gain scores and IQ change to unidirectional loss scores, no significant negative correlation was found, thus negating the prediction.

The continued presence of a retarded child in the family for the 1-year period of the project resulted in decreases in the functioning of the family and in the intellectual status of the child. The social maturity of the community children, however, did not decline significantly. The latter finding is in contradiction to Barclay and Goulet (1965), who indicated that SQ was more complexly related to family functioning whereas IQ was largely a function of CA. The results obtained in the present study suggest that IQ may also be a function of the complex interaction of family and environmental factors.

In the institution sample, separation of the retarded child from the family was related to significant increases in the functioning of the family and, contrary to the anticipated outcome, decreases in the intellectual functioning of the institutionalized child. This finding does not, however, support an "institution syndrome" as a similar decrement in IQ was found in the children who remained in their homes. Rather, the interpretation of the IQ loss in both groups appears to be the result of a complex interaction of home, institution, and child

variables. The institution "effect," in this case, was more likely to be idiosyncratic to the particular institution involved in the study than to a general factor associated with institutions per se.

DISCUSSION

It appears that family functioning, SQ, and the relationship of SQ to IQ are factors significantly related to a family's decision to admit their mentally retarded child to an institution. Among the community children, the demonstrated consistently greater SQs in comparison to their IQs suggests that a significantly greater SQ than IQ may be a determining factor in a family's decision to keep their mentally retarded child at home and/or the result of a concerned family's efforts to help their child. The distinctly different patterns of IQ/SQ discrepancy found in comparing the institution and community children indicate that reversals in IQ/SQ discrepancy with IQs greater than SQs may be symptomatic of a stressful family situation that leads eventually to admission of the retarded child to an institution. In view of the significant negative correlation in the institution sample between the children's initial SQ and subsequent family functioning pre-posttest improvement, the results also point up the stressful nature of the presence of a retarded child in the family and the important relationship between the degree of social competence of the child and the adequacy of family functioning. However, in the community sample no relationship existed between initial SQ and family de-

Table 7. Analysis of family functioning year 1–year 2 change in institution and community samples.

Group	Year 1		Year 2		Degrees of freedom	t
	Mean	SD	Mean	SD		
Institution	4.61	1.65	5.26	1.86	41	2.97*
Community	6.33	.94	5.96	.73	26	1.99*

* $p < .05$.

Table 8. IQ and SQ change from year 1 to year 2 for institution and community samples.

Analysis	Year 1		Year 2		Degrees of freedom	t
	Mean	SD	Mean	SD		
IQ—Institution	38.12	21.49	35.55	22.04	41	3.77*
IQ—Community	43.33	20.09	40.63	20.16	26	2.95*
SQ—Community	50.52	22.11	48.89	21.18	26	1.13

* $p < .05$.

creases in functional adequacy, thus cautioning against a simple explanation of social competence and family functioning change.

The predicted observed changes in both groups in family functioning may have been effected by statistical regression toward the mean, thereby limiting the finding's conclusiveness. Following a covariance analysis, the results remained significant but the extent to which the tendency toward regression entered into the pre-posttest difference is unknown.

Also, caution needs to be exercised in interpreting the decrements in functioning that were observed in the community sample as these findings cannot be generalized without reservation to families who have not approached a community facility for professional help. Well-adjusted families who have retarded children living at home may be able to cope quite successfully and, indeed, may maintain or improve in their functional adequacy over time. In addition, the degree to which clinic personnel recommendations may have influenced family decisions leading to the original selection of groups is beyond the scope of the study.

No implications from these data can be made regarding IQ as a factor in differential placement or separation of a retarded child from his family, as the groups were found not different statistically in IQ at the onset of the study.

The IQ decrement found was not significantly associated with initial CA, IQ, or with initial family functioning in either institution or community sample. In the community sample, the IQ decrement was related significantly to lowered family functioning. On the other hand, in the institution sample where IQ loss was expected to be less in families of lower family functioning, the children who decreased less did not come from families whose home environment was most unfavorable. This finding is in contrast to the Clarke and Clarke (1954) finding that children institutionalized from adverse homes fared better intellectually upon institutionalization than children from relatively good home situations.

Clearly, the continued presence of the retarded child in the family resulted in decreases in the functioning of both the child and his family. Although removal of the retarded child produced a favorable effect on family functioning, the decrement in IQ shown by the institutionalized child could not be explained adequately by the data. Institutional variables were not identified nor was a quantification of institutionalized parameters attempted. No support was found for the position that family and home factors are partial determinants of a child's subsequent intellectual development following institutional placement. This finding, however, in view of the complete lack of information regarding the institutional environment involved in the study must remain speculative.

Specific institutional and home environments need to be analyzed for their psychological contents and comparative studies initiated before it will become possible to articulate the question of institution vs. community as a series of meaningful and researchable hypotheses.

In conclusion, the results have pointed up the importance of viewing mental retardation, institutional placement vs. home care, and the intellectual and social development of the mentally retarded child in a socially relevant framework. The complex reciprocal interrelations existing between the retarded child and his environment appear to be crucial to an adequate understanding of the problems presented by families who have a mentally retarded child.

REFERENCES

Alper, A., & Horne, B. Changes in IQ of a group of institutionalized mental defectives over a period of two decades. *American Journal of Medical Deficiency*, 1959, **64**, 474-475.

Barclay, A. Longitudinal changes in intellectual and social development of noninstitutionalized retardates. *American Journal of Mental Deficiency*, 1969, **73**, 831-837.

Barclay, A., & Goulet, L. Short-term changes in intellectual and social maturity of young noninstitutionalized retardates. *American Journal of Mental Deficiency*, 1965, **70**, 257-261.

Brown, G. E. (Ed.) *The multi-problem dilemma, a social research demonstration with multi-problem families.* Metuchen, N. J.: Scarecrow Press, 1968.

Centerwall, S., & Centerwall, W. A study of children with mongolism reared in the home, compared with those reared away from home. *Pediatrics*, 1960, **25**, 678-685.

Clarke, H., & Clarke, A. Cognitive changes in the feeble-minded. _British Journal of Psychology_, 1954, **45**, 173–179.

Crane, J. Analysis of variation in ratings of family functioning. _Area Development Project_, Vancouver, 1967.

Cummings, S. T., Bayley, H. C., & Rie, H. E. Effects of the child's deficiency on the mother: A study of mothers of mentally retarded, chronically ill, and neurotic children. _American Journal of Orthopsychiatry_, 1966, **36**(4), 595.

Doll, E. A. _The measurement of social competence: A manual for the Vineland Social Maturity Scale._ Minneapolis: Educational Test Bureau, Educational Publishing, Inc., 1953.

Downey, K. J. Parents' reasons for institutionalizing severely mentally retarded children. _Journal of Health and Human Behavior_, 1965, **6**, 1963.

Fackler, E. The crisis of institutionalizing a retarded child. _American Journal of Nursing_, 1968, **68**(7), 1508.

Farber, B. _Mental retardation: Its social context and social consequences._ Boston: Houghton Mifflin, 1968.

Fowle, C. M. The effect of the severely mentally retarded child on his family. _American Journal of Mental Deficiency_, 1968, **73**, 468–473.

Geismar, L. L., & Ayres, B. _Measuring family functioning, a manual on a method for evaluating the social functioning of disorganized families._ St. Paul, Minn.: Family Centered Project, Greater Saint Paul United Fund and Council, Inc., 1960.

Geismar, L. L., & La Sorte, M. A. _Understanding the multi-problem family: A conceptual analysis and exploration in early identification._ New York: Association Press, 1964.

Hansen, D. A., & Hill, R. Families under stress. In H. T. Christensen (Ed.), _Handbook of marriage and the family._ Chicago: Rand McNally, 1964.

Hess, R. D., & Handel, G. The family as a psychosocial organization. In G. Handel (Ed.), _The psychosocial interior of the family._ Chicago: Aldine, 1967.

King, R., & Raynes, N. Patterns of institutional care for the severely retarded. _American Journal of Mental Deficiency_, 1968, **72**, 700–709.

Koch, R., Share, J., Webb, A., & Graliker, B. The predictability of Gesell Developmental Scales in mongolism. _Journal of Pediatrics_, 1963, **62**, 93–97.

Mercer, J. R. Patterns of family crisis related to reacceptance of the retardate. _American Journal of Mental Deficiency_, 1966, **71**, 19–32.

Peck, J. R., & Stephens, W. B. A study of the relationship between the attitudes and behavior of parents and that of their mentally defective child. _American Journal of Mental Deficiency_, 1960, **64**, 839.

Pringle, K. Social maturity and social competence. _Educational Review_, 1951, **3**, 183–195.

Rosen, M., Stallings, L., Floor, L., & Nowakiwska, M. Reliability and stability of Wechsler IQ scores for institutionalized mental subnormals. _American Journal of Mental Deficiency_, 1968, **73**, 218–225.

Sarason, S., & Doris, J. _Psychological problems in mental deficiency._ New York: Harper & Row, 1969.

Schaffer, H. R. The too cohesive family: A form of group pathology. _The International Journal of Social Psychiatry_, 1964, **10**, 266–275.

Shotwell, A., & Shipe, D. Effect of out-of-home care on the intellectual and social development of mongoloid children. _American Journal of Mental Deficiency_, 1964, **68**, 693–699.

Sternlicht, M., & Siegel, L. Institutional residence and intellectual functioning. _Journal of Mental Deficiency Research_, 1968, **12**, 119–127.

Stone, N. D. Family factors in willingness to place the mongoloid child. _American Journal of Mental Deficiency_, 1967, **72**, 16–20.

Stone, N. D., & Parnicky, J. J. Factors in child placement: Parental response to congenital defect. _Social Work_, 1966, **11**(2), 35.

Thurston, J. R. Attitudes and emotional reactions of parents of institutionalized retarded patients. _American Journal of Mental Deficiency_, 1960, **65**, 227–235.

Tizard, J., & Grad, J. C. _The mentally handicapped and their families. A social survey._ London: Oxford University Press, 1961.

Wallace, D., & Smith, J. _The Chemung County research demonstration with dependent multi-problem families._ New York: The State Charities Aid Association, 1965.

THE RETARDED CHILD AS A REINFORCING AGENT

Allen E. Wiesen
Gordon Hartley
Colleen Richardson
Allan Roske

Operant levels of social interaction were obtained for six young retarded children. Three pairs were formed of those children having the least interaction with one another. A "generosity" response was then shaped for both Ss of a given pair in which each child learned to give a piece of candy to his partner and in turn be reinforced by E. This technique was employed with a variable interval schedule of 50 seconds whenever both children of a pair were within 3 ft of one another and were not engaging in aggressive, antisocial behavior. Two out of three dyads increased markedly in minutes of interaction and one dyad showed only slight conditioning. Extinction procedures led to a rapid decrease in social interaction and reinstatement of the reinforcement contingency again increased minutes of interaction.

Operant conditioning has been employed successfully to modify and increase social interaction among normal children (Azrin and Lindsley, 1956) and among schizophrenic children (Hingtgen, Sanders, and DeMyer, 1965). Most of the work with severely retarded children, however, has involved the effectiveness of adults, retarded peers and normal peers as social reinforcers for essentially nonsocial, motor behavior rather than social interaction itself (Gewirtz and Baer, 1958; Hartup, 1964; Patterson and Anderson, 1964; Terrell and Stevenson, 1958). Although long acknowledged, the paucity of social interaction among severely retarded children has not been the focus of particular investigation. In view of this, the present study is concerned with the application of operant techniques in an effort to increase the social interaction of six severely retarded children.

METHOD

Subjects. Six children, five boys and one girl, were randomly selected from the ambulatory population of a residence hall to serve as Ss. The age of the Ss ranged from 5 to 9 years and length of institutionalization varied from 6 months to 2 years, one month. The children selected were in the severely retarded category of mental deficiency, with IQ's ranging from 22 to 39 and a mean of 30.3. Vocalization occurred in varying degrees among the Ss but only one spoke in coherent phrases,

Reprinted with permission of the authors and publisher from the *Journal of Experimental Child Psychology*, 1967, **5**, 109–113.

the others emitting sounds of a few disconnected words. Although these children lived on the same side of the hall, there was practically no extended social interaction among them. The few contacts that were observed prior to the study were usually very short, physically aggressive and often irrelevant to other behavior.

Procedure. Operant levels of interaction were recorded in seconds over 5 days during 1-hour periods both inside and outside the residence hall. Social interaction was defined as being within 3 ft of another child and looking at or touching him in a socially acceptable manner. Negative kinds of behavior such as hitting or pushing were not considered for the purpose of this study. Cooperative behavior such as pushing or pulling one another in wagons or swings was regarded as interaction but parallel play in which a task or game was not contingent upon the performance of both partners was not.

After operant levels were obtained for the six Ss, each was paired with the S with whom he had shown the least interaction during the operant level period. This presented no problem since only one pair showed interaction during operant level and only for a total of 20 seconds.

Three sessions of 1 hour each were then spent in shaping a "generosity" response employing each S as a reinforcing agent. In each pair of Ss, child A was reinforced for giving an M & M to child B by, in turn, receiving an M & M from one of the Es. At other times, child B was the reinforcing agent that was, in turn, reinforced by E. At first the Ss tended to consume the candy immediately upon receiving it from E. To prevent this, at the beginning of the shaping phase it was occasionally necessary to hold an agent's hand open and place an M & M in it enabling the other child to take it. The desired response was easily established by the third shaping session without any further intervention by E and was surprisingly resistant to extinction.

After each S learned to function as a reinforcing agent for his partner, intermittent reinforcement was begun. Social interaction, as defined in the operant level procedure, was first reinforced via the reinforcing agent who received an M & M from the E to dispense to his partner on a variable interval schedule of 50 seconds. The member of the pair serving as reinforcing agent was in turn immediately reinforced by *E*. The *E* for each pair of *S*s was changed every session so that experimenter variables would not influence overall rate of interaction.

Conditioning was continued for 14 days after operant level and shaping and then a 5-day extinction phase was initiated in which social interaction was not reinforced though the *E*s were present. Despite social interaction, the agents were no longer given M & M's by the *E*s to give to their partners, nor were the agents themselves reinforced by the *E*s. When extinction was apparent, social interaction was reconditioned for 4 days as a final test of the potency of the independent variable.

RESULTS

The cumulative data in Fig. 1 reflect the general effectiveness of the reinforcement of social interaction with the assistance of retarded subjects trained as reinforcing agents. For example, despite a total of only 20 seconds of social interaction during operant level, in session 18 pair D and P interacted for a considerable 25 minutes and 20 seconds and in session 19 pair R and D displayed social interaction for as long as 32 minutes and 50 seconds. Pair D and P demonstrated the greatest degree of social interaction and usually the most even rate of response acquisition. While no attempt has been made to compare this technique with the more traditional approach in which *E* reinforces both members of a pair directly, data for the two pairs that showed conditioning are reasonably consistent with what might be expected employing the usual technique.

For pairs D and P and R and D, the cumulative minutes of interaction curves rise rather expectedly in the conditioning phase, level off rapidly during extinction and resume their rise as the reinforcement contingency is reinstated during reconditioning. The similarity of the learning curves of these pairs of subjects is particularly observable during reconditioning where the curves tend to be almost perfectly parallel. Whether this is a chance occurrence or the effect of environmental factors cannot be determined due to the rather limited data obtainable during the brief reconditioning phase.

DISCUSSION

The above findings support not only the idea that relationships can be formed by reinforcing social interaction but also point out the feasibility of training retarded children to dispense primary reinforcers to other retarded children. While in these cases the child serving as the reinforcing agent was reinforced by *E* on a 1:1 schedule, it might be possible to maintain this dispensing response on a much thinner schedule and develop what appears to be "generosity."

The failure of *S*s T and K to acquire the interaction response is not surprising in light of their past behavior. Both are somewhat hyperactive children who routinely display destructive behavior toward other children and have several times engaged in fighting. It is possible, then, that the aversive quality of past interactions set the groundwork for what often appeared to be avoidance behavior. The uneven rates of conditioning that were achieved by pairs D and P and R and D were

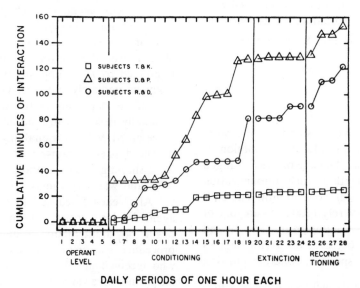

Figure 1.   Conditioning of social interaction in three pairs of retarded *S*s.

not unexpected in light of the constant environmental changes that occurred on a busy wing.

It was initially thought that some difficulty might arise in differentiating assaultive behavior from social interaction. This problem, however, did not materalize as the operational definition of social interaction was sufficiently clear to exclude questionable responses. Blows of any kind were never reinforced nor were responses such as pulling, spitting, or biting. Due to the specific limits set by the operational definition, it was indeed unlikely that assaultive behavior was ever reinforced. With the exception of pair T and K, practically all assaultive interaction discontinued as social interaction was reinforced.

Reinforcement techniques appear to be highly applicable to the socialization of even severely retarded children. The employment of a retarded S as a reinforcing agent may facilitate not only the formation of dyads as found here, but may permit extended social interaction among triads and still larger groups.

REFERENCES

Azrin, N. H., & Lindsley, O. R. The reinforcement of cooperation between children. *J. abnorm. soc. Psychol.,* 1956, **52,** 100–102.

Gewirtz, J. L., & Baer, D. M. The effect of brief social deprivation on behavior for a social reinforcer. *J. abnorm. soc. Psychol.,* 1958, **56,** 49–56.

Hartup, W. W. Friendship status and the effectiveness of peers as reinforcing agents. *J. exp. Child Psychol.,* 1964, **1,** 154–162.

Hingtgen, J. N., Sanders, Beverly, J., & DeMyer, Marian, K. Shaping cooperative responses in early childhood schizophrenics. In L. P. Ullmann and L. Krasner (Eds.), *Case studies in behavior modification.* New York: Holt, Rinehart and Winston, 1965. Pp. 130–138.

Patterson, G. R., & Anderson, D. Peers as social reinforcers. *Child Develpm.,* 1964, **35,** 951–960.

Terrell, Catherine, & Stevenson, H. W. The effectiveness of normal and retarded peers as reinforcing agents. *Amer. J. ment. Defic.,* 1965, **70,** 373–381.

Zigler, E. F., Hodgden, L., & Stevenson, H. W. The effect of support on the performance of normal and feebleminded children. *J. Pers.,* 1958, **26,** 106–122.

3
PHYSICAL HANDICAPS AND LEARNING DISABILITIES

CHAPTER FOUR

PHYSICAL HANDICAPS

Because of the diverse nature of physically handicapping conditions, exceptional persons with physical handicaps are grouped according to their particular kind of physical impairment. However, the grouping of subjects on the basis of common physical disorders in no way ensures uniformity among subjects on psychological attributes. Studies in somatopsychology indicate that the relationships between physical and psychological variables are highly complex. Further, it is probable that the emotional adjustment of individuals to their physical handicap depends in part on situational, developmental, and psychosocial factors (Newman, 1971).

The complexity of the associations existing between physical and psychological variables is illustrated in the study by Myers, Friedman, and Weiner. Myers and her colleagues found that the psychological adjustment of female adolescents to the treatment of an acquired physical disability, scoliosis, required varying durations of time. Moreover, the authors reported that success in adjustment to physical handicaps may be contingent on family as well as subject variables. They cited research indicating that children with acquired orthopedic handicaps have greater esteem for their body and can better cope with anxiety than children with congenital handicaps. Thus, combining subjects with acquired and congenital physical handicaps in the same exceptional group may contribute to individual differences in adjustment within that group.

The biasing effect of medical treatment—especially drug therapy—is likely to occur in research on physically handicapped children as well as in research on learning-disabled and emotionally disturbed children. The effects of drug therapy vary with the length of treatment. In the case of hyperactive children, drugs are administered to suppress behavior. Rawls, Rawls, and Harrison reported that students with allergic disorders were rated by their teachers as less intelligent and lower in achievement than were nonallergic children. It is possible that the performance of the children with allergies was influenced by medication.

Although it is frequently necessary to modify test-administration conditions to allow for handicapping characteristics of subjects in a study, the effects of these test adaptations on the reliability and validity of the test are generally unknown (Newland, 1971). The problem of test modification in the study of cerebral-palsied and other motorically impaired groups has been difficult to resolve. Data reported by Fair and Birch indicated that introducing a rest period between the first and second halves of a standardized test produced differential effects on the test scores of physically handicapped and nonphysically handicapped subjects. The effects of manipulating testing conditions were investigated further by Fassler, who reasoned that behavior accompanying neurological damage, especially distractability, interferes with test performance. The author's research hypothesis was supported in part by data indicating that scores of cerebral-palsied children improved under a condition of low auditory input on some, but not all, of the tasks administered. Unless controlled, the effects of multiple-handicapping factors, such as distractability in cerebral-palsied children, are confounded with the effects of the variables studied by the research worker.

AN INVESTIGATION OF SIX- TO ELEVEN-YEAR-OLD CHILDREN WITH ALLERGIC DISORDERS

Donna J. Rawls
James R. Rawls
C. Wade Harrison

The purpose of the present study was to compare children with and without allergic reactions as to their intellectual ability, academic performance, social interaction patterns, medical history, TAT responses, and scores on a number of other psychological tests. The S population, 1,190 6–11-year-old children, was provided by the National Center for Health Statistics. Placement in the allergic sample was determined by a medical history provided by the parents of each child. The allergic sample included 199 boys and 172 girls, while the nonallergic sample consisted of 419 boys and 400 girls. Results indicated that children who did not exhibit allergic reactions were otherwise healthier and were rated as superior on a number of academic, social, and emotional adjustment dimensions.

A large body of research and clinical reports on allergic disorders has been accumulated over the past 20 years. The majority of studies that have dealt specifically with children have concentrated largely on three major areas: (*a*) the relationship between psychological variables (personality traits, emotional factors, etc.) and allergic disease (largely asthma, hay fever, and skin disorders); (*b*) the relationship between certain familial variables and allergic disease; and (*c*) methods of treatment of allergic individuals (behavior therapy, drug therapy, and psychotherapy) (Freeman, Feingold, Schlesinger, & Gorman, 1964).

The most frequently investigated allergic disorder among children has been bronchial asthma. Several studies have investigated allergic disturbances within the psychosomatic frame of reference and have reported distinctive characteristics of asthmatics, including a large number of neurotic symptoms. Dependency (Fine, 1963; Neuhaus, 1958), high levels of hostility and repressed aggression (Aaron, 1967; Alcock, 1960; Bacon, 1956), parental rejection (French & Alexander, 1941; Garner & Wenar, 1959; Miller & Baruch, 1948), general emotional instability or neuroticism (Fine, 1963; Miller & Baruch, 1967; Riess & DeCillis, 1940; Schatia, 1941), and lower school achievement (Aaron, 1967) have all been ascribed to individuals suffering from asthma.

There is similar evidence for groups with other allergic symptoms. Miller and Baruch (1948, 1950) found allergic Ss (with asthma, hay fever, and/or eczema) to suffer from maternal rejection and to be less overtly hostile in their daily lives and play sessions than nonallergic children. General feelings of loneliness and rejection by parents were observed among asthmatics and children with other allergies, but not among healthy children (Aaron, 1967). Purchard (1967) found psychosomatic skin disorders such as eczema to be related to dependency conflicts with suppressed anger, guilt, and faulty self-image.

It has been consistently found that health is an important factor in social and emotional adjustment during childhood. There is, however, a paucity of data that is directly related to the adjustment of children with allergic reactions to the school environment. The present study, part of a broader inquiry into the social development of children, was designed to investigate the incidence of allergic symptoms among a large sample of 6–11-year-old children as it is related to medical history, academic performance, social interaction patterns, Thematic Apperception Test (TAT) responses, and scores on a number of other psychological tests.

METHOD

Subjects

The S population of 1,190 children was provided by the National Center for Health Statistics. There were 572 girls and 618 boys, ranging from 6 to 11 years of age.

The criterion for being classified as exhibiting allergic reactions was obtained from a medical history provided by the parents of each child. Those

From *Journal of Consulting and Clinical Psychology*, 1971, **36**, 260–264. Copyright 1971 by the American Psychological Association. Reprinted by permission.

TABLE 1

COMPARATIVE ANALYSIS OF ALLERGIC AND NONALLERGIC CHILDREN

Variable	Direction of significance[a]		
	p	Psycho-somatic	Nonpsycho-somatic
Ratings			
Health (physical examination)	.001		*
Motor activity	ns		
Intellectually gifted	.001		*
Above-average students	.001		*
Average students	.001	*	
Slow learners	.001	*	
Intellectual ability	.001		*
Academic performance	.001		*
Nursery school or kindergarten attendance	ns		
Aggression	.001		*
Disciplinary actions	.05	*	
Tension level	.001	*	
Emotional disturbance	.001	*	
Overall adjustment	.001		*
Rank when choosing sides	.001		*
Incidence of being chosen a leader	.001		*
Making new friends	ns		
Race (frequency of whites)	.05	*	
Residence location	ns		
TAT variables			
Queer or unusual verbalizations	.001	*	
Misperceptions	.001	*	
Bizarre themes	.05	*	
Religious emphasis	.001	*	
Morbid content	ns		
Fear	.001	*	
Fantasy	.001	*	
References to poverty	.001		*
Egocentrism	.001		*
Projection	.001		*
Mother–child antagonism	.001		*
Father–child antagonism	.001		*
Mother–father antagonism	.001		*
Child–sibling antagonism	.001		*
Mother–child affection	.001		*
Father–child affection	.001		*
Mother–father affection	.001		*
Child–sibling affection	ns		
Kind, loving, rewarding characters	.001		*
Mean, rejecting, punishing characters	.001		*
Psychological tests			
WRAT Reading	ns		
WRAT Arithmetic	ns		
WISC Vocabulary	ns		
WISC Block Design	ns		
Draw-a-Man	ns		

[a] Asterisk designates higher scoring group.

children who were reported as having asthma, hay fever, skin disorders (eczema, rash, etc.), or any combination thereof were defined as being allergic. The allergy sample included 199 boys and 172 girls, while the control group consisted of 419 boys and 400 girls.

Procedure

The communities from which the children were drawn were selected according to the field data collection locations of the National Center for Health Statistics. The Ss were examined on site within each community in special examination trailers.

Data collected included medical and dental examinations, medical histories, teacher ratings, and ratings by mothers. Demographic data such as socioeconomic status, income level, residential location, etc., were also gathered. Psychological tests included the Wide Range Achievement Test (WRAT) Reading and Arithmetic subtests, the Goodenough Draw-a-Man test, and the Wechsler Intelligence Scale for Children (WISC) Vocabulary and Block Design subtests. All psychological tests were administered and scored by psychologists holding at least a master's degree.

In addition, TAT protocols for Cards 1, 2, 5, 8, and 16 were tape-recorded and subsequently transcribed and scored. Protocols were scored according to a system designed by Sells and Cox (1966). This system provides for scoring of two components: structural and thematic. Structural variables, or measures of language production, are derived by counting the incidence of various parts of speech and speech patterns. Thematic variables are derived from a checklist of outcomes reflecting the S's projection content or tone.

RESULTS

The data were analyzed by means of appropriate ts and chi-squares. Results are presented in Table 1. Analyses of the physical examinations and medical histories indicated that nonallergic children were otherwise significantly healthier than allergic children ($p < .001$); however, no significant difference was found in the motor activity of the two groups.

With regard to school performance, a significantly greater number of allergic Ss were average students or slow learners as opposed to above-average and gifted ($p < .001$). Nonallergic students scored significantly higher on teacher ratings of intellectual ability ($p < .001$) and academic performance ($p < .001$). No significant differences were found between allergic and control groups in regard to nursery school or kindergarten attendance. Teacher ratings of aggression indicated that nonallergic Ss were significantly more aggressive than Ss with allergic reactions ($p < .001$). However, allergic children required more frequent disciplinary action ($p < .05$).

Mother ratings of allergic children showed them to have a higher tension level or to be more tense and nervous ($p < .001$). Teacher ratings indicated that allergic Ss were more frequently emotionally disturbed than nonallergic Ss ($p < .001$). In contrast, nonallergic Ss were rated significantly higher on overall adjustment ($p < .001$).

When choosing sides for games and activities, children in the control group were more likely to be chosen toward the first ($p < .001$). Nonallergic Ss also showed a significantly greater incidence of being chosen a leader ($p < .001$). No differences were found in mother ratings of interchild relations or frequency of making new friends.

A significantly greater number of the allergic children were whites rather than nonwhites ($p < .05$). Whether or not Ss resided in rural or urban areas made no difference.

Analysis of TAT protocols indicated that the stories of allergic children contained a significantly greater number of queer or unusual verbalizations ($p < .001$) and misperceptions ($p < .001$). Allergic Ss' stories also included more bizarre themes ($p < .05$), and there was greater religious emphasis in their stories ($p < .001$). No difference was found with regard to morbid content. Allergic Ss exhibited more fear ($p < .001$) and more fantasy in their protocols ($p < .001$). Control Ss gave more references to poverty in their stories ($p < .001$) and displayed more egocentrism in their responses ($p < .001$).

Nonallergic children showed significantly more projection in their stories ($p < .001$). They exhibited a greater frequency of mother–child antagonism ($p < .001$), father–child antagonism ($p < .001$), mother–father antagonism ($p < .001$), and child–sibling antagonism ($p < .001$) in the content of their responses. At the same time, they exhibited more mother–child affection ($p < .001$), father–child affection ($p < .001$), and mother–father affection ($p < .001$) than did those with an allergy. No difference was found in child–sibling affection.

The attributes of the characters in stories of children who did not exhibit allergic reactions were more frequently kind, loving, and rewarding ($p < .001$). However, they also included more mean, rejecting, and punishing characters in their stories ($p < .001$).

With regard to the other psychological tests, the WRAT Reading and Arithmetic subtests and the WISC Vocabulary and Block Design subtests did not differentiate the two groups. Similarly, the Goodenough Draw-a-Man test failed to discriminate children with allergic disorders from controls.

DISCUSSION

Results of the present study indicated that children who were not reported as having asthma, hay fever, or other allergies were rated as superior on a number of academic and social dimensions when compared to Ss who were reported as exhibiting these reactions. In terms of academic performance, allergic Ss were rated by their teachers as being less intelligent, poorer students, and lower achievers than control Ss. However, the WRAT Reading and Arithmetic subtests, the WISC Vocabulary and Block Design subtests, and the Goodenough Draw-a-Man test failed to differentiate the two groups. These results lend support to Aaron's (1967) conclusion that children with allergic disorders have lower motivation for school achievement. However, another possible explanation is that teachers may misperceive the intellectual ability of the allergic child, assigning lower grades to him as a function of her perception of him as "sickly," nonaggressive, less stable emotionally, etc.

Teacher and mother ratings of adjustment indicated that allergic Ss were significantly less aggressive than nonallergic Ss. This supports the hypothesis that childhood allergy is related to repressed aggression (Aaron, 1967; Alcock, 1960; Bacon, 1956; Miller & Baruch, 1950; Ziskind, 1954). Teachers also rated allergic Ss as being more frequently in need of disciplinary action. These apparently contradictory findings can probably be explained by the fact that teachers also more frequently rated allergic children as being less well adjusted, behavior problems, and less intellectually gifted. Furthermore, mothers more frequently rated allergic children as being more tense and nervous. These findings are in support of previous studies which have indicated that psychosomatic and other sickly children are not as socially or emotionally well adjusted as are healthy children (Aaron, 1967; Hurlock, 1964; Mussen, Conger, & Kagan, 1963; Neuhaus, 1968).

An alternative explanation for teachers rating allergic children as being in more frequent need of discipline may be due to the fact that the allergic child is more inhibited in the home situation, since his problems are likely to be centered around his relationships with his parents. However, when he is outside the family nucleus, he may act out certain impulses.

In terms of interchild relations, children with allergic reactions were less likely to be chosen as leaders and were not likely to be chosen toward the first for games and other activities. This supports the finding that childhood leaders are healthier than followers (Harrison, Rawls, & Rawls, 1968). No significant differences were observed between the two groups in terms of getting along with others or of making new friends.

Several differences were noted in the TAT protocols of the two groups. The stories of children with allergic disorders contained a greater frequency of unusual verbalizations, misperceptions, bizarre themes, and religious emphasis. In addition, more fear and fantasy were exhibited in the protocols of allergic Ss. This constellation of responses appears to lend support to the results of Neuhaus (1958), Bacon (1956), and others, who have found childhood psychosomaticism to be related to emotional instability or neuroticism.

Allergic children also appeared to be relatively emotionally unresponsive or low in affect. This was demonstrated by the fact that they showed significantly less projection in their stories, less mother–child, father–child, and mother–father affection and antagonism in the content of their responses. In addition, allergic Ss less frequently attributed both kind, loving, and rewarding, and mean, rejecting, and punishing traits to the characters in their stories. These data indicate that allergic children might suppress or repress both extremely positive and extremely negative emotions. It may be, as Ziskind (1954) and a number of other writers have suggested, that psychosomatics repress and turn aggression and other conflict-producing emotions inward, which contributes to the development of allergic reactions.

REFERENCES

Aaron, N. S. Some personality differences between asthmatic, allergic, and normal children. *Journal of Clinical Psychology,* 1967, **23**, 336–340.

Alcock, T. Some personality characteristics of asthmatic children. *Journal of Medical Psychology,* 1960, **33**, 133–141.

Bacon, C. L. The role of aggression in the asthmatic attack. *Psychoanalytic Quarterly,* 1956, **25**, 309–323.

Fine, R. The personality of the asthmatic child. In H. I. Schneer (Ed.), *The asthmatic child. Psychosomatic approach to problems and treatment.* New York: Hoeber, 1963.

Freeman, E. J., Feingold, B. F., Schlesinger, K., & Gorman, F. J. Psychological variables in allergic disorders: A review. *Psychosomatic Medicine,* 1964, **26**, 543–575.

French, T. M., & Alexander, F. Psychogenic factors in bronchial allergy. *Psychosomatic Medicine,* 1941, Monograph IV.

Garner, A. M., & Wenar, G. *The mother-child interaction in psychosomatic disorders.* Urbana: University of Illinois Press, 1959.

Harrison, C. W., Rawls, J. R., & Rawls, D. J. Differences between leaders and non-leaders in six to eleven year old children. Paper presented at the meeting of the Southwestern Psychological Association, New Orleans, April 1968.

Hurlock, E. B. *Child development.* (4th ed.) New York: McGraw-Hill, 1964.

Miller, H., & Baruch, D. W. Psychosomatic studies of children with allergic manifestations. I. Maternal rejections. *Psychosomatic Medicine,* 1948, **10**, 275–278.

Miller, H., & Baruch, D. W. A study of hostility in allergic children. *American Journal of Orthopsychiatry,* 1950, **20**, 506–509.

Miller, H., & Baruch, D. W. The emotional problems of childhood and their relation to asthma. In I. Frank & M. Powell (Eds.), *Psychosomatic ailments in childhood and adolescence.* Springfield, Ill.: Charles C Thomas, 1967.

Mussen, P. H., Conger, J. J., & Kagan, J. *Child development and personality.* New York: Harper & Row, 1963.

Neuhaus, E. C. A personality study of asthmatic and cardiac children. *Psychosomatic Medicine,* 1958, **20**, 181–186.

PURCHARD, P. R. Some psychiatric aspects of dermatology. *Psychiatric Quarterly*, 1967, 41, 208–285.

RIESS, B. F., & DeCILLIS, O. E. Personality differences in allergic and non-allergic children. *Journal of Abnormal and Social Psychology*, 1940, 35, 104–113.

SCHATIA, V. The incidence of neurosis in cases of bronchial asthma as determined by the Rorschach test with psychiatric examination. *Psychosomatic Medicine*, 1941, 3, 156–169.

SELLS, S. B., & COX, S. H. *Normative studies of children's performance on the Thematic Apperception Test. I. Standardized scoring and development of measurement scales.* (Institute of Behavioral Research, Texas Christian University, Final Report, Contract No. PH 86-64-103) Washington, D. C.: National Center for Health Statistics, March 1966.

ZISKIND, E. *Psychophysiologic medicine.* Philadelphia: Lea & Febiger, 1954.

PERFORMANCE OF CEREBRAL PALSIED CHILDREN UNDER CONDITIONS OF REDUCED AUDITORY INPUT

Joan Fassler

Abstract: This study investigated the task performance of cerebral palsied children under conditions of reduced auditory input and under normal auditory conditions. A nonhandicapped group was studied in a similar manner. Results indicated that under conditions of reduced auditory input, cerebral palsied children showed some positive change in performance on a recall of missing picture test, an attention test, and on parts of a learning test and digit span test. They showed no change in performance on visual-perceptual or perceptual-motor tasks. The nonhandicapped children showed no significant change in performance under conditions of reduced auditory input.

THE literature about brain damaged and cerebral palsied children often suggests that they are easily distracted by auditory and visual stimuli (Cruickshank, Bentzer, Ratzeburg, & Tannhauser, 1961; Werner & Strauss, 1941). Although research has been done in varying the visual stimuli to which such children are exposed, little has been done involving change or manipulation of the auditory environment.

Cerebral palsied children are children who suffer from brain injury and motor impairment. Other disorders frequently associated with cerebral palsy and brain injury are intellectual retardation, learning disturbances, visuomotor and cognitive disorders, restlessness, failure of concentration, emotional lability, and convulsive disorders and disorders in speech and hearing (Nielsen, 1966).

A particular emphasis on distractibility and figure background disturbances appears in the literature concerned with cerebral palsied and brain injured children. For example, Eisenberg (1964) described such children as being easily distracted by the trivial and the transient. Birch (Birch & Lefford, 1964) suggested that brain injured and cerebral palsied children apparently fail to outgrow the the initial chaos of infancy, or what James (1890) referred to as "one great blooming, buzzing confusion [p. 488]."

The present investigation was designed to examine the possibility that cerebral palsied children with normal auditory acuity may be so satiated with auditory stimuli that this stimulation or their reaction to it may be interfering with their intellectual, cognitive, and perceptual functioning.

There is evidence from the field of sensory psychology indicating that a change in stimuli received through one sense modality may affect performance or behavior involving other modalities. The sensory tonic field theory of perception (Werner & Wapner, 1956), the theory of intersensory synthesis (Birch & Lefford,

JOAN FASSLER *is Research Associate, Research and Demonstration Center, Teachers College, Columbia University, New York. The research reported herein was performed in part pursuant to a grant from the United Cerebral Palsy Research and Educational Foundation, and a grant from the US Office of Education awarded to the Research and Demonstration Center for the Education of Handicapped Children, Teachers College, Columbia University.*

From *Exceptional Children*, 1970, 37, 201-209. Reprinted by permission of The Council for Exceptional Children.

1964), and the concentration of energy theory (Hernandez-Peon & Donoso, 1959; Stern, 1938) all offer cogent evidence supporting this possibility.

Hypotheses

Accordingly, to explore the possibility noted above and to compare the performance of cerebral palsied children and the performance of noncerebral palsied children under conditions of reduced auditory input, the following hypotheses were formulated:

Hypothesis one (a): There will be a positive change in the performance of normally hearing cerebral palsied children on selected tasks of memory, attention, learning, and perceptual abilities under conditions of reduced auditory input.

Hypothesis one (b): There will be a positive change in the performance of normally hearing nonhandicapped children on selected tasks of memory, attention, learning, and perceptual abilities under conditions of reduced auditory input.

Hypothesis two: Normally hearing cerebral palsied children will show a greater amount of positive change on selected tasks of memory, attention, learning, and perceptual abilities under conditions of reduced auditory input than the amount of positive change exhibited by normally hearing children who are not cerebral palsied.

Method

Subjects

One group of subjects consisted of 30 cerebral palsied children with normal auditory acuity, ranging in age from approximately 6 to 13 years and in IQ scores from 70 to 136 (Peabody Picture Vocabulary Test). One subject was ataxic, 3 were athetoids, and the remaining 26 were spastics. The second group consisted of 35 children with normal auditory acuity who were not cerebral palsied and are referred to in this study as the nonhandicapped group. Table 1 indicates that the groups were comparable in chronological age, mental age, and IQ. The ratio of boys to girls was approximately the same for each group.

The Peabody Picture Vocabulary Test was selected for use in this study because it can be administered equally well to normal subjects and to subjects exhibiting a variety of handicapping conditions. It should be noted, however, that an IQ score obtained with this test is a receptive vocabulary score. The test author reports that Peabody mental age scores have correlated with 1960 Stanford Binet mental age scores over the range of .82 to .86 (Dunn, 1965).

TABLE 1

Means and Standard Deviations of Chronological Age, Mental Age, and IQ Score for Cerebral Palsied and Nonhandicapped Groups

	Cerebral palsied (N=30)		Nonhandicapped (N=35)	
	Mean	SD	Mean	SD
Chronological age	114.7[b]	24.3	113.0	21.4
Mental age[a]	103.9	31.4	106.3	28.4
IQ[a]	92.1	17.7	95.2	15.0

a Peabody Picture Vocabulary Test.
b In months.

However, the author also observes that there is need for additional study concerning the statistical validity of the Peabody test.

Setting and Procedure

The major purpose of this study was to ascertain if a reduction in auditory input in the usual environment to which the child was exposed would result in an increase in performance on selected tasks. It was decided, therefore, to keep the setting as natural as possible so that the child could be observed in his customary milieu.

Both groups of subjects received a series of tasks, administered on an individual basis, under two different conditions—normal auditory environment and reduced auditory input. Tasks were administered in an empty classroom with the door remaining open during the testing session. There was an interval of one week's time between the two sessions. A counter-balancing procedure was used so that one-half of all subjects were tested first under normal auditory conditions and the remaining subjects were tested first under conditions of reduced auditory input.

The condition of reduced auditory input was established by placing a set of ear protectors on the subject and allowing him to proceed with his usual routine. The ear protectors, designed to block out a certain amount of auditory stimuli, consisted of a muff type protection for the ears, attached to an adjustable vinyl head band.

Subjects wore the ear protectors for one hour before testing and during the entire testing session. Previous pilot work had shown that children could hear and understand task instructions while wearing the ear protectors.

The condition of normal auditory input included the use of a placebo mechanism that did not block out auditory stimuli, worn before and during the testing session.

Task Selection and Administration

Learning test. This test consists of 15 pictures of common objects. Pictures were selected from the easy pages of the Peabody Picture Vocabulary Test. The complete series of pictures was shown to the child, one by one. Pictures were presented at one-second intervals, each picture covered the preceding one, and each object was named by the examiner as it was shown. After all 15 pictures were shown, the pile was removed and the child was asked to name all objects he could remember. Replies were recorded. The child was shown the same series for three separate trials. The score for each trial was the total number of objects remembered on that trial. Two different sets of pictures of similar vocabulary difficulty were used for this test. One set was used at the first testing session and the second set was used at the second testing session.

To obtain reliability data, this test was administered to 30 fifth graders in an elementary school, on a test-retest basis, in a normal auditory environment. A Pearson product moment correlation coefficient of .52 was obtained from the raw scores achieved on Trial 2 of each testing session. A correlation coefficient of .69 was obtained from the raw scores achieved on Trial 3 of each testing session. A similar test had been used previously (Meyer & Simmel, 1947; Rey, 1941). More recently, a like task has been described by Taylor (1961).

Digit span test. The digit span test was administered and scored on both testing sessions according to the instructions given in the Wechsler Intelligence Scale for Children (Wechsler, 1949). Maximum score for digits forward was 9 points. Maximum score for digits backward was 8 points.

Recall of missing picture. Simple vocabulary picture cards selected from the Stanford Binet Intelligence Scale, Form L-M (Terman & Merrill, 1960) were used for this item. Three picture cards were placed in a row, one at a time, from left to right, facing the child. Each picture was identified as it was placed. The child was asked to examine the entire row. After placing the last object on the table, 10 seconds were allowed for this examination. All pictures were then screened from view, one picture was removed, and the gap closed. The child was asked to look and guess which picture had been taken away. If the response was correct, the procedure was repeated with a series of four, five, six, and additional pictures up to 12. The final score was the total number of correct guesses. Testing for this item was stopped after the first trial in which the child did not recall the missing picture.

In order to obtain reliability data for this task, the test was administered to 30 fifth graders in an elementary school setting on a test-retest basis in a normal auditory environment. A Pearson product moment correlation coefficient of .69 was obtained. A similar test item was used some time ago (Kuhlman, 1922; Terman & Merrill, 1937). A recent description of a similar task has been presented by Taylor (1961).

Attention test. Test 10 of the Hunt Minnesota Test for Organic Brain Damage (Hunt, 1943) was used for this item. The examiner read a list of numbers at the rate of about two per second. The subject was asked to tap whenever he heard the number "3." The test was scored as pass or fail according to the suggestion in the test manual. Four or more correct taps out of a possible number of six correct taps received a grade of pass. Zero, one, two, or three correct taps out of a possible number of six correct taps received a grade of fail.

Designs. Tasks selected from the 1960 Stanford Binet included copying a circle, a square, a diamond, and memory for designs. Each item was administered and scored according to the procedure described in the test manual. The maximum score possible for these tasks was 6 points.

Syracuse visual figure background test. This test consists of a series of pictures which are briefly flashed on a screen by a tachistoscope, with the exposure time controlled. The pictures consist of common everyday objects imbedded in a structured background. After each exposure, the subject is requested to indicate what he has seen. The procedure used in administering this test is described in detail in a monograph concerned with perception and cerebral palsy (Cruickshank, Bice, Wallen, & Lynch, 1965). For this item, performance was scored according to the two major categories suggested by the test authors, i.e., number of correct responses and number of background responses.

The cerebral palsied group received all of the tests described above. The nonhandicapped group, however, received only the first four tests—learning test, digit span test, recall of missing pictures, and attention test.

Analysis of Data

The data were analyzed by an examination of the difference scores* resulting from each child's performance under normal auditory conditions and his performance under conditions of reduced auditory input. The effects of order were found to be negligible. Therefore, in the analysis,

* Throughout this study, "difference score" refers to the score obtained under conditions of reduced auditory input minus the score obtained under normal auditory conditions.

simple *t* tests were used. Although the hypotheses have been stated in a positive direction, the possibility of a negative change in performance was not completely ruled out and, accordingly, two-tailed tests were performed on the data.

The statistic used to test hypothesis one (a) and hypothesis one (b) was the *t* test for paired comparisons (two-tailed). The statistic used to test hypothesis two was the *t* test for independent samples (two-tailed).

Results

Hypothesized Results

An examination of the raw scores of both the cerebral palsied and the nonhandicapped group showed that there was adequate room for improvement in performance in both groups. Table 2 reports

TABLE 2

Means, Standard Deviations, and Tests of Significance for the Difference Scores for Tests Administered to the Cerebral Palsied Group Under Two Different Auditory Conditions (N=30)

	Mean	SD	t	p
Learning test				
Trial 1	.27	2.45	.60	
Trial 2	.23	1.81	.70	
Trial 3	1.00	1.60	3.43	<.01
Total correct responses	1.50	4.25	1.93	
Trial 3 minus Trial 1	.73	2.56	1.57	
Digit span test				
Forward	.30	.84	1.96	
Backward	.30	.75	2.19	<.05
Total	.60	1.25	2.63	<.05
Recall of missing picture	.70	1.42	2.70	<.05
Designs				
Copying designs	-.10	.40	-1.36	
Memory for designs	.03	.41	.44	
Total designs score	-.07	.45	-.81	
Figure background test				
No. of correct responses	-.13	1.14	-.64	
No. of background responses	.00	2.21	.00	

difference scores that show some evidence of improvement in the cerebral palsied group. The cerebral palsied group showed a positive change in performance under conditions of reduced auditory input on the learning test (Trial 3), digit span test (backward and total), and recall of missing picture test. Hypothesis one (a), therefore, was partially supported.

On the attention test, six subjects changed from a grade of failure under normal auditory conditions to a grade of passing under reduced auditory conditions. There were no subjects who changed from a grade of failure under reduced auditory conditions to a grade of passing under normal auditory conditions. The probability of obtaining a zero to six split is 1/64 or .015. This can be judged as a significant change in performance on the attention test and offers additional support for hypothesis one (a).

It is interesting to note that the performance of the cerebral palsied children improved under conditions of reduced auditory input only on those items which involve intellectual and cognitive skills and which depend most heavily on concentration and memory abilities, i.e., the learning, digit span, recall of missing picture, and attention tests. There was no statistical evidence of improvement on tasks that depend largely on visual-perceptual skills or visual-motor skills, i.e., tasks involving figure background discrimination and tasks involving designs.

TABLE 3

Means, Standard Deviations, and Tests of Significance for the Difference Scores for Tests Administered to the Nonhandicapped Group Under Two Different Auditory Conditions (N=25)

	Mean	SD	t
Learning test			
Trial 1	.20	2.29	.52
Trial 2	.83	2.53	1.90
Trial 3	.43	2.25	1.13
Total correct responses	1.46	5.43	1.59
Trial 3 minus Trial 1	.23	2.71	.50
Digit span test			
Forward	.11	.72	.94
Backward	-.06	.84	-.40
Total	.06	1.00	.34
Recall of missing picture	.26	1.69	.90

As can be observed from Table 3, the nonhandicapped group showed no significant change in task performance under conditions of reduced auditory input on the learning, digit span, and recall of missing picture tests. Accordingly, hypothesis one (b) was not supported by the results of this study. In addition, the shift in performance on the attention test indicates that there was no significant change in the performance of the nonhandicapped children on this item under the two auditory conditions.

Hypothesis two states that cerebral palsied children will show a greater amount of improvement under conditions of reduced auditory input than will nonhandicapped children. A comparison of the performance of the two groups on the attention test indicated that the cerebral palsied group showed a greater positive change in performance on this task under conditions of reduced auditory input than the nonhandicapped group. This finding offered some support for hypothesis two. However, a comparison of the difference scores of the two groups on the learning, digit span, and recall of missing picture tests showed no significant difference in the amount of positive change shown by the two groups (Table 4).

Supplementary Analyses

A correlation matrix consisting of Pearson product moment correlations among sex, IQ, and difference scores for tests administered to the cerebral palsied group under normal auditory conditions and tests administered to the same group under conditions of reduced auditory input was prepared. A similar correlation matrix for the nonhandicapped group was also prepared. Of particular interest in these tables was the indication of a possible negative relationship between IQ and learning test mean difference scores in the nonhandicapped group; the lower IQ children in this group appeared to show greater improvement than the higher IQ children on Trial 2 of the learning test and on the total learning test score, under conditions of reduced auditory input. This suggested that the low IQ children in the nonhandicapped group might show some evidence of positive change in performance under conditions of reduced auditory input, even though the group as a whole showed no significant change in performance on any of the tasks. Accordingly, subgroups were established consisting of subjects whose IQ scores were 87 or below and subjects whose IQ scores were 88 or above. Table 5 shows mean difference scores for the two subgroups within the nonhandicapped group. This table shows some evidence of improvement in the low IQ nonhandicapped subgroup on Trial 2 of the learning test, on the total learning test, and on the recall of missing picture test. The high IQ subgroup showed no improvement under conditions of reduced auditory input.

Table 6 reports similar information for

the cerebral palsied children. In the cerebral palsied group some evidence of improvement in performance was shown in both the low IQ and high IQ subgroups.

Discussion

The results of this investigation have shown that a partial reduction in auditory input affected the task performance of cerebral palsied children. This finding can only be considered applicable to cerebral palsied children represented by the present sample group. In addition, it should be noted that only performance on certain tasks showed improvement under conditions of reduced auditory input. Performance on other tasks showed no statistical improvement under such conditions. Therefore, present findings, offering evidence of a change in performance resulting from a change in auditory input, must be considered specific to the type of tasks involved as well as to the nature of the sample group.

It is not clear from this study whether improvement in performance was due to the decrease in auditory stimuli experienced by subjects for one hour prior to the test situation or due to the wearing of ear protectors during the test situation. Additional investigation would be necessary to determine which part of the auditory reduction had the greatest effect on task performance.

The results of this study do, however, suggest several areas toward which future research might be directed. Investigation of the effects of a period of reduced auditory input on the performance or behavior of other groups might include studies involving retarded or low IQ children, brain injured children who are not classified as cerebral palsied, schizophrenics and other emotionally disturbed children, slow learning children, and, possibly, children who have been identified by their teachers as being highly distractible. Cerebral palsied

TABLE 4

Comparison of Difference Scores of Cerebral Palsied and Nonhandicapped for Learning Test, Digit Span Test, and Recall of Missing Picture Test

| | Cerebral palsied (N = 30) | | Nonhandicapped (N = 35) | | |
	Mean	SD	Mean	SD	t
Learning test					
Trial 1	.27	2.45	.20	2.28	.11
Trial 2	.23	1.81	.83	2.53	−1.07
Trial 3	1.00	1.60	.43	2.25	1.16
Total	1.50	4.25	1.46	5.43	.03
Trial 3 minus Trial 1	.73	2.56	.23	2.71	.77
Digit span test					
Forward	.30	.84	.11	.72	.96
Backward	.30	.75	−.06	.84	1.80
Total	.60	1.25	.06	1.00	1.95
Recall of missing picture	.70	1.42	.26	1.69	1.13

TABLE 5

Means, Standard Deviations, and Tests of Significance for Difference Scores of the
Low IQ [a] and High IQ [b] Subjects in the Nonhandicapped Group

	Low IQ subjects (N = 16)			High IQ subjects (N = 19)		
	Mean	SD	t	Mean	SD	t
Learning test						
Trial 1	0.44	2.31	0.76	0.00	2.31	0.00
Trial 2	2.00	2.03	3.94**	−0.16	2.52	−0.27
Trial 3	1.06	2.35	1.81	−0.11	2.08	−0.22
Total	3.50	5.16	2.71*	−0.26	5.16	−0.22
Trial 3 minus 1	0.62	3.07	0.81	−0.11	2.40	−0.19
Digit span test						
Forward	0.19	0.54	1.38	0.05	0.85	0.27
Backward	0.00	0.82	0.00	−0.11	0.88	−0.52
Total	0.19	0.83	0.90	−0.05	1.13	−0.20
Recall of missing picture	0.81	1.33	2.45*	−0.21	1.84	−0.50

[a] Peabody Picture Vocabulary Test IQ score of 87 or below.
[b] Peabody Picture Vocabulary Test IQ score of 88 or above.
* Significant at the .05 level.
** Significant at the .01 level.

children who are blind, emotionally disturbed, or affected by severe motor impairment might be studied in a similar manner. It would also be interesting to study a group of children who have been identified by suitable audiometric techniques as hyperacusic in order to explore the possibility that a reduction in auditory input might have an effect on the behavior or task performance of such children. Different means of auditory reduction might also be investigated, such as the use of a soundproof room or the introduction of white noise as a masking device. The possibility of controlling the base level of the noise to which subjects are exposed in the placebo as well as the experimental condition could also be considered.

In addition, it might be worthwhile to explore the possibility that a reduction in auditory input may also reduce anxiety levels. In the present study, a positive change in performance in the cerebral palsied group occurred on at least one task in which performance is known to be adversely affected by a high degree of anxiety—the digit span task (Siegman, 1956; Glasser & Zimmerman, 1967). Possibly, a period of reduced auditory input could reduce the level of anxiety experienced by an individual, thus making disturbed or highly anxious individuals more amenable to a therapy or learning situation.

Certain practical implications are also suggested by the results of this study. For example, it might be worthwhile to make ear protectors available for cerebral palsied children in schools or hospitals. Ear protectors could be worn at the discretion of the individual child himself. Thus, if the clatter of the dining room was particularly annoying to a child on a certain day, he might reach for a set of ear protectors. Studies could be conducted to see whether or not cerebral palsied children would, in fact, choose to wear ear protectors, how often, in what settings, and which particular children would reach for

TABLE 6

Means, Standard Deviations, and Tests of Significance for Difference Scores of the
Low IQ [a] and High IQ [b] Subjects in the Cerebral Palsied Group

	Low IQ subjects (N = 16)			High IQ subjects (N = 14)		
	Mean	SD	t	Mean	SD	t
Learning test						
Trial 1	0.19	3.04	0.25	0.36	1.65	0.81
Trial 2	0.12	2.00	0.25	0.36	1.65	0.81
Trial 3	0.81	1.72	1.89	1.21	1.48	3.08**
Total	1.12	4.91	0.92	1.93	3.47	2.08
Trial 3 minus Trial 1	0.62	3.01	0.83	0.86	2.03	1.58
Digit span test						
Forward	0.25	1.06	0.94	0.36	0.50	2.69*
Backward	0.12	0.50	1.00	0.50	0.94	1.99
Total	0.38	1.31	1.15	0.86	1.17	2.75*
Recall of missing picture	0.81	1.42	2.28*	0.57	1.45	1.47

[a] Peabody Picture Vocabulary Test IQ score of 87 or below.
[b] Peabody Picture Vocabulary Test IQ score of 88 or above.
* Significant at the .05 level.
** Significant at the .01 level.

the ear protectors most often. Studies might also be conducted to see if the availability of the ear protectors would produce a favorable effect on the actual behavior or performance of cerebral palsied children in school or hospital settings.

Results of this study also suggest certain meaningful implications for IQ testing situations. Specifically, in evaluating the intellectual potential of certain children, such as cerebral palsied or brain injured, it may be important to arrange a test setting to exclude, as much as possible, distracting stimuli. It should be noted, however, that serious concern with this attribute of a test situation is somewhat contradictory to the suggestions and advice presently being offered in testing manuals (Terman & Merrill, 1960, p. 56).

Concerning hypothesis two, it seems appropriate to consider possible explanations for the lack of significant difference in a comparison of the difference scores of the two groups. Part of this explanation may result from the fact that the difference scores for the nonhandicapped group, although showing no significant change under conditions of reduced auditory input, did move slightly in a positive direction. A test comparing two sets of difference scores always loses a certain amount of reliability and this reduction in reliability may have contributed to the lack of statistical significance noted above. The possibility should also be considered that the use of more rigorous techniques in the matching of cerebral palsied subjects with nonhandicapped subjects might have resulted in some additional statistical support for the second hypothesis. Such matching techniques might include selecting two groups within a narrow IQ and chronological age range, careful matching of the range of auditory abilities and possible sensitivity reactions within each group, pretest matching on task performance, and complete neurological examinations.

The implication from the present findings that normal nonhandicapped children are unlikely to show benefit in task performance from a period of reduced auditory input is somewhat consistent with previous findings (Slater, 1966). Accordingly, it is suggested by the present investigator that further studies concerning the task performance of school age children under conditions of reduced auditory input might produce most beneficial results by concentrating on the exceptional child.

References

Birch, H. G., & Lefford, A. Two strategies for studying perception in "brain-damaged" children. In H. G. Birch (Ed.), *Brain damage in children.* Baltimore: Williams & Wilkins, 1964. Pp. 46-60.

Cruickshank, W. M., Bentzer, F. A., Ratzeburg, F. H., & Tannhauser, M. T. *A teaching method for brain-injured and hyperactive children.* Syracuse: Syracuse University Press, 1961.

Cruickshank, W. M., Bice, H. V., Wallen, N. E., & Lynch, K. S. *Perception and cerebral palsy studies in figure-background relationship.* Syracuse; Syracuse University Press, 1965.

Dunn, L. M. *Peabody Picture Vocabulary Test.* Minneapolis: American Guidance Service, 1965.

Eisenberg, L. Behavioral manifestations of cerebral damage. In H. G. Birch (Ed.), *Brain damage in children.* Baltimore: Williams & Wilkins, 1964, Pp. 61-76.

Glasser, A. J., & Zimmerman, I. L. *Clinical interpretation of the Wechsler Intelligence Scale for Children.* New York: Grune & Stratton, 1967.

Hernandez-Peon, R., & Donoso, M. Influence of attention and suggestion upon subcortical evoked electric activity. In *International Congress of Neurological Sciences, Brussels, 21-28, July, 1957. Vol. III.* Fourth International Congress of Electro-encephalography and Clinical Neurophysiology. Eighth Meeting of the International League Against Epilepsy. London: Pergamon Press, 1959.

Hunt, H. F. *Hunt Minnesota Test for Organic Brain Damage.* Minneapolis: University of Minnesota Press, 1943.

James, W. *The principles of psychology.* New York: Holt, Rinehart & Winston, 1890.

Kuhlmann, F. *A handbook of mental tests.* Baltimore: Warwick & York, 1922.

Meyer, E., & Simmel, M. The psychological appraisal of children with neurological defects. *Journal of Abnormal and Social Psychology,* 1947, **42**, 193-205.

Nielsen, H. H. *A psychological study of cerebral palsied children.* Munksgaard, Copenhagen: Scandinavian University Books, 1966.

Rey, A. L'examen psychologique dans les cas d'encephalopathie traumatique. *Archives de Psychologie,* 1941, **28**, 286-340.

Siegman, A. W. The effect of manifest anxiety on a concept formation task, a non-directed learning task and on timed and untimed intelligence tests. *Journal of Consulting Psychology,* 1956, **20**, 176-78.

Slater, B. Effects of noise on pupil performance. Unpublished doctoral dissertation, Columbia University, 1966.

Stern, W. *General psychology from the personalistic standpoint.* H. D. Spoerl (Trans.). New York: Macmillan, 1938.

Taylor, E. M. *Psychological appraisal of children with cerebral defects.* Cambridge, Mass.: Harvard University Press, 1961.

Terman, L. M., & Merrill, M. A. *Measuring intelligence.* A guide to the administration of the new revised Stanford-Binet tests of intelligence. Boston: Houghton-Mifflin, 1937.

Terman, L. M., & Merrill, M. A. *Stanford-Binet Intelligence Scale—Manual for the third revision, Form L-M.* Boston: Houghton-Mifflin, 1960.

Wechsler, D. *Wechsler Intelligence Scale For Children.* New York: Psychological Corp., 1949.

Werner, H., & Strauss, A. A. Pathology of figure-background relation in the child. *Journal of Abnormal and Social Psychology,* 1941, **36**, 236-248.

Werner, H., & Wapner, S. Sensory-tonic field theory of perception: Basic concepts and experiments. *Review Psicologia,* 1956, **50**, 315-337.

EFFECT OF REST ON TEST SCORES OF PHYSICALLY HANDICAPPED AND NONHANDICAPPED CHILDREN

Dennis T. Fair
Jack W. Birch

Abstract. Physically handicapped children given a rest period between two sections of a standardized achievement test performed better on the second section than did handicapped children given no rest. The introduction of the rest interval had no significant effect on the performance of normal children.

Two factors which should be considered while testing the physically handicapped are increased rest periods and increased time limits. Doll (1951), Newland (1963), Johnson (1967), and Anastasi (1968) have indicated that the physically handicapped are susceptible to fatigue if they are subjected to standardized test conditions. Therefore, these researchers advocate altering the manner of test administration and the time requirements if test scores obtained by crippled individuals are to be compared with those of nonhandicapped persons.

Birch, et al. (1966) compared standardized achievement test scores of partially sighted children with scores of children who had no educationally significant visual loss. Both groups were tested with and without time limits, and it was found that the test scores of the handicapped were lowered when they were subjected to standardized time limits.

The purpose of this study was to determine if a rest period given between sections of the *Advanced Stanford Achievement Test* (ASAT) would increase the test scores of physically handicapped children.

Subjects

Ten physically handicapped subjects participated in this investigation. Their diagnoses included muscular dystrophy, arthrogryposis, cerebral palsy, hemophilia, spina bifida, and poliomyelitis. These subjects were subdivided into experimental (Hx) and control (Hy) groups.

Ten nonhandicapped subjects took part in this investigation. They were also subdivided into experimental (Nx) and control (Ny) groups.

All subjects were randomly chosen from two schools in western Pennsylvania. The variables of grade level, IQ, and CA were controlled, their ranges being 7 to 9, 96 to 130, and 12.3 to 15.8, respectively.

Procedure and Results

The Hx and Nx groups were given a 10 minute rest period between Parts A and B of the ASAT Social Studies section. The Hy and Ny groups were not given a rest between Parts A and B of that section. Since the purpose of this study was to determine if rest increased the test scores of physically handicapped children, only Part B of the ASAT was checked. The mean scores and standard deviations of all groups involved in this investigation are summarized in Table 1.

TABLE 1

Means and Standard Deviations for Experimental and Control Groups

Group	Mean	SD
Hx	30.4	3.980
Hy	21.8	3.429
Nx	30.4	2.417
Ny	29.6	3.007

The *t* test was used to determine if the mean performances of the physically handicapped and nonhandicapped subjects were significantly different ($p = .01$). The results can be found in Table 2.

From *Exceptional Children*, 1971, **38**, 335-336. Reprinted by permission of The Council for Exceptional Children.

TABLE 2
t Test for Physically Handicapped
and Nonhandicapped Groups

Groups	Mean differences	df	t	Level of significance
Hx Hy	8.6	8	3.274	.01
Nx Ny	0.8	8	0.415	< .01

Conclusion

There was a significant difference ($p = .01$) between the means of the Hx and Hy groups, but there was not a significant difference between the means of the Nx and Ny groups. Thus, it seems appropriate to conclude that rest periods or extended time arrangements should be provided when physically handicapped pupils are taking standardized tests in order that their total potential ability can be demonstrated.

References

Anastasi, A. *Psychological testing.* (3rd ed.) New York: MacMillan Co., 1968.

Birch, J. W., Tisdall, W. J., Peabody, R., & Sterrett, R. *School achievement and effect of type size on reading in visually handicapped children.* Cooperative Research Program, US Office of Education, Department of Health, Education, and Welfare. Cooperative Research Project No. 1766, Final Report, 1966.

Doll, E. A. Mental evaluation of children with expressive handicaps. *American Journal of Orthopsychiatry,* 1951, **21**, 148-154.

Johnson, G. O. Guidance for exceptional children. In W. M. Cruickshank and G. O. Johnson (Eds.), *Education of exceptional children and youth.* (2nd ed.) Englewood Cliffs, N.J.: Prentice-Hall, 1967.

Newland, T. E. Psychological assessment of exceptional children and youth. In W. M. Cruickshank (Ed.), *Psychology of exceptional children and youth.* Englewood Cliffs, N.J.: Prentice-Hall, 1963.

COPING WITH A CHRONIC DISABILITY: PSYCHOSOCIAL OBSERVATIONS OF GIRLS WITH SCOLIOSIS TREATED WITH THE MILWAUKEE BRACE

Beverly A. Myers
Stanford B. Friedman
Irving B. Weiner

The adjustment to wearing a Milwaukee brace for scoliosis was studied in 26 girls and their mothers. Sixteen girls were able to adjust well after an initially difficult period, seven had behavioral symptoms which interfered with their adaptation, and two refused to wear the brace. The frequency of problems is probably due to 6 of 25 girls being referred because of management difficulty. Factors contributing positively to coping included intellectual understanding of scoliosis and bracing, optimistic view of outcome, active decision to wear brace, and support of family and medical staff. Negative factors included poor intellectual understanding, denial of deformity, conflicts between mother and daughter, family problems, and long duration for the brace. There were no significant associations between the girls' adjustment to the Milwaukee brace and indications of distorted body imagery on projective testing.

The psychosocial implications of wearing the Milwaukee brace for scoliosis have been commented upon by orthopedic surgeons. Riseborough[1] summarizes: "Patients adapt to the brace rapidly, but the initial experience may provoke an emotional storm." Harrington[2] points out that a major alteration in daily living is involved and that patient-parent co-operation is critical for successful treatment. He groups brace wearers into three types: (1) brace riders (who develop ulcers on the chin and avoid exercises), (2) habit formers (who twist their necks and hence avoid the therapeutic forces of the brace), and (3) ideal patients. This paper represents a more detailed examination of how adolescent girls and their mothers psychologically adjust to the girl having to wear a Milwaukee brace.

The effectiveness of the Milwaukee brace in the treatment of mild to moderate idiopathic scoliosis has been demonstrated over the past 10 to 15 years.[1] With early detection, the brace, in conjunction with prescribed exercises,[3] will prevent the progression of the curve in the majority of those children treated.[4] At the University of Rochester Medical Center, one orthopedic surgeon, Louis Goldstein, MD, has extensive experience in the management of scoliosis.[5] In his treatment program, children with curves under 20° are generally observed, while the Milwaukee brace (Figure) is recommended in children under 15 years (bone age) who have curves between 20° and 50°. In the 50° to 70° more

Reprinted with permission of the authors and publisher from *American Journal of Diseases of Children*, 1970, **120**(3), 175-181.

mobile curves, the Milwaukee brace also is recommended, but surgery is the treatment of choice when the spinal deformity is rigid and more than 70°. The Milwaukee brace, in conjunction with prescribed exercises, initially is worn 24 hours a day (a few do not wear the brace to school). If the curve is controlled with the brace and exercise management, it is worn until the spine is mature by radiologic criteria. The duration of wearing the brace is then gradually decreased. If, during the course of this treatment, the progress of the curve is not controlled, surgery is recommended.

Method

The principal author (B.A.M.) interviewed 25 girls, 9 to 16 years of age, and their mothers. Nineteen of these 25 girls were selected randomly from the total group of patients with scoliosis seen by the orthopedic surgeon and his staff. Six girls were referred to us because they presented problems in cooperating with the treatment program.

Each mother was interviewed to explain the study and to obtain information regarding her daughter's experience in adjusting to the Milwaukee brace. General background information on the girls' behavior at home, with peers, and at school was also obtained from each mother. Approximately one month later, the girl was interviewed and three projective tests administered (Holtzman inkblot, Draw-A-Person, and Miale-Holsopple Sentence Completion tests). Most of the girls also were observed during at least one physical therapy session. Further data were obtained from their medical records regarding diagnosis and response to orthopedic table management. The Table summarizes the clinical data on the girls included in the study.

Results and Comment

General Findings.—At the time the brace was recommended by the orthopedic surgeon, 15 of the 25 girls were noted to express overt distress, as manifested by tears and an expression of feeling unable to wear the brace. The setting for this "breakdown" was variable in that it sometimes occurred in the physician's office, later at home, in the

brace shop to get the mold for the brace, or upon getting the brace itself. A few expressed no overt negative response to having to wear a brace per se, but cried at some initial frustration, such as having difficulty entering a car for the first time wearing the brace. The first night in the brace was spontaneously mentioned by three mothers as a frightening event for their daughters, their fears being related to falling out of bed or choking. Despite their initial distress, all but five of the girls regularly wore the brace within two to four weeks and, for the most part, were able to resume their usual daily routine.

The task of facing friends, school, and the public in a brace was difficult, but not insurmountable. The brace, in drawing attention to a deformity not previously conspicuous, altered the girls' relationships to the outside world and commonly resulted in a tendency to withdraw. Five of the 25 girls persisted in their refusal for several weeks or longer, but eventually three of these five agreed to wear the brace. Facing the public alone with the brace outside of the school was more difficult. For example, the girls preferred to go shopping with their mothers, rather than alone, and preferred not to wear their braces for church. Thus, although they were able to resume their usual school and extracurricular activities, the majority exhibited some avoidance of being seen in public in the brace.

The girls' compliance with the exercise program, an essential aspect of the treatment, was noted to be related to the nature of their relationship to their mothers. Twelve of the girls, who were judged to have a good relationship with their mothers, were able to take responsibility for doing the exercises with minimal need to be reminded. On the other hand, 11 girls judged to be overly dependent on their mothers, relied heavily on them to carry out the exercises, as well as to help with many

other aspects of their daily life. (In two cases it was not possible to judge the mother-child relationship from the information obtained.) The treatment program went well as long as mothers did not resent this marked dependence on them. However, a previous pattern of over-dependence and mutual resentment, identified in 4 of the 11, was exaggerated by the demands of the exercise program, and the conflict resulted in haphazard, intermittent attempts at the exercises.

It was our impression that those girls who displayed overt crying and what appeared to be a period of withdrawal and depression followed by a conscious decision to wear the brace and do the exercises showed a better ability to tolerate the brace than those girls who did not show this type of initial response. The active decision of both daughter and parents to follow through with the recommended program seems essential to effective results, and when either was not convinced of the need for the brace, difficulties arose. However, this impression that better cooperation and follow through actually led to better correction of the curvature could not be measured objectively in this study.

Families' continued support and praise for their daughters was crucial in keeping the girls wearing their braces and continuing their usual activities. This support was noted to be impaired by serious personality problems in the parents or marital conflicts. Such parental problems were noted in six of nine having difficulties in wearing the brace, but were not identified in any who wore the brace without difficulty.

The support of the staff involved (orthopedic surgeon, physical therapist, bracemaker, secretaries, school nurses) was also important to the continued wearing of the brace. The physical therapist played a key role in encouraging the girls, as well as in detecting those who were having difficulties. Likewise, regular ortho-

Summary of Clinical Data

Case	Age (Yr)	Duration/ Wearing Brace (Mo)	Degrees of Curvature Before	Change	Problems With Brace and Exercises	Adjust-ment
1	12	10	18	−13	Not doing exercises regularly	G
2	12½	4	18	0	Overly dependent on mother	G
3	13½	6	36	0	None	G
4	13	48	40	−15	Out of brace often; problems with exercises; overly dependent on mother	P
5	12½	2	25	0	Initial refusal; later worn 18 hr/day*	G
6	12½	10	54	−34	None	G
7	13	12	31	−4	None	G
8	14	4	36	−9	None	G
9	15½	10	30	−15	None	G
10	12	33	29	−16	None	G
11	12½	8	54	−12	Overly dependent on mother	G
12	12	3	52	−16	None	G
13	12½	1	21	−3	None	G
14	15	33	65	−25	Out of brace often; problems with exercises	G
15	9	8	38	−20	Problems with exercises; enuresis*†	P
16	13	6	25	−14	Problems with exercises	P
17	14	Data not available	40	Data not available	Refused brace; doing exercises; withdrawn*	P
18	13½	4	48	−8	Not doing exercises; school phobia	P
19	12½	7	60	+2		G
20	13½	16	30	−18	None	G
21	13½	24	51	−19	Problems with exercises for six months; dependent on mother	P
22	13	6	61	−24	None	G
23	10	25	34	−8	Congenital scoliosis; +33° in three weeks out of brace; wearing and doing exercises*†	P
24	13	6	Data not available	Data not available	Problems wearing brace and doing exercises; mental retardation	P
25	14	Data not available	Data not available	Data not available	Muscular dystrophy; refused brace*†	P

* Referred because of problems.
† Projective tests not given.

pedic visits facilitated coordination and communication between staff and families, as problems related to the brace could be raised and handled jointly by the orthopedic surgeon, bracemaker, and physical therapist.

Families with previous experience with the brace were able to support others who were just starting out. A visit to meet a girl currently wearing a brace was sometimes suggested and was of considerable help to a family in making a decision about their own commitment to this corrective procedure.

Stabilization or improvement in the curvature, usually achieved within the first three to six months, was gratifying to the girl and her family. However, as the months and years went on, problems appeared. The brace, viewed more as a "prison," was worn less often and exercises were done less regularly. Of the four girls who had worn the brace more than two years, three were having increasing difficulty in complying with wearing the brace 24 hours a day and doing the exercises.

An overall assessment of the adaptation, or "adjustment," of the girls studied was made with placement into one of two groups: (1) "good" adaptation (G) was defined as the ability to wear the brace and do the exercises, a good attendance record at school, the presence of positive family and peer relationships, and the identification of few or no emotional problems, and (2) "poor" adaptation (P) was defined as the presence of serious problems in wearing the brace and doing exercises, difficulties attending school, poor peer and family relationships, and the presence of behavioral or emotional symptoms. Of the 25 girls, 16 were judged to have made a good adaptation, and nine were judged to have made a poor adjustment. It should be noted that six of these nine girls were specifically referred to the authors because of behavioral problems, and, thus, this sample does not reflect a nonbiased population of girls wearing Milwaukee braces.

Coping Behavior.—The process of adaptation to a brace for a disability may be viewed from the point of view of psychological stress and the coping process. Lazarus[6] defines *coping behavior* as "those means utilized by an individual to tolerate a threat without disruptive anxiety or depression." After the recognition of a threat to himself or to his motives, the individual may be observed to respond to this stress in one or more of several ways: (1) intrapsychic defense mechanisms or maneuvers in which the individual deceives himself about the actual conditions of the threat (eg, denial, intellectualization); (2) motor-behavioral reactions to reduce the threat (including actions aimed at strengthening the individual's resources against harm, attack, or avoidance); (3) disturbed affect of varying degrees (including anxiety, anger, guilt, depression). The first two categories, intrapsychic defense mechanisms and motor behavioral reactions, comprise the *coping process*, the means by which anticipated threat or harm is reduced or eliminated.

The coping process may be judged as effective with reference to the degree to which it protects the individual from overwhelming psychological distress, regardless of whether the behavior is socially or medically desirable. Thus, for example, complete denial of the threat of a deformity may protect an individual from experiencing extreme distress, though it may also prevent him from seeking the appropriate medical help. Coping behavior also may be judged in terms of the individual's ability to carry out socially desirable goals, irrespective of the distress he experiences psychologically. Thus, for example, a mother who is able to tend to her chronically handicapped child, no matter how distressed she feels, may be viewed as coping successfully. Optimal coping, therefore, protects the individual from being psychologically overwhelmed, yet allows for sufficient recognition of the illness to seek medical help.

Coping behavior depends upon many variables, including the nature and duration of the threat, the personality resources and past experience of the individual involved, and the resources available in the environment. Coping under severe stress situations has been studied in patients with severe burns,[7] polio patients with respiratory paralysis,[8] parents of fatally ill children,[9] as well as chronic physical disabilities.[10] The following is an examination of the coping process of girls and their mothers to the girl wearing the Milwaukee brace for scoliosis.

Intrapsychic Defense Mechanisms.
—The process of identification, or the perception of another as an extension of oneself, was a prominent feature of all mothers interviewed. In fact, during the interview with the mothers, it was often difficult to have them describe their daughters' reactions as separate

from their own. The threat to the daughter seemed to be an identical threat to the mother. This was reflected in such statements by the mother as: "I didn't think it would happen to *us*" and "How can *we* live with this." Several mothers commented on their need to make a conscious effort not to do everything for their daughters and to recognize them as separate individuals. Moreover, the girls' expressed attitudes toward the brace were usually identical to those of their mothers. Their ability to cope with the brace well (or poorly) seemed so closely tied with their mothers' attitudes that it was impossible to attribute strength to either independently. At times, the strength to cope with this chronic disability seemed to be increased by the support that was gained via this identification process, even when marked, as in the following example:

> A mother with an only daughter actually performed the exercises herself regularly with her daughter and constantly wished there was something more she could do for her. This obese girl was able to cope with the brace both at school and in public, and had even begun to lose weight. Thus, the mother's identification with her daughter aided rather than impaired the girl's ability to function independently at school (case 11).

Denial was recognized frequently as a coping mechanism in the group of mothers and their daughters. It was usually not so pervasive that it interfered significantly with the ability to follow the treatment recommendations. The process of *denying the feelings* or distress (isolation of affect) was observed in most mothers. They showed no overt distress at critical times in their daughters' course, and several mothers commented about feeling an initial "shock" or numbness when first informed about the seriousness of their daughter's deformity. This absence of experiencing the full emotional impact upon hearing the diagnosis and treatment can easily be misinterpreted as lack of concern, rather

than a protective mechanism. At least some of the girls experienced the same initial "shock" which later gave way to the overt distress and tears.

Most families *denied the threat* of the deformity by minimizing the problem before seeing the orthopedic surgeon, eg, "I didn't think it was serious." This tendency to minimize the seriousness of the handicap and the wearing of the brace protected the individual from overwhelming distress, whereas total denial of the threat can lead to rejection of medical help:

> A 14-year-old girl who refused to wear the brace, despite a 40° curve, denied the threat of scoliosis in such comments as "I don't have to look at it. . . . (her back). There's something wrong with it, but it's not that bad. I do my exercises. That's enough. . . . I just don't want to hear about them (the possible long-term effects of ignoring the scoliosis) . . . it's none of my business. . . ." This girl had difficulty in complying with the orthopedic management and was specifically referred to the authors because of her refusal (case 17).

The inability to admit the very existence of an obvious deformity is a severe distortion of reality and an indication of little personal resources to cope with threat. It is frequently accompanied by an intense expression of anger at those who attempt to point out the presence of this deformity. This degree of denial was observed only in one family, and such denial seriously interfered with the treatment plan:

> A father of a 9-year-old girl had considerable difficulty accepting her severe deformity, and, according to mother, felt "the defect doesn't exist if he doesn't think about it." He felt the brace was of no use and discouraged his daughter from wearing the brace. It took several attempts to have him talk over his daughter's management with the physician, and thus support her to wear the brace. A deterioration of 33° in the curvature in three weeks out of the brace "because she was ill" may have helped convince him,

yet some weeks later, the author met this girl without her brace at a store (case 23).

Intellectualization, or the process of analyzing a situation rationally, was used frequently as a means of reducing the threat. Almost all mothers rationalized by saying that "the brace is better than surgery." Understanding scoliosis and the therapeutic program greatly helped both the girls and their families in tolerating the long orthopedic program. Conversely, the inability to understand, because of communication difficulties, as observed in cases due to mental retardation, deafness, or the inability to speak English, seriously interfered with the comprehension of the back deformity and compliance with the treatment program.

A 13-year-old mentally retarded girl with epilepsy had little understanding of her deformity and the reason for the brace. She seemed to feel her mother "didn't love" her and made her wear the brace as punishment. Mother felt intensely distressed and guilty by this and found it difficult to insist that her daughter wear the brace.

Reaction formation is an action, feeling, or opinion which is the opposite to what would commonly be expected and may help the individual master a stressful situation. This process was seen in a few families where the commonly expected responses seemed to be intolerable or unacceptable. When not extreme, this process served to diminish the anticipated threat and increase the sense of mastery.

A mother of a 13-year-old girl was persistently upset that her daughter had to wear "one of those awful things," took her daughter out to a concert shortly after getting the brace "to prove we could do it" (case 1).

Displacement is the transfer of a feeling away from the individual or situation to which it was originally attached to another individual or situation. It was impossible for some families to express anger or distress

directly in response to an emotionally arousing event. For example, rather than express anger directly at the current medical staff, previous physicians were blamed for disappointments about progress. In addition, there were complaints about the school not being helpful, when in reality, the hospital was the source of the difficulty. In this way, the possible disruption of the necessary relationship with the physician and paramedical staff was avoided.

Motor Activity.—Motor-behavioral interactions with the individual's environment were observed to be part of the coping process and served to reduce the threat of this deformity. Most important, obviously, were wearing the brace and doing the exercises. These activities had both direct medical benefit and also the psychological assurance that something was actively being done to deal with the threat of an increasing back deformity. By their actions, mothers also were able to help their daughters adapt to the brace. For instance, they were quite imaginative in finding clothing to make the girls feel more attractive. Parents created various adaptations to enable the girls to see down to what they were eating or writing while at a desk or table. A preparatory visit to school after hours with a parent to make desk rearrangements also was noted to be helpful. By these and other ways, the girls and their families were able to take appropriate action to reduce the threat of the deformity and of the wearing of the brace.

Avoidance of the brace itself may be the only alternative to avoidance of society and overwhelming distress. Occasionally, but rarely, the brace may be too much to ask of an adolescent girl, given her particular life situation:

A 13-year-old girl with progressive muscular weakness as a young child had been thought by her family to have a fatal illness. Although her weakness did not progress or alter ambulation, she later had to cope

with the loss of her mother. When a progressive scoliosis developed, her new stepmother was quite unable to support the girl in wearing the Milwaukee brace. The girl stated, "I don't care what the future holds. I want to enjoy myself now and the brace makes me miserable. I am going to high school next year (instead of a class for physically handicapped) and I don't want to be different from the other kids." The many prior stresses left this girl little reserve to cope with the superimposed stress of a developing scoliosis (case 25).

Projective Testing.—Because of the adolescent youngster's usual concern about the appearance of his body and his heightened sensitivity to deviations from the ideal, it was expected that these girls' adjustment to their scoliosis would be reflected in their perception of their body. The projective test data were accordingly analyzed primarily for indications of disturbed body imagery and inordinate concerns about physical disability.

Fisher and Cleveland,[11-13] in their extensive explorations of the relation of body image to other personality factors, have developed two major body boundary indices that can be scored from the Holtzman inkblot test: the Barrier index, which refers to definiteness of body boundaries, and the Penetration index, which measures a lack of disruption of a perceived discrete body exterior. A number of studies have demonstrated an association between increasing boundary definiteness, diminished likelihood of psychosis, and enhanced ability to deal effectively with difficult disturbing experiences, especially those involving body disablement.[11] Thus, higher Barrier scores have been observed to be directly related to the ability to adjust to the stress of body disablement as measured in paraplegic men and pregnant women.[14] High Penetration scores, on the other hand, are associated with schizophrenia and have also been observed in individuals several years after colostomy. Fisher[11] also suggests that Penetration scores are particularly sensitive to immediate situational conditions.

The Barrier scores of these girls wearing the Milwaukee brace for scoliosis ranged from 0 to 7 with a median of 3.6. This median value closely resembled the median Barrier score of 3 observed in normal populations of adults and adolescent girls. Indeed, the Barrier scores of the girls with satisfactory adjustment did not differ significantly from those of the girls with adjustment problems. In contrast to the normally observed median Penetration score of 1, however, these girls had a Penetration range of 0 to 10, with a median of 5.5. This median value for the whole group was comparable to the level seen in schizophrenic groups. One interpretation of this finding would be that the whole experience of wearing a Milwaukee brace, even though there is no actual penetration of the skin, constituted a threat to the perception of bodily integrity and is reflected in these high Penetration scores. With respect to recency to the traumatic event, however, no significant differences in median Penetration score were found between those girls who had recently begun to wear the brace (six months or less) and those who had worn it for a relatively long time (more than six months).

The Draw-A-Person and Sentence Completion tests did not contribute further to the demonstration or problems with body image. With only one exception (a girl with onset of scoliosis in early childhood), none of the girls drew human figures containing significant body distortions reflecting disturbed body imagery. The Sentence Completion protocols were strikingly free from references to disability, and the most that could be concluded from them was the girls, as noted above, probably had significant needs to deny their deformities.

Conclusions

The majority of the girls observed were able, after an "initial storm,"[1] to cope with wearing a Milwaukee brace and carry on their usual daily lives. This was in spite of a biased sample which included an inordinate number of girls having problems wearing the brace. In this study it was possible to identify a number of the factors existing in the girl and her family, as well as in their environment (including the medical milieu), which influenced the manner and success of coping with a chronic disability. Those factors contributing positively to the girls' ability to cope included: (1) the girls' and their mothers' intellectual understanding of scoliosis and the reason for the bracing procedure; (2) the girls' and her parents' active decision to wear the brace; (3) the family's continuing support and encouragement; (4) the relatively optimistic view of outcome with a definite termination time; (5) the support, coordination, continuity and interest of the regular visits with the medical staff.

Another possible factor may be the fact that these girls had a handicap appearing later in childhood, rather than one existing from birth. Although there are few studies comparing acquired versus congenital handicaps, it is interesting to note a study by Kimmel[15] who suggests that children with acquired orthopedic handicaps have a greater esteem for their bodies and can cope with more anxiety than can children with congenital handicaps. In agreement with this, the two girls who had handicaps dating from early childhood (case 23 and 25) were observed to have especially serious problems in adapting to the brace in contrast to the majority of the others whose deformity developed much later. The minimal disturbance of body image in the majority of girls, as measured by the projective tests, may reflect the later onset of scoliosis.

Among those factors which contributed to difficulties in coping were: (1) limitations in intellectual understanding of scoliosis and the brace (eg, mental retardation, language barriers); (2) total denial of the deformity or the threat it posed; (3) daughters' excessive dependence leading to conflict with mother, particularly around exercises; (4) marital conflicts and other personality problems in the parents leading to little support for the daughters; (5) the long duration of wearing the brace; and (6) increasing threat of surgery, indicating the failure of the brace.

There are several implications in our data for the physician and other professionals dealing with children with chronic handicaps. While each individual's manner of coping is unique and related to his personality structure and available resources, there are nevertheless certain patterns common to many. Awareness and understanding to these patterns can facilitate the effectiveness of any professional dealing with the chronically handicapped. Green and Haggerty[16] emphasize this in discussing the general principles of management of long-term, non-life-threatening illness in children, which include continuity of care, individualization of care, and awareness of parental reactions. Coping mechanisms should be viewed not only as protection from intolerable anxiety or depression, but also in terms of how such behavior contributes to, or interferes with, cooperation with the treatment program for the handicapped child.

The pediatrician, in addition to his early detection of the scoliosis, can help the family by his continuing interest and support and by his preparation of the family for referral. Some explanation of the problem and the possible means of management can facilitate understanding and hence a greater ability to adjust to the therapeutic program. This anticipatory guidance by the referring physician may be extremely helpful in that the expected psychosocial problems can be discussed with the family. Such advanced warning, if not in itself made overwhelming, promotes subsequent mastery of the task the adolescent must face in wearing the Milwaukee brace.

This investigation was supported by Children's Bureau grant 148 and Public Health Service grant K3-MH-18, 542 (Dr. Friedman) from the National Institute of Mental Health.

References

1. Riseborough EJ: Current concepts: Treatment of scoliosis. *New Eng J Med* **276**:1429-1431, 1967.

2. Harrington PR: Nonoperative treatment of scoliosis. *Texas Med* **64**:54-65, 1958.

3. Blount WP, Bolinske J: Physical therapy in the nonoperative treatment of scoliosis. *Phys Ther* **47**:919-923, 1967.

4. Blount WP: Scoliosis and Milwaukee brace. *Bull Hosp Joint Dis* **19**:152-165, 1968.

5. Goldstein AL: Surgical management of scoliosis. *J Bone Joint Surg* **48**:167-180, 1966.

6. Lazarus RS: *Psychological Stress and the Coping Process*. New York, McGraw-Hill, 1966.

7. Hamburg DA, Hamburg B, deSozer S: Adaptive problems and mechanisms in severely burned patients. *Psychiatry* **16**:1-20, 1953.

8. Visotsky HM, Hamburg DA, Goss MA, et al: Coping behavior under extreme stress. *Arch Gen Psychiat* **5**:423-488, 1961.

9. Friedman SB, Chodoff P, Mason JW, et al: Behavioral observations on parents anticipating the death of a child. *Pediatrics* **32**:610-625, 1963.

10. Wright B: *Physical Disability: A Psychological Approach*. New York, Harper & Row, 1960.

11. Fisher S: A further appraisal of the body boundary concept. *J Consult Psychol* **27**:62-70, 1963.

12. Fisher S: Body image psychopathology. *Arch Gen Psychiat* **10**:519-529, 1964.

13. Fisher S, Cleveland SE: *Body Image and Personality*. Princeton, NJ, D Van Nostrand, 1958.

14. Landau, quoted by Wiener I: *Psychodiagnosis of Schizophrenia*. New York, John Wiley, 1966, p 132.

15. Kimmel J: A comparison of children with congenital and acquired orthopedic handicaps on certain personality characteristics. *Dissertation Abstracts* **19**:3023, 1959.

16. Green M, Haggerty R: *Ambulatory Pediatrics*. Philadelphia, WB Saunders, 1968, p 443.

CHAPTER FIVE

LEARNING DISABILITIES

Learning disabilities represent a relatively new area of emphasis in the study of exceptionality. However, the work under way stems from several decades of research on brain-damaged children. The influence of prior research is reflected in the conditions that are now associated with learning disabilities: minimal brain dysfunction, hyperactivity, perceptual deficits, dyslexia, maturational lag, and reading disability. Learning disabilities have been attributed to a variety of etiological sources, none of which can be regarded as definitive in light of existing research.

Educators tend to agree that the learning-disabled child is a low achiever who is either average or above average in intelligence. At the outset, then, researchers attacking the problem from an educational standpoint are faced with a complex performance criterion as well as an imperfect predictor variable (IQ test score). Unfortunately, the current literature on learning disabilities is replete with studies in which the author failed to identify explicitly the psychological, educational, or medical criteria used in sample selection. Terms such as dyslexia, maturational lag, and hyperactivity may be diagnosed in divergent yet legitimate ways. The lack of precision found in research on hyperactivity is discussed by Keogh. The more general issue of problem definition is raised by Brabner. Although educators tend

to regard learning disabilities as a child-centered problem, Brabner argues that learning disabilities may be teacher-centered or instructional in origin. As pointed out by Caplan and Nelson (in Chapter Eight in this book), the way in which researchers define a socially relevant problem determines what, if anything, is done to solve that problem.

Given the relatively recent development of learning disabilities as a phenomenon for study, the research completed to date tends to be descriptive in nature. Case-study techniques have been popularly used to investigate the characteristics of the learning-disabled child as well as to search for hypotheses regarding effective remedial treatment. This approach is exemplified in the paper by Wadsworth. Researchers also frequently use the prescriptive technique, or medical model, which consists of introducing a training program designed to correct one or more learning deficits that have been diagnosed through testing. However, even if the learning deficits can be removed through training, positive transfer to the academic criterion of interest is not ensured. In other words, it is necessary to ask whether removal of the presumed cause of the learning deficit results in improved academic performance. The application of the medical model is illustrated in the field experiment by Jacobs, Wirthlin, and Miller.

LEARNING DISABILITIES OR INSTRUCTIONAL PROBLEMS?

George Brabner, Jr.

The roles and functions of learning disability teachers will not be clearly defined until a more basic issue is resolved: namely, should teacher training conform to the traditional clinical or disease model, or should it be based on a natural science approach? Some of the implications for teacher training for each approach are discussed.

In considering the possible roles and functions of learning disability teachers, a starting point may lie in one of the conclusions reached by the participants in the

Reprinted with permission of the author and publisher from the *Journal of Learning Disabilities*, 1971, **4**, 592–593.

Institute for Advanced Study dealing with definitions of learning disabilities: ". . . typical educational manipulations of the environment and of experience are not adequate approaches to remediation" (Kass & Myklebust, 1969, p. 378).

What are typical and what are atypical educational manipulations of the environment is a moot point; however, it seems evident that—apart from the effects of prescribed pharmacological treatment—consistently significant gains in learning efficiency are going to occur in these difficult cases only as a result of the systematically applied skill of a teacher trained to search for *functional* relationships among external variables. Thus, a teacher preparation approach which advocates that teachers be trained to search for underlying "causes" or "correlates" of the child's "symptoms" is open to serious question.

To a large extent, a clear delineation of the roles and functions of learning disability teachers will ultimately hinge on the resolution of a more fundamental issue—namely, will the preparation of these teachers be based on the traditional clinical model imported into education and psychology from the medical profession, or will it be based on a natural science approach similar to that proposed by Bijou (1963) and others?

Teachers schooled in the first approach will tend to employ constructs that are unobservable and will tend more often to search for the causes of learning deficiencies within the child and in his past and present extramural experience rather than to focus on functional relationships among variables in the instructional environment. Because a definitive understanding of the nature of many learning disorders must await further investigation, such a viewpoint may divert the attention of the teacher from an exploration of potentially significant environmental variables, or de-emphasize the importance of such an exploration. As Lovitt et al. have pointed out, "Many children fail to attain academic skills at rates which permit them to remain in the mainstream of education. Often these children are labeled 'learning disabled,' implying failure is inherent in the child rather than in the teaching situation. Whether a given failure stems from a learning disability or a teaching disability is a question for which final answers are not readily available" (1968, p. 710).

In any event, a teacher trained to regard a child exhibiting learning *irregularities* as presenting instructional problems rather than as inherently "disabled"

would probably view her role and functions somewhat differently from one who was not so trained. In all likelihood, the former teacher would be less prone to "blame" the child for what may often be shortcomings or limitations in her repertoire of instructional techniques. This assumption appears to be plausible in view of the fact that the difficult problems presented by learning disabled children can intensify any inclination on the part of the teacher to place more of the responsibility for failure on the child himself.

In this context, an instructional problem might be defined as: any obstacle to learning resulting from or perpetuated by the absence of those modifications of the instructor's behavior and/or other controlling variables (such as parental understanding, administrative cooperation, available facilities) in the learning environment which would lead to the elimination of the obstacle.

In the long run it may be scientifically sounder and professionally less confusing to refrain entirely from talking about children with learning disabilities. Rather, one might talk of teachers with instructional problems of a unique and difficult type but still to be dealt with and understood in terms of the same behavior principles—perhaps applied in unique ways—that we employ with any learner.

REFERENCES

Bijou, S. W. Theory and research in mental (developmental) retardation. *Psychol. Record,* 1963, **13,** 95–110.

Kass, C. E., and Myklebust, H. R. Learning disability: an educational definition. *J. Learning Disabil.,* 1969, **2,** 377–379.

Lovitt, T. C., et al. The dimensions of classroom data. *J. Learning Disabil.,* 1968, **1,** 710–721.

A MOTIVATIONAL APPROACH TOWARD THE REMEDIATION OF LEARNING DISABLED BOYS

H. G. Wadsworth

Abstract: A group of unmotivated third grade boys was diagnosed as having learning disabilities and was taught under three conditions. The boys served as their own controls. The dependent variables were reading level and school behavior. The independent variables were, in order of presentation, reading tutoring at a private clinic, reinforcement techniques in a self contained classroom, and intermittent reinforcement (via a resource room) during reintegration into a regular classroom. Clinic tutoring resulted in no significant gains in reading; reinforcement approaches, however, produced significant gains. Appropriate school behavior was significantly related to reading level.

THERE is little debate that schools across the nation are generally unsuccessful with significant proportions of the children they serve. On the whole, school personnel are dissatisfied with the inability to change seemingly intractable characteristics of children whose performance is academically and socially inadequate. There are various areas of exceptionality under which many school children with problems have been subsumed.

An apparent new malady has emerged and is known by such names as perceptual handicap, minimal brain dysfunction, learning disability, etc. (Reger, Schroeder, & Uschold, 1968). The most popular label seems to be "learning disability" and has been adopted by the Department of Health, Education, and Welfare. The National Advisory Committee on Handicapped Children (1968) says, "A learning disability refers to one or more significant deficits in essential learning processes requiring special educational techniques for its remediation [p. 34]." Programs for children with learning disabilities are springing up in many communities to reach those children who are not best served by other special education programs. There is probably also a significant number of parents who prefer their children to be called "learning disabled" rather the more stigmatized "emotionally disturbed" or "mentally retarded"; thus they are pushing for this new classification. Actually this "new malady" is not new but represents an attempt to encompass and cover all the previously existing problems.

This study examined a remediation approach which has received scant attention in the learning disability field (McCarthy & McCarthy, 1969). The central feature of the approach was to utilize knowledge from learning theory (behavior modifica-

tion) for the benefit of 15 elementary school boys who had learning disabilities. These boys were diagnosed by a certified school psychologist as having visual-motor integration difficulties, auditory discrimination problems, reading disabilities, and other related disorders.

Overview of Learning Disabilities

Teachers and parents have long been concerned about the considerable percentage of children who have difficulty learning for one reason or another. A diagnosis of "learning disabilities" provides a vindication for many school failures. Some pediatricians (de la Cruz & La Veck, 1965) explain that learning disorders are symptoms of a great variety of functional and organic conditions. They say that various disciplines have approached the problem, each with their special viewpoints, "and findings have not been integrated into a rational and workable form [p. 31]." The pediatrician remains the key to any successful effort since the causes are primarily motor and sensory deficit, malnutrition, organicity, diseases, and metabolic disturbances. Michal-Smith and Morgenstern (1965) give more credit to the ego and therefore emotional factors in the discussion of causes.

Clements (1964) is well noted for his work with learning disorders and considers this problem within the area of minimal brain dysfunction. Children with this impairment are of at least average intelligence and have mild to severe genetically and neurologically based school problems. Clements reports that in the past these children have shown up in psychiatric clinics or classes for the retarded, or were retained as children who were simply lazy. Graduate schools of psychology, social work, education, and medicine are faulted

From *Exceptional Children*, 1971, **38**, 33–42. Reprinted by permission of The Council for Exceptional Children.

for not having provided information in this area. The diagnosis of the learning disordered child, which Clements considers crucial, is made on the basis of clinical behavior, history, psychological evaluation, and neurological signs. Treatment depends on proper medication and educational planning along with psychotherapy where indicated. However, Haring and Hauck (1969) are not concerned about causes. They feel that by the time reading behavior, for example, becomes important for children, it is too late to be concerned about etiology. Johnson (1968) shows some disfavor with the diagnostic process because he feels such terms as "perceptually handicapped" are frequently and unfortunately used as "global explanations of complex behavior [p. 62]."

Kephart (1960) says about this type of child that he needs to have experiences which train his perceptual-motor skills and that he needs to practice these experiences often. It can also be said, and this was our implicit supposition, that the child needs to first have an orderly educational plan and then to have *motivation to practice,* because he may regard as monotonous the experiences which are necessary in order to improve. This statement is at issue with Edgington (1968) when she comments on the child with reading disabilties. "He is not lazy; he is not retarded; he is not able to do better if he just would; he is not likely to outgrow his disability without special help [p. 7]. . . ." The author contends that he *is,* in a sense, lazy and is able to do better if he wants to. His "wanting to" depends on motivating factors, and motivation does not come from within the child; it comes from experiences and environmental manipulation.

Setting of the Study

The learning disabilities (LD) program in the district chosen for this study is large and serves a school system of 12,000 children in 20 buildings (grades K-8). Each building has its own LD teacher who is permitted a maximum enrollment of 10 children. These children go to a resource room for periods varying from 20 to 45 minutes per day for remedial work pertaining to their disability as diagnosed by a student-services team (nurse, psychologist, social worker). The primary treatment mode is the use of special materials including such things as pegboards, lacing cards, blocks, tracing items, shape patterns, walking boards, and Language Masters.

The program assumed that lack of experience in certain areas causes the child to do poorly in reading, arithmetic, and writing, and auditory difficulties hamper oral understanding. Likewise, it is assumed that emotional factors enter into a child's school performance and his parents' reac-

tion to it. Unfortunately, the success of this approach has not been validated because of a lack of research on it in the district. It is known, however, that some LD teachers are unsure of their effectiveness, that some do not feel the child benefits significantly, and that some regular classroom teachers are dubious about the program and its carryover for the child in the regular classrooms.

Because of an interest in the above mentioned concerns, one of the LD teachers agreed to participate in a small project. One of the central premises of the project was that it is not necessary to be concerned with extensive diagnostic findings regarding the causes of the disability, but to view the problem as an educational one and to seek better programing and motivating factors for the children.

A Motivational Approach

Behavior modification had been used in the school district in classes for the emotionally disturbed and the socially maladjusted, with individual children in regular classrooms, and with individual children through their parents at home. (For a fuller understanding of behavior modification, see Thomas, 1967; Ullmann & Krasner, 1965; Ulrich, Stachnik, & Mabry, 1966). In using these methods for children with learning disabilities, it is necessary to consider two broad types of maladaptive behavior—social and academic. Social maladaptive behavior includes such things as hitting or talking without permission. Academic maladaptive behavior covers such responses as pronouncing words incorrectly or misspelling words.

The LD teacher wanted to try a motivational approach on half of her children with whom she worked individually. (The terms behavior modification and operant conditioning were avoided because of their negative connotations to some.) A point exchange system was set up with the children earning points for such behaviors as reading, sounding out words, and working with flash cards. In an attempt to transfer the children's gains to the regular classroom, they were also reinforced for correct answers on spelling and math tests and for turning in assignments. The points, which were accompanied by praise, were exchangeable for primary reinforcers such as toys and candy. Criticism or calling attention to poor work was avoided. The LD teacher worked with these five children on this basis for the last 3 months of the school year. She and the regular classroom teachers felt the results were good. These subjective feelings were substantiated by the objective data of better grades, more assignments turned in, and a higher achievement level. The extra cost for this experiment was very small—less than $25.

Other researchers (McKenzie, Clark, Wolf, Kothera, & Benson, 1968) comment on token systems straining school budgets. This project demonstrates however, that it is not so much the retail value of the items that motivates children, but the aspect of a consistent, positive approach including verbal and tactile praise with the relative immediacy of reinforcement for their accomplishments.

It was unusual to see five children who had been classified as perceptually handicapped significantly improve upon or even overcome their "learning disability" so rapidly. Therefore, a more sophisticated project was instituted involving better controls. The director of special education authorized a self contained LD class, with eligibility for the class being determined by the severity of the child's disability and concomitant behavioral problems.

Evolution of the LD Class

Subjects and their history. The subjects were 10 boys of middle class, suburban background who were in the third grade and were 8 and 9 years old. When these boys entered the third grade in the fall of 1968, they were quickly identified by the teacher as children who had severe reading problems.

Midway in the third grade their teacher requested special help since she was not being successful within the regular classroom. She felt the children's academic problems far exceeded any she had ever experienced. A number of behavior problems were also surfacing. However, the academic difficulties—especially reading— were such that the teacher believed the 10 boys would not be able to pass the third grade academic requirements and should therefore be retained at the end of the year.

Reading disability is probably the most difficult problem facing schools. The consequences of being unable to read can be everlasting to the individuals involved— not to mention to society. School systems are concerned for at least three reasons. One is that poor reading reflects on the effectiveness and efficiency of the educators. Second, difficulties in reading frequently lead to behavioral problems which upset teachers and parents. Third, educators are dedicated to help children have happy and successful school experiences. During the last months of the school year, special education services were approved. The school staff obtained agreement from the district administration that the district would assume responsibility to help these boys despite budget limitations.

Procedure

Efforts with the subjects were divided into four stages. The boys were used as their own controls, and reading performance was a dependent variable throughout the entire project. School behavior was not a dependent variable for Stage II as will be explained later. The stages are outlined as follows:

Stage I : LD consultation, April, 1969– June, 1969.

Stage II : reading clinic, June, 1969–September, 1969.

Stage III: self contained LD class, September, 1969–December, 1969.

Stage IV: resource room, December, 1969– May, 1970.

Stage I. This stage did not involve a major effort by the specialists and covered a 2 month period from April to June, 1969. Baseline measurements were taken in April. After extensive observation the LD teacher rated the 10 boys with the *School Behavior Test* (see chart 1) and the social worker administered the *Slosson Oral Reading Test* (SORT). During the 2 month period, the only intervention was the LD teacher's consultation with the regular classroom teacher.

Stage II. Before Stage II began, the SORT and *School Behavior Test* (SBT) were administered again. Stage II extended from June to September during which time the boys received tutoring—three 45 minute sessions per week—from a reading clinic (paid for by the district). Just prior to the tutoring, the boys were tested by the reading clinic, using various psychological and reading tests including the *Wechsler Intelligence Scale for Children* (WISC). the *Bender-Gestalt Test for Young Children,* and the *Wide Range Achievement Test* (WRAT). (The SORT significantly correlated with the reading section of the WRAT: rho = .65, $p < .05$, means identical.)

Stage III. The SORT was administered again during early September before Stage III began. However, the children were not rated with the SBT because they had not been in school during the summer months and the LD teacher had no information on which to rate them. Stage III involved the self contained LD class beginning in early September and ending in early December, 1969. The purpose of this 3 month period was to determine if significant change could result over a short period of time.

Before the class began at the start of the school year, the social worker met casually with the boys' parents both individually and in groups to inform them of the nature of the class and to determine if there were any significant home problems. No important problems were uncovered through this approach, i.e., there were no discoveries of severe medical problems or family disorganization. After these initial meetings, no further counseling or psychotherapeutic

CHART 1

School Behavior Chart

Student_____   Teacher_____   Date_____

Behavior	Almost Always (0)	Frequent (1)	Occasional (2)	Seldom (3)	Almost Never (4)
1. Stays in seat, moves around with permission.					
2. Does not hit, push, disturb others.					
3. Talks with permission.					
4. Quiet, does not cry, scream, whistle, or make other oral noise (excluding talking).					
5. Does not make noise deliberately with objects.					
6. Pays attention.					
7. Turns in homework and assignments.					
8. Prepared for classwork (paper, pencils, etc.).					
9. Answers teacher's questions and follows directions.					
10. Participates in class.					

sessions were scheduled with parents or children.

The class was organized to focus on the amelioration of reading and school behavior problems. Other necessary school subjects were also taught. Traditional LD materials (e.g., pegboards) were not used. The teacher drew on the existing school environment to provide perceptual training and experiences. A point exchange system provided the motivation. The procedure included:

1. Outline for the children (on a blackboard or poster) the rules or social and academic behavioral expectations.
2. Reinforce with points (and praise) behavior according to the rules. Points are later exchangeable for tangible items.
3. Give little or no attention to the breaking of rules unless the child becomes exceedingly disruptive whereupon he could be given a "time-out" and sent into the hall for 2 to 5 minutes. The breaking of rules is, in a sense, self punishing in that the child loses the opportunity to be positively reinforced.
4. Reintegration into the regular classroom, when ready, is the ultimate goal for this class. This is accomplished through gradual exposure to regular classrooms and through the gradual termination of tangible reinforcers.

Behaviors to be reinforced and the corresponding points given are shown in Chart 2.

Points were recorded on 200 point cards which were placed on each child's desk. The value of tangible items was determined by their retail value, for example

CHART 2

Point Exchange System for LD Class

Behaviors to be Reinforced	Points
Social:	
Being on time	5, morning and following breaks
Talking with permission	Maximum of 3 per hour (use timer)
Moving around with permission	Maximum of 2 per hour (use timer)
Academic:	
Spelling worksheets (10 per week)	4 per page
Handwriting worksheets (5 per week)	4 per page
Reading worksheets (15 per week)	4 per page
Spelling test (20 words per week)	3 per correct word
Reading out loud	3 per page
Phonic questions	1 per correct answer

100 points equaled a 5 cent value; 1,000 points equaled a 50 cent value. Free time privileges were also earned. For example, if an assignment was to be finished within a 15 minute time period and the child finished within 10 minutes (the assignments could always be finished much faster than the allowed time period), the balance of time could be used to draw, read a book of his choice, or play quiet games.

Initially, the social worker observed frequently in the classroom to work out problems that might arise. For example, one boy approached the teacher's desk several times an hour and bothered her with meaningless questions. The technique used to extinguish this behavior was to compliment the child whenever he was appropriately sitting at his desk working, and to totally ignore him when he tried to get the teacher's attention at her desk. Since the attention he got was achieved while he was at his desk and none was achieved when he went without permission to the teacher's desk, this behavior was almost totally eliminated within 2 days.

Stage IV. In December Stage IV began and SBT and SORT scores were again obtained. Following these measurements, a reintegration process (into the regular fourth grade) was begun. When the boys spent time in the regular class, they were not reinforced with points. However, reinforcers were continued in the resource room. The resource room was actually the same as the LD self contained room (same teacher, etc.), but the boys only visited this room for a short time each day. By January the group was spending only 80 minutes per day in the resource room, and by the end of March, they had all been completely reintegrated. In a sense, then,

they were being intermittently reinforced from December through March. Furthermore, the points became increasingly more difficult to earn as determined by the LD teacher's judgment of each child's need for tangible reinforcers for motivation. In early May the final SORT and SBT posttests were administered.

What was primarily investigated in this study was the influence of behavior modification techniques to overcome the effects of "learning disabilities" on behavior and reading. Therefore, this aspect (Stages III and IV) was emphasized rather than the tutoring program.

Results

Reading. Table 1 shows the changes in reading level. The rate of learning (Libaw, Berres, & Coleman, 1966), based on past learning speed, was used to measure the boys against themselves. The nonparametric t test and Wilcoxon were utilized for statistical verification. Improvement in reading level was not statistically significant ($p < .05$) during Stages I and II. Significant differences were found for Stages III and IV. In the 3 month span of Stage III, the group gained 8 months in reading performance. During the 5 month period of Stage IV, a gain of 9 months in reading level was made.

The last phase of intermittent reinforcement generated significant results. Even if a new expectation baseline had been calculated as of December, 1969 (increasing the group's rate of learning from .62 in April, 1969 to a new rate of .84), the Wilcoxon would indicate significant changes between December and May ($p < .005$). However, there were not significant differences between December and

TABLE 1

Expected and Actual Reading Levels of the 10 Boys

Boys	Reading level base	Rate of learning[a]	Stage I Expected	Actual	Reading level Stage II Expected	Actual	Stage III Expected	Actual	Stage IV Expected	Actual
1	2.6	.70	2.7	2.7	2.8	3.1	3.0	3.7	3.4	4.3
2	1.3	.35	1.4	2.2	1.4	2.1	1.5	2.9	1.7	3.8
3	2.2	.60	2.3	2.3	2.4	2.7	2.6	3.2	2.9	4.5
4	3.1	.84	3.3	2.6	3.4	2.4	3.6	2.8	4.0	3.7
5	3.0	.80	3.2	3.1	3.2	3.6	3.4	4.9	3.8	5.2
6	2.6	.70	2.7	3.4	2.8	3.6	3.0	4.4	3.4	5.9
7	2.0	.54	2.1	1.9	2.2	2.1	2.4	2.1	2.6	3.0
8	1.5	.41	1.6	2.1	1.6	2.4	1.8	3.2	2.0	3.9
9	2.2	.60	2.3	2.4	2.4	2.4	2.6	3.5	2.9	4.3
10	2.1	.57	2.2	3.9	2.3	3.8	2.5	5.3	2.7	6.4
Mean	2.3	.62	2.4	2.7	2.5	2.8	2.6	3.6	2.9	4.5
SD	.56		.58	.60	.61	.62	.62	.94	.70	.97
Wilcoxon			NS		NS		$p = .01$		$p < .005$	
t			$1.07 \, p > .10$		$1.03 \, p > .10$		$2.25 \, p < .025$		$4.05 \, p < .005$	

[a] Base level divided by population norm level (3.7); expected levels determined by this rate.
Note: One-tailed tests used, nonparametric.

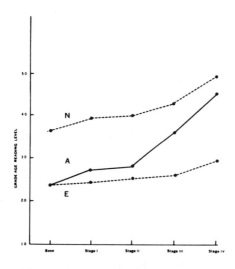

FIGURE 1. Comparison of the boys' expected (E) and actual (A) reading levels with population grade norms (N) for children their age.

May scores according to the t test (1.06, $p > .10$).

Figure 1 reflects the gains and the narrowing of disparity between the actual and norm reading levels. Although all boys were fully reintegrated in May, 1970, the individual results of two boys (numbers 4 and 7) warranted some reading assistance when they entered the fifth grade.

School behavior. All of the boys were not behavior problems as can be noted in Figure 2. The Wilcoxon, nevertheless, was used to determine if there were significant positive directional changes in behavior as measured by the SBT. This was administered by the LD teacher based solely on her observations of the boys in regular and special classes. It was expected that with no intervention, behavior would do no better than remain the same (and probably worsen). There were statistically significant differences in the direction of improvement during Stages I and III (see Table 2). Behavior was not considered a problem at the end of Stage III. Thus, no further improvement was expected or achieved in Stage IV. Incidentally, although only three social behaviors were specifically reinforced (see Chart 2), there appeared to be effective generalization to other behaviors.

Association between behavior and reading. The SBT and SORT correlated significantly initially (April, 1969) and before Stage II began (June, 1969).* (See Table 2.) Subjects with lower reading levels tended to have more behavior problems.

* Note that the correlations between the SBT and SORT as of December, 1969 and May, 1970 were not significant. It is assumed that the lack of association is due to the factor that behavior was no longer a problem.

It may be concluded, at least for this study, that poor behavior is associated with poor reading level. Bateman (1966) states that since boys outnumber girls 10 to 1 in primary reading retardation, a sex-linked factor is strongly indicated. On the other hand, it could be hypothesized that boys, who generally have more behavior problems than girls, are retarded in reading because of behavioral interferences rather than from hereditary disadvantages attributed to their sex (e.g. slower maturation). McCarthy and McCarthy (1969) in their review point out that disturbed behavior is not the direct consequence of brain damage but is the result of patterns developed in the course of a typical relations with the developmental environment. Likewise it is presumed, but not known for certain, that the behavioral problems were not a direct result of the learning disability but did develop because of frustrations associated with learning and emanating from the disability.

Diagnostic appraisal. The results of this study appear to be important in light of the lack of understanding about what approaches are best for the "learning disability" child. Consequently, it would not be unreasonable to question the original diagnoses. Were these children representative of the learning disordered? During Stage I the boys were given a battery of psychological tests by a certified school psychologist to help assess the nature of their problems. WISC scores ranged from 89 to 110 with a mean of 100. There were no significant correlations between the Verbal Scale, Performance Scale, and Full Scale of the WISC and reading level. There were also no significant differences between Performance Scale (mean = 102) and Verbal Scale (mean = 95). The three following sum-

TABLE 2

School Behavior Test Scores of the 10 Boys

Boys	SBT Scores			
	Base	Stage I	Stage III	Stage IV
1	0	0	0	0
2	33	26	2	4
3	35	22	6	9
4	23	20	1	4
5	25	18	3	3
6	5	4	1	0
7	26	23	5	4
8	27	27	0	1
9	0	1	0	0
10	26	21	2	1
Mean	20.0	16.2	2.0	2.6
Wilcoxon[a]		$p < .01$	$p < .005$	NS
rho[b]	$-.60, p < .05$	$-.65, p < .05$	$-.17,$ NS	$-.21,$ NS

[a] Wilcoxon tested the two adjacent scores i.e., Base with Stage I, Stage I with Stage III, etc.
[b] Spearman rank correlation coefficient of subjects' SBT scores with SORT scores.
Note: One-tailed tests used, nonparametric.

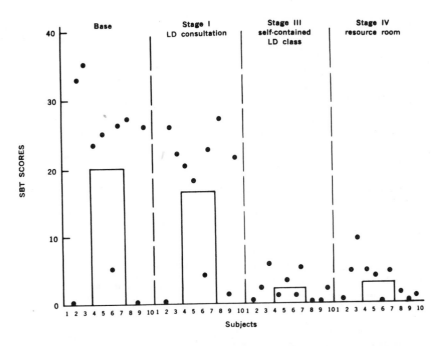

FIGURE 2. Illustration of group average (bars) and individual scores (dots) on the *School Behavior Test.*

maries by the psychologist further substantiate the learning disability diagnoses:

Billy exhibits reading performance a full three grade levels below his potential ability as demonstrated by listening comprehension. Basic word attack skills appear to be missing. Performance on the *Wepman Auditory Discrimination Test* was poor. Analyzing parts auditorily and visually seemed to be a problem area. Billy's left to right working direction is inconsistent. Reversal patterns occurred several times. He performed better in most sections of the *Gates Test* but exhibited difficulty in recognizing and blending common word parts.

Mark is a boy of average intelligence with a reading disability. Oral reading is at least one grade level below school placement and two levels below his potential level as demonstrated by listening comprehension. Mark's distractibility and short attention span further complicate his reading efforts. Testing reveals weakness in auditory discrimination skills and possible difficulties in eye-motor coordination. Mark has a medical history of allergies and asthma and has been treated with hormones for a thyroid problem. He is easily discouraged and lacks confidence with new learning tasks.

Joe's testing indicates problems in visual and auditory perception. Reversal rotation problems, incorrect working directional sense, with very slow progress in formal reading activities further suggest that there may be deep seated, neurologically based problems. Indicative of good potential are his superior performance in some areas of the WISC and good listening comprehension. He has a wandering right eye which,

according to an oculist, needs fusion training.

Discussion

This project attempted to investigate the application of reinforcement techniques to learning disabilities. Although the design of this project was not ideal, it is a beginning in an area which is in the incipient stages.* It can be argued that variables other than the primary one discussed (reinforcement techniques) accounted for the significant improvements in the boys' reading level and social behavior. The improvements could have been attributed to the small classroom setting, the teacher's personality, the newly found enjoyment of school, or parental support via the home. Improvement could also have occurred because of high experimenter expectations: "When programs of change or treatment are instituted, expectations for their effectiveness are very likely to be involved . . . [Rosenthal & Jacobson, 1968, p. 166]." The success with the original five boys increased the confidence toward the program with the 10. It is likely that the positive changes were due to several variables; however, most of the credit is given to the motivational approach.

There is no effort to interpret the data as giving support to the "special education" classroom. The author's bias is that chil-

* Behavior modification researchers will need to give, where possible, greater emphasis to designs which are more methodologically tight than the one used here. Essentially this involves randomization of subjects to treatment and control groups.

dren's problems can be solved as well or better in the regular classroom or on a resource room basis (Wadsworth, 1970), but perhaps a short period of intensive work in a self contained atmosphere provides a strong counteractive foundation. The results after a year's duration appear significant, but the stability of the subjects' progress continues to be checked.

The educational programing of disabled learners is crucial. The tutoring given these children from an outside clinic was presumed to have been unsuccessful because of unsatisfactory motivating techniques. Once children become interested in learning—have a reason that is valid to them, e.g., pleasant things happen when they work—then they can learn at an accelerated pace. As they spend more time on their tasks, less time is available for maladaptive behavior. There is, of course, wide disagreement on how to solve reading difficulties. Nevertheless, Haring and Hauck (1969) are speaking for a growing number of specialists when they say the etiology of the problem should be ignored and emphasis should be given to the improvement of instructional conditions.

References

Bateman, B. Learning disorders. *Review of Educational Research*, 1966, **36**, 93–119.

Clements, S. The child with minimal brain dysfunction—A profile. In S. Clements, L. Lehtin, and J. Lukens (Eds.), *Children with minimal brain injury*. Chicago: National Society for Crippled Children and Adults, 1964. Pp. 1–15.

de la Cruz, F., & La Veck, G. The pediatricians' view of learning disorders. In J. Hellmuth (Ed.) *Learning disorders*. Seattle: Straub and Hellmuth, 1965. Pp. 31–47.

Edgington, R. *Helping children with reading disability*. Chicago: Developmental Learning Materials, 1968.

Haring, N., & Hauck, M. Improved learning conditions in the establishment of reading skills with disabled readers. *Exceptional Children*, 1969, **35**, 341–352.

Johnson, O. Testing the educational and psychological development of exceptional children. *Review of Educational Research*, 1968, **38**, 61–70.

Kephart, N. *The slow learner in the classroom*. Columbus: Charles E. Merrill, 1960.

Libaw, F., Berres, F., & Coleman, J. Evaluating the treatment of learning difficulties. In N. J. Long, W. C. Morse, and R. G. Newman (Eds.), *Conflict in the classroom: The education of emotionally disturbed children*. Belmont, Cal.: Wadsworth Publishing, 1966. Pp. 505–508.

McCarthy, J. J., & McCarthy, J. F. *Learning disabilities*. Boston: Allyn & Bacon, 1969.

McKenzie, H., Clark, M., Wolf, M., Kothera, R., & Benson, C. Behavior modification of children with learning disabilities using grades as tokens and allowances as back up reinforcers. *Exceptional Children*, 1968, **34**, 745–752.

Michal-Smith, H., & Morgenstern, M. Learning disorders—An overview. In Jerome Hellmuth (Ed.), *Learning disorders*. Seattle: Straub and Hellmuth, 1965. Pp. 171–196.

National Advisory Committee on Handicapped Children. *Special education for handicapped children*. First annual report. Washington, D. C.: Department of Health, Education, and Welfare, Office of Education, 1968.

Reger, R., Schroeder, W., & Uschold, K. *Special education: Children with learning problems*. New York: Oxford University Press, 1968.

Rosenthal, R., & Jacobson, L. *Pygmalion in the classroom*. New York: Holt, Rinehart & Winston, 1968.

Thomas, E. (Ed.) *The socio-behavioral approach and applications to social work*. New York: Council on Social Work Education, 1967.

Ullmann, L., & Krasner, L. (Eds.) *Case studies in behavior modification*. New York: Holt, Rinehart & Winston, 1965.

Ulrich, R., Stachnik, T., & Mabry, J. *Control of human behavior*. Glenview, Ill.: Scott Foresman, 1966.

Wadsworth, H. Initiating a preventive-corrective approach in an elementary school system. *Social Work*, 1970, **15** (3), 60–66.

HYPERACTIVITY AND LEARNING DISORDERS: REVIEW AND SPECULATION

Barbara K. Keogh

Abstract: Research on hyperactive children was reviewed in order to define and clarify relationships and interactions between hyperactivity and learning disorders. Despite agreement on maladaptive social and behavioral characteristics associated with hyperactivity, findings specifying the nature of educational deficits are inconsistent and inconclusive. Three hypotheses are proposed to explain learning problems of hyperactive children. The first represents the medical-neurological syndrome explanation; the second suggests that activity disrupts attention and the information acquisition stages of learning; the third implicates impulsivity in decision making. Although neither exhaustive nor mutually exclusive, the hypotheses differ in remedial and treatment implications. Evidence is reviewed under each hypothesis.

CLASSROOM teachers have long been concerned with learning and behavior problems of hyperactive children, those children identified in school programs by such traditional labels as "acting out," "aggressive," and "conduct disordered." Since children with learning problems have become the concerns of physicians and psychologists as well as of educators, there has been a notable increase in the amount and scope of research relating to hyperactivity. Several comprehensive reviews of medical and psychological aspects of this problem are available (Knobel, 1962; Werry, 1968a, 1968b; Werry & Sprague, 1969). Less is known of the educational aspects of hyperactivity. The present article is a selective review of research on hyperactivity. The selection was determined according to two major purposes: (a) to summarize and clarify the evidence relating hyperactivity and learning problems, and (b) to propose some reasonable theoretical explanation for the learning disturbances of hyperactive children.

Definitions and Confusions

Hyperactivity is a general and emotionally laden word; it is a catchall for many descriptive terms, a construct lacking in precision or in specificity of defining parameters. Most investigators focus on the symptomatology of the condition without defining the construct. Definitions and descriptions emphasize two major aspects of symptom patterns: first, those which have to do with the extent and kind of motor activity; second, those which have to do with associated behavioral, social, and psychological characteristics.

Many investigators refer to persistent, heightened, and sustained activity levels, and/or increased speed of movement (Chess, 1960; Ounstead, 1955; Werry, 1968b; Werry, Weiss, & Douglas, 1964; Werry, Weiss, Douglas, & Martin, 1966). Despite clinical observations of the increased quantity and speed of motoric action, there is only limited evidence to document quantitative differences in activity levels of hyperactive and normal children. Schulman, Kaspar, and Throne (1965) monitored activity levels of children using Schulman's actometer (Schulman & Reisman, 1960). They reported consistencies of individual activity levels over time, but noted marked within-group and within-child variations. Hutt and Hutt (1964) found hyperactive children less able than normal children to modify their behavior and activity levels in relation to differing physical and social aspects of the experimental environment. The important point is that it is not just the amount of motor activity, but also the character of the activity which defines hyperactivity.

A critical characteristic of the motor activity of hyperactive children is that it is situationally or socially inappropriate (McConnell, Cromwell, Bialer, & Son, 1964; McFarland, Peacock, & Watson, 1966; Werry, 1968a, 1968b). Werry and Sprague (1969) concluded that the hyperactive child's activity level may be at "the upper end of the distribution of this behavioral trait in the population. . ." But that there is also "a qualitative element of situational inappropriateness, thus bringing the child into conflict with his sociofamilial environment [p. 2]."

From the practical point of view, it is likely that the higher the level of motor activity, the greater the probability of inappropriate behavior: The child who does

From *Exceptional Children*, 1971, **38**, 101–109. Reprinted by permission of The Council for Exceptional Children.

more is apt to make more mistakes than is the child who does little. High activity level per se may contribute to the maladaptive behavior pattern of hyperactive children, but activity level alone does not provide a satisfactory explanation for the behavior or for the learning problems. Indeed, chronic high activity levels may also be characteristic of some high achieving individuals. In such cases, adjectives such as vigorous, hard working, enthusiastic, and energetic are apt to be applied. Differences in motor activity of hyperactive and hypersuccessful children thus may be qualitative as well as quantitative.

Symptoms confounded. Part of the confusion in definition of this term is that the major presenting symptom—hyperactivity—is often confounded with other behavioral psychological, and/or medical-neurological conditions. In a well known study of educational management of brain injured and hyperactive children, Cruickshank, Bentzen, Ratzeberg, and Tannhauser (1961) emphasized motor activity but broadened their definition of hyperactivity to include "emotional disturbances and gross manifestations of behavior disorders, . . . short attention span, visual and auditory distractibility, and disturbances in perception leading to dissociative tendencies [p. 10]." This description is consistent with the symptom patterns included in the various hyperkinetic syndromes (Burks, 1960; Knobel, 1962; Knobel, Wolman, & Mason, 1959; Laufer & Denhoff, 1957; Laufer, Denhoff, & Solomons, 1957; Stewart, Pitts, Craig & Dieruf, 1966; Wunderlich, 1969), in syndromes of developmental delay (Bakwin & Bakwin, 1966), or in minimal cerebral dysfunction (Anderson, 1963; Clements & Peters, 1962; Ingram, 1956; Lytton & Knobel, 1959; Pincus & Glaser, 1966; Thelander, Phelps, & Kirk, 1958).

Despite consistent reports that hyperactivity is characteristic of children otherwise diagnosed as having cerebral dysfunction conditions, it is unclear whether characteristics of perceptual disorganization, attentional defects, distractibility, excitability, and the like are defining parameters or are correlates of hyperactivity. Furthermore, there is solid evidence that the relationship between hyperactivity and cerebral dysfunction is in no sense one to one (Eisenberg, 1957; Freibergs & Douglas, 1969; Herbert, 1964; Reger, 1963; Werry, 1968a, 1968b; Werry, Weiss, & Douglas, 1964). Hertzig, Bortner, and Birch (1969) found that only 19 of 90 children placed in a special school for brain damaged children evidenced signs of the hyperkinetic behavior syndrome. They stress the "neurologic heterogeneity" of such a group. All hyperactive children are not brain damaged, and all children who are brain damaged are not hyperactive (Birch, 1964; Birch, Thomas, & Chess, 1964; Schrager, Lindy, Harrison, McDermott, & Wilson, 1966). Hyperactivity and cerebral dysfunction are neither synonomous nor mutually exclusive.

Characteristic behaviors. Despite agreement that there is imprecision of definition of hyperactivity, professionals and parents also agree that "they know it when they see it." In a survey by Schrager et al. (1966), pediatricians, teachers, psychologists, psychiatrists, and social workers concurred that the six behaviors most characteristic of hyperactive children were: fidgety and restless; inattentive; hard to manage; cannot sit still; easily distracted; cannot take frustration. Stewart et al. (1966) interviewed mothers of 37 hyperactive elementary school children and found that over two-thirds of these children were described as: cannot sit still; talks too much; wears out toys and furniture; fidgets; does not complete projects; does not stay with games. Professionals and parents apparently react to similar behaviors. Furthermore, descriptive terms on which professionals and parents agreed were for the most part negative. Such terms reflect irritation on the part of adults and support Werry and Sprague's (1969) point as to the importance of qualitative aspects of hyperactivity in bringing about disruption of the social and personal adjustment of the child.

Characteristics of Learning Problems

It is well substantiated that many hyperactive children have learning problems and are poor achievers in school (Chess, 1960; Cruickshank, et al., 1961; Knobel, 1959, 1962; Menkes, Rowe, & Menkes, 1967; Millichap, Aymat, Sturgis, Larsen & Egan, 1968; Stewart et al., 1966; Werry, 1968a, 1968b; Wunderlich, 1969). However, relatively little empirical evidence has been reported as to the nature of the educational deficits. Clinical and educational observers have noted that hyperactive children are variable in learning performance, with variability evident in day to day and task to task performance (Thelander et al., 1958; Newman, 1956).

Teachers report that hyperactive children sometimes do excellent work and sometimes fail completely. In addition to within-subject variability, there is well documented within-group variability. Chess (1960) analyzed a sample of 82 hyperactive children seen in private consultative practice. She noted that the incidence of serious learning problems differed among five etiological groups: All children in the organic brain damage group had educational deficits, but incidence and kind of **learning problems for the other groups varied. Elementary age children evidenced problems of school behavior; adolescents had poor school achievement. Chess' findings may be interpreted to question whether learning problems are a necessary and invariant correlate of hyperactivity, or whether the often observed educational deficits are more accurately explained as an interaction effect.**

Varying educational deficits. Findings regarding the nature of educational deficits of hyperactive children are inconsistent, to say the least. Laufer and Denhoff (1957) and Laufer, Denhoff, and Solomons (1957) reported that overall achievement was low for the hyperkinetic children in their studies. They pinpointed problems of arithmetic, handwriting, and reading reversals. Freibergs and Douglas (1969), however, found that hyperactive children in their study did not have particular difficulty with attainment of arithmetic or number concepts.

A number of investigators have identified visual motor functions as contributing to learning problems of hyperactive children (Cruickshank et al., 1961; Laufer, et al., 1957; Strauss & Lehtinen, 1947; Thelander et al., 1958; Werry, 1968b; Werry & Sprague, 1969; Werry et al., 1966). In most cases neither the particular educational skills affected nor the specific mechanisms responsible have been verified. Anderson (1963) reported special problems in reading, e.g. reversals and mirroring, as did Burks (1960). Burks noted also that hyperkinetic children performed badly on achievement tests, whereas Chess (1960) observed that a number of her hyperactive subjects did adequately on such tests even though they did not perform well on a daily basis. It seems safe to say that there is agreement that hyperactive children often have learning problems. It is also safe to say that the educational expression of these problems is unclear and needs investigation.

Three Speculative Hypotheses

Three hypotheses appear tenable in clarifying the relationships and interactions between hyperactivity and learning problems. These hypotheses are in no sense exhaustive nor mutually exclusive but do have different theoretical and remedial implications.

Hypotheses 1 represents the medical-neurological syndrome explanation: Learning problems, distractibility, perceptual problems, and motor hyperactivity are perceived as caused by a common underlying condition, that is, neurological impairment. Symptoms are considered interacting but not in any necessary functional relationship. Hypothesis 2 suggests that learning problems of hyperactive children are a result of increased motor activity which disrupts attention to task and thus prevents accurate intake of information. Hypothesis 3 suggests that learning problems of hyperactive children are a function of hasty, impulsive decisions in learning situations.

Hypothesis 1: Neurological Impairment

This explanation of the learning problems of hyperactive children assumes that there are a number of maladaptive symptoms which have as their basis some kind of neural impairment. Issues and controversies surrounding the brain damage concept have been argued extensively and intensely (Bax & MacKeith, 1963; Birch, 1964). Some of the definitional considerations and confusions have been summarized already in this article.

Medically oriented investigators are convinced of the organic etiology of the hyperactivity syndrome; yet, there are differences of opinion as to the mechanisms involved (Anderson, 1963; Ayers, 1964; Laufer & Denhoff, 1957) or the most effective therapeutic programs (Hartlage, 1965; Lytton & Knobel, 1959; Werry & Sprague, 1969). There can be little doubt that a significant number of children with signs of neurological dysfunction are found in atypical groups (Bakwin, 1968; Burks, 1960, 1965; Hertzig, Bortner, & Birch, 1969). However, symptom patterns are variable, and the relationships of symptomatology to learning and behavior are unclear (Beck, 1961; Birch, 1964; Graham & Berman, 1961; Hartlage, 1965). Bateman (1967) and Birch and Bortner (1968) have questioned whether etiological preoccupations and specification of neurological correlates of learning problems have value for educational remediation.

Effects of drugs on learning. Treatment of hyperactivity with medication is common and provides a kind of indirect support for the neurological hypothesis. There is, however, considerable controversy regarding effects of drugs on learning (Freeman, 1966, 1969; Hartlage, 1965; Weiss, 1969). A number of investigators (Conners & Eisenberg, 1963; Conners, Eisenberg, & Sharpe, 1965; Freed, 1957; Freed & Peifer, 1956; Helper, Willicott, & Garfield, 1963; Knobel, 1962; Millichap et al., 1968; Werry et al., 1964) have attempted to specify effects of particular drugs on various aspects of children's learning. Conners and Rothschild (1968) concluded that functions which improved under one medication (dextroamphetamine) were attention, new learning, school and home behavior, and an ability to "plan" rather than to respond hastily or impulsively. Measures of visual and auditory perception, motor inhibition, general intelligence, and short term memory were not significantly affected by the medication.

In Freeman's (1966) detailed review, only 10 of 32 controlled studies demonstrated improvement in learning related to medication, whereas 22 of 45 studies reported improvement in behavior. Furthermore, some drugs may have a negative effect on learning (Hartlage, 1965). It appears likely that medication may affect change in level of motor activity and in attention, but that the direct effect of medication on learning is unclear. Change in behavior in a more socially compatible direction, however, may be an extremely significant factor in learning success. In this sense medication may indirectly facilitate improvement in learning.

It seems reasonable to conclude that there are a number of children whose hyperactivity and learning problems are symptomatic of some neurological impairment. However, functional interaction among symptoms is unknown, and specific therapeutic implications are unclear. The neurological hypothesis may reasonably be called upon to explain the behavior of hyperactive children. Evidence does not allow acceptance of this hypothesis as a definitive and broadly encompassing explanation for the learning problems of hyperactive children.

Hypothesis 2: Information Acquisition

The second hypothesis concerning hyperactivity and learning problems assumes that the hyperactive child may be neurally intact, but that the nature and extent of his motor activity disrupts the accurate acquisition of information. Motor activity is seen as interfering with attention to task, failure to learn—in part at least, a function of disruptive activity in the information acquisition stages of problem solving. Werry and Sprague (1969) noted that a good deal of time in learning new tasks is spent in information seeking. Interference with the information seeking process limits the amount of information acquired; heightened and/or inappropriate motor activity may be a powerful interference. Evidence consistent with the hypothesis comes from a number of sources.

Grinsted (1939) reported a negative correlation ($r = -.52$) between measures of intellectual ability and activity level for groups of normal children in first through seventh grades and in eleventh grade. Other investigators have confirmed this relationship in various mentally retarded samples (Cromwell, Palk, & Foshee, 1961; Foshee, 1958). Carrier, Malpass, and Orton (1961) monitored the behavior of intellec-

tually bright, normal, and educable mentally retarded children while they performed various learning and problem solving tasks. They found that the educable retarded group had significantly higher numbers of head and hand movements than did the other groups while solving problems. Overall, there was an inverse relationship between improvement over trials and number of head movements. Tasks involving new learning were more affected than tasks requiring utilization of already learned information. Findings of Sprague and Toppe (1966) are compatible with those of Carrier et al. (1961), in that they found high and low activity levels of trainable mentally retarded children were maintained throughout an experimental session, but low activity children learned and high activity children did not.

Movement during crucial points of learning. Confirming data are found in studies of children of normal intelligence. Turnure (1970) reported a significant, inverse relationship between amount of presolution glancing and learning success on a concept attainment task. Massari, Hayweiser, and Meyer (1969) demonstrated the influence of increased motor control on young children's performance on a standard intelligence test. Maccoby, Dowley, Hagen, and Degerman (1965) argued that successful and unsuccessful preschool problem solvers do not necessarily differ in amount of total body activity, but that the successful problem solver "modulates, or regulates, his activity, so that expressive activity is inhibited during crucial points of problem-solving where it might constitute an interference . . . [p. 763]." These investigators cited further evidence from Grinsted's (1939) work demonstrating that amount of movement varies at different stages of problem solving, with the least activity occurring at the time of solution. Maccoby and her colleagues considered it reasonable to conclude that some kind of inhibition of activity is essential for successful problem solving. A "crucial point" in problem solving may be the information acquisition stage.

Finally, recent work of Freibergs and Douglas (1969) may be cited to support the information input hypothesis. These investigators found that hyperactive children were as successful as normal children on a concept attainment task under certain conditions of reinforcement. The fact that hyperactive children could learn suggests that their learning problems were not due to underlying deficit or impairment. Although not necessarily the authors' interpretation, Freibergs and Douglas' (1969) findings may be interpreted to suggest that if the hyperactive child can get the information into the system, he can learn successfully.

In summary, excessive, extraneous movements, especially of the head and eyes, appear associated with learning difficulties. Heightened motor activity may disrupt learning by interfering with the accurate intake of information. New learning has been shown to be negatively affected in high activity retarded subjects; new learning is sometimes benefited by medication. It seems possible that regardless of the particular therapeutic agent, i.e. medication or behavioral management (Doubros & Daniel, 1966; Patterson, Jones, Whittier, & Wright, 1965), decrease in motor activity allows more accurate intake of information and therefore increases the probability of successful learning. The remedial and educational management implications of this position focus on control of motor activity at the information acquisition stage of the learning process.

Hypothesis 3: Decision Process

The third hypothesis proposed to delineate the relationship between hyperactivity and learning disorders is that hyperactive children have disturbed and speeded up decision making processes. Rather than pinpointing directly the information acquisition stage of learning, this hypothesis implicates the decision process in explaining learning problems of hyperactive children. Simply stated, this hypothesis says that hyperactive children make decisions too rapidly. Obviously, the effect of rapid decision and response is to cut down the amount of information acquired; acquired information is presumed to be accurate, however. It is speed of decision which is considered responsible for poor problem solving. Under this hypothesis, hyperactive children might be considered extreme examples of the impulsive children described by Kagan and his collaborators (Kagan, 1965, 1966; Kagan, Pearson, & Welch, 1966a, 1966b; Kagan, Rosman, Day, Albert, & Phillips, 1964).

Impulsivity/reflectivity. Impulsivity and reflectivity have to do with individual differences in tendency toward fast or slow decision time. Kagan and his colleagues have found impulsivity and reflectivity to be relatively stable across time and task and refer to a cognitive style or conceptual tempo (Kagan, 1966). The impulsive child characteristically makes rapid decisions and many errors; the reflective child takes longer to make decisions and makes fewer errors. Reflectivity is clearly more compatible with school learning requirements than is impulsivity.

Kagan's formulation of the impulsivity/reflectivity dimension provides a reasonable framework to explain the learning problems of hyperactive children. Hyperactive children are considered to lack thoughtfulness, to respond too quickly, to lack ability to think things through, and to be unable to delay response. Palkes, Stewart, and Kahana (1968) described hyperactive behavior as "heedless and slapdash [p. 817]." Kagan et al. (1964) have hypothesized that cognitive impulsivity may be part of a larger syndrome of impulsivity which includes high motor activity and short attention span. Ward's (1968) findings with kindergarten children are compatible with this interpretation.

Speed of response. A number of investigators of impulsivity/reflectivity have provided evidence which is relevant to hyperactivity. Massari et al. (1969) found that increased response time affected preschool children's performance on the Stanford-Binet. Zucker and Stricker (1968) report positive relationships between response time and accuracy in perceptual tasks for young children; differences in reflectivity/impulsivity were demonstrated for middle and lower socioeconomic status groups.

Kagan (1965) found that impulsive elementary school children made more reading errors than did reflective children of the same age. By definition (Kagan, 1965), reflective children took longer than impulsive children to respond on the measure of perceptual style, the *Matching Familiar Figures Test.* Of particular interest was the finding that reflective children also made more eye movements than did impulsive children in comparing the standard stimulus figure to the possible choices. The seeming inconsistency with findings of Turnure (1970) and Carrier et al. (1961) is explained when it is noted that in the latter studies, poor learners had higher rates of diffuse or extraneous head and eye movements than did good learners. The reflective children in Kagan's study were able to regulate and direct their motor behavior and to delay response, apparently allowing them opportunity to maximize information input and/or hypothesis testing. Supporting evidence comes from the recent work of Drake (1970) who found reflective children directed more of their regard and looked at a larger portion of stimulus material than did impulsive children. Such findings are consistent with the interpretation of Maccoby et al. (1965) and support the interrelation of conceptual style and motor regulation.

Further support for a relationship between conceptual style (impulsivity) and hyperactivity comes from the work of Palkes et al. (1968) who trained hyperactive boys to use self directed verbal commands to "slow down" while solving problems. Training resulted in improved performance on the Porteus Maze, an independent (untrained) measure, and increased ability to "stay put" and pay attention to the task. Meichenbaum and Goodman's (1969) findings with kindergarten children were in general consistent with Palkes et al. (1968). It is unclear whether improved problem solving under verbal self instructions resulted from delay of decision which allowed intake of more information or whether there was an increase in number of hypotheses considered before decision was reached. In either case, the findings suggest that speed of response is important in learning situations.

Effect of reinforcement. In one of the few studies dealing directly with learning characteristics of hyperactive children, Freibergs and Douglas (1969) found that hyperactive boys were as successful as normal boys in learning a new concept under 100 percent reinforcement but were debilitated under a 50 percent schedule of reinforcement. The authors interpreted their results within a motivational framework, implicating arousal level of hyperactive children. An alternative explanation might be in terms of an impulsive conceptual style. Kagan et al. (1966a) suggest that the impulsive child has difficulty solving inductive reasoning problems because he acts on the first relatively reasonable inference he thinks of, failing to evaluate the quality of his choice or to consider other possible solutions. One hundred percent reinforcement not only serves to increase attention to task but reduces the number of possible hypotheses to be considered in solving the problem. A 50 percent schedule of reinforcement increases the number of possible hypotheses, i.e., increases uncertainty or ambiguity and thus predictably would disrupt learning of impulsive, hyperactive children.

Ambiguity. It is interesting to speculate that if the hyperactive child has inconsistent perceptual functioning, he probably confronts extreme and pervasive ambiguity in interactions with his environment. If impulsivity is heightened in situations of high response uncertainty, the hyperactive child may, indeed, be caught in a circular situation: his hyperactivity disrupts the development of consistent and stable percepts and concepts; lack of stability of percepts and concepts leads to heightened motor activity; and heightened motor activity increases the disruption of stability of percepts and concepts. Much of the touching, manipulating behavior of hyperactive children may be efforts to achieve perceptual confirmation or constancy and thus reduce ambiguity (Wedell, 1971).

Conclusions

On the basis of evidence reviewed, it may be concluded that there is agreement that hyperactivity is associated with a wide range of social, behavioral, and maladaptive characteristics. Educational implications of hyperactivity have not been clearly specified however. Three hypotheses have been proposed to explain the relationships and interactions of hyperactivity and learning problems. These hypotheses are neither exhaustive nor mutually exclusive, but imply different remedial approaches and treatment plans. Determination of power of theoretical position or of effective use of treatment procedure awaits careful empirical research.

References

Anderson, W. W. The hyperkinetic child: A neurological appraisal. *Neurology*, 1963, **13**, 968-973.

Ayres, A. J. Tactile functions: Their relation to hyperactive and perceptual motor behavior. *American Journal of Occupational Therapy*, 1964, **18**, 6-11.

Bakwin, H. (Ed.) The pediatric clinics of North America. *Developmental disorders of motility and language*, 1968, **75**, 565-567.

Bakwin, H., & Bakwin, R. M. *Clinical management of behavior disorders in children.* Philadelphia: W. B. Saunders, 1966.

Bateman, B. Three approaches to diagnosis and educational planning for children with learning disabilities. *Proceedings of international convocation on children and young adults with learning disabilities.* Pittsburgh, Pa.: Home for Crippled Children, 1967.

Bax, M., & MacKeith, R. C. (Eds.) *Minimal cerebral dysfunction: Papers from the international study group held at Oxford, September, 1962.* London: Heinemann, 1963.

Beck, H. S. Detecting psychological symptoms of brain injury. *Exceptional Children*, 1961, **28**, 57-62.

Birch, H. G. *Brain damage in children: The biological and social aspects.* Baltimore: Williams & Wilkins, 1964.

Birch, H., & Bortner, M. Brain damage: An educational category? In M. Bortner (Ed.), *The evaluation and education of children with brain damage.* Springfield, Ill.: Charles C Thomas, 1968.

Birch, H. G., Thomas, A., & Chess, S. Behavioral development in brain-damaged children. *Archives of General Psychiatry*, 1964, **11**, 596-603.

Burks, H. F. The hyperkinetic child, *Exceptional Children*, 1960, **27**, 18-26.

Burks, H. F. Effects of amphetamine therapy on hyperkinetic children. *Archives of General Psychiatry*, 1965, **11**, 604-609.

Carrier, N. A., Malpass, L. F., & Orton, K. D. Responses of bright, normal, and retarded children to learning tasks. Office of Education Cooperative Research Project No. 578. Carbondale, Ill.: Southern Illinois University, 1961.

Chess, S. Diagnosis and treatment of the hyperactive child. *New York State Journal of Medicine*, 1960, **60**, 2379-2385.

Clements, S. D., & Peters, J. Minimal brain dysfunctions in the schoolage child. *Archives of General Psychiatry*, 1962, **6**, 185-197.

Conners, C. K., & Eisenberg, L. The effects of methylphenidate on symptomatology and learning in disturbed children. *American Journal of Psychiatry*, 1963, **120**, 458-464.

Conners, C. K., Eisenberg, L., & Sharpe, L. A controlled study of the differential application of outpatient psychiatric treatment for children. *Japanese Journal of Child Psychiatry*, 1965, 6, 125-132.

Conners, C. K., & Rothschild, G. Drugs and learning in children. In J. Hellmuth (Ed.), *Learning disorders*. Vol. 3. Seattle: Special Child Publications, 1968.

Cromwell, R. L., Palk, B. E., & Foshee, J. G. Studies in activity level: V. The relationships among eyelid conditioning, intelligence, activity level, and age. *American Journal of Mental Deficiency*, 1961, 65, 744-748.

Cruickshank, W. M., Bentzen, F. A., Ratzeburg, F. H., & Tannhauser, M. T. *A teaching method for brain-injured and hyperactive children: A demonstration pilot study*. Syracuse, New York: Syracuse University Press, 1961.

Doubros, S. G., & Daniels, G. J. An experimental approach to the reduction of overactive behavior. *Behavior Research and Therapy*, 1966, 4, 251-258.

Drake, D. M. Perceptual correlates of impulsive and reflective behavior. *Development Psychology*, 1970, 2, 202-214.

Eisenberg, L. Psychiatric implications of brain damage in children. *Psychiatric Quarterly*, 1957, 31, 72-92.

Foshee, J. G. Studies in activity level: I. Simple and complex task performance in defectives. *American Journal of Mental Deficiency*, 1958, 62, 832-836.

Freed, H. The tranquilizing drugs and the school child. *American Practitioner and Digest of Treatment*, 1957, 8, 377-380.

Freed, H., & Peifer, C. A. Some considerations on the use of chlorpromazine in a child psychiatry clinic. *Journal of Clinical and Experimental Psychopathology*, 1956, 17, 164-169.

Freeman, R. D. Drug effects on learning in children: A selective review of the past thirty years. *Journal of Special Education*, 1966, 1, 17-44.

Freeman, R. D. Review of drug effects on learning in children. In J. Arena (Ed.), *Selected papers in learning disabilities*. Proceedings of International Conference of the Association for Children with Learning Disabilities, Boston, 1969. San Rafael, Cal.: Academic Therapy Publications, 1969.

Freibergs, V., & Douglas, V. L. Concept learning in hyperactive and normal children. *Journal of Abnormal Psychology*, 1969, 74, 388-395.

Graham, F. K., & Berman, P. W. Current status of behavioral tests for brain damage in infants and preschool children. *American Journal of Orthopsychiatry*, 1961, 31, 713-727.

Grinsted, A. D. Studies in gross bodily movement. Unpublished doctoral dissertation, Louisiana State University, 1939.

Hartlage, L. C. Effects of chlorpromazine on learning. *Psychological Bulletin*, 1965, 64, 234-245.

Helper, M. M., Wilcott, R. C., & Garfield, S. L. Effects of chlorpromazine on learning and related processes in emotionally disturbed children. *Journal of Consulting Psychology*, 1963, 27 (1), 1-9.

Herbert, M. The concept and testing of brain-damage in children: A review. *Journal of Child Psychology and Psychiatry*, 1964, 5, 197-216.

Hertzig, M. E., Bortner, M., & Birch, H. G. Neurologic findings in children educationally designated as "brain-damaged." *American Journal of Orthopsychiatry*, 1969, 39, 437-446.

Hutt, S. J., & Hutt, C. Hyperactivity in a group of epileptic (and some non-epileptic) brain-damaged children. *Epilepsia*, 1964, 5, 334-351.

Ingram, T. T. S. A characteristic form of overactive behavior in brain-damaged children. *Journal of Mental Science*, 1956, 102, 550-558.

Kagan, J. Reflection-impulsivity and reading ability in primary grade children. *Child Development*, 1965, 36, 609-628.

Kagan, J. Reflection-impulsivity: The generality and dynamics of conceptual tempo. *Journal of Abnormal Psychology*, 1966, 71, 17-24.

Kagan, J., Pearson, L., & Welch, L. Conceptual impulsivity and inductive reasoning. *Child Development*, 1966, 37, 583-594. (a)

Kagan, J., Pearson, L., & Welch, L. The modifiability of an impulsive tempo. *Journal of Educational Psychology*, 1966, 57, 359-365. (b)

Kagan, J., Rosman, B. C., Day, D., Albert, J., & Phillips, W. Information processing in the child: Significance of analytic and reflective attitudes. *Psychological Monographs*, 1964, 78 (1, Whole No. 578).

Knobel, M. A. A syndromic approach to "acting-out" children. *Diseases of the Nervous System*, 1959, 20, 80-87.

Knobel, M. Psychopharmacology of the hyperkinetic child. *Archives of General Psychiatry*, 1962, 6, 198-202.

Knobel, M., Wolman, M. B., & Mason, E. Hyperkinesis and organicity in children. *Archives of General Psychiatry*, 1959, 1, 310-321.

Laufer, M. W., & Denhoff, E. Hyperkinetic behavior syndrome in children. *Journal of Pediatrics*, 1957, 50, 463-473.

Laufer, M. W., Denhoff, E. D., & Solomons, G. Hyperkinetic impulse disorder in children's behavior problems. *Psychosomatic Medicine*, 1957, 19 (1), 38-49.

Lytton, G. J., & Knobel, M. Diagnosis and treatment of behavior disorders in children. *Diseases of the Nervous System*, 1959, 20, 334-345.

Maccoby, E. E., Dowley, E. M., Hagen, J. W., & Degerman, R. Activity level and intellectual functioning in normal preschool children. *Child Development*, 1965, 36, 761-770.

Massari, D., Hayweiser, L., & Meyer, W. J. Activity level and intellectual functioning in deprived preschool children. *Developmental Psychology*, 1969, 1, 286-290.

McConnell, T. R., Cromwell, R. L., Bialer, I., & Son, C. D. Studies in activity level: VII. Effects of amphetamine drug administration on the activity level of retarded children. *American Journal of Mental Deficiency*, 1964, 68, 647-651.

McFarland, J. N., Peacock, L. J., & Watson, J. A. Mental retardation and activity level in rats and children. *American Journal of Mental Deficiency*, 1966, 71, 376-380.

Meichenbaum, D., & Goodman, J. Reflection-impulsivity and verbal control of motor behavior. *Child Development*, 1969, 40, 785-798.

Menkes, M. M., Rowe, J. S., & Menkes, J. H. A twenty-five year follow-up study on the hyperkinetic child with minimal brain dysfunction. *Pediatrics*, 1967, 39, 398-399.

Millichap, J. G., Aymat, F., Sturgis, L. H., Larsen, K. W., & Egan, R. A. Hyperkinetic behavior and learning disorders. *American Journal of Diseases of Children*, 1968, 116, 235-244.

Newman, R. G. The acting-out boy. *Exceptional Children*, 1956, 22, 186-190, 204-206.

Ounsted, C. The hyperkinetic syndrome in epileptic children. *The Lancet*, 1955, 269, 303-311.

Palkes, H., Stewart, M., & Kahana, B. Porteus maze performance of hyperactive boys after training in self-directed verbal commands. *Child Development*, 1968, 39, 817-826.

Patterson, G. R., Jones, R., Whittier, J., & Wright, M. A. A behavior modification technique for the hyperactive child. *Behavior Research and Therapy*, 1965, 2, 217-226.

Pincus, J. H., & Glaser, G. H. The syndrome of "minimal brain damage" in childhood. *New England Journal of Medicine*, 1966, **275**, 27-35.

Reger, R. Stimulating the distractible child. *Elementary School Journal*, 1963, **64**, 42-48.

Schrager, J., Lindy, J., Harrison, S., McDermott, J., & Wilson, P. The hyperkinetic child. *Journal of American Academy of Psychiatry*, 1966, **5**, 526-533.

Schulman, J. L., Kaspar, J. C., & Throne, F. M. *Brain damage and behavior: A clinical-experimental study.* Springfield, Ill: Charles C Thomas, 1965.

Schulman, J. L., & Reisman, J. M. An objective measure of hyperactivity. *American Journal of Mental Deficiency*, 1960, **64**, 455-456.

Sprague, R. L., & Toppe, L. K. Relationship between activity level and delay of reinforcement in the retarded. *Journal of Experimental Child Psychology*, 1966, **3**, 390-397.

Stewart, M. A., Pitts, F. N., Craig, A. G., & Dieruf, W. The hyperactive child syndrome. *American Journal of Orthopsychiatry*, 1966, **36**, 861-867.

Strauss, A. A., & Lehtinen, L. E. *Psychopathology and education of the brain injured child.* New York: Grune & Stratton, 1947.

Thelander, H. E., Phelps, J. K., & Kirk, E. W. Learning disabilities associated with lesser brain damage. *Journal of Pediatrics*, 1958, **53**, 405-409.

Turnure, J. E. Children's reactions to distractors in a learning situation. *Developmental Psychology*, 1970, **2** (1), 115-122.

Ward, W. C. Reflection-impulsivity in kindergarten children. *Child Development*, 1968, **39**, 867-874.

Wedell, K. Early identification of children with potential learning problems: Perceptuo-motor factors. In B. Keogh (Ed.), Early identification of children with potential learning problems. *Journal of Special Education*, 1970, **4**, 323-331.

Weiss, G. C. Review of the effects of drugs on children's behavior. In J. Arena (Ed.), *Selected papers in learning disabilities*. Proceedings of International Conference of the Association for Children with Learning Disabilities, Fort Worth, 1968. San Rafael Cal.: Academic Therapy Publications, 1969.

Werry, J. S. The diagnosis, etiology, and treatment of hyperactivity in children. In J. Hellmuth (Ed.), *Learning disorders*. Vol. 3. Seattle: Special Child Publications, 1968. (a)

Werry, J. S. Developmental hyperactivity. *Pediatric Clinics of North America*, 1968, **15**, 581-599. (b)

Werry, J. S., & Sprague, R. L. Hyperactivity. In C. G. Costello (Ed.), *Symptoms of psychopathology*. New York: John Wiley & Sons, 1969.

Werry, J. S., Weiss, G., & Douglas, V. Studies on the hyperactive child: I. Some preliminary findings. *Canadian Psychiatric Association Journal*, 1964, **9** (2), 120-130.

Werry, J. S., Weiss, G., Douglas, V., & Martin, J. Studies on the hyperactive child: III. The effect of chlorpromazine upon behavior and learning ability. *American Academy of Child Psychology Journal*, 1966, **5**, 292-312.

Wunderlich, R. C. Hyperkinetic disease. *Academic Therapy*, 1969, **5** (2), 99-108.

Zucker, J. S., & Stricker, G. Impulsivity-reflectivity in preschool headstart and middle class children. *Journal of Learning Disabilities*, 1968, 578-583.

A FOLLOW-UP EVALUATION OF THE FROSTIG VISUAL-PERCEPTUAL TRAINING PROGRAM

James N. Jacobs
Lenore D. Wirthlin
Charles B. Miller

INTRODUCTION

During the 1965–66 school year an evaluation of the Frostig Visual-Perceptual program was conducted.[1] Subjects were in prekindergarten, kindergarten, and first grade. In general, it was found that children taking the Frostig program did better on the Frostig Visual-Perceptual Test than did controls. Largest gains were registered by first graders. After initial differences in Frostig scores were cancelled out, no significant differences in end-of-year reading readiness scores were found among kindergarten pupils in Frostig and non-Frostig classes. Finally, subtest analyses were made and revealed that practically all the differences in Frostig total test scores noted above were due to one subtest; i.e., Form Constancy.

Readers who are not acquainted with the Frostig Visual-Perceptual program or the instrument, are referred to the original study or to the Frostig manual.[2]

The purpose of this study is to replicate[3] as much as possible the former study and to follow up the chil-

Reprinted with permission of the Association for Supervision and Curriculum Development and the authors from *Educational Leadership Research Supplement*, 1968, **2**(2), 169-175. Copyright © 1968 by the Association for Supervision and Curriculum Development.

[1]James N. Jacobs. "An Evaluation of the Frostig Visual-Perception Training Program." *Educational Leadership*, **25**(4), 332-340. January 1968.

[2]M. Frostig, P. Maslow, W. LeFever, and J. R. B. Whittlesey. *The Marianne Frostig Developmental Test of Visual Perception*. Palo Alto, California: Consulting Psychologists Press, 1964. (Standardization.)

[3]Errors in generalization are common to studies of this type. Before practical decisions regarding the use of the treatment are made, replication studies should be made.

dren in the study to determine the predictive validity of the Frostig tests as well as to study the cumulative effects of the Frostig program upon future reading achievement.

Specifically, this study is designed to answer the following questions:

1. Do children in prekindergarten, kindergarten, and grade one who take the Frostig program achieve better than controls on the Frostig Visual-Perception Tests? Is the benefit uniform among grades tested?

2. Do kindergarten "Frostig" children achieve higher on the Metropolitan Reading Readiness Test at the end of their kindergarten year as compared to controls?

3. What is the predictive validity of the Frostig test as compared to the Metropolitan Reading Readiness Test?

4. Do Frostig trained children achieve better on reading tests as compared to controls?

5. Do children exposed to two years of the Frostig program achieve better on reading tests as compared to one-year Frostig children and controls? That is, is there a cumulative effect due to Frostig involvement in reading achievement?

The first two questions were pursued in the initial study and are partially replicated in this study. The last two questions had to be delayed until Frostig program children last year advanced in grade.

DESIGN AND METHODS OF ANALYSIS

The pupils used in this study were identified as experimental (Frostig) or control. They attended five different schools and were in intact classes. For most comparisons, controls were drawn from the same schools as experimental classes. Further, the pupils may be considered "disadvantaged" since they attend schools designated as "primary target" schools under the Education Act. Education Act services, which may bias results, are considered to be present in equal force with experimental and control children. Thus, no systematic bias is expected.

In answering the first two questions, the Frostig tests and the Metropolitan Reading Readiness Test were administered to experimental and control children in May only. The initial study included beginning-of-year Frostig testing as well as end-of-year testing. This feature could not be replicated this past year. The analysis consisted simply of a two-way analysis of variance of grade by treatment using total Frostig test score as the criterion. For reading readiness comparisons only kindergarten children were tested. Thus, a one-way analysis of variance was applied. All experimental children in

this phase of the study took the Frostig program one year only.

The last three questions were studied by administering the Gates-MacGinitie test to first-grade children in May and the Stanford Primary I at the end of grade two. Since the Gates produces two subtest scores, i.e., vocabulary and comprehension, separate analyses on these two tests were made. The first-grade experimental children tested with the Gates were subdivided into two groups: one group having taken the Frostig program during the first grade only; and the second group who had taken the Frostig program during their kindergarten year as well as during the first grade. These two groups were in turn compared with control children who did not have the Frostig program either year.

The question of the effects of the Frostig program on reading achievement was studied in another context. Second-grade children in 1966-67 who were involved in the initial experiment as first graders in 1965-66 were identified and compared with respect to end-of-year (May) reading achievement using the Stanford Primary I battery. The pupils used in this phase had taken the Frostig program only during the first grade last year as compared to controls who did not have the Frostig program.

RESULTS

Question 1: Do Frostig program children achieve better than controls on the Frostig Visual-Perception Test? A summary of the Frostig test results is seen in Table 1. The children in the experimental group took the Frostig program only for the given year.

Results of the analysis of variance showed significant differences between treatments and among grades, but no significant interaction between treatments and grades. Thus, we observe an average difference of 2.73 in favor of experimental pupils on the Frostig test. In the absence of interaction we conclude further that the benefits accruing from the Frostig program on the Frostig test score are equal to prekindergarten, kindergarten, and first grade pupils.

These results bear out the initial study with one exception: significant interaction was noted in the initial study, with first-grade pupils showing significantly more gain than prekindergarten or kindergarten children. This same result occurred but lacked statistical significance. Most important, however, is determination that the Frostig program does produce higher Frostig scores in comparison to controls. The difference noted in interaction probably is the result of the fact that a covariance analysis was applied in the initial study using Frostig pre-test scores as a control measure while this could not be done in this investigation. Since there is little reason to believe that the experimental pupils began the year at a higher pre-test level than controls, we may interpret the higher post-test scores as responding to the Frostig program.

Question 2: Do kindergarten "Frostig" children achieve higher on the Metropolitan Reading Readiness Test at the end of their kindergarten years as compared to controls? Most of the children at the kindergarten level whose Frostig scores are reported in Table 1 also took the Metropolitan Reading Readiness Test at the end of the school year. The mean raw score made on the reading readiness test for experimental pupils was 37.22 and a standard deviation of 14.4. Kindergarten control pupils had a mean raw score of 29.90 on the reading readiness and a standard deviation of 15.2. The difference of 7.32 favoring the experimental pupils was found to be significant (t=2.63, df. 112).

Essentially the same comparison was made in the initial study. The results showed the experimental group to be higher than control but did not reach a statistically significant difference. In view of this replication, it seems safe to say that kindergarten pupils who take the Frostig program generally will show higher Metropolitan Reading Readiness scores.

Since pupils who take the Frostig program achieve higher on both the Frostig test and on the Metropolitan Reading Readiness Test in comparison to control, it seems reasonable to conclude that there is a correlation between the two tests. The correlation co-efficient obtained between the Frostig test score and the Metropolitan Reading Readiness raw score was .556 among the experimental pupils and .659 among controls. These correlations are not significantly different and reflect a moderate degree of relationship between the two tests.

Question 3: What is the predictive validity of the Frostig test as compared to the Metropolitan Reading Readiness Test? The first-grade pupils used in the initial study were in the second grade in 1966-67. The Frostig scores of these pupils obtained in September of the first grade and again in May of the first grade were both correlated against Stanford Primary I reading subtests. The Metropolitan Reading Readiness Test scores, obtained by essentially the same pupils at the end of the kindergarten year, were also correlated with the Stanford reading subtests. The results of these correlations are seen in Table 2.

It should be borne in mind that both Frostig tests were given on dates *closer* to the administration of the criterion reading tests than was the Metropolitan Reading Readiness Test. It is well known that the closer the time between test administrations, the more probable is a high correlation. Thus, one would expect lower correlation of the Metropolitan Reading Readiness Test with the reading tests scores than either Frostig test since it was given four months before the Frostig pre-test and twelve months before the Frostig post-test.

The correlations shown in Table 2 reflect the degree to which reading achievement can be predicted from a knowledge of the Frostig and Metropolitan Reading Readiness scores. The general picture shows rather low correlation between both Frostig and Metropolitan with the reading tests. Of the eighteen correlations reported, only eight are significantly different from zero and then only barely significant.

The Frostig test given at the end of the first grade appears to be a slightly better predictor than the Frostig test given at the beginning of the first grade. There seems to be no pattern of one reading subtest being better predicted than any other. There seems to be a unique pattern of slightly better than average correlation of the Metropolitan Reading Readiness with reading test scores within the control group. All three of these correlations are seen to be significantly different from zero. One wonders why the latter correlations are systematically higher than the other Metropolitan correlations within the experimental group.

Table 1. Average scores on the Frostig Visual-Perception Test* administered in May for experimental and control pupils.

Group	Experimental		Control		Diff. (X-C)	Grade means
Prekindergarten	X̄	39.00	X̄	38.53	+ .47	38.77
	(N)	(36)	(N)	(34)		
Kindergarten	X̄	41.78	X̄	38.69	+3.09	40.30
	(N)	(67)	(N)	(67)		
First	X̄	48.68	X̄	44.06	+4.62	45.04
	(N)	(78)	(N)	(61)		
Unweighted Treatment Means	43.15		40.42		+2.73	

* The scores reported are the sums of five scale scores each of which is defined as perceptual age divided by chronological age, multiplied by 10. A total scale score of 50 is equivalent to a perceptual quotient of 100.

Table 2. Correlations of the Frostig and Metropolitan Reading Readiness Tests with second grade reading achievement as measured by the Stanford Primary I Battery.

Stanford Subtest (a)		*Frostig Visual-Perception Test*		*Metropolitan Reading Readiness Test (d)*
		(b)	(c)	
		N = 37	N = 37	N = 28
Within	Word reading	.219	.361*	.273
experimental	Paragraph meaning	.144	.309*	.042
group	Vocabulary	.539*	.154	.197
		N = 29	N = 29	N = 25
Within	Word reading	.342*	.164	.432*
control	Paragraph meaning	.192	.084	.442*
group	Vocabulary	.044	.324*	.494*

* Significantly different from 0 at 5% level.
(a) Stanford reading tests given at end of second grade, May 1967.
(b) Frostig pre-test given at beginning of first grade, September 1966.
(c) Frostig post-test given at end of first grade, May 1966.
(d) Metropolitan Reading Readiness Test given at end of kindergarten, May 1966.

One could infer that when children go through the Frostig program their reading readiness pattern is changed somewhat, resulting in lower correlation between the reading readiness score and reading achievement later on. Thus, one may interpret this to mean that the Frostig program does *something* to the reading readiness of pupils but this "something" does not necessarily operate with equal intensity for children with low or high Frostig scores. If the latter were the case, the correlations would be maintained and only the means would be affected.

It is difficult to explain the relatively high correlation (.539) between the Frostig pre-test score and the Stanford vocabulary score within the experimental group. This correlation seems to stand alone and there appears to be no good explanation as to why this particular relationship should be higher than any other. It is presumed that this higher correlation is simply a matter of chance.

Considering the fact that the Metropolitan test was given earlier than either Frostig test and considering the fact that the highest group of correlations was between the Metropolitan Reading Readiness Test and the reading test within the control group, one may conclude that the Metropolitan tests seem to be better predictors of reading achievement than the Frostig tests.

Question 4: Do Frostig trained children achieve better on reading tests than controls? This question was pursued by studying the average reading scores of the same pupils on whom the correlations in Table 2 were based. It should be borne in mind that these reading tests were given at the end of grade two while the experimental pupils were defined as pupils having one year of the Frostig program in the *first grade* as compared

to controls who did not take the Frostig program in the first grade. Summary of the results is shown in Table 3.

The data shown in Table 3 bear out what was learned previously, i.e., that there is little relationship between Frostig scores and reading achievement. Thus we note that, while the Frostig scores of the experimental group exceed those of the controls by 3.55, nevertheless the reading subtest scores are consistently in favor of the control group. Two of the three subtests show significant differences favoring the control group. In all probability the reading differences favoring controls are due to initially higher levels of achievement by the control group. Thus it is apparent that high Frostig test performance is no guarantee of higher reading achievement.

Question 5: Do children exposed to two years of the Frostig program achieve better on reading tests as compared to one-year Frostig children and controls? First-grade Frostig children in 1966-67 were divided into two groups, one group who had taken the Frostig program as kindergarteners and a second group who were beginning the Frostig program for the first time in the first grade. End of first-grade Frostig scores were compared between the two-year and one-year Frostig pupils as well as against controls. In addition, this first-grade group was given the Gates-MacGinitie test at the end of their first grade, thus permitting comparison of reading achievement of two-year Frostig pupils, one-year Frostig program pupils, and controls. These results are shown in Table 4.

Inspection of Table 4 reveals immediately that the two-year Frostig group, i.e., pupils who took the Frostig program in kindergarten *and* in grade one performed

Table 3. Average Stanford Primary I grade scores obtained at the end of grade two and summary statistics for Frostig trained pupils and controls.

Stanford Subtest	Experimental Frostig group N = 37	Control group N = 29	Diff. (X-C)	t-ratio
Word reading	2.12	2.44	− .32	2.13*
Paragraph meaning	2.17	2.47	− .30	2.26*
Vocabulary	1.96	2.13	− .17	1.77
Average end of first grade Frostig score	53.14	49.59	+ 3.55	

* Significant beyond 5% level.

higher on the Frostig test (51.57) than did pupils who took the Frostig program in grade one only (48.68). Both of the Frostig groups in turn scored higher on the Frostig test than did the control pupils who had a mean Frostig score of 44.06. Thus, it is apparent that the Frostig program does have cumulative effects on the Frostig test score—the longer a pupil is in the program, the higher is his Frostig test score.

Comparison of the Gates reading scores shows a picture favorable to the Frostig groups. In both the vocabulary and comprehension subtests both Frostig groups scored higher than did the controls. One-year and two-year Frostig program pupils tend to score similarly on both vocabulary and comprehension while both score comparatively higher than controls. For both subtests, however, analysis of variance showed no significant difference among the three groups on either the vocabulary or the comprehension subtests. The lack of significant difference revealed by the analysis of variance was a result of large variation within each of the three groups.

In view of the comparative achievement of Frostig and control pupils on reading tests at the end of grade two (reported earlier), one is inclined to accept the analysis of variance at face value and conclude that there is no significant difference in the achievement of Frostig program pupils and controls on reading tests at the end of grade one.

DISCUSSION

The results of this study may be summarized briefly as follows:

1. Pupils who take the Frostig program in prekindergarten, kindergarten, or first grade tend to show higher levels of visual-perceptual performance on the Frostig test in comparison to control pupils.

2. There is a moderate degree of correlation between Frostig scores and the Metropolitan Reading Readiness scores resulting in the fact that higher scoring Frostig pupils tend to be higher scoring pupils in terms of reading readiness tests.

3. The predictive validity of both the Frostig test and the Metropolitan Reading Readiness Test is quite low using standardized reading tests as criteria.

4. Pupils who take the Frostig program seem to have no particular advantage as far as future reading achievement is concerned as compared to pupils who do not take the Frostig program.

5. Pupils who take the Frostig program for two consecutive years achieve higher on the Frostig test compared to pupils who take the Frostig program for one year, who in turn achieve better than pupils who do not take the Frostig program in either grade.

One other finding, not discussed in the body of this report, relates to subtest analyses. In the original study, the only subtest which showed a significant difference

Table 4. Average Frostig and Gates reading scores obtained at the end of grade one for one-year and two-year Frostig program pupils and controls.

Test comparison	Two year Frostig group N = 30	One year Frostig group N = 78	Controls N = 67
Gates Reading Tests			
Vocabulary (raw scores)	28.67	27.17	24.80
Comprehension (raw scores)	18.91	19.14	16.25
Frostig (total score)	51.57	48.68	44.06

favoring Frostig pupils was the Form Constancy subtest. This finding was disturbing in that we could not explain why this should happen. In the present study, however, we found that experimental pupils in general performed higher on *all* of the five subtests than did the controls. The differences favoring the experimental Frostig group on each test were as follows: Eye-Motor Coordination, +.81; Figure-Ground, +.61; Form Constancy, +.62; Position in Space, +.82; Spatial Relations, +.35. These results are much more reasonable and highlight the importance of replication in studies of this type.

One could argue that the differences in mental ability of the comparison groups could account for any observed differences in criterion measures. In this regard, it is interesting to note that the mean IQ's as measured by the Pintner Cunningham Mental Ability Tests of the groups shown in Table 4 were 92 for the two-year Frostig group, 91 for the one-year Frostig group, and 88 for the control group. Since these mental tests were given at the end of the year or at the same time that the criterion tests were administered, one might argue that the differences in IQ were a response to the Frostig program. One could also argue that these differences in mental ability, while small, may account for the slight advantage seen for the Frostig groups over the control groups on the reading tests.

One may ask whether it is beneficial to offer the Frostig Visual-Perceptual Training Program to primary-grade children. If one's goal is simply to increase the visual-perceptual quotient of children, the answer is obviously "yes" since the program does tend to increase visual-perceptual scores. If, however, the goal is to increase reading achievement beyond the normally expected, the evidence obtained from this study would not tend to support the notion that this will occur. Whether reading criterion tests were administered at the end of the first grade or at the end of the second grade, the results were consistent, showing that experimental Frostig pupils achieved approximately the same as controls. While there is some *inclination* for Frostig pupils to show higher reading achievement at the end of grade one, this tendency is counterbalanced by the fact that control pupils achieved higher than Frostig pupils on reading tests administered at the end of grade two.

4
CULTURAL AND SOCIAL DIFFERENCES

CHAPTER SIX

CULTURAL DIFFERENCES

Terms such as "culturally different" or "culturally disadvantaged" signify that the group under study differs from a comparative majority group in one or more ways. The connotation of "disadvantaged" has arisen because environmental variables have been identified that correlate simultaneously with social grouping (for example, socioeconomic status and race) and functional impairment (for example, poor academic achievement). Some of these environmental variables are housing conditions (deteriorating versus sound), amount of education desired for the child by his parents, number of children in the home (membership in a large family tends to be associated with low academic achievement), and conversation versus no conversation with parents during dinner (Deutsch & Whiteman, 1968).

Three major approaches to the problem of educating the culturally disadvantaged have emerged over the past decade. These are (1) the deficit model, which assumes that the children of the poor are limited intellectually and require remedial or preventive intervention to attain middle-class levels of achievement; (2) the school-disparity model, which assumes that children of the poor differ culturally but not intellectually from their peers and that the schools must change their present ineffective approaches to maximize achievement and maintain subcultural identity; and (3) the deactualization model, which assumes that the disadvantaged child is restricted in self-actualizing his potential and needs a program that allows him to develop to the fullest extent possible (Cicirelli, 1972). The deficit model underlies a variety of home- and school-based intervention programs, including those reported by Levenstein and Sunley and by Plant and Southern. This model is also supported by Hess and Shipman, who observed that the lack of cognitive meaning in the mother-child communication system is central to the effects of cultural deprivation. The study reported by Marwit, Marwit, and Boswell is consistent with the rationale underlying the school-disparity model—that is, that subcultural differences, particularly in language, do exist and should be considered in educational programs.

Variables contributing to the development of racial attitudes have also been of interest to researchers who study cultural differences. Williams and Edwards, for example, investigated the relationship between color connotations and racial attitude in a laboratory setting.

The relationships observed in basic and applied research on culturally different children have attracted the attention of persons interested in the resolution of social problems. However, the problems associated with external validity are difficult to answer—even for the research scientist. The theoretical discussion of the effects of early experience on school achievement mean one thing to the psychologist and quite another to the person involved in the problematic situation (see the Caplan & Nelson article in Chapter Eight of this book). In general, the issue of the proper relation between science and environmental change calls for a reconsideration of the relationship between psychology and society (Haskett, 1973).

EARLY EXPERIENCE AND THE SOCIALIZATION OF COGNITIVE MODES IN CHILDREN

Robert D. Hess
Virginia C. Shipman

This paper deals with the question: what is cultural deprivation and how does it act to shape and depress the resources of the human mind? The arguments presented are: first, that the behavior which leads to social, educational, and economic poverty is socialized in early childhood; second, that the central quality involved in the effects of cultural deprivation is a lack of cognitive meaning in the mother-child communication system; and, third, that the growth of cognitive processes is fostered in family control systems which offer and permit a wide range of alternatives of action and thought and that such growth is constricted by systems of control which offer predetermined solutions and few alternatives for consideration and choice.

The research group was composed of 160 Negro mothers and their 4-year-old children selected from four different social status levels.

The data are presented to show social status differences among the four groups with respect to cognitive functioning and linguistic codes and to offer examples of relations between maternal and child behavior that are congruent with the general lines of argument laid out.

THE PROBLEM

One of the questions arising from the contemporary concern with the education of culturally disadvantaged children is how we should conceptualize the effects of such deprivation upon the cognitive faculties of the child. The outcome is well known: children from deprived backgrounds score well below middle-class children on standard individual and group measures of intelligence (a gap that increases with age); they come to school without the skills necessary for coping with first grade curricula; their language development, both written and spoken, is relatively poor; auditory and visual discrimination skills are not well developed; in scholastic achievement they are retarded an average of 2 years by grade 6 and almost 3 years by grade 8; they are more likely to drop out of school before completing a secondary education; and even when they have adequate ability are less likely to go to college (Deutsch, 1963; Deutsch & Brown, 1964; Eells, Davis, Havighurst, Herrick, & Tyler, 1951; John, 1963; Kennedy, Van de Riet, & White, 1963; Lesser, 1964).

This research is supported by the Research Division of the Children's Bureau, Social Security Administration; Department of Health, Education, and Welfare; Ford Foundation for the Advancement of Learning; and grants-in-aid from the Social Science Research Committee of the Division of Social Sciences, University of Chicago.

For many years the central theoretical issues in this field dealt with the origin of these effects, argued in terms of the relative contribution of genetic as compared with environmental factors. Current interest in the effects of cultural deprivation ignores this classic debate; the more basic problem is to understand how cultural experience is translated into cognitive behavior and academic achievement (Bernstein, 1961; Hess, 1964).

The focus of concern is no longer upon the question of whether social and cultural disadvantage depress academic ability, but has shifted to a study of the mechanisms of exchange that mediate between the individual and his environment. The thrust of research and theory is toward conceptualizing social class as a discrete array of experiences and patterns of experience that can be examined in relation to the effects they have upon the emerging cognitive equipment of the young child. In short, the question this paper presents is this: what *is* cultural deprivation, and how does it act to shape and depress the resources of the human mind?

The arguments we wish to present here are these: first, that the behavior which leads to social, educational, and economic poverty is socialized in early childhood—that is, it is learned; second, that the central quality involved in the effects of cultural deprivation is a lack of cognitive meaning in the mother-child communication system; and, third, that the growth of cognitive processes is fostered in family control systems which offer and permit a wide range of alternatives of action and thought and that such growth is constricted by systems of control which offer predetermined solutions and few alternatives for consideration and choice.

In this paper we will argue that the structure of the social system and the structure of the family shape communication and language and that language shapes thought and cognitive styles of problem-solving. In the deprived-family context this means that the nature of the control system which relates parent to child restricts the number and kind of alternatives for action and thought that are opened to the child; such constriction precludes a tendency for the child to reflect, to consider and choose among alternatives for speech and action. It develops modes for dealing with stimuli and with problems which are impulsive rather than reflective, which deal with the immediate rather than the future, and which are disconnected rather than sequential.

This position draws from the work of Basil Bernstein (1961) of the University of London. In his view, language structures and conditions what the child learns and how he learns, setting limits within which future learning may take place. He identifies two forms of communication codes or styles of verbal behavior: *restricted* and *elaborated*. Restricted codes are stereotyped, limited, and condensed, lacking in specificity and the exactness needed for precise conceptualization and differentiation. Sentences are short, simple, often unfinished; there is little use of subordinate clauses for elaborating the content of the sentence; it is a language of implicit meaning, easily understood and commonly shared. It is the language form often used in impersonal situations when the intent is to promote solidarity or reduce tension. Restricted codes are nonspecific clichés, statements, or observations about events made in general terms that will be readily understood. The basic quality of this mode is to limit the range and detail of concept and information involved.

Elaborated codes, however, are those in which communication is individualized and the message is specific to a particular situation, topic, and person. It is more particular, more differentiated, and more precise. It permits expression of a wider and more complex range of thought, tending toward discrimination among cognitive and affective content.

The effects of early experience with these codes are not only upon the communication modes and cognitive structure—they also establish potential patterns of relation with the external world. It is one of the dynamic features of Bernstein's work that he views language as social behavior. As such, language is used by participants of a social network to elaborate and express social and other interpersonal relations and, in turn, is shaped and determined by these relations.

The interlacing of social interaction and language is illustrated by the distinction between two types of family control. One is oriented toward control by *status* appeal or ascribed role norms. The second is oriented toward *persons*. Families differ in the degree to which they utilize each of these types of regulatory appeal. In status- (position-) oriented families, behavior tends to be regulated in terms of role expectations. There is little opportunity for the unique characteristics of the child to influence the decision-making process or the interaction between parent and child. In these families, the internal or personal states of the children are not influential as a basis for decision. Norms of behavior are stressed with such imperatives as, "You must do this because I say so," or "Girls don't act like that," or other statements which rely on the status of the participants or a behavior norm for justification (Bernstein, 1964).

In the family, as in other social structures, control is exercised in part through status appeals. The feature that distinguishes among families is the extent to which the status-based control maneuvers are modified by orientation toward persons. In a person-oriented appeal system, the unique characteristics of the child modify status demands and are taken into account in interaction. The decisions of this type of family are individualized and less frequently related to status or role ascriptions. Behavior is justified in terms of feelings, preference, personal and unique reactions, and subjective states. This philosophy not only permits but demands an elaborated linguistic code and a wide range of linguistic and behavioral alternatives in interpersonal interaction. Status-oriented families may be regulated by less individuated commands, messages, and responses. Indeed, by its nature, the status-oriented family will rely more heavily on a restricted code. The verbal exchange is inherent in the structure—regulates it and is regulated by it.

These distinctions may be clarified by two examples of mother-child communication using these two types of codes. Assume that the emotional climate of two homes is approximately the same; the significant difference between them is in style of communication employed. A child is playing noisily in the kitchen with an assortment of pots and pans when the telephone rings. In one home the mother says, "Be quiet," or "Shut up," or issues any one of several other short, preemptory commands. In the other home the mother says, "Would you keep quiet a minute? I want to talk on the phone." The question our study poses is this: what inner response is elicited in the child, what is the effect upon his developing cognitive network of concepts and meaning in each of these two situations? In one instance the child is asked for a simple mental response. He is asked to attend to an uncomplicated message and to make a conditioned response (to comply); he is not called upon to reflect or to make mental discriminations. In the other example the child is required to follow two or three ideas. He is asked to relate his behavior to a time dimension; he must think of his behavior in relation to its effect upon another person. He must perform a more complicated task to follow the communication of his mother in that his relationship to her is mediated in part through concepts and shared ideas; his mind is stimulated or exercised (in an elementary fashion) by a more elaborate and complex verbal communication initiated by the mother. As objects of these two divergent communication styles, repeated in various ways, in similar situations and circumstances during the preschool years, these two imaginary children would be expected to develop significantly different verbal facility and cognitive equipment by the time they enter the public-school system.

A person-oriented family allows the child to achieve the behavior rules (role requirements) by presenting them in a specific context for the child and by emphasizing the consequences of alternative actions. Status-oriented families present the rules in an assigned manner, where compliance is the *only* rule-following possibility. In these situations the role of power in the interaction is more obvious, and, indeed, coercion and defiance are likely interactional possibilities. From another perspective, status-oriented families use a more rigid learning and teaching model in which compliance, rather than rationale, is stressed.

A central dimension through which we look at maternal behavior is to inquire what responses are elicited and permitted by styles of communication and interaction. There are two axes of the child's behavior in which we have a particular interest. One of these is represented by an *assertive*, *initiatory* approach to learning, as contrasted with a *passive*, *compliant* mode of engagement; the other deals with the tendency to reach solutions impulsively or hastily as distinguished from a tendency to *reflect*, to compare alternatives, and to choose among available options.

These styles of cognitive behavior are related, in our hypotheses, to the dimensions of maternal linguistic codes and types of family control systems. A status-oriented statement, for example, tends to offer a set of regulations and rules for conduct and interaction that is based on arbitrary decisions rather than upon logical consequences which result from selection of one or another alternatives. Elaborated and person-oriented statements lend themselves more easily to styles of cognitive approach that involve reflection and reflective comparison. Status-oriented statements tend to be restrictive of thought. Take our simple example of the two children and the telephone. The verbal categoric command to "Be quiet" cuts off thought and offers little opportunity to relate the information conveyed in the command to the context in which it occurred. The more elaborated message, "Would you be quiet a minute? I want to talk on the phone" gives the child a rationale for relating his behavior to a wider set of considerations. In effect, he has been given a *why* for his mother's request and, by this example, possibly becomes more likely to *ask* why in another situation. It may be through this type of verbal interaction that the child learns to look for action sequences in his own and others' behavior. Perhaps through these more intent-oriented statements the child comes to see the world as others see it and learns to take the role of others in viewing himself and his actions. The child comes to see the world as a set of possibilities from which he can make a personal selection. He learns to role play with an element of personal flexibility, not by role-conforming rigidity.

RESEARCH PLAN

For our project a research group of 163 Negro mothers and their 4-year-old children was selected from four different social status levels: Group A came from college-educated professional, executive, and managerial occupational levels; Group B came from skilled blue-collar occupational levels, with not more than high-school education; Group C came from unskilled or semiskilled occupational levels, with predominantly elementary-school education; Group D from unskilled or semiskilled occupational levels, with fathers absent and families supported by public assistance.

These mothers were interviewed twice in their homes and brought to the university for testing and for an interaction session between mother and child in which the mother was taught three simple tasks by the staff member and then asked to teach these tasks to the child.

One of these tasks was to sort or group a number of plastic toys by color and by function; a second task was to sort eight blocks by two characteristics simultaneously; the third task required the mother and child to work together to copy five designs on a toy called an Etch-a-Sketch. A description of various aspects of the project and some preliminary results have been presented in several papers (Brophy, Hess, & Shipman, 1965; Jackson, Hess, & Shipman, 1965; Meyer, Shipman, & Hess, 1964; Olim, Hess, & Shipman, 1965; Shipman & Hess, 1965).

RESULTS

The data in this paper are organized to show social-status differences among the four groups in the dimensions of behavior described above to indicate something of the maternal teaching styles that are emerging and to offer examples of relations between maternal and child behavior that are congruent with the general lines of argument we have laid out.

SOCIAL-STATUS DIFFERENCES

Verbal codes: restricted versus elaborated.—One of the most striking and obvious differences between the environments provided by the mothers of the research group was in their patterns of language use. In our testing sessions, the most obvious social-class variations were in the total amount of verbal output in response to questions and tasks asking for verbal response. For example, as Table 1 shows, mothers from the middle-

Table 1. Mean number of typed lines in three data-gathering situations.

	Upper Middle N = 40	Upper Lower N = 40	Lower Lower N = 36	ADC N = 36
School situations	34.68	22.80	18.86	18.64
Mastery situations	28.45	18.70	15.94	17.75
CAT card	18.72	9.62	12.39	12.24
Total	81.85	51.12	47.19	48.63

class gave protocols that were consistently longer in language productivity than did mothers from the other three groups.

Taking three different types of questions that called for free response on the part of the mothers and counting the number of lines of typescript of the protocols, the tally for middle-class mothers was approximately 82 contrasted with an average of roughly 49 for mothers from the three other groups.

These differences in verbal products indicate the extent to which the maternal environments of children in different social-class groups tend to be mediated by verbal cue and thus offer (or fail to offer) opportunities for labeling, for identifying objects and feelings and adult models who can demonstrate the usefulness of language as a tool for dealing with interpersonal interaction and for ordering stimuli in the environment.

In addition to this gross disparity in verbal output there were differences in the quality of language used by mothers in the various status groups. One approach to the analysis of language used by these mothers was an examination of their responses to the following task: They were shown the Lion Card of the Children's Apperception Test and asked to tell their child a story relating to the card. This card is a picture of a lion sitting on a chair holding a pipe in his hand. Beside him is a cane. In the corner is a mouse peering out of a hole. The lion appears to be deep in thought. These protocols were the source of language samples which were summarized in nine scales (Table 2), two of which we wish to describe here.

The first scale dealt with the mother's tendency to use abstract words. The index derived was a proportion of abstract noun and verb types to total number of noun and verb types. Words were defined as abstract when the name of the object is thought of apart from the cases in which it is actually realized. For example, in the sentence, "The lion is an *animal*," "animal" is an

Table 2. Social status differences in language usage (scores are the means for each group).

	Social status			
Scale	Upper Middle N = 40	Upper Lower N = 42	Lower Lower N = 40	ADC N = 41
Mean sentence length[a]	11.39	8.74	9.66	8.23
Adjective range[b]	31.99	28.32	28.37	30.49
Adverb range[c]	11.14	9.40	8.70	8.20
Verb elaboration[d]	.59	.52	.47	.44
Complex verb preference[e]	63.25	59.12	50.85	51.73
Syntactic structure elaboration[f]	8.89	6.90	8.07	6.46
Stimulus utilization	5.82	4.81	4.87	5.36
Introduced content	3.75	2.62	2.45	2.34
Abstraction[g]	5.60	4.89	3.71	1.75

[a] Average number of words per sentence.
[b] Proportion of uncommon adjective types to total nouns, expressed as a percentage.
[c] Proportion of uncommon adverb types to total verbs, adjectives, and adverbs, expressed as a percentage.
[d] Average number of complex verb types per sentence.
[e] Proportion of complex verb types to all verb types, simple and complex.
[f] Average number of weighted complex syntactic structures per 100 words.
[g] Proportion of abstract nouns and verbs (excluding repetitions) to total nouns and verbs (excluding repetitions), expressed as a percentage.

abstract word. However, in the sentence, "This animal in the picture is sitting on his throne," "animal" is not an abstract noun.

In our research group, middle-class mothers achieved an abstraction score of 5.6; the score for skilled work levels was 4.9; the score for the unskilled group was 3.7; for recipients of Aid to Dependent Children (ADC), 1.8.

The second scale dealt with the mother's tendency to use complex syntactic structures such as coordinate and subordinate clauses, unusual infinitive phrases (e.g., "To drive well, you must be alert"), infinitive clauses (e.g., "What to do next was the lion's problem"), and participial phrases (e.g., "Continuing the story, the lion . . ."). The index of structural elaboration derived was a proportion of these complex syntactic structures, weighted in accordance with their complexity and with the degree to which they are strung together to form still more complicated structures (e.g., clauses within clauses), to the total number of sentences.

In the research group, mothers from the middle class had a structure elaboration index of 8.89; the score for ADC mothers was 6.46. The use of complex grammatical forms and elaboration of these forms into complex clauses and sentences provides a highly elaborated code with which to manipulate the environment symbolically. This type of code encourages the child to recognize the possibilities and subtleties inherent in language not only for communication but also for carrying on high-level cognitive procedures.

Control systems: person versus status orientation.—Our data on the mothers' use of status- as contrasted with person-oriented statements comes from maternal responses to questions inquiring what the mother would do in order to deal with several different hypothetical situations at school in which the child had broken the rules of the school, had failed to achieve, or had been wronged by a teacher or classmate. The results of this tally are shown in Table 3.

As is clear from these means, the greatest differences between status groups is in the tendency to utilize person-oriented statements. These differences are even greater if seen as a ratio of person-to-status type responses.

The orientation of the mothers to these different types of control is seen not only in prohibitive or reparative situations but in their instructions to their children in preparing them for new experiences. The data on this point come from answers to the question: "Suppose your child were starting to school tomorrow for the first time. What would you tell him? How would you prepare him for school?"

One mother, who was person-oriented and used elaborated verbal codes, replied as follows:

"First of all, I would remind her that she was going to school to learn, that her teacher would take my place, and that she would be expected to follow instructions. Also that her time was to be spent mostly in the classroom with other children, and that any questions or any problems that she might have she could consult with her teacher for assistance."

"Anything else?"

"No, anything else would probably be confusing for her at her particular age."

In terms of promoting educability, what did this mother do in her response? First, she was informative; she presented the school situation as comparable to one already familiar to the child; second, she offered reassurance and support to help the child deal with anxiety; third, she described the school situation as one that involves a personal relationship between the child and the teacher; and, fourth, she presented the classroom situation as one in which the child was to learn.

A second mother responded as follows to this question:

"Well, John, it's time to go to school now. You must know how to behave. The first day at school you should be a good boy and should do just what the teacher tells you to do."

In contrast to the first mother, what did this mother do? First, she defined the role of the child as passive and compliant; second, the central issues she presented were those dealing with authority and the institution, rather than with learning; third, the relationship and roles she portrayed were sketched in terms of status and role expectations rather than in personal terms; and, fourth, her message was general, restricted, and vague, lacking information about how to deal with the problems of school except by passive compliance.

A more detailed analysis of the mothers' responses to this question grouped their statements as *imperative* or *instructive* (Table 4). An imperative statement was defined as an unqualified injunction or command, such as, "Mind the teacher and do what she tells you to do," or "The first thing you have to do is be on time," or "Be nice and do not fight." An instructive statement offers information or commands which carry a rationale or justification for the rule to be observed. Examples: "If you are tardy or if you stay away from school, your marks will go down"; or "I would tell him about the importance of minding the teacher. The teacher needs his full cooperation. She will have so many children that she won't be able to pamper any youngster."

Status differences in concept utilization.—One of the measures of cognitive style used with both mothers and children in the research group was the S's mode of classificatory behavior. For the adult version (Kagan, Moss & Sigel, 1963), S is required to make 12 consecu-

Table 3. Person-oriented and status-oriented units on school situation protocols (mothers).

A. Mean number

Social class	Person-oriented	Status-oriented	P/S ratio	N
Upper middle	9.52 (1–19)	7.50 (0–19)	1.27	40
Upper lower	6.20 (0–20)	7.32 (2–17)	0.85	40
Lower lower	4.66 (0–15)	7.34 (2–17)	0.63	35
ADC	3.59 (0–16)	8.15 (3–29)	0.44	34

B. Mean per cent

Social class	Person-oriented	Status-oriented	N
Upper middle	36.92	27.78	40
Upper lower	31.65	36.92	40
Lower lower	26.43	40.69	35
ADC	20.85	51.09	34

tive sorts of MAPS figures placed in a prearranged random order on a large cardboard. After each sort she was asked to give her reason for putting certain figures together. This task was intended to reveal her typical or preferred manner of grouping stimuli and the level of abstraction that she uses in perceiving and ordering objects in the environment. Responses fell into four categories: descriptive part-whole, descriptive global, relational-contextual, and categorical-inferential. A descriptive response is a direct reference to physical attributes present in the stimuli, such as size, shape, or posture. Examples: "They're all children," or "They are all lying down," or "They are all men." The subject may also choose to use only a part of the figure—"They both have hats on." In a relational-contextual response, any one stimulus gets its meaning from a relation with other stimuli. Examples: "Doctor and nurse," or "Wife is cooking dinner for her husband," or "This guy looks like he shot this other guy." In categorical-inferential responses, sorts are based on nonobservable characteristics of the stimulus for which each stimulus is an independent representative of the total class. Examples:

"All of these people work for a living" or "These are all handicapped people."

As may be seen in Table 5, relational responses were most frequently offered; categorical-inferential were next most common, and descriptive most infrequent. The distribution of responses of our status groups showed that the middle-class group was higher on descriptive and categorical; low-status groups were higher on relational. The greater use of relational categories by the working-class mothers is especially significant. Response times for relational sorts are usually shorter, indicating less reflection and evaluating of alternative hypotheses. Such responses also indicate relatively low attention to external stimuli details (Kagan, 1964). Relational responses are often subjective, reflecting a tendency to relate objects to personal concerns in contrast with the descriptive and categorical responses which tend to be objective and detached, more general, and more abstract. Categorical responses, in particular, represent thought processes that are more orderly and complex in organizing stimuli, suggesting more efficient strategies of information processing.

Table 4. Information mothers would give to child on his first day at school.

Social status	Imperative	Instructive	Support	Preparation	Other	N
			% of total statements			
Upper middle	14.9	8.7	30.2	8.6	37.6	39
Upper lower	48.2	4.6	13.8	3.8	29.6	41
Lower lower	44.4	1.7	13.1	1.2	39.6	36
ADC	46.6	3.2	17.1	1.3	31.8	37
		% of mothers using category				
Upper middle	48.7	38.5	76.9	33.3	87.2	—
Upper lower	85.4	17.1	39.0	19.5	70.7	—
Lower lower	75.0	5.6	36.1	8.3	77.8	—
ADC	86.5	16.2	43.2	8.1	86.5	—

Table 5.   Mean responses to adult Sigel Sorting Task (maps).

	Social status			
Category	Upper Middle N = 40	Upper Lower N = 42	Lower Lower N = 39	ADC N = 41
Total descriptive	3.18	2.19	2.18	2.59
Descriptive part-whole	1.65	1.33	1.31	1.49
Descriptive global	1.52	0.86	0.87	1.10
Relational-contextual	5.52	6.79	7.38	6.73
Categorical-inferential	3.30	3.00	2.23	2.66

The most striking finding from the data obtained from the children's Sigel Sorting Task was the decreasing use of the cognitive style dimensions and increasing nonverbal responses with decrease in social-status level. As may be seen in the tables showing children's performance on the Sigel Sorting Task (Tables 6 and 7), although most upper middle-class children and a majority of the upper lower-class children use relational and descriptive global responses, there is no extensive use of any of the other cognitive style dimensions by the two lower lower-class groups. In looking at particular categories one may note the relative absence of descriptive part-whole responses for other than the middle-class group and the large rise in nonverbal responses below the middle-class level. These results would seem to reflect the relatively undeveloped verbal and conceptual ability of children from homes with restricted range of verbal and conceptual content.

Relational and descriptive global responses have been considered the most immature and would be hypothesized to occur most frequently in preschool children. Relational responses are often subjective, using idiosyncratic and irrelevant cues; descriptive global responses, often referring to sex and occupational roles, are somewhat more dependent upon experience. On the other hand, descriptive part-whole responses have been shown to increase with age and would be expected to be used less frequently. However, these descriptive part-whole responses, which are correlated with favorable prognostic signs for educability (such as attentive-

Table 6.   Children's responses to Sigel Sorting Task (means).

	Social status			
Category	Upper Middle N = 40	Upper Lower N = 42	Lower Lower N = 39	ADC N = 41
Descriptive part-whole	2.25	0.71	0.20	0.34
Descriptive global	2.80	2.29	1.51	0.98
Relational-contextual	3.18	2.31	1.18	1.02
Categorical-inferential	2.02	1.36	1.18	0.61
Nonscorable verbal responses	5.75	6.31	6.64	7.24
Nonverbal	3.00	6.41	7.08	8.76
No sort	1.00	0.62	2.21	1.05

Table 7.   Percentage of four-year-old children responding in each of the categories.

	Social status			
Category	Upper Middle N = 40	Upper Lower N = 42	Lower Lower N = 39	ADC N = 41
Descriptive part-whole	40.0	28.6	18.0	14.6
Descriptive global	70.0	54.8	53.8	31.7
Total descriptive	80.0	66.7	59.0	39.0
Relational-contextual	77.5	66.7	41.0	43.9
Categorical-inferential	52.5	45.2	30.8	24.4
Nonscorable verbal	85.0	88.1	92.3	85.4
Nonverbal	52.5	66.7	82.0	87.8
No sort	12.5	7.1	25.6	19.5

ness, control and learning ability), were almost totally absent from all but the upper middle-class group. Kagan (1964) has described two fundamental cognitive dispositions involved in producing such analytic concepts: the tendency to reflect over alternative solutions that are simultaneously available and the tendency to analyze a visual stimulus into component parts. Both behaviors require a delayed discrimination response. One may describe the impairment noted for culturally disadvantaged children as arising from differences in opportunities for developing these reflective attitudes.

The mothers' use of relational responses was significantly correlated with their children's use of nonscorable and nonverbal responses on the Sigel task and with poor performance on the 8-Block and Etch-a-Sketch tasks. The mothers' inability or disinclination to take an abstract attitude on the Sigel task was correlated with ineffectual teaching on the 8-Block task and inability to plan and control the Etch-a-Sketch situation. Since relational responses have been found (Kagan, Moss, & Sigel, 1963) to be correlated with impulsivity, tendencies for nonverbal rather than verbal teaching, mother-domination, and limited sequencing and discrimination might be expected and would be predicted to result in limited categorizing ability and impaired verbal skills in the child.

ANALYSIS OF MATERNAL TEACHING STYLES

These differences among the status groups and among mothers within the groups appear in slightly different form in the teaching sessions in which the mothers and children engaged. There were large differences among the status groups in the ability of the mothers to teach and the children to learn. This is illustrated by the performance scores on the sorting tasks.

Let us describe the interaction between the mother and child in one of the structured teaching situations. The wide range of individual differences in linguistic and interactional styles of these mothers may be illustrated by excerpts from recordings. The task of the mother is to teach the child how to group or sort a small number of toys.

The first mother outlines the task for the child, gives sufficient help and explanation to permit the child to proceed on her own. She says:

"All right, Susan, this board is the place where we put the little toys; first of all you're supposed to learn how to place them according to color. Can you do that? The things that are all the same color you put in one section; in the second section you put another group of colors, and in the third section you put the last group

of colors. Can you do that? Or would you like to see me do it first?"

Child: "I want to do it."

This mother has given explicit information about the task and what is expected of the child; she has offered support and help of various kinds; and she has made it clear that she impelled the child to perform.

A second mother's style offers less clarity and precision. She says in introducing the same task:

"Now, I'll take them all off the board; now you put them all back on the board. What are these?"

Child: "A truck."

"All right, just put them right here; put the other one right here; all right put the other one there."

This mother must rely more on nonverbal communication in her commands; she does not define the task for the child; the child is not provided with ideas or information that she can grasp in attempting to solve the problem; neither is she told what to expect or what the task is, even in general terms.

A third mother is even less explicit. She introduces the task as follows:

"I've got some chairs and cars, do you want to play the game?" Child does not respond. Mother continues: "O.K. What's this?"

Child: "A wagon?"

Mother: "Hm?"

Child: "A wagon?"

Mother: "This is not a wagon. What's this?"

The conversation continues with this sort of exchange for several pages. Here again, the child is not provided with the essential information he needs to solve or to understand the problem. There is clearly some impelling on the part of the mother for the child to perform, but the child has not been told what he is to do. There were marked social-class differences in the ability of the children to learn from their mothers in the teaching sessions.

Each teaching session was concluded with an assessment by a staff member of the extent to which the child had learned the concepts taught by the mother. His achievement was scored in two ways: first, the ability to correctly place or sort the objects and, second, the ability to verbalize the principle on which the sorting or grouping was made.

Children from middle-class homes were well above children from working-class homes in performance on these sorting tasks, particularly in offering verbal explanations as to the basis for making the sort (Tables 8 and 9). Over 60 per cent of middle-class children placed the objects correctly on all tasks; the performance of working-class children ranged as low as 29 per cent correct. Approximately 40 per cent of these middle-class children who were successful were able to verbalize the

Table 8.   Differences among status groups in children's performance in teaching situations (Toy Sort Task).

Social status	Placed Correctly (%)	Verbalized Correctly (%)		N
A. Identity sort (cars, spoons, chairs):				
Upper middle	61.5	28.2	45.8[a]	39
Upper lower	65.0	20.0	30.8	40
Lower lower	68.4	29.0	42.3	38
ADC	66.7	30.8	46.2	39
B. Color sort (red, green, yellow):				
Upper middle	69.2	28.2	40.7[a]	39
Upper lower	67.5	15.0	22.2	40
Lower lower	57.9	13.2	22.7	38
ADC	33.3	5.1	15.4	39

[a] Per cent of those who placed object correctly.

Table 9.   Differences among status groups in children's performance in teaching situations (8-Block Task).

Social status	Placed correctly (%)	One-dimension verbalized (%)		Both verbalized (%)		N
A. Short O:						
Upper middle	75.0	57.5	57.5[a]	25.0	33.3[a]	40
Upper lower	51.2	39.0	43.2	2.4	4.8	41
Lower lower	50.0	29.0	33.3	15.8	31.6	38
ADC	43.6	20.5	22.2	2.6	5.9	39
B. Tall X:						
Upper middle	60.0	62.5	64.1[a]	27.5	45.8[a]	40
Upper lower	48.8	39.0	42.1	17.1	35.0	41
Lower lower	34.2	23.7	26.5	7.9	23.1	38
ADC	28.2	18.0	20.0	0.0	0.0	39

[a] Per cent of those who placed object correctly.

sorting principle; working-class children were less able to explain the sorting principle, ranging downward from the middle-class level to one task on which no child was able to verbalize correctly the basis of his sorting behavior. These differences clearly paralleled the relative abilities and teaching skills of the mothers from differing social-status groups.

The difference among the four status levels was apparent not only on these sorting and verbal skills but also in the mother's ability to regulate her own behavior and her child's in performing tasks which require planning or care rather than verbal or conceptual skill. These differences were revealed by the mother-child performance on the Etch-a-Sketch task. An Etch-a-Sketch toy is a small, flat box with a screen on which lines can be drawn by a device within the box. The marker is controlled by two knobs: one for horizontal movement, one for vertical. The mother is assigned one knob, the child the other. The mother is shown several designs which are to be reproduced. Together they attempt to copy the design models. The mother decides when their product is a satisfactory copy of the original. The products are scored by measuring deviations from the original designs.

These sessions were recorded, and the nonverbal interaction was described by an observer. Some of the most relevant results were these: middle-class mothers and children performed better on the task (14.6 points) than mothers and children from the other groups (9.2; 8.3; 9.5; [Table 10]). Mothers of the three lower-status groups were relatively persistent, rejecting more complete figures than the middle-class mothers; mothers from the middle-class praised the child's efforts more than did other mothers but gave just as much criticism; the child's cooperation as rated by the observer was as good or better in low-status groups as in middle-class pairs (Table 11); there was little difference between the groups in affect expressed to the child by the mother (Brophy et al., 1965).

In these data, as in other not presented here, the mothers of the four status groups differed relatively little, on the average, in the affective elements of their interaction with their children. The gross differences appeared in the verbal and cognitive environments that they presented.

Against this background I would like to return for a moment to the problem of the meaning, or, perhaps more correctly, the lack of meaning in cultural depriva-

Table 10. Performance on Etch-a-Sketch Task (means).

	Social status			
	Upper Middle N = 40	Upper Lower N = 42	Lower Lower N = 40	ADC N = 41
Total score (range 0–40)	14.6	9.2	8.3	9.5
Average number of attempts	12.7	17.2	12.2	15.1
Complete figures rejected	2.3	3.6	3.5	3.4
Child's total score	5.9	4.0	3.4	4.0
Child's contribution to total score (per cent)	40.4	43.5	41.0	42.1

tion. One of the features of the behavior of the working-class mothers and children is a tendency to act without taking sufficient time for reflection and planning. In a sense one might call this impulsive behavior—not by acting out unconscious or forbidden impulses, but in a type of activity in which a particular act seems not to be related to the act that preceded it or to its consequences. In this sense it lacks meaning; it is not sufficiently related to the context in which it occurs, to the motivations of the participants, or to the goals of the task. This behavior may be verbal or motor; it shows itself in several ways. On the Etch-a-Sketch task, for example, the mother may silently watch a child make an error and then punish him. Another mother will anticipate the error, will warn the child that he is about to reach a decision point; she will prepare him by verbal and nonverbal cues to be careful, to look ahead, and to avoid the mistake. He is encouraged to reflect, to anticipate the consequences of his action, and in this way to avoid error. A problem-solving approach requires reflection and the ability to weigh decisions, to choose among alternatives. The effect of restricted speech and of status orientation is to foreclose the need for reflective weighing of alternatives and consequences; the use of an elaborated code, with its orientation to persons and to consequences (including future), tends to produce cognitive styles more easily adapted to problem-solving and reflection.

The objective of our study is to discover how teaching styles of the mothers induce and shape learning styles and information-processing strategies in the children. The picture that is beginning to emerge is that the meaning of deprivation is a deprivation of meaning—a cognitive environment in which behavior is controlled by status rules rather than by attention to the individual characteristics of a specific situation and one in which behavior is not mediated by verbal cues or by teaching that relates events to one another and the present to the future. This environment produces a child who relates to authority rather than to rationale, who, although often compliant, is not reflective in his behavior, and for whom the consequences of an act are largely considered in terms of immediate punishment or reward rather than future effects and long-range goals.

When the data are more complete, a more detailed analysis of the findings will enable us to examine the effect of maternal cognitive environments in terms of individual mother-child transactions, rather than in the

Table 11.[a] Mother-child interaction on Etch-a-Sketch Task (means).

	Social status			
	Upper Middle N = 40	Upper Lower N = 41	Lower Lower N = 39	ADC N = 39
Praises child	4.6	6.9	7.2	7.5
Criticizes child	6.4	5.5	6.4	5.9
Overall acceptance of child	2.2	3.2	3.4	3.6
Child's cooperation	5.6	5.3	4.5	5.1
Level of affection shown to child	4.8	5.4	5.2	5.8

[a] Ratings made by observer; low number indicates more of the quality rated.

gross categories of social class. This analysis will not only help us to understand how social-class environment is mediated through the interaction between mother and child but will give more precise information about the effects of individual maternal environments on the cognitive growth of the young child.

REFERENCES

Bernstein, B. Social class and linguistic development: a theory of social learning. In A. H. Halsey, Jean Floud, & C. A. Anderson (Eds.), *Education, economy, and society*. Glencoe, Ill.: Free Pr., 1961.

Bernstein, B. Family role systems, communication, and socialization. Paper presented at Conf. on Develpm. of Cross-National Res. on the Education of Children and Adolescents, Univer. of Chicago, February, 1964.

Brophy, J., Hess, R. D., & Shipman, Virginia. Effects of social class and level of aspiration on performance in a structured mother-child interaction. Paper presented at Biennial Meeting of Soc. Res. Child Develpm., Minneapolis, Minn., March, 1965.

Deutsch, M. The disadvantaged child and the learning process. In A. H. Passow (Ed.), *Education in depressed areas*. New York: Columbia Univer. T. C., 1963. Pp. 163-180.

Deutsch, M., & Brown, B. Social influences in Negro-white intelligence differences. *J. soc. Issues,* 1964, **20** (2), 24-35.

Eells, K., Davis, Allison, Havighurst, R. J., Herrick, V. E., & Tyler, R. W. *Intelligence and cultural differences*. Chicago: Univer. of Chicago Pr., 1951.

Hess, R. D. Educability and rehabilitation: the future of the welfare class. *Marr. fam. Lvg,* 1964, **26,** 422-429.

Jackson, J. D., Hess, R. D., & Shipman, Virginia. Communication styles in teachers: An experiment. Paper presented at Amer. Educ. and Res. Ass., Chicago, February, 1965.

John, Vera. The intellectual development of slum children: some preliminary findings. *Amer. J. Orthopsychiat.,* 1963, **33,** 813-822.

Kagan, J., Moss, H. A., & Sigel, I. E. Psychological significance of styles of conceptualization. *Monogr. Soc. Res. Child Develpm.,* 1963, **28,** No. 2.

Kagan, J. Information processing in the child: significance of analytic and reflective attitudes. *Psychol. Monogr.,* 1964, **78,** No. 1 (Whole No. 578).

Kennedy, W. A., Van de Riet, V., & White, J. C., Jr. A normative sample of intelligence and achievement of Negro elementary school children in the southeastern United States. *Monogr. Soc. Res. Child Develpm.,* 1963, **28,** No. 6.

Lesser, G. Mental abilities of children in different social and cultural groups. New York: Cooperative Research Project No. 1635, 1964.

Meyer, Roberta, Shipman, Virginia, & Hess, R. D. Family structure and social class in the socialization of curiosity in urban preschool children. Paper presented at APA meeting in Los Angeles, Calif. September, 1964.

Olim, E. G., Hess, R. D., & Shipman, Virginia. Relationship between mothers' language styles and cognitive styles of urban preschool children. Paper presented at Biennial Meeting of Soc. Res. Child Develpm., Minneapolis, Minn., March, 1965.

Shipman, Virginia, & Hess, R. D. Social class and sex differences in the utilization of language and the consequences for cognitive development. Paper presented at Midwest. Psychol. Ass., Chicago, April, 1965.

NEGRO CHILDREN'S USE OF NONSTANDARD GRAMMAR[1]

Samuel J. Marwit
Karen L. Marwit
John J. Boswell

Two Negro and two white examiners presented 93 Negro and 108 white second graders with a task requiring them to derive the present, plural, possessive, and time extension forms of nonsense syllables. The hypothesis that white subjects would supply more standard English forms and Negro subjects more nonstandard English forms was supported. The hypothesized characteristics of nonstandard English were upheld in all but one category. The possibility of Negro nonstandard English being a distinct "quasi-foreign" language system and its implications were discussed.

It has been noted for a long time (Klineberg, 1935; Pasamanick & Knobloch, 1955) that Negro children, primarily those of lower socioeconomic status, appear deficient in language functioning. Many of these linguistic "deficiencies" are similar to those noted among white children of low socioeconomic status (Bernstein, 1961; Templin, 1957); others appear specifically related to race (Deutsch, 1965). Most of the literature to date has been focused either on the relationship of these deficits to specific cognitive impairments (Deutsch, 1965; John, 1963; John & Goldstein, 1964; Klineberg, 1935) or to those social conditions that might be responsible for the manifestation of such problems (Gray & Klaus, 1963; McCarthy, 1961; Milner, 1951; Nisbet, 1961). Regardless, the traditional view of Negro children's language is that it represents a "substandard" language relative to white middle-class norms and expectations (S. Baratz, 1968).

Recently, however, some linguists and educators (Bailey, 1968; J. Baratz, 1969; S. Baratz, 1968; Labov, 1967; Stewart, 1967, 1968; Vetter, 1969) have come to regard "black language" as a uniquely different linguistic system from that of standard American English. Instead of considering it *sub*standard American English, they have come to view it as *non*standard American English. They point out that black lan-

guage follows a consistent and predictable set of phonological and grammatical rules that are highly elaborated and sophisticated, and different from those governing the standard English used by most white Americans. If this is the case, Negro children are approaching the traditional school situation with the overwhelming disadvantage of speaking a "quasi-foreign language" (Stewart, 1968) which is neither fully recognized nor openly accepted. The problems this poses in holding one's own in reading, writing, communication, and concept formation have been clearly illustrated by Bailey (1968) and Vetter (1969). These problems, according to Deutsch (1965), are "cumulative" and therefore increase over the child's academic career.

Using standard English as a reference point, the major distinguishing syntactical features of Negro nonstandard English are (a) the zero copula (absence of the verb "is" in the present tense); (b) singularization of plural objects; (c) the zero possessive (lack of a morphological possessive); and (d) the use of "be" to represent time extension. Examples of each of these, respectively, are, "He go," "There are two hat," "The man hat," and "He be going."

Unfortunately, most of the literature pertaining to these nonstandard patterns has been descriptive and observational. Few attempts, if any, have been made to study them empirically. If Negro nonstandard English is, in fact, a well-ordered, highly structured, highly developed language system, we must assume, as does J. Baratz (1969), that by the time the Negro child is

[1] This research was supported by United States Department of Health, Education, and Welfare, Office of Education Grant No. OEG-6-70-0041(509) and by funds supplied by Office of Research Administration, University of Missouri–St. Louis.

5, he has learned the rules of *his* linguistic environment. The present study investigates this by employing a design similar to that used by Berko (1958) in studying white children's acquisition of the rules of standard English. Negro and white second graders were required to transform nonsense syllables in ways designed to represent each of the above four distinguishing grammatical features. Nonsense syllables were used to insure that the child was responding in terms of internalized rules and not in terms of familiarity with preexisting vocabulary. It was hypothesized that for each category, white children would supply significantly more standard English forms and Negro children significantly more nonstandard English forms of the variety described above.

METHOD

Subjects

A total of 229 second graders from 10 classrooms of four elementary schools in a St. Louis County public school system were tested by two Negro and two white examiners. Nineteen of these subjects were discarded because of an examiner's failure to present standard instructions, 8 because information relevant to socioeconomic status could not be obtained, and 1 because of oriental origin. The remaining sample consisted of 93 Negro subjects, 38 of whom were tested by Negro examiners, 55 by white examiners; and 108 white subjects, 49 tested by Negro examiners, 59 by white examiners. Subjects were further subdivided into high, middle, and low socioeconomic status by applying Hollingshead's (1958) Occupational scale from his Two Factor Index of Social Position to subjects' parents' occupation. High, middle, and low were arbitrarily represented by Categories 1–3, 4, and 5–7, respectively. Unfortunately, parental occupation was the only demographic datum provided by the schools. The absence of supportive educational and/or income information necessarily reduces the validity of the scale (Light & Smith, 1969) and any effects due to socioeconomic status must be interpreted with this in mind.

Apparatus

Each subject was administered a test consisting of 24 ambiguous drawings each accompanied by sentences read by the examiner describing the drawing as either an object or a person engaged in some action. In all cases, the object or action was labeled by a nonsense syllable and presented to the subject in such a way that he was required to derive the present, plural, possessive, or time extension form of the nonsense syllable. The first four items were sample items offered to (a) familiarize the subject with the task and (b) to assure the examiner that his subject understood and was able to perform it. These were followed by 20 test items arranged sequentially such that each of the 5 items assessing present tense was followed by one testing the formation of plural objects, followed by possessive, followed by time extension. This order was chosen to minimize the generalization of a set established on one item to any of the four related items. Examples of each test item and the order of presentation are given below:

(1) Present tense. Stick figure reclining with legs crossed and head on hand. "This is a man who knows how to pid. /þɪð/. What is he doing now? Now he _____."
(2) Pluralization. One, then two figures resembling musical notes. "This is a lun /lʌɲ/. Now there is another one. There are two of them. There are two _____."
(3) Possessive. Cup, lun holding cup. "This is a cup that belongs to the lun. Whose cup is it? It is the _____."
(4) Time extension. Stick figure positioned for throwing. "This is a man who knows how to mork /mɔrk/. He does this *all the time. All the time*, he _____."

The 18 nonsense syllables employed for the total 24 items (12 used only once as in 1 and 4 above, 6 duplicated as in 2 and 3 above) were selected from a total of 25 nonsense syllables on the basis of association values obtained from an independent sample of 60 Negro and 22 white second graders from a school system other than the one under study (J. J. Boswell, K. L. Marwit, & S. J. Marwit, unpublished data, 1970). Those 15 syllables which had the lowest association value and the highest frequency of independent responses were employed as test stimuli. The next three highest in "nonsensibility" were employed as sample items. The remaining six were discarded from study.

All sessions were recorded on Ampex 641-1/4-1800 tape using a Wollensak 1500 tape recorder at $3\frac{3}{4}$ inches per second.

Testing Procedure

Prior to testing, examiners attended four 2-hour training sessions, half of each being devoted to the practice testing of children (four per examiner) from schools other than those used in the study, and half devoted to a discussion of problems in test administration and to practice in the verbatim recording of subjects' responses. Examiners were told that they were participating in a study of language development but were never informed of the hypotheses being tested. They were instructed to accept all subject responses as being "inherently correct for that particular child at his particular stage of linguistic development." Posttest interviews confirmed each examiner's ignorance of the purpose of the research.

Testing for data collection was performed in rooms set aside by each school for the express purpose of conducting this study. Each subject was tested individually. Each was seated at a table opposite the examiner and told that he was "about to play a little word game using a tape recorder" and that he was to speak directly into the microphone placed before him. The task was then introduced to the child as follows:

We are going to play a silly word game with a bunch of silly words that somebody made up. I think you will find this a lot of fun. What I am going to do is this. I am going to say some sentences but I will leave off the last part. What you are to do is finish the last part for me. OK? (Answer any questions that might arise). Now let's practice.

The examiner then administered the four sample items which could be repeated for the child, if necessary. Examiners were not permitted, however, to repeat anything more than the sentence stem. Most children comprehended the task by Item 2, all by Item 3. Practice was followed by the examiner's presentation of the 20 test items, for which no repetition was permitted. Each subjects' responses were recorded verbatim in a test booklet which also provided space for his name, sex, age, race, and "comments."

Rating Procedure

All tapes of all sessions were given to two student speech clinicians who independently recorded all subjects' responses verbatim in test booklets identical to those used by examiners. It was felt that "trained ears" whose sole task was to listen and record would provide an accurate assessment of each subject's responses as well as a reliability check on the examiners' ability to record these responses. Responses recorded by examiners and speech clinicians were then rated by the three principal investigators blind to subjects' identifying information. The rating scale provided categories for standard English, nonstandard English as hypothesized, and nonstandard English other than hypothesized. This scale and examples utilizing sentence stems from the sample items above are included in Table 1.

A kappa coefficient (k) of agreement for nominal scale data (Fleiss, Cohen, & Everitt, 1969) was used to test interrecorder reliability. All ks were highly significant ($p < .001$). Tests of significance between ks were nonsignificant. While the vast majority of test items showed triple agreement, those that did not showed at least double agreement. Thus, the "best two out of three" was defined as the criterion for obtaining scores for the final data analyses.

RESULTS

Individual Differences between Examiners

It was decided, a priori, to initially test for differences between examiners. Univariate analyses of variance comparing all examiners for each rating category for each of the four tasks revealed only one significant main effect. That was for the number of standard English forms elicited on the present tense task ($F = 2.86$, $df = 3/197$, $p < .05$). A Duncan multiple-range test (Winer, 1962) showed this to be the result of differences between Negro and white examiners and not between examiners of the same race. On this basis, both Negro examiners' scores were combined as were both white examiners' scores. All ensuing analyses of variance, therefore, employed two levels of examiner race in addition to the two levels of subject race and three levels of subject socioeconomic status.

TABLE 1

RATING SCALE AND EXAMPLES OF STANDARD ENGLISH, NONSTANDARD ENGLISH AS HYPOTHESIZED, AND NONSTANDARD ENGLISH OTHER THAN HYPOTHESIZED

Task and category	Rating	Example
Present tense		Now he_____.
SE	1	is pidding, pids
NSE as hypothesized	2	pid
NSE other than hypothesized	3	is pid
NSE other than hypothesized	4	pidding
No response	5	
Pluralization		There are two ____.
SE	1	luns
NSE as hypothesized	2	lun
No response	5	
Possessive		It is the _____.
SE	1	lun's
NSE as hypothesized	2	lun
No response	5	
Time extension		All the time, he _____.
SE	1	is morking, morks
NSE as hypothesized	2	be morking
NSE other than hypothesized	3	mork
NSE other than hypothesized	4	morking
No response	5	

Note.—Abbreviations: SE = standard English, NSE = nonstandard English.

Standard English

The multivariate analysis of variance used to test the hypothesis that white subjects supply significantly more standard English forms than Negro subjects on all four tasks is presented in Table 2. The mean number of standard English endings supplied by both races on all tasks can be obtained from Table 3. While all four mean comparisons are in the hypothesized direction and a strongly significant effect of subject race was obtained, a Subject Race ×

TABLE 2

ANALYSIS OF VARIANCE OF NUMBER OF STANDARD AMERICAN ENGLISH FORMS SUPPLIED BY NEGRO AND WHITE SUBJECTS ON FOUR TASKS

Source	df	MS	F
Between			
Examiner race (A)	1	6.22	.55
Subject race (B)	1	140.07	12.45**
Subject socioeconomic status (C)	2	34.96	3.11
A × B	1	1.48	.13
A × C	2	3.40	.30
B × C	2	12.08	1.07
A × B × C	2	3.47	.31
Error	189	11.25	
Within			
Task (D)	3	62.84	64.58***
A × D	3	1.76	1.80
B × D	3	5.17	5.31**
C × D	6	1.37	1.41
A × B × D	3	2.73	2.80*
A × C × D	6	.73	.75
B × C × D	6	2.97	3.05*
A × B × C × D	6	.59	.60
Error	378	.97	

* $p < .05$.
** $p < .01$.
*** $p < .001$.

Task interaction was also obtained indicating significant race effects on certain tasks only. Univariate analyses of variance analyzing each task separately indicate significant effects of subject race on the plural ($F = 7.78$, $df = 1/189$, $p < .005$), possessive ($F = 12.11$, $df = 1/189$, $p < .0001$), and time extension ($F = 20.03$, $df = 1/189$, $p < .0001$) dimensions but not on the present tense task.

Two significant triple interactions were obtained. Observation of the relevant means indicates that the Examiner Race × Subject Race × Task interaction is the result of Negro examiners eliciting more standard English from Negro subjects on all but the time extension task and from white subjects on all but the plural task.

Whether this is primarily an examiner effect with Negro examiners facilitating or white examiners suppressing the occurrence of standard English regardless of subject race, or an interactive effect dependent upon particular examiner—subject combinations cannot be ascertained from the present design, nor can the reason for the reversal of these effects in one of four cases. The Subject Race × Subject Socioeconomic Status × Task interaction was analyzed by applying Scheffé's (1953) test to all pairs of mean differences in the amount of standard English endings supplied by each race on each task at each socioeconomic level ($k = 24$). In all comparisons, white subjects supplied more standard English than Negro subjects. Neither Negro and white subjects of high socioeconomic status nor Negro and white subjects of middle socioeconomic status differed in their relative rates of supplying standard English endings to each of the four tasks. In other words, the functions depicting both races' performances across the four tasks at these socioeconomic levels were essentially parallel. On the other hand, a significant difference was obtained when comparing Negro and white subjects of low socioeconomic status in their relative rates of responding to the present and time extension tasks as vs. the plural and possessive tasks ($F = 53.27$, $F'_{(.01)} = 43.31$). Plotting the means for these groups across tasks indicates nonparallel functions and suggests that the major contributing factor in the triple interaction is the differential rate of responding on the time extension task. Whether white subjects are overproducing or Negro subjects underproducing standard English forms on this task relative to their performance on the other three tasks cannot be determined, nor can the reason for this discrepancy occurring among subjects of one socioeconomic level only.

Nonstandard English

Inherent in the white subjects' significantly greater productivity of standard English is the implication that Negro subjects respond significantly more with either one or a number of nonstandard English forms. To determine whether these are of the variety hypothesized, a multivariate analysis of variance, similar in structure to that found in Table 2, was run for the total number of hypothesized nonstandard English forms obtained from subjects of both races on the present, plural, and possessive tasks. Time extension was omitted from

TABLE 3

MEAN NUMBER OF STANDARD AMERICAN ENGLISH AND NONSTANDARD AMERICAN ENGLISH AS
HYPOTHESIZED FORMS SUPPLIED BY NEGRO AND WHITE SUBJECTS ON PRESENT, PLURAL,
POSSESSIVE, AND TIME EXTENSION TASKS

Form	Race	n	Task							
			Present		Plural		Possessive		Time extension	
			M	SD	M	SD	M	SD	M	SD
Standard	White	108	2.65	1.94	3.91	1.81	3.93	1.75	4.00	1.78
	Negro	93	1.80	1.80	2.89	2.01	2.73	1.93	2.45	2.11
Nonstandard	White	108	1.15	1.83	1.06	1.78	1.04	1.71	.90ᵃ	1.71
	Negro	93	1.75	1.92	2.04	1.99	2.25	1.95	2.43ᵃ	2.14

ᵃ No nonstandard English as hypothesized, rated 2, was obtained for time extension. Scores entered represent the mean number of 3 ratings obtained.

analysis because no nonstandard English as hypothesized was obtained. In other words, no subject responded to the sentence stem "All the time, he _____" by supplying "be" followed by the gerund form of the nonsense syllable.

As can be seen in Table 3, all means for the three comparisons are in the predicted direction. The analysis of variance displayed a significant effect of subject race $(F = 8.80, df = 1/189, p < .01)$ and a significant Subject Race × Task interaction $(F = 3.18, df = 2/378, p < .05)$ which complements results obtained in the analysis of standard English forms described above. Univariate analyses of variance analyzing each task separately again showed significant effects of subject race for the plural $(F = 8.10, df = 1/189, p < .005)$ and possessive $(F = 12.92, df = 1/189, p < .0005)$ tasks and again failed to reach significance for the present tense variable. Regarding time extension, while no hypothesized nonstandard English forms were obtained, Negro subjects did consistently offer a nonhypothesized nonstandard English form. Significantly more Negro than white subjects responded to the time extension stem by supplying the stimulus syllable, without modification $(F = 20.07, df = 1/189, p < .0001)$ thereby obtaining a rating of 3 (see Table 1).

DISCUSSION

In general, the results support the hypothesis that white children supply more standard English endings to nonsense syllables designed to represent the plural and possessive of nouns and the present and time extension forms of verbs, and that Negro subjects, consequently, supply more nonstandard English forms. Significant syntactical differences due to subject race were obtained on all but the present tense task. The hypothesized characteristics of Negro nonstandard English were supported for all but the time extension dimension.

The failure to obtain significant subject race differences on the present tense task was a particularly unexpected finding. While it is possible that, in actuality, no differences exist, it is unlikely since it is this category, more than any other, that is referred to in the literature when documenting racial differences in language functions. A second possibility is that differences do exist but that the grammatical rules involved are particularly difficult to learn and are not incorporated by the time children reach second grade. However, this too is unlikely since it is hard to see what is more difficult about learning these rules than those governing the other three tasks for which significant differences were obtained. More likely, the failure to obtain significance resulted from the investigators' poor assignment of nonsense stimuli to this task. Of the five words used to test present tense, one was ris, another zub. To the first, subjects could respond with ris which would be rated nonstandard English as hypothesized or risses, rated standard English. The final s on the stimulus syllable makes the auditory discrimination of these forms difficult, especially if the response is slurred or spoken rapidly. Similarly, with zub, subjects could respond with either, "Now he's zubbing," a standard English form, or "Now he zubbing," a nonstandard English form. Research now in progress has substituted more easily discriminable stimuli; that is, nonsense syllables not containing sibilants in the initial or final position, and should help determine whether or not the hypothesized differences exist.

Regarding the preponderance of nonstandard English given by Negro subjects, the hypothesized form was given to a significant degree on the plural and possessive tasks. A noteworthy but nonsignificant trend in this direction was also obtained for the present tense task. The failure to reach significance in this latter case is probably the complementary result of the poor choice of present tense nonsense syllables discussed above. The complete failure of the time extension task to elicit any nonstandard English as hypothesized was surprising. Either the hypothesized form was incorrect or the sentence stem was improperly structured to elicit it. According to J. Baratz (1969) and others, "be" followed by the "ing" form of the verb in and of itself denotes time extension for the Negro child. It is therefore possible that the authors' use of the stem "all the time" obviated the Negro subjects' need to supply "be-ing." To do so would have simply been redundant and poor grammatical form in any man's language. Just what stimulus, if any, is required to elicit the hypothesized nonstandard form of time extension must remain a question for future investigation. More important for the present hypothesis, however, is recognition of the fact that even though Negro subjects failed to respond with the hypothesized nonstandard form, they did supply an alternate nonstandard form with significant regularity.

The consistent use of nonstandard English forms by Negro subjects is probably the most remarkable finding of this study. It lends empirical support to those who have claimed that "black language" is a separate, highly consistent language with fixed grammatical rules that differ in particular ways from the rules governing the language used by most white Americans. If black language were nothing more than a substandard form of standard English, a sloppy array of nonstandard forms should have emerged. Instead, well-defined nonstandard forms differing in set ways from standard English were elicited for the most part by each sentence stem. The problems inherent in a culture supporting languages differing in grammar yet sharing the same vocabulary are too immense to be elaborated upon here. Yet, it seems imperative to note, in conclusion, that unless the distinguishing features of one language are recognized and accepted by speakers of the other, no one stands to gain.

REFERENCES

BAILEY, B. L. Some aspects of the impact of linguistics on language teaching in disadvantaged communities. *Elementary Education*, 1968, **45**, 570–579.

BARATZ, J. C. Language and cognitive assessment of Negro children: Assumptions and research needs. *Asha*, 1969, **11**, 87–91.

BARATZ, S. S. Social science strategies for research on the Afro-American. Paper presented at the meeting of the American Psychological Association, San Francisco, September, 1968.

BERKO, J. The child's learning of English morphology. *Word*, 1958, **14**, 150–177.

BERNSTEIN, B. Social structure, language, and learning. *Educational Research*, 1961, **3**, 163–176.

DEUTSCH, M. The role of social class in language development and cognition. *American Journal of Orthopsychiatry*, 1965, **35**, 78–88.

FLEISS, J. L., COHEN, J., & EVERITT, B. S. Large sample standard errors of kappa and weighted kappa. *Psychological Bulletin*, 1969, **72**, 323–327.

GRAY, S. W., & KLAUS, R. Early Training Project: Interim report. Murfreesboro, Tenn.: The City Schools and George Peabody College for Teachers, November, 1963. (Mimeo)

HOLLINGSHEAD, A. B., & REDLICH, F. C. *Social class and mental illness.* New York: Wiley, 1958.

JOHN, V. P. The intellectual development of slum children: Some preliminary findings. *American Journal of Orthopsychiatry*, 1963, **33**, 813–822.

JOHN, V. P., & GOLDSTEIN, L. S. The social context of language acquisition. *Merrill-Palmer Quarterly*, 1964, **10**, 265–276.

KLINEBERG, O. A. *Negro intelligence and selective migration.* New York: Columbia University Press, 1935.

LABOV, W. Some suggestions for teaching standard English to speakers of nonstandard urban dialects. In *New Directions in Elementary English.* Champaign, Ill.: National Council of Teachers of English, 1967.

LIGHT, R. J., & SMITH, P. V. Social allocation models of intelligence: A methodological inquiry. *Harvard Educational Review*, 1969, **39**, 484–510.

McCARTHY, D. A. Affective aspects of language learning. (Presidential address, Division of Developmental Psychology, American Psychological Association, September, 1961.) APA *Newsletter*, Division of Developmental Psychology, Fall, 1961, 1–11.

MILNER, E. A study of the relationship between reading readiness in grade one school children and patterns of parent-child interaction. *Child Development*, 1951, **22**, 95–112.

NISBET, J. P. Family environment and intelligence. In A. H. Halsey, J. Floud, & C. A. Anderson (Eds.), *Education, economy, and society.* New York: Free Press of Glencoe, 1961.

PASAMANICK, B., & KNOBLOCH, H. Early language behavior in Negro children and the testing of intelligence. *Journal of Abnormal and Social Psychology*, 1955, **50**, 401–402.

SCHEFFÉ, H. A method for judging all contrasts in the analysis of variance. *Biometrika*, 1953, **40**, 87–104.

Stewart, W. A. Sociolinguistic factors in the history of American Negro dialects. *The Florida FL Reporter*, 1967, *5* (No. 2, 1–4).

Stewart, W. A. Continuity and change in American Negro dialects. *The Florida FL Reporter*, Spring, 1968.

Templin, N. C. *Certain language skills in children.*

Minneapolis: University of Minnesota Press, 1957.

Vetter, H. J. *Language behavior and communication.* Itasca, Ill.: Peacock Publishing Company, 1969.

Winer, B. J. *Statistical principles in experimental design.* New York: McGraw-Hill, 1962.

STIMULATION OF VERBAL INTERACTION BETWEEN DISADVANTAGED MOTHERS AND CHILDREN

Phyllis Levenstein
Robert Sunley

The verbal IQ's of two matched groups of disadvantaged preschoolers were compared before and after the Experimental Group was exposed for four months to stimulation of verbal interaction with their mothers through home visits and play material. There was a significant rise in the verbal IQ of the Experimental Group.

Can the verbal intelligence of socially disadvantaged two-year-old children be fostered by encouraging their mothers to play and talk with them? This was the question posed by the investigation to be described in this paper.

It is a question growing out of the recognition that, although in America the acquisition of education can be the road to upward mobility, yet the cognitive impoverishment linked to economic poverty can limit the utilization of education. Current understanding of the role of experience in cognitive growth,[4, 7] with identification of the preschool years as those most favorable for adding cognitively enriching experience,[2] raises the hope that this link can be broken.

Investigators in the area of cognitive impoverishment of disadvantaged children have emphasized the crucial role of language development in the intellectual growth of these children.[2, 3] And it has been noted that children in our society appear to develop normally, regardless of class or ethnic origin, until about the period when speech begins to be established.[1, 9] Yet by the time socially disadvantaged children enter kindergarten, their cognitive lags, including verbal deficiencies, are apparent. A major factor in this lag seems to lie in the minimal verbal communication by the mother of a "pattern of sequential meaning," to use Hess and Shipman's phrase.[5]

The current study was a limited empirical exploration of the possibility of increasing in preschool children the capacity for verbal symbolization, or verbal intelligence, by encouraging meaningful verbal interaction between very young children and their mothers, organized around toys and books. The research involved an experimental approach to disadvantaged two-year-old children and their mothers together in their own homes, the most natural setting for mother-child interaction. Thus the independent variable was a compensatory enrichment program in the family, with the mother as the ultimate agent of intervention and with motivational factors for the child intrinsic to the relationship and to the play materials chosen for the project.[10, 11]

DESIGN AND PROCEDURE

The research program, called Project Verbal Interaction, was experimental in design. It compared the verbal intelligence of two groups of two-year-old disadvantaged children—one the Experimental Group, the other the Control Group. The children in both groups lived at home and were equated for ethnicity, housing, socioeconomic class, and verbal intelligence of themselves and their mothers. Their verbal intelligence was compared after the Experimental Group had been exposed for four months to a stimulation of verbal interaction with the mothers. The hypothesis for the experiment was that the verbal intelligence of the Experimental Group would rise after this exposure as compared with that of the Control Group.

The subjects were 12 lower-class,[6] Negro, mother-child dyads. They all lived in a predominantly Negro,

The pilot project reported in this paper was followed by more extensive research. For example, see Levenstein, P. Cognitive growth in preschoolers through verbal interaction with mothers. *American Journal of Orthopsychiatry*, 1970, *40*, 426–432.

low income public housing project in a New York City suburb. The choice of ethnic variable was determined by the overrepresentation of Negroes in economic and thus in cognitive impoverishment.[8] Of the 12 dyads, one from the Control Group moved from the housing project before the retesting, so only five Control dyads were available for comparison with the six Experimental dyads.

The 12 mothers were interviewed to elicit background variables of the child's exact age in months; the child's birth-weight; number of siblings at home; the education, age, and occupation of both parents; and whether the father was living at home. The mother-child dyads were then observed in a short unstructured verbal interaction play session.

Both the 12 mothers and the 12 children were pre-tested on the Peabody Picture Vocabulary Test (Form A for the children and Form B for the mothers) to determine their verbal IQ's. The mother-child dyads were then paired as equally as possible for the IQ's of both, and randomly separated into the Experimental and Control Groups. This resulted in an initial mean IQ of 75.8 for the children in the Experimental Group and a higher initial mean IQ of 80.8 for those in the Control Group. The verbal IQ's of the mothers were somewhat higher, with a mean IQ of 83.5 for the Experimental Group and 86 for the Control Group.

The mother-child dyads were then exposed to the independent variable. Trained social workers visited them in their homes 15 times over a four-month period. Each time, the social worker brought with him, as gifts for the child, one or two new Verbal Interaction Stimulus Materials (VISM) to "demonstrate" to the child and mother together. The VISM were commercially available toys and books carefully chosen for their verbal, perceptual, conceptual, and motor stimulus properties and were of increasing complexity. The length of each VISM Session was flexible, with a range from 20 to 55 minutes but averaging 32 minutes. During the session the social worker encouraged the mother to exploit the stimulus properties of the materials for verbal interaction. He used principles of positive reinforcement in building a sense of competence in both mother and child and served as a model to the mother in interacting with the child. The VISM were then left with the dyad for daily use of the mother and child together. At each visit the social worker "reviewed" VISM previously assigned and emphasized the importance of mother-child play interaction with verbalization between visits. By the end of four months, each Experimental child had received 23 VISM—16 toys and 7 books—the same for each child in approximately the same order.

The social workers tried to convey to the mothers respect for their importance in this project, which was explained in terms of helping the child's future school adjustment. The mother's needs and the life style of the family were primary considerations in all arrangements; for example, the home visits were made only at a time of day acceptable to the mother, and a criterion for the VISM was "no hardship for the mother" (no small parts or messy materials). The emphasis was on the project as a team effort in behalf of the child, with the social worker and mother working together almost in peer relationship.

There was no contact with the Control Group during this four month period except to present one gift to the Control dyads in appreciation of their cooperation and to arrange for the retest.

At the end of four months all Experimental and Control subjects were retested on the original instrument, using alternate forms of the Peabody. The resulting data were tabulated and compared with the original data.

ATTITUDES AND BEHAVIOR

With the exception of the one Control mother who eliminated herself and her child from the research by moving out of the housing project before the end of the experiment, and only thus could be said to be "uncooperative," all of the subjects lent full cooperation. Sometimes this was in the face of serious life problems for the Experimental mothers, spontaneously described to the social workers.

All of the children produced full pre- and post-test protocols and participated willingly in the VISM Sessions. Generally there was great and lasting interest in almost every toy and book, and this appeared to confirm the original conjecture that materials rich in features feeding into the developmental needs of the child would be intrinsically interesting. The children's reaction to the VISM were compiled (mainly from behavioral cues) from VISM session records. Out of a total of 138 child-VISM reactions, 113 VISM were "Liked," 19 elicited "Indifferent" reactions, and only 6 were "Disliked" (three negative reactions each for the same toy and book).

Perhaps the most unforeseen finding was the interest of some of the mothers in the VISM themselves. Mothers described themselves as challenged by puzzles and other toys and played with some of them alone, after the child was in bed. One mother called in the social worker assigned to her for a VISM Session after her two-year-old had been put to sleep for a nap!

TEST FINDINGS

The results before and after testing the mothers and children are presented in Tables 1 and 2. As is apparent from Table 1, the mean IQ of the Experimental Group rose 13.7 points as compared with a fractional loss of .4 points from the initial mean IQ of the Control Group. The Experimental Group began the experiment with a mean IQ of 75.8 and ended it with a mean IQ of 89.5. The Control Group started off with a higher IQ, 80.8, but ended the experiment with a slightly lower IQ, 80.4. The difference between the two final means is thus 14.1 points, in favor of the Experimental Group, a difference significant at the .05 level of confidence (t test).

As indicated in Table 2, there was no significant change in the mean verbal IQ's of the two groups of mothers, although it is interesting to note that very small but almost equal gains were made in the mean IQ's of both groups from the initial testing. There was a mean rise of 3.5 points in the Experimental Group of mothers (from 83.5 to 87) and of 3.8 points in the Control Group (from 86 to 89.8).

There are no significant relationships between IQ rise and differences in background variables among the Experimental children. The only variable with which the rise in verbal IQ is significantly associated is the independent variable to which the Experimental Group was exposed. Thus there appears to be support for the hypothesis that the verbal intelligence of two-year-old disadvantaged children will increase if there is stimulation of verbal interaction between them and their mothers, utilizing selected play materials as a focus of interaction.

DISCUSSION

This outcome suggests not only that environmental enrichment can raise the verbal intelligence of two-

Table 1. Verbal IQ's* of experimental and control children before and after experimental group's exposure to independent variable.

		Experimental group					Control group		
Child	Sex	IQ before	IQ after	Difference	Child	Sex	IQ before	IQ after	Difference
DG	F	94	110	+ 16	CL	M	100	105	+ 5
SB	M	82	95	+ 13	CB	F	82	66	− 16
DF	F	73	89	+ 16	BJ	M	73	73	0
DV	M	69	98	+ 29	MH	F	69	72	+ 3
LS	F	71	73	+ 2	JD	M	80	86	+ 6
AH	F	66	72	+ 6					
Mean:		75.8	89.5	+ 13.7	Mean:		80.8	80.4	− .4

Difference between means of Experimental and Control differences = 14.1.
t = 2.6.
P < .05 (difference between means significant at .05 level of confidence).
* On Peabody Picture Vocabulary Test.

Table 2. Verbal IQ's* of experimental and control mothers before and after experimental group's exposure to independent variable.

	Experimental group				Control group		
Mother of:	IQ before	IQ after	Difference	Mother of:	IQ before	IQ after	Difference
DG	99	101	+ 2	CL	106	110	+ 4
SB	99	106	+ 7	CB	99	111	+ 12
DF	80	90	+ 10	BJ	85	86	+ 1
DV	67	72	+ 5	MH	74	68	− 6
LS	61	57	− 4	JD	66	74	+ 8
AH	95	96	+ 1				
Mean:	83.5	87	+ 3.5	Mean:	86	89.8	+ 3.8

* On Peabody Picture Vocabulary Test.

year-old children, but that the children's mothers can be effective agents of such intervention. Furthermore, such a mother can be of low SES and of low verbal intelligence; even with such handicaps, she is apparently able to retain the dignity of having an effective role in one aspect of her own child's cognitive growth, with probable benign effects on her own self-esteem. The interest shown in the VISM not only by the children but also by their mothers suggests that the materials were fortuitously chosen as a natural focus of mother-child verbal interaction, and it is perhaps a happy note in our instrumentally oriented society that toys and books used for play—expressive needs—should be a means to the intellective growth so important to upward mobility in that society.

But caution should be exercised in generalizing from the results of this study. For one thing, the variety of lower-class family life was not represented in the small group of Experimental families; for example, there were no working mothers in this group, and all fathers were living in the home. Perhaps more important, the small number of subjects sets a narrow limit on generalization, however promising the current results may seem to be.

The test effect of the intervention does suggest further similar experimental exploration, with a larger group of subjects, of several questions besides the one implied above. Does a gain in verbal intelligence indicate a similar gain in general cognitive ability? Will the gains be held over a period of time? Would a later subject age than two years yield equally good results? Can the independent variable be defined more accurately? These questions will be among the basic formulations of our currently planned research.*

REFERENCES

1. Bayley, N. 1965. Comparisons of mental and motor test scores for ages one to fifteen months by sex, birth order, race, geographic location, and education of parents. Child Development. 36:379.
2. Bloom, B. S. 1964. Stability and Change in Human Characteristics. John Wiley and Sons, New York.
3. Deutsch, M. 1963. The disadvantaged child and the learning process. *In* Education in Depressed Areas. A. H. Passow, ed. Teachers College, New York. 163–179.
4. Hebb, D. O. 1949. The Organization of Behavior. John Wiley and Sons, New York.
5. Hess, R. D., and V. C. Shipman. 1965. Early blocks to children's learning. Children. 12:189–194.
6. Hollingshead, A. B., and F. C. Redlich. 1958. Social Class and Mental Illness. John Wiley and Sons, New York.
7. Hunt, J. MCV. 1961. Intelligence and Experience. Ronald Press, New York.
8. Orshansky, M. 1965. Counting the poor: another look at the poverty profile. *In* Poverty in America. J. L. Kornbluh and A. Haber, eds. University of Michigan, Ann Arbor. 42–82.
9. Pasamanick, B. 1946. A comparative study of the behavioral development of negro infants. J. Genetic Psychol. 69:3–44.
10. Piaget, J. 1945. Play, Dreams and Imitation in Childhood. Norton Library, 1962, New York.
11. White, R. W. 1963. Ego and Reality in Psychoanalytic Theory. International Universities Press, New York.

*Under a U.S. Children's Bureau Grant, Project No. R-300.

THE INTELLECTUAL AND ACHIEVEMENT EFFECTS OF PRESCHOOL COGNITIVE STIMULATION OF POVERTY MEXICAN-AMERICAN CHILDREN[1]

Walter T. Plant
Mara L. Southern

I. INTRODUCTION

Since the middle of the 1960's there has been widespread implementation of preschool programs for the disadvantaged. Great hopes have rested on the premise that if children are prepared for school they will succeed in academic affairs, remain in the school setting for longer periods of time, and eventually

[1] A modification of the Final Report for Project 5-0590, Contract OE-6-10-118, Bureau of Research of the United States Office of Education, October 1965 through September 1970.

become productive, participating citizens. Most efforts to reverse the spiraling trend of greater poverty and less education for the disenfranchised segments of our population have not been successful. No wonder that so many have grasped at the notion that to reverse the syndrome, one must begin at the beginning. Thus, preschool education has been considered almost a panacea for the ills of the disadvantaged.

The literature concerned with ameliorative programs for the disadvantaged has recently burgeoned. Yet, there is little that is highly organized so that conclusions as to the effectiveness of such projects may be evaluated. Many groups of the disadvantaged have been studied (e.g., American Indian, Negro, Appalachian Whites, Mexican-American). Treatment foci and structures of the various programs are different. Evaluation of the enrichment programs is not systematic, and different evaluation instruments and techniques have been employed. Conclusions as to the effectiveness of these various programs are in conflict.

Many of the programs that have been developed to provide preschool education for the disadvantaged young have had Negro children as targets. In recent years the plight of the American Negro has become widely known and strong social and political support for projects aimed at the Negro has arisen. Few attempts have been made to reach another segment of the disinherited in America: namely, the Mexican-American. Yet there is ample documentation that the Mexican-American youth is in dire need of academic attention and help (3, 11, 12, 33, 53). The effects of the progressive academic retardation of culturally disadvantaged Mexican-American children has led to (*a*) a greater proportion of Mexican-American children than what would be expected in school remedial programs of all kinds at all levels, (*b*) a greater proportion than to be expected in special education classes for the mentally retarded, (*c*) a greater proportional dropout rate in junior and senior high schools for Mexican- compared with Anglo-American students, (*d*) a greater proportional rate of school failure and retention in grade for Mexican- over Anglo-American students, and (*e*) a disproportionate number of Mexican- over Anglo-American people in unskilled occupational groups or the unemployed. Samora's (40) analysis of the 1960 census data revealed that the median number of school grades completed by Mexican-Americans in California was 8.6 in contrast to the median number of 12.1 for Anglo-Americans. Other data having to do with percentages of Mexican-Americans *versus* Anglo-Americans and education are as dismal. For example, in a local study reported by Baker (3), among a group of high school students studied, 43 percent of the total number of dropouts were from Mexican-American bilingual homes, while only 12.3 percent of the graduating class were Mexican-American. Such data strongly support the need for ameliorative efforts in the low income Mexican-American community.

The present investigation was concerned with providing and evaluating a highly cognitively structured preschool experience for very young disadvantaged Mexican-American children. Rather than a usual summer training before school entrance, the project provided two full summers of treatment. Rather than evaluating the effects of the project in terms of performance the first year of preschool only, a longitudinal design was used. Evaluations of in-school performance were made through kindergarten, first, and second grade. Samples of intellective functioning and in-school achievement were collected and analyzed.

II. REVIEW OF THE LITERATURE

Preschool education for the disadvantaged was begun on a massive scale in 1965 when the Federal program Operation Head Start was implemented.

Other Federally sponsored programs of preschool enrichment for the disadvantaged were begun even before the onset of Operation Head Start programs (2, 20, 47). Early programs, as well as subsequent ones, have tended to have two sets of goals. The immediate goals have been to establish good attitudes towards school and also to help the involved children enter school with a more highly developed cognitive system for learning. Also involved in the immediate goal have been higher levels of academic performance, usually defined as performance during the first year of school.

The ultimate goals have been to offset many of the cultural and social ills associated with school failure and dropout, and the resulting impact of low educational attainment levels upon subsequent employment and income. Implicit in the ultimate goal has been the notion that success in school throughout the learning process is necessary for the ultimate end to be reached. Presently, it has been well-documented that low socioeconomic status (SES) children do not reach the performance levels of middle SES children. Deutsch (14) has said that by the time low SES children reach first grade they are already "preprogrammed for failure." Initial school failure has been interpreted to lead to a greater probability of later school failure and early termination of education. Thus, many members of the growing low SES population now reach maturity without the developed ability or skills required to leave the ghettoes.

The position of the sponsors and workers in preschool training for the disadvantaged has been one of "intervene before the effects of deprivation are irreversible." This position may be traced specifically to the work of Hunt (25) and of Piaget (35). Both Hunt and Piaget have suggested that very early experiences, especially in terms of variety of environmental stimuli and verbal interaction, are extremely important in later cognitive growth. Piaget's theory of intellectual development states that before a child can move to a new learning plateau, he must first have mastered concepts on the lower plateau. Jensen's (29) theory on Levels I and II of intellectual development is similar to Piaget's in this respect. According to Piaget, concepts are most easily mastered by having a variety of exemplars of the concept available. In effect, the environment stimulates the child to explore, assimilate, and master.

Writing from essentially the same position, Hunt (24, 25) suggests that intellectual development is dependent upon a rich and varied sensory input. Children who lack such an environment or who are unable to interact effectively with the environment will be inadequate in intellectual functioning. It follows that children who are not restricted continue to seek sensory input. Mildly incongruous input will provide motivation to seek further stimulation, thus motivation becomes an integral part of cognitive development. Hunt contends that stimuli restriction or enrichment in the first few years of life may be the most important. He also argues that the duration of environmental sensory deprivation will determine the severity of deficits incurred.

Children from low SES families frequently do not have the varied and rich environments thought important in intellectual growth. Thus, by the time the culturally disadvantaged child reaches school, there may be little correspondence between what the child has assimilated from his environment and the sensory input provided by the school. Such a situation may lead to disruption in cognition and negative motivation. This would suggest that ameliorative programs should be designed to decrease the incongruity between the child's early sensory experience and that which he would encounter in the school environment. Assimilation of sensory input congruent with later school experience should provide a foundation for appropriate development. Such sensory stimulation, then, should occur prior to school entrance and as early in the child's life as possible.

These two developmental positions have been the leading force in planning enrichment programs for preschool disadvantaged. Numbers of different kinds of preschool programs have been implemented which follow, to a greater or lesser extent, the suggestions and conclusions of Hunt and Piaget.

The literature on preschool intervention among the disadvantaged is familiar to almost all now. Thus, an extensive review of the literature is unnecessary today. There is, however, some necessity for making some gross distinctions about the kinds of preschool programs which have been developed.

Weikart (50) has suggested that there are two main classifications which may be used to distinguish preschool programs. His classification system is based upon the teaching method employed rather than overall project services rendered. The first type of preschool program may be called "traditional." In this class of programs the teacher watches and waits for the child's preferences to emerge, and that determines the timing of different activities. This "traditional" program is one most familiar to middle SES parents who send their children to preschool or nursery school. The primary goals are for social, emotional, and motor development to be accomplished through rather unstructured activities.

The second class of preschool programs, according to Weikart, may be called a "highly cognitively structured" program. This type of program rests upon carefully planned presentations of activities that are based on a specific developmental theory. Traditional nursery or preschool materials are used, but the primary goals are always stated in intellectual and language development terms. Many of the preschool programs for young disadvantaged children have used the "structured" model (7, 15, 20, 31, 37, 44), while many other efforts have been made with the use of the "traditional" model (1, 10, 22, 41). Weikart has suggested that the "structured" programs typically yield more favorable outcomes than do the "traditional" programs.

Implicit in the "structured" preschool model is use of a learning theory in preparation of program materials and teaching methods, as well as a developmental theory. Modification of many behaviors including intellectual behaviors may be enhanced by the use of reinforcements during the training process. Two different learning theories make use of systematic reinforcements. The first is the well-known instrumental conditioning paradigm (43). The second is called a social learning theory (6). Both models call for the S to be rewarded, either concretely or verbally, when the behavior desired is either approximated or emited.

Skinner (43) has suggested that reinforced behavior is more likely to recur than is nonreinforced behavior. Further he suggests that behavior that has been systematically rewarded may become intrinsically rewarding in and of itself. These principles are used unsystematically by most parents in child rearing. These principles are used more or less systematically in the learning process in the schools. Bandura and Walters (6) have refined the early principles of Skinner so that the concept of reinforcement and its resulting impact on behavior has been broadened. The use of systematic reinforcement has been shown to be effective in the modification of the syntactic style of children (4), the modification of children's moral judgments (5), and in traditional learning tasks (45). The application of reinforcements during acquisition of appropriate learning skills should result in both shortening the time required for completion, and also mastery of the skill learned. Reinforcement principles were systematically used in the present study.

Only one specific program employing the "structured" preschool model will be reviewed in detail here. This program was chosen for careful analysis because of its similarities to the current study. The Early Training Project (20,

30, 31) was developed to provide preschool enrichment for culturally disadvantaged Negro children in Tennessee. Two experimental groups of children had two or three summers of a 10-week preschool plus weekly meetings with a home visitor prior to entrance into first grade. Two control groups were included; one in the same area and one in a town 60 miles away. The treatment centered around efforts to instill achievement motivation, to encourage persistence and ability to delay gratification, and to help Ss to identify with achieving role models. This project stressed acquisition and the development of language skills. This was done by having a high ratio of adults to children, and by encouraging oral language throughout the preschool classes. Highly individualized instructional techniques were used, and every attempt was made to plan the activities for each S according to the S's particular needs.

To the point of Ss' entry into school, the project was considered very successful. Using conventional intelligence tests, the investigators reported that the experimental Ss showed positive and significant changes in IQ scores. The control Ss, on the other hand, showed progressive retardation, a frequently observed phenomenon among young culturally disadvantaged. During the first year of school, the experimental Ss did not maintain their accelerated growth but, rather, tended to remain at the level at which they were functioning during the first school year. During the second year of schooling there was a decline in intellective functioning, as measured by intelligence tests, for both control and experimental Ss.

These kinds of outcomes have been reported by other investigators who have attempted evaluation of the long-term effects of preschool training of disadvantaged children. DiLorenzo and Salter (16) reported that at the end of preschool training, significant differences were observed between experimental and control Ss on various IQ measures. However, when the Metropolitan Readiness Test was administered to all Ss at the end of kindergarten, it was revealed that the kindergarten experience did not build on the differences associated with the preschool experience. In particular, it was found that the nonwhite experimental Ss lost any advantage whatever, while white experimental Ss maintained their prekindergarten advantage. The conclusions drawn by DiLorenzo and Salter were that programs of longitudinal effectiveness for nonwhites more than whites require the continuation of special programming to counteract the adverse effects of their environment.

Similar findings were reported by Wilkerson (52) in a two-year evaluation of the Perry Preschool Project (51). After one year of training, experimental Ss earned significantly higher IQ scores than did control Ss. This was not found at the end of the second year after preschool training.

Likewise, the early encouraging results of evaluation of Operation Head Start programs were reversed when time had intervened between training and evaluation. For example, Eisenberg and Conners (18) initially evaluated the effects of Head Start training at the beginning of kindergarten. Head Start Ss were found to have earned significantly higher scores on intelligence tests than comparable control Ss. A follow-up study of the same groups was performed by Waller and Connors (48) after nine months of kindergarten. The average gain over the school year by the control group exceeded that made by the Head Start group.

A recent unpublished study (9) was concerned with first-grade children who had had Head Start experience. After a year of kindergarten and first grade, the Head Start children were behind their matched comparison group in scores from the Stanford Achievement Test. Many other examples of the "wash-out" phenomenon have been reviewed by Shriver (42).

It appears that the early promise associated with preschool education for the disadvantaged has not been realized. Initial positive effects have been shown to fade after just a year or two in the regular school system. Further longitudinal research is needed to determine what lasting effects, if any, are associated with specific preschool programs for specific subgroups of the disadvantaged. This is one such investigation.

III. METHOD

A. Subjects

Seven different groups of Ss were involved during the five years of the investigation. In all cases the groups were composed of children identified as Mexican-American on the basis of surname. Five of the seven groups of Ss resided within the school attendance areas of Mayfair and San Antonio Schools in the Alum Rock Union Elementary School District, San Jose, California.

1. *Training Unit Subjects*

a. Training Unit 1 (T1) Subjects. During the Spring of 1966, 51 Mexican-American children born between December 3, 1961, and December 2, 1962, were selected for participation in the project. All Ss resided within the school attendance areas of Mayfair and San Antonio Schools. This geographic location has been described elsewhere (12) as a badly blighted poverty pocket. These Ss were pretested with the Stanford-Binet, L-M (SBLM) and the Peabody Picture Vocabulary Test (PPVT) prior to entry into the project program.

All T1 Ss attended 10, five-day weeks of preschool training during the summer of 1966. At the end of the summer session only 40 of the original T1 Ss remained in the community. All T1 Ss still residing within the school attendance area in June of 1967 ($N = 29$) returned for a second 10-week summer session. At the end of the second summer training session, 26 T1 Ss remained. These Ss entered kindergarten in the fall of 1967.

b. Training Unit 2 (T2) Subjects. During the Spring of 1967, 57 Mexican-American children born between December 3, 1962, and December 2, 1963, were selected for participation in the project. T2 Ss resided in the same geographic area as T1 Ss. All T2 Ss were tested with the SBLM and PPVT prior to beginning the project program.

The T2 Ss attended 10, five-day weeks of preschool training during the summer of 1967. At the end of this first summer session, 53 T2 Ss remained in the community. All T2 Ss still residing within the school attendance areas in June of 1968 ($N = 38$) returned for a second 10-week summer session of preschool training. At the end of the second summer training session, 32 T2 Ss remained. These Ss entered kindergarten in the Fall of 1968.

2. *Comparison Group Subjects*

The phenomenon of the extended family in the Mexican-American community and its resulting effect upon inter- and intrafamily decisions and communication (12, 27) made it necessary to provide for an extramural comparison group. Two "outside-the-area" comparison groups were formed to control for possible contaminating effects of communication between and within families residing within the experimental locale. These comparison Ss were selected from available Mexican-American children of the appropriate ages in the Mexican-American community in Healdsburg, California.

a. Outside-area Comparsion Group, 1966 (CG'66). Twenty Mexican-American children from Healdsburg, California were identified and tested in the Spring of 1966 with the SBLM and PPVT. None of these Ss was exposed to preschool experiences during this summer. Like their comparable T1 Ss, the CG'66 Ss were all born between December 3, 1961, and December 2, 1962. At the end of the summer of 1966 there were 17 CG'66 Ss remaining in the community; they were retested with the dependent variable instruments.

b. Outside-area Comparison Group, 1967 (CG'67). Twenty-one Mexican-American children from Healdsburg, California, were identified and tested in the Spring of 1967 with the SBLM and PPVT. Like their comparable T2 Ss, the CG'67 Ss were all born between December 3, 1962, and December 2, 1963. None of the CG'67 Ss was exposed to preschool experiences during the 1967 summer. At the end of the summer of 1967 there were 16 CG'67 Ss remaining in the community; they were retested with the dependent variable measures.

There were many Mexican-American children residing in the same school attendance area as T1 and T2 Ss who would have been eligible for participation in the project program, but were not identified and selected for participation. Such eligible Ss provided the comparison groups for both experimental samples. In addition a "front-wave" comparison group was selected from the kindergarten classes at the Mayfair School in 1965, prior to the possibility of their participation in the project.

c. In-school Front-wave Comparison Group, 1965 (C'65). All Mexican-American children attending kindergarten classes at the Mayfair School in the Fall of 1965 served as C'65 Ss. The C'65 group was comprised of 69 children. Dependent variable measures were administered to C'65 Ss during the early part of the 1965-1966 academic year.

d. In-school Comparison Group, 1967 (C'67). All 64 Mexican-American children enrolled in the kindergarten classes at Mayfair and San Antonio Schools in the Fall of 1967, but who had not participated in the project preschool program, served as comparison Ss for T1 Ss. All C'67 Ss were tested with the dependent variable measures at the same time as were the T1 Ss. Examiners had no knowledge of why they were testing Ss, so they had no knowledge of which Ss were T1 Ss and which were C'67 Ss.

e. In-School Comparison Group, 1968 (C'68). All 63 Mexican-American children enrolled in the kindergarten classes at Mayfair and San Antonio Schools in the Fall of 1968 who had not participated in the project preschool program served as comparison Ss for T2 Ss. All C'68 Ss were tested with the dependent variable measures at the same time as were the T2 Ss. Examiners had no knowledge of why they were testing Ss, so they had no knowledge of which Ss were T2 Ss and which were C'68 Ss.

B. Experimental Personnel

Two different teaching staffs were utilized in the project. Professional school district kindergarten teachers planned broad objectives and activities during the summer, and they supervised the daily teaching of Mexican-American Small Group Leaders (SGLs) who were all nonprofessionals with no formal teaching experience.

1. Training Unit Master Teachers

For both T1 and T2 groups one experienced kindergarten teacher was assigned to each 25-30 children. Four different training unit teachers participated in the summer sessions. All teachers had been nominated by school district personnel as being one of the best primary teachers in the district. Two teachers were assigned to work with T1 Ss and SGLs during the summer of 1966. One of these teachers returned to work with the T1 *S*s in the summer of 1967. Two teachers were assigned to work with T2 *S*s both summer of 1967 and summer of 1968.

2. *Small Group Leaders*

Since all children to be treated were of Mexican-American origin, and few *S*s were fluent in English at the beginning of the project, high school students of Mexican-American background were assigned many of the actual teaching duties. These "learning teachers" or Small Group Leaders (SGLs) were identified from the Mexican-American students attending Overfelt High School, San Jose, California. All SGLs had been nominated by members of the high school counseling staff as achievement-oriented and interested young people. There were, in all, 19 such SGLs selected, nine of whom were male and 10 of whom were female.

Each SGL was assigned to teach five or six experimental *S*s each summer. The SGL had the responsibility of planning, executing, and evaluating the daily lessons under the supervision of the Training Unit Master Teachers.[2]

C. Training Program

The basic treatment for all training unit *S*s took place over a 15-month period prior to *S*s' entry into kindergarten. Each group of training *S*s attended two, 10-week summer sessions, and nine one-day meetings (once a month over nine months) during the time intervening between the two summer treatment programs. Thus, each *S* spent as many as 109 days in the experimental program. Absenteeism among *S*s was fairly high, and so few *S*s attended more than 100 training days in the program.

The training sessions were highly structured and cognitively oriented. The primary focus of all activities was one of *S*s mastering and using concepts and skills thought to be important in the formal education process. Development of three different categories of cognitive skills served as the core around which specific activities were planned. The skill categories were (*a*) perceptual and motor abilities; (*b*) concept formation and attainment; and (*c*) language fluency.

Perceptual and motor abilities tasks emphasized the *S*s' gaining ability to discriminate figure and ground relationships and to develop spatial orientation. These two abilities are thought to be particularly important in the early stages of reading. In addition, perceptual and motor tasks designed to enhance the *S*s' perception of numerosity, color discrimination, and development of hand-eye coordination were undertaken.[3]

The category of concept formation and attainment was broadly defined. Initial procedures concentrated on development of *S*s' knowledge of their immediate environment. School environmental structure was provided by the staff in an attempt to offset the inconsistent objects and people in the *S*s' home environments. Family, self, and the everyday world provided many of the concepts to be mastered. The main stress was placed, however, upon color and number concepts and language development. Following Irwin's (28) lead, emphasis was placed on a wide content of reading materials.[4]

Language fluency was frequently the very heart of treatment lessons. It has been suggested that a relatively high ratio of adults to children fosters a climate that promotes increased language usage. Milner (34) demonstrated that wide participation in adult conversations is a crucial variable in good language

[2] Sample lessons and typical activities may be obtained by writing either author.
[3] See footnote 2.
[4] See footnote 2.

development. The adult to child ratio in the present project was quite high and the staff worked intensively to elicit appropriate verbalizations from *S*s in all activities. Constant effort was made throughout the program to make verbalization the instrumental act leading to reinforcement. For example, *S*s were encouraged to state verbally their desires (what paint color to use, which book to look at, etc.) rather than to use a simple pointing response. Strict reinforcement procedures were employed to help *S*s improve in their verbalizations.

In all activities both concrete and secondary reinforcements played large roles. It has been amply demonstrated that behavior may be modified through the judicious use of reinforcers. Appropriate reinforcers in the school setting are, of course, various forms of verbal praise. At the outset of the current project, tangible rewards, such as M&M candies, paper stickers, and animal stamps, were used whenever *S*s were successful (or approximated success) on tasks. These concrete rewards were always paired with verbal praise and physical contact. Gradually (by the end of the third week of the first summer session) the concrete rewards were dropped as *S*s learned to accept verbal reinforcers for their achievements.

The pairing of consistent reinforcements with cognitively oriented task completion was designed to produce positive attitudes toward school activities. Development of appropriate attitudes is related to the concept that the sensory input must not be too disparate from that which the child has already assimilated (24, 25, 35). Thus the content was graded or programmed to insure success experiences for all *S*s. Success was denoted at first by concrete rewards. Continued success met with verbal praise after the relationship between tangible reward and verbal praise was established. The continuation of verbal praise for success was designed not only to be effective for maintaining successful performance, but also to reinforce attitudes of persistence, increase levels of aspiration, and desire to achieve. Thus, positive attitudes toward school and school activities were encouraged.

Each day of the treatment program a variety of activities were planned and executed.[5] The school day was split into seven different activity periods. At the beginning of each school day, approximately 20 minutes was spent with all training *S*s, their SGLs, and their master teachers together for a general content lesson. These lessons were broad in scope and typically served to introduce the specific activities that followed.

After the total group of experimental *S*s met for the major content lessons, small groups of four to six *S*s and the assigned SGL began a variety of tasks designed to relate to the major content lesson, but using a wide range of materials and techniques. There were five different activity "stations" available for use by the small groups. These were (*a*) "art" station for using paints, color crayons, papier mâché, clay, etc.; (*b*) "audio visual and music" station wherein film strips, tape recordings, records, and real rythmn musical instruments were used; (*c*) "block and wheel toy" station where toy trucks and cars, tricycles, and wagons could be used, as well as large kindergarten blocks; (*d*) "idea" station wherein books, flannel boards, and the like were used; and (*e*) "action" station where parquetry blocks, beads, peg boards, primary puzzles, etc. were employed.

Only four of these five different "stations" were used by any one small group each day. Attempts were made to relate the activities in each of the stations to the major content lesson provided by the training unit master teacher. The lessons taught by SGLs during these activity periods were all cognitively oriented; that is, all lessons involved teaching for the mastery of

---

[5] See footnote 2.

some skill. Complete and accurate verbalizations by *S*s which related to lessons were always encouraged and rewarded. Only incidentally during the lessons were specific social and personal skills stressed. The major objective during the small group activities was cognitive stimulation and growth.

After the fourth activity lesson of the day, *S*s were served lunch in the school cafeteria. Variety in the lunch menu was provided so that *S*s' exposure to new stimuli could continue even during lunch. Labeling of the various foods was encouraged and *S*s were urged to continue verbal exchange among themselves and with their SGL during the lunch time.

After the lunch period a short time (about 15 minutes) was spent on the school playground. Organized games, as well as free play, took place. Games which were designed to aid in the development of gross motor skills were organized and led by the staff. As in the other activity periods throughout the day, verbalizations by *S*s were encouraged and rewarded.

After the playground session, *S*s, their SGLs, and master unit teachers reconvened for a final content lesson. Generally, this last lesson of the day was designed to remind *S*s of what they had learned during the day. Efforts were made to have the *S*s themselves provide a recapitulation of the day's events. Content for the next day was suggested, and then *S*s were returned home by school bus.

This pattern of activities in large and small groups was followed throughout the 10 weeks of summer session. Slight changes in daily routine were made for field trips to the airport, for a train ride, and to go to the beach.

D. Dependent Variable Measures

Several dependent variable measures were used to test the hypotheses concerning increased cognitive skills of treated *S*s. Three different types of abilities were assessed. The following tests were employed to measure the intellectual skills of experimental and comparison *S*s: (*a*) the Stanford-Binet, form L-M: SBLM (46), (*b*) the Peabody Picture Vocabulary Test: PPVT (17), (*c*) the Pictorial Test of Intelligence: PTI (19), (*d*) the Wechsler Preschool and Primary Scale of Intelligence: WPPSI (49).[6] Scores from each of these measures have been shown to correlate positively with indices of school achievement for disadvantaged *S*s (36).

Oral language functions were assessed with two subtests from the Illinois Test of Psycholinguistic Abilities: ITPA (32). The Auditory-Vocal Automatic (A-V) subtest was used to sample *S*'s abilities to predict future linguistic events and to sample understanding of underlying grammatical structure of English. The Vocal-Encoding (V-E) subtest was employed to assess an *S*'s ability to generate descriptions, functions, and properties of common objects.

In addition to the above measurements, indices of school achievement were also gathered. The instruments used to evaluate school achievement were the Metropolitan Readiness Test and two forms (Primary I and Primary II) of the Metropolitan Achievement Tests.

E. Hypotheses

The research hypotheses and the variables employed in testing each are listed below.

1. *Hypothesis 1*

Training group *S*s (T1 and T2) will earn significantly higher short-term criterion gain scores on the SBLM and PPVT than will "outside-the-area"

[6] Though the WPPSI was not published until 1967, six sets of it were made available through the late Harold Seashore, Ph.D. and David Herman, Ph.D. of the Psychological Corporation.

comparison group (CG'66 and CG'67) *S*s. To test this hypothesis, the two tests were administered to T1 and CG'66 *S*s in April and May of 1966, and again in August and September of 1966. The two instruments were also administered to T2 and CG'67 *S*s April and May of 1967, and again in August and September of 1967.

2. *Hypothesis 2*

Training group *S*s (T1 and T2) will earn significantly higher short-term criterion scores at entry into kindergarten than will similar *S*s in the "front-wave comparison group" (C'65 *S*s). To test this hypothesis, the SBLM, PPVT, WPPSI, and PTI were administered to C'65 *S*s in the Fall of 1965; to the T1 *S*s in the Fall of 1967; and to the T2 *S*s in the Fall of 1968.

3. *Hypothesis 3*

Training group *S*s (T1 and T2) will earn significantly higher short-term criterion scores at entry into kindergarten than will similar *S*s (C'67 and C'68) in the same classes. To test this hypothesis, the SBLM, PPVT, WPPSI, and PTI were administered to T1 and C'67 *S*s in the Fall of 1967, and to the T2 and C'68 *S*s in the Fall of 1968.

4. *Hypothesis 4*

Training group *S*s (T1 and T2) will earn significantly higher scores on selected oral language measures at the end of kindergarten than will similar *S*s in the same classes (C'67 and C'68). To test this hypothesis, two subtests from the ITPA were administered to T1 and C'67 *S*s in May of 1968, and to T2 and C'68 *S*s in May of 1969. The subtests used were the Auditory-Vocal Automatic (A-V) and the Vocal Encoding (V-E) subtests.

5. *Hypothesis 5*

Training group *S*s (T1) will earn significantly higher reading readiness test scores at the beginning of first-grade than will similar *S*s in the same classes (C'67 *S*s). To test this hypothesis, the Metropolitan Readiness Test was administered to T1 and C'67 *S*s in the early part of the 1968 school year.

6. *Hypothesis 6*

Training group *S*s (T1 plus T2) will earn significantly higher school achievement test scores at the end of first-grade than will similar *S*s in the same classes (C'67 plus C'68). To test this hypothesis, the Metropolitan Achievement Test, Primary Battery I was administered to T1 and C'67 *S*s in May of 1969, and to the T2 and C'68 *S*s in May of 1970.

7. *Hypothesis 7*

Training group *S*s (T1) will earn significantly higher school achievement test scores at the end of second-grade than will similar *S*s in the same classes (C'67). To test this hypothesis, the Metropolitan Achievement Test, Primary Battery II was administered to T1 and C'67 *S*s in May of 1970.

Because of extreme attrition among the "outside-the-area comparison group" *S*s (CG'66 and CG'67), it was not possible to obtain long-term criterion scores from them for comparison purposes. Indeed, the attrition among all groups studied was quite high, and terminal results are based upon relatively small samples.

IV. RESULTS

The results of the present investigation are reported in terms of analyses designed to test each of the seven research hypotheses. Where the number of training group *S*s was large, separate analyses for T1 and T2 are reported. Where the number of training group *S*s is relatively small, the two groups, and their relevant comparison groups, were collapsed.

Hypothesis 1 was tested by administering the SBLM and PPVT to T1 and CG'66 *S*s just before and after the first 10-week training sessions. The time span was constant for T2 and CG'67 *S*s, but occurred one calendar year later. The correlated *t*-test results for within-group change for all groups are found in Table 1. The changes in mean scores from first to second testing for both T1 and T2 *S*s were significant beyond the .01 level on both criterion measures. The CG'66 *S*s earned significantly higher SBLM scores at the second testing over the first ($p < .05$), but showed no significant change in mean PPVT scores. The mean CG'67 *S*s' scores on both the SBLM and PPVT were significantly higher upon retesting ($p < .05$).

Because there were large differences between mean SBLM and PPVT scores of T1 or T2 and CG'66 and CG'67 *S*s at initial testing, analyses of covariance for differences between terminal means adjusted for initial scores were computed. The resulting *F* ratios are also reported in Table 1. Each of the four comparisons between groups (T1 *vs.* CG'66 and T2 *vs* CG'67) was significant beyond the .01 level. Each of the adjusted mean comparisons favored training group *S*s; thus, Hypothesis 1 was supported.

Hypothesis 2 was tested with data from four separate dependent variable measures. To determine whether training group *S*s earned higher short-term criterion scores than either the "front-wave comparison group" (C'65) or "in the same classes" comparison groups (C'67 and C'68), four measures were used. These were the SBLM, PPVT, WPPSI, and PTI. All tests were administered individually to *S*s during the first few months of kindergarten.

The results of between-group uncorrelated *t* tests for differences between means are found in Table 2 for the T1 comparisons, and in Table 3 for the T2 comparisons.

Criterion scores of T1 were compared with C'65 *S*s and it was found that T1 *S*s earned significantly higher scores on four of the six comparisons. Differences significant beyond the .01 level were observed on the SBLM, and PTI, while differences beyond the .05 levl were observed on the WPPSI Performance and Full Scale *IQ* measures. No significant differences between these two groups were observed on the PPVT or Verbal *IQ* measure of the WPPSI.

The short-term criterion score comparisons of T1 and C'67 *S*s yielded significant differences on all six measurements. Differences beyond the .01 level were found on the SBLM, PPVT, PTI, WPPSI Verbal *IQ*, and WPPSI

TABLE 1
COMPARISONS OF SHORT-TERM CRITERION GAIN SCORES FOR TREATMENT
AND OUTSIDE-THE-AREA COMPARISON *S*s

Test	Group	*N*	Time 1 Mean	Time 1 Sigma	Time 2 Mean	Time 2 Sigma	*t*	Adj.[a] mean	*F*-ratio[b]
SBLM	T1	41	85.6	16.6	94.4	16.2	6.13**	91.9	
	CG'66	17	75.9	16.2	80.2	19.9	2.04*	86.4	4.19**
	T2	51	85.0	16.4	95.8	15.7	7.55**	81.3	
	CG'67	16	66.4	13.6	74.3	11.8	2.51*	84.4	6.62**
PPVT	T1	39	71.5	16.9	83.9	18.8	6.75**	81.3	
	CG'66	17	62.1	16.6	65.1	8.9	1.03	71.2	8.23**
	T2	51	69.2	17.0	81.5	18.6	6.61**	78.8	
	CG'67	16	55.4	5.4	59.9	10.6	2.89*	68.5	8.06**

* $p < .05$.
** $p < .01$.
[a] Retest means adjusted by covariance procedures for initial scores.
[b] *F*-ratio for testing homogeneity of adjusted means.

TABLE 2
COMPARISONS OF MEAN SBLM, PPVT, PTI, AND WPPSI *IQs* OBTAINED IN THE
FIRST MONTHS OF KINDERGARTEN FOR T1 *VS.* C'65 AND C'67 COMPARISON GROUPS

Variable	Group	N	Mean	Sigma	$\overline{X}$ diff.	t
SBLM	C'65	69	85.8	12.3	13.4	4.04**
	T1	26	99.2	14.8		
	C'67	64	84.2	13.5	15.0	4.33**
PPVT	C'65	69	83.1	18.4	4.5	1.07
	T1	26	87.6	17.5		
	C'67	64	73.6	16.8	14.0	3.41**
PTI	C'65	60	88.1	15.1	11.3	3.30**
	T1	25	99.4	12.4		
	C'67	73	87.9	15.0	11.5	3.43**
WPPSI-VIQ	C'65	60	85.4	14.0	6.2	1.87
	T1	25	91.6	14.1		
	C'67	73	82.0	12.0	19.6	3.32**
WPPSI-PIQ	C'65	60	90.8	14.4	7.5	2.33*
	T1	25	98.3	11.0		
	C'67	73	91.6	13.6	6.7	2.24*
WPPSI-FSIQ	C'65	60	86.9	14.4	7.3	2.21*
	T1	25	94.2	11.9		
	C'67	73	85.2	11.6	9.0	3.25**

* $p < .05$.
** $p < .01$.

Full Scale *IQ* measures. The scores earned by the two groups on the Performance *IQ* from the WPPSI were significantly different at the .05 level.

Similar results were obtained when comparisons of scores earned by T2, C'65, and C'68 *S*s were made. Eleven of the 12 comparisons were significantly different from zero. Three comparisons between T2 and C'65 *S*s were significant beyond the .01 level; these comparisons were for the SBLM, WPPSI Performance *IQ*, and WPPSI Full Scale *IQ* scores. The comparisons significant beyond the .05 level were for the PPVT and WPPSI Verbal *IQ* scores.

The short-term criterion score comparisons of T2 and C'68 *S*s yielded significant differences on all six measurements. Significant differences beyond the .01 level were observed on the PPVT, WPPSI Verbal *IQ*, WPPSI Performance *IQ*, and WPPSI Full Scale *IQ*. Differences significant beyond the .05 level were for the SBLM and PTI comparisons. Hypothesis 2 was supported.

TABLE 3
COMPARISONS OF MEAN SBLM, PPVT, PTI, AND WPPSI *IQs* OBTAINED IN THE
FIRST MONTHS OF KINDERGARTEN FOR T1 *VS.* C'65 AND C'68 COMPARISON GROUPS

Variable	Group	N	Mean	Sigma	$\overline{X}$ diff.	t
SBLM	C'65	69	85.8	12.3	8.2	2.94**
	T2	35	94.0	14.8		
	C'68	63	85.4	15.5	8.6	2.53*
PPVT	C'65	69	83.1	18.4	9.7	2.27*
	T2	35	92.8	20.9		
	C'68	56	70.9	26.9	21.9	4.28**
PTI	C'65	60	88.1	15.1	5.8	1.89
	T2	35	93.9	14.0		
	C'68	56	86.9	12.9	7.0	2.39*
WPPSI-VIQ	C'65	60	85.4	14.0	7.8	2.40*
	T2	35	93.2	15.7		
	C'68	63	83.1	15.3	10.1	3.04**
WPPSI-PIQ	C'65	60	90.8	14.4	10.3	3.70**
	T2	35	101.1	11.8		
	C'68	63	94.8	13.6	6.3	2.34**
WPPSI-FSIQ	C'65	60	86.9	14.4	9.1	2.98**
	T2	35	96.0	14.0		
	C'68	63	85.0	12.0	11.0	3.87**

* $p < .05$.
** $p < .01$.

Hypothesis 3 was concerned with differences in language usage of training group *S*s and comparison *S*s. The A-V and V-E subtests of the ITPA were administered to T1, T2, C'67, and C'68 *S*s in May of *S*s' kindergarten year. Because the number of *S*s in each group was relatively small, the two training group samples were combined as were the two comparison group samples. The results of uncorrelated *t* tests of differences between means are listed in Table 4. Both comparisons yielded significant differences beyond the .01 level and favored the training over the comparison groups.

While means on both variables, for both groups, were below the normative sample means, it is interesting to note that training group *S*s' mean on the V-E subtest was very close to the expected normative mean. The results of these two tests support research Hypothesis 4.

Hypothesis 5, concerning differences between reading readiness test scores at the beginning of first grade for training group and comparison *S*s, was tested with the use of only T1 and C'67 *S*s' scores. In September of 1968, the Metropolitan Readiness Test (MRT) was administered in the participating schools. The results of the comparisons of MRT raw scores for T1 and C'67 are presented in Table 5.

Mean score differences on the seven MRT subparts favored T1 over C'67 *S*s in five comparisons. On two of these variables, Alphabet and Numbers, the T1 means were significantly higher than C'67 means at the .01 level. At best, Hypothesis 5 was only partially supported; the most conservative interpretation is that Hypothesis 5 was rejected.

Hypothesis 6 was concerned with school achievement at the end of first grade for training *S*s *vs.* comparison *S*s. The Metropolitan Achievement Test, Primary Battery I (MAT) was administered to remaining T1 and C'67 *S*s in May of 1969, and to remaining T2 and C'68 *S*s in May of 1970. Due to at-

TABLE 4
END OF KINDERGARTEN ORAL LANGUAGE PERFORMANCE OF 49 TREATMENT (T1 AND T2) *vs.* 98 COMPARISON (C'67 AND C'68) SUBJECTS

Variable	Group	N	Mean	Diff.	Sigma	t
ITPA A-V (z + 4.00)	T	49	3.3		1.1	
	C	98	2.6	.7	1.2	3.45**
ITPA V-E (z + 4.00)	T	49	3.9		1.0	
	C	98	3.4	.5	.8	3.05**

** *p* < .01.

TABLE 5
COMPARISONS OF METROPOLITAN READINESS TEST RAW SCORES FOR T1 AND C'67 *S*s OBTAINED AT THE BEGINNING OF FIRST GRADE

Variable	Group	N	Mean	Sigma	t
Word meaning	T1	20	7.4	3.4	1.57
	C'67	37	6.1	2.1	
Listening	T1	20	8.6	2.5	.16
	C'67	37	8.5	1.9	
Matching	T1	20	5.5	3.0	—.12
	C'67	37	5.6	2.8	
Alphabet	T1	20	5.8	3.6	4.05**
	C'67	37	4.5	3.8	
Numbers	T1	20	8.7	3.7	2.47**
	C'67	37	7.9	3.5	
Copying	T1	20	5.1	3.7	—.31
	C'67	37	5.2	3.7	
Total MRT score	T1	20	40.9	18.4	.95
	C'67	37	36.4	14.4	

** *p* .01.

trition from all four groups, the T1 and T2 samples were combined as were the C'67 and C'68 samples for the analyses. The uncorrelated *t* test results of mean MAT raw scores for training *vs.* comparison Ss are found in Table 6.

No differences were found between mean scores for training unit Ss and comparison group Ss. The number of Ss per group for this set of analyses varied for each of the subtests due to the need for the MAT to be administered during several sittings. Absenteeism accounts for the small differences in numbers in the group. Additionally, one teacher refused to administer the Reading subtest to her pupils because it would interfere with other planned activities. Five T2 and two C'68 Ss were enrolled in that classroom. Research Hypothesis 6 was rejected.

Hypothesis 7 dealt with school achievement at the end of second grade for training *vs.* comparison Ss. The Metropolitan Achievement Test, Primary Battery II was administered to all remaining T1 and C'67 Ss in May of 1970. Further attrition resulted in very small numbers of Ss in either group, and thus a Wilcoxon Rank-Sum Test (8) was computed to determine differences in central location of the distributions of the two groups. The means, standard deviations, and W_n statistics for MAT-variable raw scores are reported in Table 7.

None of the comparisons for differences in location parameter of the two distributions was significant. In terms of raw score means, the C'67 group had higher mean scores on three of the five subtests, while the T1 group had higher mean scores on but two of the battery subtests. However, the W_n statistic results revealed that there were no real differences between the scores from the two samples. Thus, Hypothesis 7 was not supported.

TABLE 6

COMPARISONS OF METROPOLITAN ACHIEVEMENT TEST RAW SCORES FOR TRAINING UNIT (T1 + T2) AND COMPARISON (C'67 + C'68) GROUPS AT THE END OF FIRST GRADE

MAT variable	Group	N	Mean	Sigma	t
Word knowledge	T	43	22.6	7.99	.36
	C	56	22.0	7.36	
Word discrimination	T	44	20.9	7.23	.16
	C	56	20.6	7.49	
Reading	T	39	18.3	9.11	—.07
	C	54	18.4	8.20	
Arithmetic concepts & skills	T	44	47.9	10.56	—.12
	C	56	48.2	10.37	

TABLE 7

RANK SUM COMPARISONS OF METROPOLITAN ACHIEVEMENT TEST RAW SCORES OBTAINED AT END OF SECOND GRADE FOR 12 T1 AND 18 C'67 SUBJECTS

MAT variable	Group	Mean	Sigma	W_n*
Word knowledge	T1	15.7	7.62	167
	C'67	16.9	6.22	
Word discrimination	T1	23.3	7.78	174
	C'67	20.9	9.58	
Reading	T1	20.0	8.02	180
	C'67	19.8	7.86	
Spelling	T1	12.3	9.60	189
	C'67	14.2	7.98	
Arithmetic total	T1	49.2	12.18	199
	C'67	51.2	13.05	

* $p < .05$ when $W_n = 146$ (one-tailed test).

V. DISCUSSION

Initial results of the present study were very encouraging. Indeed all hypotheses concerning differences between the scores of training unit *S*s and comparison *S*s on traditional measures of intellectual functioning were supported. At the time T1 and T2 *S*s entered kindergarten they outperformed comparable age peers on all the tests administered. While prediction of school success from intelligence test scores obtained at an early age is not accurate, there is generally a positive relationship between the two kinds of performances (36). It was expected that T1 and T2 *S*s would maintain their advantages over their comparison group. *S*s.

Of particular interest were the differences observed between the oral language measurements collected at the end of kindergarten. Again training unit *S*s significantly outperformed comparison *S*s. It is assumed that the constant urging of training *S*s to verbalize during the preschool training accounted for this difference. Performance of training *S*s on the Vocal Encoding subtest of the ITPA was "normal" in the sense that the mean score for T1 plus T2 *S*s was at the normative sample mean. There was, it appears, internal maintenance within experimental *S*s to make verbalizations about the things in their environment. This skill was one that was especially stressed during the summer treatment sessions. Apparently, however, superior skills in the sampled oral language did not transfer to tasks of reading and simple arithmetic.

None of the school achievement hypotheses was supported. There are many possible explanations for the lack of support of these "in-school achievement" hypotheses, and at least three possibilities are deemed worth considering.

First, there were really no differences between intellectual functioning level of training and comparison *S*s even at the beginning of kindergarten. The tests used in kindergarten were all individually administered instruments, and training group *S*s had been exposed to two individual testing sessions prior to entrance into kindergarten. Comparison group *S*s had not been so exposed. Some of the in-kindergarten differences could be due to facilitory practice effects and familiarity with individual testing procedures gained by training *S*s and not comparison *S*s. However, two of the tests employed in kindergarten were unknown to experimental *S*s. These were the last measurements to be taken. Thus no practice effects could be operating during the use of the Wechsler Preschool and Primary Scale of Intelligence and the Pictorial Test of Intelligence. Additionally, comparison *S*s had, by the time these two scales were administered, experience with two recent individual testing sessions. Since significant score differences were observed on these two dependent variable measures, as well as on the other two measures, it is unlikely that practice and familiarity with procedures accounted for a very large portion of the differences in performance by the two groups of *S*s.

A second possible explanation is that comparison *S*s received more individual attention and assistance during kindergarten than did training unit *S*s. It is possible that those children in kindergarten who were not functioning at as high a level as training *S*s were the recipients of more of the teachers' time. Teachers may be likely to help those children who need help the most, and overlook the children who are already performing adequately. In the overcrowded classrooms in the schools in which training and comparison *S*s were enrolled this is a very plausible possibility. In addition to the possibility of differential teacher attention, it is possible that training unit *S*s experienced a sort of "cultural shock" by moving from the situation of one adult to five children to a situation of one adult to 35 children. Adequate transfer from the preschool to the school setting probably did not take place.

A third possible explanation for the lack of differences in school achievement between the experimental and comparison Ss by the time of first grade has to do with possible selective attrition over a two- or three-year period. Frequently it is the case that children from upwardly mobile families perform better in school than children from stationary families. It is possible that more of the training Ss who were performing well than similar comparison Ss left the participating schools. At any rate, attrition of both experimental and comparison Ss may have had some unknown effect upon the terminal samples when achievement test data were gathered.

While the results of the Early Training Project (31) are mixed, the authors suggest that results are still encouraging. Like many of the other preschool intervention studies which have been reported, the Ss in the Klaus and Gray project have been Negro. Perhaps one of the reasons why Ss in the present study did not enjoy even the mixed greater school success of that reported by Klaus and Gray is due to the greater disparity between the Mexican-American cultural background and white middle-class background than is the case between the Negro and white cultural background. In order to enjoy school success, children must internalize and work easily within the so-called "middle-class ethos" of the school. Young Mexican-American children may find it more difficult than Negro children to accept and use the needed middle-class values and attitudes. Thus, it may be the case that more intensive preschool training, or longer periods of preschool training are required to bring the lower SES Mexican-American child to the point of being able to cope with quite different demands of the middle-class school system.

In general, the overall results of the present longitudinal study are strikingly similar to those reported by other investigators involved in the follow-up of children participating in preschool intervention programs (16, 26, 31, 52). The results of the present and other studies may be clearly divided into two parts.

First, the preschool experience gained by the training unit Ss apparently was effective in modifying cognitive performance in kindergarten as measured by traditional tests of intellectual ability. Experimental Ss earned significantly higher scores on the dependent variable measures designed to sample level of cognitive functioning, than did comparable age peers in the same classrooms.

Second, the early school advantages apparent in kindergarten did not result in improved performance on indices of school achievement in first or second grade. At the beginning of the first grade, treated Ss did not perform differently from comparison Ss on measures of reading readiness. By the end of first grade, no differences between the two groups were observed on a battery of academic achievement measures.

Intervention, by making available a highly structured, cognitively oriented two-year preschool program succeeded in reaching a set of "first goals" for Mexican-American disadvantaged children. Superior performance on tasks thought to be highly related to school success at the outset of formal schooling were, indeed, observed. Subjects with the intensive preschool experience did excel their age peers on the tests which sampled intellective functions. These "first goals," outlined in the present study by the first four research hypotheses, were met. The results were very encouraging.

Initial evaluations of other preschool programs, including Operation Head Start, have pointed to great promise for the effectiveness of preschool experience among the disadvantaged. Howard and Plant (23) reported that Operation Head Start Ss earned significantly higher scores than a matched comparison group on such indices as the Pictorial Test of Intelligence, Peabody Picture Vocabulary Test, and the Performance Scale of the Wechsler Preschool and

Primary Scale of Intelligence. Similar results were reported for children participating in Operation Head Start Classes by Eisenberg and Conners (18) and by Riley and Epps (39). These initial school advantages were presumed to be lasting and it was hoped that subsequent higher academic achievement would result.

Other studies, wherein much time was spent with young disadvantaged children prior to school entry, initially led to the conclusion that intensive preschool experience for the disadvantaged might be extremly beneficial in reversing the frequent school failure observed among such children. Gray and Klaus (21) reported that *IQ* gains for their sample of disadvantaged black *S*s lasted up to 39 months. Wilkerson (52) reported that children enrolled in the Perry Preschool Project earned significantly higher scores on cognitive measures during their first year of school.

Once the move was made to sample school achievement rather than abstract cognitive functioning, the supposed advantages were no longer apparent. In most of the longitudinal studies, including the present one, initial advantages associated with preschool education disappeared as the children continued in school and actual achievement rather than aptitude was evaluated. Part of the discrepancy between scores earned on intelligence tests and on school achievement tests lies in the less than perfect relationship between the two kinds of measurements. While *IQ* scores tend to be good predictors of school performance, it is rare that performance on intelligence tests account for more than 50 percent of the variance of school achievement test scores (13). Scores on a test like the Stanford-Binet might well be interpreted as an index of potentiality for performance in academic tasks; there may be a great difference between the "potential" and the "actual."

It has been suggested that part of the reason that the early promise associated with preschool training has not borne fruit has to do with the lack of follow-up with the training once *S*s enter school. Shriver (42) has pointed out that the disadvantaged child with the typical preschool experience moves from a setting where the adult to child ratio is favorable to one where there is one teacher for 30 or 40 children. Thus the individual attention to which the child eagerly responded during preschool is unavailable; the assistance he individually needs to maintain his initial interest and performance is impossible to achieve.

An example of the difficulties experienced by the *S*s in the present study at the kindergarten level illustrates well the point made by Shriver. Training group *S*s had experience with a 1:5 teacher-to-children ratio in preschool. The kindergarten classes at one of the schools attended by *S*s were overcrowded to the point that one teacher had 42 children enrolled in a morning class and 38 children enrolled in an afternoon class. Such a teacher-to-children ratio made it almost impossible for the teacher to attend to the learning needs of any one specific child. Where primary classrooms have such a large enrollment, the teacher's function may well become one of custodian rather than one of facilitator in the learning process. Stress necessarily will be placed on quietness and good citizenship and probably at the expense of making the learning process exciting and stimulating.

It is not, however, entirely the fault of the schools when such dismal events take place. Schools do not and cannot provide preschool education for the large numbers of the disadvantaged. Special programs can probably better provide such services. But, as Reissmann (38) has indicated, the special programs are stopped too soon. Shriver (42) has forcefully stated that special training for disadvantaged children cannot terminate just because the children enter kindergarten or first grade. And, as Klaus and Gray (31) wrote, it would seem most peculiar and naive to think that limited preschool training (in the current investigation about 100 days) can offset the years of deprivation the child has had up to and during the first few school years. These investigators, including the present ones, suggest that special assistance for the disadvantaged must not only start early, but also continue beyond the time of entry into school if early training effects are to be lasting.

VI. SUMMARY

This is the report of the rationale, design, and execution of a longitudinal investigation of the intellectual and achievement effects of a two-year cognitively oriented preschool for disadvantaged Mexican-American children.

Seven different groups of Mexican-American children from very low socioeconomic family backgrounds were studied. Two groups were each exposed to two, 10-week successive summer sessions of cognitively oriented preschool prior to entry into kindergarten. These training Ss were exposed to a wide variety of cognitively structured activities daily in small groups of five or six Ss. The small groups were led by Mexican-American high school students under the supervision of experienced primary teachers. All activities were designed to facilitate Ss in gaining relevant school-related abilities and experience.

The other five groups were comparison groups; two were from outside the geographical area of residence of the treatment Ss, and three from the school attendance areas of the treatment Ss.

Seven hypotheses were tested through gathering samples of intellectual or school achievement abilities. Psychometrics utilized were (*a*) the Stanford-Binet, form L-M (SBLM), (*b*) the Peabody Picture Vocabulary Test (PPVT), (*c*) the Pictorial Test of Intelligence (PTI), (*d*) the Wechsler Preschool and Primary Scale of Intelligence (WPPSI), (*e*) the Auditory-Vocal (A-V) and Vocal-Encoding (V-E) subtests of the Illinois Test of Psycholinguistic Abilities (ITPA), (*f*) the Metropolitan Readiness Test (MRT), and (*g*) two forms (Primary I and Primary II) of the Metropolitan Achievement Test (MAT). All hypotheses tested involved comparing performance of treatment group Ss *vs.* that of appropriate comparison group Ss.

Hypothesis 1 was that training group Ss would earn significantly higher short-term criterion gain scores on the SBLM and PPVT than would outside-the-area comparison group Ss. Hypothesis 1 was supported.

Hypothesis 2 was that training group Ss would earn significantly higher short-term criterion scores at entry into kindergarten on the SBLM, PPVT, WPPSI, and PTI than would Ss in the "front-wave" comparison group. Hypothesis 2 was supported.

Hypothesis 3 was that training group Ss would earn significantly higher short-term criterion scores at entry into kindergarten on the SBLM, PPVT, WPPSI, and PTI than would similar Ss in the same kindergarten classes. Hypothesis 3 was supported.

Hypothesis 4 was that training group Ss would earn significantly higher scores on oral language measures ITPA A-V and V-E at the end of kindergarten than would similar Ss in the same kindergarten classes. Hypothesis 4 was supported.

Hypothesis 5 was that training group Ss would earn significantly higher reading readiness test scores on the MRT at entry into the first grade than would similar Ss in the same classes. At best, Hypothesis 5 was partially supported, but to be conservative Hypothesis 5 was judged to be not supported.

Hypothesis 6 was that training group Ss would earn significantly higher school achievement test scores on the MAT at the end of first grade than would similar Ss in the same classes. Hypothesis 6 was not supported.

Hypothesis 7 was that training group Ss would earn significantly higher school achievement test scores on the MAT at the end of second grade than would similar Ss in the same classes. Hypothesis 7 was not supported.

The results of this longitudinal investigation were compared with those reported by others particularly with reference to the early advantage of training group Ss over comparison Ss until entry into first grade. Additionally, as with reports by others, the lack of "in-school" achievement differences between training and comparison Ss was discussed with reference to possible reasons for the apparent loss of early advantage by training group Ss.

REFERENCES

1. ALPERN, G. D. The failure of a nursery school enrichment program for culturally disadvantaged children. *Amer. J. Orthopsychiat.*, 1966, **36**, 244-245.

2. AMETJIAN, A. The effects of a pre-school program upon the intellectual and social competency of lower-class children. Unpublished Doctoral dissertation, Stanford University, Stanford, California, 1965.

3. BAKER, W. P. A high school program evaluation by means of a cooperative follow-up study. Unpublished Doctoral dissertation, Stanford University, Stanford, California, 1956.

4. BANDURA, A., & HARRIS, M. B. Modification of syntactic style. *J. Exper. Child Psychol.*, 1966, **4**, 341-352.

5. BANDURA, A., & MacDONALD, F. J. The influence of social reinforcement and the behavior of models in the shaping of children's moral judgments. *J. Abn. & Soc. Psychol.*, 1963, **67**, 274-281.

6. BANDURA, A., & WALTERS, R. H. Social Learning and Personality Development. New York: Holt, Rinehart & Winston, 1963.

7. BEREITER, C., & ENGELMANN, S. Teaching Disadvantaged Children in the Pre-school. Englewood Cliffs, N. J.: Prentice-Hall, 1966.

8. BRADLEY, J. V. Distribution Free Statistical Tests. Englewood Cliffs, N.J.: Prentice-Hall, 1968.

9. BROUSE, D. Evaluation of an Operation Head Start program in terms of reading achievement two years later. Unpublished Masters thesis, San Jose State College, San Jose, California, 1969.

10. CAPOBIANCO, R. J. A pilot project for culturally disadvantaged preschool children. *J. Spec. Educ.*, 1967, **1**, 191-194.

11. CARLSON, H. B., & HENDERSON, N. The intelligence of American children of Mexican parentage. *J. Abn. & Soc. Psychol.*, 1950, **45**, 544-551.

12. CLARK, M. Health in the Mexican-American Culture: A Community Study. Berkeley, Calif.: Univ. Calif. Press, 1959.

13. CRONBACH, L. J. Essentials of Psychological Testing (3rd ed). New York: Harper & Row, 1970.

14. DEUTSCH, M. Early social environment and school adaptation. *Teach. Coll. Rec.*, 1965, **66**, 699-706.

15. DiLORENZO, L. T. Effects of year-long pre-kindergarten programs on intelligence and language of educationally disadvantaged children. *J. Spec. Educ.*, 1968, **36**, 36-39.

16. DiLORENZO, L. T., & SALTER, R. An evaluative study of prekindergarten programs for educationally disadvantaged children: Followup and replication. *Except. Child.*, 1968, **35**, 111-117.

17. DUNN, L. M. Peabody Picture Vocabulary Test: Manual. Nashville, Tenn.: Amer. Guid. Serv., 1959.

18. EISENBERG, L., & CONNERS, C. K. The effect of Headstart on developmental processes. Paper presented at Joseph P. Kennedy, Jr. Foundation Scientific Symposium on Mental Retardation, Boston, April, 1966.

19. FRENCH, J. L. Pictorial Test of Intelligence: Manual. Boston: Houghton-Mifflin, 1964.

20. GRAY, S. W., & KLAUS, R. A. An experimental preschool program for culturally deprived children. *Child Devel.*, 1965, **36**, 887-898.

21. ————. The Early Training Project: An intervention study and how it grew. *J. Sch. Psychol.*, 1966, **4**, 15-20.

22. HITTINGER, M. S. Decategorizing the disadvantaged. In J. C. Gowan & G. D. Demos (Eds.), The Disadvantaged and Potential Dropout. Springfield, Ill.: Thomas, 1966. Pp. 30-42.

23. HOWARD, J. L., & PLANT, W. T. Psychometric evaluation of an Operation Headstart program. *J. Genet. Psychol.*, 1967, **111**, 281-288.

24. HUNT, J. McV. Experience and the development of motivation. *Child Devel.*, 1960, **31**, 489-504.

25. ————. Intelligence and Experience. New York: Ronald Press, 1961.

26. HYMAN, I. A., & KILMAN, D. S. First-grade readiness of children who have had summer Head Start programs. *Train. Sch. Bull.*, 1967, **63**, 163-167.

27. IMMACULATE, SISTER M. Mexican cultural patterns. In J. Boyd, *et al.* (Eds.), *Proceedings of Workhsop on Low Socio-economic and Spanish Cultural Patterns.* Denver, Colo.: Denver Commission on Community Relations, 1959. Pp. 1-18.

28. IRWIN, O. C. Infant speech: Effect of systematic reading of stories. *J. Speech & Hear. Res.*, 1960, **3**, 187-190.

29. JENSEN, A. R. How much can we boost *IQ* and scholastic achievement? *Harvard Educ. Rev.*, 1969, **39**, 1-123.

30. KLAUS, R. A., & GRAY, S. W. Early Training Project: Interim Report. Nashville, Tenn.: George Peabody Coll., 1963.

31. ————. The Early Training Project for Disadvantaged Children: A report after five years. *Monog. Soc. Res. in Child Devel.*, 1968, **33**, Whole No. 1.

32. McCARTHY, J. J., & KIRK, S. A. Illinois Test of Psycholinguistic Abilities: Examiner's manual. Urbana, Ill.: Univ. Illinois Press, 1963.

33. MILLER, J. O., & PLANT, W. T. Mexican-American *vs.* Anglo-American mean differences in ability and achievement test scores for 1st, 3rd, 5th, and 8th grade samples. Unpublished study, San Jose State College, San Jose, California, 1964.

34. MILNER, E. A study of the relationship between reading readiness in grade one school children and patterns of parent-child interaction. *Child Devel.*, 1951, **22**, 95-112.

35. PIAGET, J. The Origins of Intelligence in Children (trans. by M. Cook). New York: Internat. Univ. Press, 1952.

36. PLANT, W. T., & SOUTHERN, M. L. First grade reading achievement predicted from WPPSI and other scores obtained 18 months earlier. *Proc. 76th Ann. Conv. Amer. Psychol. Assoc.*, 1968, **3**. 593-594.

37. RADIN, N., & WEIKART, D. A. A home teaching program for disadvantaged preschool children. *J. Spec. Educ.*, 1967, **1**, 183-187.

38. REISSMAN, F. Teachers of the poor: A five point plan. In C. W. Hunnicutt (Ed.) *Urban Education and Cultural Deprivation.* Syracuse, N.Y.: Syracuse Univ. Press, 1964.

39. RILEY, C. M., & EPPS, F. M. J. Head Start in Action. West Myack, Calif.: Parker, 1967.

40. SAMORA, J. The education of Spanish-American in the Southwest: An analysis of the 1960 census materials. Unpublished study (mimeo.), University of Notre Dame, Notre Dame, Indiana, 1964.

41. SEIDEL, H. E., JR., BARKLEY, M. J., & STITH, D. Evaluation of a program for Project Head Start. *J. Genet. Psychol.*, 1967, **110**, 187-197.

42. SHRIVER, R. S. After Head Start—what? *Childhood Educ.*, 1967, **44**, 2-3.

43. SKINNER, B. F. Science and Human Behavior. New York: Holt, Rinehart & Winston, 1953.

44. SOUTHERN, M. L. Language-cognitive enhancement of disadvantaged preschool children through modeling procedures. Unpublished Doctoral dissertation, Stanford University, Stanford, California, 1969.

45. STAATS, A. W., & STAATS, C. K. Complex Human Behavior. New York: Holt, Rinehart & Winston, 1964.

46. TERMAN, L. M., & MERRILL, M. Stanford-Binet Intelligence Scale: Manual for the Third Revision, Form L-M. Boston: Houghton-Mifflin, 1960.

47. VANCE, B. The effects of preschool group eperience on various language and social skills in disadvantaged children. Unpublished Doctoral dissertation, Stanford University, Stanford, California, 1967.

48. WALLER, D. A., & CONNERS, C. K. A follow-up study on intelligence changes in children who participated in Project Headstart. Unpublished study (mimeo.), Johns Hopkins University School of Medicine, Baltimore, Maryland, undated, received 2-19-1967.

49. WECHSLER, D. Wechsler Preschool and Primary Scale of Intelligence: Manual. New York: Psychological Corp., 1967.

50. WEIKART, D. P. Pre-school programs: Preliminary findings. *J. Spec. Educ.*, 1967, **1**, 163-181.

51. WEIKART, D. P., KAMII, C. K., & RADIN, N. Perry Preschool progress report. Unpublished report (mimeo.), Ypsilianti Public Schools, Ypsilianti, Michigan, 1964.

52. WILKERSON, D. A. Review of pre-school programs from "Programs and practices in compensatory education for disadvantaged children." *Rev. Educ. Res.*, 1965, **35**, 240-246.

53. YOUNG, J. M. Lost, strayed, or stolen. *Clearing House*, 1954, **29**, 89-92.

AN EXPLORATORY STUDY OF THE MODIFICATION OF COLOR AND RACIAL CONCEPT ATTITUDES IN PRESCHOOL CHILDREN

John E. Williams
C. Drew Edwards

Previous studies demonstrated that preschool Caucasian children have learned the concept attitude of the color black as negatively evaluated and the color white as positively evaluated, and also have learned the racial concept attitude of Negro figures as negatively evaluated and Caucasian figures as positively evaluated. In the present study, laboratory reinforcement procedures were employed to weaken the naturally formed black-white concept attitudes of 5-year-old Caucasian *S*s. Subsequently, some evidence was found for a reduction in the tendency to attribute negative adjectives to pictures of Negroes and positive adjectives to pictures of Caucasians. The findings were viewed as consistent with the theory that the color concept attitude acts as one support for the racial concept attitude.

Among the many studies of concept formation in young children, a number have been concerned with what Rhine (1958) has called "concept attitudes," that is, concepts with strong evaluative meaning components. The available concept-attitude studies have dealt either with the acquisition and extinction of concept attitudes under laboratory conditions (e.g., Eisman 1955; Rhine & Silun 1958) or with the development and change of concept attitudes under real-life conditions (e.g., Kowitz & Tigner 1961; Weinstein 1957). No studies have been found in which laboratory methods have been employed in an attempt to modify concept attitudes which have been acquired by the child under real-life reinforcement conditions.

Previous studies (Renninger & Williams 1966; Williams & Roberson 1967) have demonstrated that one concept attitude developing naturally among Caucasian children during the preschool years is the conception of the color white as positively evaluated and the color black as negatively evaluated. Since it is generally recognized that racial attitudes are being formed during the same period, the question arises as to the possible relation of the black-white concept attitude to the development of concept attitudes toward Negro and Caucasian persons. It might be hypothesized that the black-white concept attitude is established first and serves as a gen-

eral framework for the learning of concept attitudes toward racial groups color-coded by our culture as "black" and "white." When this sequential development hypothesis was tested (Williams & Roberson 1967), it was not supported since the black-white and racial concept attitudes were found to be developing together during the preschool years. This demonstration of concurrent development provides no evidence that the two concept attitudes are functionally related, since many other, presumably unrelated, concepts also are developing during the same period. If, however, it could be demonstrated that by altering the child's evaluations of black and white one obtained a corresponding alteration in racial attitude, one could be more confident of a functional relation between the two. This would be particularly true if it were also shown that the treatment employed did not result in the modification of some unrelated control concept, such as the child's conception of appropriate sex-role behaviors. In addition, the demonstration of changes in concept attitudes would be more impressive if the modifications were shown to persist across significant time intervals, rather than being assessed in a single session.

The present study was conducted to explore the following questions: Can the naturally formed black-white concept attitudes of Caucasian preschool children be weakened by laboratory reinforcement procedures? Will any modifications in the black-white concept attitude be found to persist during a period of approximately 2 weeks? Following an additional 2-week interval, will children's racial concept attitudes be found to have been significantly altered, with no corresponding effect upon the children's sex-role concepts?

METHOD

SUBJECTS

The *S*s were 84 Caucasian preschool children (46 boys; 38 girls) enrolled in two church-affiliated kindergartens in Winston-Salem, North Carolina. They ranged in age from 5-0 to 5-11 at the time the experiment began, and were judged informally to be generally from middle-class families.

This study was supported by grants to the senior author from the National Institute of Child Health and Human Development (HD-02821-01), the Wake Forest University Graduate Council, and the Piedmont University Center.

From *Child Development*, 1969, **40**, 737–750. © 1969 by the Society for Research in Child Development, Inc. Reprinted by permission.

APPARATUS

Two sets of materials were employed in this study. The first was the picture-story procedure originally designed by Renninger and Williams (1966) for use in assessing connotative meanings of black and white, and later revised by Williams and Roberson (1967). The second set of materials was the picture-story technique designed by Williams and Roberson (1967) to provide a measure of attitude toward dark-skinned (Negro) and light-skinned (Caucasian) persons, as well as a measure of knowledge of sex-role behaviors. The two sets of stimulus pictures have been described in detail by Williams and Roberson (1967).

Revised Color Meaning Picture Series

Each 11 × 14-inch picture card presented drawings of two animals or toys, identical except for color, side by side. Table 1 describes the content of the nonblack and nonwhite filler (F) pictures and the black and white test (T) pictures. Table 1 also gives the key questions asked by E after she displayed the picture and told a two- or three-sentence story to provide context. A typical F story was "One of these planes carries a lot of packages from one city to another. Which one carries the packages?" A typical T story was "One of these rabbits is *good*. He helps mother rabbit care for all his little brothers and sisters. Which one is the *good* rabbit?" Four story questions are given for each of the 12 pictures, since the procedure involved displaying the series a total of four times, each time in the same order but with different stories and, for the test pictures, with different evaluative adjectives. Thus, S had a total of 24 opportunities to respond to the black and white test pictures in indicating positive or negative evaluation. The evaluative adjectives employed are indicated in italics in the key question at the right of Table 1. The positive evaluative adjectives (PEAs) were *clean, nice, good, pretty, smart,* and *kind;* the negative evaluative adjectives (NEAs) were *dirty, naughty, bad, ugly, stupid,* and *mean.*

Racial Attitude—Sex-Role Picture Series

This series, designed along the same general lines as the revised color-meaning series, has been described in detail elsewhere (Williams & Roberson 1967, table 2). Here, racial attitude test cards and evaluative stories occupied even-numbered positions, while the odd-numbered positions contained sex-role items. Each of the twelve 9 × 12-inch stimulus cards consisted of two full-length drawings of human figures of the same age level. The six racial attitude test cards displayed two figures which were identical except for hair and skin color; one figure (Caucasian) had light yellow hair and pinkish-tan skin, while the other figure (Negro) had black hair with medium-brown skin. The figures, drawn with minimal facial characteristics, were posed in neutral standing, walking, or sitting positions on a plain white background. A typical racial attitude story was, "Here are two girls. Everyone says that one of them is very *pretty.* Which is the *pretty* girl?" Each of the six sex-role pictures consisted of two figures, one male and one female, with the same hair and skin color. A typical sex-role story was, "After every meal, one of these two people clears the table and washes the dirty dishes. Which person washes the dishes?"

The 12 pictures in the combined racial attitude—sex-role procedure were administered twice in the same order, with a different story told each time for a given picture. The adjectives used in the key questions of the racial attitude test stories were the same 12 evaluative adjectives which were employed in the test items of the revised color-meaning test.

PROCEDURE

The 84 Ss were divided in a random manner into four groups, with care being taken to maintain approximately equal mean age and sex ratio in each group. The groups were: PR (positive reinforcement only, N = 21); NR (negative reinforcement only, N = 20); PR-NR (positive and negative reinforcement, N = 23); and C (control, no reinforcement, N = 20).

The Es were two female Caucasian college students. Each S was seen by one of the Es individually for a 20–30-minute session, on three different occasions, at intervals of approximately 2 weeks. The S was seen by the same E each time, with each E seeing approximately half of the Ss in each of the four groups.

Experimental Groups

Session 1: learning phase: color-meaning procedure. The S was taken from his classroom to a private room, seated at a table across from E, and told that he would be shown some pictures, hear a story about each one, and be asked to guess the ending of the story. The PR Ss were informed that a correct guess would result in the receipt of candy; NR Ss were told that an incorrect guess would result in the loss of two of the 30 pennies which had been given them at the outset; and PR-NR Ss were told that they would get candy for a correct guess and would lose pennies for an incorrect one. The Ss in groups PR and NR were also told that they would receive some pennies or candy, respec-

Table 1. Summary of color-meaning procedure, describing picture content and key questions for text (T) and Filler (F) items.

Picture number and type	Picture content		Story number and key question ("Which one. . .")
	Left	*Right*	
1 (F)	Brown plane	Green plane	1. . . . got caught up in the tree?
			13. . . . would fly the fastest?
			25. . . . did Johnny want?
			38. . . . carries the packages?
2 (T)	White dog	Black dog	2. . . . is the *clean* doggy?
			14. . . . is the *bad* doggy?
			26. . . . is the *pretty* doggy?
			38. . . . is the *naughty* doggy?
3 (F)	Brown phone	Red phone	3. . . . of these would you like to have?
			15. . . . would your mommy choose?
			27. . . . does Mary's mother have?
			39. . . . is the loud phone?
4 (T)	Black teddy bear	White teddy bear	4. . . . is the *dirty* teddy bear?
			16. . . . is the *nice* teddy bear?
			28. . . . is the *bad* teddy bear?
			40. . . . is the *kind* teddy bear?
5 (F)	Red wagon	Blue wagon	5. . . . of these will go the fastest?
			17. . . . would be safe for the baby?
			29. . . . do you guess is Bobby's wagon?
			41. . . . has the broken wheel?
6 (T)	Black kitten	White kitten	6. . . . is the *pretty* kitty?
			18. . . . is the *naughty* kitty?
			30. . . . is the *smart* kitty?
			42. . . . is the *dirty* kitty?
7 (F)	Green top	Orange top	7. . . . is the broken top?
			19. . . . will spin the fastest?
			31. . . . can spin the longer?
			43. . . . doesn't spin well?
8 (T)	White rabbit	Black rabbit	8. . . . is the *mean* rabbit?
			20. . . . is the *smart* rabbit?
			32. . . . does Pam think is *ugly*?
			44. . . . is the *good* rabbit?
9 (F)	Brown butterfly	Gray butterfly	9. . . . was caught by the girl?
			21. . . . did Susie see in the garden?
			33. . . . likes daisies the most?
			45. . . . is hurt?
10 (T)	White horse	Black horse	10. . . . is the *good* horse?
			22. . . . is the *ugly* horse?
			34. . . . is the *clean* horse?
			46. . . . is the *stupid* horse?
11 (F)	Green scooter	Red scooter	11. . . . do you think Billy will choose?
			23. . . . would you pick?
			35. . . . is George's scooter?
			47. . . . do you guess belongs to Jimmy?
12 (T)	Black cow	White cow	12. . . . is the *stupid* cow?
			24. . . . is the *kind* cow?
			36. . . . is the *mean* cow?
			48. . . . is the *nice* cow?

tively, at the end of the session "just for playing the game." This was done so that each child would return to his classroom with the same things "to show" for his session with *E*.

The *S* was then shown the series of 12 pictures four times in the order indicated in table 1. For each of the even-numbered color-meaning pictures, *E* told a brief story ending with the key question containing the evaluative adjective, recorded whether *S* chose the black or the white figure, and, as appropriate, delivered positive reinforcement (spoken word "fine" or "all right" and receipt of three M&M candies) or negative reinforcement (spoken word "no" and loss of two pennies). Since the intent of the procedure was to modify *S*s' customary responses to black and white, positive reinforcement (groups PR and PR-NR) was given for choosing a black animal in response to a story containing a positive evaluative adjective (PEA) or a white animal in response to a story containing a negative evaluative adjective (NEA); negative reinforcement (groups NR and PR-NR) was given for the choice of a white figure to a PEA story or a black figure to a NEA story. On the odd-numbered picture presentations, S was shown a filler (F) picture and told a nonevaluative story. The PR and NR Ss received their type of reinforcement on alternate F pictures regardless of the response made. For PR-NR Ss, responses to all F pictures were reinforced with alternate positive and negative reinforcement.

At the completion of the 48 picture-story presentations, S collected his candy and pennies, was asked to keep the game a secret, and was told that E would return in a couple of weeks to see how much S remembered of what had been done.

Session 2: retention and relearning: color-meaning procedure. Approximately 2 weeks after Session 1, S was seen again by the same E, who informed him that he would be shown the same pictures as before to see how many correct guesses he remembered, and that he would not be told which guesses were correct (or incorrect) at first but that he would be told later. Then S was readministered the first fourth (12 pictures and stories) of the Session 1 procedure with no reinforcement of responses. Following this, E told S that he would now be told when he was guessing correctly (group PR), incorrectly (NR), or correctly and incorrectly (PR-NR), as in Session 1. Then E readministered the remaining three-fourths of the Session 1 procedure, giving the reinforcement appropriate to the group. Again, at the conclusion of the session, S collected his candy and pennies, was sworn to secrecy, and told that E would see him in a couple of weeks to play a different game.

Control Group

Session 1: color-meaning procedure. The S was told that he would play a game with E in which pictures would be shown, a story told about each, and guesses made as to the story ending. He was also informed that candy and pennies would be given at the end "just for playing the game." However, no mention was made of right or wrong guesses, and no reinforcement, either positive or negative, was given. At the end, E gave S pennies and candy, asked him to keep the game a secret, and told him she would return in a couple of weeks to play the game again.

Session 2: color-meaning procedure. After the 2-week interval, E told S that they would play the same game as last time and that candy and pennies would be given at the end "just for playing the game." Everything else followed as in Session 1.

All Groups

Session 3: transfer phase: racial attitude-sex role procedure. Each S returned for Session 3 approximately 2 weeks after Session 2 and was told, "You remember the last time I showed you some pictures of animals and toys and things like that. Well, this time the pictures I have are very different. They are pictures of people. Now, I'll tell you a little story and I want you to help me by pointing to the person in the pictures that you think the story is about." For groups PR, NR, and PR-NR, E continued, "Now the last time, I told you which ones you were getting right/wrong/[right or wrong] as we went along. This time, I'm not going to tell you how you did until we finish. If you do all right, I'll give you some candy." For group C, E simply continued, "When we finish, I'll give you some candy for playing the game."[1] The series of 12 racial attitude and sex-role pictures were administered twice, in the same order (see Williams & Roberson 1967, table 2), thus providing 12 opportunities to assess racial attitude (RA) and 12 to assess sex-role (SR) awareness. It should be stressed that no reinforcement was given to any response: E simply recorded S's response and went directly to the next picture. At the end, each S was told that he had done "fine" and was given a small package of M&M candies. The Ss were again encouraged not to talk to their friends about what they had done.

RESULTS

The principal data analyses were as follows: (a) determining the effectiveness of the reinforcement procedures in modifying the black-white concept attitude; (b) testing for the retention of any observed changes in this concept attitude; (c) observing whether additional learning trials led to further concept-attitude modification; and (d) determining whether there were transfer effects to the racial concept attitude and to the sex-role concept employed as a control. Since the principal interest was in the general effects of reinforcement, the rela-

---

[1]The instructions for experimental and control Ss were designed to preserve continuity with instructions received in Sessions 1 and 2. It might be argued that the slight variation here was unnecessary and that all Ss should have been given the same instructions, simply promising candy at the end of the session.

tive efficacy of the different reinforcement procedures having only empirical interest, the general analysis scheme at any given point was first to analyze the data for possible differences among the three experimental (reinforcement) groups. If no differences were found, the three would then be pooled into a single experimental group, designated as pooled group E ($N = 64$), which would be compared with group C, the nonreinforced control group ($N = 20$). If reliable differences were found among the experimental groups, individual comparisons with group C would be made. In carrying out this plan of analysis, only one of the numerous comparisons among experimental groups was found significant at the .05 level and this result seemed most reasonably attributable to chance. For this reason, only the analyses concerned with pooled group E versus group C are reported below.

SESSION 1: LEARNING PHASE

Initial Response Level

Since the reinforcement procedures for the black-white pictures were not instituted until after Ss' responses to the first evaluative picture-story combination, performance on this trial was used as a check on the equivalence of the initial level of the color-meaning concept attitude in the research groups. This was done by computing the percentage of Ss responding to the evaluative adjective *clean* by making the customary color-meaning (CM) response, that is, indicating the white dog. This analysis indicated that the customary response had been given by 84 percent of Ss in pooled group E and by 70 percent of the Ss in group C, a nonsignificant difference as judged by a proportion test (Guilford 1965). It may be noted that the higher observed percentage in the pooled reinforcement group constituted, if anything, a conservative error, since the reinforcement group percentage later had to fall significantly *below* that of the nonreinforcement group if an effect of reinforcement was to be demonstrated.

A similar analysis of the percentage of Ss giving customary CM responses on trials 2–6 revealed a generally decreasing trend in pooled group E with the 49.63 percent of this group on trial 6 being significantly ($p < .05$) lower than the 75.00 percent of group C on trial 6.

An additional analysis supplied further support for the presence of differential changes in pooled group E and group C over trials 1–6. For each S, the number of customary CM responses given on trials 5 and 6 (2, 1, or 0) was subtracted from the number given on trials 1 and 2 (2, 1, or 0). Of interest was the percentage of

Ss in each group giving fewer customary responses on trials 5 and 6 than on trials 1 and 2. In pooled group E, 53 percent of the Ss gave a reduced number of customary responses compared with only 25 percent of group C, a statistically significant ($p < .05$) difference. From these analyses, it appeared that, over the first six trials, the reinforcement procedures were reducing Ss' tendency to give customary CM responses.[2]

In order to study the performance of the research groups during the remainder of Session 1, the data for all 24 color-meaning trials were grouped into four blocks of six trials each. For each block, a CM score was computed by counting the number of times out of six opportunities that S gave a customary (positive → white, negative → black) CM response. The mean CM scores for the three reinforcement groups (PR, NR, PR-NR), the pooled reinforcement group (E), and the nonreinforced control group (C) are presented in table 2. Figure 1*A* displays the means for pooled group E and for group C across the four blocks of trials. A Lindquist (1953) Type I analysis revealed a significant main effect of groups ($p < .005$), a significant main effect of trials ($p < .001$) and a nonsignificant interaction ($p > .20$). This analysis, while confirming that pooled group E had generally lower CM scores, provided no evidence of a differential rate of score change across these blocks of trials, an effect which would have been reflected in a significant interaction.

In summary, the analysis of results for the learning phase of the study provided evidence of a learning effect among reinforced Ss during the first six trials, with no statistical evidence of any further differential effect of reinforcement during the remaining 18 trials.

SESSION 2: RETENTION AND RELEARNING PHASES

Retention

In this session, responses to the first 12 stimulus presentations, containing the first six black-white trials, were not reinforced and were used to study the retention of the changes in CM scores observed during Session 1. The mean CM score for each group on the block of six retention trials is presented on the left in table 3, with the pooled group E and group C means displayed in figure 1*B*. The mean CM score of 2.74 for pooled group E was significantly ($p < .01$) lower than the mean of 3.85 in group C. In neither group was there a significant difference between this mean retention CM score

[2]Had such an immediate effect of reinforcement procedures been anticipated, the picture-story combinations would have been counterbalanced across the first six trials.

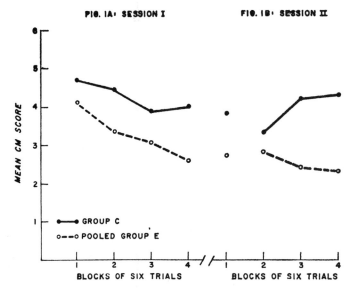

Figure 1. Mean color-meaning (CM) scores during Session 1 learning trials and Session 2 retention and relearning trials for pooled experimental group (E) and control group (C).

and the mean CM score from the last block of trials in Session 1 (see table 2). From these analyses, it was concluded that the effects of reinforcement in Session 1 had been retained across the 2-week interval between sessions.

Relearning

Starting with the thirteenth stimulus presentation, the reinforcement procedures used in Session 1 were resumed and continued through the remaining 36 presentations, thus providing 18 additional reinforcement opportunities for the black-white stimulus cards. Table 3 displays the mean CM scores of each group across the three blocks of six relearning trials. A Lindquist Type I analysis of the pooled group E and group C means across the three relearning trial blocks revealed a significant ($p < .001$) groups effect (pooled E lower) and a significant ($p < .001$) interaction effect. While the latter effect provides evidence of differential change in the two groups, an inspection of the means seen in Figure 1B suggests that this is partially attributable to

an increase in scores in group C, while the scores for pooled group E continued downward.

Since the evidence to this point for additional learning beyond the first six trials of Session 1 was equivocal, an additional overall analysis was made. For each S, a CM score was computed, based on his performance on the first 12 test trials of Session 1, with a second CM score computed for the last 12 trials of Session 2. Using these scores, a Lindquist Type I analysis of variance comparing pooled group E and Group C revealed a significant interaction ($p < .01$), which was interpreted as indicating that significant learning had taken place through the latter portion of the learning phase and the early portion of the relearning phase (the means were: 7.56 and 4.72 for pooled group E; and 9.15 and 8.60 for group C).

SESSION 3: TRANSFER PHASE

Attention centered upon the racial attitude (RA) and sex-role (SR) measures obtained from S's responses to the 24 picture-story presentations. The RA score was

Table 2. Session 1 mean color-meaning (CM) scores for reinforcement and control groups.

		Block of six trials			
Group	N	1	2	3	4
PR	21	4.38	3.90	3.52	3.09
NR	20	3.90	3.15	2.60	2.15
PR-NR	23	3.95	3.04	2.95	2.56
E	64	4.13	3.35	3.08	2.60
C	20	4.70	4.45	3.91	4.05

Table 3. Retention and relearning data: Mean color-meaning (CM) score for each group on the block of retention trials (trials 1–6) and the three blocks of relearning trials (trials 7–24) in session 2.

Groups	Retention	Relearning		
		1	*2*	*3*
PR	3.57	3.00	2.99	2.52
NR	2.15	2.70	1.55	2.00
PR-NR	2.40	2.70	2.65	2.40
E	2.74	2.84	2.45	2.35
C	3.85	3.35	4.25	4.35

obtained from the even-numbered presentations by counting the number of times S indicated the yellow-haired, pinkish-tan-skinned figure when a positive adjective was used plus the number of times S indicated the black-haired, brown-skinned person when a negative adjective was used. The SR score was obtained from the odd-numbered presentations by counting the number of times that S indicated the male figure when a masculine activity was mentioned plus the number of times S indicated the female figure when a feminine activity was mentioned. With 12 response opportunities for each, the RA and SR scores had a possible range of 0–12 with 6 as a neutral midpoint indicating lack of consistent response.

The mean RA scores in the three reinforcement groups were PR = 8.67, NR = 8.60, and PR-NR = 6.83. Analysis of variance revealed that the differences among the reinforcement groups were statistically nonsignificant. Accordingly, the three were combined into pooled group E with a mean of 7.98, which was found to be significantly ($p < .05$) lower than the group C mean of 9.60, via a single tailed t test. (The median score for pooled group E was 8.25, while that for group C was 10.30.)

The mean SR scores in the experimental groups were PR = 11.38, NR = 11.75, and PR-NR = 10.25. The respective medians were 12.00, 11.87, and 12.00. Since an inspection of the RA score distributions indicated that the assumption of normality was questionable, the Kruskal-Wallis nonparametric analysis of variance (Siegel 1956) was performed for the three experimental groups with no significant differences found. Accordingly, the three were combined into pooled group E with a mean score of 11.09 and a median score of 11.80. These compared with group C's mean of 10.70 and median of 11.78. A comparison of the pooled group E and group C data via Mann-Whitney U test (Siegel 1956) was not statistically significant. Thus, the results from the transfer phase can be summarized by noting that some evidence was found for lower RA scores in pooled group E than group C, while the mean SR scores of these two groups did not differ.

DISCUSSION

The reinforcement procedures of the study seemed to bring about significant and persisting changes in the children's tendency to associate white with positive evaluation and black with negative evaluation. This represents, to our knowledge, the first demonstration that a concept attitude which preschool children have learned under natural conditions can be modified by laboratory learning procedures. In this regard, it can be noted that the procedures did not often lead to the reversal of color connotations which would have maximized positive reinforcement and/or minimized negative reinforcement. In the typical case, the procedures merely weakened the customary connotations of white as good and black as bad, and left the child with no consistent evaluative response to the colors.

The study can be viewed as providing evidence in support of the hypothesis concerning a functional link between the black-white concept attitude and the racial concept attitude; children whose black-white concept attitude had been weakened subsequently showed somewhat less tendency to evaluate Negroes negatively and Caucasians positively. The change in racial attitude attributable to the experimental treatment, however, was not great; the mean RA score was 7.98 in the pooled experimental group and 9.60 in the control group. Another way to summarize this change is by noting that 70 percent of the individuals in the control group displayed a significant ($p < .05$) degree of anti-Negro, pro-Caucasian prejudice (i.e., made RA scores of 9 and up) compared with only 48 percent of the individuals in the pooled experimental group. These results are considered consistent with the theory that the black-white concept attitude serves as one support for the racial concept attitude.

In view of the general similarities between the learning procedures of Sessions 1 and 2 and the racial attitude test procedure of Session 3, it seems rather straightforward to attribute the racial attitude effects to primary stimulus generalization based on the similarity of the light-dark human figures to the white-black animal figures. It should be noted, however, that the instructions to *S* were deliberately designed to establish a discrimination between the learning situation and the racial attitude test situation ("You remember that last time I showed you some pictures of animals and toys and things like that. Well, this time the pictures I have are very different. They are pictures of people, etc."). Thus, the observed generalization effects occurred in spite of the child having been urged not to generalize and, hence, would seem to represent a conservative estimate of the degree of relation between the two concept attitudes. In addition, the fact that the sex-role scores in Session 3 were unaffected by the earlier experimental treatments indicates that the racial attitude effects were not attributable to *S*s having learned a general tendency toward the reversal of any concept employed in the experimental situation.

The study also provided some incidental information concerning semantic generalization—a problem which has received little attention in studies of preschool children. The data for trials 1–6 of Session 1 suggested that the reinforcement procedures applied following the use of certain adjectives early in the series were modifying the child's use of *other* adjectives occurring for the first time later in the series. While the confounding of adjectives with order of presentation prevents a careful assessment of this effect, this finding suggests that the general method employed in this study might provide a fruitful approach to the investigation of semantic generalization in preschool children.

Because of the social significance of racial attitudes, one must guard against the overgeneralization of results which appear to be encouraging with respect to the amelioration of racial prejudice. In this regard, the results of this study should be interpreted quite cautiously and only taken as indicating one possible line of approach to the solution of this critical social problem.

REFERENCES

Eisman, B. S. Attitude formation: the development of a color-preference response through mediated generalization. *Journal of Abnormal and Social Psychology*, 1955, **50**, 321–326.

Guilford, J. P. *Fundamental statistics in psychology and education.* New York: McGraw-Hill, 1965.

Harbin, S. P., & Williams, J. E. Conditioning of color connotations. *Perceptual and Motor Skills*, 1966, **22**, 217–218.

Kowitz, G. T., & Tigner, E. J. Tell me about Santa Claus: a study of concept change. *Elementary School Journal*, 1961, **62**, 130–133.

Lindquist, E. F. *Design and analysis of experiments in psychology and education.* Boston: Houghton Mifflin, 1953.

Renninger, C. A., & Williams, J. E. Black-white color connotations and racial awareness in preschool children. *Perceptual and Motor Skills*, 1966, **22**, 771–785.

Rhine, R. J. A concept-attitude approach to attitude acquisition. *Psychological Review*, 1958, **65**, 362–370.

Rhine, R. J., & Silun, B. A. Acquisition and change of a concept-attitude as a function of consistency of reinforcement. *Journal of Experimental Psychology*, 1958, **55**, 524–529.

Siegel, S. *Nonparametric statistics for the behavioral sciences.* New York: McGraw-Hill, 1956.

Weinstein, E. A. Development of the concept of flag and the sense of national identity. *Child Development*, 1957, **28**, 167–174.

Williams, J. E. Connotations of color names among Negroes and Caucasians. *Perceptual and Motor Skills*, 1964, **18**, 721–731.

Williams, J. E. Connotations of racial concepts and color names. *Journal of Personality and Social Psychology*, 1966, **3**, 531–540.

Williams, J. E., & Carter, D. J. Connotations of racial concepts and color names in Germany. *Journal of Social Psychology*, 1967, **72**, 19–26.

Williams, J. E., & Foley, J. W. Connotative meanings of color names and color hues. *Perceptual and Motor Skills*, 1968, **26**, 499-502.

Williams, J. E., Morland, J. K., & Underwood, W. L. Connotations of color names in the United States, Europe, and Asia. *Journal of Social Psychology*, in press.

Williams, J. E., & Roberson, J. K. A method for assessing racial attitudes in preschool children. *Educational and Psychological Measurement*, 1967, **27**, 671–689.

CHAPTER SEVEN

EMOTIONAL DISTURBANCE

The role of environmental versus organic factors in the development of emotional disturbance has long been a controversial topic in exceptionality. While some theorists propose that such conditions as childhood psychosis and hyperactivity can be attributed to neurological damage, biochemical malfunction, or maturational lag, others speculate that emotional disorders are primarily the consequence of unfavorable social relationships. The results of the Lovaas, Schreibman, Koegel, and Rehm study are consistent with an organic interpretation of autistic behavior. The autistic subjects, in contrast with retarded and normal subjects, attended to only one attribute of a complex stimulus in a learning task. Disturbances of attention have long been regarded as one of the consequences of brain injury. Closely allied with the organic view is the developmental hypothesis, which suggests that certain conditions, such as hyperactivity, disappear at puberty. This hypothesis was not supported by the relationships observed by Minde, Lewin, Weiss, Lavigueur, Douglas, and Sykes. Instead, postpubertal hyperactive children were found to manifest many academic and behavioral problems.

Evidence supporting the "double-bind" hypothesis, an environmental point of view, was reported by Bugental, Love, Kaswan, and April. The double-bind hypothesis suggests that one becomes emotionally disturbed because of an inability to satisfy the conflicting demands imposed by others (for example, family members) in his immediate environment. Another aspect of the environmental point of view is finding the treatment that best remediates the emotionally disturbed condition.

Special-class placement has the advantage of eliminating the disruptive effects of the emotionally disturbed child from the regular classroom and the disadvantage of exposing the child to the deviant behavior modeled by his emotionally disturbed peers. Thus, the current trend is toward educational placement in a regular classroom with assignment to a resource room for part of the school day. The effectiveness of regular class-resource room placement for emotionally disturbed children was investigated by Glavin, Quay, Annesley, and Werry.

Although the problem of emotional disturbance has long been of interest to educators and psychologists, few objective measures of the condition exist. By and large, persons who are regarded as emotionally disturbed are diagnosed by projective and objective personality devices after they are referred (probably by the classroom teacher) for clinical assessment. Subjects in the Minde, Lewin, Weiss, Lavigueur, Douglas, and Sykes study were selected on the basis of clinical referral, whereas subjects in the studies by Glavin and his colleagues and Bugental and her colleagues were selected by teacher referral. Teachers base referrals on informal observation, anecdotal records, checklists of descriptive adjectives, and behavioral rating scales. Hence, the validity of the referral depends in part on the observational skill of the teacher. Although personality tests and projective techniques are regarded as highly valuable by some psychologists, others view these measures as unreliable and invalid (Woody, 1969).

SELECTIVE RESPONDING BY AUTISTIC CHILDREN TO MULTIPLE SENSORY INPUT[1]

O. Ivar Lovaas
Laura Schreibman
Robert Koegel
Richard Rehm

Three groups of children (autistic, retarded, and normal) were reinforced for responding to a complex stimulus involving the simultaneous presentation of auditory, visual, and tactile cues. Once this discrimination was established, elements of the complex were presented separately to assess which aspects of the complex stimulus had acquired control over the child's behavior. We found that: (*a*) the autistics responded primarily to only one of the cues; the normals responded uniformly to all three cues; and the retardates functioned between these two extremes. (*b*) Conditions could be arranged such that a cue which had remained nonfunctional when presented in association with other cues could be established as functional when trained separately. The data failed to support notions that any one sense modality is impaired in autistic children. Rather, when presented with a stimulus complex, their attention was overselective. The findings were related to the literature on selective attention. Since much learning involves contiguous or near-contiguous pairing of two or more stimuli, failure to respond to one of the stimuli might be an important factor in the development of autism.

The unresponsivity of autistic children serves as one of the main criteria for their diagnosis. This unresponsiveness is typically apparent in a child during the first year of life when he behaves as if he were blind and deaf, causing his parents to seek professional opinion. Kanner (1944) describes such behavior in one of his patients as follows:

When spoken to, he went on with what he was doing as if nothing had been said. Yet one never had the feeling that he was willingly disobedient or contrary. He was obviously so remote that the remarks did not reach him. [p. 212].

Rimland (1964, cf. pp. 94–96) has presented several other illustrations of such unresponsivity. Description of the phenomenon points to a large variability which can be observed within a particular modality. For example, it may be impossible to observe a response in these children to a very loud (100-db.) sound, yet they may respond excessively to a barely audible siren. The child who behaves as if he does not see the person who greets him, or other objects in his environment, may spot a sugar-coated corn flake some 20 ft. away. There also exists some speculation (Rimland, 1964) that the unresponsiveness may vary across modalities, such that visual, auditory, and pain stimulation are less likely to elicit a response than tactual, gustatory, or olfactory stimuli.

An example from our own laboratory serves to illustrate how such unresponsivity interferes with these children's treatment. We attempted to teach mute autistic children language by beginning with a program on the teaching of verbal imitation (Lovaas, Berberich, Perloff, & Schaeffer, 1966). We have tried to facilitate such imitations by providing the child with visual cues as well as auditory ones. Thus, the child can clearly see the teacher's face when she presents the various sounds, such as "mm," which has auditory and visual cues quite distinct from "ah." The child will learn under these conditions; that is, he comes to reliably emit the vocal response in apparent imitation of the teacher. Following this, the teacher presents the sounds while the child is looking away, or while she is purposely covering her face. Strikingly, the child remains mute. He only attended to the visual cues. It is as if he had never heard the sounds despite thousands of trial exposures.

Figure 1 presents an example from a large number of such instances in our speech training program. The figure is based on data from a patient, Johan, an 8-yr.-old mute boy diag-

[1] This investigation was supported by United States Public Health Service Research Grant 11440 from the National Institute of Mental Health.

nosed as a "textbook example of autism." He was trained to imitate the sound "ah" with full visual exposure to the teacher's face. Percentages of correct reproductions (S's "ah" to E's "ah") are given on the ordinate, and trials are given along the abscissa. The S had 1,180 trials preceding those which are plotted here, but his performance reflected no learning until after 1,400 trials. At this point he improved, and by Trial 1,740 he gave an onlooker the impression that he was listening to E and imitating what he had heard. However, when E removed the visual cues associated with the sound (Trials 1760–1780, 1800–1820, and 1840–1860), S's performance fell to zero. It is as if he had never heard E's voice.

The insert in the figure shows the same loss when visual cues are removed from the training of Johan's second sound, "mm." Eventually, as in the case of gutteral sounds (e.g., "g," "k") without distinct visual components, the child learns to discriminate (imitate) the auditory cues. This acquisition is very slow. These observations raise several questions. Are the children particularly unresponsive to auditory cues? Are they unresponsive to auditory cues when these are presented together with visual cues? Do they have difficulty attending to any one cue in a multiple cue input, etc.?

The clinical observations that these children respond to cues in a particular modality on one occasion while not responding to these cues on another occasion have led to inferences regarding deficiencies in attentional, rather than sensory, mechanisms. These deficiencies in attentional mechanisms have been given a central, explanatory role in the child's failure of cognitive, social, or emotional development. For the reader who feels that there may be a similarity between attentional deficit in adult and childhood schizophrenia, excellent reviews of theories of attentional deficit in adult schizophrenia have been provided by Buss and Lang (1965), Lang and Buss (1965), and Feigenberg (1969).

There are two main etiologies which have been proposed to underlie the attentional deficiencies in autism. One of these is based on developmental models and draws heavily on Sherrington's work (1906). He postulated a transition from near-receptor dominance in lower organisms to far-receptor dominance in higher organisms. He considered, furthermore, that the far receptors are prerequisite for the development of complex psychological processes. This conceptualization has been employed by Goldfarb (1964) in his postulation of a distorted hierarchy of receptor dominance in autistic children, with motor-tactile orientation dominating auditory and visual inputs. Subsequent experimental studies (cf. Schopler, 1966) have failed to verify the propriety of this model in describing receptor orientation in autistic children.

The other proposed etiology of these attentional deficits is based on hypothesized deviations in their social history and draws heavily on psychodynamic formulations. The children's primary difficulty is seen to arise from inadequate early mother-child interactions, with a consequent failure in the

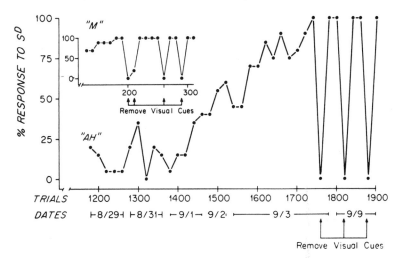

FIG. 1. Acquisition of "Ah" and "Mm" trained with auditory and visual cues. (Percentages of correct reproductions of E's presentations are plotted on the ordinate with trials plotted along the abscissa. Arrows indicate trials where visual cues were removed.)

development of perceptual activity, or it may be selective, largely restricted to social stimuli. As was the case with the developmental theories based on Sherrington's work, there has been a similar failure for research to confirm psychodynamic interpretations.

Much of the empirical work here has been carried out by Hermelin and O'Connor (summarized by Hermelin, 1966) and usually involved exposing the children to various stimulus displays, obtaining preferences for certain inputs as a function of the amount of their visual or tactual attending behavior. The conclusion which can be drawn from these studies is that, in contrast to normals, autistic children look less at the experimental stimuli, but do not selectively avoid social ones. Young (1969) found that they may attend proportionately less to complex, incongruous stimuli.

Although descriptions of visual attending behavior, which comprise the bulk of research in this area, may provide leads in understanding the psychopathology, such studies are quite inferential. That is, they require a model which relates visual attending to learning, or to some other behavior change. This is feasible since a person can visually attend to an environment without learning anything about it. Receptor orientation is necessary, but not sufficient, for learning. Viewed in that context, a discrimination learning situation may be a superior procedure for the study of attentional deficits, since it incorporates learning. We have employed such a procedure in the study we shall describe below.

The situation we constructed was as follows: the child was reinforced for responding in the presence of a stimulus display and was not reinforced for responding in the absence of that display. One can argue that the child attends to (is controlled by) certain stimuli when independent variation of these stimuli is associated with concurrent change in the child's behavior. We employed a multidimensional stimulus display, that is, a display which contained auditory, visual, tactual, and temporal cues. The study was designed such that, after the child's behavior was brought under the control of the display, separate components of that display could be presented singly so as to assess to which aspects the child was responding. One could then find out if certain components of the display were more functional than others, how many components had become functional, whether certain components had failed to acquire any function, etc.

METHOD

Subjects

We ran three groups of Ss. The autistic group consisted of five boys and one girl, with mean CA of 7.2 yr. (range of 4–10 yr.). These children had been diagnosed by agencies not associated with the experiment. Four of the Ss were mute and would utter only unintelligible sounds without communicative intent. They gave sporadic response to the most elementary commands (e.g., "sit down," "close the door"). They were untestable on standard psychological tests. Two of the Ss were not toilet-trained, and other social and self-help skills were minimal. For example, they did not dress themselves; they did not play with toys; and they did not play with peers. Three had early histories of suspected deafness. They were inpatients, and in all likelihood faced permanent hospitalization. In short, they were extremely regressed and fell within the lower third of the psychotic continuum. The fifth child, Danny, differed from the rest in that he was echolalic, expressed simple demands, and was behaviorally more advanced so that he remained at home and made a marginal adjustment to a class for severely retarded children. Like the others, he would frequently act as if he did not see or hear adults. All Ss demonstrated bizarre self-stimulatory behavior (stereotyped motor acts).

The second group contained five mentally retarded children, four boys and one girl, with a mean CA of 8 yr. (range of 7–10 yr.) and a mean MA of 3.7 yr. (range 3.5 to 4.0 yr.). Four of these Ss were institutionalized. Two had been diagnosed as Mongoloid, two as retarded due to birth trauma, and one as retarded from an unknown genetic origin. One of the retarded Ss had a history of suspected (but unconfirmed) deafness, while all other Ss had displayed normal responsiveness to external stimulation.

A normal control group consisted of five children with mean CA of 6.4 yr. (range of 6.0–7.5 yr.). These Ss, two boys and three girls, were obtained from parents working at the university.

Apparatus

The S was seated in a 7 × 8 ft. experimental room in front of a $2\frac{1}{2}$-ft.-high table holding a box with a 3-in. bar protruding from its front. The box also housed a Davis Model 310 universal feeder which delivered candy, potato chips, etc., to S through a chute at the left side of the box. Sound equipment and one-way vision screens connected the experimental room to an observation room from which E would present the various experimental manipulations. The experimental room was lighted by a 40-w. light, giving a dim illumination level of .50 ftc. The room was sound attenuated.

We employed four kinds of stimuli. (a) A visual stimulus, which consisted of a 150-w. red floodlight, was mounted on the ceiling behind S's back and out of his view. This light raised the room illumination level from .50 to 2.50 ftc. as measured by a Weston illumination meter, Model 756 (these readings were made on the front panel of the box which faced S). (b) An auditory stimulus, consisting of white noise, was fed from a tape recorder into a speaker located above S. The noise level generated was 63 db. (measured by a General Radio Co. sound-level meter, Type No. 1551-B, set at 20-kc. weighting). Since white noise consists of all frequencies, the possibility of *S*s being differentially sensitive to particular frequencies was eliminated. (*c*) A tactile stimulus was applied by forcing air into a blood pressure cuff fastened around *S*'s left calf. The cuff was attached by a rubber tube to an automobile tire pump operated by *E*. The arrangement allowed *E* to deliver a rather discrete tactile pressure (20 mm. of mercury), retain that pressure for the desired interval, and instantly remove (deflate) it. (*d*) A temporal cue was arranged by presenting all the stimuli for a 5-sec. interval every 20 sec. That is, *S* could obtain reinforcement simply by hitting the bar as a function of time elapsed since last reinforcement (a temporal cue) rather than on the basis of the three other cues.

The *S* was run in two kinds of sessions, training and testing. During training sessions, he was taught a discrimination where his bar presses were brought under the control of the stimulus complex. During the subsequent test sessions, he was presented with the various components of the stimulus complex to assess which one(s) had acquired functional control.

Training

The *S* was seated before the bar and instructed that if he pressed it he would get candy. If *S* failed to respond to the instructions, *E* prompted the response manually. As soon as *S* had emitted two unassisted bar presses within 1 min., he was left alone in the experimental room and presented with the S^D (stimulus complex). The S^D was presented for 10 sec. or until it was terminated by a single bar press. When *S* had responded to the S^D on three successive presentations, the duration of the S^D period was gradually decreased in 1-sec. units to the ultimate 5-sec. S^D interval. At the same time, the reinforcement schedule was gradually changed from FR-1 to FR-4. In the final stages of training, *S* would eventually respond with a burst of four bar presses within the 5-sec. S^D period. The fourth bar press terminated the S^D. S^Δ was set to last for 20 sec. When *S* failed to give any evidence of decreased rate of response during the S^Δ interval after the first training session, *E* would deliver a loud "no" over the intercom contingent on such response. All steps, including the onset and timing of the S^D and S^Δ intervals, operation of the feeder, recording of the bar presses, etc., were carried out automatically through Davis relay programming equipment and a Davis Model CRRC 133 cumulative recorder. Session lengths, which varied between 20 and 50 min., were determined by the length of time it required *S* to obtain 36 reinforcements (which emptied the dispenser). The *S*s received not more than two sessions per day, not more than 3 days apart. The discrimination training was considered complete, and test trials were begun, when *S* had completed two consecutive sessions in which at least 90% of his bar presses fell within the S^D interval.

Testing

Upon completion of the training phase, each autistic and retarded *S* received 10 test sessions. Testing for the normal *S*s was terminated after two successive tests showing 100% response to the auditory, visual, and tactile cues. The test sessions were of the same duration as the training sessions and were distributed such that *S* received no more than two tests a day nor less than one every third day. In the test trials, the single stimuli were randomly interspersed between training trials (trials with all the stimulus components present) except that: (*a*) each test trial was always preceded and followed by at least one training trial, and (*b*) *E* did not run more than three training trials in a row. The density of the training trials helped to maintain the discrimination. The *S* was reinforced if he responded correctly on a test trial. To test for temporal discriminations, the S^Δ interval was altered from 20 to 10, 15, 25, and 30 sec. The intervals with presentations occurring prior to 20 sec. potentially provided evidence for responses to individual stimuli in the absence of the normal temporal cue. The intervals greater than 20 sec., however, allowed *S* to respond on the basis of a temporal cue without the influence of the external stimuli. The *S* received, on the average, seven presentations of each individual stimulus in a test session. The temporal intervals were randomly selected among the 10, 15, 25, and 30 sec. Altogether, he received approximately 70 test trials on any one stimulus, distributed over 10 sessions.

RESULTS

There was a great deal of variability in the acquisition of the discrimination. The normal *S*s learned to respond to the complex input within a matter of minutes. The retarded *S*s required, on the average, less than five 30-min. training sessions, while the autistic group required approximately twice as many sessions as the retardates. One autistic child, Leslie, was run for a total of 3 mo., five sessions a week, and still could not maintain the discrimination (she responded less than 80% of the time to the S^D, and had large bursts of S^Δ responding). Her discrimination of the complex input was so poorly maintained that tests for component control were meaningless; hence her data are not included.

Once *S* had learned to discriminate the stimulus complex, the main question became centered on which stimuli within the complex were controlling his responding. The *S*'s responding to the separate components will be presented as a percentage derived from the number of actual responses to a given stimulus over the total number of opportunities to respond to that stimulus. For example, if in a particular test session *S* gave eight bar presses to the tactile stimulus, and that stimulus was presented eight times during that session, which would allow for 32 possible responses (4 responses per presentation), his score would equal 25%. This value is used as an index of *S*'s sensitivity to a particular stimulus element. There will be no discussion of the temporal cue since no evidence for a temporal discrimination was observed for any of the *S*s.

The most general conclusion which can be made from the data is that autistic *S*s respond primarily to one stimulus component, retardates to two, and normals to all three.

We derived this conclusion from a statistical analysis which was carried out as follows: we divided the *S*s' responses into three levels—high, medium, and low—on the basis of the amount of responding to the separate stimuli. High was the stimulus component to which *S* responded most (was most functional), medium was the next most functional, and low the least functional. The magnitude of these differences was tested as follows. If there was no significant difference in the amount of responding between these levels, then it could be inferred that *S* had not responded differently to the three stimuli. On the other hand, a significant difference between these levels would indicate differential control by the stimulus components. For example, a significant difference between high and medium and a lack of difference between medium and low would indicate that only one cue had acquired control.

The statistical analysis was performed on the first test session only. We limited the analysis to this test session because with additional sessions *S* received increasing reinforcement for responding to single cues.

Table 1 shows the analysis of variance. There was a significant ($p < .01$) interaction between diagnosis (autistic, retarded, and normal) and level of responding (high, medium, and low). There was no significant difference in regard to overall level of responding. A Newman-Keuls test on the means enabled a closer analysis of the individual populations. The result of that analysis has been presented in Table 2.

As Table 2 shows, there was no significant difference in the amount of responding to the separate stimuli for the normal *S*s. The normals gave no evidence for a preference among the cues, or that they were selectively attending to some cues and not others. For the autistics, the significant difference between the high and medium cues and lack of significant difference between the medium and low cues show the dominance of one cue. The retardates differ from the autistics in that

TABLE 1

ANALYSIS OF VARIANCE ON LEVEL OF RESPONDING TO THE SINGLE CUES

Source	df	MS	F
Diagnosis (D)	2	1217	.548
*S*s within groups	12	2218	
Level of responding (L)	2	9487	43.1*
D × L	4	1677	7.62*
L × *S*s within groups	24	220	

*p < .005.

TABLE 2

RESULTS OF THE NEWMAN-KEULS TEST ON THE MEAN LEVELS OF RESPONDING FOR AUTISTIC, RETARDED, AND NORMAL *S*s

*S*s	Level of response	*p* <
Autistics	High vs. medium	.05
	Medium vs. low	ns
	High vs. low	.01
Retardates	High vs. medium	ns
	Medium vs. low	.01
	High vs. low	.01
Normals	High vs. medium	ns
	Medium vs. low	ns
	High vs. low	ns

they responded to two of the cues. They did not show a significant difference between the two most functional cues (high versus medium), while the difference between these cues and the third cue (medium versus low) was significant.

The data from all the test sessions for the autistic *S*s are presented in Figure 2. Percentages of correct responding are presented on the ordinate, while the test sessions are plotted along the abscissa. It is perhaps best to split these data into two parts. The first part can be limited to Test Session 1 and provides data on which cues had acquired control over *S* during training, when he was reinforced for responding to the stimulus complex. The second part of the data provides information about change in *S*'s responding to the separate stimuli with continuation of testing conditions, when *S* was reinforced for responding to the separate presentations of these stimuli.

If we inspect the data from Test Session 1 in Figure 2, we observe that the performance on only one of the single cues lies close to the complex cue, and the response to the remaining two cues is very weak or absent altogether. This is clearly shown in regard to the tactile cue for all *S*s. It is also apparent in Elmer and Kurt's minimal response to the visual cue, while Marty and Brian responded minimally to the auditory cue.

If we now look at the data with continuation of testing (Session 2 on), one can observe much variability in *S*s' response to the separate stimuli. Elmer's record is the least variable. He was initially under auditory control only, but as he received reinforcement for responding to the separate presentation of the visual cue, that cue acquired control. Similar effects can be observed in Brian's and Marty's records. They were initially under

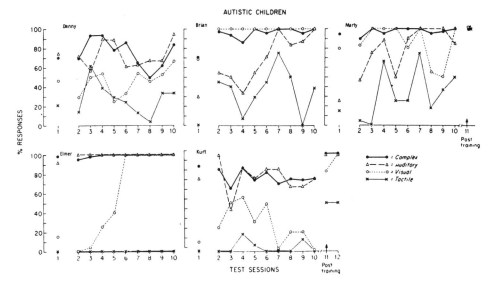

FIG. 2. Test sessions for the autistic Ss. (Percentages of correct response to the stimuli are plotted on the ordinate and test sessions are plotted along the abscissa.)

visual control and later began responding to the auditory stimulus. This effect, however, is unpredictable. Thus, despite Kurt's reinforcement for responding to the visual cue, that cue eventually ceases to control him. Similar failures of separate elements to acquire control, despite reinforcement for responding in their presence, can be observed in Danny's response to the visual cue, and in Brian's, Marty's, and Danny's response to the tactile cue.

Since we were testing for the possible acquisition of temporal cues, we could not maintain the conditions for the suppression of S^Δ responding. One may therefore question whether response to the least functional cue(s) reflects control by that cue, or random responding. We attempted to answer this question by examining the correlation between S^Δ responding preceding an S^D trial and response during that trial. This analysis was performed on the data of three of the autistic Ss. For each S, we correlated S^D and S^Δ to the two least functional stimuli and to the complex stimulus. This was done for five of the tests of each of the three Ss. Of the 45 correlations, only 6 were significant. However, these 6 were based on few observations, thus increasing the possibility of the analysis reaching significance by chance. We therefore concluded that S^Δ responding was not an important factor in determining S's level of responding to the least functional stimuli.

At the end of the test sessions, we took the cue which had not become functional in the earlier training (visual for Kurt, tactile for Marty) and attempted to establish it as functional by presenting it repeatedly with a variable S^Δ interval. Thus, in contrast to the test sessions, reinforcement could only be obtained by responding to the nonfunctional cue since none of the other cues were presented. Upon reaching criterion, S was reintroduced to the test sessions as before. The data from this training are presented as Posttraining Trial 11 for Marty on the tactile cue and Posttraining Trials 11 and 12 for Kurt on the visual cue. When the previously nonfunctional cues are trained separately, they do acquire control.

Data from the normal Ss are presented in Figure 3. The normal Ss differed from the autistics in three ways. First, they quickly acquired the discrimination and, second, their data show little variability. Third, while the autistic Ss responded differentially to certain components of the complex, the normals responded uniformly to all. Four of the normal Ss appeared to have formed a pattern discrimination, treating the separate components as different from the complex. With continuation of testing, this discrimination is broken, allowing for a demonstration of the equal control acquired by the separate cues.

Individual responding of the retarded Ss is presented in Figure 4. David's (Mongoloid), Tony's (genetic origin), and Colleen's (birth trauma) responding conform to the statistical analysis (Table 1) in that their response to two of the cues parallels their response to the complex. By the end of testing, Jeffrey's (only outpatient) record resembles a normal child, while Roberto's (Mongoloid) graph most closely resembles that of an autistic in

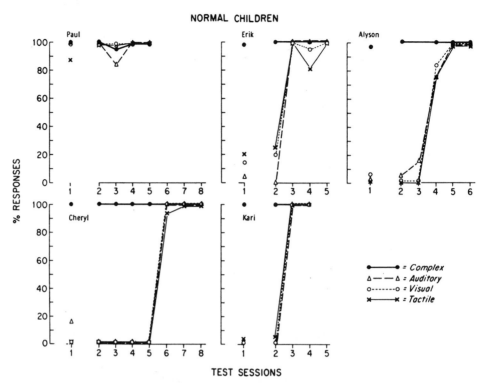

FIG. 3. Test sessions for the normal Ss. (Percentages of correct response to the stimuli are plotted on the ordinate and test sessions are plotted along the abscissa.)

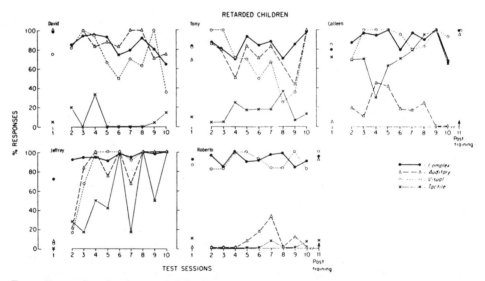

FIG. 4. Test sessions for the retarded Ss. (Percentages of correct response to the stimuli are plotted on the ordinate and test sessions are plotted along the abscissa.)

that he responded to only one of the cues. These children, like most retardates, present heterogenous behavioral repertoires, and we have no way of accounting for the variability in their performance.

At the end of testing, we trained a nonfunctional stimulus separately (the auditory stimulus for Colleen and Roberto) in the same manner as we had for the autistic chil-

dren. The data are presented in Session 11 for both children. The separate training established the cues as functional and allows us to rule out more easily understood problems in sensory deficiency.

DISCUSSION

Three groups of children were reinforced for responding to a complex stimulus involving the simultaneous presentation of auditory, visual, and tactile cues. Once this discrimination was established, elements of the complex were presented separately to assess which aspects of the complex stimulus had acquired control over the child's behavior. We found that (a) the autistics responded primarily to only one of the cues; the normals responded uniformly to all three cues; and the retardates functioned between these two extremes. (b) Conditions could be arranged such that a cue which had remained nonfunctional when presented in association with other cues could be established as functional when trained separately.

Our data failed to support notions that any one sense modality is impaired in autistic children, or that a particular sense modality is the "preferred" modality. Our data can perhaps best be understood as the autistics' problem of dealing with stimuli in context, a problem of quantity rather than quality of stimulus control. One can call this a problem of *stimulus overselectivity*.

There are some obvious qualifications which one has to impose upon these data. One pertains to the potentially unstable nature of Ss' responding with increased exposure to the training stimuli. This is left unclear in our experiment, since the stimuli were taken out of context and presented singly (from Test Session 1 on). But one may observe different results with different amounts of training prior to testing.

Perhaps the most important qualification centers on the choice of Ss and the bases of their diagnoses. It is noteworthy that we have worked with the most regressed of autistic children, and that different results may have been obtained had we used children who were more advanced, having, for example, speech development. This problem may be even more pronounced with the retarded Ss who show much heterogeneity. Roberto, for example, though he was diagnosed as retarded, responded like an autistic.

Similarly, we may qualify our data in regard to the *intensity* of the stimuli. Prior to the experiment we attempted to correct for unequal subjective intensities by choosing intensities which college students had rated as having "equal impact." It would have been more ideal to have autistic Ss perform this task, but that would be extremely difficult to do. The results could also be a function of the particular *kind* of stimuli we employed. Perhaps it is the tactile cue which blocks response

to other cues. One can also think of other qualifications, such as Ss' motivational level, except that the retarded Ss appeared motivated, yet show parts of the deficiency. Training under more stress, however, as when the child is anxious or inhibiting self-stimulation, may wipe out the effect.

Although these results could be interpreted in several ways, the data conform closely to a selective attention, or stimulus selection, hypothesis. Selective attention refers to the process in which an organism, when presented with multiple cues, attends to, or comes under the control of, only a portion of the available stimuli. This fact has led to the distinction between "nominal" or perceived stimulus variables which consist of the total set of available elements and "functional" or effective stimuli which are those elements actually controlling behavior.

There has been a great deal of research on this differentiation, and excellent reviews of such research are available in recent texts by Fellows (1968) and Trabasso and Bower (1968). A comprehensive presentation will not be attempted here, but a short comment is appropriate.

Long ago, Pavlov (1927) found that the conditioned response to one element (the dominant) of a complex stimulus was as large as the response to the complex, leaving the response to the other elements negligible. Warren (1953) taught monkeys to discriminate between two objects differing in size, color, form, two, or all three of these dimensions. He found that although learning was facilitated by the inclusion of more relevant cues, the color cue alone was the most dominant. Similar results have been reported in other studies with animals (Harlow, 1945; Warren, 1954) and with children (Suchman & Trabasso, 1966). Studying nursery and kindergarten children, Suchman and Trabasso found that when color, size, and form cues were simultaneously available for discrimination, younger children preferred the color cue while the older children preferred the form cue. Working within the operant training paradigm presented here, Reynolds (1961) trained two pigeons to discriminate two white forms on differently colored backgrounds (red or green). In extinction test periods, it was found that one pigeon responded only to the white form and the other pigeon responded only to the colored background. Orlando (1961) reported similar instances of stimulus selection in the learning of retarded children. In a task in which a cue for S^D and S^Δ

periods was employed, he found that one of these cues was not only sufficient, but exclusively functional in maintaining the discrimination.

There have been various mechanisms thought to underlie selective responding in normals. Sometimes the underlying mechanism is considered genetic, in that a particular cue emerges as the dominant for the great majority of members within a species. One can also manipulate learning experiences in such a fashion as to render a cue dominant. Both Kamin (1968) in a classical conditioning paradigm and Trabasso and Bower (1968) in a redundant relevant cue (RRC) paradigm have demonstrated blocking effects, finding that a first-learned cue blocks the learning of anothter relevant cue which was added during overtraining.

"Stimulus blocking" is said to occur when attention to one stimulus in a complex stimulus situation blocks or inhibits the attention to another cue also present. Trabasso and Bower (1968) suggested that the observed dominance or selection in RRC tasks could be due to the blocking of a slower learned cue by a faster learned cue when both cues are present from the beginning of training. They see overshadowing as resulting when an S by chance responds to a particular cue and because he is reinforced does not broaden his learning to the other relevant cues.

One conclusion from all the work on normal children using RRC procedures is that normal children display stimulus selection and thus often come under the control of only a portion of the available stimuli. It is important, therefore, to use a control group of normal Ss to better assess selective responding in autistics. Our failure to observe selective responding in the normal children, which others so often report, was probably based on the nature of the task. In most RRC tasks all the elements fall within one modality, rather than being distributed across modalities as was the case in our study. We also kept the number of stimuli small. Levine (1967) and Eimas (1969) have presented data which suggest that by the time normal children have reached the age of the Ss in this experiment, they will generally attend to about three or four simultaneous cues during discrimination learning. In contrast to the normal children, the autistic children showed an extreme degree of stimulus selection, leaving large segments of their environment essentially neutral.

Perhaps the first questions to be raised by this study regard a more accurate description of the stimulus overselectivity. For example,

one may wonder whether the selectivity is a function of the kinds and number of cues in the complex stimulus; whether it is present also when all cues are presented in one modality; or whether it also presents itself when the cues are nonoverlapping but closely spaced in time. Studies are now in progress in our laboratory to investigate some of these questions.

The second line of questions deals with assessing some of the mechanisms which may underlie stimulus overselectivity. Perhaps the autistics tend to respond only to one cue because of a failure in "switching" behavior. Lindsay, Taylor, and Forbes (1968) and Treisman (1969) have suggested that normals seem to attend to only one stimulus component at a time and analyze complex cues by very rapidly switching attention to different aspects of the complex, going quickly through sets of "alternative analyzers." Autistics may not adequately sample stimuli, but settle on one stimulus which "blocks" the others. The problem with this line of reasoning can be easily seen when one considers the possibilities that inadequate switching may result in stimulus blocking, or, conversely, that stimulus blocking may result in inadequate switching. Either direction seems equally plausible.

A third line of questions may be directed toward a better description of stimulus selectivity among groups with different pathology. We included a retarded group to help isolate those peculiarities associated with autistic functioning. The retarded Ss showed less stimulus selectivity than the autistics. They also showed less behavioral deficiency (higher IQ scores, social adjustment, etc.). Perhaps future research will suggest that this kind of discrimination task differentiates between children with different degrees of behavioral deficiencies.

It may be of interest to speculate on how our findings may relate to the pathology in autistic children. Before we present this speculation, two considerations must be made. First, the pathology in autism is so profound and extensive that it is unlikely any one finding will provide insight into it all. Second, the speculations we make presuppose that our inference of stimulus overselectivity best describes the data. Additional studies will be needed to strengthen this inference.

Implications for Understanding Autism

A necessary condition for much learning involves a contiguous or near-contiguous presentation of two stimuli. Such contiguous stimulus presentations are clearly present in classical conditioning when the CS is presented in close proximity to the UCS. In fact, this is a necessary condition for optimal learning. Contiguous presentations are also present in those aspects of operant conditioning where one seeks a shift in stimulus control. In these instances the training stimulus is presented simultaneously with a prompt. Since this contiguous presentation of two stimuli involves presenting the child with a stimulus complex, it may be assumed that the autistics' response to one of these stimuli is blocked, overshadowed, or otherwise has failed to occur. Let us consider some of the implications of this assumption for certain kinds of learning.

1. One can consider that the acquisition of most human behavior, like language, interpersonal, and intellectual behavior, is based on the prior acquisition of conditioned reinforcers. A failure in this acquisition would lead to a failure in behavioral development (Ferster & DeMyer, 1962). If it is the case that conditioned reinforcers acquire strength by contiguous association with primary ones, then our finding should help to further describe the failure for such conditioning to take place in autistic children (Lovaas, Freitag, Kinder, Rubenstein, Schaeffer, & Simmons, 1966).

2. The autistic child's failure to give appropriate affect is well-known. The mechanisms for establishing appropriate affect may well be very similar to those involved in establishing conditioned reinforcers: contiguous presentation of two stimulus events which enables the affect, elicited by one of these events (the UCS), to be elicited by the other (the CS).

3. Many autistic children have topographically elaborate speech (echolalia), but it appears without "meaning." One can argue that the speech exists without meaning to the extent it has an impoverished context. The acquisition of a context for speech probably involves a shift in stimulus control. To the extent that this involves simultaneous presentations of auditory with visual, tactile, or some other cue, one may expect that the autistic child would "overselect" and fail to learn.

4. From a consideration of the data in Figure 1, which illustrates the difficulties in the establishment of imitative behavior, it is also possible that such stimulus overselectivity as we have described might contribute importantly to the autistic child's failure in the acquisition of new behavioral topographies. In fact, the usual way we train new skills is to "aid" the child by adding large numbers of extra cues to the training situation. This, of course, may be exactly what makes it so difficult for the autistic child to learn what we want him to.

5. Whenever one postulates blocking of incoming stimuli, learning as well as performance should be impaired. Stimulus overselectivity may also be a factor which underlies the sporadic, highly variable nature of these children's responses to already functional stimuli. A number of other possibilities suggest themselves, which probably are best discussed in light of more extensive data.

REFERENCES

Buss, A., & Lang, P. Psychological deficit in schizophrenia. I. Affect, reinforcement, and concept attainment. *Journal of Abnormal Psychology,* 1965, **70,** 2–24.

Eimas, P. Multiple-cue discrimination learning in children. *Psychological Record,* 1969, **19,** 417–424.

Feigenberg, I. Probabilistic prognosis and its significance in normal and pathological subjects. In M. Cole & I. Maltzman (Eds.), *A handbook of contemporary Soviet psychology.* New York: Basic Books, 1969.

Fellows, B. J. *The discrimination process and development.* London: Pergamon Press, 1968.

Ferster, C. B., & DeMyer, M. A method for the experimental analysis of the behavior of autistic children. *American Journal of Orthopsychiatry,* 1962, **32,** 89–98.

Goldfarb, W. An investigation of childhood schizophrenia. *Archives of General Psychiatry,* 1964, **11,** 620–634.

Harlow, H. F. Studies in discrimination learning in monkeys. VI. Discriminations between stimuli differing in both color and form, only in color, and only in form. *Journal of General Psychology,* 1945, **33,** 225–235.

Hermelin, B. Recent psychological research. In J. K. Wing (Ed.), *Early childhood autism.* London: Pergamon Press, 1966.

Kamin, L. J. Attention-like processes in classical conditioning. In M. R. Jones (Ed.), *Miami Symposium on the Prediction of Behavior, 1967: Aversive stimulation.* Miami: University of Miami Press, 1968.

Kanner, L. Early infantile autism. *Journal of Pediatrics,* 1944, **25,** 211–217.

Lang, P. J., & Buss, A. H. Psychological deficit in schizophrenia. II. Interference and activation. *Journal of Abnormal Psychology,* 1965, **70,** 77–106.

Levine, M. The size of the hypothesis set during discrimination learning. *Psychological Review,* 1967, **74,** 428–430.

Lindsay, P. H., Taylor, M. M., & Forbes, S. M. Attention and multidimensional discrimination. *Perception and Psychophysics,* 1968, **4,** 113–117.

Lovaas, O. I., Berberich, J. P., Perloff, B. F., & Schaeffer, B. Acquisition of imitative speech in schizophrenic children. *Science,* 1966, **151,** 705–707.

LOVAAS, O. I., FREITAG, G., KINDER, M. I., RUBEN-STEIN, B. D., SCHAEFFER, B., & SIMMONS, J. Q. Establishment of social reinforcers in schizophrenic children using food. *Journal of Experimental Child Psychology,* 1966, **4,** 109–125.

ORLANDO, R. The functional role of discriminative stimuli in free operant performance of developmentally retarded children. *Psychological Record,* 1961, **11,** 153–161.

PAVLOV, I. P. Lectures. In, *Conditioned reflexes.* Oxford: University Press, 1927.

REYNOLDS, G. S. Attention in the pigeon. *Journal of the Experimental Analysis of Behavior,* 1961, **4,** 203–208.

RIMLAND, B. *Infantile autism.* New York: Appleton-Century-Crofts, 1964.

SCHOPLER, E. Visual versus tactual receptor preference in normal and schizophrenic children. *Journal of Abnormal Psychology,* 1966, **71,** 108–114.

SHERRINGTON, C. S. *The integrative action of the nervous system.* London: Cambridge University Press, 1906.

SUCHMAN, R. G., & TRABASSO, T. Color and form preference in young children. *Journal of Experimental Child Psychology,* 1966, **3,** 177–187.

TRABASSO, T., & BOWER, G. H. *Attention in learning.* New York: Wiley, 1968.

TREISMAN, A. Strategies and models of selective attention. *Psychological Review,* 1969, **76,** 282–299.

WARREN, J. M. Additivity of cues in visual pattern discrimination by monkeys. *Journal of Comparative and Physiological Psychology,* 1953, **46,** 484–488.

WARREN, J. M. Perceptual dominance in discrimination learning in monkeys. *Journal of Comparative and Physiological Psychology,* 1954, **47,** 290–292.

YOUNG, S. Visual attention in autistic and normal children: Effects of stimulus novelty, human attributes, and complexity. Unpublished doctoral dissertation, University of California, Los Angeles, 1969.

THE HYPERACTIVE CHILD IN ELEMENTARY SCHOOL: A 5 YEAR, CONTROLLED, FOLLOWUP

K. Minde
D. Lewin
Gabrielle Weiss
H. Lavigueur
Virginia Douglas
Elizabeth Sykes

Abstract: The study examines the academic performance of 37 school-children, diagnosed as hyperactive 4 to 6 years previously, and compares it with the performance of an equal number of nonhyperactive classmates. The results indicate that hyperactive youngsters have a significantly higher failure rate in all academic subjects and are rated by their teachers as displaying far more behavioral problems than their controls. While the hyperactive children showed an increase in learning disorders and did poorer on a group IQ test than their peers, intelligence alone was ruled out as the main contributor to their academic failure.

THE present study is part of a continuing investigation by the individual authors on the hyperactive child of normal intelligence; other reports have appeared elsewhere (Werry, Weiss, & Douglas, 1964; Werry, Weiss, Douglas, & Martin, 1966; Douglas, Werry, & Weiss, 1965; Minde, Webb, & Sykes, 1968; Weiss, Minde, Werry, Douglas, & Sykes, 1971b). Most investigations of this group of children have dealt with short term behavioral or cognitive changes following treatment with either phenothiazines or the amphetamine group of drugs (Cytryn, Gilbert, & Eisenberg, 1960; Grant, 1962; Conners & Eisenberg, 1963; Eisenberg, 1965; Werry et al., 1966; Weiss et al., 1971b). Only recently have careful studies on the long term outcomes of this condition been published (Laufer, 1962; Menkes, 1967; Weiss, Minde, Werry, Douglas, & Nemeth, 1971a).

These followup studies suggest that hyperactive children may calm down some-

From *Exceptional Children,* 1971, **38,** 215-221. Reprinted by permission of The Council for Exceptional Children.

what after the age of 12. However they continue to show moderately severe defects in their general behavior (Laufer, 1962) and have severe academic difficulties (Laufer, 1962; Weiss et al., 1971a). In addition, Weiss and her group (1971a) reported that a clinical psychiatric evaluation of 65 hyperactive children 4 to 6 years after their initial assessment showed the majority to have a low self image which often appeared to be related to great apprehension about personal and academic failure.

The present article attempts to investigate school performance in more detail by comparing a group of hyperactive children with their classmates on a variety of academic and behavioral tasks.

Method

Subjects

The present study examined 37 children (35 boys and 2 girls) who attended regular primary school classes within the Protestant or Catholic school boards of Greater Montreal and had 4 to 6 years earlier been diagnosed as hyperactive by two of the authors using criteria quoted in detail elsewere initially seen at the outpatient clinic 1965). Briefly, they were children who were initially seen at the out patient clinic of the department of psychiatry of the Montreal Children's Hospital. Their most conspicuous symptomatology consisted of severe sustained hyperactivity which caused significant and continued complaints both at home and at school. All children had an IQ of at least 85 on the *Wechsler Intelligence Scale for Children,* lived at home with at least one parent, and were free from overt physical (including neurological) and mental illness.

There had initially been 62 children, but 25 had to be excluded from the present analysis for the following reasons:

Family had moved out of town	9
School did not send sufficient information	7
Child was placed in boarding school out of town	3
Child had left primary school	3
Child was placed in special class for slow learners	3

The 25 excluded children did not differ in age (mean age 12.03 years, $SD = 2.1$) or sex ratio (24 boys, 1 girl) from the rest of the group. They did however include more children from upper socioeconomic groups. Eight of the nine families who had moved out of town (mainly because of job promotions and transfers) and the three children placed in boarding schools came from upper middle class families.

Procedure

To facilitate comparisons between the hyperactive and control children, each of the hyperactive children was paired with a child of the same sex immediately following him or her alphabetically in the classroom list.

The following measures were obtained for both hyperactive and control children:

1. The school report from the previous school year, including academic ratings in individual school subjects and conduct items.
2. Scores on the behavioral checklist designed by the authors and completed by the classroom teacher. This questionnaire recorded age and grade of the child, number of grades repeated, and number of days absent during the most recently completed school year. It also contained a 3 point (no problem, mild problem, real problem, i.e. among the three or four worst children in the class) rating scale on eight behavioral items dealing with restlessness, level of concentration, daydreaming, peer relationships, motivation, aggression, delinquent behavior, and general approach toward work (possible total score range 8-24).
3. All scores of standardized group tests performed in the school.
4. Any other information the school had on the individual child, e.g. notes of psychiatric assessments, possible court referrals, or other nonacademic matters.

After this information was received, the marks on the report cards were transformed into number scores. Each academic mark (excellent, very good, good, fair, unsatisfactory) was given a score of 1 to 5, with 5 denoting unsatisfactory and 1 denoting excellent. Since each child had been marked on 12 subjects, total scores could range from 12 to 60.

Each of the 9 conduct items (e.g. neatness, courtesy, work habits) was scored as 2 when the report card contained any positive comments or the marks "excellent," "very good," or "good," and as 1 if it contained negative remarks or denoted "fair" or "unsatisfactory." Possible scores thus ranged from 9 to 18.

After each youngster's report card had been converted into number scores, one way analyses of variance comparing the hyperactive to the control group were performed.

Results

Background variables. As can be seen from Table 1, hyperactive and control children differ significantly in the number of grades repeated, indicating that hyperactive children do less well academically than their nonhyperactive peers. The table also indicates that the two groups did not differ significantly in the sex distribution or the number of school days missed. The trend for hyperactive children to be older than their control peers can be explained by the greater number of repeaters among the former group.

As the control children were only labeled by their initials to preserve anonymity, no statistical intergroup comparisons for socioeconomic class standing could be made. This was felt to be a justified sacrifice, since there is evidence (Eisenberg, 1959) that children attending the same class and hence living in the same neighborhood usually come from a similar social environment.

Academic conduct and behavior ratings. Table 2 presents a comparison on the most recent individual academic ratings of the hyperactive children and their control group. The hyperactive children scored significantly lower than their peers on all subjects except art and handwork, and physical activity.

Similar results were obtained on the most recent report card ratings pertaining to conduct and on the behavioral checklist ratings from the present teachers. On both evaluations the hyperactive children scored significantly lower than their control peers.

Intellectual functioning. The possibility arose that the results indicating such wide group variations in academic and behavioral functioning were due to a difference in intelligence between the hyperactive and control children. In order to investigate this a comparison was made of the *Henmon-Nelson Tests of Mental Ability* administered to the groups. The normal

children scored significantly higher than their hyperactive classmates (IQ 112.0 vs 101.5, $p<.001$) on this test. The scores for the controls, though high, were comparable to the city average of all fourth and sixth grade children ($N = 9,734$; average IQ = 110) and thus conformed to a truly randomly selected group.

The question remained whether the sample group of hyperactive children was genuinely less intelligent than the control group or whether they had been penalized by (a) the group test procedure, (b) their grossly deviant behavior in the class, which could have caused the teachers to mark them lower, or (c) a higher incidence of specific learning difficulties.

To rule out the first possibility, the results of the WISC which all hyperactive

TABLE 1

Background Variables of Hyperactive and Control Subjects

Variables	Group Control ($N = 37$)	Group Hyperactive ($N = 37$)	Significance
Age [a]			$<.1$
Mean	11.03	11.96	
SD	1.9	2.0	
Sex			NS
Boys	34	34	
Girls	3	3	
Grades repeated [b]			$<.001$
None	31	16	
One or more	6	21 [c]	
School days missed [d]	10.2	11.1	NS
SD	9.4	13.9	

[a] $t = 1.69$, $df = 72$.
[b] $X^2 = 13.12$, $df = .1$.
[c] Three failed twice, one failed three times.
[d] $t = 0.1$, $df = 72$.

TABLE 2

Comparison Between Hyperactive and Control Group on Most Recent Academic Ratings

Rating	F	df	Significance
Oral reading	26.04	1.60	$<.01$
Silent reading	14.79	1.60	$<.01$
Language	18.00	1.62	$<.01$
Literature	10.23	1.50	$<.01$
Spelling	11.06	1.62	$<.01$
Arithmetic	3.41	1.64	$<.01$
French	8.01	1.58	$<.01$
Handwriting	13.29	1.64	$<.01$
Health & safety	7.81	1.56	$<.01$
Music	8.85	1.56	$<.01$
Art & handwork	2.98	1.58	NS
Physical activity	.04	1.50	NS

children had received within the previous 12 months were compared to the individual's group test scores. The hyperactive children fared significantly better on this individually administered test (WISC IQ 105.4 vs Henmon-Nelson IQ 101.5; $t = 2.17$, $p < .05$), but still scored significantly lower than their control group on the Henmon-Nelson. As WISC data on the control subjects were not available and the literature does not report any studies which systematically compare children's IQ scores on the WISC and the Henmon-Nelson group test, no final interpretation can be given to this finding, except to say that the hyperactive children in this sample scored significantly lower on a standard group IQ test than did a normal group of youngsters.

The second possibility—that teachers would give the worst mark to the most poorly behaved child—was tested by performing Spearman's coefficient of rank correlation *rho* (Ferguson, 1966), ranking academic standing versus the nine conduct items on the report card for both hyperactive and control children. No significant correlation ($r = 0.159$ for the hyperactive group and $r = 0.231$ for the control group) between academic performance and conduct of the children appeared. This implies that the teachers did not automatically give poor academic marks to a badly behaved child.

The last possibility—that hyperactive children have a higher incidence of specific learning disabilities which in turn contribute to their academic failure and reduce their scores on an intelligence test—proved difficult to assess because there is no unanimous agreement in the literature on the definition of a learning disability and the tests best suited to detect it (Wittenborn, 1949). The criterion of some workers (Michael-Smith & Morgenstern, 1965; Bateman, 1965; Johnson & Myklebust, 1967) has been to include all children in this category who despite average work perform significantly worse in school than their general intelligence suggests.

While this definition embraces a great number of children, Clements and Peters (1962) have argued that specifically a wide discrepancy between verbal and performance IQ on the WISC is indicative of some learning impairment. This has been questioned by Seashore (1951). In the authors' opinion, the majority of the sample hyper-

active children had done poorer in school than their IQ would warrant. Therefore, the 10 academically most successful ones (as rated by their last annual report card) were selected and compared with the 10 academically least successful children.

As can be seen in Table 3 the two subgroups differed in many respects, including a discrepancy between their verbal and performance score on the WISC (8 of 10 unsuccessful, 6 of 10 successful children scored higher on the performance scale), suggesting at least a greater variability in the performance of the unsuccessful group.

A further, rather crude test to discover possible problems in learning was done by presenting to an experienced clinical psychologist the results of a battery of tests which all hyperactive children had taken within the previous 12 months. The battery consisted of the *Lincoln-Oseretsky Motor Development Scale*, the *Bender Visual-Motor Gestalt Test*, a *Test for Primary Mental Abilities*, and the *Goodenough Draw-A-Man Test*. The psychologist, who was unaware of the academic standing of the individual child, reviewed the material and recorded clinically moderate to severe visual-spatial problems, verbal (e.g. vocabulary, speech defects) difficulties, and a standing below the 20th percentile on the *Lincoln-Oseretsky Motor Developmental Scale*. In 19 of 20 cases, the rater predicted correctly the successful or failing child. The academically very poor children with one exception showed gross deficiencies in

TABLE 3

Comparison of the Academically Most and Least Successful Hyperactive Children

Variables	Group Successful (N = 10)	Unsuccessful (N = 10)	Significance
Grades repeated [a]			< .01
None	6	0	
One or more	4	10 [b]	
WISC IQ score [c]			< .05
Mean	108.7	95.9	
SD	7.1	8.2	
Verbal-Performance [d] Score			< .01
difference	5.7	13.4	
SD	2.5	7.9	

[a] $X^2 = 8.6$, $df = 1$.
[b] Three failed twice.
[c] $t = 2.24$, $df = 18$.
[d] $t = 2.95$, $df = 18$.

two of the three areas recorded, whereas the successful children showed either no abnormality (5 cases) or performed poorly in only one of the measured areas.

These data then give some evidence that a fairly high percentage of hyperactive children, in addition to their restlessness and inattention, also have uneven cognitive patterns which may further penalize them in their academic and IQ test performance.

Comparison of control and hyperactive children matched for IQ on most recent academic and behavior ratings. Having documented the importance of intelligence as a variable for scholastic success, the authors sought to determine to what extent hyperactivity with its possible associated features (e.g. decreased attention and distractibility) would influence academic success. To this effect every hyperactive child was matched with a control child within ±3 points on the Henmon-Nelson score alone. Children were matched irrespective of the school attended. Only 23 of the original 37 children remained in the sample because the control children with the highest IQ scores and the hyperactive children with the lowest IQ scores could not find equivalent partners.

Table 4 reflects the results of this investigation. The groups do not differ in age, present grade, or number of repeated grades. The Henmon-Nelson IQ scores were 104.3 for the control group and 103.5 for the hyperactive children. Nevertheless, the hyperactive children's performance was significantly inferior ($t = 3.74, p < .001$) on the 10 purely academic subjects (art and handwork and physical activity were excluded as they had previously been found to contribute nothing to academic excellence). In addition the hyperactive group was rated as presenting far more behavior problems by their present teachers ($t = 6.3, p < .001$).

The final variable investigated was the consistency of the hyperactive child's failure in school. Two of the authors visited individual schools and collected the report card marks from 3 previous calender years for 23 pairs of the original sample. These then were the grades obtained by the children approximately 1 year after they had initially been referred to the Montreal Children's Hospital. Data were not available on the remaining 14 pairs.

TABLE 4

Comparison of Background Variables and Academic and Behavioral Standing of Groups Matched for IQ

Variables	Group Control (N = 23)	Hyperactive (N = 23)	Significance
Age [a]			NS
Mean	10.9	11.5	
SD	1.8	1.4	
Grade [b]			NS
Mean	5.3	5.7	
SD	1.4	1.2	
Grades repeated [c]			> .20
None	17	10	
One or more	6	13	
Academic standing [d]			< .001
Mean score	22.7	28.5	
SD	4.7	5.2	
Behavioral standing [e]			< .001
Mean checklist score	9.5	15.7	
SD	2.4	4.1	

[a] $t = 1.37, df = 44.$
[b] $t = 0.97, df = 44.$
[c] $X^2 = 1.17, df = 1.$
[d] $t = 3.74, df = 44.$
[e] $t = 6.3, df = 44.$

One way analyses of variance were performed on the difference scores of the hyperactive-control pairings 3 years previous, compared with the difference scores of the hyperactive-control pairings on the most recent report card. All academic and conduct ratings were included. There was no statistically significant change in the standing of the hyperactive child to his control partner on any academic or conduct rating. Hence, hyperactive children 4 years after initial diagnosis were as poor in classroom performance as they had been 1 year after diagnosis.

Discussion

The data present a number of points worth consideration. A hyperactive child selected by our criteria is frequently characterized by extremely poor advancement in the average school environment. This point has been stressed before by Burks (1960) who found 11 year old hyperactive children to be academically 1 year behind the control group, though they showed no difference in IQ scores.

Other investigators (Paine et al., 1968; Clements & Peter, 1962) who observed this phenomenon clinically claimed that the academic retardation is related to poor reading ability or to general difficulties in visual-motor coordination and spatial relationships. Their data, however, is based on clinical evidence and with the exception of Burks is devoid of a control group.

The present findings indicate without a doubt that the sample group of hyperactive children is inferior academically and has inferior scores on a group IQ test. However even when a selected group of hyperactive children was matched on IQ with a control group, the hyperactive children still did much poorer in class. The academically worst children are in addition penalized by uneven cognitive patterns and a preponderance of verbal difficulties including actual speech defects. These difficulties are frequently of such magnitude that instruction within a normal class setting is unlikely to produce any academic progress. Yet only one of the children in the academically worst group had received extended help with his learning problems because adequate facilities were not available.

On the other hand the hyperactive group did not score lower on art and handwork, physical activity, and arithmetic, although the latter test for significance ($F = 3.401$) approaches the .05 level ($F = 3.994$, $p < .05$). A possible reason why art and handwork did not differentiate the control from hyperactive group may be because this subject traditionally is considered a practical rather than an academic subject. Hence marks here may reflect faculties other than those tapped by reading, writing, or arithmetic.

It is of further interest to note that physical activity marks are not affected by hyperactivity, despite the known poor motor coordination of hyperactive youngsters (Douglas et al., 1965). The results suggest that such a disability is more in the fine motor area and does not affect the gross motor coordination called for in physical activity class. Clinical findings (Weiss et al., 1971a) confirmed that by age 12 the hyperactive children often excelled in activities such as swimming and skiing, yet scored poorly on the *Lincoln-Oseretsky Motor Developmental Scale* (13.7 percentile) because the scale at this age primarily measures fine motor control.

It is also interesting to see how consistently the hyperactive group at age 12 was still seen as behaviorally deviant. They fared poorer than their peers on all of the rated behavior characteristics in spite of the fact that 20 percent of the sample had remained on some kind of medication (chlorpromazine or dextroamphetamine) for periods varying from 6 months to 4 years.

This finding is in contrast with the popularly held concept that hyperactivity and all its associated problems disappear around age 12. On the contrary, the data suggest that in addition to difficulties primarily related to hyperactivity (lack of concentration, distractibility), behavior characteristics not primarily associated with hyperactivity (e.g. daydreaming, delinquent behavior) occur. This is in agreement with the psychiatrists' personal reassessments of these children (Weiss et al., 1971a) where some 25 percent of the children had a history of acting out or antisocial behavior and 15 percent had "court referrals." This number appears much higher than one would expect in a control population and far exceeds the reported data in one other reported study (Robins, 1966) where only 2 percent of the control children had appeared in court up to age 15.

One reason for this high incidence of disturbance is undoubtedly the fact that many of these youngsters have experienced years of failure, both academically and socially, and that some have learned to withdraw from conflicting situations, whereas others have attempted success through acting out and delinquency.

A further interesting finding is that teachers, at least within the Montreal school system, do not appear to confuse the behavioral and academic evaluations of hyperactive children. Thus a halo effect (a poorly behaving child also receiving poor academic ratings) is not evident from the data, indicating high professional attitudes on the part of the average teacher.

Finally, this investigation clearly demonstrates that hyperactive children do not improve academically up to age 12. This finding has support in the literature: Both Laufer (1962) and Menkes (1967) who followed hyperactive children for longer periods reported that poor school performance persists far beyond latency. This may be due to the increasing emphasis placed on abstract concepts, the need in the higher grades to reflect and attend rather than act impulsively on presented academic material, and the deficiency of the sample group in precisely these areas (Campbell, Douglas, & Morgenstern, 1969; Sykes, Douglas, Weiss, & Minde, 1971). On the other hand, the clinicians on the team have repeatedly noted how multiple failures have tended to undermine individual children's ambition and caused a profound sense of failure and lack of motivation—facts hardly conducive to learning. In addition, the previously reported high rate of specific cognitive disabilities, mostly untreated, may well forestall improvement and thus compound the above mentioned difficulties.

The findings demonstrate that hyperactivity as defined by the authors is a condition which profoundly affects the personal and academic life of the individual child and requires long term psychological, academic, and remedial assistance.

References

Bateman, B. An educator's view of a diagnostic approach to learning disorders. In J. Helmuth (Ed.), *Learning disorders.* Vol. 1. Seattle: Special Child Publications, 1965. Pp. 219-239.

Burks, H. F. The hyperkinetic child. *Exceptional Children*, 1960, **27**, 18-26.

Campbell, S., Douglas, V., & Morgenstern, G. Cognitive styles in hyperactive children and the effect of methylphenidate. Paper read at Canadian Psychological Association Meeting, Toronto, 1969.

Clements, S. D., & Peters, J. E. Minimal brain dysfunction in the school-age child: Diagnosis and treatment. *Archives of General Psychiatry,* 1962, **6**, 185-197.

Conners, C., & Eisenberg, L. The effects of methylphenidate on symptomatology and learning in disturbed children. *American Journal of Psychiatry*, 1963, **120**, 458-464.

Cytryn, L., Gilbert, A., & Eisenberg, L. The effectiveness of tranquilizing drugs plus supportive psychotherapy in treating behavior disorders of children: A double-blind study of eighty outpatients. *American Journal of Orthopsychiatry,* 1960, **30**, 113-129.

Douglas, V., Werry, J., & Weiss, G. Hyperactive behavior in children: Some findings regarding aetiology and treatment. *Canadian Psychology,* 1965, **6**, 219. (Abstract)

Eisenberg, L. Basic issue in drug research with children: Opportunities and limitations of a pediatric age group. In S. Fisher (Ed.), *Child research in psychopharmacology.* Springfield, Ill.: Charles C Thomas, 1959.

Eisenberg, L., Conners, C. K., & Sharpe, L. A controlled study of the differential application of

outpatient psychiatry treatment for children. *Japanese Journal of Child Psychiatry*, 1965, **6**, 125-132.

Ferguson, G. H. *Statistical analysis in psychology and education.* (2nd ed.) New York: McGraw-Hill, 1966.

Grant, G. Psychopharmacology in childhood emotional and mental disorders. *Journal of Pediatrics,* 1962, **61**, 626-637.

Johnson, D. J., & Myklebust, H. R. *Learning disabilities, educational principles and practices.* New York: Grune & Stratton, 1967.

Laufer, M. W. Cerebral dysfunction and behavior disorders in adolescents. *American Journal of Orthopsychiatry,* 1962, **32**, 501-506.

Menkes, M. M., Rowe, J. S., & Menkes, J. H. A twenty-five year follow-up study on the hyperkinetic child with minimal brain dysfunction. *Pediatrics,* 1967, **39**, 393-399.

Michael-Smith, H., & Morgenstern, G. Learning disorders: An overview. In J. Helmuth (Ed.), *Learning disorders.* Vol. 1. Seattle: Special Child Publications, 1965. Pp. 169-196.

Minde, K., Webb, G., & Sykes, D. Studies on the hyperactive child VI. Prenatal and paranatal factors associated with hyperactivity. *Developmental Medicine and Child Neurology,* 1968, **10**, 355-363.

Paine, R. S. Snydrome of "minimal cerebral damage." *Paediatric Clinics of North America,* 1968, **15**, 779-801.

Robins, L. N. *Deviant children grown up.* Baltimore: Williams & Wilkins, 1966.

Seashore, H. G. Differences between verbal and performance I.Qs. on the Wechsler Intelligence Scale for Children. *Journal of Consulting Psychology,* 1951, **15**, 62-67.

Sykes, D., Douglas, V., Weiss, G., & Minde, K. Attention in hyperactive children and the effect of methylphenidate. *British Journal of Medical Psychology,* 1971, in press.

Weiss, G., Minde, K., Werry, J., Douglas, V., & Nemeth, E. Hyperactive children—Five years later. *Archives of General Psychiatry,* 1971, **24**, 409-414. (a)

Weiss, G., Minde, K., Werry, J., Douglas, V., & Sykes, D. A comparison of the effects of chlorpromazine, dextroamphetamine and methylphenidate on the behaviour and intellectual functioning of the hyperactive child. *Canadian Medical Association Journal,* 1971, **104**, 20-25. (b)

Werry, J., Weiss, G., & Douglas, V. Studies on the hyperactive child: I. Some preliminary findings. *Canadian Psychiatric Association Journal,* 1964, **9**, 120-130.

Werry, J. S., Weiss, G., Douglas, V., & Martin, J. Studies on the hyperactive child: III. The effect of chlorpromazine upon behaviour and learning ability. *Journal of American Academy of Child Psychiatry,* 1966, **5**, 292-312.

Wittenborn, J. R. Bellevue subtest scores as an aid in diagnosis. *Journal of Consulting Psychology,* 1949, **13**, 433-439.

AN EXPERIMENTAL RESOURCE ROOM FOR BEHAVIOR PROBLEM CHILDREN

John P. Glavin
Herbert C. Quay
Frederick R. Annesley
John S. Werry

Abstract: The Temple Resource Room Project represents an attempt to develop, refine, and evaluate an alternative to special class placement for behavior problem children in the public school. Children in the experimental group were scheduled for a resource room program during those periods of the day in which they were functioning least effectively in the regular class. Since the majority were also performing below expected grade level academically, the program emphasized academic remediation with the use of response-reinforcement contingencies in a structured classroom situation. The experimental group made significantly greater gains in reading vocabulary and arithmetic fundamentals than did a comparison group. Behavioral changes also occurred, with the greatest improvement being noted with the experimental group when in the resource room.

THE basic goal for public school special education programs for the behaviorally disordered should be the reintegration of the child functioning behaviorally and academically at a level within the range which the regular class program accommodates. Historically, most programs for the disturbed have been based either on theories of counseling and psychotherapy or on techniques of remedial education. More recently, a great deal of research has focused on the use of techniques derived from reinforcement theory to bring classroom behavior under control and to upgrade academic functioning (O'Leary & Becker, 1967; Walker, Mattson, & Buckley, 1969; Glavin, Quay, & Werry, 1971).

No matter which set of techniques are adopted, a number of problems must be considered in the provision of services to restore the behaviorally deviant child to the academic mainstream. While deviant classroom behavior usually triggers the referral process, recent research (Stone & Rowley, 1964; Graubard, 1964; McCaffrey & Cumming, 1967) suggests that such children will also have academic deficiencies, either as the cause or the effect of the deviant behavior. Thus, a successful program must also aim at upgrading academic skills as well as eliminating deviant behavior.

A second consideration relates to the cost of the intervention program. The usual self contained special class for behaviorally disordered children serves 8 to 10 pupils and frequently employs both a teacher and an aide. The cost per child is obviously high. Because of cost factors and a shortage of qualified teachers, many children who need help cannot be served—particularly those whose behavior may not be so grossly deviant as to completely preclude regular class attendance.

A third consideration relates to the effects of labeling and extrusion and the way in which these effects operate to make re-entry into the regular class more difficult. It appears that any intervention which removes the basic responsibility for the child from the hands of the regular class teacher serves to make reintegration of the child more difficult.

A final consideration relates to the pervasiveness and persistence of deviant behavior itself. It has been observed for some time that many children who are referred for disruptive and otherwise deviant behavior are problems in the regular class for only a part of the school day (Kounin, Friesen, & Norton, 1966; Long, Morse, & Newman, 1965). These disruptive episodes may, in fact, be related to the child's academic difficulties. It should also be noted that behavior problems in a significant number of children do not persist over time even in the absence of formal intervention (Glavin, 1968; Shepherd, Oppenheim, & Mitchell, 1966). Both of these factors make questionable the need for full-time placement outside the regular class with the concomitant labeling and extrusion phenomena.

The research reported herein was performed pursuant to Grant No. G3-6-062063-1559, U.S. Office of Education, Department of Health, Education, and Welfare.

From *Exceptional Children*, 1971, **38**, 131–137. Reprinted by permission of The Council for Exceptional Children.

A consideration of all of these factors led to a decision to adopt the resource room as an alternative setting to the special class, to attempt to develop a remedial program within that context, and to use the principles of reinforcement theory to provide positive consequences for appropriate responses to the program.

Method

Selection of Children

Faculty members of the three participating elementary schools were asked to complete the Behavior Problem Checklist (Quay & Peterson, 1967) for any child the teacher felt was either extremely disruptive or overly withdrawn. Teachers also completed a form which requested information on the child's most disruptive times of the day, classroom activity and achievement at those times, and reinforcement preferences of the child.

Between 40 and 50 children were referred from each school; this represented approximately 4 or 5 percent of the total population. From the pool of referrals, half of the children were randomly selected for parttime participation in the resource room; the remainder continued in their regular class and comprised the comparison group.

Children were from the second through the sixth grades, though their academic achievement seldom matched their grade placement (approximately 90 percent were academically retarded). All had an IQ of at least 70. In two schools in low socioeconomic areas the majority of the children were Afro-American; the remaining children were Puerto Rican. The third school had an all Caucasian population and was located in a more stable and slightly higher socioeconomic area.

Table 1 provides data on the characteristics of those children in both groups on whom achievement and behavior gains were compared. None of these characteristics were significantly different between groups with the exception of intelligence, which was significantly higher in the comparison group. However, correlations obtained later between intelligence and gain

scores ranged from 0 to .26 with none approaching statistical significance for the associated numbers of subjects. Table 1 also indicates how the children were distributed in terms of participation in either reading or arithmetic instruction in the resource room. Of the 27 children in the experimental group who met the criteria for the analysis of academic gains, 14 attended the resource room for 2 periods a day and received instruction in both subjects, 11 attended for 1 period per day and were instructed in reading only, and 2 attended 1 period per day and received instruction in arithmetic only.

Although each experimental child was scheduled to attend the resource room for either 1 or 2 periods a day, responsibility for the child remained with his regular class teacher. The resource rooms were not available for random problems at other times of the day. Instead, it was believed that the resource room teacher would be able to provide concrete suggestions and support in minimizing and handling behavioral crises in the regular classroom. In turn, the resource room teacher would rely on the regular teacher for many types of information as well as for a periodic check of the child's performance to determine if transference of results was accomplished from the resource room to the regular class.

It was also intended that the staff of the resource room see itself not only as operating an intervention setting, but also as operating a laboratory in which techniques for teaching adaptive behavior in a group setting could be developed and communicated to teachers in the regular class. In order that these objectives might be carried out, each school had a specific period of the day (usually morning recess) when the resource room was not in use. During this time the resource room personnel had time to locate absent children, arrange interviews with parents, or discuss problems with the regular class teachers. The remainder of the daily resource room schedule consisted of four 45-60 minute teaching segments with from 7 to 10 children attending each period.

TABLE 1

Characteristics of Control and Experimental Groups

Group variables	CA	Behavior Problem Checklist Score[a]				IQ	Grade	Pretest Achievement	
		I	II	III	IV			Reading	Arithmetic
Experimental									
Mean	10.0	11.2	5.3	4.1	1.9	84.5	4.3	2.2	2.1
SD	1.7	5.1	4.0	2.2	1.8	7.9	1.3	1.2	0.76
N	27	27	27	27	27	27	27	25	16
Control									
Mean	9.4	9.9	5.8	3.5	1.2	91.7	4.2	2.6	2.1
SD	1.5	4.7	4.4	2.6	1.9	11.1	1.5	1.6	0.96
N	34	34	34	34	34	34	34	29	13

[a] I : Conduct problem; II : personality problem; III : inadequate-immature; IV : socialized delinquent.

Classroom Organization

The environment of the resource rooms varied in each of the three participating schools depending largely upon whatever free room was available at the beginning of the school year. One resource room was located in a church rectory office across the street from the school. Otherwise, an attempt was made to keep the room as uniform as possible. The nature of the classroom and the educational materials may be found in detail in Glavin, Quay, and Werry (1971).

Reinforcement System

Poker chips used as secondary reinforcers were employed to reinforce starting, maintaining, and completing assigned work—a sequence following that of Hewett, Taylor, and Artuso (1969). When a pupil started his work quickly, he received one chip. If he continued to work, he could receive a maximum of two chips. Completion of the task enabled the child to earn one or two chips depending on the accuracy of his work. A bonus of two poker chips was allotted for task completion before a timing bell sounded ending each 15 minute work segment. The pupil worked for three 15 minute work segments in each 60 minute period. A fourth, optional, free time segment was used so that the pupil could either "buy into" an activity corner (games, phonograph and records, comic and library books, magazines, tape recorder, etc.) or continue working in order to achieve extra points for other reinforcers. Thus, a maximum of either 21 or 28 chips could be earned each period depending on the child's performance on any given day.

At the end of his last work section, the pupil would count his chips, report the total to the resource room teacher, and enter his chip total on a personal graph. The teacher would exchange 10 chips for a card which could then be spent immediately or saved for a higher valued item. While it was hoped to move the children from immediate to delayed reinforcers, the basic principle was to make desirable objects available for every child on both a short and long term basis. The card value or price of reinforcers changed as the time progressed, requiring greater performance for the same rewards. The distribution and exchange of points for reinforcers was accompanied with a brief, positive verbalization by the teacher. Extra praise was given to the child who delayed cashing in his points until he could buy a more expensive reinforcer.

A large store of toy reinforcers was maintained ranging from 5 cent "monster people" and toy finger rings (1 card) to 55 cent car and airplane plastic model kits (11 cards). When it was observed that many of the pupils came to school without breakfast, primary reinforcers of cookies, crackers, and fruit punch (1 card) were introduced. The popularity of manipulable reinforcers diminished in two schools located in very economically deprived area once the edible reinforcers were introduced. At the third school which was situated in a stable upper lower class environment, the manipulable reinforcers continued to be preferred.

The reinforcement system was used for behavioral management control. When classroom rules were violated, the child would be given a warning which might consist of a look, restraining touch, question, or some other means of communication. If the behavior perished, the child was removed from the opportunity to receive reinforcements by being sent to the time-out room (cloak room). He could return to the resource room after being quiet for a minute or two. Teachers were encouraged to return the children as quickly as possible.

Staff Training

Two of our teachers had less than 1 year of substitute teaching prior to joining our staff; the third teacher had 11 years' experience. Each teacher was supported by a teacher assistant. One parttime teacher assistant had 13 years teaching experience while the other 3 parttime assistants had none.

During the first weeks of the project, teachers and one of the project directors met regularly to discuss the operating strategies to be used in the resource rooms. After classes commenced, a weekly meeting was conducted for teaching personnel by a project director. Behavior modification, classroom structure, and particularly difficult management problems dominated the discussions. Other problems often discussed included individualizing curriculum, reinforcement problems, resource room and regular teacher relationships, and methods of handling chronic absentees.

Each resource room was visited by a project director approximately once a week. This visit usually involved a short discussion with the school principal. In addition, three times during the year the authors held meetings with the entire regular classroom faculty to describe the rationale of the project, to clarify and modify the role of classroom observers (some of whom had become a problem to the faculty), and finally to communicate the results of the first year of the research to the regular class teachers. Several other small group meetings were held by a project director, resource room personnel, and regular class teachers who continued to have management problems with children referred to the resource room.

Classroom observers were trained to time sample the children's classroom behavior using a technique described previously (Werry & Quay, 1969). Throughout the research the observers were given a review of procedures, feedback concerning their problems in carrying out the data collection, and reliability trials.

Criterion Measures

One aim of the research was to compare overt behavior change in the resource room as compared to the control group. Observers gathered counts on three classes of observations: deviant behavior, on-task behavior, and teacher-pupil contact. Observing was to be done in a task situation where the rules were clearly defined. In general, this was during individual, academic seat work where there was a minimal amount of pupil-teacher interaction (Werry & Quay, 1969).

Children in the control group were observed in the regular classroom setting while the experimental group was observed in both regular classrooms and resource rooms. Observations were made throughout the school year. Spot checks were taken of the observers at irregular intervals to insure reliability. A mean percentage ratio agreement (Werry & Quay, 1969) was computed for each behavioral category between all pairs of observers. This was continued until the mean percentage ratio agreement for all categories exceeded 80 percent.

A second research aim was to evaluate academic gain. Different forms of the *California Achievement Test* were used for pre- and posttesting all children referred.

Results

Academic Achievement

School personnel were encouraged to make referrals to the resource room throughout the year as well as to participate in deciding when a child in a resource room should be returned fulltime to the regular classroom. Because of this service aspect and the typically high movement rate between schools in the inner city, there was a high turnover of pupils in the resource rooms throughout the year. Providing an open-ended program in terms of student admissions and discharges enabled the resource rooms to function in a service role but added many difficulties to the collection and analysis of the data.

In order to assess the effect of the program and to compare children participating in the experimental program with a group who did not, the following criteria were established to define participation:

1. At least 6 months between pre- and posttests for both experimental and control groups.

2. At least 5 months in the experimental program for experimental children.
3. No more than 30 school days between pretest and program admittance for the experimental group.

Thus, while a total of 55 children received some service in the resource rooms, only 27 children met the above criteria; the following analyses are restricted to that group. The actual length of time of exposure to the experimental program ranged from a minimum of 5 months to a maximum of 6.5 months with a mean of 5.8 months.

The experimental and comparison groups were compared on four achievement gain scores as shown in Table 2. Two comparisons produced significant results. The experimental group improved significantly more in reading comprehension and arithmetic fundamentals.

Classroom Behavior

Observations were analyzed in two ways. In the first, a simple pre versus post split by date of admission to the resource room was made for the experimental group. For the control group, the pre versus post point was fixed as the median date of admission of the experimental children to the resource room in the same school. Using a two-way analysis of variance technique (pre-post-admission) for the treatment group, two separate analyses were made to compare changes in behavior of subjects in the resource room and subjects in the regular class during the time they were attending the resource room, with that of control subjects in the regular class. The results of this analysis are summarized in Table 3.

These data suggest that in their behavior in the regular classroom both control and experimental subjects show an equal amount of significant improvement after the admission date to the resource room or the equivalent date for the control subjects. Since there is no difference in this respect between experimental and control subjects, the improvement could not have been influenced by the resource room program and hence must be termed "spontaneous improvement." Neither does the amount or kind of teacher attention seem to be a factor in this spontaneous improvement since this remained constant. However, while there is no difference between experimental and control subjects in the regular class situation, there was a significantly greater degree of improvement in children observed in the resource room when compared with control subjects. It is also noteworthy that there was a significantly greater amount of positive teacher-

TABLE 2

Gain Scores for Experimental and Control Groups on Achievement Tests

Subject		Experimental			Control			
	N	Mean	SD	N	Mean	SD	t	p
CAT Reading								
Vocabulary	25	0.63	0.71	29	0.51	0.58	0.70	NS
Comprehension	25	0.74	0.69	29	0.21	0.89	2.41	< .02
CAT Arithmetic								
Reasoning	16	1.00	0.70	13	0.75	0.61	1.04	NS
Fundamentals	16	1.55	0.53	13	0.61	0.69	4.47	< .001

pupil ratios in the resource room. This could be one of the factors responsible for the significantly better behavior in the resource room.

The data would suggest that while the program was effective in improving the children's behavior in the resource room, this improvement does not appear to generalize into the regular classroom and is thus linked to the stimulus conditions and consequential events in the resource room. However, the lack of data necessitated comparison on a simple pre-post-admission split; if treatment in the resource room program had a considerable latency before becoming effective, this simple split might have obscured any treatment effect.

For this reason, a second analysis was done to examine behavioral changes as a function of time, using resource room subjects only since too few control subjects had sufficient data. The behavior observations were subdivided into pre-entry, early resource room (during the first month), late resource room (during the third month), early postadmission in the regular class, and late in the regular class. The results of this analysis (one-way ANOVA) are shown in Table 4. The Scheffé (1953) method was used for the posthoc analysis of difference between means.

It can be seen that, as in the first analysis, behavior is significantly better in the resource room than in the regular class either pre-entry or postadmission to the resource room situations. Most of this improvement occurs immediately (within the first month); the small subsequent improvement in the third month does not

support the notion that the failure to find differences between resource room and control subjects in the first analysis was due to slow program effectiveness. Under these circumstances it appears wisest to conclude that while the children's behavior can be changed rapidly and dramatically in the resource room situation, generalization into the regular classroom does not occur automatically, but requires deliberate attempts to generalize this improvement into the regular classroom. A further incidental finding is that all children improve as the school year goes on, independent of what treatment they get; this emphasizes once again the necessity for control groups in evaluating any remedial interventions.

Discussion

The effect of resource rooms on academic achievement was encouraging, with significant results shown in two of the four comparisons. The magnitude of the gains themselves are even more encouraging in light of the fact that the average exposure to the resource room program was under 6 months. Increases in attending and decreases in deviant behaviors in the resource rooms appeared immediately after admission and showed little increase thereafter —perhaps due to the rapid approximation to the desired terminal goal.

The data suggest that generalization does not occur fortuitously; it has to be engineered. The current program is being improved in this respect along several dimensions. It is understandable that with less than 1 year of teaching experience for two of the three resource room teachers,

TABLE 3

Mean Percent Occurrence of Behaviors in Control and Experimental Subjects Before and After Admission

Item	Control group (N = 14)		Experimental group (N = 15)		
	Pre	Post	Pre	Regular class	Resource room
No deviant behavior [a]	22.8	44.7	23.9	41.9	60.2 [b]
On-task [a]	43.2	60.6	46.2	52.0	77.2 [b]
Positive teacher-pupil interaction	10.2	8.5	8.3	7.9	22.0 [b]

[a] Significant ($p \lesssim .05$) "spontaneous improvement" effect in both groups on this item.
[b] Significant ($p \lesssim .05$) difference between experimental and control groups.

TABLE 4

Early and Late Classroom Behavior—Observations of Experimental Children in Resource Room and Regular Class

Item	Pre-entry (P)	Resource room (R) 1/12	3/12	Regular class (C) 1/12	3/12	Significance
No deviant behavior	22.5	58.8	66.3	32.1	41.1	<.001 PvR RₐvC₁
On-task	44.0	76.6	79.1	42.7	47.5	<.001 PvR PvC
Positive teacher-pupil interaction	7.7	17.8	20.4	5.9	7.8	<.001 PvR RvC PvC₁

they may have been hesitant to suggest needed changes to the regular class teachers. In addition, all teachers had much to learn this first year concerning reinforcement principles, resource room operation, and behavior problem children.

A second factor concerns the regular classroom teacher. There was found to be no halo effect from teacher attention in the regular class situation as a result of a child being admitted to the resource room. This would suggest that given the number of children in a regular class or the current mode of teaching style, it is probably impossible for a teacher to significantly increase her amount of positive attention to a given child unless specific techniques can be developed, communicated, and implemented.

References

Glavin, J. P. "Spontaneous" improvement in emotionally disturbed children. *Selected convention papers: 46th Annual International Convention 1968.* Washington, D.C.: The Council for Exceptional Children, NEA, 1968. Pp. 295-304.

Glavin, J. P., Quay, H. C., & Werry, J. S. Behavioral and academic gains of conduct problem children in different classroom settings. *Exceptional Children,* 1971, 37, 441-446.

Graubard, P. S. The extent of academic retardation in a residential treatment center. *Journal of Educational Research,* 1964, 58, 78-80.

Hewett, F. M., Taylor, F. D., & Artuso, A. A. The Santa Monica project: Evaluation of an engineered classroom design with emotionally disturbed children. *Exceptional Children,* 1969, 35, 523-529.

Kounin, J. S., Friesen, W. V., & Norton, A. E. Managing emotionally disturbed children in regular classrooms. *Journal of Educational Psychology,* 1966, 57, 1-13.

Long, N. J., Morse, W. C., & Newman, R. G. *Conflict in the classroom: The education of emotionally disturbed children.* Belmont, Cal.: Wadsworth Publishing, 1965.

McCaffrey, I., & Cumming, J. *Behavior patterns associated with persistent emotional disturbances of school children in regular classes of elementary grades.* Onondaga County: Mental Health Research Unit, New York State Department of Mental Hygiene, 1967.

O'Leary, K. D., & Becker, W. C. Behavior modification of an adjustment class: A token reinforcement program. *Exceptional Children,* 1967, 33, 637-642.

Quay, H. C., & Peterson, D. R. *Manual for the behavior problem checklist.* Champaign: Children's Research Center, University of Illinois, 1967. (Mimeo)

Scheffé, H. A method for judging all contrasts in the analysis of variance. *Biometrika,* 1953, 40, 87-104.

Shepherd, M., Oppenheim, A. N., & Mitchell, S. Childhood behavior disorders and the child-guidance clinic: An epidemiological study. *Journal of Child Psychology and Psychiatry,* 1966, 7, 39-52.

Stone, F. B., & Rowley, V. N. Educational disability in emotionally disturbed children. *Exceptional Children,* 1964, 30, 423-426.

Walker, H. M., Mattson, R. H., & Buckley, N. K. Special class placement as a treatment alternative for deviant behavior in children. In F.A.M. Benson (Ed.), *Modifying deviant social behaviors in various classroom settings.* Eugene: University of Oregon, Department of Special Education, 1969.

Werry, J. S., & Quay, H. C. Observing the classroom behavior of elementary school children. *Exceptional Children,* 1969, 35, 461-470.

VERBAL-NONVERBAL CONFLICT IN PARENTAL MESSAGES TO NORMAL AND DISTURBED CHILDREN[1]

Daphne E. Bugental
Leonore R. Love
Jaques W. Kaswan
Carol April

An analysis was made of videotaped parent-child communication within 20 families containing a "disturbed" child (referred by schools for chronic behavior or emotional problems) and 10 "normal" control families. Parental messages were judged for evaluative content in verbal (typescript of message), vocal (tone of voice), and visual (facial expressions, gestures, etc.) channels. Significantly more ($p = .05$) disturbed mothers (59%) produced messages containing evaluative conflict between channels than did normal mothers (10%); no difference was found between normal and disturbed fathers. The sons of mothers producing conflicting messages were found to be higher on school aggressiveness than the sons of "nonconflicting" mothers ($p = .05$).

This study is concerned with the presence of conflict between communication channels in parental messages to normal and disturbed children. Considerable theoretical speculation and research has focused on the relationship between conflicting parental communication and psychopathology in children. Most of such research has been directed toward a test of the double-bind hypothesis with respect to schizophrenia (Bateson, Jackson, Haley, & Weakland, 1956; Weakland, 1961), but increasingly there has been an interest in communication conflict as related to more general disturbances (e.g., Beakel & Mehrabian, 1969). The double-bind hypothesis has received little empirical support (Schuham, 1967), and the presence of conflict in parental messages to disturbed children still rests heavily on anecdotal evidence.

The interpretation of noncongruent and conflicting messages has revealed developmental differences in responses to three communication channels (Bugental, 1966; Bugental, Kaswan, & Love, 1970; Bugental, Kaswan, Love, & Fox, 1970); young children have been observed to give less weight to facial expressions than do older children or adults. Additionally, adults have been found to give differential weight to verbal, vocal, and visual channels in resolving conflicting messages (Bugental, Kaswan, & Love, 1970; Mehrabian & Ferris, 1967; Mehrabian & Wiener, 1967). These studies suggest the importance of comparing different types of channel conflict in exploring the relationship between parental messages and the psychopathology of their children. Beakel and Mehrabian (1969) focused on the relationship between psychopathology in adolescents and parental evaluative incongruence in verbal and postural communication components. They observed greater negativity in parental messages to more disturbed adolescents in comparison with less disturbed adolescents, but failed to observe any relationship between psychopathology and incongruity. The present study is concerned with the presence of evaluative conflict (friendliness or approval versus unfriendliness or disapproval) between verbal content, vocal intonation, and visual components (facial expression, gestures, etc.).

The "disturbed" group studied here consisted of the families of children (aged 8–12 yr.) referred by their school to the University of California, Los Angeles, Psychology Department Clinic because of serious and chronic behavior or emotional problems. This group was compared with a set of matched "normal" control families. All families were videotaped as part of a larger clinical project (Kaswan & Love, 1969). The videotapes were subsequently subjected to a detailed analysis of channel content in parent-child communication.

[1] This study was supported by United States Public Health Service Grant 1R01-MH-14770.

METHOD

Sample

The original groups from which we drew samples included 87 disturbed and 30 normal control families. The disturbed group included children, aged 8–12, referred by school personnel as demonstrating behavioral or emotional disturbances in the classroom and playground. Disturbed children were of normal intelligence but were typically underachievers in school performance; all children in our sample were, however, attending regular classes in the public school system. Normal control children were selected by asking one-third of the referring teachers (randomly selected) to select a child in the same classroom (matched for sex with the referred child) who did not demonstrate significant or chronic problems at school. School referrals constituted the only basis for assigning children to disturbed or normal control groups.

For this study, 20 disturbed and 10 normal control families were selected from the total sample for detailed analysis of their videotaped interaction. The two groups were matched on the basis of sex of child and socioeconomic level. Table 1 summarizes information on both samples with respect to these and other potentially relevant variables. It can be seen that the two groups did not differ in terms of sex, IQ, or socioeconomic level. As a chance selection factor, a trend appeared for disturbed children to be older than normal control children. The only significant difference between groups was in family composition: 9 out of the 20 disturbed families contained only one parent, whereas all normal control families contained two parents. This difference reflected the generally higher incidence of broken homes in the background of disturbed children in our sample.

All children were rated on a 9-point scale on four independent[2] behavior dimensions: aggressiveness (expresses anger physically; is hostile, disruptive, uncooperative; defies authority); poor attention control (poor work habits, immaturity, distractibility); fearful (anxious, insecure, low in self-confidence, dependent on teacher); and hyperactivity (restless, compulsive talker with poor peer relations). Ratings were based on statements made by the child's teachers (contained in the child's cumulative school record and in referring statements made by the current teacher). Ratings of these statements, in terms of referral categories, were made by two clinical psychologists. Interjudge reliability coefficients were .85 on aggressiveness, .91 on poor attention control, .71 on fearfulness, and .86 on hyperactivity. Six children in the disturbed sample presented a primary problem of "aggressiveness" (i.e., ratings on this dimension were higher than ratings on other dimensions), six had a primary problem of "poor attention control," four were primarily "fearful," and two were primarily "hyperactive."

Videotaped Messages

All families were videotaped (from an adjacent room) in a standardly equipped waiting room; all knew they would be observed and recorded. The family interactions recorded included a planned sequence arranged for all families: their free interaction during a 5-min.

[2] There were no significant correlations (or trends) between these four dimensions.

TABLE 1

COMPARISON OF DISTURBED AND NORMAL CONTROL SAMPLES

Item	Disturbed	Normal	Difference
Child IQ			
$\bar{X}$	120	125	$t = 1.02$
SD	(12)	(12)	
Child age			
$\bar{X}$	9.85	8.90	$t = 1.79^*$
SD	(1.15)	(1.38)	
Child sex			
% male	85	70	$X^2 = .23^a$
Family composition			
% one-parent	45	00	$X^2 = 4.46^{**}$
Occupation of household head[b]			
$\bar{X}$	4.11	4.22	$t = .17$
SD	(1.51)	(1.48)	
Education of household head[b]			
$\bar{X}$	3.41	3.40	$t = .02$
SD	(1.15)	(1.11)	

Note.—Child IQ was measured by Ammons Full-Range Picture Vocabulary Test; this instrument was used in order to reduce academic and cultural weightings even though it gives inflated IQ values.
[a] Adjusted by Yates' correction for small samples.
[b] Hollingshead (Hollingshead & Redlich, 1958) 7-point scales (1 = high status; 7 = low status) for occupational and educational status.
* $p = .10$.
** $p = .05$.

wait; brief dyadic interactions between specified members; and a problem definition period in which the family was asked to discuss among themselves what they would like changed in their family.

Scenes for subsequent analysis were chosen by starting each tape at a random point and selecting those parent-child messages in which (a) the person speaking was visible; (b) only one person was speaking and the words could be clearly understood; and (c) the message was rated independently by two judges[3] as positive or negative in total evaluative content. Whenever possible, one positive and one negative scene were obtained for each parent.[4] Not all parents produced both positive and negative scenes, but there were no group differences in average number of positive or negative scenes.

The following scenes are typical for length and type of message:

Encoder	Verbal Message
Normal father	"I asked you to sit down. Now I won't ask you again."
Disturbed father	"How's your breathing today? Is your cold better today"?
Normal mother	"Lookit—lookit that. Look at the other one. Those are not your socks."
Disturbed mother	"And then they'll take me and then you'll be left by yourself, Jimmy."

[3] In addition, the message was cross-verified by a previous rating of total scenes by four judges rating the evaluative content of the entire tape, subdivided into 30-sec. periods (as part of another study in progress).

[4] One normal and two disturbed parents produced no messages with agreed-upon evaluative content.

Judges

Five parent-aged women were selected as judges on the basis of their maturity (for rating privileged data) and their consensual accuracy in rating social interaction. Applicants who made deviant ratings on a set of acted messages (with respect to previous ratings of the same messages by experienced raters) were screened out. Judges were trained by making repeated ratings of practice videotaped messages and received feedback on the ratings made by others. Interjudge agreement (for the 5 judges selected) was measured on the basis of their ratings of actual family tapes, made subsequent to preliminary selection and training procedures. Interjudge agreement was estimated by $1 - \dfrac{MS \text{ within scenes}}{MS \text{ between scenes}}$ (Winer, 1962, p. 128). This formula is equivalent to the Spearman-Brown prediction formula. Reliability coefficients (based on a sample of 67 independent messages) were .93 for verbal content, .81 for vocal content, and .93 for visual content.

The judges were unaware of the purpose of the project or the nature of the families. None of the judges had a background in psychology.

Channel Ratings

Independent channel ratings were made for all scenes on an evaluative scale from +6 to −6 with a neutral 0 point between. The dimension was initially defined for the judges by repeated showing of videotaped, acted scenes which demonstrated the two extremes and the neutral point. The judges were asked to use these polar scenes as scale anchors. Brief verbal descriptions of the anchors were used to help define them; for example, positive evaluative behavior was defined as "friendly, approving, or considerate."

Ratings of the verbal content of scenes were obtained by having the judges rate typescripts of all scenes. For vocal ratings, the audio portion of the tape was played with the intelligible portion of speech effectively eliminated by means of a band-pass filter. For visual ratings, the TV picture was turned on but the sound was turned off.

Any channel input rated as positive (or negative) by four out of five judges was considered to be positive (or negative) in subsequent analyses. Any scene containing a consensually established positive message in one channel and a consensually established negative message in another channel was accepted as representing a conflicting message. For example, if four out of five judges rated the picture in a given scene as positive, four out of five judges rated the script as negative, but failed to agree (or gave neutral ratings) to the voice, the scene was categorized as demonstrating visual-verbal conflict; if, on the other hand, four out of five judges rated the voice as negative, the scene was categorized as demonstrating visual-vocal conflict as well as visual-verbal conflict.

RESULTS

A comparison was made of the number of parents who produced conflicting messages, as shown in Table 2, in the disturbed and normal groups. A higher proportion of disturbed parents produced conflicting messages than did normal parents. This difference, however, was only a trend ($\chi^2 = 2.40$, $p < .20$). A partitioning

TABLE 2

PROPORTION OF DISTURBED AND NORMAL FAMILIES PRODUCING CONFLICTING MESSAGES

Family	Conflict	No conflict	Total
Disturbed			
f	12	8	20
Proportion	.67	.33	
Normal			
f	3	7	10
Proportion	.30	.70	
Total	15	15	30

Note.—A family was categorized as "conflicting" if either parent produced at least one conflicting message (there were potentially four messages per family, two for each parent); a family was categorized as "nonconflicting" if neither message by either parent contained channel conflict. The unit of analysis was the family, not the message.

of groups by parent sex (see Table 3) reveals that there is a significant difference between normal and disturbed *mothers* (χ^2, adjusted by Yates' correction for small samples, $= 4.32$, $p = .05$) but not between normal and disturbed fathers (corrected $\chi^2 = .13$). A much greater proportion of disturbed mothers produced conflicting messages than did normal mothers. This difference did not appear to be influenced by the presence or absence of a father in the home, that is, "conflicting" mothers were just as common in two-parent disturbed families (60%) as in "father-absent" disturbed families (57%). Consequently, the difference in composition between our disturbed and normal samples does not appear to have influenced our findings. The conflicting messages produced by disturbed mothers included conflict between verbal content and facial expression, and

TABLE 3

PROPORTION OF DISTURBED MESSAGES PRODUCED BY MOTHERS AND FATHERS (DISTURBED VERSUS NORMAL GROUPS)

Parents	Conflict	No conflict	Total[a]
Mothers			
Disturbed			
f	10	7	17
Proportion	.59	.41	
Normal			
f	1	9	10
Proportion	.10	.90	
Total	11	16	27
Fathers			
Disturbed			
f	2	10	12
Proportion	.17	.83	
Normal			
f	3	6	9
Proportion	.33	.67	
Total	5	16	21

Note.—A parent was categorized as "conflicting" if he produced at least one conflicting message; a parent was categorized as "nonconflicting" if neither of his messages contained channel conflict. The unit of analysis was the individual parent.
[a] Frequencies do not add to the total N (30 sets of parents) because (a) 9 families contained only one parent and (b) 3 parents produced no agreed-upon evaluative messages.

between verbal content and tone of voice (but not between face and voice); there were, however, no significant differences between groups in specific types of channel conflict manifested.

An analysis was made within the disturbed group of the referral categories of the children whose mothers produced conflicting messages versus those whose mothers did not produce conflicting messages. There was a trend ($U = 20$, $p = .20$, two-tailed test) for the ratings on "aggressiveness" to be higher for the children of conflicting mothers than for the the children of "nonconflicting" mothers. When comparisons were limited to boys, the difference between groups of mothers was statistically significant ($U = 6.5$, $p = .05$, two-tailed test). No other relationships were found between referral category ratings and the presence of conflict in parental messages.

DISCUSSION

A much higher proportion of the mothers of disturbed children was observed to produce conflicting messages than of the mothers of normal control children. No equivalent difference was found between the fathers of disturbed and normal control children. Our findings provide evidence that the mothers of disturbed children simultaneously give conflicting evaluative messages in different communication channels. This is consistent with the double-bind hypothesis, but suggests that conflicting communication is not limited to schizophrenogenic mothers.

A common type of conflicting message produced by the mothers of disturbed children contained a critical or disapproving statement spoken in a positive voice. For example, one mother typically cooed all here criticisms, for example, "That's not n-i-ce," in a "syrupy" voice. If the mother is attempting to soften or deny the negative component in one channel by the positive component in another, her message is likely to be decoded much more negatively by the child than she would anticipate. Some of our previous data (Bugental, Kaswan, & Love, 1970) suggest that young children resolve all conflicting messages by accepting the negative component and totally or partially discounting any positive component (in particular for messages from women).

An analysis of the observed trends in the type of referral problem manifested by the children of conflicting mothers may offer some explanatory leads. There was a trend for the children of conflicting mothers to be more aggressive in school than the children of non-

conflicting mothers (within the disturbed sample); this difference was statistically significant when comparisons were limited to boys. The teachers of these boys complained of their fighting, defiance of authority, and general disruptiveness in the classroom and on the playground. The conflicting communication pattern of their mothers may have the effect of arousing the negative feelings of the child (due to the negative evaluative component) while simultaneously inhibiting a direct negative response to her (because of the positive component). By giving, for example, a positive nonverbal message along with a verbal criticism, the mother is saying, "I'm criticizing you but you shouldn't get angry at me because I'm really being nice." When children responded negatively to disapproval, no matter how nicely stated, the mother often countered by telling the child he should not be resentful because she had his best interests at heart. The child is effectively constrained from responding with anger toward his mother but may subsequently express his aggression in the "safer" school environment. This speculative interpretation is, of course, related to the frustration-aggression hypothesis. The relationship between maternal punitiveness and child aggressiveness outside the home is well-established (e.g., Becker, 1964; Sears, Whiting, Nowlis, & Sears, 1953). In this case we are referring less to maternal punitiveness than to the expression of negative evaluation in such a way as to preclude or limit an immediate negative response.

This approach to the study of contradictory messages seemed to be a fruitful avenue to an issue which has previously defied empirical analysis. When clinicians have reported contradictions in interpersonal messages as characteristic of interaction in families with disturbed children, it has been extremely difficult to specify empirically testable criteria for such messages (e.g., Mishler & Waxler, 1968, pp. 274–275). In large part, this difficulty seems to be due to the typical focus on linguistic patterns of contradiction which, because of problems like change in context and multiple levels of meanings, are virtually impossible to classify into a manageable number of nontrivial categories. While our approach leaves out much of the richness which context provides, it does refer to clinically meaningful aspects of contradiction in communication. In fact, recognition that divergent meanings are often conveyed in different channels is basic to the increasing use of videotapes as a method for client-feedback and self-confrontation in a variety of clinical interventions (Kaswan & Love, 1969).

REFERENCES

BATESON, G., JACKSON, D. D., HALEY, J., & WEAK-LAND, J. Toward a theory of schizophrenia. *Behavioral Science*, 1956, 1, 251–264.

BEAKEL, N. G., & MEHRABIAN, A. Inconsistent communications and psychopathology. *Journal of Abnormal Psychology*, 1969, 74, 126–130.

BECKER, W. C. Consequences of different kinds of parental discipline. In M. L. Hoffman & L. W. Hoffman (Eds.), *Review of child development research.* Vol. 1. New York: Russell Sage Foundation, 1964.

BUGENTAL, D. E. Characteristics of interpersonal messages in families. In D. J. Kincaid (Chm.), Communication patterns in the family and the school as related to child adjustment. Symposium presented at the meeting of the American Psychological Association, New York, September 1966.

BUGENTAL, D. E., KASWAN, J. W., & LOVE, L. R. Perception of contradictory meanings conveyed by verbal and nonverbal channels. *Journal of Personality and Social Psychology*, 1970, 16, 647–655.

BUGENTAL, D. E., KASWAN, J. W., LOVE, L. R., & FOX, M. N. Child versus adult perception of evaluative messages in verbal, vocal, and visual channels. *Developmental Psychology*, 1970, 2, 367–375.

HOLLINGSHEAD, A. B., & REDLICH, F. C. *Social class and mental illness: A community study.* New York: Wiley, 1958.

KASWAN, J. W., & LOVE, L. R. Confrontation as a method of clinical intervention. *Journal of Nervous and Mental Disease*, 1969, 148, 224–237.

MEHRABIAN, A., & FERRIS, S. R. Inference of attitudes from nonverbal communication. *Journal of Consulting Psychology*, 1967, 31, 248–252.

MEHRABIAN, A., & WIENER, M. Decoding of inconsistent communications. *Journal of Personality and Social Psychology*, 1967, 6, 109–114.

MISHLER, E. E., & WAXLER, N. E. *Interaction in families.* New York: Wiley, 1968.

SCHUHAM, A. I. The double-bind hypothesis a decade later. *Psychological Bulletin*, 1967, 68, 409–416.

SEARS, R. R., WHITING, J. W. N., NOWLIS, V., & SEARS, P. S. Some child-rearing antecedents of aggression and dependence in children. *Genetic Psychology Monographs*, 1953, 47, 135–236.

WEAKLAND, J. H. The "double-bind" hypothesis of schizophrenia and three-party interaction. In D. D. Jackson (Ed.), *The etiology of schizophrenia.* New York: Basic Books, 1961.

WINER, B. J. *Statistical principles in experimental design.* New York: McGraw-Hill, 1962.

CHAPTER EIGHT

DELINQUENCY

There have been numerous investigations and speculations about the antecedents of delinquent behavior. As indicated by Caplan and Nelson, the variables hypothesized to account for delinquency are more likely to be person- rather than situation-oriented. The articles in this chapter provide information on three of the many factors that have been found to correlate with delinquency: poor parent-child relationships (Dietz), an inability to delay gratification (Erikson and Roberts), and little facilitation of learning through punishment (Schlichter and Ratliff).

It has been hypothesized that a poor parent-child relationship may contribute to the development of a negative self-concept and low self-acceptance in delinquents. Dietz investigated this problem by comparing lower-class male nondelinquents with lower-class male delinquents on several personality scales that defined the concepts of interest. The composition of the delinquent sample studied by Dietz reflects the fact that lower-class males from minority groups are more likely to be labeled delinquent than are middle-class Caucasian males. In addition, institutionalized delinquents, such as those studied by Dietz, are known to have a higher recidivism rate than noninstitutionalized delinquents. Consequently, one must avoid generalizing the results of this study beyond the population defined. Many delinquents appear to engage in impulsive behavior without regard for the consequences of that behavior. The results of the Erikson and Roberts study support the relationship between delinquency and an inability to delay gratification. Schlichter and Ratliff studied the effects of reward and punishment on learning in delinquent versus nondelinquent subjects. Data indicated that punishment facilitated learning significantly less in the delinquent than in the nondelinquent group.

The investigator interested in the study of delinquent groups is faced with difficulty in obtaining accurate data from subjects. However, this difficulty is not unique to research on delinquency. Whenever subjects classified as "exceptional" have experienced frustration and failure with authority figures, their motivation for cooperating with a research worker may be markedly reduced.

ON BEING USEFUL: THE NATURE AND CONSEQUENCES OF PSYCHOLOGICAL RESEARCH ON SOCIAL PROBLEMS

Nathan Caplan
Stephen D. Nelson

Abstract. Analysis of research reports summarized in *Psychological Abstracts* over a six-month interval indicates that psychologists engaged in the study of social problems tend to blame existing difficulties on the personal characteristics of subjects rather than on situational factors in the environment. Further, the assumptions made about the source of the problem (person versus situation) determine the direction of remediation and even whether remedial attempts are undertaken. The need for redefinition of the proper role of both science and individual scientists in research on social issues is considered.

There is considerable encouragement, support, and pressure today for behavioral scientists to direct their attention away from the preoccupations of their vigorously irrelevant past and to engage in work with more obvious social utility. This move from peripheral functions at the edge of society to the more central activities of organized social planning enjoys the official sanction of two important study groups (Brim et al., 1969; National Academy of Sciences, 1969) and the promise of favorable future financial support as exemplified by the National Science Foundation (RANN). Increased federal funding for "applied" research is already evident. Riecken (1972) reported that from fiscal year 1968 to 1971, the total federal expenditures for "basic" research in the social sciences grew from $116 to $141 million, while federal expenditures for "applied" research during that same period grew from $134 to $257 million.

Those of us who have long felt that the social sciences have not met their social responsibility welcome this upsurge of interest in the problems of society. On the other hand, becoming useful is not as simple a matter as it might first appear. The application of psychological findings and thought to the improvement of societal functioning and human welfare is fraught with many potential problems. Our purpose here is to discuss some meta-issues that raise doubts and uncertainties about the possible consequences of applying psychological

The article is supported in part by Grant MH 19313 to the authors from the National Institute of Mental Health, United States Public Health Service.

thought and research—and the behavioral sciences in general—to the problems of society. We do this in hopes that both psychology as a profession and society as a whole may avoid potential pitfalls and unanticipated negative consequences that may ensue from injudiciously moving the orientation of psychology as a science into the public arena as a means for dealing with the problems that beset society.

To delimit the domain of "relevancy" with which this article is concerned we should emphasize three tnings: (*a*) in this article we deal with *social* policy and not other types of public policy issues; (*b*) our interest is in social policy at the national level, with nationwide implications; and (*c*) we are concerned with social problems and problem behavior—various kinds of so-called "social pathology."

The discussion of these issues is organized into two parts. The first part deals with what may be called the "person-blame" causal attribution bias in psychological research on social problems. By this we mean the tendency to hold individuals responsible for their problems. Our concern is with (*a*) psychologically oriented research that focuses on "person-centered" characteristics (those that lie within the individual), while ignoring situationally relevant factors (those external to the individual); and (*b*) the tendency to attribute *causal* significance to person-centered variables found in statistical association with the social problem in question. Published research reports are used to illustrate

From *American Psychologist*, 1973, **28**, 199–211. Copyright 1973 by the American Psychological Association. Reprinted by permission.

this bias. In this section of the article we also discuss the social action implications of this person-blame bias and two major reasons for its prevalence among psychologists.

In the second part of the discussion we explore the utility and applicability of psychological thought and research to social problems within the framework of the issues raised in the first part of the discussion. Particular attention is given to the political implications and partisan advantages of person-blame interpretations and how unintended functions served by such a bias in causal attribution may become ends in themselves if well-meaning researchers continue to regard social research as if it were a neutral competency.

Problem Definitions and Causal Attribution Bias in Psychological Research

THE IMPORTANCE OF PROBLEM DEFINITIONS: PERSON VERSUS SITUATION

We have chosen to concentrate on problem-defining activities for three closely linked reasons.

1. First, what is done about a problem depends on how it is defined. The way a social problem is defined determines the attempts at remediation— or even whether such attempts will be made—by suggesting both the *foci* and the *techniques* of intervention and by ruling out alternative possibilities. More specifically, problem definition determines the change strategy, the selection of a social action delivery system, and the criteria for evaluation.

Problem definitions are based on assumptions about the causes of the problem and where they lie.[3] If the causes of delinquency, for example, are defined in *person-centered* terms (e.g., inability to delay gratification, or incomplete sexual identity), then it would be logical to initiate *person-change* treatment techniques and intervention strategies to deal with the problem. Such treatment would take the form of counseling or other person-change efforts to "reach" the delinquent, thereby using his potential for self-control to make his behavior more conventional. Or if it seemed that person-centered impediments at the root of such "antisocial" behavior were too deeply ingrained or not amenable to routine help (e.g., causes such as birth order position or an extra Y chromosome), it would then follow that coercive external control techniques (e.g., confinement or possibly medical solutions) could be instituted. Under such circumstances, it could be argued with impunity that those officially defined as delinquent would have to relinquish autonomous control over their behavior and other rights in the service of the common good. Thus, where person-centered interpretations provide the foundation on which corrective intervention is based, little need be done about external factors since they would presumably be of lesser or no etiological significance in the determination of such behavior.

If, on the other hand, explanations are *situation centered*, for example, if delinquency were interpreted as the substitution of extralegal paths for already preempted, conventionally approved pathways for achieving socially valued goals, then efforts toward corrective treatment would logically have a *system-change* orientation. Efforts would be launched to create suitable opportunities for success and achievement along conventional lines; thus, existing physical, social, or economic arrangements, not individual psyches, would be the targets for change.

The way a problem is defined determines not only what is done about it, but also what is *not* done—or what apparently need not be done. If matrifocal family structure is argued to be the

[3] The reader should be forewarned that in the discussion to follow, a constant-sum model of causality is used, which assumes in its weakest form that person-centered causes and situation-centered causes are inversely related (i.e., the more one type of causal factor is shown to operate, the less the other type is assumed to operate, in bringing about particular outcomes). In its most extreme form, this model would assume that person-centered and situation-centered causal factors are dichotomous and mutually exclusive (i.e., if one type of factor is shown to be causally operative, it is assumed that the other type does not operate at all). The authors labor under no such simplistic notions and are well aware of the complexities of causal interpretation and multidetermined outcomes. The arguments in this article follow this simpler model, however, because of (a) the tendency of the public to think in such either–or terms with respect to causality, and (b) the eagerness of political actors to take advantage of that tendency.

Further, because we are dealing with the public phenomenology of causality, the article necessarily blurs two con-

cepts that would be carefully distinguished in a more rigorously analytical article. These are the concepts of (a) the *cause* of an event or condition, which according to the scientific ideal can be factually and empirically ascertained and then communicated in a purely descriptive, nonevaluative fashion; and (b) *responsibility* for an event or condition, which includes both credit and blame and, as these words suggest, is more evaluative and value laden, based on certain normative assumptions including an evaluation of the event and, in the case of personal or group agents, intentionality. There is an even sharper analytical and often empirical distinction between these two concepts and a third, that of responsibility for changing an undesirable event or condition.

basis for deviancy, nonachievement, and high unemployment, then opportunity structure, discriminatory hiring practices, and other system defects would appear less blameworthy as the causes of poverty. Likewise, if it can be shown that the use of nonstandard speech interferes with the ability to mediate thought and consequently is the cause of poor performance on formal academic tasks, then such a person-blame explanation would remove pressure for structural and institutional changes in the educational system to raise the educational levels of persons from "linguistically deficient" backgrounds. If leniency during child rearing could be shown to be characteristic of student activists, then their system-antagonistic actions could be discredited as the ravings of immature and spoiled children. If, on the other hand, we found that the dissidents are more likely to be cognitively correct about the issues in question than nondissidents or counterdissidents, then there would be reason to seriously consider their recommendations for change.

Whether the social problem to be attacked is delinquency, mental health, drug abuse, unemployment, ghetto riots, or whatever, the significance of the defining process is the same: *the action (or inaction) taken will depend largely on whether causes are seen as residing within individuals or in the environment.* Thus, because the remedies proposed reflect the definition of the problem, it is crucial that the causal inferences made by problem identifiers, social policy planners, and professional change agents—anyone who plans and guides large-scale action programs—be based on accurate and comprehensive information. Sartre, in *Saint Genet,* said it in a way that illustrates not only that how you define something determines what you do about it, but also that what you do about a problem also defines it: "Action, whatever it be, modifies that which is in the name of that which is not yet."

2. Such definitions, once legitimated and acted upon, tend to define the problem indefinitely, irrespective of their validity. Once in effect, they resist replacement by other definitions. Program administrators and professional change agents develop a vested interest in maintaining established definitions since their very jobs, status, power, and the employment of subordinates may depend on those definitions being accepted as correct. If intervention fails, the problem definition and the delivery system are seldom held responsible. Instead, the responsibility for failure may be avoided by locating blame in the target group and by interpreting that failure as a further sign of the seriousness of the "pathology" being dealt with. As far as we know, no recent large-scale action program has been put out of business because research has shown its failure to fulfill its intended goals.

Also, to the extent that a problem definition conforms to and reinforces dominant cultural myths and clichés (e.g., Horatio Alger), as indeed most definitions must in order to become widely accepted, its change or replacement will be stubbornly resisted. Furthermore, people tend to conform to public definitions and expectations; even if there are doubts regarding their accuracy, they at least provide people with a publicly defined role and definite image of who they are and what is expected of them. Still further, of course, many groups have economic and political interests in seeing that certain definitions are accepted over others (e.g., the business community with regard to the causes of unemployment). In the context of such pressures, an invalid person-centered problem definition often has its most pernicious effect: it can convince the target population of its blameworthiness as alleged.

Thus, problem definitions take on a life of their own; they set in motion a variety of social and psychological forces which give them important functional significance. Consequently, to question established definitions is to challenge important institutions and belief systems that have their origins in those definitions.

3. In view of the federal funds being invested in evaluations of social intervention efforts, it bears emphasizing that effective evaluation depends on linking program outcomes to the presumed causes of the problem behavior. Thus, a precise and explicit diagnosis of the problem is an indispensable preliminary to good program evaluation. Many different forces shape human behavior, and if remedial intervention fails to produce intended effects, it may be impossible to know the reasons for failure, that is, whether because of the limited changeability of the target population, whether the level of intensity of the treatment was inadequate to produce an effect, or whether the treatment program was inappropriate because it was premised on invalid problem definitions and incorrect assumptions about the causal factors involved.

In the foregoing we have described why problem definitions are crucial in determining what is done or not done about social problems and, more specifically, how person-blame definitions may deflect attention and energies away from important situational determinants, often to the detriment of those supposedly being helped. The significance of this discussion resides in the fact that regardless of the type of problem and the intent of the investigator, the findings of psychologically oriented research lend themselves more easily to person-blame than to system-blame interpretations of the problem. In consequence, such research frequently plays an integral role in a chain of events that results in *blaming people in difficult situations for their own predicament*. This article focuses on the processes by which this takes place and the implications for "problem" subgroups, the profession, and society as a whole.

PERSON-CENTERED PREOCCUPATION AND CAUSAL ATTRIBUTION BIAS OF PSYCHOLOGICAL RESEARCH

It is often at the problem definition stage in the social policy formulation process that social scientists either volunteer, or are called on, to be helpful. It is expected that we will provide expert and unbiased information, but the meaning of "unbiased" is not identical for the consumers and the producers of social science information. To the knowledge user, it may mean (*a*) that the problem will be viewed from all vantage points and that the interpretation offered will depend on an assessment of a sufficient variety of competing hypotheses that reflect the complexity of the issues, and/or (*b*) that the new information does not challenge established definitions.

To the social science knowledge producer, on the other hand, "unbiased" is defined in terms of the canons of scientific methodology. However, there is a characteristic that distinguishes psychology from other disciplines, and while this distinction may or may not be a bias in a technical, methodological sense, the fact that the chief focus of interest for psychologists is on person-centered variables has a definite biasing effect on the *inferential potential* of the findings when used as a premise on which to base later action for "corrective" change. Psychologists study individuals and in particular their mental states: their thoughts, attitudes, motives, intrapsychic equilibrium, etc. Moreover, we prefer to view these factors as independent variables, that is, antecedent and causal in relation to other behavior; and while we may pay lip service to external factors influencing behavior and agree that man to a large degree is a simulator of his environment, when it comes to the actual study of that man and why he behaves as he does, we are more likely to limit our search for etiological evidence to what goes on between his ears and to ignore or exclude from consideration a multitude of

external impingements that could justifiably be hypothesized as causal.[4]

The law of the instrument. When psychologists turn their attention to social problems, we see something akin to what Archibald (1970) called the "clinical orientation" to the utilization of social scientific knowledge, which she characterizes as assuming that "if the shoe doesn't fit, there's something wrong with your foot." The reasons for this parochial perspective are understandable. To begin with, it is an occupational expectancy that the psychologist would want to demonstrate the applicability of his skills and services. Kaplan (1964) called this widely observed tendency the Law of the Instrument: give a small boy a hammer, and suddenly he discovers that everything needs hammering. Train a person in psychological theory and research, and suddenly a world disastrously out of tune with human needs is explained as a state of mind. As we shall see presently, the probability of locating cause in variables outside one's area of familiarity or expertise is not great. "It comes as no particular surprise to discover that a scientist formulates problems in a way which requires for their solution just those techniques in which he himself is especially skilled [Kaplan, 1964, p. 31]." The difficulty is that, as Kaplan says, "The price of training is always a certain 'trained incapacity': the more we know how to do something, the harder it is to learn to do it differently [p. 31]."

Evidence of the person-centered bias in psychology with regard to social problems. To illustrate the intrapersonal preoccupation of psychologists studying social problems, we examined the first six months' issues of the 1970 *Psychological Abstracts* (Volume 44, Numbers 1–6, plus the semiannual index). We took as an example the research dealing with black Americans, who represent the largest, most visible, and most frequently studied group in a problematic relationship to the rest of society.

The following criteria were used for deciding

---

[4] Our assertion is not inconsistent with, nor should it be confused with, Carlson's (1971) recent claim of a "generalist" bias in personality research (i.e., the tendency to concentrate on the effect of different experimental conditions on individuals, irrespective of individual differences). Her claim is relevant to a particular area of academic psychology, while we are concerned with the psychologist's research orientation to social problems. While the claim of her insightful and persuasive paper may be valid for the area to which she refers, we are convinced that quite another viewpoint is adopted when the psychologist turns toward the real world and its problems.

whether a particular abstract should be included in the categorization:

1. We selected those items that either mentioned blacks specifically or were included under the index heading "Negro."

2. Abstracts from clearly nonpsychological journals (such as those for sociology, political science, etc.) were excluded, not because such journals are not of interest to psychologists, but because psychologists are less likely to publish in them.

3. Because our interest is in American psychology, abstracts were included only if they appeared in a journal published in the United States or if the author was based in the United States.

4. PhD dissertations were excluded.

5. Because we are concerned with psychological research, only data-based research studies were used. We excluded case reports, review articles, and general discussions of the topic.

We sorted each abstract that met the above criteria into categories based on (*a*) the types of variables studied (i.e., person versus situation) and (*b*) the causal relationships between them as interpreted by the authors. We found a total of 69 items that could be meaningfully categorized. The categories, together with the percentage of the

abstracts that fell into each of them, are presented in Table 1.

Authors of Category 1 studies, containing 15% of the research articles, reported an association between a problem characteristic and a personal characteristic and concluded that the personal characteristic is the cause of the problem. Thus, this category of studies lends itself most readily to person-blame interpretations. Category 2, containing 19% of the studies, also permits such interpretations, especially among those readers (whether social scientists or not) who do not concern themselves with the finer points of the logic of causal proof. While the authors of such studies make no explicit causal inferences regarding two correlated variables, the nature of the person-centered variables is such that a causal relation seems so plausible that the reader is easily led to conclude that the cause of the problem is psychological. Studies of the kind in Category 8, into which 48% of the studies fall, can also be pressed into service for person-blame interpretations of social problems, especially in view of the fact that a majority of such studies which could be compared cross-racially put blacks in an unfavorable light. Of the 33 abstracts which fell into this category, 14 reported unfavorable

TABLE 1   *Distribution of Types of Causal Attribution in Research on Black Americans Found in* Psychological Abstracts, *1970,* **44,** *No. 1–6*

Category	Variable type	Type and direction of association	Variable type	% of abstracts
1	Personal characteristic[a]	Causal →→→→	Problem characteristic[b]	15
2	Personal characteristic	Correlation	Problem characteristic	19
3	Personal characteristic[b]	←←← Causal	Problem characteristic[a]	0
4	Situational or environmental characteristic[a]	Causal →→→→	Problem characteristic[b]	16
5	Situational or environmental characteristic	Correlation	Problem characteristic	0
6	Situational or environmental characteristic[b]	←←← Causal	Problem characteristic[a]	3
7	Both personal and situational characteristics[a]	Causal →→→→	Problem characteristic[b]	0
8[c]	Group membership (e.g., black or white)	Correlation	Personal characteristics	48
9	Group membership (e.g., black or white)	Correlation	Situational characteristics	0

[a] Independent variable.
[b] Dependent variable.
[c] To illustrate the difference between Category 8 and Categories 1 and 2, let us take a hypothetical example. If a study merely documented the existence of an alleged "deficit" in blacks as compared to whites, it would fall into Category 8. If, however, the study tried to relate an alleged "deficit" among blacks (e.g., in standard English language skills) to another socially relevant "problem" of blacks (e.g., educational underachievement), then it fell into either Category 1 or 2 depending on whether a causal relation was specified or not.

comparisons of blacks to whites, 2 showed blacks' performance as better than whites', and 6 reported no differences. (Eleven could not be evaluated cross-racially.)

Categories 4, 5, and 7 are amenable to system-blame interpretations of social problems. Of these, only Category 4, with 16% of the articles, contains any entries. It is noteworthy that no studies were found in Category 7, which is often held up as a model for social psychologists to follow.[5]

[5] Despite our emphasis on the necessity of acknowledging the causal role played by environmental factors, we do not believe that this is enough, for even explanations that employ situational factors can be twisted into playing a person-blaming role. Ryan (1971) eloquently described such interpretations:

> Victim-blaming is often cloaked in kindness and concern, and bears all the trappings and statistical furbelows of scientism; it is obscured by a perfumed haze of humanitarianism . . . and those who practice this art display a deep concern for the victims that is quite genuine. . . . Its adherents include sympathetic social scientists with social consciences in good working order, and liberal politicians with a genuine commitment to reform. . . . They indignantly condemn any notions of innate wickedness or genetic defect. "The Negro is *not born* inferior," they shout apoplectically. "Force of circumstance," they explain in reasonable tones, "has *made* him inferior" [pp. 6–7].

Whereas earlier, more conservative ideologies attributed the position of blacks in society to intrinsic or inherent defects, the new ones described by Ryan stress environmental causation.

> The new ideology attributes defect and inadequacy to the malignant nature of poverty, injustice, slum life, and racial difficulties. The stigma that marks the victim and accounts for his victimization is an acquired stigma, a stigma of social, rather than genetic, origin. But the stigma, the defect, the fatal difference—though derived in the past from environmental forces—is still located within the victim, inside his skin. With such an elegant formulation, the humanitarian can have it both ways. He can, all at the same time, concentrate his charitable interest in the defects of the victim, condemn the vague social and environmental stresses that produced the defect (some time ago), and ignore the continuing effect of victimizing social forces (right now). It is a brilliant ideology for justifying a perverse form of social action designed to change, not society, as one might expect, but rather society's victim [pp. 6–7].

Ryan argues persuasively that it is not personal defects produced by past environmental influences that account for blacks' social and economic position in society, but rather the present and continuing effects of situational forces acting upon individuals who, given the same opportunities as most of the rest of us, would do equally well or poorly. This is certainly a credible hypothesis and one as worthy of scientific testing as any other.

Another closely related question demonstrates the inadequacy of simply acknowledging that situational forces play determining roles in the emergence of social problems. This is the question of whether particular problems produced by the social structure are inherent in that structure and occur inevitably because of internal contradictions

Although this is admittedly a crude way of measuring fairly complex phenomena, the picture that emerges is one of psychologists investing disproportionate amounts of time, funds, and energy in studies that lend themselves, directly or by implication, to interpreting the difficulties of black Americans in terms of personal shortcomings. Combining Categories 1, 2, and 8, we see that 82% of the classifiable psychological research dealing with black Americans reported in the six months of *Psychological Abstracts* under study are of this sort. It should be clearly understood that we do not condemn this preoccupation in and of itself, but rather because it overlooks the importance of other kinds of forces that operate on black Americans, and thereby reinforces the negative labeling of a group already politically and socially vulnerable.[6]

within the structure, or whether instead they are merely mistakes or unforeseen consequences, perhaps caused by significant but essentially random processes. The answer to this question will have profound implications for the policies proposed, for if the problems are seen as manifestations of the essential nature of the system as it normally operates, then policies that go farther to fundamentally restructure the system will be proposed.

[6] As with telephone books, reading *Psychological Abstracts* can be instructive in ways not intended by those who compiled or organized it. Some peripherally relevant observations: (a) Although *Psychological Abstracts* abstracts articles from the journal *Social Problems* (roughly, sociology's counterpart to SPSSI's *Journal of Social Issues*), there is no category by that name or any variation of it in the subject index. (b) In the format outline used by *Psychological Abstracts,* the areas of crime, juvenile delinquency, and drug addiction are among those grouped under the subheading of Behavior Disorder within the division of Clinical Psychology—again illustrating the bias of the field. (c) Perhaps reflecting their missionary zeal, Mental Health and Psychological Services listings can be found under the index heading Social Movements. (d) Even in the act of trying to select social problem areas with which to illustrate our thesis, our assertion was substantiated. Almost all "problems" listed are those of individuals or conventionally defined categories of persons. One searches in vain for serious treatment—whether as dependent, independent, or merely correlated variables—of social *system* variables as they may relate to those psychological variables with which psychologists ordinarily concern themselves. Examples of social system variables that one might expect to play a role of some consequence are the following: the concentration of wealth and power, unequal educational or occupational opportunity, particularistic dispensation of justice at the hands of the police and the judicial system, national budgetary priorities for destructive as compared to social welfare purposes, and the militarization of the economy. (Psychologists should not be singled out for criticism on this point, since until recently the standard sociological works on "social problems," "deviance," and the like, have also focused to a large extent on individuals, for example, crime, juvenile delinquency, alcoholism, suicide, etc.) Possible exceptions might include organizational (i.e., business and industrial) analysis and occasional use of variables that represent summaries of individual "problems" or

The occupational orientation of psychologists and its effects. A second major reason for this preoccupation with person-centered variables pertains to career gains. There is little chance for a career-conscious psychologist to become successful by helping people who are not. But it is possible to enhance one's own position among colleagues by conducting "relevant" research as a means for pursuing theoretical rather than applied interests, while at the same time contributing to the profession as a whole by offering explanations and solutions within the paradigms of a particular discipline.

It is the good will and approval of our colleagues in the scientific community, not that of the target population members affected by our work, that get us ahead. A social scientist's findings may provide or influence the underlying assumptions on which

problem behavior (e.g., crime rates, the magnitude of poverty in the United States, etc.). Another possible exception involves the uncharacteristic analysis of certain kinds of problem behavior (e.g., riots) in terms of a "system breakdown." For cogent critiques of this often misused concept, see Coser (1956) and Buckley (1967).

Finally, we share with the reader a few items which came to our attention in our search of the abstracts. Admittedly, these are the more extreme examples of the tendencies to which this article refers, but it must be recognized that they differ only in degree and not in kind. The subject index description of a dissertation study (No. 564) concerned with attitudes toward "handicapped groups" reads as follows: "public vs. private attitudes toward stutterers & cerebral palsied & blind & Negroes." A study of conscientious objectors (No. 677) belonging to a fundamentalist religious sect showed "extraordinary inhibition of aggression" on their part, on the basis of MMPI scale scores which were "higher than *other* federal prisoners or *non*criminals" (authors' italics). A shallow understanding of the roots of urban disorders was evident in two other reports. One author investigating "use patterns & the effects of mass media" on black ghetto residents (No. 3570) stated that his results support the hypothesis that "open communication channels would lessen the tendency to riot." The second report (No. 2248), summarizing four studies of the Detroit riots, reported that results "revealed an obvious lack of communication between the black and the power structures. . . . It is suggested that psychiatry be used to further understand these matters." Showing that no bit of common wisdom is immune from the scrutiny of empirical investigation, another author (No. 2191) evaluated inner-city black youths' sense of rhythm, tonal memory, and other musical talents, finding them "markedly deficient" by test standards (although he holds out the possibility that such "standardized testing programs" may be inappropriate for such populations). "Suicide, and white reformatory girls' preference for Negro men" was the subject of an article (No. 8798) which concluded that this preference results from both groups' rejection by society and feelings of worthlessness. The abstract of an article entitled "The Irrational in Economic Behavior" (No. 6825), although vague, suggested a focus on the individual consumer's irrationality and contained no hint of any recognition of such forces as ubiquitous advertising and a need-creating, redundant economy which may induce persons to act counter to their own best interests.

"corrective" programs affecting thousands or perhaps millions of persons will be predicated. It is ironic, then, that his career gains will depend more on his contribution to the advancement of his discipline from studying applied problems than on the success or failure of those programs.

This would not be a cause for such serious concern if, as tends to be the case in academic psychology, the only risk is that of bad or incorrect theory. But, what is good for science and the individual scientist may not be good for those on whom the research is based. As we have recently seen, to talk of hereditary and environmental effects on intelligence (long a concern of psychologists) means one thing when discussed in terms of its relevance to psychological theory, but quite another when applied to those in a problematic relationship to the rest of society (cf. Jensen and his critics in *Environment, Heredity, and Intelligence*). Similarly, to focus on the role of different nuclear family units and their consequences on childhood development is one thing when discussed on theoretical grounds and another when applied to real groups living under extraordinarily difficult circumstances (cf. Moynihan's *The Negro Family* and the ensuing controversy).

The repercussions of our research findings—the views of the world they inspire or perpetuate—may seem like epiphenomena to us, but they are often painfully real for those affected by them. Thus, psychology as a profession has special reason to consider a more balanced approach in the selection of variables for the study of social problems. In addition to the usual reason for acknowledging the necessity of such an approach, namely, that any discipline-bound approach to any given social problem is at best only partially correct and at worst just plain wrong, psychologists have added reason to show caution: person-blame explanations of social problems, *whether valid or not*, hold the potential for reinforcing established stereotypes and thereby perpetuating the condition of the "problem" group.

A closely related set of incentives further contributes to the psychologist's bias toward person-centered research on social problems. It is based, in part, on Becker's (1970) notion of a "hierarchy of credibility":

In any system of ranked groups, participants take it as given that members of the highest group have the right to define the way things really are. . . . From the point of view of the well socialized participant in the system, any tale told by those at the top intrinsically deserves to be regarded as the most credible account obtainable. . . . And since . . . matters of rank and status are contained in the mores, this belief has a moral quality. We are, if we are proper members of the group, morally bound to accept the definition imposed on reality by a superordinate group in preference to the definitions espoused by subordinates. . . . By refusing to accept the hierarchy of credibility, we express disrespect for the entire established order [p. 18].

Thus, when authorities offer person-blame explanations for particular social problems and make research funds available, suddenly one's disciplinary outlook, career gains, and socially acceptable behavior all converge for the psychologist. By investigating a social problem in terms given him, a *mutually beneficial exchange relationship* is established: the researcher is rewarded both materially and in terms of prestige (in addition to remaining a "proper member of the group") by using the tools of his trade; while on the other side of the exchange, officialdom stands to have its preferred interpretation buttressed by the respectability of "scientific data."

Little has been said in this section about the political and social context of psychological research on social problems for the purpose of illustrating the implications of such research, independent of other considerations. Even under the most ideal conditions of a conscientious, well-meaning, responsive government and populace, on the basis of psychological research, person-blame definitions of social problems would be the likely outcome. Given the actual nature of government and the political process, however, this outcome is made even more certain, except that the consequences are likely to be less benign for the "problem" group. In the next section we will consider these broader issues in order to understand (*a*) why person-centered research findings lead so quickly to person-blame public interpretations, and, in turn, (*b*) the social and political conditions favorable for the emergence of, and the uncritical willingness among policy planners to embrace, person-blame interpretations.

Utility of Person-Blame Problem Definitions

PROBLEM IDENTIFICATION

Every society attempts to characterize its deviant segments as problematic, and therefore as candidates for change, sometimes because they represent a breach of norms and folkways, and at other times for purely political or interest-based reasons. But the social scientist who becomes "relevant" seldom questions already established problem definitions,

or the wisdom behind the process that leads to the identification of so-called social problems. Nor does he question whose ends are served by the entire definitional process and by his participation in that process. Instead he waits in the wings until the problems have been selected for attention. Only then does he become involved, as if accepting as given that (*a*) whatever becomes identified publicly as a social problem is a genuine problem, derived from universally recognized truths; and (*b*) the problem is of such priority that it deserves attention over other problems that go unattended or unrecognized.

Why does one kind of poverty concern us, and another does not? Why do we constantly study the poor rather than the nonpoor in order to understand the origins of poverty? Why do we study nonachievement among minority group members as undesirable behavior, but do not study exaggerated profit motive among "successful" businessmen as a form of deviance? Why do we study the use of marijuana as a "drug problem," but not federal government involvement in the drugging of "minimal brain dysfunction" (MBD) children in our grammar schools? Why is it illegal to be a "wetback" but not to hire one (cf. Bustamante, 1972)?

These kinds of questions are rarely raised. Yet the social scientist should understand that by his involvement *qua* scientific authority in research, treatment, and planning operations, he has—consciously or unconsciously, explicitly or implicitly—lent credibility and legitimation to a given problem as publicly defined and the treatment program launched to deal with that problem.

Certain groups within society become continually stigmatized as problem groups (e.g., migratory workers, mental patients, blacks, the poor) because they are visible and accessible, but, most especially, because they are vulnerable to the social scientist for research purposes. In this sense the criteria by which social scientists select "problem" groups for study are not unlike the criteria by which the wider culture selects certain groups as scapegoats. Indeed, the former process often follows the lead of the latter. Nonachieving lower income children are more identifiable and accessible as a research population than are greedy "entrepreneurially motivated" slum landlords, for example, and they command far less countervailing power and resources than do the landlords. Thus, there is much person-centered research data to justify initiating a program such as Head Start (all of the data suggesting, essentially, that it is the child who fails, rather than the school and the educational system). But, by contrast, there is a lack of data on landlords, bankers, and city officials who permit building code violations that would justify using them as targets for person-change treatment efforts.

Moreover, just as we must concern ourselves with whose problem definition we are being asked to validate, we must constantly examine what is *not* being done. Social ills which are ignored through oversight, ignorance, or deliberate non-issue-making may be as important as those "problems" that become issues. Dubos (1970) said:

> The greatest crime committed in American cities may not be murder, rape, or robbery, but rather the wholesale and constant exposure of children to noise, ugliness and garbage in the street, thereby conditioning them to accept public squalor as the normal state of affairs [p. 14].

These issues are of particular concern at this time because of the rise of interest in social indicators. It would be expected that those charged with the responsibility of conducting such research would use this opportunity to participate in identifying social problems and thereby make the study of social indicators something more than social seismology. But this seems unlikely, judging from Bauer (1969), one of the movement's main advocates:

> The decision to observe a phenomenon implies a decision to be responsible for it, if such responsibility is within one's own power. . . . It is wisdom, not cynicism, to urge caution in extending diagnostic measures of social phenomena beyond the system's capacity to respond to the problems which are unveiled [p. 67].

Contrary to the Dubos position, Bauer implies that something becomes a social problem only if it is politically feasible to deal with it. As long as such attitudes prevail among the leaders of the social indicator movement, there should be no question as to whose welfare and interests—dominant political and economic interests, or the wider society—will be served by the selection and gathering of social indicators. If social scientists choose to be morally indifferent social bookkeepers and leave the selection of indicators and their use in the hands of others, then, to use Biderman's (1966) term, social "vindicators" would be a better name for such measures. If our apprehensions are confirmed, these vindicators will take the form of person-blame data collected for the political management of guilt and culpability.

BLAME DISPLACEMENT AND THE USE OF SOCIAL SCIENTISTS

Whether or not the problems we study are true social problems, or whether they deserve the at-

tention that they receive vis-à-vis other social ills, is open to debate. However, a more serious and less obvious danger is *the use of social science and social scientists to displace the blame for prior political and technological failures.* Such failures are often the end result of a series of short-run political and technological accommodations for which there may no longer be either short- or long-term political, technological, or social solutions. But because breakdowns in the political-economic system produce serious social *consequences,* social scientists are called on to deal with these so-called "social" problems. Their involvement carries with it the implication that socially undesirable behavior *is the problem,* rather than the inevitable by-product of political trade-offs and technological fixes, thereby distracting attention from the real causes. Kramer (1970) succinctly warned: "Never forget that your research may seem like an end in itself to you, but to rank outsiders with other agendas, it may be a means to other goals [p. 32]."

To a substantial extent, transportation, public housing, education, environmental pollution, possibly even drugs, and many other such problems associated with the management of urban life fall into this category. Public housing problems provide a good example. At the early planning stages the important decisions about such housing are often based solely on political and technological grounds, for example, the level and timing of appropriations, the selection of sites, the choice of building materials and design, and production methods. It is only after the housing is completed and people do not want to live in it, or are afraid to live in it, or those who live in it do not behave in some desired way, that public housing becomes viewed as a problem requiring social science expertise, and thereafter becomes publicly defined as a "social" problem. The "problem" behavior may in fact be a straightforward reaction to external realities in the immediate environment. But, by a process of causal inversion, the victims of poor planning become treated as if they were the cause of the situation in which they find themselves.

THE NEGOTIATION OF REALITY [7]

Perhaps one of the more important but subtle political advantages of person-blame research is that it can permit authorities to control troublesome segments of the population under the guise of being helpful, even indulgent. Normally one would expect that those who control power and resources

[7] The phrase is borrowed from Scheff (1968).

would be unrelentingly noncooperative with system-antagonistic "problem" groups. "Cooperation" with such groups is possible, however, if a person-blame rather than system-blame action program can be negotiated. Thus, they can be "helpful" as long as the way in which the target group is helped serves the interests of those offering assistance. Under these circumstances the definitional process remains in the control of the would-be benefactor, and "help" will be forthcoming as long as the public definitions of the real problem behind the system-antagonistic ·acts are explained in person-centered terms.[8] The system-antagonistic poor become "deserving" of help only if they accept personal blame for their social and economic position in society; that is, because of personal impediments, they would be unable to effectuate personal and social goals even under the most ideal conditions. Otherwise, they remain "undeserving" of help and are ignored or controlled through the exercise of negative sanctions.

For example, in 1969, a group of Indians occupied and attempted to reclaim Alcatraz Island shortly after its use as a prison facility had been discontinued. They argued that it should rightfully be returned to them since it was in effect surplus federal land. The government refused to recognize the legitimacy of their claim and made it exceedingly difficult for the group to survive on the island. Finally, after two years, the Indians were forcibly removed.

These events in San Francisco Bay contrast with a similar incident on the opposite coast. In the summer of 1970, a small group of blacks landed on Ellis Island in New York Harbor and attempted to claim it because, like Alcatraz, it was federal land no longer being used. They were immediately threatened with expulsion, and the illegality of their actions was made public. After several days of negotiation, however, authorities agreed to provide a major drug rehabilitation center on the island, and the dispute was thus settled.

The outcomes on Alcatraz and Ellis Island might have been reversed, however, if the Indians had agreed to the establishment of a treatment center for alcoholism among Indians (thus adding credibility to a stereotyped person-blame explanation to account for their social and economic position in America), and if the blacks had denounced white repression and demanded to use Ellis Island as the base for establishing an independent black nation.

We do not mean to appear unduly alarmist by implying that every problem group, particularly those who are system antagonistic, has a rendezvous with a deviancy label, nor that the social sciences will inevitably become insidious political arms of the state, nor that the government will go to the extreme of hospitalizing its political opponents as mentally ill. We have not come to that, nor are we likely to, at least not in the near future. We should realize, however, that the potential for manipulation of problem definitions for purely political ends, while now only partially realized, could become a fully exploited reality.

Summary and Conclusions: Truth or Consequences

CAUSAL ATTRIBUTION BIAS

We have demonstrated the existence of a person-centered preoccupation and causal attribution bias in psychological research which, when applied to social problems, favors explanations in terms of the personal characteristics of those experiencing the problem, while disregarding the possible influence of external forces. Because of the ominous prospects that can ensue from the narrowly circumscribed range of action possibilities derivable from person-centered data, there is reason to question whether such findings would be a suitable foundation for the development and promulgation of ameliorative programs.

Because these issues are complex and their implications are far reaching, we should caution the reader against possible misinterpretations. First, we are not concerned with which academic disciplines have a hegemony over truth. We are not saying that person-centered variables are less valid or etiologically less important than situational variables in accounting for social problems. Second, we do not object to psychologically oriented research on social problems because it offends our sense of egalitarianism by documenting individual or group differences. Such differences may or may not exist, but that alone is not our concern here. Third, the reader should not conclude that we are blindly enamored of an approach that stresses environmental factors to the exclusion of person-centered factors. That would be an error in the opposite direction.[9] Instead, our concern is not

[8] Scheff (1968) discussed analogous relationships between psychotherapists and their patients, and between defense lawyers and their clients.

[9] A dogmatic system-blame orientation has its own dangers, in addition to also being part of the truth. Just as such an orientation once liberated man from supernatural or biological conceptions of his destiny, it may now become increasingly repressive of man's initiative and spirit. Reifying environmental factors as causal agents

with the truth of propositions about human behavior so much as with their social, political, economic, and human consequences.

FUNCTIONS OF PERSON-BLAME RESEARCH

Although the initial intent behind the use of psychological research and analysis on social problems may have been an effort of responsible government to be responsive to human needs, because the data psychologists provide stress person-centered impediments to account for societal problems, they serve other ends as well. We have distinguished at least five latent functions of person-blame interpretations of social problems.

1. They offer a convenient apology for freeing the government and primary cultural institutions from blame for the problem.

2. Since those institutions are apparently not the cause of the problem, it may be legitimately contended that they cannot be held responsible for amelioration. If they do provide such help, they are credited with being exceedingly humane, while gaining control over those being helped, through the manipulation of problem definitions in exchange for treatment resources.

3. Such interpretations provide and legitimate the right to initiate person-change rather than system-change treatment programs. This in turn has the following functions: (*a*) it serves as a publicly acceptable device to control troublesome segments of the population, (*b*) it distracts attention from

may deny, and thus have the effect of dampening, the autonomy and dynamism of the individual (Gouldner, 1970). This raises the serious question of people's attitudes toward their responsibility for their behavior. Unless counteracted in some way, an excessively system-blame perspective carries with it the potential for providing the individual with a ready explanation for avoiding responsibility for his own behavior.

One of the most serious philosophical and psychological problems of our age may be to provide a view of man and his surroundings that recognizes the validity of situational causality without leaving the individual feeling helpless and unable to shape his fate. Part of that view will have to contain a more complex and sophisticated view of causality than the implicit constant-sum model that most people seem to hold (i.e., the more my environment is responsible for my outcomes, the less responsible I am, and vice versa). But until that state is reached, social scientists, especially those concerned with environmental determinants of behavior and thought, have a responsibility: we must recognize that much of our work holds the potential for further eroding an already changing social order and crumbling value system; and, therefore, it may be argued that we have an obligation to put something better in the place of that which we help destroy. It is in this spirit that Miller (1969) suggested that perhaps the most radical activity that psychology can undertake is to build a new image of man, more valid and hopeful than those of the past, and to freely dispense that image to anyone who will listen.

possible systemic causes, and (*c*) it discredits system-oriented criticism. Some of these functions were illustrated in a recent, much publicized address to correctional psychologists by Judge David Bazelon (1972):

Why should we even consider fundamental social changes or massive income redistribution if the entire problem can be solved by having scientists teach the criminal class—like a group of laboratory rats—to march successfully through the maze of our society? In short, before you respond with enthusiasm to our pleas for help, you must ask yourselves whether your help is really needed, or whether you are merely engaged as magicians to perform an intriguing side-show so that the spectators will not notice the crisis in the center ring. In considering our motives for offering you a role, I think you would do well to consider how much less expensive it is to hire a thousand psychologists than to make even a minuscule change in the social and economic structure [p. 6].[10]

4. The loyalty of large numbers of the well-educated, melioristic-minded nonneedy is cemented to the national structure by means of occupational involvement in "socially relevant" managerial, treatment, and custodial roles required to deal with those persons designated as needing person-centered correction.

5. Person-blame interpretations reinforce social myths about one's degree of control over his own fate, thus rewarding the members of the great middle class by flattering their self-esteem for having "made it on their own." This in turn increases public complacency about the plight of those who have not "made it on their own."

The major conclusion that can be drawn from the above is that *person-blame interpretations are in everyone's interests except those subjected to analysis.*

Assuming that person-blame interpretations can produce the political benefits described above, the provocative question of function versus intent must be considered. Are these effects merely unforeseen consequences of decisions made for purely humanitarian reasons, or are they the products of decisions made deliberately with these political gains in mind? The more conspiratorial view would argue

[10] A few academics have pointed with undisguised glee at what they perceive to be an inherent contradiction in claims variously attributed to radicals, students, and various other critics. On the one hand, they assert, the social sciences are accused of being "irrelevant" and inconsequential; yet, on the other hand, they are also accused of being power serving. How can these both be possible? The apparent inconsistency vanishes when one recognizes that the two charges pertain to different domains, the first to those academic and theoretical issues that occupy most of the space in journals and many texts, and the second to the realm of social problems and public issues, in the ways demonstrated by this article. We regard both charges as being more accurate than false.

that such outcomes are intended, while the more benign view would hold that they are both unintended and unanticipated. Both views probably have elements of truth, but each misses the mark to some degree.

Unquestionably, conscious and deliberate use has been made of person-blame arguments, buttressed by psychologically oriented research, with a view toward protecting the established order against criticism. Although those who have relied on person-blame arguments in these ways have been associated with dominant economic, social, and political institutions, it must be emphasized that others in these same institutions have not been and would not be engaged in such activities.

Following Ryan (1971), we suggest that for most persons (including psychologists and other social scientists) who subscribe to person-blame interpretations of social problems, the functions that such explanations serve are indeed unintended and probably even unsuspected as yet. These interpretations derive largely from epistemological biases and "blinders" deeply embedded in cultural beliefs that favor person-centered interpretations of either success or failure. Citing Mannheim (1936), Ryan states that while such belief systems distort reality and serve specific functions (namely, maintaining the status quo in the interests of particular groups), the distortion is neither conscious nor intentional. Thus, in the main, person-blame interpretations have the function, but not necessarily the intent, of serving the interests of the relatively advantaged segments of the society.

In conclusion, we would like to turn our attention to the legitimacy and appropriateness of the volatile issues raised in this article, such as (*a*) what is the relative emphasis the social sciences should place on the truth of propositions about human behavior, on the one hand, and the action implications, often political, that flow from them, on the other; (*b*) to whom are social scientists responsible and to whom should they be responsible; and (*c*) more generally, what is the proper role of science and of individual scientists with regard to research on "relevant" social issues? Increasingly we will have to face such issues, both as individuals and as a profession, and the quality of our solutions will not be improved by postponing the discussion. The purpose of this article was to show why we must be wary of uncritically accepting the idea that the promotion and dissemination of social science knowledge are intrinsically good, moral, and wise. The sooner we recognize that such knowledge is not truth divorced from the realities of time, place, or *use*, the better will be our chances of making a truly responsible contribution to societal improvement.

REFERENCES

ARCHIBALD, K. Alternative orientations to social science utilization. *Social Science Information*, 1970, 9(2), 7–34.

BAUER, R. Societal feedback. In B. Gross (Ed.), *Social intelligence for America's future*. Boston: Allyn & Bacon, 1969.

BAZELON, D. L. Untitled. Address to the American Association of Correctional Psychologists' Conferences on "Psychology's Roles and Contributions in Problems of Crime, Delinquency and Corrections." Lake Wales, Florida, January 20, 1972. (Mimeo)

BECKER, H. S. Whose side are we on? In W. J. Filstead (Ed.), *Qualitative methodology: Firsthand involvement with the social world*. Chicago: Markham, 1970. (Orig. publ. in *Social Problems*, 1967, **14**, 239–247.)

BIDERMAN, A. D. Social indicators and goals. In R. Bauer (Ed.), *Social indicators*. Cambridge: M.I.T. Press, 1966.

BRIM, O. G., JR., ET AL. *Knowledge into action: Improving the nation's use of the social sciences*. (Report of the Special Commission on the Social Sciences of the National Science Board) Washington, D.C.: National Science Foundation, 1969.

BUCKLEY, W. *Sociology and modern systems theory*. Englewood Cliffs, N.J.: Prentice-Hall, 1967.

BUSTAMANTE, J. A. The "wetback" as deviant: An application of labelling theory. *American Journal of Sociology*, 1972, **77**, 706–718.

CARLSON, R. Where is the person in personality research? *Psychological Bulletin*, 1971, **75**, 203–219.

COSER, L. *The functions of social conflict*. Glencoe, Ill.: Free Press, 1956.

DUBOS, R. Life is an endless give-and-take with earth and all her creatures. *Smithsonian*, 1970, 1, 8–17.

Environment, heredity, and intelligence. (Compiled from the *Harvard Educational Review*. Reprint Series No. 2) Cambridge: Harvard Educational Review, 1969.

GOULDNER, A. Toward the radical reconstruction of sociology. *Social Policy*, 1970, May/June, 18–25.

KAPLAN, A. *The conduct of inquiry*. San Francisco: Chandler, 1964.

KRAMER, J. R. The social relevance of the psychologist. In F. Korten, S. W. Cook, & J. I. Lacey (Eds.), *Psychology and the problems of society*. Washington, D.C.: American Psychological Association, 1970.

MANNHEIM, K. *Ideology and utopia*. (Trans. by L. Worth & E. Shils) New York: Harcourt, Brace & World, 1936.

MILLER, G. A. Psychology as a means of promoting human welfare. *American Psychologist*, 1969, **24**, 1063–1075.

NATIONAL ACADEMY OF SCIENCES, Behavioral and Social Sciences Survey Committee. *The behavioral and social sciences: Outlook and needs*. Englewood Cliffs, N.J.: Prentice-Hall, 1969.

RIECKEN, H. W. Social change and social science. Address in the Science and Public Policy Series, Rockefeller University, January 26, 1972. (Mimeo)

RYAN, W. *Blaming the victim*. New York: Pantheon, 1971.

SCHEFF, T. J. Negotiating reality: Notes on power in the assessment of responsibility. *Social Problems*, 1968, **16**, 3–17.

A COMPARISON OF DELINQUENTS WITH NONDELINQUENTS ON SELF-CONCEPT, SELF-ACCEPTANCE, AND PARENTAL IDENTIFICATION

George E. Deitz

Abstract. The contention of this study was that delinquents are in conflict with themselves, parents, and society and that their aggressive activities are manifestations of subjectively felt frustration and anxiety. It was found that although delinquents do not have a lower self-concept or rate themselves lower as seen by parents, they do identify less closely with their parents (particularly the father), they are less self-accepting, and they feel less understood by their parents than do nondelinquents. The results imply that delinquents, because of disturbed relationships with their parents, are self-dissatisfied and project self-rejection and rejection of others through aggressive behavior.

A. Introduction

Sociologically, juvenile delinquency is regarded as an expression of the internalized norms of a deviant subculture which places the individual in conflict with the values of society proper.

This view is more descriptive and global in nature than explanatory. It does not provide a meaningful basis for understanding the delinquent as an individual nor does it explain why only a fraction of those from subcultural and lower socioeconomic living conditions become delinquent. Also unexplained is the fact that many individuals representative of higher socioeconomic strata become delinquent. It is imperative that essential distinctions be made between delinquent and nondelinquent behavior irrespective of demographic variables but with reference to dimensions of personality.

It is the position of this study that delinquents are partly the by-products of disturbed family relationships and that they act out their frustrations against society.

The term "juvenile delinquency" often conveys disparate meanings. To the psychologist, delinquency is seen essentially as aggressive "acting out" in a maladaptive manner. Since the occurrence of aggression usually presupposes the existence of frustration (13), it can be assumed that delinquent acts are manifestations of frustration more intense than that of their nondelinquent agemates. This is not tantamount to suggesting that aggression is the inevitable result of all frustration. Not only may some responses incompatible with aggression occupy a more dominant position on one's hierarchy, but the tendency exists for some personality types to vent hostility through indirect channels or to reverse it intropunitively. Because delinquents characteristically discharge hostility in socially unapproved ways, inner conflict is suspected. Therefore, juvenile delinquency will be construed to represent a loosely formulated syndrome of emotionally disturbed behaviors that arise out of faulty interpersonal relationships originating within the family complex. Internalized dispositions in the form of attitudes toward both oneself and others assume fundamental importance in the emotional and social adjustive potential

Reprinted with permission of the author and publisher from *Journal of Genetic Psychology*, 1969, **115**, 285–295. Copyright 1972 by the Journal Press.

of the developing human organism. The value assigned to oneself inheres within interpersonal relationships; it reflects the individual's interpretations of how he is regarded by others and determines, in turn, both his attitudes and behavior toward them.

Rogers (9) defines the "self" as a differentiated portion of the phenomenal field consisting of a pattern of conscious perceptions and values of "I" or "ME." The self develops out of the organism's interaction with the environment and introjects the values of other people. It strives for both intrapersonal and interpersonal consistency, and experiences not consistent with the self are perceived as threats.

Studies anchoring self-acceptance within social and emotional adjustment are numerous (2, 3, 5, 7, 8, 16, 19, 20). To the extent that one lacks an acceptable self-image, he perceives rejection in the actions of others toward him and responds to them accordingly.

Since one's personal frame of reference, which includes self-oriented attitudes, emanates from the process known as parental identification, it seems plausible that the degree to which one is identified with his primary models might also function as an index of personal and social adjustment (4, 11, 12, 15, 18).

It should be explained that it is not the lack of identification with parents *per se* that engenders maladjustment; but, rather, it is the more basic negative perception of oneself fostered by nonnurturant parents. To the extent that the child perceives rejection in the manner by which his parents relate to him, the identification process is stinted. This is, of course, not an all or none process. As a result of having been rejected, he will come to reject himself. In part, he will also reject those by whom he has been rejected, as well as others symbolizing their image and that of his own. Thus, self-rejection would appear to be the connecting link with behavioral impairment, as one relates both to himself and to others.

Since the basic assumption is that juvenile delinquency is a manifestation of personal and social maladjustment residing within family processes, this study predicts that delinquents will (*a*) have negative self-concepts; (*b*) be self-rejecting; (*c*) have weak identification with parents; (*d*) perceive parental rejection; and (*e*) believe themselves misunderstood by parents in comparison with nondelinquents of similar socioeconomic status.

B. Method

1. *Subjects*

The delinquent group (D group) was composed of 86 delinquents from Juvenile Hall, San Jose, California. These (*S*s) were males ranging in age from 14 to 18 with a median age of 16 years. The range in level of education was from grades 9 to 12 with a median grade of 10.

Sixty-four nondelinquent male pupils ranging in age from 14 to 18 with a median age of 15 years, from Santa Clara High School, Santa Clara, California, constituted the nondelinquent group (*N* group). The range in level of education was from 9 to 12 with a median grade of 9. This particular high school was chosen because its students, as is the case with the majority of delinquents, come disproportionately from lower socioeconomic levels.

2. *Instruments*

The primary instrument used was the Semantic Differential (S-D) developed by Osgood, Suci, and Tannenbaum (14). The S-D consists of nine scales of bipolar adjectives, such as valuable-worthless; active-passive; strong-weak. Each of the pairs of adjectives occurs on a seven-point dimension to which a rating is assigned. The nine scales are subdivided into three, each of which is represented by a single factor.

The Two-Factor Index of Social Position (T-FISP) designed by Hollingshead and Redlich (10) was used to assess social class affiliation on the basis of the S's father's education and occupation.

3. *Procedure*

The S-D was administered to all Ss on a voluntary basis in which concepts appropriate to the stated hypotheses were rated.

Differences between the two groups on the concept ME AS I REALLY AM provided a measure for Hypothesis 1.

The differences between ME AS I REALLY AM and ME AS I WOULD LIKE TO BE and between ME AS I REALLY AM and the combined concepts of FATHER AS HE REALLY IS and MOTHER AS SHE REALLY IS were tests of Hypotheses 2 and 3, respectively.

Hypothesis 4 was measured by combining the concepts ME AS MY FATHER SEES ME and ME AS MY MOTHER SEES ME which the Ss were required to rate themselves on. Hypothesis V was tested by determining the difference between the concepts ME AS I REALLY AM and the combined concepts of ME AS MY FATHER SEES ME and ME AS MY MOTHER SEES ME.

When the Ss finished rating the concepts, they were instructed to write the answers to the following three questions on the back of the test: (*a*) the occupation and education of father; (*b*) the S's own age and education; and (*c*) whether or not the S was living with both parents at the present time (in the case of the D group, prior to incarceration). The information from the first question was used in conjunction with the T-FISP to control for social class position which ranges from I to V.

The second question provided the necessary information for determining age and education homogeneity between the two groups. If question three was answered in the negative, the test was disqualified. It was felt that the S's responses to the concepts FATHER and MOTHER would be contaminated if the S did not live with both parents because of death, divorce, or miscellaneous reasons.

Both the D and N groups were administered the same tests and given the same set of instructions. The N group was tested during regular school day while attending a scheduled study period. The records of the Ss were screened by the school principal prior to the actual testing session in order to disqualify anyone who had been charged with juvenile delinquency. In addition to one test rejected for this reason, 21 were eliminated due to disqualifying responses on question three which resulted in 42 that were used for the N group.

The D group was tested during a free period at Juvenile Hall and, except for age and sex, were unselected. Of the original 86 Ss tested, 40 tests were used as 46 were eliminated for disqualifying responses given on question three.

4. *Scoring*

The raw data from the S-D are a collection of check marks on the bipolar scales. To each of the seven positions a digit, ranging from 1 to 7, is assigned. To judge the similarity between two different concepts, discrepancy scores (D scores) are used which result from determining the square root of the sum of the squared differences between concepts on each factor.

The D scores between groups were ranked and checked for significance by the nonparametric Mann Whitney U Test. For checking the difference between the two groups on the same concept, the medians of the sums of factor scores were used.

C. Results

1. Socioeconomic Distribution

One of the basic assumptions to be met prior to testing the main hypotheses is that of social class homogeneity between the two samples.

The two groups were found to be perfectly matched on all but level II in which there were two Ss in the N group. Whatever other differences exist with regard to the stated hypotheses are thus not attributable to differential class membership.

2. Self-attitudes

Hypothesis 1. The first hypothesis predicted that the D group will rate themselves lower on the concept ME AS I REALLY AM than the N group. The raw scores ranging from 1 to 7 were compared for the two groups. Low scores are indicative of a positive self-concept and high scores of a negative self-concept. In a one-tailed test, the ranked scores between the two groups produced a U of 799 which lacks significance ($Z = -.38$; $p = .3520$). Thus the D group was found not to have a lower self-concept than the N group.

Hypothesis 2. The second hypothesis stated that the D group will have greater discrepancy between the concepts ME AS I REALLY AM and ME AS I WOULD LIKE TO BE than the N group. The results were significant as the U obtained from the ranked scores was $Z = -2.16$; $p = .0154$. This discrepancy between the real and ideal self is used as an index of self-acceptance and implies that delinquents are less self-accepting than nondelinquents.

Because the D group did not rate themselves significantly lower on self-concept and yet did exhibit greater self-dissatisfaction than the N group, the ideal self-concept scores were compared. The U of 589 was highly significant ($Z = -2.33$; $p = .0099$), indicating that the self-expectations of the D group were greater than for the N group.

3. Parental Identification

The following hypotheses were concerned with the assumed similarity between the subject and his parents. The comparison was made between self-descriptions and descriptions of parents made by the subject.

Hypothesis 3. The third hypothesis stated that the D group will have a greater D score between the concept ME AS I REALLY AM and the concept of both parents AS THEY REALLY ARE than will the N group. When the D scores for ME-MOTHER and ME-FATHER were combined and ranked for the two groups, a U of 581.5 was obtained which is significant ($Z = -2.39$; $p = .0084$). Thus, nondelinquents identify more closely with their parents than do delinquents.

Because such a large difference occurred in the degree to which the two groups identify with their parents, it seemed appropriate to examine the strength of identification with each of the individual parents. The D scores for ME-FATHER were significantly greater for the D group than they were for the N group ($Z = -2.66$; $p = .0039$); however, the D scores for ME-MOTHER did not significantly differentiate the two groups ($Z = -1.56$; $p = .0594$). Although the .05 level has been used to determine significance, this latter finding is sufficiently strong to imply a relationship.

4. *Perceived Parental Attitudes*

Hypothesis 4. The fourth hypothesis stated that the D group will rate themselves lower on the concept ME AS MY PARENTS SEE ME than the N group. The results failed to confirm the prediction as the U of 761.5 lacked significance ($Z = -.73$; $p = .2327$). A closer inspection showed that the D group neither rated themselves significantly different as seen by father ($Z = -1.1$; $p = .1357$) nor as seen by mother ($Z = -.46$; $p = .3238$) than the N group.

Hypothesis 5. The fifth hypothesis stated that the D group will have significantly greater D score between the concept ME AS I REALLY AM and the concept ME AS SEEN BY BOTH PARENTS than will the N group. This hypothesis was confirmed as the difference in the D scores yielded a significant U of 477 ($Z = -3.37$; $p = .0003$). When the score for each parent was treated separately, it was found that the D score for ME-SEEN BY FATHER was significantly larger for the D group than for the N group ($Z = -3.31$; $p = .0005$). This was also true of the D score for ME-SEEN BY MOTHER ($Z = -2.17$; $p = .01500$). Thus, delinquents believe themselves to be less accurately perceived by their parents than nondelinquents.

D. DISCUSSION

The sociological approach which views delinquency as basically a lower socioeconomic or subcultural problem fails to explain why not all juvenile members of lower class status become delinquent and why conditions which supposedly give rise to delinquency also generate responsible, productive behavior.

It is evident that the task of "explaining" delinquency must center upon concepts dealing with psychological phenomena and the probability of personality disorganization. The basic assumption of this investigation is that delinquents represent internalized conflict which disturbs their relations with themselves and with members of society. In conjunction with this notion several hypotheses were tested.

The first hypothesis which states that delinquents would exemplify self-concepts lower than that for nondelinquents failed to be confirmed. This could mean that in terms of self-concept, the behavioral dichotomy delinquency-nondelinquency is either unrealistic or possibly that other sources of explanation exist. Reckless, Dinitz, and Kay (16) contend that the two groups can be distinguished from one another on the basis of self-concept. Unfortunately, the criteria used in evaluation were not described. Indications are, however, that they were measuring "social self-concept" which is a construct somewhat different from self-concept *per se*. Although Davids and Lawton (5) demonstrated that emotionally disturbed subjects do have lower self-concepts than normals, they were using a projective device. It is possible that since the purpose of the S-D used in the present study is relatively obvious, the delinquent defense system failed to be penetrated. If the assumption of their pathology is valid, the defense system might tend to be more impermeable and rigid than for the nondelinquents.

The tendency to give socially desirable responses is an additional consideration (6). Due to the guilt inducing effects of incarceration and social ostracism, delinquents might be inclined to project a favorable self-image as a means for expiating anxiety. This assumption would be consistent with the incidental finding that delinquents also tend to have unusually high self-expectations (ME AS I WOULD LIKE TO BE). In aspiring to an elevated self-ideal they are able to rationalize and atone for the fact of their misconduct. This is precisely what nondelinquents are not forced to do, since their actual self-image is not an uncomfortable burden to them. Since the behavior of delinquents by definition is nonconstructive, it can either be assumed that an unrealistically high self-ideal is defensive in nature: i.e., an attempt to bolster the actual self-image by creating standards leading to self-improvement, or that it possibly represents an image sought for itself with no secondary rewards other than its own actualization. Either way, the unquestionable net effect is subjectively felt frustration and anxiety.

In relation to the confirmation of the second hypothesis, delinquent self-dissatisfaction seems crucial to the understanding of the dynamics underlying their interpersonal relationships. More important than the level of self-concept is the degree of self-acceptance. It is entirely conceivable that minimal self-dissatisfaction represents better adjustment independent of the level at which one construes his actual self. Self-acceptance is basic both to emotional adjustment (2, 3) and to the acceptance of others (8, 20). Whether or not the nonacceptance of others can be translated into a need for aggression toward others or possibly symbolically toward society remains conjectural. Other factors must be considered such as competing responses, exposure to aggressive models, and the extent to which one needs the dependent support and acceptance of an aggressive peer group. Nevertheless, it seems altogether plausible that frustration, anxiety, and instigation to aggression can be quite intense in a self-rejecting individual who rejects those in whom he has perceived rejection.

The results of the third hypothesis suggest disturbed parent-child relationships to have some possible etiological relevance in the development of the delinquent syndrome. Many studies have shown a strong positive relationship between parental identification and personal and social adjustment. In the case of male children, the father-son attachment appears crucial (11, 18). The family is an interrelated, interdependent system of roles. The removal or malfunctioning of one of the component parts stultifies the internal regulation of the system as a whole in which certain anomalies may arise. The father-absent home, for example, has been known to foment abnormal characteristics in male offspring, mainly in the form of untypical male-type traits, which may not be reversible in later years (17). The normal process includes identification with both mother and father but with slightly greater emphasis on the parent of the same sex. Many factors affect the identification process. Parents should be nurturant, competent, noncompetitive with one another, approximate to the ideal type, and should manifest sexually appropriate traits. Culturally, behavior is sex-typed and we are expected to conform to the limitations of stereotypic ideals. Since one's self-concept is infused with sexual components, it is necessary for males in relating both to women and men in adult life to have the benefit of internalized dispositions that result from close and intimate interaction with a competent and rewarding father whose behavior approximates the socially desired role. The mother is an equally important participant in this enterprise. Through the personification of a misinterpreted role she can debilitate the father-son attachment and undermine the son's self-identity to the extent that it may result in unstable interpersonal relationships.

In relation to the above, the lack of confirmation for Hypothesis 4 was not anticipated. Paternal rejection would be one of the suspected reasons for the lack of parental identification, and yet delinquents do not perceive themselves as being more rejected by their fathers than do nondelinquents. A tentative explanation is that rejection is only one of the conditions of weak parental identification. The image of competence that the father presents in this ongoing process is equally important. Thus even in lieu of perceived paternal rejection, a lack of competence or mastery could weaken the father-son attachment. Another possibility is that delinquents could be protecting themselves in a way similar to their presumed tendency to evaluate themselves more favorably and thus deny the reality of paternal rejection. The parental identification ratings themselves are more subtle and do not activate the defense system. Finally, if we can assume the self-ideal ratings to be partly due to interpreted parental expectations, then the inferred paternal judgments would constitute rejection, since wide disparity exists between the two.

The confirmation of Hypothesis 5 sheds some light on the matter. Individuals desire to be understood and accepted for themselves. To be construed differently from the person one believes himself to be might constitute a possible basis for the perception of rejection. If so, rejection in the form of parental-misunderstanding may function as a determinant of nonself-acceptance and weak parental-identification.

A pattern of delinquent dynamics begins to take shape. Delinquents are less self-accepting, identify less with parents, and feel less understood by parents than nondelinquents. The final question is, "how do these variables translate themselves into aggressive, destructive activity?" Weak parental identification results in the inculcation of an underdeveloped set of predispositions to behave in socially desirable ways. When combined with dependent attachment to an aggressive peer group, it might form the nucleus of aggressive acting out. However, even though aggressive responses can be of an imitative nature (1), the fact is they are not intrinsically rewarding. Since aggression is a manifestation of, and tends to reduce frustration, it must be assumed that delinquents are experiencing internalized conflict and anxiety. The very core of this conflict would appear to be self-rejection. Because they perceive parental rejection they tend to reject both their parents and themselves and act out towards those who are generalized extensions of each. Since aggression would invite actual rejection we have the catalyst of inexorably discharged hostility which denotes the substance of the delinquent pattern.

E. Summary

Sociological approaches at best can only describe certain observable characteristics of juvenile delinquency. Explanation, however, necessitates recourse to psychic factors and personality dynamics.

The contention of this study was that delinquents are in conflict with themselves, parents, and society and that their aggressive activities are manifestations of subjectively felt frustration and anxiety.

Since previous studies have shown relationships between emotional and social stability on one hand and self-acceptance and parental identification on the other, it was predicted that delinquents would have lower self-concepts; be less self-accepting; identify less with parents; rate themselves lower as seen by parents; and feel less understood by their parents than nondelinquents.

The *S*s consisted of 40 delinquent and 42 nondelinquent males who were matched on socioeconomic status and who were living with both parents.

The procedure consisted of the administration of the Semantic Differential to all *S*s who rated six concepts (ME AS I AM; FATHER AS HE IS; MOTHER AS SHE IS; ME AS FATHER SEES ME; ME AS MOTHER SEES ME; ME AS I WOULD LIKE TO BE) according to nine scales.

It was found that while delinquents do not have a lower self-concept or rate themselves lower as seen by parents, they do identify less closely with their parents (particularly father) ; are less self-accepting; and feel less understood by their parents than nondelinquents.

The results imply that delinquents, because of disturbed relationships with their parents, are self-dissatisfied and project self-rejection and rejection of others through the medium of aggressive behavior.

REFERENCES

1. BANDURA, A., ROSS, D., & ROSS, S. Transmission of aggression through imitation of aggression models. *J. Abn. & Soc. Psychol.,* 1961, **63,** 575-582.
2. BLOCK, J., & HOBART, T. Is satisfaction with self a measure of adjustment? *J. Abn. & Soc. Psychol.,* 1955, **51,** 254-259.
3. BROWNFAIN, J. J. Stability of the self-concept as a dimension of personality. *J. Abn. & Soc. Psychol.,* 1952, **47,** 597-606.
4. CAVA, E. F., & RAUSH, H. L. Identification and the adolescent boy's perception of his father. *J. Abn. & Soc. Psychol.,* 1952, **47,** 855-857.
5. DAVIDS, A., & LAWTON, M. J. Self-concept, mother concept, and food aversions in emotionally disturbed and normal children. *J. Abn. & Soc. Psychol.,* 1961, **62,** 309-316.
6. EDWARDS, A. L. Social Desirability Variables in Personality Assessment and Research. New York: Dresden, 1957.
7. ENGEL, M. The stability of the self-concept in adolescence. *J. Abn. & Soc. Psychol.,* 1959, **58,** 211-215.
8. FEY, W. F. Acceptance by others and its relation to acceptance of self and others. *J. Abn. & Soc. Psychol.,* 1955, **50,** 274-276.
9. HALL, C., & LINDZEY, G. Theories of Personality. New York: Wiley, 1957.
10. HOLLINGSHEAD, A. B., & REDLICH, F. C. Social Class and Mental Illness. New York: Wiley, 1958.
11. LAZOWICK, L. M. On the nature of identification. *J. Abn. & Soc. Psychol.,* 1955, **51,** 175-183.
12. MANIS, M. Personal adjustment, assumed similarity to parents, and inferred parental evaluations of the self. *J. Consult. Psychol.,* 1958, **22,** 481-485.
13. MILLER, N. E., SEARS, R., MOWRER, O. H., DOBB, L. W., & DOLLARD, J. Frustration-aggression hypothesis. *Psychol. Rev.,* 1941, **48,** 337-342.
14. OSGOOD, C., SUCI, G., & TANNENBAUM, P. The Measurement of Meaning. Urbana, Ill.: Univ. Illinois Press, 1957.
15. PAYNE, D., & MUSSEN, P. H. Parent-child relations and father identification among adolescent boys. *J. Abn. & Soc. Psychol.,* 1956, **52,** 358-362.
16. RECKLESS, W. C., DINITZ, S., & KAY, B. The self-component in potential delinquency and potential nondelinquency. *Amer. Sociolog. Rev.,* 1957, **22,** 566-570.
17. SEARS, R. R., PINTLER, M. M., & SEARS, P. S. Effect of father separation on preschool children's doll play aggression. *Child Devel.,* 1946, **17,** 219-243.
18. SOPCHAK, A. Parental identification and tendency toward disorders as measured by the MMPI. *J. Abn. & Soc. Psychol.,* 1952, **47,** 159-165.
19. STOCK, D. An investigation into the interrelationships between the self-concept and feelings directed toward other persons and groups. *J. Consult. Psychol.,* 1949, **13,** 176-180.
20. SUINN, R. The relationship between self-acceptance and acceptance of others: A learning theory analysis. *J. Abn. & Soc. Psychol.,* 1961, **63,** 37-42.

SOME EGO FUNCTIONS ASSOCIATED WITH DELAY OF GRATIFICATION IN MALE DELINQUENTS[1]

Robert V. Erikson
Alan H. Roberts

Two groups of institutionalized adolescent delinquent males were individually matched on age and IQ and compared on measures of foresight and planning ability, impulsiveness, verbal delay of gratification, internal versus external control, and adjustment ratings. The experimental group consisted of boys who had chosen to live in a special cottage and attend public school even though this choice was made with the understanding that it would delay their release from the institution. The control group consisted of boys from the remaining cottages. The two groups differed in the hypothesized direction on measures of impulsiveness, verbal delay of gratification, and internal versus external control, but not on measures of foresight and planning ability or adjustment ratings.

Several recent studies of disturbed or delinquent children and adolescents have focused on ego functions (Davids, 1969; Davids, Kidder, & Reich, 1962; Davids & Parenti, 1958; Levine, Spivack, Fuschillo, & Tavernier, 1959; Spivack, Levine, & Sprigle, 1959). Singer (1955) reviewed several theories of ego development and indicated the clinical and experimental implications of these theories. Generally, the studies support the hypotheses that basic ego functions tend to be less well developed in younger children than in older children and that at any particular development level, disturbed or delinquent children demonstrate less adequate ego functioning than do less disturbed children.

Roberts and Erikson (1968) and Erikson and Roberts (1966) have demonstrated that subgroups of delinquents can be differentiated in terms of the ability to delay gratification, foresight and planfulness, and impulsivity. They also found a relationship between behavioral adjustment ratings in a training school situation and delay of gratification and impulsiveness. Their findings demonstrated a high degree of communality among these ego functions grouped around the concept of delay of gratification.

The present study was conducted in order to extend these findings by contrasting two groups of institutionalized adjudicated delinquent males. The first group consisted of all Caucasian students at a state youth develop-

ment center who lived in a special cottage and attended public school off the grounds. This experimental group is defined by a selection process which includes a staff decision that a boy is likely to succeed in a public school and the boy's agreement to live in the cottage even though this is likely to delay his release from the institution for several months or years until graduation from high school. Boys are selected to live in the cottage by a committee of the staff which is asked to decide whether the student is likely to succeed in a public school both behaviorally and academically. However, no boy is selected unless he agrees with that decision together with the clear understanding that he will probably delay his release from the institution. This is understood to be the case by all students asked to live in the cottage even though a few may ultimately leave the institution in six months or less. In the present study, 16 of the 20 experimental *S*s actually remained in the cottage for more than six months. It is understood by the staff that no boy will be coerced into making the decision to live in the cottage.

Aside from attendance in public school together with the schedule changes required by this, there are no major differences in the programs of boys living in this cottage and boys living in other cottages at the institution. There is, however, an implied emphasis on individual initiative and responsibility which complicates our operational definition of "delay of gratification" but which is consistent with it. All of the boys in this cottage have demonstrated their willingness to delay

[1] This investigation was supported in part by Social Rehabilitation Services, Research and Training Grant RT-2.

more immediate gratification (leaving the center) for future goals (attending and graduating from an outside school program) and have agreed to accept some initiative and responsibility consistent with this decision.

The boys in this group were compared with a matched sample of boys from the remaining cottages in the center and the following hypotheses were tested: (a) Ss in the special program (delayers) will demonstrate less impulsivity than will a matched group of boys from the remaining institutionalized population (controls), (b) delayers will demonstrate greater foresight and planfulness than controls, (c) delayers will demonstrate greater ability or willingness to delay gratification than controls on an independent verbal measure of delay, and (d) delayers will see their behavior as having been determined by "internal" rather than "external" controls more often than control Ss.

METHOD

Subjects

This study compared two groups of adolescent delinquent males committed to a state youth development center, an open residential institution for delinquent youths located in central Pennsylvania. The center consists of seven cottages with a combined capacity of 150 boys. In six of the cottages, boys are placed according to size and maturation level. All of these boys attend school on the grounds or participate in a work experience program such as, for example, maintenance or kitchen work. The seventh cottage houses those boys who have agreed to attend school off the grounds even though this will delay their release from the center.

The first group of Ss consists of 20 of the 27 boys living in this latter cottage (hereafter referred to as the delay group). Three of the remaining seven boys could not be matched on relevant variables with the other boys in the school, three were Negro students, and one of the boys left the school before data collection was completed. The remaining 20 Ss were matched with 20 others from the school on the basis of age (within at least four months) and IQ (within at least five points) in order to form a control group. IQ was determined by an appropriate individual intelligence test (the Stanford-Binet, WAIS, or WISC).[2] In matching the two samples, length of institutionalization was also a consideration; if there was a choice between two or more boys for the control group, the one with the longer length of stay was selected. There were no significant differences between the two groups in age, IQ, and length of stay (see Table 1).

As part of the testing procedures used, all Ss were asked the following question: "If a boy were to be released next week and he could be guaranteed that

[2] It is recognized, of course, that IQ scores from these three different tests are not precisely comparable. However, it is felt that they can be treated as though they were similar for the rough purpose of matching, even though such a procedure would be unacceptable if IQ were a dependent variable.

TABLE 1

SAMPLE CHARACTERISTICS AND PORTEUS SCORES
OF DELAYERS AND CONTROLS

Item	Delayers[a]		Controls[b]		t (df = 19)
	M	SD	M	SD	
Age (in months)	192.8	15.45	191.6	16.35	1.82
IQ	104.4	10.08	103.6	10.58	1.14
Length of stay (months)	13.7	7.53	11.2	7.85	1.08
Porteus TQ	120.4	17.34	119.1	18.85	.24
Porteus Q	20.7	14.76	39.0	21.79	3.13*

[a] N = 20.
[b] N = 20.
* p < .01.

he would not get into any further difficulty if he remained at Loysville for six more months, what do you think he would do? Leave next week or stay six more months?" Responses were categorized in terms of whether or not Ss would stay or leave. Two judges blindly and independently scored the responses with no scoring disagreements. In the delay group, 65% of the 20 Ss said they would stay, while only 20% of the 20 control Ss gave this answer. This difference is significant at the .05 level of confidence ($\chi^2 = 6.55$) and further defines the dimension upon which the two groups are being compared.

Measures

The Ss were seen individually and the following procedures were administered.

The Porteus Maze Tests. Measures of foresight and planfulness, as well as impulse control, were derived from the nonverbal Porteus Maze Tests (Porteus, 1965). This test provides two scores: a Test Quotient (TQ) which appears to measure nonverbal foresight and planning ability and a Qualitative (Q) score which is a measure of impulse control and has been demonstrated to differentiate between various groups differing in impulsiveness (Docter & Winder, 1954; Fooks & Thomas, 1957). Erikson and Roberts (1966) and Roberts and Erikson (1968) demonstrated that the TQ was significantly related to adjustment ratings of delinquents during a short two- or three-week stay in a reception center, while no relationship was found between TQ and ratings of adjustment during a much longer period of time in a training school dormitory. In the present study, the correlation between TQ and IQ was .03 while the correlation between Q and IQ was .00, both obviously not significantly different from zero. TQ and Q correlated .31 ($df = 39$, $p < .05$). The Porteus Maze Test was scored in the standard fashion (Porteus, 1965) by two independent scorers with virtually no disagreement.

Verbal delay of gratification. Each S was individually asked the following question: "A boy won $1,000 in a contest. What do you think he did with it?" and E wrote down the responses. The question was scored independently by two judges with only two disagreements. These two disagreements were resolved by a third judge. The question was scored in terms of whether S delayed spending the money or spent it immediately for some immediate gratification.

Internal versus external control. The Ss were also asked, "Why is a boy transferred to 'ZB' [the name of the delayer's cottage] cottage?" The question was designed to determine whether or not Ss perceived this experience as resulting from personal internal decisions and controls or from external decisions and controls made by others. Responses were classified as "internal" (e.g., "The boy wants to go to an outside school"), "external" (e.g., "They think he should go to an outside school"), or "neutral" (e.g., "If the boy is smart, he goes to an outside school"). There were seven disagreements between the two judges in scoring this question and these were solved by a third rater.

Adjustment. Previous studies (Erikson & Roberts, 1966; Roberts & Erikson, 1968) demonstrated that supervisor's ratings of adjustment to a training school situation are related to a verbal measure of delay of gratification, a behavioral measure of delay of gratification, and impulsiveness. These ratings were also related to foresight and planfulness when the adjustment rated is for a relatively short period of time but not for adjustment over longer periods of time. Because of this, ratings of adjustment were obtained in order to determine whether differences between the two groups could be accounted for on the basis of differences in adjustment to the school situation.

Good adjustment was defined as "obeying the rules and regulations as well as showing responsibility, maturity, and participating in the general school processes." After reviewing the meaning of the term "good adjustment" with the cottage supervisors, they were asked to rate Ss as having "good adjustment" or "poor adjustment." Those boys who could not be easily rated were placed in an intermediate category. Following this, the supervisors were asked to rate those boys in the intermediate category as either being "good" or "poor" on a forced-choice basis. All of the data were analyzed for both sets of ratings and the findings were the same in both instances. Therefore, only the dichotomous ratings which include the forced choices will be reported.

RESULTS

Porteus Maze Tests

As shown in Table 1, there is no significant difference between the Porteus TQ scores of the delay group ($M = 120.4$) and the control group ($M = 119.1$). Contrary to the hypothesis, the two groups do not differ on this measure of foresight and planfulness. In contrast to this, the control group had a significantly higher Q score ($M = 39.0$) than the delay group ($M = 20.7$) as shown in Table 1. Since higher Q scores indicate greater impulsiveness, it would seem that Ss who make a decision to attend public school and delay release from the center are less impulsive than the average student who has not made this decision.

Verbal Delay of Gratification

The frequencies of response to the verbal delay of gratification question are shown in Table 2. When asked what they would do with $1,000 they had won in a contest, 80% of the delay group responded with answers

indicating they would delay spending the money while only 35% of the control group responded in this fashion. This difference is significant at the .05 level of confidence.

Internal versus External Control

Responses to the question about why a boy goes to the special cottage are shown in Table 2. While 25% of the Ss in both groups gave responses scored as "External Control," 40% of the delay group gave "Internal Control" answers as contrasted to only 5% of the control group. Thirty-five percent of the delay group and 70% of the control group gave neutral answers. The overall chi-square (7.78) is significant beyond the .05 level of confidence.

Adjustment Ratings

There was no significant difference between the two groups on adjustment ratings. As shown in Table 2, 60% of the delay group and 50% of the control group were rated as having "good" adjustment by the cottage supervisors. Further, 2×2 analyses of variance, corrected for disproportional frequencies, were performed using the delay and control groups, and good and poor adjustment as independent variables. No significant differences on Porteus TQ or Q could be attributed to adjustment, and no significant interactions were found.

As shown in Table 3, adjustment was not significantly related to answers to the verbal delay question ($\chi^2 = 1.41$, $df = 1$). There was, however, a significant relationship ($p < .05$) between ratings of adjustment and answers to the internal versus external control question ($\chi^2 = 6.70$, $df = 2$). The findings of differ-

TABLE 2

COMPARISON OF DELAY GROUP AND CONTROL GROUP ON VERBAL DELAY OF GRATIFICATION, INTERNAL OR EXTERNAL CONTROL, AND ADJUSTMENT RATINGS

Ratings	Delay group[a]	Control group[b]	χ^2
Verbal delay			
Save	16	7	6.55*
Spend	4	13	
Internal or external control			
Internal	8	1	7.78*
External	5	5	
Neutral	7	14	
Adjustment			
Good	12	10	.10
Poor	8	10	

[a] $N = 20$.
[b] $N = 20$.
* $p < .05$.

TABLE 3

Comparison of Subjects Rated "Good" or "Poor" in Adjustment on Verbal Delay of Gratification and Internal or External Control

Rating	Good adjustment[a]	Poor adjustment[b]	χ^2
Verbal delay			
Save	15	8	1.41
Spend	7	10	
Internal or external control			
Internal	8	1	6.70*
External	6	4	
Neutral	8	13	

[a] $N = 22$.
[b] $N = 18$.
* $p < .05$.

ences in ego functions between delayers and controls in this study apparently cannot be accounted for by differences in adjustment ratings with the one exception of the perception of internal versus external control.

DISCUSSION

The findings of this study demonstrate that delinquent males who make a choice which implies an ability or willingness to delay immediate gratification for a future goal differ from other delinquents on measures of impulsiveness, verbal delay of gratification, and internal versus external control, but not on measures of foresight and planning ability or adjustment ratings. Several variables which have been demonstrated to relate to delay of gratification in previous studies were either controlled by matching or shown not to differentiate between the two groups in the present study. These include age and intelligence (Bialer, 1961; Mischel & Metzner, 1962) and ratings of institutional adjustment (Roberts & Erikson, 1968).

The nonverbal Porteus Maze TQ, used as a measure of foresight and planning, did not differentiate the two groups. While contrary to the hypothesis, the present findings are consistent with a previous study (Roberts & Erikson, 1968) which showed it to be uncorrelated with both a verbal and a behavioral measure of delay of gratification. However, there is considerable evidence that TQ is often related to social adjustment or social effectiveness (e.g., Cooper, York, Daston, & Adams, 1967; Erikson & Roberts, 1966; Karpeles, 1932; Poull & Montgomery, 1929). Apparently, when social adjustment does not vary, foresight and planning ability may be independent of delay of gratification.

However, these relationships need further investigation and clarification.

The Porteus Q score, a measure of impulsiveness, does differentiate between the two groups. The institutional control Ss were significantly higher on this measure of impulsiveness than were Ss in the delay group. This is in line with previous findings demonstrating impulsiveness to be an important factor contributing to the ability or willingness to delay gratification (Roberts & Erikson, 1968), and extends these findings by demonstrating that this relationship holds up even when the groups do not differ in ratings of adjustment. Davids' (1969) measure of motor inhibition is quite possibly related to the Porteus Q score used in this study, and he has demonstrated a similar relationship between his motor inhibition measure and a measure of delay of gratification in groups of normal and emotionally disturbed children.

The two groups differ also in the verbal measure of delay of gratification, suggesting that the behavioral delay demonstrated in making the choice to go to a public school is generalizable and is not specific to the independent variable of this study.

The delaying group also appears to feel more personally responsible for the decisions they make. The decision to go to public school is more often seen to be a function of personal control and choice by the delaying group, while neutral, impersonal reasons are given more often by the control group. These two delinquent groups did not seem to differ in the degree to which they perceive their behavior to be determined by others.

According to Freud (1953), the development of the ability to delay gratification is a major step in the shift from chaotic, diffuse primary-process thinking to synthetic, goal-directed, reality-oriented, secondary-process thinking. A major function of the ego is to synthesize, organize, and integrate past, present, and future in the service of a healthy and rewarding life. Impulsivity must often be inhibited if the individual is to attain the gratification of long-term future goals. The ability to delay gratification seems to be a critical explanatory concept for the development of socialization, and the present study comparing two groups of institutionalized delinquents provides further support for this view.

REFERENCES

Bialer, I. Conceptualization of success and failure in mentally retarded and normal children. *Journal of Personality*, 1961, **29**, 303–319.

COOPER, G. D., YORK, M. W., DASTON, P. G., & ADAMS, H. B. The Porteus Tests and various measures of intelligence with southern Negro adolescents. *American Journal of Mental Deficiency,* 1967, 71, 787–792.

DAVIDS, A. Ego functions in disturbed and normal children: Aspiration, inhibition, time estimation, and delayed gratification. *Journal of Consulting and Clinical Psychology,* 1969, 33, 61–70.

DAVIDS, A., KIDDER, C., & REICH, M. Time orientation in male and female juvenile delinquents. *Journal of Abnormal and Social Psychology,* 1962, 64, 239–240.

DAVIDS, A., & PARENTI, A. N. Time orientation and interpersonal relations of emotionally disturbed and normal children. *Journal of Abnormal and Social Psychology,* 1958, 57, 299–305.

DOCTER, R. F., & WINDER, C. L. Delinquent vs. nondelinquent performance on the Porteus Qualitative Maze Test. *Journal of Consulting Psychology,* 1954, 18, 71–73.

ERIKSON, R. V., & ROBERTS, A. H. A comparison of two groups of institutionalized delinquents on Porteus Maze Test performance. *Journal of Consulting Psychology,* 1966, 30, 567.

FOOKS, G., & THOMAS, R. Differential qualitative performances of delinquents on the Porteus Maze. *Journal of Consulting Psychology,* 1957, 21, 351–353.

FREUD, S. The interpretation of dreams. In, *The standard edition of the complete psychological works of Sigmund Freud.* Vol. 5. London: Hogarth Press, 1953.

KARPELES, L. M. A further investigation of the Porteus Maze Test as a discriminative measure in delinquency. *Journal of Applied Psychology,* 1932, 16, 427–437.

LEVINE, M., SPIVACK, G., FUSCHILLO, J., & TAVERNIER, A. Intelligence and measures of inhibition and time sense. *Journal of Clinical Psychology,* 1959, 15, 224–226.

MISCHEL, W., & METZNER, R. Preference for delayed reward as a function of age, intelligence, and length of delay interval. *Journal of Abnormal and Social Psychology,* 1962, 64, 425–431.

PORTEUS, S. D. *Porteus Maze Tests: Fifty years' application.* Palo Alto, Calif.: Pacific Books, 1965.

POULL, L. E., & MONTGOMERY, R. P. The Porteus Maze test as a discriminative measure in delinquency. *Journal of Applied Psychology,* 1929, 13, 145–151.

ROBERTS, A. H., & ERIKSON, R. V. Delay of gratification, Porteus Maze Test performance, and behavioral adjustment in a delinquent group. *Journal of Abnormal Psychology,* 1968, 73, 449–453.

SINGER, J. L. Delayed gratification and ego development: Implications for clinical and experimental research. *Journal of Consulting Psychology,* 1955, 19, 259–266.

SPIVACK, G., LEVINE, M., & SPRIGLE, H. Intelligence test performance and the delay function of the ego. *Journal of Consulting Psychology,* 1959, 23, 428–431.

DISCRIMINATION LEARNING IN JUVENILE DELINQUENTS

K. Jeffrey Schlichter
Richard G. Ratliff

Forty-five delinquent and 45 nondelinquent males were run in a two-choice discrimination task with either reward for correct responses, punishment for incorrect responses, or reward and punishment for correct and incorrect responses, respectively. The results indicated a significant Group × Reward interaction in which nondelinquent Ss learned best for punishment and delinquent Ss learned best for reward. The results were interpreted as reflecting possible group differences in reward expectancies.

In a series of recent studies, Hare (1965a, 1965b, 1965c, 1966, 1968) has found punishment to be much less effective in facilitating the learning of avoidance responses for psychopaths than for normals. If degree of social deviance and frequency of occurrence of antisocial behavior can be placed on a continuum from nondelinquent to psychopathic, it would seem reasonable to assume that the behavior of delinquent adolescents would appear between the two extremes. Thus, one might hypothesize that punishment may be a less effective means of facilitating the learning in delinquents than of facilitating the learning on the part of normals. Stated simply, the behavior of normals may be more readily controlled by punishment than the behavior of delinquents.

In order to test this notion, delinquent and nondelinquent Ss were run in a two-choice

From *Journal of Abnormal Psychology,* 1971, 77, 46–48. Copyright 1971 by the American Psychological Association. Reprinted by permission.

discrimination task with either positive reinforcement for correct responses, punishment for incorrect responses, or a combination of both positive reinforcement for correct responses and punishment for incorrect responses, respectively.

METHOD

Subjects

The Ss were 90 male students, 45 of whom were randomly selected from the population at Loysville Youth Development Center (YDC), Loysville, Pennsylvania, and 45 of whom were randomly selected from Roosevelt Junior High School, Altoona, Pennsylvania. The criteria for selection of Ss were: no record of brain damage; IQ scores between 70 and 125; ages ranging from 11 to 16; and environments financially poor and culturally deprived. In addition, the nondelinquents had no history of delinquency; and the delinquents had been incarcerated for less than 12 mo. The 45 Ss in each group were randomly assigned to one of the three experimental conditions, with an equal number of Ss at each age level in each condition. The three experimental conditions were reinforcement (R) for correct responses, punishment (P) for incorrect responses, and reinforcement-punishment (RP) for correct and incorrect responses, respectively. There were 15 Ss per cell.

Apparatus

A modified Wisconsin General Test Apparatus (WGTA), measuring 22 × 26 in., was used. In the center was a vertical masonite divider, 19 in. wide and 22 in. high. In the center of the divider was a one-way vision mirror measuring 2½ × 11 in. The entire surface area of the mirror was exposed on S's side of the screen; but only two small square openings each ½ × ½ in. were exposed on E's side of the screen. A flourescent lamp, 14 in. in length, was mounted on S's side of the apparatus 17 in. above the base of the WGTA. The manually operated tray on which the discriminanda were placed could be moved under the divider from one side to the other.

At the top of the divider above S and on his side of the WGTA were two Bogen speakers (Model D-35, 35 w.), each directed at one ear of the S from a distance of approximately 18 in. Two side shields, each 20 in. high × 34 in. long, were mounted into place after S was seated in order to prevent him from visually attending to other stimuli.

The discriminanda were two 3½-in. Masonite squares, ¼ in. thick. Each was composed of two right-angle triangles, one black and the other white. The squares were placed over the two reward wells, and S was to learn that the correct response was to choose the block that had been placed so that the base of the white triangle was down and, therefore, facing him. For Ss in the R and RP groups, a plastic poker chip 1½ in. in diameter was placed in the reward well under the correct discriminanda, thus constituting the reward for Ss in these groups. Punishment for Ss in the P and RP groups consisted of a 98-db., 2,000-cps tone, .1 sec. in duration, which was delivered immediately for incorrect responses. The tone was produced by an Eico audio generator (Model 378), amplified with a Challanger amplifier (Model CHB50) and emitted through the two speakers. The left-right positioning of the correct discriminanda was determined by a Gellerman series.

Procedure

All Ss were scheduled for individual participation in the experiment in a random order. Due to absences and other typical school problems, the schedule was flexible enough for substitution by other Ss when any given S was not available. Five minutes previous to each S's time of participation, his teacher informed him privately that he would take part in the experiment. Each S was then sent immediately to the experimental room.

When the S entered the room, E asked him to be seated at the apparatus and moved the side shields of the WGTA into place. The Ss in the R and RP group were then given the following instructions:

What I have for you today is a learning problem. In this problem you have to learn to pick up the correct block—the block with the chip under it [E showed S a chip]. You can win a chip every time, and at the end of the time you can trade in your chips for some money. The more chips you win, the more money you will get.

(The Ss were not told how much their chips were worth.) Group RP was then given the following additional instructions: "But this noise means you are wrong and losing" (tone was sounded for .1 sec.). The following instructions were given to Ss in the P group:

What I have for you today is a learning problem. In this problem you have to learn to pick up the correct block. This noise means you are wrong and losing (tone was sounded for .1 sec.).

For all Ss, E demonstrated the task twice, once for a correct response and once for an incorrect response, and then continued to S:

Now its your turn to try it. We'll do this a number of times, and each time you will have about 10 sec. to make your choice. Do you have any questions?

Following the reading of the instructions, which was done in a businesslike tone, E reread the appropriate part of the instructions if S had any questions. The E then began the 60 acquisition trials.

RESULTS

Two separate sets of analyses were performed. First, the age and the IQ scores for each group were submitted separately to a simple analysis of variance. These analyses revealed no significant differences between the groups on either age or IQ (in both instances, $F < 1$, $df = 5/84$). Also, a 2×3 repeated-measures analysis of variance was performed on the mean number of correct responses in each of the 12 blocks of five trials. This analysis revealed a significant main effect of reward conditions ($F = 4.46$, $df = 2/84$, $p < .05$) and a significant main effect of trials ($F = 6.08$, $df = 11/924$, $p < .001$). More important was the significant Group X Reward interaction ($F = 4.88$, $df = 2/84$, $p < .01$. This interaction is shown in Figure 1.

As Figure 1 shows, P produced significantly more correct responses than R ($p < .01$) and

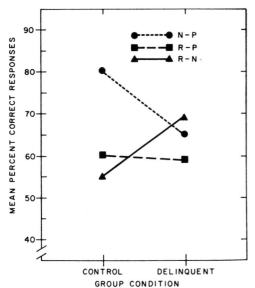

FIG. 1. Mean percent correct response as a function of group and reward conditions.

R-P ($p < .01$) for the nondelinquent group as determined by Scheffé's test for multiple contrasts (Winer, 1962). There were no significant differences between the R and R-P groups. For the delinquent Ss, Scheffé's test revealed no significant differences in performance between the P and R conditions. Similarly, there were no differences between the P and R-P groups, but the R group did show a significantly greater number of correct responses than the R-P group in the delinquent sample.

Of more interest are comparisons between delinquents and nondelinquents. Scheffé's test revealed that nondelinquents performed better in the P condition than did delinquents ($p < .01$), whereas delinquents performed better in the R condition than nondelinquents ($p < .01$). There were no significant differences between the two R-P groups.

DISCUSSION

The results of the present study support the hypothesis that punishment may facilitate learning significantly less in incarcerated delinquents than in nondelinquents. Further, the performance of delinquents was more effectively controlled by reward, whereas reward had no discernible effect on the performance of nondelinquents. Finally, neither the delinquents nor the nondelinquents showed evidence of learning in the reward-punishment condition. No explanation for this finding is readily available, but it is conceivable that the amount of information provided by combining reward and punishment may have distracted Ss from the task.

More important are possible explanations for the differences between the delinquent and nondelinquent groups. Any explanation suggesting the possibility of covert social approval of the E for Ss in either punishment group seems unlikely since interaction between Ss and E was kept at a minimum throughout the experiment—instructions were read in a businesslike tone, E was shielded behind a one-way-vision screen, S was shielded behind the side panels of the apparatus, and Ss and E had no verbal exchange throughout the trials.

Perhaps a more plausible conjecture is the probable reinforcement histories of each group with authority figures. Since S was aware that E was working with the approval of the authorities of his institution, we can assume that S regarded E as an authority. If we also assume that delinquents have experienced fewer positive reinforcements and nondelinquents, fewer punishments from authorities, it follows that positive reinforcement for delinquents and punishment for normals may represent unusual events which are contrary to their expectancies and, therefore, serve to heighten attention to the task itself. Such heightened attention should serve to facilitate performance for delinquents in the reward condition and performance for nondelinquents in the punishment condition.

For whatever reason, the finding of increased effectiveness of reward and decreased effectiveness of punishment in controlling the performance of delinquents suggests that concern should be directed toward establishing, yet more fully, the limits and determinants of the delinquents' marked responsivity to positive reinforcement so that more effective methods of prevention and treatment can be developed.

REFERENCES

HARE, R. D. Acquisition and generalization of a conditioned fear response in psychopathic and non-psychopathic criminals. *Journal of Psychology*, 1965, 59, 367–370. (a)

HARE, R. D. A conflict and learning theory analysis of psychopathic behavior. *Journal of Research in Crime and Delinquency*, 1965, 2, 12–20. (b)

HARE, R. D. Temporal gradient of rear arousal in psychopaths. *Journal of Abnormal Psychology*, 1965, 70, 442–445. (c)

HARE, R. D. Psychopathy and choice of immediate versus delayed punishment. *Journal of Abnormal Psychology*, 1966, 71, 25–29.

HARE, R. D. Psychopathy, autonomic functioning, and the orienting response. *Journal of Abnormal Psychology* 1968, 73 (3, Pt. 2).

WINER, B. J. *Statistical principles in experimental design.* New York: McGraw-Hill, 1962.

5
COMMUNICATION DISORDERS

CHAPTER NINE

VISUAL IMPAIRMENT

Several problems confront the researcher seeking accurate and generalizable information about visually impaired individuals. These problems include the operational definition of the impairment, the use of subjects from a restricted segment of the population, and the lack of control over variability in age at the onset of the condition.

Legal definitions are used to classify persons according to visual acuity and field of vision, whereas functional definitions are used to classify persons according to effective use of residual vision. Nolan (1967) observed that only about 22 percent of the persons classified as legally blind are functionally blind. Hence, contradictory research results may reflect disparate subject characteristics—that is, differences between the functional and legal levels of vision in the subjects studied.

Residential schools for the blind provide the only convenient source of visually impaired subjects for the research worker. Relative to day schools, residential institutions attract persons who have more serious visual handicaps, multiple handicaps, poorer family relationships, and lower socioeconomic status. Consequently, the generalization of relationships from residential to nonresidential visually impaired subjects requires an empirical test. Tisdall, Blackhurst, and Marks included samples of blind students from both residential and day schools and a sample of children with normal vision in their study on divergent-thinking abilities.

The integration of information from the various sensory modalities is a popular area of research on visually impaired populations. Jones studied the localization of information obtained from the visual, cutaneous, and kinesthetic senses, and Brodlie and Burke studied the presence of letter reversals and confusion in letter placement in visual and tactual word reading. The comparative study of visually impaired versus sighted groups on the understanding of concepts (for example, color, objects too large for tactual exploration, and geographical features) is another popular area of investigation. Tisdall and his colleagues reported no significant difference between blind and sighted groups on divergent-thinking tests that did not require visual familiarity with test stimuli. Further, Franks and Baird studied geographical concept attainment in visually handicapped students as a basis for improving the ability of the students to interpret embossed maps.

PERCEPTUAL LEARNING DISABILITIES IN BLIND CHILDREN

Jerome F. Brodlie
John Burke

Summary.—119 totally blind and 81 legally blind children were observed for perceptual problems in learning to read and write. Error patterns analogous to those found in sighted 'dyslexic' children were observed in about 15% of both groups. These legally blind children with perceptual deficits were first taught to read and write by sighted methods before learning Braille. A child had similar errors when learning to read or write Braille and when learning by the traditional sighted method.

Although reading difficulties may result from any one of a number of factors (e.g., emotional block, deprived educational setting), recent research efforts have focused on reading problems associated with perceptual deficit. The term dyslexia has been used to describe this pattern, although much confusion exists as to specific definitions or whether a pattern of errors characterizes all dyslexic children. A few symptoms, however, appear most often mentioned in the literature (2). Among these are: letter reversals (e.g., confusion of b for d and p for q), confusion of letter placement in words (e.g., reading 'saw' for 'was,' 'roof' for 'for'), mirror writing, right-to-left reversal of writing on paper. The dyslexic child is said to be of at least normal intelligence and to manifest weak lateralization. Although these patterns have been identified in many dyslexic children, research is needed to clarify the number and types of errors, perceptual dysfunctions, and lateralization problems found in dyslexic children.

Three major positions have been taken as to the etiology of dyslexia, i.e., dyslexia is essentially associated with a visual problem involving the mechanisms of the eye or eye muscles (3), a result of a specific lesion most likely located in that brain area responsible for perceptual functions (1), a central nervous system deficit, which is diffuse and related to a general integrative problem in perceptual and conceptual functions (4).

The present pilot study was undertaken to help clarify the etiology of learning disability in the reading skill area. A sample of 200 blind children, ages 5 through 12 yr., were classified as totally blind ($N = 119$) or incapable of any sight and as legally blind ($N = 81$) or able to see large figures and in some instances learning to read according to standard visual methods except that they read books having special large type.

Standardized interviews and questionnaires were presented to the teaching staff. Observations of all 200 students learning to read occurred in normal classroom settings and during special sessions held by a remedial reading teacher for 33 of these students. The observations were made by the authors who walked around the classroom while class was in session and watched each of the children working on normal reading and writing units. In addition, we asked each child to read and write (through sighted method or with Braille) a few sentences which permitted reversals, such as: "I saw the boy run on the roof." Also, the teachers permitted us to look over some previously produced work by each child and gave us her evaluation of the child's progress in language skills as well as psychometric and neurological evaluations where these were on file. One author was present with the teacher and student for at least one full remedial reading session for each of the children receiving this additional help.

Results.—Approximately 15% of the totally blind children who were learning to read Braille, evidenced patterns of errors analogous to those found in sighted children often classified as dyslexic. For example, (a) letter reversals, e.g., .·. for ·.· or ∴ for ∴, (b) confusion of letter placement in words, (c) poor orientation of fingers on the paper. Included in the 15% are only those who made all three types of errors and with sufficient frequency as to impede their reading progress. For all but 4 of these children the errors appear in typing Braille and in reading Braille. Except, of course, in typing Braille a machine is used so that error (c) is not found. In some instances the child's difficulties were so marked as to make reading an almost impossible task in spite of S's normal intelligence.

Reprinted with permission of the authors and publisher: Brodlie, J. F. & Burke, J. Perceptual learning disabilities in blind children. *Perceptual and Motor Skills*, 1971, **32**, 313-314.

Some children who are admitted to schools for the blind are diagnosed as legally but not totally blind. Many of these children suffer from degenerative conditions and because of increasing blindness are also taught Braille. In learning Braille, they are required to learn by touch alone. It was noted that a small percentage of the 81 legally blind children we observed while they were learning by traditional visual method were diagnosed by the school's consulting psychologist and neurologist as having perceptual problems in learning. Here, too, the standard letter and word reversals, etc., were noted. These children were referred by classroom teachers to reading specialists for remedial work which seemed to be accomplished with varying degrees of success.

These 81 legally blind children were taught Braille. After first learning according to the sighted method, (with the book having large type) those children who showed problems while learning when they were sighted had similar difficulties with Braille. The children who had frequent reversal problems with large type also had frequent letter reversals with Braille. Likewise, those children who showed orientation difficulties while they were partially sighted showed the same difficulties using Braille. This pattern was true of all of the aforementioned error patterns. Most teachers we interviewed also remarked that an unusually high percentage of blind children showed marked problems in learning and evidenced some confused laterality.

Because the present study was exploratory, these observations are quite tentative. The authors are now devising perceptual tasks not dependent upon vision for administration to matched samples of blind and sighted children to assess the nature of dyslexia in depth.

REFERENCES

1. CRITCHLEY, M. Isolation of the specific dyslexic. In A. Keeney & V. Keeney (Eds.), *Dyslexia.* St. Louis: Mosby, 1968. Pp. 17-20.
2. EISENBERG, L. Introduction. In J. Money (Ed.), *Reading disability.* Baltimore: Johns Hopkins Press, 1962. Pp. 1-3.
3. KIRSCHNER, R. Word blindness: neuro-opthalmologic implications. In A. Keeney & V. Keeney (Eds.), *Dyslexia.* St. Louis: Mosby, 1968. Pp. 69-71.
4. THOMPSON, L. *Reading disability.* Springfield, Ill.: Thomas, 1966.

DEVELOPMENT OF CUTANEOUS AND KINESTHETIC LOCALIZATION BY BLIND AND SIGHTED CHILDREN

Bill Jones

Seventy-eight blind and 160 sighted subjects in the age range 5–12 years were compared in cutaneous and kinesthetic localization. There were two experimental conditions for both types of localization. In Condition 1, both blind and sighted subjects made a localizing response without the aid of visual cues. Sighted subjects only were tested in Condition 2 which was like Condition 1 except subjects opened their eyes while making the localization response. Cutaneous and kinesthetic localization by blind subjects was superior to that by sighted subjects under Condition 1. Localization by sighted subjects under Condition 2 was superior to localization by both groups under Condition 1. The results are discussed in terms of the interactive effects of sensory systems.

Comparisons of blind and sighted people often aim at elucidating the effects of vision on functioning in other modalities. Gomulicki (1961) compared 163 blind children with 170 sighted children between the ages of 5 and 16 years. He found that tactual perception of three-dimensional objects (stereognosis) by blind subjects was slower and less accurate than by sighted subjects of the same age. Axelrod (1959), on the other hand, found that cutaneous discriminations measured by 2-point thresholds were finer in blind children than in sighted. Also, Hunter (1953), in a comparison of the kinesthetic perception of straightness in blind and sighted adolescents, found that the blind have a lower threshold for the detection of curvature and were also less variable than

From *Developmental Psychology,* 1972, **6,** 349–352. Copyright 1972 by the American Psychological Association. Reprinted by permission.

the sighted. However, 6 out of 20 of Hunter's blind subjects had had considerable visual experience until at least the sixth year. This is an important point since children who lose their sight after the fifth or sixth year often retain considerable visual memory (Schlaegel, 1953), which may influence their performance when blind. There is, in fact, considerable evidence that the late blinded are superior to the congenitally or early blinded in a wide variety of tasks (Axelrod, 1959; Hatwell, 1959; Worchel, 1962).

Renshaw and his colleagues (Renshaw, 1930; Renshaw & Wherry, 1931; Renshaw, Wherry, & Newlin, 1930) studied cutaneous localization of a point on the hand or forearm of a small number of blind and sighted children and adults. Two methods of localizing were used by sighted subjects. In the first, the "tactile method," the subject was blindfolded so that he did not see the point touched by the experimenter and the localizing response was made without vision. In the second, the "visual method," the subject had his eyes closed when he was stimulated and opened them and looked at his hand or arm to make the localizing response. Localization was superior under the visual method until the twelfth year, at which time there was a reversal of relative accuracy under the two methods (Renshaw & Wherry, 1931). The authors argued that there must be a period of tactual followed by later visual dominance in normal perceptual development. However, there was no statistical treatment of the data, and only a small number of subjects was used.

The present study is, in part, a replication of Renshaw's work. The processing of cutaneous and kinesthetic information by blind and sighted children was compared to elucidate the effect of vision on the cutaneous and kinesthetic modalities.

Method

Subjects

All subjects were in the age range of 5–12 years. Blind children were pupils at schools for the blind in either Sheffield (Tapton) or Liverpool (The Royal School and St. Vincents), England. The schools draw from a large part of the United Kingdom and from all socioeconomic groups.

The 78 blind subjects were either totally blind or had at the most perception of light. All but two had been blind since birth. The number of blind subjects and their mean chronological ages (in years and months) are presented in Table 1. Many causes of blindness were associated with the sample, though optic atrophy, buphthalmos, and

TABLE 1

MEAN CHRONOLOGICAL AGE AND NUMBER OF BLIND AND SIGHTED SUBJECTS AT EACH AGE LEVEL

Age level	Blind		Sighted	
	M	N	M	N
5	5–4	9	5–6	20
6	6–4	9	6–10	20
7	7–7	8	7–6	20
8	8–5	13	8–7	20
9	9–5	7	9–6	20
10	10–3	7	10–4	20
11	11–8	15	11–5	20
12	12–7	10	12–6	20

retinoblastoma accounted, respectively, for 20%, 14%, and 14% of the cases. All children with multiple defects and those of subnormal intelligence were not included in the sample.

The sighted comparison group was composed of 20 randomly selected children from each of the age levels 5–12 years (see Table 1). They were drawn from three day schools in predominantly middle-class areas of Sheffield.

Procedure

Each subject performed a cutaneous and a kinesthetic localizing task in a random order.

Cutaneous localization. A matrix of squares, each .01 square inch in area, was rubber stamped on the inner surface of the subject's nonpreferred arm. The whole matrix was 2 × 4 inches, giving a total of 800 squares. So that failures of localization could be measured within the matrix, only an area, .6 × 2.6 inches, in the center of the matrix was chosen for stimulation. Within this area 10 squares were randomly selected to serve as stimulus points. The stimulus points were the same for each subject. Using a sharpened pencil point the experimenter touched at random one of the previously chosen squares. The child, also using a pencil, moved his preferred arm through a distance of 12 inches and tried to locate exactly the same spot. Whichever square he touched was marked on a sheet of graph paper drawn to the same dimensions as the matrix on his arm. The distance between the point stimulated and the point touched by the child could thus be later measured by the experimenter.

Two experimental conditions were used. Under Condition 1 the subject closed his eyes and was stimulated by the experimenter. The subject then made a localizing response without opening his eyes. Blind subjects were tested only under Condition 1. Sighted subjects were additionally tested under Condition 2, a visual method of localizing. The subject closed his eyes and was stimulated by the experimenter. The subject then opened his eyes, looked at his arm, and made the localizing response with vision. Sighted children were stimulated once on each of the 10 selected squares under Condition 1 and once on each under Condition 2. There were thus 10 trials per condition for the sighted subjects. Blind children were stimulated twice on each of the 10 squares so that they received 20 trials under Condition 1.

Kinesthetic localization. The subject put the index finger of his preferred hand in a thimble mounted on a rail. He then slid the thimble along the rail in an extensor movement until he came to a stop set by the experimenter. The subject then went back to the starting point and tried to reproduce as accurately as possible his previous movement, the experimenter meanwhile having removed the stop. A pointer attached to the thimble was moved along a scale below the slide thus enabling the experimenter to read off the distance that the child had moved his arm. Absolute error of movement duplication was recorded.

There were two experimental conditions corresponding to those used in the cutaneous localization procedure. Blind children were tested only under Condition 1, in which the sighted subjects had their eyes closed throughout the procedure described. Under Condition 2, the sighted subject closed his eyes, moved to the stop and back to the starting point. He then opened his eyes and attempted to duplicate the previous movement with visual guidance. Five standard stimulus distances of 6, 8, 10, 12, and 14 inches long were used. Each distance was presented to the sighted subject twice in a random order under each condition. There were thus 10 trials per condition. Each standard was presented four times in a random order to each blind subject, who consequently had 20 trials on Condition 1.

Since blindfolds had an upsetting effect on some of the younger children, they were not used. The experimenter did not observe any of the sighted subjects opening their eyes at inappropriate times.

Results and Discussion

Results for cutaneous localization by blind and sighted subjects under Condition 1 are presented in Table 2. The blind were more accurate and less variable than the sighted at every age level, though this difference was only significant at 11 years ($t = 1.86$, $df = 33$, $p < .05$). Overall, however, cutaneous localization by the blind was significantly more accurate than by the sighted ($t = 2.50$, $df = 236$, $p < .01$). In order to check how far accuracy of cutaneous localization represents mere guesswork the following check was devised. The distance between the 10 squares selected for stimulation was measured and the mean taken. If the subject's average error score was lower than the average of the distance between the stimulus squares (1.09 inches), that is, if on the average he was nearer the stimulated square than any of the nonstimulated ones, his performance was regarded as nonrandom. According to this criterion, cutaneous localization by only two of the sighted 5-year-olds under Condition 1 could be described as random.

TABLE 2

MEAN ERRORS AND STANDARD DEVIATIONS IN INCHES FOR CUTANEOUS LOCALIZATION UNDER CONDITION 1

Age level	Blind		Sighted	
	M	*SD*	*M*	*SD*
5	.80	1.58	.86	1.85
6	.61	1.36	.78	1.73
7	.64	1.39	.78	1.69
8	.55	1.31	.63	1.46
9	.50	1.30	.55	1.39
10	.41	1.22	.50	1.08
11	.43	1.09	.56	1.43
12	.40	1.15	.49	1.40

Results for kinesthetic localization by blind and sighted subjects under Condition 1 are presented in Table 3. As for cutaneous localization the blind were more accurate and less variable than the sighted at each age level, and these differences were significant between 8 and 11 years ($ts \geq 2.08$, $dfs \geq 25$, $p < .05$). Overall, the difference between the blind and sighted was highly significant ($t = 6.75$, $df = 236$, $p < .001$).

Clearly both blind and sighted subjects improve with age in the ability to make both cutaneous and kinesthetic localization without vision, and localization by blind subjects is more accurate in both modalities. The demonstration by Gomulicki (1961) that stereognostic perception is more accurate in sighted subjects indicates that sensory processing by the blind may be comparable to that of patients with lesions of the posterior parietal lobe in whom stereognosis may be

TABLE 3

MEAN ERRORS AND STANDARD DEVIATIONS IN INCHES FOR KINESTHETIC LOCALIZATION UNDER CONDITION 1

Age level	Blind		Sighted	
	M	*SD*	*M*	*SD*
5	1.80	2.10	1.99	2.10
6	1.21	2.10	1.48	2.42
7	1.09	2.06	1.31	2.34
8	.91	2.02	1.26	2.20
9	.90	1.80	1.16	1.97
10	.84	1.53	1.07	1.83
11	.83	1.66	.99	1.79
12	.83	1.31	.91	1.72

affected out of proportion to the basic cutaneous and kinesthetic deficits (Ruch, 1965). It may also be noted that Tees (1968) has shown visual deprivations in rats to have no effect on the discrimination of simple orientation. Only the visual perception of patterns is affected. The blind person may have little difficulty in performing simple sensory discriminations and matchings in the modalities available to him, but he is not able to combine and use these sensations with anything like the efficiency of the sighted person.

The performance of sighted subjects under Condition 2 is given in Table 4. Visually guided sighted were more accurate than the blind for both cutaneous ($t = 1.97$, $df = 236$, $p < .05$) and kinesthetic ($t = 5.06$, $df = 236$, $p < .001$) localizations.

The errors of the combined age groups of sighted subjects were analyzed by means of t tests for correlated measures. The results indicated that visually guided localization was significantly more accurate than localization without vision for both cutaneous ($t = 2.06$, $df = 159$, $p < .05$) and kinesthetic ($t = 3.20$, $df = 159$, $p < .001$) localization. It is obvious from these results that no evidence is provided for the contention of Renshaw and Wherry (1931) that tactile dominance is succeeded by visual dominance. Visually guided localization by subjects in the present study demonstrates no marked change with age between 5 and 12 years. Cutaneous (and kinesthetic) localization on the other hand, improves consistently throughout this age range. These results provide some confirmation of the suggestion by Bryant (1968) that developmental increases in visual-tactual cross-

modal accuracy in sighted children may depend largely on tactual improvements rather than some developing ability to integrate visual and tactual information. However, sighted children are presumably better able to integrate cutaneous and kinesthetic information than are blind children (Gomulicki, 1961). It may be that developmental improvements in stereognosis by blind children depend upon improvements in the ability to integrate skin sensation with knowledge of movements. More work is needed in which cutaneous and kinesthetic processing is specifically compared to stereognostic abilities in blind and sighted children.

REFERENCES

Axelrod, S. *Effects of early blindness.* New York: American Foundation for the Blind, 1959.

Bryant, P. Comments on the design of developmental studies of cross-modal matching and cross-modal transfer. *Cortex,* 1968, **4,** 127–137.

Gomulicki, B. R. The development of perception and learning in blind children. Unpublished manuscript, University of Cambridge, 1961.

Hatwell, Y. Perception tactile des formes et organisation spatiale tactile. *Journal of Psychology,* 1959, **56,** 187–204.

Hunter, I. M. L. Tactile-kinaesthetic perception of straightness in blind and sighted humans. *Quarterly Journal of Experimental Psychology,* 1953, **6,** 149–154.

Renshaw, S. The errors of localisation and the effect of practice on the localising movement in children and adults. *Journal of Genetic Psychology,* 1930, **38,** 223–238.

Renshaw, S., & Wherry, R. J. Studies in cutaneous localisation: III. The age of onset of ocular dominance. *Journal of Genetic Psychology,* 1931, **39,** 493–496.

Renshaw, S., Wherry, R. J., & Newlin, J. C. Cutaneous localisation in congenitally blind versus seeing children and adults. *Journal of Genetic Psychology,* 1930, **38,** 239–248.

Ruch, T. C. Somatic sensation. In T. C. Ruch & M. D. Patton (Eds.), *Physiology and biophysics.* Philadelphia: Saunders, 1965.

Schlaegel, T. F. The dominant method of imagery in blind as compared to sighted adolescents. *Journal of Genetic Psychology,* 1953, **83,** 265–277.

Tees, R. C. Effects of early restrictions on later form discrimination in the rat. *Canadian Journal of Psychology,* 1968, **22,** 294–301.

Worchel, P. Space perception and orientation in the blind. In E. P. Trapp & P. Himelstein (Eds.), *Readings on the exceptional child.* London: Methuen, 1962.

TABLE 4

Mean Errors and Standard Deviations in Inches for Cutaneous and Kinesthetic Localizations under Condition 2

Age group	Cutaneous Localization		Kinesthetic Localization	
	M	SD	M	SD
5	.54	1.73	1.30	1.83
6	.56	1.30	.87	1.39
7	.47	1.31	.96	1.39
8	.54	1.33	.80	1.17
9	.52	1.20	.74	1.24
10	.48	1.10	.70	1.30
11	.42	1.05	.81	1.11
12	.54	1.01	.76	1.14

DIVERGENT THINKING IN BLIND CHILDREN

William J. Tisdall
A. Edward Blackhurst
Claude H. Marks

The purpose of this investigation was to study the influence of visual deprivation upon divergent thinking dimensions of intelligence. Six divergent thinking tests were administered to 76 seeing children, 76 blind children in residential schools, and 76 blind children in day school programs. It was concluded that (*a*) blind children exhibit more verbal fluency than do seeing children; (*b*) visual familiarity with the environment allows seeing children advantage over the blind in a small number of divergent thinking activities; (*c*) blind and seeing children (CA 10–12) generally do not differ in the ability to think divergently; (*d*) blind children in residential and day school settings are equally capable of thinking divergently; and (*e*) seeing and day school blind males tend to be more divergent than their female classmates.

The phenomenon of divergent thinking has received considerable attention in the research literature of education and psychology in recent years. The formulation of Guilford's (1960) theoretical model of the Structure of Intellect has provided researchers with new avenues for more penetrating scrutiny of previously unexplored aspects of intellectual functioning. In the present study, divergent thinking is defined as that kind of thinking in which new information, or new combinations of ideas, are generated out of given or known information and which represents a respondent's performance on purported verbal measures of originality, fluency of ideas, flexibility of thought, and elaboration of ideas. According to Guilford's theory, divergent thinking is a vital prerequisite to creativity which in turn is an important part of intelligence.

The general purpose of this investigation was to study the influence of visual deprivation upon the verbal divergent thinking dimension of intelligence. Specifically, the primary objectives were to study differences which may exist in the divergent thinking abilities of (*a*) blind children and seeing children, (*b*) residential school and day school blind children, (*c*) both blind and seeing males and females, and (*d*) children

of varying ages of onset of blindness. For purposes of this investigation, blindness was defined as residual vision of light perception or less (Jones, 1963).

Although some research has been conducted on the creative expressions of blind children Lowenfeld (1952), it was done through the artistic medium of modeling. The need remains for an examination of the creative abilities of blind children along the intellectual, in addition to the artistic, dimension. The effect which blindness has on the development of divergent thinking abilities of blind children is not known. Yet, there is some support for the contention that the blind do possess the ability to think divergently. Guilford (1959), for example, argued that all persons possess the various abilities defined in his theoretical model in differing degrees since the abilities are assumed to be continuously distributed variables. In addition, the work of Wilson, Guilford, and Christensen (1952) led to the conclusion that the intellectual component of originality is a continuous variable which is possessed by all individuals to some degree.

Lowenfeld (1959) presented a strong argument for the existence of creative ability in everyone. He maintained that man possesses the ability to create intentionally while the animal does not. Thus, it follows that every man is a potential creator. At the same time, Lowenfeld indicated that the

Supported by Grant Number 32-27-0350-6003, Bureau of Education for the Handicapped, United States Office of Education.

extent to which the creative ability is developed varies among individuals. Each person, he claimed, has functional and potential creative abilities. The former is that which is used by the individual while the latter is that portion of the person's creative ability which remains unused. Some individuals, because of their early training and experiences, have matured into essentially functional creators. Others, not having gained an awareness of their potential, have remained uncreative.

While Guilford's theoretical explanation of the nature of intelligence posits the potentiality of all individuals to think divergently, Lowenfeld implies that deterrents to an awareness of that potential would lead to a truncation of divergent thinking ability. Since the severe sensory impairment of blindness leads to a supression of interaction with the environment, blind individuals may be more likely to develop as potential, rather than functional, divergent thinkers. Seeing children, on the other hand, having use of the visual sense modality, may be more likely to have greater and more varied opportunities to become functional divergent thinkers. The present study was designed to determine if this is the case.

METHOD

Subjects

The sample consisted of 76 seeing children (40 males, 36 females), 76 blind children enrolled in public day schools (39 males, 37 females), and 76 blind children in residential schools for the blind (34 males, 42 females). All subjects were between 10 and 12 years of age and were enrolled in school programs in the Eastern half of the United States. The characteristics of the groups selected for the investigation are reported in Table 1.

For purposes of determining group comparability, analyses were conducted between groups on the independent variables. All analyses were two-tailed t tests for differences between means (Guil-

ford, 1956). The .05 level of significance was preset as the criterion for rejecting the null hypotheses.

It was found that there were no differences between the two blind groups on the independent variables. However, the seeing group was significantly superior to both blind groups in MA and IQ. Even though these differences were found, because of the low correlation reported between intelligence and tests of divergent thinking (Torrance, Yamamoto, Schenitzki, Palamutlu, & Luther, 1960), it was felt that these differences would not differentially affect the divergent thinking test scores. Furthermore, and more important, the intelligence criterion was construed for purposes of this study as a screening device only in order to ascertain that no mentally retarded subjects were included in the sample. In addition, IQ comparisons between the blind and seeing subjects in this study were viewed with caution, since the same tests were not used with all subjects.

It was found that there were significant differences among the three groups with respect to grade level in school. Seeing children tended to be in higher grade levels than both groups of blind children. These differences in grade level could be a function of learning difficulties encountered by the blind children—particularly in the residential schools. This is supported by the fact that years in school corresponded exactly to grade level for the seeing subjects, whereas the blind children were placed in grade levels lower than would be expected on the basis of the number of years they had been in school. This is consistent with the findings reported by Lowenfeld (1963) that blind children are overage for their grade levels.

Instrumentation

Six tests of verbal divergent thinking were administered to each subject. From the 17 subtests, 41 separate divergent thinking scores were derived. The following tests were administered:

1. *Word Fluency* (Christensen & Guilford, 1958) yielded a total fluency score in addition to scores on Subtests B and T.

2. Fluency, Flexibility, Originality, and Elaboration were assessed with the *Product Improvement* test (Torrance & Palamutlu, 1960).

3. The Brick, Heat, and Water Subtests of the *Unusual Uses* (Undated) battery yielded Fluency, Flexibility, and Breadth scores as well as a total Unusual Uses Fluency score.

4. Fluency, Flexibility, Breadth, Remote, and Obvious scores were obtained on each of the Food, Reading, and Writing, and Balance items of the *Consequences Test* (Christensen, Merrifield, & Guilford, 1958). A total Consequences Fluency Score was also derived.

5. The Drink, Sweet, Smooth, and Green Subtests were administered to determine *Ideational Fluency* (Christensen & Guilford, 1957). These also yielded a total Ideational Fluency Score.

6. Scores were also obtained on the Hammer, Wind, and Glue Subtests of the *Seeing Problems Test* (Undated).

A brief pilot study was conducted for the purpose of determining whether or not blind children could respond meaningfully to the tests of divergent thinking which were used in this study. The tests were administered to 10 blind children, between the ages of 10 and 12. It was found that blind subjects were capable of providing meaning-

TABLE 1

MAJOR CHARACTERISTICS OF THE SAMPLE

Variable	Seeing children		Day school blind children		Residential school blind children	
	M	*SD*	*M*	*SD*	*M*	*SD*
CA (in months)	141.2	8.4	140.0	10.0	140.2	9.2
MA (in months)	163.8	18.9	149.0	23.6	149.5	27.2
IQ	116.1	12.9	106.5	14.8	106.3	16.6
Years in school	6.08	0.67	5.93	1.0	5.81	1.15
Grade	6.08	0.67	5.47	1.0	5.17	1.3

ful and relevant responses to these verbal tests of divergent thinking.

Methods of Analysis

When scoring the tests of divergent thinking, it was found that the scoring criteria proposed by the authors of the tests were not, in a number of cases, sufficiently broad enough to permit categorization of the subjects' responses. It was therefore necessary to revise the scoring criteria.

Upon revision, the extent of agreement among scorers as to the application of the criteria was determined. The test papers of 15 subjects were randomly selected for each of the six tests of divergent thinking. Three members of the project staff scored each test independently according to the revised scoring criteria. The total number of responses was then computed for each of the tests as was the number of instances in which the scorers did not agree. The percentage of interscorer agreement was then calculated.

In 10 of the 17 subtests the interscorer agreement was 90% or higher. The lowest percentage of agreement was 85.2. Provisions were then made to assure the accuracy and consistency of the scoring. That is, test scorers were instructed to discuss questionable responses which arose during the scoring process and reach agreement before assigning that response to a category.

To guard against scorer bias, all test papers were assigned random numbers prior to scoring by a person not associated with the project. Thus, the scorers were not aware whether the tests which they corrected were those of day school blind, residential school blind, or seeing children.

To test for significant differences between groups, means scores on each of the variables were computed for each group. Comparisons between means were then performed using *t* tests. The following comparisons were made: (*a*) seeing versus day school blind subjects, (*b*) seeing versus residential school blind subjects, and (*c*) day school blind versus residential school blind subjects. Differences between mean scores of males and females in each of the three groups received similar analysis. The .05 level of significance was set as the criterion for rejecting the null hypotheses. All statistical analyses were performed using raw-score data.

Results and Discussion

Mean divergent thinking test scores and standard deviations for the three groups are presented in Table 2.[1] It was found that day school blind children scored significantly higher than both seeing and residential school blind subjects on the two subtests and on total score of the Word Fluency test. This is consistent with earlier findings of greater fluency in day school blind children (Kenmore, 1965; Lax, 1953; Maxfield, 1936; Payne, 1931). No differences in word fluency existed between the residential blind subjects and seeing subjects.

[1]Complete data on results of the statistical analyses are contained in the original report of the study (Tisdall, Blackhurst, & Marks, 1967).

TABLE 2
DIVERGENT THINKING TEST SCORE MEANS
AND STANDARD DEVIATIONS

Test	Day school blind children		Residential school blind children		Sighted children	
	M	*SD*	*M*	*SD*	*M*	*SD*
Word Fluency						
B	17.29	6.28	14.97	6.37	14.53	4.20
T	18.53	7.18	16.13	6.51	16.47	4.27
Total	35.83	12.55	31.11	12.17	31.00	7.48
Product Improvement						
Fluency	10.61	6.18	9.19	5.49	11.96	6.26
Flexibility	4.44	3.06	4.05	2.73	5.69	2.97
Originality	16.04	10.35	14.72	9.54	19.97	11.50
Elaboration	12.71	8.08	10.61	6.33	13.56	7.43
Unusual Uses						
Brick						
Fluency	6.51	3.17	6.55	3.11	7.13	2.97
Flexibility	3.87	2.69	3.99	2.29	4.87	2.22
Breadth	3.73	1.72	3.76	1.48	4.59	1.42
Heat						
Fluency	8.25	3.76	7.53	3.30	8.31	3.02
Flexibility	5.35	2.76	5.05	2.56	5.67	2.24
Breadth	5.17	1.96	5.03	1.83	5.36	2.00
Water						
Fluency	7.12	3.68	7.35	3.24	6.92	2.54
Flexibility	4.81	2.96	5.11	2.62	4.88	2.10
Breadth	4.73	2.26	5.04	1.93	5.31	1.72
Total Fluency	21.00	8.85	21.44	7.99	22.43	7.35
Consequences						
Food						
Fluency	8.93	4.42	8.19	3.17	7.36	2.81
Flexibility	4.33	2.77	4.05	2.33	4.37	2.41
Breadth	3.68	1.50	3.43	1.38	3.75	1.14
Remote	1.60	1.72	1.56	1.62	1.97	1.83
Obvious	7.33	4.25	6.56	3.14	5.39	2.99
Read and write						
Fluency	8.85	3.44	8.47	3.65	7.69	3.02
Flexibility	3.95	2.59	3.51	2.67	3.60	2.03
Breadth	3.39	1.48	3.16	1.56	3.21	1.30
Remote	1.95	1.59	2.07	2.26	1.75	1.45
Obvious	6.89	3.06	5.40	2.94	6.01	3.00
Balance						
Fluency	6.13	3.29	6.79	3.42	6.45	2.68
Flexibility	3.48	2.29	3.61	2.35	3.89	2.28
Breadth	3.52	1.60	3.53	1.45	3.72	1.55
Remote	1.37	1.61	1.93	2.03	1.56	1.53
Obvious	4.76	2.95	4.87	2.65	4.89	2.19
Total Fluency	23.92	8.87	23.44	8.60	21.51	7.40
Ideational Fluency						
Drink	10.72	5.27	9.73	4.56	8.71	3.29
Sweet	8.72	5.07	7.79	5.22	6.37	3.78
Smooth	10.20	5.75	11.05	5.70	10.67	4.85
Green	5.79	5.37	6.00	4.26	4.17	3.61
Total	35.44	17.29	34.56	15.09	29.96	11.79
Seeing Problems						
Hammer	2.08	1.59	2.71	1.30	2.87	1.45
Wind	2.93	1.46	2.92	1.20	3.51	1.00
Glue	2.51	1.56	2.99	1.27	3.23	1.31

The seeing subjects scored significantly higher than the residential blind on all subtests of the Product Improvement test and significantly higher than the day school blind on the flexibility and originality dimensions. These differences could be a function of the test item itself. The test required that the student describe ways to improve the toy dog in order to make it more fun to play with. It is possible that seeing subjects were utilizing visual cues which triggered further responses, thus inflating their scores.

Of the 30 comparisons made on the Unusual Uses tests, 4 yielded significant differences, all of which were in favor of the seeing group. These subjects scored significantly higher than the day and residential blind subjects on both the flexibility and breadth dimensions of the Brick Subtest. The breadth score on this subtest reflected the number of different categories of uses named, and flexibility was determined by the number of shifts between different categories. It could be postulated that seeing subjects scored higher on these items because they have seen bricks used in different ways in their environment. This might be construed as an accumulation of incidental knowledge that would not be available to the blind by virtue of their visual handicaps. However, it is interesting to note that the blind did not differ from the seeing children on the fluency score of the Brick item. This is fairly consistent with the earlier fluency findings and indicates that the blind were inferior in the quality, but not quantity, of their responses.

Sixteen scores were derived from the Consequences test battery. The day school blind children scored significantly higher than the seeing children on the fluency dimensions of the Food and Read-Writing Subtests and the obvious responses on the Food Subtest. Residential school blind children scored higher than the day school blind group on the remote score of the Balance Subtest, and higher from seeing children on the obvious score of the Food Subtest. All other differences in Consequences were nonsignificant.

Day school blind subjects scored significantly higher than seeing subjects on the Drink, Sweet, and Green Subtests, and on the total Ideational Fluency score. Residential blind subjects scored significantly higher than the seeing subjects on the Green Subtest and on the total ideational Fluency score. Thus, the greater fluency of the blind subjects was again in evidence.

On the Consequences test battery, seeing children scored significantly higher than both groups of blind children on the Wind Subtest. Both the seeing and residential school blind children obtained significantly higher scores on the Hammer and Glue subtests than did the day school blind subjects.

Seeing males scored significantly higher than females on 11 of the 41 tests of divergent thinking. Likewise, day school blind males scored significantly higher than females on eight of the subtests. No pattern for these differences emerged. The only instance of demonstrated superiority of fe-

males on the tests of divergent thinking was in the residential school group on the breadth dimension of the Unusual Uses-Brick subtest. All other differences in the residential group were nonsignificant.

An attempt was made to examine differences which may have existed in the divergent thinking abilities of children according to varying ages of onset of blindness. The range of onset of blindness could not be anticipated prior to the selection of the sample. Consequently, there was no initial guarantee that this variable would be manifest in enough subjects of various onset ages to extract meaningful information.

It was found that of the 152 blind subjects, 134 were congenitally blind, 10 were blinded between birth and 1 year of age, 3 became blind between the ages of one and five, and 5 became blind after the age of five. In attempting to analyze these data, it was decided that an insufficient number of adventitiously blind subjects precluded the drawing of sound conclusions regarding the divergent thinking abilities of the blind subjects. This decision was further supported by the fact that many of the children in the birth to 1 year onset range became blind within a few weeks or months of birth. The high incidence of congenitally blind children is explained by the etiological data which indicated that most of these subjects suffered retrolental fibroplasia.

On the basis of this investigation, it was concluded that blind children exhibit more verbal fluency in the divergent thinking dimension of intelligence than do seeing children. Visual familiarity with the environment, as opposed to inherent intellectual disparity, allows seeing children some advantage over blind children on a few divergent thinking tasks; however, more often than not, blind and seeing children in the 10 to 12 year age range do not differ in the ability to think divergently. Blind children in residential and day school settings are equally capable of thinking divergently; although there is a slight tendency for those in day school programs to be more verbally fluent.

When sex differences appear on the dimensions of divergent thinking, seeing and day school blind males tend to be more divergent than their female classmates. There are essentially no differences in the divergent thinking abilities of blind males and females who are enrolled in residential school programs.

REFERENCES

CHRISTENSEN, P. R., & GUILFORD, J. P. *Ideational fluency.* Beverly Hills, Calif.: Sheridan Supply Company, 1957.

CHRISTENSEN, P. R., & GUILFORD, J. P. *Word fluency.* Beverly Hills, Calif.: Sheridan Supply Company, 1958.

CHRISTENSEN, P. R., MERRIFIELD, P. R., & GUILFORD, J. P. *Consequences.* Beverly Hills, Calif.: Sheridan Supply Company, 1958.

GUILFORD, J. P. *Fundamental statistics in psychology and education.* New York: McGraw-Hill, 1956.

GUILFORD, J. P. Traits of creativity. In H. H. Anderson (Ed.), *Creativity and its cultivation.* New York: Harper, 1959.

GUILFORD, J. P. *The structure of intellect model: Its uses and implications.* (University of Southern California Report from the Psychological Laboratory) April, 1960.

JONES, J. W. Problems in defining and classifying blindness. *Research Bulletin.* New York: American Foundation for the Blind, August, 1963, 123–129.

KENMORE, J. R. Associative learning by blind versus sighted children with words and objects differing in meaningfulness and identifiability without vision. Unpublished doctoral dissertation, University of Minnesota, 1965.

LAX, B. A. A comparison of the imaginative productions of congenitally blind and seeing children to structure auditory stimulation. Unpublished master's thesis, University of Texas, 1953.

LOWENFELD, V. *Creative and mental growth.* New York: MacMillan, 1952.

LOWENFELD, V. What is creative teaching? In E. P. Torrance (Ed.), *Creativity: Proceedings of the second Minnesota conference on gifted children.* Minneapolis: University of Minnesota Press, 1959.

LOWENFELD, V. Psychological problems of children with impaired vision. In W. M. Cruickshank (Ed.), *Psychology of exceptional children and youth.* Englewood Cliffs, N.J.: Prentice Hall, 1963.

MAXFIELD, K. E. The spoken language of the blind pre-school child, *Archives of Psychology.* 1936, **29**, 53.

PAYNE, S. Free association in blind children. Unpublished master's thesis, Columbia University, 1931.

SEEING PROBLEMS TEST, Aptitudes Research Project, Department of Psychology, University of Southern California, Los Angeles, California, Undated.

TISDALL, W. J., BLACKHURST, A. E., & MARKS, C. H. *Divergent Thinking in Blind Children.* United States Office of Education, Grant Number 32-27-0350-6003, 1967.

TORRANCE, E. P. & PALAMUTLU, N. Product improvement task. In E. P. Torrance, K. Yamamoto, D. Schenetzki, N. Palamutlu, and B. Luther (Eds.), *Assessing the creative thinking abilities of children.* Minneapolis: Bureau of Educational Research, University of Minnesota, 1960.

TORRANCE, E. P., YAMAMOTO, K., SCHENETZKI, D., PALAMUTLU, N., & LUTHER, B. *Assessing the creative thinking abilities of children.* Minneapolis: Bureau of Educational Research, University of Minnesota, 1960.

UNUSUAL USES TEST. Aptitudes Research Project, Department of Psychology, University of Southern California, Los Angeles, California, Undated.

WILSON, R. C., GUILFORD, J. P., & CHRISTENSEN, P. R. The Measurement of Individual Differences in Originality, *Psychology Bulletin*, 1953, **50**, 362–370.

GEOGRAPHICAL CONCEPTS AND THE VISUALLY HANDICAPPED

Frank L. Franks
Richard M. Baird

Abstract. Visually handicapped Braille and large-print readers from a residential school were taught geographical concepts using eight raised-surface landforms, which were both tactually and chromatically coded. Large-print readers learned more of the concepts than Braille readers, and tenth-grade children performed better than sixth-grade children. Some Braille readers were able to use the chromatic cues in inspection of the landforms.

This study, along with the others in a series, explored geographical concept attainment in visually handicapped students as a basis for improving their ability to interpret embossed maps. The limited quantity of research in map reading has focused on such problems as the perception of tactile forms, textures, and symbols as they appear on embossed maps, with little emphasis on the development of basic geographical concepts by the students who are to use these maps. It was felt that more information on geographical concept attainment of visually handicapped students would add a basic, but so far overlooked, dimension to studies in map design and map legibility.

Summary of First Studies

The first two studies are summarized briefly to provide background information relevant to the study reported here:

Study 1. In an exploratory study of the development of geographical concepts in blind students, Franks and Nolan (1970) identified 70 geographical terms through curriculum analysis of fourth, fifth, and sixth grade social studies textbooks. These terms were administered as a test to 75 braille students to determine their knowledge of basic geographical concepts. It was found that:

1. A number of the concepts tested were relatively unknown at several grade levels.
2. Higher scores at some grade levels appeared as a result of repetition of the terms.

3. Overall gains due to repetition were short lived and decreased when repetition was reduced.

When used as a test, these 70 items were administered orally and individually to each student tested. The student defined, identified, or explained the terms, and the examiner recorded responses on a separate answer sheet. This process was laborious and time consuming. The need for a short-form group test for research and educational purposes was indicated.

Study 2. The purpose of the second study (Franks & Nolan, 1971) was to develop a short-form instrument for measuring geographical concept attainment of visually handicapped students. The test developed in the study consisted of 40 items and allowed visually handicapped students to record their own responses. The test was then administered to 48 visually handicapped students, 8 braille and 8 large print readers from each of grades 6, 8, and 10. It was found that:

1. The short test is practical to administer to groups of visually handicapped students and provides a reliable measure of their level of geographical concept attainment.
2. The short test revealed the same pattern of performance as the original 70 item test.
3. No significant differences were found between braille readers and large print readers.
4. A number of geographical concepts were again largely unknown at the grade levels tested.

From *Exceptional Children*, 1971, **38**, 321–324. Reprinted by permission of The Council for Exceptional Children.

Purpose

Since the 40 items on the short-form test represented fundamental geographical concepts, it was felt that if these terms could be presented and taught more concretely, existing deficits in geographical concept attainment could be greatly reduced. These 40 terms all represent specific land and water areas. Accordingly, three dimensional raised surface models (landforms) were developed to tactually and chromatically represent these concepts.

It was the purpose of this study to test a set of eight landforms to determine the ability of braille and large print readers to identify and locate tactual and chromatic representations of basic geographical concepts as they appear on the landforms.

Subjects

A total of 48 visually handicapped students from grades 6, 8, and 10 in two residential schools were selected. Eight braille readers and 8 large print readers from each grade were included. IQ scores for the total test sample ranged from 84 to 137 with an overall mean of 99.2. All students were enrolled in academic programs and ranged in age from 12 to 20 years. No students were included for whom onset of visual impairment occurred after the age of 5 years. All were in the regular school program and none were receiving psychological or psychiatric services for emotional disorders. None had any apparent sensory-motor dysfunction of the hands. Mean age and IQ scores for braille readers and for large print readers are presented for each grade level in Table 1.

TABLE 1

Mean Age and IQ for Braille and Large Print Readers

Grade	Braille (N = 24) Age	IQ	Large print (N = 24) Age	IQ	Overall Age	IQ
6 (N = 16)	15	95	13	97	14	96
8 (N = 16)	14	102	15	99	15	101
10 (N = 16)	17	102	17	100	17	101

Materials

Eight raised surface landforms were constructed of 15 mil high impact styrene using a Thermoform process and were designed to provide the best possible tactual and chromatic discrimination for use by visually handicapped students.

Tactual Coding

Precisely defined scaling of elevations of land areas and of sizes of various land and water areas was not maintained when it was necessary to exaggerate an area to increase contrast and/or tactual discrimination of the geographical concepts represented. However, the following general guidelines were observed:

1. Tactual and chromatic symbols on a landform represented real things on the earth. Small symbols on the landform represented big things on the earth.
2. General overall size perspective, however, was maintained although not to scale. Oceans were larger than lakes; mountains were higher than hills.
3. Water areas (oceans, lakes, rivers) were represented on landforms by a level rippled surface that varied 1 mm. and was very different tactually from the raised smooth surface of land areas.
4. Boundaries between adjacent land areas and between water areas (mountain, hill, gulf, bay) were made as discriminable as possible.

Each landform measured 8 inches square. Water areas were represented by a rippled surface that varied 1 mm. All land areas were smooth surfaced with a maximum rise of 2⅜ inches. Landforms were numbered in braille and large print in the lower right hand corner.

Chromatic Coding

Colors used on the landforms were blue for water, yellow for lowlands, green for hills, red for mountains, white for snow-capped peaks, and black for dams and dikes. The exact hues and color scheme were selected according to the following guideline:

1. Primary hues were used when possible. Mixtures of colors were avoided.
2. The number of hues utilized was limited to the minimum number actually necessary.
3. Chromatic contrast was maximized.
4. Reflectance (luminance) contrast also was maximized to facilitate visual inspection of the landforms by low vision students.

5. Within the above restriction, hues selected were as consistent as possible with the existing color scheme used on maps and globes produced by the American Printing House for the Blind.

Table 2 presents the color scheme used and the reflectance values for each hue.

Concepts Introduced on Landforms

The purpose of each landform and the geographical concepts illustrated are included below.

- Landform 0—Introduction
  Purpose: To introduce the chromatic and textural differences in land and water as indicated on landforms and to determine whether the student uses residual vision, tactual discrimination, or a combination of these in identifying land and water areas.

  Geographical concepts: land and water.

- Landform I—Simple Land and Water Masses
  Purpose: To introduce to visually handicapped students the concepts of land and water as they appear on landforms.

  Geographical concepts: ocean, island, lake, seashore (coast, coastline), and beach.

- Landform II—Simple Land Masses
  Purpose: To introduce visually handicapped students to chromatic and tactual differences in elevation of simple land masses on landforms.

  Geographical concepts: hill, mountain, valley, canyon, and reservoir.

- Landform III—Open Land Areas
  Purpose: To introduce to visually handicapped students concepts of space and open areas on landforms.

  Geographical concepts: basin, plain, prairie, and plateau.

- Landform IV—Water Areas
  Purpose: To teach visually handicapped students relative sizes and outlines of partially enclosed bodies of water as they may appear on landforms.

  Geographical concepts: channel, canal, gulf, bay, harbor, and port.

- Landform V—River Areas
  Purpose: To teach visually handicapped students the origin and directional flow of rivers and related concepts.

  Geographical concepts: river, tributary, source of a river, mouth of a river, delta, and river basin.

- Landform VI—Hills and Mountains
  Purpose: To give visually handicapped students more experience in discriminating various levels of elevation on landforms.

  Geographical concepts: volcano, mountain peak, range of mountains, highland, foothills, divide, and timberline.

- Landform VII—Additional Land and Water Areas
  Purpose: To give visually handicapped students wider exposure in discriminating additional land and water areas which are illustrated on landforms.

  Geographical concepts: peninsula, cape, isthmus, strait, sound, inlet, and dike.

Procedure

An introductory landform with a small island (a smooth, raised yellow area) located in an ocean (a textured, level blue area) was presented to each student for examination. Texture and color coding was explained. Opportunity to ask questions was given. Additional color coding was explained when landform II was presented. Landform II contained all of the colors used in coding the landforms.

The following procedure was used in testing the landforms:

1. Each student was tested individually.
2. The list of terms to be identified on each landform was read aloud as the student made a gross exploration of the landform.
3. The definition of each item to be identified was read and the student was

TABLE 2

Color Reflectance Values

Area identified	Color shade used	Reflectance value
Water (oceans, lakes, etc.)	blue	17%
Lowland areas (first land level)	yellow	85%
Hills and mountains (second land level)	green	33%
Mountains (third land level)	red	15%
Mountain peaks (fourth land level)	white	87%

asked to find its representation on the landform.

4. Each item was read twice and was repeated on request.
5. Respones were recorded by the examiner.
6. The landforms were tested sequentially from landform I through landform VII.

Overall percentage of correct identification of the features illustrated on the landforms was 83.5 percent. The mean and percentage scores for all subjects in this experiment are presented in Table 3.

TABLE 3

Mean and Percentage Scores

Grade	Braille	Large print	Combined
6	28.13 (70.3%)	34.75 (86.9%)	31.44 (78.6%)
8	29.88 (74.7%)	33.00 (82.5%)	31.44 (78.6%)
10	36.13 (90.3%)	38.50 (96.3%)	37.32 (93.3%)
Total	31.38 (78.5%)	35.43 (88.6%)	33.40 (83.5%)

An analysis of variance was conducted on the number of correct identifications made by each subject. The analysis indicated significant effects due to grade level ($p<.01$) and mode of reading ($p<.01$) and a significant interaction ($p<.01$). Table 4 presents the analysis of variance.

TABLE 4

Summary Analysis of Variance

Source	df	MS	F
Reading mode (A)	1	196.02	11.72*
Grade (B)	2	122.72	7.34*
A × B	2	302.67	18.11*
Error	42	16.71	
Total	47		

*$p < .01$

Discussion

The generally high level of performance of all groups on the identification task indicates that the geographical concepts illustrated on each landform were legible and readily identifiable. The significant differences between braille and large print readers was probably due to the effectiveness of the chromatic coding scheme in facilitating the performance of the subjects with some residual vision. The efficacy of the chromatic cues was not limited to large print readers, however. It was observed that a number of braille readers (who were educated as blind and had used braille exclusively in written communication) made almost exclusive use of visual cues in inspecting the landforms. Apparently, the chromatic and reflectance contrasts were such that they provided important information even for those braille readers with very limited residual vision.

It is also possible that the high contrast values of the hues used on the landforms will facilitate inspection of the landform with an audible photoconductive light probe such as the one available through the Royal National Institute for the Blind (catalog no. 9432). This may be of significant value to those students who actually are totally blind. Increased use of the light probe by visually handicapped students was recommended by the Institute on Instructional Materials Development in Science for Visually Handicapped (Franks, 1970).

Conclusion

The results of this study indicate that the series of three dimensional raised surface landforms reported here provide highly discriminable illustrations of 40 basic geographical terms for use by visually handicapped students. The system of tactual coding which was developed provides easily discriminable surface areas. The chromatic coding system utilized on the landforms also provides effective, highly discriminable cues, even for some braille readers with extremely limited residual vision. The use of these materials should greatly facilitate both instruction and evaluation of geographical concept attainment of the visually handicapped student. Implications for use with exceptional children other than visually handicapped students should be investigated.

References

Franks, F. L. Institute report on instructional materials development in science for visually handicapped. Unpublished manuscript, American Printing House for the Blind, Louisville, Kentucky, 1970.

Franks, F. L., & Nolan, C. Y. Development of geographical concepts in blind children. *Education of the Visually Handicapped,* 1970, **2,** 1-7.

Franks, F. L., & Nolan, C. Y. Measuring geographical concept attainment in visually handicapped students. *Education of the Visually Handicapped,* 1971, **3,** 11-17.

CHAPTER TEN

AURAL IMPAIRMENT

Many of the problems encountered in seeking knowledge about blind and partially sighted persons are intensified in the study of the deaf and hard of hearing. For example, questions arise regarding the use of legal versus functional definitions of hearing impairment, controlling for congenital versus acquired sources of hearing loss, and the selection of subjects from residential versus day schools. In addition, young deaf children are difficult to differentiate from children with delayed speech or from those who are mentally retarded, aphasic, or severely emotionally disturbed.

The article by Balow, Fulton, and Peploe illustrates the modification in testing procedures required for administering reading achievement tests that have been standardized on normally hearing children to subjects with a hearing loss. The need for control over testing conditions is demonstrated by the results of the Goldman and Sanders study. Data indicated that many culturally disadvantaged children who failed an auditory screening test administered under normal classroom noise levels passed the test when it was administered in a soundproofed room.

Professionals who work with hearing-impaired persons have benefited from basic research in the areas of memory and learning. Allen found that aurally handicapped children learned written pairs of words that "looked alike" more readily than pairs that "sounded alike" and that this difference was greatest among children with very mild hearing losses. Subjects with normal hearing learned both types of word pairs with equal ease.

Since the beginning of education for the deaf, scholars have debated the relative merits of the "oral" and "manual" methods of instruction. Proponents of the oral method (lipreading and oral speech) have stressed the importance of acquiring verbal and social contact with the normally hearing population. Advocates of the manual method (signing and finger spelling) have emphasized the rapid progress in language development realized by even very young deaf children through this method. Russian pedagogues use both methods simultaneously and claim highly successful results (Telford & Sawrey, 1972). Sharp observed that good lipreaders performed significantly better than poor lipreaders on measures of visual closure, movement closure, and short-term memory. Future research may indicate that direct training in the foregoing skills can facilitate the acquisition of lipreading.

A higher percentage of hearing-impaired than normally hearing persons have been classified as emotionally disturbed. Neuhaus hypothesized that emotional maladjustment among the aurally impaired may be due to the negative attitudes of parents toward children or toward disability in hearing. A relationship was observed between a negative parental attitude toward children and an emotional disturbance in the child; however, maternal and paternal attitudes toward disability were not related to the emotional adjustment of the deaf child. These relationships lend some support to the view that the home environment contributes to the social adjustment of the hearing-impaired child.

CULTURAL FACTORS AND HEARING

Ronald Goldman
Jay W. Sanders

Abstract. This study reviews the results of several recent investigations on the hearing acuity of normal and culturally disadvantaged children and adults. Findings suggest that the hearing impairments reported among the culturally disadvantaged may reflect the testing conditions used rather than loss of hearing.

In recent years the culturally disadvantaged have been the subject of investigation in many areas of learning disability. Attention has been given to various aspects of learning such as speech, language, intelligence, and perception, as well as motoric behavior. Even more recently, interest has developed in the relationship between hearing and cultural limitation. Specifically, a reported characteristic of the culturally disadvantaged is their inability to discriminate differences in auditory stimuli. Deutsch (1964) has suggested that discrimination difficulties may exist even in the presence of an intact end organ in the child from an environment of limited meaningful auditory experience. According to Deutsch, although the home may be noisy, meaningful verbal interaction may be severely restricted.

Clark and Richards (1966) have recently reported a significant auditory deficiency in an economically disadvantaged population. A comparison of children from this group with a control group of advantaged children on the Wepman Test of Auditory Discrimination revealed the disadvantaged children to be significantly poorer in the ability to differentiate between phonemically similar words.

Results obtained by the present investigators suggest that this same dysfunction may occur in the culturally disadvantaged for auditory stimuli that are far less complex. In this survey, 226 recent high school graduates selected by Fisk University for a US Office of Education project were seen for hearing evaluation. The group was unique in that the criteria for selection were intellectual potential for successful academic achievement at the college level combined with a culturally and economically limited background.

The hearing evaluation consisted of pure tone screen testing in small groups at Fisk University. The noise level in the test room was found by measurement to be entirely adequate for screen testing. Students failing the initial screen test were retested one week later in a sound isolated room at the Bill Wilkerson Hearing and Speech Center.

Although a total of 25 students, 11.1 percent of the population, failed the initial test, only one student was found on retest to have an actual hearing loss, and the remaining 24 students passed a rescreen at 0 dB hearing level re the 1951 ASA standards. Thus, more than 10 percent of this population was unable to respond to pure tones at suprathreshold levels in the screen test situation.

These findings are certainly provocative in view of the results reported previously by Deutsch (1964) and by Clark and Richards (1966). One can speculate with these investigators that the limited verbal interaction in the presence of high noise levels frequently found in the disadvantaged home environment might interfere with the acquisition by the child of the ability to extract an auditory signal from a competing background. Clearly, the 24 students described here had difficulty in this task. Although they were unable to respond to pure tones at hearing levels of 15 to 20 dB re the 1951 ASA standards amid the distractions of the screen test situation, they responded easily at 0 dB hearing level when alone in the sound isolated test room. The question may be raised, of course, as to wheth-

From *Exceptional Children,* 1969, **35**, 489–490. Reprinted by permission of The Council for Exceptional Children.

er the distractions present were auditory, visual, or a combination of these two factors. It should be reiterated here that the noise level in the screen room was not high enough to interfere with perception of the test tones.

Results similar to those reported here were obtained in a recent school hearing survey in Sarasota County, Florida (McAdoo, 1967). A total of 3,634 second, fourth, and sixth grade pupils were evaluated. Of this number, 12 percent failed the initial pure tone screen test. Although this percentage is somewhat higher than that usually found in a school survey, it is certainly not phenomenal. A breakdown of the schools according to area, however, does produce some startling results. In only those schools in nondisadvantaged areas, the percentage of screen test failure was only 5.6, whereas the percentage of failure in the disadvantaged neighborhood schools was 41.4. Furthermore, on followup testing, almost all of the latter group were found to have normal hearing. The similarity to the results reported here for college age students is striking. One can at least speculate that the variable in both surveys was a significant disability in responding to a simple stimulus in a dis-

traction situation. Spurious screen test failure rates as high as 10 and 40 percent in culturally disadvantaged populations force one to wonder about the relationship between cultural background and auditory perception.

Previous studies have differentiated between disadvantaged and nondisadvantaged children in their ability to discriminate between speech sounds. The findings reported in the present study and the Florida survey suggest difficulty with a much simpler auditory task, the detection of pure tones.

The need for further study is clearly indicated. If this auditory disability does exist, procedures for overcoming the problem must be developed to minimize or eliminate a serious obstacle to learning in the culturally disadvantaged.

References

Clark, A. D., & Richards, C. J. Auditory discrimination among economically disadvantaged and nondisadvantaged preschool children. *Exceptional Children*, 1966, **33**, 259-262.

Deutsch, C. Auditory discrimination and learning: Social factors. *Merrill-Palmer Quarterly*, 1964, **4**, 277-296.

McAdoo, D. *Hearing screening summary: Sarasota County Schools, 1966-67.*

MODALITY OF SIMILARITY AND HEARING ABILITY*

Doris V. Allen

Paired-associate lists differing in implicit modality of cue (auditory or visual) and in response mode (written or oral) were learned by five groups of children differing in hearing ability (normal to deaf). Overall, visual cues were easier than auditory cues, but cues interacted with hearing ability such that implicit auditory cues (rhymes) contributed less to the performance of Ss with impaired hearing.

Early severe hearing impairment manifests itself primarily in later retarded language skills. This relationship is generally taken to mean that loss in hearing ability interferes quantitatively with the development of language. That is, the language of the hearing-impaired is regarded as representing some less well-developed immature stage of verbal functioning through which all persons pass.

*The work reported herein was performed pursuant to Grant No. OEG-0-8-07837-1858 from the U.S. Office of Education, Department of Health, Education, and Welfare.

Reprinted with permission of the author and publisher from *Psychonomic Science*, 1971, **24**(2), 69-71.

In contrast to this quantitative view, a qualitative explanation should be explored. An early hearing loss may alter the perception, so that primary emphasis is placed upon sense modalities other than audition as information-gathering channels. Thus, the dimensions underlying cognitive processes might be visual-tactile rather than auditory-visual, which probably best describes the process in normal-hearing individuals. Numerous studies of short-term memory (e.g., Conrad, 1964; Wickelgren, 1965) suggest that the hearing person transforms written verbal material to

its auditory equivalents during storage and retrieval. This transformation probably reflects the fact that oral language precedes the written mode in time. If this is so, the hearing-handicapped person would not be expected to make the same kind of transformation, since oral language is not as "basic" to him, generally being acquired later in life. It is for this reason that qualitatively different strategies in processing verbal material are expected as a function of hearing ability.

Conrad & Rush (1965) provide evidence supporting qualitative differences as a function of hearing ability in their study of short-term memory in the deaf. They found that deaf and normals differed in the manner in which they stored letters of the alphabet; normals apparently used auditory encoding, while the deaf did not. The fact that errors were consistent among the deaf led Conrad and Rush to conclude further that some other encoding system was being used which they were unable to identify. Similarly, Odom & Blanton (1967) varied word order in phrases and found that recall by normal Ss was adversely affected by unusual word orders, while recall by the deaf was not affected by this factor. They suggested that the linguistic structure of sign might be more important for understanding how the deaf learn word phrases. Pronunciability of trigrams presented for recognition (Blanton & Nunnally, 1967) or for recall (Blanton & Odom, 1968) has been studied using normal and deaf Ss. In both instances, the deaf were unaffected by the pronunciability ratings, while normal-hearing Ss showed a deterioration in performance for the items rated more difficult to pronounce. Allen (1970) used acoustic similarity to produce interference in a paired-associate task and reported a positive relationship between amount of hearing loss and resistance to interference. The deaf also exhibit less interference on the color-word task of the Stroop test than do normals (Allen, 1971). Thus, a number of studies suggest that hearing-impaired Ss do not handle verbal material internally in the same fashion as do normals.

Unpublished Research by McLinden (1959) gives additional support for qualitative differences in learning as a function of hearing. She provided auditory or visual cues for learning printed word pairs and found that printed word pairs which sounded alike (ROUGH-CUFF) were easier to learn for normal-hearing children, while printed word pairs which looked alike (LOST-MOST) were easier for hearing-loss Ss. However, all of her Ss responded orally, a fact which could explain the performance of the normals. Speaking the answers might encourage the use of acoustic attributes for storage, since the information would be retained in the form needed for responding. While this explanation for her findings is possible, it is weakened by the fact that the short-term memory studies demonstrating acoustic encoding have generally employed written responses. Thus, acoustic memory seems to be characteristic of normal-hearing Ss regardless of response mode. It is predicted that performance in McLinden's study would not be different if written response modes were used.

The present study was designed to confirm the findings of McLinden regarding an interaction between nature of cue and hearing ability and to examine the effects of a written response mode upon performance. While a significant interaction between hearing ability and modality of cues was expected, no interaction between modality of cues and response mode was predicted.

MATERIALS

The materials consisted of two lists of eight word pairs which rhyme but are spelled differently (auditory lists), two lists of eight word pairs which are spelled similarly but differ in pronunciation (visual lists), and a list of four unrelated word pairs (practice list). An example of an auditory pair would be SIGN-LINE, while CAVE-HAVE would be a visual pair. All words were rated A or AA in frequency (Thorndike & Lorge, 1944) and were monosyllabic.

SUBJECTS

A total of 45 children were tested. Five groups were established on the basis of hearing ability, using the average pure-tone threshold for 500, 1,000, and 2,000 Hz in the better ear. One group had normal hearing, while four had some degree of sensorineural hearing impairment: 0-25 dB ISO (mild or nonsignificant losses), 26-60 dB (moderate losses or "hard of hearing"), 61-90 dB (severe losses), and 91+ dB (profound losses or "deaf"). In addition, all Ss were required to have grade-equivalent reading scores of 3.5 to 6.0 (Iowa Test of Basic Skills).

PROCEDURE

Visual presentation was used for all conditions. A Tel-n-See film-strip projector (with an inbuilt synchronized tape recorder) and a lenticular screen were used; letter height in the projected image was 8 in. The materials were photographed on 16-mm film strips in reverse image; 2-sec presentation intervals were controlled by tape-recorded signals.

One each of the auditory and visual lists was assigned to a written response condition, the other to an oral; the combination changed for each child. In this manner, four experimental conditions were formed: oral auditory (OA), oral visual (OV), written auditory (WA), and written visual (WV). Order of administration of the four lists was counterbalanced, and each S was assigned to an order at the first session.

Initially, the practice list was administered in the same response mode as the first test list; for example, if the first test condition was to use written responses, practice was also written. Practice continued until the S understood the task. Usually only a

few trials were needed. This was followed by the first test list; alternate study and test trials were administered until the S achieved one errorless trial. Booklets with separate pages for each trial were used for written responses, and a cassette tape recorder was used during oral responding. The remaining three lists were administered at separate sessions. At no time was attention directed to the relevant dimension for the cues; each subsequent session was begun with a statement to the effect that another list of word pairs was to be learned, and the response mode was defined.

RESULTS

The mean number of trials to a criterion of one errorless trial for the five groups and the four experimental conditions are summarized in Table 1. As shown there, the auditory lists were more difficult than the visual for all the hearing-loss groups but not for normal-hearing Ss, while the groups all performed alike on the visual lists. Modality of response apparently did not contribute differentially to learning. These trends were supported statistically. The only significant sources of variance were cues [$F(1,40) = 28.40$, $p < .01$] and Cues by Hearing Ability interaction [$F(4,40 = 3.44$, $p < .05$]. A posteriori tests using the Scheffé procedure (Winer, 1962) showed the 0-25 dB group to be significantly poorer, as compared with normals, on the auditory lists. None of the differences among groups for the visual lists was significant. Simple effects for cues showed that visual cues were significantly easier for the 0-25 dB and 91+ dB hearing-loss groups.

Learning curves for the groups for each condition were also examined, with points representing mean number of trials needed to learn the first word pair (regardless of which pair it was), the second pair, etc. The curves for the two auditory conditions, OA and WA, were much alike, as were the curves obtained for the two visual conditions, OV and WV; only one of each set is presented here. The learning curves for both auditory conditions showed a marked spread among the five groups, as illustrated by Fig. 1 (Condition OA). The poorest performance on practically all auditory pairs was shown by the 0-25 dB group, while the normal-hearing group showed the best performance. These data are in marked contrast to the two visual conditions. As seen in Fig. 2 (Condition OV), there is little spread among the curves for the groups. The normal group was now the slowest, with the deaf group fastest in acquiring each visual pair. Since repeated measurements were used, differences must be attributed to

Table 1
Mean Trials to Criterion (TTC) and Standard Deviations (SD) in Four
Experimental Conditions for Five Hearing Categories

Hearing Category	N		OA	OV	WA	WV
Normal	13	TTC	4.77	4.92	4.69	4.15
		SD	1.74	2.84	1.97	1.68
0-25	7	TTC	8.14	3.57	7.29	4.43
		SD	3.02	1.14	4.82	1.27
26-60	8	TTC	6.38	4.75	5.50	4.13
		SD	2.93	2.25	2.33	2.17
61-90	8	TTC	5.50	3.63	5.63	3.75
		SD	1.31	1.30	3.11	1.49
91+	9	TTC	7.00	3.56	6.11	3.44
		SD	2.55	1.60	1.69	1.60

materials and not to sampling differences. Also, order of presentation of the lists had been counterbalanced to offset any bias due to sequencing effects.

Since the groups were controlled on reading ability, they necessarily differed in age. To evaluate whether or not this variable contributed to the obtained differences, correlations between age and performance were calculated for the 32 Ss with impaired hearing. These values ranged in magnitude from .03 to −.12 for the four conditions and were not significant.

DISCUSSION

The two hypotheses in this study were supported by the data. The fact that we failed to reject the null hypothesis for the interaction between modality of cues and response mode is interpreted as indicating that no such practical relationship exists, fully recognizing the philosophical problems inherent in such a conclusion. Greater confidence in this interpretation is obtained from the very small F ratio for this source of variance. As for the other hypothesis in this study, a significant Cues by Hearing Ability interaction was obtained, with differences somewhat in the predicted direction, i.e., the visual material was learned more rapidly than the auditory by the hearing-impaired, while normal Ss learned all lists at the same time. These data are consistent with the results obtained by McLinden, who also found a significant interaction between cues and hearing ability, and reinforce the theory that a congenital hearing loss results in different strategies' being used in learning verbal materials.

Since cues for learning word pairs are constant within a list, it might be suspected that differences in trials to criterion merely reflect differences in the trials needed to recognize the relevant dimension. If this were so, then the learning curves should show the groups to be separated on the number of trials needed to learn the first pair and should be negatively accelerated thereafter. In fact, just the opposite was observed. The groups did not differ in trials to acquire the first item but did diverge on subsequent pairs with more trials needed to learn successive pairs. In particular, the curves for the 0-25 dB group with Conditions OA and WA suggest a laborious trial-by-trial acquisition of materials similar to what one might see with unrelated word pairs. Thus, the learning-curve data serve to demonstrate further the hypothesized qualitative differences in approach to verbal material by hearing and hearing-impaired children.

The fact that the 0-25 dB group showed the greatest effect of modality of cues is intriguing. This group is usually considered to be most like normal-hearing Ss yet performed least like the normal group in this study. Possibly auditory training, generally recommended for more severe losses, could be of benefit to these Ss also. Obviously, further research with hearing losses of this magnitude is needed.

REFERENCES

ALLEN, D. V. Acoustic interference in paired-associate learning as a function of hearing ability. Psychonomic Science, 1970, 18, 231-233.

ALLEN, D. V. Color-word interference in deaf and normal children. Paper presented at 43rd annual meeting of Midwestern Psychological Association, Detroit, Michigan, May 1971.

BLANTON, R. L., & NUNNALLY, J. C. Retention of trigrams by deaf and hearing subjects as a function of pronunciability. Journal of Verbal Learning & Verbal Behavior, 1967, 6, 428-431.

BLANTON, R. L., & ODOM, P. B. Some possible interference and facilitation effects of pronunciability. Journal of Verbal Learning & Verbal Behavior, 1968, 7, 844-846.

CONRAD, R. Acoustic confusions in immediate memory. British Journal of Psychology, 1964, 55, 75-84.

CONRAD, R., & RUSH, M. L. On the nature of short-term memory encoding by the deaf. Journal of Speech & Hearing Disorders, 1965, 30, 336-343.

McLINDEN, M. M. C. Learning with different associative cues by normal-hearing and hearing-impaired children. Unpublished data, Wayne State University, 1959.

ODOM, P. B., & BLANTON, R. L. Phrase-learning in deaf and hearing subjects. Journal of Speech & Hearing Research, 1967, 10, 600-605.

THORNDIKE, E. L., & LORGE, I. The teacher's word book of 30,000 words. New York: Bureau of Publications, Teachers College, Columbia University, 1944.

WICKELGREN, W. A. Acoustic similarity and intrusion errors in short-term memory. Journal of Experimental Psychology, 1965, 70, 102-108.

WINER, B. J. Statistical principles in experimental design. New York: McGraw-Hill, 1962.

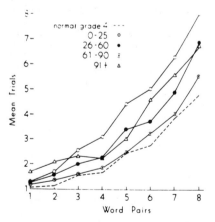

Fig. 1. Learning curves for five categories of hearing ability for Condition OA.

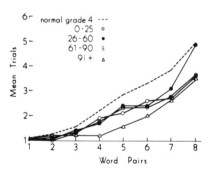

Fig. 2. Learning curves for five categories of hearing ability for Condition OV.

READING COMPREHENSION SKILLS AMONG HEARING IMPAIRED ADOLESCENTS

Bruce Balow
Helen Fulton
Ella Peploe

One hundred fifty-seven hearing impaired adolescents in Minnesota, who attend residential schools or special day school programs for the hearing impaired, were given two reading tests, the New Developmental Reading Test *and the* Metropolitan Reading Test *to determine their reading levels. Comparisons were made between scores of various age groups (ranging from age 13 to age 21); between scores obtained under standard time limits and those attained under unlimited time conditions; and between literal reading comprehension skills and interpretative reading comprehension skills. Implications of these comparisons and additional descriptive information are discussed.*

DEFICIENCIES in the reading skills of hearing impaired children have been documented in the literature over the past 50 years. Pintner and Patterson in 1917 reported that median reading scores of deaf people at any age never reached the median of 8-year-old hearing children and that deaf children of ages 14 to 16 had median reading scores equal to hearing children of age 7. More recently, Pugh (1946) reported that none of her groups obtained median scores at sixth grade level on the *Iowa Silent Reading Test.* She also reported only limited improvement in reading achievement between the seventh and 13th years of schooling. Fusfeld (1955) reported median scores of approximately grade eight in paragraph reading and grade six in word meaning on the *Advanced Stanford Achievement Test* among 18- and 19-year-old deaf students entering Gallaudet. Goetzinger and Rousey (1959) found residential school deaf children of average ability reading at fourth to fifth grade level throughout the age range of 14 to 21. Magner (1964), reporting on *Stanford Achievement Test* scores among deaf pupils at Clarke School, showed 8- to 10-year-olds having average reading scores at second to third grade level while 17- and 18-year-olds were reading at sixth grade level on the average.

The major survey of reading abilities among deaf children is that of Wrightstone *et al.* (1962) in which 5307 deaf children between the ages of 10 and 16 were tested on the elementary level of the *Metropolitan Achievement Test.* Consistent with most previous findings on all but highly selected hearing impaired groups, according to Furth's (1966) calculations with the Wrightstone data, roughly 8 percent of those tested read above fourth grade level. At age 11 the mean reading score was mid-second grade; five years later, at age 16, the mean was only one grade higher, at mid-third grade.

This is a dismal record. The search for more detailed description, causes, explanations, and corrections needs to be continued. The present study contributes some detail to previous descriptions of the problem.

population and sample

The population for this study was comprised of non-mentally retarded hearing impaired adolescents attending

Reprinted with permission of the authors and publisher from *Volta Review,* 1971, **73**, 113–119. © The Alexander Graham Bell Association for the Deaf.

special education programs in the State of Minnesota. Forty-nine students were dropped from the analysis of results because they were absent at one or more of the various testing sessions. Thus, the sample reported on here is 157 adolescents (70 girls; 87 boys), approximately two-thirds of whom attended residential schools, and one-third attended day school special programs at the time of testing. These special educational settings included the state residential school for the deaf, special day classes for the hearing impaired housed in public junior and senior high schools, a private day school, and a private residential school. Table 1 portrays the age and sex distribution of the sample.

description of hearing

Air conducted, pure tone, audiometric evaluation was available on all of the subjects in this study. Measurements were made at 500, 1000, and 2000 cycles in both ears. Measurements of discrimination scores, speech reception thresholds, speech awareness thresholds, and evaluation of functioning ability of the subject with a hearing aid were recorded by authorized audiologists within a period of two years preceding the reading testing. The etiology and history of hearing loss in many cases was recorded as "unknown," especially for the older age groups; therefore, it was not included in the variables of this study.

Three arbitrary categories of hearing level were chosen by the advising audiologist. Group I, mild impairment, had losses of 40 to 60 decibels; Group II, severe impairment, had losses of 65 to 95 decibels; and Group III, profound impairment, showed losses of 100 or more decibels. All measures were by ISO standards. The distribution of subjects in these categories is shown in Table 1.

Students with milder losses than Group I were not found in these educational settings.

procedure

The subjects were tested with the five parts of the *New Developmental Reading Tests, Intermediate Level* (1968). These five sections measure reading vocabulary and four types of reading comprehension; however, the comparison of primary interest in this study was between the two parts that test literal comprehension and the two parts that test inferential comprehension. Test administration was usually handled by the teacher. Directions were a slightly simplified form of the standard directions for hearing children.

Table 1

Distribution of the Sample by Age, Sex, and Hearing Impairment

| Age* | Male | Female | Total | ISO Standards | | |
				100+	95-65	60-40
−21	4	4	8	7	1	0
−20	13	9	22	13	9	0
−19	11	8	19	11	6	2
−18	10	17	27	12	14	1
−17	17	7	24	7	15	2
−16	16	9	25	10	14	1
−15	9	11	20	4	15	1
−14	6	5	11	5	6	0
−13	1	0	1	1	0	0
N	87	70	157	70	80	7

* Age is to the nearest 6 months, thus age 21 includes pupils 20-7 to 21-6.

Transparencies of the directions were used with an overhead projector to ensure understanding of the task by the hearing impaired pupils and to provide uniform administration from one classroom to another. Additionally, when the normal time limit expired, the subjects were instructed to mark the item just completed and then to continue with the test until they reached either a power limit or the end of the test. Finally, to provide an independent measure of reading skills, the vocabulary and paragraph reading sections of the *Metropolitan Achievement Test, Intermediate,* were administered with standard time limits.

results and implications

Most of the subjects were found to be in the profound and severe hearing loss categories; approximately five percent were in the mild impairment category. Inasmuch as the sample was obtained from special programs for hearing impaired pupils, this finding simply confirms the expected degree of impairment.

Mean scores in this sample, at about mid-fourth grade in vocabulary and early fifth grade in comprehension, were approximately equivalent to those reported in other studies of unselected hearing impaired adolescents. It is difficult to explain fully these results since they are somewhat more sanguine than certain other surveys have indicated. It is likely that the use of unlimited time on the *New Developmental Reading Tests* provided a "maximum power" score rather than a "usual efficiency" score such as might be obtained from time limits. However, the *Metropolitan Reading Test* was administered with standard time limits, and although the obtained scores were slightly lower than those obtained in standard time limits on the *New Developmental Reading Test,* they also tended to be above previous reported results and confirm the *New Developmental Reading Test* findings. Because many of the highest achieving hearing impaired students in Minnesota may be

fully integrated in regular classes and therefore not included in this sample, there is some likelihood that the mean scores for the total Minnesota population of pupils with severe or profound hearing impairment are even higher than those reported here.

As has been observed consistently in previous research, there was only limited improvement in the mean scores from younger to older age groups. Over the six years, from the two youngest age groups (13 - 14 - 15) to the two oldest groups (20 and 21), the growth reflected in Table 2 is roughly half of one year.

Table 3 shows that on the total sample, the Literal Comprehension mean grade equivalent score was significantly higher than the Creative Comprehension mean. The difference of almost one full grade was a practical difference, in addition to being statistically significant. Even with unlimited time, these hearing impaired pupils were unable to accomplish inferential-interpretive reading nearly as well as they could read for specific factual information.

It is interesting to note in Table 4 that on the *New Developmental Reading Tests* there is little difference in the timed and unlimited scores on the Creative Comprehension tests, but there is a distinct tendency for extended time to improve the Literal Comprehension scores. This finding, together with the above finding, may be a reflection of the tendency to "concreteness" in the language and reasoning of pupils with severe hearing impairment. The reading comprehension skills required in the Literal Comprehension subtests are those of acquiring and associating factual information explicitly stated in the material. Such skills are highly related to the study-type reading a pupil is normally expected to do in school content subjects in order to learn factual information.

The Creative Comprehension sub-

Table 2

Mean Grade Equivalent Scores by Age Groups on Selected Parts of
the New Developmental Reading Tests* and
on the Metropolitan Reading Tests**

Age	N	New Developmental Reading Tests *			Metropolitan Reading Tests * *	
		Vocabu-lary	Literal Compre-hension	Creative Compre-hension	Vocabulary	Paragraph Reading
		Mean	Mean	Mean	Mean	Mean
21	8	4.3	5.8	4.9	4.7	4.4
20	22	5.1	6.6	5.5	5.0	4.8
19	19	5.5	7.0	5.9	5.2	5.4
18	27	4.5	5.8	5.1	4.6	4.6
17	24	4.8	6.2	5.4	4.5	4.9
16	25	4.2	5.6	4.7	3.9	4.4
15	20	4.5	5.9	5.2	4.0	4.5
13 & 14	12	4.0	5.5	4.9	3.7	4.2
	N=157	$\overline{X}$=4.7	$\overline{X}$=6.1	$\overline{X}$=5.2	$\overline{X}$=4.5	$\overline{X}$=4.7

* Administered under conditions of unlimited time.
** Administered with standard time limits.

Table 3

Difference Between the Unlimited Time Mean Scores for
Literal Comprehension and
Creative Comprehension on the Total Sample

Literal Comprehension	Creative Comprehension		
Mean	Mean	t Value	P
6.1	5.2	1.82	.05>p>.025

N = 157

Table 4

Differences Between the Means of Standard Time Limit and
Unlimited Time Conditions for Literal Comprehension and
Creative Comprehension on the Total Sample

	Standard Time	Unlimited Time	t value	P
Literal Com-prehension	5.6	6.1	.959	.25>p>.10
Creative Com-prehension	5.0	5.2	.429	.40>p>.25

N = 157

tests, by contrast, require the pupil to make inferences, judgments, and conclusions from information provided, as well as to make interpretations of the feeling, tone, mood, and literary qualities of the material. The pupil must "read between the lines," understand subtle nuances, and reflect on what he has read. That pupils with severe hearing impairments find this type of reading much more difficult than reading in factual content is not surprising. However, the actual demonstration of this often noted difference is hard to find in the research literature. Additionally, this result may be taken as validation that the *New Developmental Reading Tests* do indeed measure the two types of comprehension indicated.

The small group of seven pupils with mild impairment is of special interest. However, its small size makes its validity questionable, and great caution should be taken in making statements which are more than questions for further investigation. In this particular group, the mean Literal Comprehension "maximum power" score on the *New Developmental Reading Tests*

was 7.4; the Creative Comprehension mean was 6.6; the mean "usual efficiency" score on the *Metropolitan Reading Test* paragraph test was 6.3. These scores are more than one grade above the same test means of the total hearing impaired sample shown in Table 2.

Because of the very small number included in this group, and the critical questions regarding factors other than hearing loss which contribute to the decision to place a pupil in a residential program (or even a special day school program), these data can do no more than reinforce the importance of further research appropriately designed to answer the question of whether severity of hearing loss reflects anything of consequence about reading skill.

Table 5 shows good agreement between the mean vocabulary scores on the two separate tests; but a higher mean score for General Comprehension is shown on the *New Developmental Reading Tests* than on the *Metropolitan Reading Test*.

Table 5

Total Sample Mean Reading Scores of the Metropolitan Reading Test and the New Developmental Reading Test With Standard Time Limits

Test	Vocabulary	Comprehension*
New Developmental Reading Test	4.7	5.3
Metropolitan	4.5	4.7

N = 157

* The comprehension score for the New Developmental Reading Test in this table is the mean combined score of the two literal and two creative comprehension tests. The comprehension score for the Metropolitan Reading Test is the Paragraph Reading Test mean score.

References

Bond, Guy L., Balow, Bruce, and Hoyt, Cyril J., *New Developmental Reading Tests, Intermediate Level*, Chicago: Lyons and Carnahan Co., 1968.
Furth, Hans G., "A Comparison of Reading Test Norms of Deaf and Hearing Children," *American Annals of the Deaf*, 111: 461-462, March 1966.
Fusfeld, Irving A., "The Academic Program of Schools for the Deaf," *The Volta Review*, 57:63-70, February 1955.
Goetzinger, C. P., and Rousey, E. I., "Educational Achievement of Deaf Children," *American Annals of the Deaf*, 104:221-224, 1959.
Magner, Marjorie E., "Reading: Goals and Achievements at Clarke School for the Deaf," *The Volta Review*, 66:464-468, September 1964.

Pintner, R. and Patterson, D. G., "The Ability of Deaf and Hearing Children to Follow Printed Directions," *American Annals of the Deaf*, 62:448-472, 1917.

Pugh, Gladys S., "Summaries from Appraisal of the Silent Reading Abilities of Acoustically Handicapped Children," *American Annals of the Deaf*, 91:331-349, 1946.

Wrightstone, J. Wayne, Aronow, Miriam S., and Moskowitz, Sue, "Developing Reading Test Norms for Deaf Children," *American Annals of the Deaf*, 108:311-316, 1963.

THE RELATIONSHIP OF VISUAL CLOSURE TO SPEECHREADING

Elizabeth Y. Sharp

Abstract: This study investigated the relationship of visual closure to speechreading ability among young deaf children. Tests of visual closure, movement closure, and short term memory were administered to a group of deaf 7, 8, and 9 year old good speechreaders (N = 18) and to a group of poor speechreaders (N = 19) as determined by a speechreading test. Performances were compared using the Mann-Whitney U Test of Significance. Results indicated that good speechreaders are significantly superior to poor speechreaders on tests of visual closure, movement closure, and short term memory.

A MAJOR problem that has confronted educators of the deaf for many years is why some deaf children become proficient speechreaders and some do not, even though they have been exposed to the same instructional methods. In attempting to determine the factors that enchance or inhibit the learning of speechreading by deaf children, researchers have studied such variables as chronological age, length of speechreading training, intelligence, rate of speech, age of onset of concept formation, educational achievement and grade placement, visual memory span, stimulus material, and synthetic ability. Reviews of these studies have indicated that there is no significant relationship between speechreading and chronological age (Utley, 1946; Reid, 1947), length of speechreading training (Heider & Heider, 1940), intelligence (Pintner, 1929; Reid, 1947; Simons, 1959; Quigley & Frisina, 1961), concept formation (Simons, 1959), or rate of speech (Byers & Lieberman, 1959). Utley (1946) found that speechreading ability cannot be predicted from the age of onset of deafness. Heider and Heider (1940) stated that the relationship between speechreading and age of onset is difficult to

determine statistically as each case must be studied individually.

The studies on educational achievement (Pintner, 1929; Reid, 1947; Simons, 1959; Quigley & Frisina, 1961) have shown that speechreading and educational achievement are related. This is understandable since educational achievement is a measure of vocabulary and language development and hence should correlate with speechreading ability, which is partially contingent upon language development.

Simons (1959) and Costello (1964) found that visual memory span is related to proficient speechreading. However, it should be noted that the subjects in both studies were adults.

It would appear that what is referred to as visual synthesis in the literature is the same as visual closure, the integration of parts to form a whole. Studies investigating visual synthetic ability and its relationship to speechreading have been limited to hearing and hearing impaired adult subjects.

Research on synthetic ability (Kitson, 1915; Göpfert, 1923; Sanders & Coscarelli, 1970) has shown a relationship between proficient speechreading and synthetic ability.

The fact that research has indicated that proficient speechreading ability is related to visual closure among adults suggests

From *Exceptional Children*, 1972, **38**, 729-734. Reprinted by permission of The Council for Exceptional Children.

that this relationship should be investigated among young deaf children. The present study attempted to answer the following question: Are visual closure, movement closure, and short term memory related to proficient speechreading among young deaf children?

Procedure

The experimental design included a comparison of 18 deaf children who were good speechreaders (age 7 to 9 years) with 19 deaf children who were poor speechreaders (age 7 to 9 years) on eight tests of visual closure, movement closure, and short term memory.

Subjects

Subjects were selected from the population of 7, 8, and 9 year old children at the Arizona State School for the Deaf, Tucson, Arizona, and from the California School for Deaf, Riverside, California.

Eligible subjects met the following criteria: (a) chronological ages of 7, 8, or 9 years, (b) incurred hearing loss at the age of 3 or before, (c) sensory-neural loss of 75 decibels or more in the better ear averaged across the speech range, and (d) no visual defects that would impede academic learning.

A speechreading test consisting of words, number phrases, and commands was given to 91 children meeting the study criteria. To establish greater reliability, the speechreading test was first administered by a qualified teacher of the deaf and after a 3 week interval administered by another qualified teacher of the deaf. The examiners were not familiar with the children. Tests were scored by the investigator.

The good speechreaders were defined as those children who scored in the upper third of the sample on the speechreading test given by two examiners, 3 weeks apart, and the poor speechreaders as those who scored in the lower third by each examiner, 3 weeks apart. Thus, 18 good and 19 poor speechreaders were examined.

Measuring Instruments

A speechreading test consisting of 36 items was constructed by the experimenter (Sharp, 1970). From the scores of the first 43 children to which it was administered at the Arizona State School for the Deaf,

an internal consistency correlation coefficient was computed yielding an r of .94. An internal consistency correlation coefficient was not computed on eligible subjects at the California School for the Deaf.

Since the test was administered to the children by two examiners with a 3 week interval between testing, test-retest reliability was computed separately for the Arizona State School for the Deaf and the California School for the Deaf. Test-retest reliability by the two examiners yielded an r of .90 for the 43 children at the Arizona State School for the Deaf and an r of .88 for 48 children at the California School for the Deaf. It was felt that the correlation coefficients were sufficiently high to warrant its use in the selection of good and poor speechreaders.

Elements of Thurstone's (1940) factorial study of perception were used as a starting point for the selection and development of the closure tests. He described three kinds of visual closure: (a) visual closure involving the ability to form or infer a meaningful whole from a visual presentation which initially appears unorganized and scattered, (b) visual closure that is obtained by inferring a whole from only some elements of the visual presentation, and (c) visual closure involving the selection of a figure embedded in what appears at first glance to be a total configuration.

Tests administered in this study attempted to assess the three types of visual closure described by Thurstone (1940), visual closure with movement, and the memory component of visual closure. All tests were administered by the investigator without the use of verbal communication.

Visual closure as described by Thurstone was tested by: (a) Picture Completion Subtest of the *Hiskey-Nebraska Test of Learning Aptitude* (Hiskey, 1966), (b) Visual Closure Subtest of the *Illinois Test of Psycholinguistic Abilities*, (c) *Porteus Maze Test* (Porteus, 1950), (d) Hidden Object Test, and (e) Hidden Figure Test. The Hidden Object Test was developed by the investigator and consists of two demonstration pictures and four test pictures in which a number of objects are imbedded. In order to close, the subject must discard the whole picture and find the objects. The Hidden Figures Test is a 20 item test also developed by the investigator. The figures in the test are nonmeaningful and were selected from the Gottschaldt figures.

The subject must discard the whole figure and find a specific figure within the larger one in order to obtain closure.

Movement closure tests were the Rhythm Pattern: A Test of Movement Closure and the Slide Test: A Test of Movement Closure. The Rhythm Pattern Test, developed by the investigator, consists of six patterns of gestures of increasing length. First, the complete pattern is executed by the examiner, and then it is repeated by the examiner and the subject. Each time it is repeated, the examiner omits a pair of gestures, allowing the subject to finish the pattern. The subject needs not only visual closure ability, speed of perception, and short term memory but movement closure to succeed on this test. The rationale behind this test lies in the fact that speech is movement and has rhythm and the speechreader must fill in the movements that are either missed or not visible. The Slide Test, developed by the investigator, involves a series of incidents of increasing complexity with the outcome left incomplete to be filled in by the subject. To obtain closure the subject must select the proper outcome. The situations become more complex, yet the number of clues remain the same. This test also assesses speed of perception and short term visual memory. Each event is on a series of slides and the subject selects the correct outcome from a multiple choice sheet of sketches placed in front of him.

The Visual Sequential Memory Subtest of the *Illinois Test of Psycholinguistic Abilities* was used to assess visual memory.

Results

Table 1 presents the means and standard deviations for chronological age, the two speechreading tests, and the visual closure tests for the 18 good speechreaders and the 19 poor speechreaders. It can be noted from Table 1 that:

1. The mean chronological ages of the good speechreaders (106.2 months) and the poor speechreaders (102.5) differed by only 4 months.
2. On both speechreading tests there is a marked difference between the mean scores of good speechreaders constituting the upper third of the sample of the 83 deaf children tested. Test scores were higher on the second administra-

tion than on the first, possibly due to practice effect which was assumed to be equal for both groups.
3. The mean raw scores on all eight closure tests were higher for good speechreaders than for poor speechreaders.
4. The standard deviations of scores for good and poor speechreaders appear to show some similarity with the exception of the Rhythm Pattern Test in which poor speechreaders have a standard deviation of 14.66 as compared to the standard deviation of 5.3 for the good speechreaders.

Table 2 presents the comparisons of the performances of good and poor speechreaders on the tests of visual closure, movement closure, and short term visual memory using the Mann-Whitney U Test of Significance.

It will be noted from Table 2 that (a) good speechreaders were superior to poor speechreaders on Rhythm Pattern: A Test of Movement Closure, the *Porteus Maze Test*, the Hidden Figure Test, Visual Sequential Memory Subtest of the ITPA, and the Hidden Object Test; (b) there was a marginal difference between the performance of good speechreaders on the Visual Closure Subtest of the ITPA; and (c) there was no difference between the performance of good speechreaders and poor speechreaders on the Slide Test: A Test of Movement Closure and the Picture Completion Subtest of the *Hiskey-Nebraska Test of Learning Aptitude*.

Discussion

Rhythm Patterns: A Test of Movement Closure. On this test the performance of good speechreaders was significantly superior to that of poor speechreaders (.002). An analysis of the components of this test indicates that the test might be measuring movement closure, visual sequential memory, speed of perception, and rhythm perception. It should be pointed out that movement closure was not included in Thurstone's (1940) factorial study of perception. However, speech has movement, and for the purpose of this research movement closure was considered as a possible factor.

The Porteus Maze Test. On this test the performance of good speechreaders was significantly superior to that of poor speechreaders (.02). The *Porteus Maze Test*

TABLE 1

**Mean Scores and Standard Deviations for Good and Poor Speechreaders
for CA, Speechreading, and Visual Closure Tests**

Test	Good speechreaders ($N=18$)		Poor speechreaders ($N=19$)	
	X̄	SD	X̄	SD
CA in months	106.2	8.4	102.5	9.1
Speechreading Test I	57.7	5.86	21.6	2.18
Speechreading Test II	67.4	3.20	28.6	5.71
Picture Completion	16.1	3.31	15.0	4.85
Visual Closure (ITPA)	28.7	6.87	24.6	8.02
Porteus Maze Test	7.4	4.00	3.5	2.66
Hidden Objects	28.0	5.78	22.5	6.96
Hidden Figures	16.0	3.32	11.2	6.71
Rhythm Patterns	47.1	5.32	21.8	14.65
Slide Test	11.1	2.94	10.1	3.22
Visual Sequential Memory (ITPA)	21.0	3.49	18.1	3.39

exemplifies the third type of visual closure described by Thurstone (1940) which requires that, after perceiving a presentation which at first glance is complete, the subject must discard the total configuration in order to perceive something else within the total configuration. In the *Porteus Maze Test* the subject first perceives the complete maze, then he must mentally analyze the parts to find the correct path.

The relationship between this kind of visual closure and speechreading suggested here may be that the proficient speechreader first perceives the total word sentence and/or paragraph. Next, he automatically investigates the parts (syllables or key words) to gain comprehension.

Hidden Figure Test. On this test the performance of good speechreaders was significantly superior to that of poor speechreaders (.02). The Hidden Figures Test also exemplifies the third type of visual closure, described by Thurstone (1940), in which the parts are analyzed. The objects embedded in the visual field have meaning, and similarity is seen between this and the visual perception of whole words within a sentence.

Visual Sequential Memory Test of the ITPA. The performance of good speechreaders on sequential memory was superior to that of poor speechreaders (.02) on this test. The relationship of short term visual sequential memory to proficient speechreading becomes apparent from these results. The symbols on the test are nonmeaningful and could be considered similar to speech sounds as seen on lips, which in isolation are nonmeaningful. However, if they are not remembered in the correct sequence to form a word, they remain meaningless.

Hidden Object Test. On this test the performance of good speechreaders was superior to that of poor speechreaders (.05). The Hidden Object Test also exemplifies the third type of visual closure described by Thurstone (1940) in which the whole configuration is perceived first, then discarded while the parts are analyzed. The object embedded in the visual field has meaning, and similarity is seen between this and the visual perception of words within a sentence.

Visual Closure Subtest of the ITPA. On this test the difference between the performance of good speechreaders and that of poor speechreaders was marginal (.10). An analysis of the factors evaluated by this test indicated that it measures (a) visual closure in determining the whole from the

TABLE 2

**A Comparison of Good and Poor Speechreaders
on the Mann-Whitney U Test**

Test	U	Significance level
Rhythm Patterns: A Test of Movement Closure	27.5	.002
Porteus Maze Test	67.5	.02
Hidden Figures Test	73.0	.02
Visual Sequential Memory Subtest of the ITPA	90.0	.02
Hidden Objects Test	95.0	.05
Visual Closure Subtest of the ITPA	114.5	.10
Slide Test: A Test of Movement Closure	140.5	NS
Picture Completion Subtest of the *Hiskey-Nebraska Test of Learning Aptitude*	157.5	NS

parts; (b) an element of figure-ground perception in which the background must be blotted out to perceive the object; and (c) speed of perception since the test is timed. It therefore cannot be considered a pure test of visual closure.

Slide Test: A Test of Movement Closure. There was no difference between the performance of good speechreaders and poor speechreaders on this test. The responses of the children indicated that it was unreliable. Further analysis of the test led to the conclusion that it probably measured problem solving ability as each sequence presented an incomplete situation and the subject was required to select the logical outcome. The examiner failed to note this fact in a pilot study.

Picture Completion Subtest of the Hiskey-Nebraska Test of Learning Aptitude. There was no difference between the performance of good speechreaders and poor speechreaders on this test. An analysis of the characteristics of the test reveals that the task involved is to supply missing parts which requires analyzing the picture. This may be the opposite of visual closure which involves synthesis. It appears that this test may not be a measure of synthetic or visual closure ability but rather a test of missing parts, which is analytic, not synthetic.

Implications

The above results suggest that good speechreaders have the capacity for visual closure, movement closure, and short term memory, while poor speechreaders do not. Most of the tests that showed significance are all type three visual closure described by Thurstone (1940) which is primarily a figure-ground function. These tests include the selection of a figure and the blotting out of the background.

Speechreading is the selection of the relevant elements (lip movement, facial expressions, and gestures) that relate to communication—in other words, the selection of the relevant and the blotting out of the irrelevant which is analogous to a figure-ground operation. When speechreading is considered from this viewpoint it becomes more apparent why speechreading is a figure-ground closure phenomenon.

The role of short term visual memory in proficient speechreading becomes increasingly obvious. To obtain meaning from the lip movements, they must be remembered in the correct sequence. Syllables are meaningless unless remembered in the right order which leads to a whole word or phrase. Also, key words must be recalled in the correct sequential pattern.

Movement closure and its correlates, rhythm perception, speed of perception, and short term visual memory, appear to be highly related to proficient speechreading. This is understandable as speech is movement, has rhythm, and is rapidly produced.

From the analysis of the test results it would appear that children who have good figure-ground closure, short term visual memory, and movement closure are proficient speechreaders. The reader should be cautioned that the results of this study can be interpreted only as a test of concurrent validity. It should not be interpreted as evidence of the predictive validity of closure abilities. However, a hypothesis that these factors will predict speechreading ability can be made.

The results of the study imply the possibility of developing a test that would assess the potential of young deaf children to learn speechreading. Such a test would measure the closure factors that were found to be significantly related to good speechreading. It would include experimentation with different forms of figure-ground visual closure tests and visual sequential memory tests similar to those administered in this study.

In view of the fact that there are different methods of teaching speechreading, the results of the study can provide a criterion upon which an analysis of speechreading methods can be made. This may be accomplished by analyzing speechreading instructional methods in terms of their emphasis on training visual closure, movement closure, and short term visual memory.

References

Byers, V., & Lieberman, L. Lipreading performance and the rate of the speaker. *Journal of Speech and Hearing Research*, 1959, 2, 271-276.

Costello, M. R. Individual differences in speechreading. In the *Report of the International Congress on Education of the Deaf*. Washington, D.C.: USGPO, 1964. Pp. 317-321.

Göpfert, H. Pshchologische untersuchungen uber das ablesen vom munde, bei ertaubten and horenden. Z. *Kinderforsch*, 1923, 28, 315-367.

Heider, F. K., & Heider, G. M. An experimental investigation of lipreading. *Psychological Monograph*, 1940, 52, 124-153.

Hiskey, M. S. *Hiskey-Nebraska Test of Learning Aptitude*, Lincoln, Neb.: Union College Press, 1966.

Kitson, H. D. Psychological tests for lipreading ability. *Volta Review*, 1915, 17, 471-476.

Pintner, R. Speech and speech-reading tests for the deaf. *Journal of Applied Psychology*, 1929, 13, 220-225.

Porteus, S. D. *The Porteus Maze Test and Intelligence.* Palo Alto, Cal.: Pacific Books, 1950.

Quigley, S. P., & Frisina, D. R. *Institutionalization and psychoeducational development of deaf children.* (CEC Research Monograph A3) Washington, D.C.: The Council for Exceptional Children, 1961.

Reid, G. A preliminary investigation in the testing of lipreading achievement. *Journal of Speech Disorders*, 1947, 12, 77-82.

Sanders, J. W., & Coscarelli, J. E. The relationship of visual synthesis to lipreading. *American Annals of the Deaf*, 1970, 1, 23-26.

Sharp, E. Y. The relationship of visual closure to speechreading among deaf children. Unpublished doctoral dissertation, University of Arizona, Tucson, 1970.

Simmons, A. A. Factors related to lipreading. *Journal of Speech and Hearing Research*, 1959, 4, 340-352.

Thurstone, L. L. *A factorial study of perception.* (Psychometric Monographs) Chicago: The University of Chicago Press, 1940.

Utley, J. A test for lip reading ability. *Journal of Speech Disorders*, 1946, 11, 109-116.

PARENTAL ATTITUDES AND THE EMOTIONAL ADJUSTMENT OF DEAF CHILDREN

Maury Neuhaus

Abstract: The parents of 84 deaf children of 3 age levels (3 to 7, 8 to 12, and 13 to 19) were administered instruments designed to assess their attitudes toward children and toward disability. The results of this study indicated that there is a significant relationship between maternal and paternal attitudes toward children and the child's emotional adjustment at all 3 age levels, with one exception: the father's attitudes toward children between ages 3 to 7. No significant relationship was found between parental attitudes toward disability and the child's emotional adjustment. Parental attitudes toward children did not vary with the age of the child, while parental attitudes toward disability did.

IN the literature, there is a conspicuous dearth of material regarding the deaf child's relationship with his family, the effects of deafness upon parental attitudes toward the child, and how these attitudes affect the emotional adjustment of the child. Nearly all of the studies have investigated the effects, generally negative, of auditory deprivation on personality structure, tacitly implying that a cause and effect relationship exists. The preponderance of available evidence suggests such personality traits for the deaf as feelings of inferiority, depression, poorly controlled emotions, immature emotional life, inadequate flexibility in everyday functioning, and egocentricity. It is not the intention of the writer to evaluate critically the experimental design of previous research studies, but to point up the paucity of inquiry into the possible causes for or determinants of the aforementioned personality traits. The typical research has consisted mainly of comparing deaf and hearing groups; the conclusions have been drawn with relatively no explanation of these determinants other than the prima causa of deafness itself in the deaf groups.

There can be little hope for a constructive and concerted effort to alleviate or reduce the degree of emotional maladjustment in a deaf child if this conclusion—that the maladjustment is caused by deafness—is maintained, since at the present time sensorineural deafness is irreversible. However, psychologists will be able to understand and eventually assuage problems relating to the personality of the deaf individual if they apply the knowledge derived from the study of parent-child relationships of hearing individuals to the un-

From *Exceptional Children*, 1969, 35, 721-727. Reprinted by permission of The Council for Exceptional Children.

derstanding of the family constellation of a deaf child.

The specific hypotheses tested were:

1. A deaf child's emotional adjustment is positively related to expressed maternal and paternal attitudes toward children and toward disability (deafness).
2. Deaf children whose parents are classified as expressing congruent positive attitudes toward children and disability will be rated as better emotionally adjusted than those children whose parents express congruent negative attitudes.
3. Where expressed parental attitudes toward children and disability are noncongruent, the combination of positive maternal-negative paternal attitudes will result in the deaf child's better emotional adjustment than will positive paternal-negative maternal attitudes.
4. There will be no differences between expressed parental attitudes toward children and disability, and among the relationships between these attitudes and the deaf child's emotional adjustment, for parents of children at various age levels.

Method

Subjects. Subjects in this study involved a sample of 84 deaf children who met the following criteria:

1. Performance Scale IQ score of at least 90 as measured by the Wechsler-Bellevue Scale, Wechsler Adult Intelligence Scale, or the Arthur Adaptation of the Leiter International Performance Scale, depending upon the age of the subject.
2. No severe secondary physical handicap.
3. Both parents living, neither deaf, no foreign language handicap, and educational level at least at eighth grade.

The subjects included (a) children who were randomly selected from a group of children who met the aforementioned criteria, and (b) their parents. The children were divided into three age groups, with 28 in each group: ages 3 to 7, 8 to 12, and 13 to 19.

Instruments. Shoben's University of Southern California (USC) Parent Attitude Survey (1949) was used to ascertain the expressed attitudes of the fathers and mothers toward their children.

The Attitude Toward Disabled Persons Scale (ATDP) (Yuker, Block, & Campbell, 1960), Form A was administered to the parents of the deaf children to measure their attitudes toward physical disability (deafness).

Haggerty-Olson-Wickman Behavior Rating Schedules (1930) were used to evaluate the child's emotional adjustment to the school situation. Three staff members who had had the opportunity to observe the child for at least 6 months were asked to rate the behavior of each pupil.

Treatment of the data. In the treatment of the data, the analysis of variance and product moment correlation coefficients were used to ascertain if there was a significant relationship between parental attitudes and the deaf child's emotional adjustment at the three age levels. *T* tests were performed between parents expressing congruent positive and congruent negative attitudes and between parents expressing noncongruent attitudes toward children and disability. In order to ascertain whether parental attitudes toward the child and his disability and the relationship between these attitudes and the child's emotional adjustment differ for parents of children at various age levels, correlation coefficients were converted into Fisher's transformation and the difference computed.

Results

Maternal and paternal attitudes and emotional adjustment.

1. Expressed maternal and paternal attitudes toward children significantly affected the emotional adjustment of the deaf child.
2. There was a significant relationship between maternal attitudes toward children and the deaf child's emotional adjustment for children between ages 3 to 7, 8 to 12, and 13 to 19.
3. There was a significant relationship between paternal attitudes toward children and the deaf child's emotional adjustment between ages 8 to 12, and 13 to 19; this relationship was not found to be significant for deaf children between ages 3 to 7.
4. Maternal and paternal attitudes toward disability did not significantly affect the emotional adjustment of the deaf child.

These results are presented in Tables 1 and 2.

TABLE 1

Analysis of Variance of the Influence of Parental Attitudes Toward Children upon the Child's Emotional Adjustment

Source of Variation	Sum of Squares	Degrees of Freedom	Mean Square	F
Father's attitude	19,140.750	1	19,140.750	16.646**
Mother's attitude	39,606.850	1	39,606.850	34.445**
Residual	74,459.640	81		
Total	133,207.240			

** Significant beyond the .01 level.

TABLE 2

Correlations Between Haggerty-Olson-Wickman Behavior Rating Schedules and the USC Parent Attitude Survey—Total Score

Ages	Maternal attitudes	Paternal attitudes
3 to 7 Boys and girls	.70**	.31
8 to 12 Boys and girls	.62**	.50**
13 to 19 Boys and girls	.55**	.49**
3 to 19 Boys and girls	.60**	.44**
3 to 19 Boys	.58**	.45**
3 to 19 Girls	.63**	.43**

** Significant beyond the .01 level.

Congruent parental attitudes and emotional adjustment of deaf children.

1. Deaf children whose parents expressed congruent positive attitudes toward children were rated as better emotionally adjusted than those deaf children whose parents expressed congruent negative attitudes.

2. No statement could be made regarding the effects of congruent positive and negative attitudes toward disability upon the deaf child's emotional adjustment, since no significant relationship was found between these two variables.

These results are presented in Table 3.

Noncongruent parental attitudes and emotional adjustment of deaf children.

1. Deaf children of parents with the combination of positive maternal-negative paternal attitudes towards children were rated as better emotionally adjusted than those deaf children of parents with positive paternal-negative maternal attitudes.

2. No statement could be made regarding the effects of noncongruent parental attitudes towards disability upon the deaf child's emotional adjustment, since no significant relationship was found between these two variables.

These results are presented in Table 4.

Consistency of parental attitudes.

1. Only one significant difference was found between maternal and paternal attitudes toward children of various levels, which is the number expected by chance in this many comparisons. Therefore, no significant differences were found between expressed parental attitudes toward children for parents of deaf children of age levels 3 to 7, 8 to 12, and 13 to 19.

TABLE 3

t Tests Between Positive Mothers-Positive Fathers and Negative Mothers-Negative Fathers (Congruent Attitudes Toward Children)

	Numbers	*Mean*	*Standard Deviation*
Positive Mothers-Positive Fathers	32	98.250	29.995
Negative Mothers-Negative Fathers	32	146.563	40.957
t (Positive Parents versus Negative Parents)			5.384**

** Significant beyond the .01 level.

TABLE 4

t tests Between Positive Mothers-Negative Fathers and Positive Fathers-Negative Mothers (Noncongruent Attitudes Toward Children)

	Numbers	*Mean*	*Standard Deviation*
Positive Mothers-Negative Fathers	10	107.80	27.361
Positive Fathers-Negative Mothers	10	135.60	24.405
t (Positive Mothers-Negative Fathers and Positive Fathers-Negative Mothers)			2.396*

* Significant beyond the .05 level.

2. Three significant differences were found between maternal and paternal attitudes towards disability for deaf children of various age levels. These differences indicated that mothers of deaf children between ages 3 to 7 were more accepting of disability than mothers of deaf children between ages 8 to 12, and that fathers of deaf children between the ages 3 to 7 and 8 to 12 were more accepting of disability than fathers of deaf children between the ages 13 to 19.

3. No significant differences were found between the relationship between parental attitudes toward children and the deaf child's emotional adjustment for parents of children of various age levels.

Discussion

This study was able to measure the degree of significant relationship which exists between expressed maternal and paternal attitudes toward children as measured by the University of Southern California Parent Attitude Survey, and the deaf child's emotional adjustment as measured by the Haggerty-Olson-Wickman Behavior Rating Schedules.

The results of the study also showed that this significant relationship existed for mothers of children for all three age levels, and for fathers of children for two age levels, 8 to 12 and 13 to 19. This relationship between pater-

nal attitudes toward children and the child's emotional adjustment was not found significant for children between ages 3 to 7. Most studies dealing with child development, thus far, have neglected the father; Schaefer and Bayley (1963) have suggested that paternal as well as maternal behavior should be investigated to obtain information relating to parent-child interaction.

This study was not able to determine the degree of significant relationship which exists between parental attitudes toward disability as measured by the Attitude Toward Disabled Persons Scale, Form A, and the deaf child's emotional adjustment. While there was a trend at some age levels, the lack of a significant relationship suggests that attitudes towards disability cannot be classified with other parental attitudes such as dominating and possessive attitudes towards children as an important determinant in the child's emotional adjustment.

Where parental attitudes were noncongruent, it is the author's opinion that the maternal attitude, either positive or negative, outweighs the paternal attitude in its effect upon the deaf child's emotional adjustment. In evaluating the relationship of parental attitudes toward children, the results indicated that the deaf children with a positive mother-negative father combination were better emotionally adjusted than those deaf children with a positive father-negative mother combination. It may be concluded, therefore, that maternal attitudes towards children play a more significant role in the emotional adjustment of the deaf child than paternal attitudes. While this finding supports the contention that in our society the mother's role in child rearing is more important than that of the father's, there has been little investigation into the effects of noncongruent parental attitudes upon the emotional adjustment of the child.

The assumption was made that parental attitudes towards deaf children would be consistent at the three age levels of the children. The results indicated that no significant differences were found between expressed parental attitudes toward children for parents of deaf children of age levels 3 to 7, 8 to 12, and 13 to 19. In the literature there is some disagreement as to the longitudinal continuity of parental attitudes. On one hand, Lasko (1952) and Baldwin (1946) have stated that parental attitudes change during different periods of growth for the child. On the other hand, in agreement with the results of this study, Ausubel (1958) stated that, despite the paucity of systematic empirical evidence,

> since a parent's child rearing attitudes might be expected to remain as stable as his personality it is plausible to suppose that within certain limits of variation a given parent tends to manifest the same kinds of rearing attitudes throughout his parental tenure [p. 355].

Regarding parental attitudes towards disability between parents of deaf children of various age levels, three significant differences were found. These differences indicated that mothers of deaf children between ages 3 to 7 were more accepting of disability than mothers of deaf children between ages 8 to 12 and 13 to 19, and fathers of deaf children between ages 3 to 7 and 8 to 12 were more accepting of disability than fathers of deaf children between ages 13 to 19. The results obtained may best be explained by the fact that attitudes, once formed, differ in their ability to be modified. Parental attitudes towards disability, therefore, are more easily modified than their attitudes towards children. It should also be noted that parental attitudes towards disability became less accepting as the child grew older. This finding can be attributed to (a) the fact that the Lexington School for the Deaf has insti-

tuted a program for the parents of young deaf children designed to bettter enable parents to understand their child's disability, and (b) that as the deaf child grows older, his parents become more aware of the limitations that deafness imposes upon the individual and their attitudes become less accepting or perhaps, more realistic.

It was also reasonable to assume that once this parent child relationship had been established, it would not change significantly as the child grew older. The results indicated that no significant differences existed between the relationship between parental attitudes toward children and the child's emotional adjustment for parents of children of the three age levels. This finding is in accord with Schaefer and Bayley (1963) and with studies in child guidance clinics which have reported that mothers who reject their children are resistant to treatment and that significant changes in attitude are rare.

Conclusions and Implications

The results of this study, which are in accord with those studies involving hearing children, indicate that a relationship exists between the deaf child's emotional adjustment and the attitudes of his parents towards children. If a stereotyped pattern of behavior did exist for deaf children it seems reasonable to conclude that the relationship found in this study would not have been significant, for then deaf children would have been so similar in their overt behavior that differences between them would hardly have been discernible or of course measurable. This situation was found not to be the case; deaf children are, as a group, as similar and dissimilar as hearing children.

Education of the deaf. With the results of this study in mind, perhaps two areas of serious concern can be markedly improved by educators and psychologists working with the deaf. One is the education of the deaf child. Nearly all deaf children are educationally retarded from 3 to 5 years as compared with their hearing peers. The nature of their disability causes learning to be slow and tedious. Unless they are proficient readers, which few are because of their poor language development, deaf children learn either at school or at home. The difficulty in being able to concentrate on the teacher's lips for 5 hours a day,

5 days a week is almost indescribable to those unfamiliar with the education of the deaf.

If, in addition, the child is emotionally disturbed, learning will be seriously impaired. The deaf child cannot, as can his hearing peers, daydream or concentrate on his emotional difficulties while listening for key words or phrases to obtain the general meaning of the lesson. Unless he concentrates on the teacher's lips, he will learn relatively little. Moreover, if the deaf child is emotionally disturbed, there will also be friction in his relationships at home with his parents. Since the home is one of the two main environs in which a deaf child acquires knowledge, his learning potential will be adversely affected.

Counseling of the deaf. The second area of concern is that of counseling the deaf child who has exhibited emotional problems at school. Due to the fact that a deaf child does not acquire much language before adolescence, regular counseling techniques are not applicable with deaf children until the age of 14 or 15. Before this age, modified play therapy techniques might be somewhat helpful, although they are quite time consuming since there is almost a total lack of trained personnel in this area. Moreover, Rainer, Altshuler, and Kallman (1963) expressed a very pessimistic attitude toward counseling with deaf of any age. They wrote:

When it comes to therapy, however, the subject is usually dismissed with a brief reference or two. Emphasis is placed on preventive measures or direct counseling, conveying a general sense of pessimism about psychiatric efforts made in the face of the limitations imposed by deafness. Indeed, there exists no scientific body of normative data as a baseline for psychiatric treatment of the deaf. In the case of the deaf, all these factors play a role in complicating the task of effective psychotherapy. Severe pathology, psychotic or psychopathic in nature, may not be evident to the psychiatrist who is unfamiliar with the methods of differential diagnosis in the deaf. Also, the conceptual immaturity of many deaf patients may affect motivation for treatment and entail modification of treatment plans based on insight and self-reliance. . . . Finally, the most obvious hindrance to effective diagnosis and psychotherapy lies in the difficulty of communication between psychotherapist and patient [p. 182].

The findings of this study suggest that improved parent child relationships will result in the deaf child's better emotional adjustment, which will ultimately result in the deaf child being able to utilize more fully his intellectual endowment at school. Based upon the results of this study, programs planned for parent education have been started at the Lexington School with these goals in mind. These programs take the form of discussion groups, in which the parents learn through their participation in the group process. The group leader uses his knowledge of individual behavior and of group dynamics in order to help the parents share their feelings about problems they have in common so that they may become more mature and responsible parents. Group guidance has been widely offered to parents of mentally and physically handicapped children, where feelings of ambivalence, bitterness, and disbelief have been shared.

This study has also revealed that it would be more expedient to include mothers rather than fathers in these groups, and that it would be beneficial for mothers of children of all age levels to participate.

The results of this study have opened up new areas for research. It would be important to conduct followup studies of these parent groups at different time intervals to determine whether significant changes had taken place in the attitudes of the parents, and to investigate whether these changes were reflected in the child's emotional adjustment at school. Other areas that would shed additional light on family interaction would be determination of the role normally hearing siblings play in the emotional adjustment of their deaf brothers and sisters and exploration of the effects of the birth of a deaf child upon parent interaction. Finally, it is important to determine whether better adjusted deaf children learn better than do their less well adjusted deaf peers. Except for the relationship between parental attitudes and the deaf child's emotional adjustment as discussed in this article, little is known regarding other areas of family interaction in families with a deaf child.

References

Ausubel, D. P., *Theory and problems of child development.* New York: Grune & Stratton, 1958.

Baldwin, A. L. Differences in parent behavior toward three and nine year old children. *Journal of Personality Research*, 1946, 15, 143-165.

Haggerty, M. E., Olson, W. C., & Wickman, E. K. Manual of directions. *Behavior Rating Schedules.* New York: World Book, 1930.

Lasko, J. K. Parent-child relationships: Report from the Fels Research Institute. *American Journal of Orthopsychiatry,* 1952, **22**, 300-304.

Rainer, J. D., Altshuler, K. Z., & Kallmann, F. J. Psychotherapy for the deaf. In Rainer et al. (Eds.), *Family and mental health problems in a deaf population.* New York: Columbia University, 1963. Pp. 182-192.

Schaefer, E. S., & Bayley, N. Maternal behavior, child behavior and their intercorrelations from infancy through adolescence. *Monographs of Social Research and Child Development,* 1963, **28**, 3 (Serial No. 87).

Shoben, E. J., Jr. The assessment of parental attitudes in relation to child adjustment. *Genetic and Psychological Monographs,* 1949, **39**, 101-148.

Yuker, H. E., Block, J. R., & Campbell, W. J. A scale to measure attitudes toward disabled persons. *Human Resources Study,* 1960, **5**, 1-14.

CHAPTER ELEVEN

SPEECH HANDICAPS

Many factors have been hypothesized to account for the development of inadequate speech. These include impairment of the speech centers of the brain and other physiological systems involved in speech, hearing loss, severe mental retardation, developmental lag, emotional disturbance, exposure to poor speech models, and reinforcement administered by hypercritical parents. One of the foremost tasks of the speech clinician is to determine whether any of the foregoing factors appears to contribute to speech disability and, if so, to refer the client to an appropriate agency or diagnostic center. Hopefully, then, any contributing variables are treated in conjunction with therapy in speech. Unfortunately, specific conditions associated with speech impairment are difficult to isolate and even more difficult to remediate. One advantage of the behavior-modification techniques investigated by Ryan lies in their independence from the etiological sources presumed to contribute to a given speech handicap.

The nature of the relationship between emotional disturbance and speech problems has long been of concern to researchers. Bloch and Goodstein reviewed and critiqued a decade of research on the personality characteristics of persons with functional speech disorders. In addition, research workers have investigated the hypothesis that hypercritical parents inadvertently precipitate stuttering in their children. Contrary to previous research, Bourdon and Silber found that stuttering children did not rate their parents as hypercritical.

The numerous difficulties encountered in conducting longitudinal follow-up research on speech-impaired children (and other groups of exceptional children) are evident in the work of Beagley and Wrenn. Whenever longitudinal research is carried out, unknown and uncontrolled variables are likely to influence the dependent variable of interest. Too, at least some of the subjects participating in the original study cannot be located at the time of follow-up. To investigate the effectiveness of remedial speech training, one could establish a series of experimental groups—each receiving varying amounts of treatment. It would then be possible to relate the amount of treatment to the amount of improvement in speech. This technique would permit one to determine whether treatment administered beyond a certain point contributed to further improvement in speech or whether additional therapy had little or no positive effect (Travers, 1965).

FUNCTIONAL SPEECH DISORDERS AND PERSONALITY: A DECADE OF RESEARCH

Ellin L. Bloch
Leonard D. Goodstein

This paper summarizes and evaluates the research literature published between 1958 and 1968, relating measured personality and adjustment to the functional (nonorganic) speech problems of articulation, delayed speech, voice, and stuttering. For each of these disorders, a review and evaluation of the research is presented on the personality and adjustment of (1) children suffering from that disorder; (2) their parents; and, where appropriate, (3) adults with that disorder. Methodological and conceptual problems are discussed in the context of the studies.

The literature reviewed has yielded few conclusive findings and few new perspectives regarding the role of personality variables in the four major functional speech disorders. The methodological and conceptual inadequacies of most studies have been striking, and steady research efforts have yielded no firm evidence that differentiates speech-defective persons and their parents from normal speakers and their parents in terms of general adjustment or broadly identifiable personality patterns. It would be profitable to concentrate future research on specific within-group variables, such as improvement in therapy, rather than to continue the present focus.

Psychological variables in speech disorders have been considered as etiological, concomitant, or consequential factors of importance both in formulating descriptions of the speech-disordered individual and in therapeutic planning. A considerable body of research has developed over a 40-year period, focusing upon the personality and adjustment of speech-handicapped individuals and their parents. This research has been developed from diverse sources: medical and psychological histories; clinical observations of the speech-disordered individual in interaction with his parents and with his peers; and the testing and application of a number of different personality theories for the purposes of diagnosis and treatment. These sources of information have suggested to many investigators that the personalities of individuals with speech problems may be aberrant along one or in several dimensions, differing in important ways from those of normal-speaking individuals. In an earlier review of the literature relating personality variables and functional speech pathology, Goodstein (1958a) concluded that research evidence of personality differences was largely inconsistent and provided no support for the contention that either the parents or the speech-disordered individuals themselves were severely maladjusted or had a distinctive personality pattern. Goodstein further concluded that the implications of these studies were difficult to assess because the "methodological and conceptual limitations were so important that few, if any, generalizations were clearly suggested . . ." (1958b).

This paper summarizes and evaluates research relating measured personality and adjustment to the functional (or nonorganic) speech problems of articulation, delayed speech, voice, and stuttering. The literature that appeared in *Dissertation Abstracts, Journal of Speech and Hearing Disorders, Journal of Speech and Hearing Research,* and *Psychological Abstracts* from January 1958 through December 1968 is reviewed. Earlier literature has been comprehensively reviewed by Goodstein (1958a); several of these earlier papers, however, are included in the current review as important reference studies. Not included here are studies dealing with organic speech disorders, disorders of hearing,[1]

---

[1] See Berlinsky (1952) for an excellent summary of this literature.

Reprinted with permission of the authors and publisher from
Journal of Speech and Hearing Disorders, 1971, **36**(3), 295–314.

disorders of speech resulting from severe psychopathology, stage fright, or the relationship between expressive speech and personality in normal people. This report includes only those investigations which have reported some empirical relationships between personality variables and the four major functional disorders of speech.

DESIGN CHARACTERISTICS OF THE RESEARCH

The greatest proportion of studies relating personality variables to functional speech disorders has been directed toward exploring the hypothesis that particular personality and adjustment characteristics distinguish speech-disordered and normal-speaking individuals. For purposes of comparison, most investigators have employed a control group, usually matched in age, sex, and intelligence to an experimental group of speech-disordered subjects. Personality assessment techniques, including interviews, personality inventories, projective tests, and behavior ratings, have been used to provide measures of similarities and differences between the two subject groups. Some studies, using similar assessment techniques, have approached psychological variables without the use of comparison groups. Still another approach—used by only a few researchers—has involved treatment of the speech-impaired child or adult, with an attempt at isolating personality and environmental factors operative in symptom removal or improvement.

Three major problems recur in these studies. First, the criteria for classifying subjects as, for example, "stutterers" or "articulartory-impaired" differ among the investigators and are rarely specified in such a way as to permit valid generalizations to be drawn from the findings of different researchers. This problem is of particular importance in stuttering research and will be further elaborated. Secondly, any conclusions drawn from this body of research must take into account differences in the reliability and validity of the many assessment techniques. It is beyond the scope of this paper to discuss in depth the basic issues involved in personality measurement or the typical instruments used. Briefly, however, it can be noted that *reliability* refers to the stability or repeatability of an obtained measure. *Validity* refers to the degree to which the obtained measure has been shown to be related to other indices of the same behavior. Comprehensive discussions of these critical issues involved in all personality assessment are provided in Lanyon and Goodstein (1971), Anastasi (1968), and Cronbach (1970). The third problem is assessing the cause-effect relationship, that is, whether psychological factors cause functional speech disorders, or vice versa. Studies of the relationship between anxiety and stuttering illustrate the complexity of this problem. Even where clear differences in anxiety level are obtained between stutterers and fluent speakers, the investigator is left with the interpretative problem of whether these differences were critical factors in the development of the stuttering or, rather, are consequences of the stuttering. There is much data to support the notion that any handicapping condition, especially one as obvious and interfering as stuttering, is anxiety-arousing. Indeed, one could argue that these positions are not mutually exclusive but that some degree of anxiety is necessary for the development of stuttering and this anxiety is consequently intensified. Obviously, the simple demonstration of group differences in anxiety does little to unravel this dilemma. More sophisticated studies, such as those relating anxiety level to the degree of severity of stuttering or tracing changes in anxiety level to reductions in stuttering, are necessary to fully understand this issue. It should be noted that the cause-or-consequence dilemma is not unique to the area of speech dysfunction, but is also important in a variety of other disorders, for example, in schizophrenia (Buss, 1966) and in allergic disorders (Freeman, Feingold, Schlesinger, and Gorman, 1968). Wherever appropriate, we shall comment on these and other methodological and conceptual problems in the context of the studies reviewed.

ARTICULATION DISORDERS

Those who do research in the area of functional speech disorders and personality seem typically to regard functional disorders of articulation as a consequence of (1) inadequate speech models, (2) a lack of stimulation in and motivation for adequate speech, or (3) some more basic emotional disturbance; however, neither the specific mechanisms involved in the formation of functional disorders nor the criteria for deciding the relative contribution of these three factors are ever clearly spelled out. Since such etiological factors are seen as operating in the home environment in the typical developmental sequence, parent-child interactions have been the focus of a number of investigations.

Personality and Adjustment of the Parents. The seminal study by Wood (1946a, b) represents the earliest and most comprehensive investigation of the relationship between parental adjustment and the presence of functional articulatory defects in children. Psychological tests, including the California Test of Personality (CTP), the Bernreuter Personality Inventory, and the Thematic Apperception Test (TAT), were administered to parents of 50 articulatory-disordered children, and their scores were compared with the test norms. The results indicated considerable emotional maladjustment of one or both parents, with more maladjustment found for the mothers than for the fathers. The data also showed that these parents were ignorant of good child-rearing practices and used overly severe techniques of child discipline.

The 50 children were later divided into two matched groups for a program of therapeutic procedures. For one group of 25 children, ordinary remedial articulation procedures were followed; for the other 25, extensive parental counseling was carried on in addition to the speech training. Children in the second group improved more rapidly in their speech than did those whose mothers were not treated. Wood concluded that parental emotional factors are important not only in the etiology of articulation defects but also in any corrective treatment.

Two recent studies (Berlin, 1958; Moll and Darley, 1960) have used parental attitude scales in comparing one or both parents of articulatory-defective children, of normal-speaking children, and of a second speech-defective group. The use of dual comparison groups, representing a refinement of Wood's design, yielded findings similar to those of Wood; both studies indicated poorer attitudes toward child-rearing among parents of children with articulation problems.

Wood's conclusions appear to be further supported in a study by Andersland (1961), who investigated the relationship between the effects of a kindergarten speech improvement program and maternal personality and attitudes. This study, unlike Wood's, used a control group of mothers of normal-speaking children. In agreement with Wood, Andersland found that mothers of children with articulation problems resistant to treatment scored lowest on a personality adjustment scale.

Andersland reported, however, that mothers of children with articulation problems were not more maladjusted than mothers of children with superior speech. Mothers of children who did not receive improvement lessons, but who later achieved errorless articulation, were reported to have provided a family atmosphere of acceptance. Similar findings also have been reported by Dickson (1962). Using the Minnesota Multiphasic Personality Inventory (MMPI), he compared the emotional adjustment of parents of children who spontaneously outgrew articulation errors with adjustment of parents of children who retained such errors. No significant differences in adjustment were found between either group of parents and the adult "normal" standardization group. Although there was a tendency among mothers of children who retained articulation errors to exhibit more neuroticism than mothers of spontaneously recovered children, there was no evidence that severe maladjustment existed within this group.

Personality and Adjustment of the Children. Prior to 1958, research dealing with the personality and adjustment of the articulatory-defective child was designed mainly to establish differences in personality test scores between groups of speech-defective children and normal-speaking control groups. Many studies reported a positive relationship between functional articulation disorders and personality, while a nearly equal number of studies found few, if any, differences between the experimental and control groups. These inconsistencies have been due in part to poorly controlled investigations, based on small numbers of subjects and using unvalidated personality measures (Goodstein, 1958a, b).

While the reliability and validity of the personality tests used in more current research are open to question, and while sampling size remains small, nevertheless a number of investigators have recognized the importance of examining within-group variables. Recent research, unlike earlier studies, has supplemented the simple differentiation of articulatory-defective and normal-speaking children with investigation of the relation between the severity of articulation disorder and the severity of personality maladjustment.

A carefully designed study by Trapp and Evans (1960) illustrates the use of within-group variables. They investigated the severity of articulation disorder as a function of anxiety level $(N = 34)$. Using the Wechsler Digit Symbol Test, they found that normal-speaking children performed less well (that is, exhibited greater anxiety) than children with mild articulation disorders, but performed better than those whose disorders were severe. Trapp and Evans stress that, had the scores of the mildly and severely disordered children been combined and compared with the scores of the normal-speaking children, no differences between the groups would have been demonstrable. They have suggested that previous inconclusive findings with regard to personality differences between articulatory-defective and normal-speaking children may have existed in part because level of severity was not a variable.

Two studies have reported a positive relationship between functional articulation disorders and personality maladjustment. Butler (1965) administered the Bender-Gestalt Visual Motor Test to 15 articulatory-defective children, concluding that more than half of this group showed a high degree of emotional disturbance. These results are to be interpreted with a great deal of caution, since Butler used a small number of subjects, compared speech-disordered subjects with the normative test sample, and found neurological impairment in the emotionally disturbed children. Solomon (1961), using parental interview data, compared the personality adjustment of 49 articulatory-defective children with that of a matched control group of normal-speaking children. He reported greater tension and anxiety and poorer overall adjustment among the children with articulation problems, concluding nevertheless that "this was by no means typical of every child in the experimental group" and that the "slight" problems that did exist within this group were unrelated to the severity of articulatory disorder. Wylie, Feranchak, and McWilliams

(1965), in a comparison of several groups of speech-defective children, found that children with articulation problems ($N = 12$) resembled most closely the normal-speaking population.

Several studies have examined the social and self-perceptions of articulatory-defective children. Perrin (1954), in an important sociometric study, found that more of the isolates came from the speech-defective group ($N = 37$) and that the speech-defective child was not readily accepted into the classroom group. Lerea and Ward (1966), interested in the child's own perceptions of himself in relation to his parents and peers, reported that children with articulation problems ($N = 20$) indicated greater reluctance to interact with others. On the other hand, Sherrill (1967) reported internally contradictory results in a study dealing with peer-, teacher-, and self-perceptions of articulatory-defective children ($N = 53$). These children were perceived by others and by themselves as less effective in verbal communication skills, but as similar to their normal-speaking peers in social acceptance characteristics. Sherrill noted, however, that the degree of social acceptance appeared to decline as the severity of the articulation disorder increased.

Personality and Adjustment of the Adult. There is only a single study reporting on the personality characteristics of adults with articulation disorders. Sergeant (1962) used a test battery, consisting in part of the Bell Adjustment Inventory and the Bernreuter Personality Inventory, to compare the personality traits and emotional adjustment of each of five groups of speech-defective adults with those of a group of normal-speaking adults. In comparison with normal speakers, the articulation group ($N = 45$) exhibited less self-confidence and less satisfactory social adjustment. No significant differences between the two groups, however, were found in anxiety level or degree of emotional stability. The results of this study remain somewhat obscure because each of the several measures yielded different findings.

Evaluation of the Studies with Articulatory Disorders. Generalizations to be drawn from this group of studies are limited, due to the inconsistencies in reported results. There appears to be some evidence indicating personality differences between parents of children with articulation disorders and parents of normal-speaking children, and even stronger evidence pointing to the role of parental personality and adjustment in determining the degree of speech improvement of the children with articulation disorders.

Studies of articulatory-disordered children—particularly those concerned with both social and self-perceptions—have yielded largely contradictory findings with regard to personality traits and emotional adjustment. A similar conclusion has been reached by Goodstein (1958a). These contradictions have more recently been noticeable within, as well as among, the several studies. Even when statistical analyses have established intergroup differences, at least one investigator (Solomon, 1961) expressed reluctance to accept his findings.

Some, but by no means all, of these inconsistencies may be partially resolved when level of severity is considered a variable. The inclusion of within-groups variables, however, cannot counteract inconsistencies arising from the use of a small number of subjects and poorly standardized and validated personality measures. Newly devised rating scales and questionnaires (Solomon, 1961; Wylie, Feranchak, and McWilliams, 1965; Sherrill, 1967), while in some cases better adapted to the researcher's hypotheses than the more customary assessment techniques, are nevertheless of questionable validity and reliability and must be interpreted with caution.

As yet, no studies have examined the relationship between the personality characteristics of the articulatory-defective child or adult and speech improvement. In spite of the current interest shown in a new population—spontaneously recovered individuals—investigations of these subjects have been confined to examining parental attitudes and adjustment (Andersland, 1961; Dickson, 1962). No study directly comparing therapeutic and extratherapeutic progress in the speech-defective individuals themselves has been undertaken.

DELAYED SPEECH

The surveyed literature over a 40-year period contained only four studies dealing with the personality factors involved in psychogenically delayed speech. Three of these studies (Beckey, 1942; Peckarsky, 1953; Moll and Darley, 1960) have examined hypotheses which stress the importance of materal influence and personality in the etiology of the disorder.

Both Beckey and Peckarsky reported deviant personality characteristics and attitudes among mothers of speech-retarded children ($N = 50$ and 52, respectively). Mothers of the delayed-speech group in Peckarsky's study were evaluated on the Fels Rating Scales as overprotective, rigid individuals who outwardly seemed devoted to their children but were actually very critical of them. On the other hand, Moll and Darley, using the Parental Attitude Research Instrument and Wiley's Attitude Scale, found that mothers of speech-delayed children ($N = 30$) differed from mothers of normal-speaking children and of articulatory-disordered children only in that they offered their children less encouragement to talk. But, while mothers of articulatory-impaired children were found to be critical and disapproving of their children's behavior, there was no evidence that these attitudes were present to any significant degree among mothers of the speech-retarded group.

The inability of these researchers to cross-validate earlier findings has been due in part to the low reliability and uncertain validity of the personality measures. In addition, the Parental Attitude Research Instrument encourages an acquiescence-response set; since agreement with most of the items represents "unhealthy" attitudes, a high (or low) score may reflect a subject's (parent's) consistent tendency to agree (or disagree) with assertions, rather than with the actual item content (Cronbach, 1946). Finally, in consideration of the fact that the delayed-speech group in this study also included children with deviant articulation—that is, subject selection was not limited to children presenting only speech-delayed behavior—parental personality and attitudinal differences may have been further obscured.

Personality disturbances in the speech-retarded children themselves have been reported by Wylie, Feranchak, and McWilliams (1965) in the single study of personality factors and adjustment in these children. Of five speech-defective groups studied, children with delayed speech ($N = 11$) least resembled the control group of normal-speaking children; they exhibited particularly the symptoms of tantrums and bed-wetting to a greater degree than any of the other groups. These symptoms might be interpreted as indicative of emotional disorder.

Although these four studies have reported findings of some interest and importance, it is clear that work in the area of delayed speech and personality remains largely in a rudimentary stage and that much additional research is required. A few studies have suggested that parental personality and attitudes, particularly overprotectiveness, may play an important role in the etiology of speech retardation; it would be equally valid, however, to conclude from the same findings that mothers of speech-delayed children develop these attitudes in response to the retarded speech behavior of their children. Overprotectiveness in particular would be expected if absent or retarded speech signified to the mother that the child were incapable of adequately communicating his needs to others.

Because the problem of psychogenically delayed speech typically disappears before an age when adequate measures for personality and adjustment are available, standard psychological inventories and projective tests cannot be used with these children. There seem to be other avenues of research, however, that are open to the investigator of the speech-retarded child and his parents. One of these is the direct observation of the mother-child interaction; findings from this method may supplement or amend results obtained from the mother's written responses to attitude inventories. The need for research dealing with the personalities and attitudes of fathers of speech-retarded children also seems clear. Additionally, no study has yet examined the personality factors—in both the parents and the children—relevant to the development of adequate speech in these children.

VOICE DISORDERS

Functional voice disorders, characterized by marked deviations in loudness, pitch, quality, or flexibility, are frequently explained as a result of psychological disturbance or maladjustment. Voice disorders, in contrast to both articulatory disorders and delayed speech, are frequently found in both adolescents and adults. Since good voice quality is an important factor in social interaction, it may be assumed that personality and adjustment factors would be of interest in the understanding of voice problems and their treatment.

The surveyed literature contained few studies dealing with this type of speech disorder. Aronson, Peterson, and Litin (1964, 1966) and Aronson, Brown, Litin, and Pearson (1968) have reported a series of studies examining the personality characteristics of female patients with voice symptoms. The investigators initially reported that the MMPI profiles obtained from these patients ($N = 25$) were more like those of psychiatric patients than like those of general medical patients. From these profiles and clinical impressions, the voice-disordered group was described as using predominately hysteroid defenses, as being immature in dealing with feelings of anger, and as showing relatively long-standing patterns of dependency. Slightly more than half the patients were judged to have made a "truly neurotic life adjustment," yet no patient was found to be in need of immediate psychiatric attention. In a later study (Aronson, Brown, Litin, and Pearson, 1968), contradictory results were reported; a greater incidence of abnormal MMPI profiles was found among general medical patients than among voice-disordered patients ($N = 49$). An inability to cross-validate the initial findings may be traced to a number of methodological problems involved in these studies. The disproportionate size of comparison groups, and conclusions drawn largely from visual inspection of percentages rather than from statistical analysis, render both sets of findings extremely dubious. Perhaps the most serious criticism to be made of these studies is their use of unmatched controls. It should be clear that two sets of results cannot be adequately compared when important characteristics of the control groups remain unspecified.

Sergeant (1962), using the Bell Adjustment Inventory and the Bernreuter Personality Inventory, reported that, in comparison with the subjects in four other speech-defective groups and a group of normal-speaking controls, subjects with voice disorders ($N = 29$) obtained scores indicating the most satisfactory home adjustment. In addition, voice-disordered subjects were found to be superior to all other groups in overall social adjustment. Voice cases, however, were reported to be less self-confident than normal-speaking controls;

but, like the normal speakers, were more ego-defensive than matched groups of stutterers or individuals with cleft palates. This experimental design would appear to be of much value in determining the personality characteristics both unique to voice-disordered individuals and shared by them with other speech-defective groups.

The research investigating the relationship between voice disorders and personality is necessarily limited by the small number of cases, the generally inadequate composition of control groups, and the reliance on personality measures of somewhat dubious validity. In particular, the validity of the Bell Adjustment Inventory is open to question (Ferguson, 1952). The conclusion reached by Goodstein (1958a) in his review of the previous literature is applicable in the present context: the number of studies in this area is very few, and little remains known about personality as an etiological, consequential, or therapeutic factor in voice disorders.

STUTTERING

Of all the functional pathologies of speech, the phenomenon of stuttering has received the greatest attention from researchers. This severely hesitant, spasmodic attempt at speech is often explained in terms of psychological or personality factors either in the stutterer himself or in his background (Bluemel, 1960; Freund, 1966). The disorder also has been widely recognized as an important factor in the consequent development of personality and adjustment, thus influencing therapeutic planning.

Stuttering has been variously described as a narcissistic neurosis, a pregenital conversion neurosis (Bluemel, 1960), an "expectancy neurosis," and a "social neurosis" (Freund, 1966). Whatever the definition, however, many clinicians have viewed stuttering either as essentially neurotic or as a symptom of some underlying personality disturbance. Bluemel (1960) noted that "in clinical observation the disorganization is not limited to speech; it involves the speaker as well as the speech." From a historical standpoint, clinical descriptions of the stutterer's personality—insecurity, shyness, excitability, oversensitivity—have varied little and have led many to the belief that personality disturbances inevitably accompany this disturbance in speech.

Personality and Adjustment of the Parents. The causes of stuttering have often been sought in psychosocial factors. Many formulations have stressed family and parent-child interactions in describing the etiology of the disorder. Since parental influence is most pervasive prior to and during the years of the onset of stuttering, studies of the stutterer's parents and the home environment should cast much light on the development of the stuttering phenomenon.

Personality inventories have been used in three studies assessing parental personality and attitudes. Berlin (1958), using the Wiley Inventory of Parent Attitudes, and Thile (1967), using the Research Inquiry Form, reported no significant differences between parents of stuttering and non-stuttering children ($N = 67$ and 90, respectively). Berlin, however, found a conflict in attitudes between stutterers' parents that was not present between parents of normal-speaking children. This attitudinal conflict was found also between parents of articulatory-defective children. He further reported that fathers of stutterers and articulatory cases responded with consistently poorer attitudes than the mothers of these children; indeed, mothers of stutterers were found to most closely resemble mothers of normal-speaking children. Kinstler (1961), in the only inventory study reporting parental intergroup differences, compared the responses of mothers of stuttering and nonstuttering children ($N = 30$ in each group) on the USC Maternal Attitude Scale. Unlike the control group, mothers of stutterers appeared to be outwardly accepting of their children, while implicitly conveying a great deal of rejection.

Robbins (1962[2], 1964), utilizing clinical interview material, has investigated parental attitudes as part of a uniquely comprehensive study of 1056 children and adults who stutter. Few parents of the young stutterers suggested that they themselves played a role in the onset of stuttering, attributing this onset to a bad fall, severe fright, or hospitalization of the child. Yet a greater percentage of adult nonstutterers reported these "trauma" occurring in their childhood than did the stutterers. Unfortunately, this interesting study did not use a parent control group or statistical analysis of data.

The assessment procedures used in the foregoing studies—personality inventories and clinical interview data—involve the subject's personal report of a wide range of feelings, ideas, and experiences. Still another method available to the investigator of parental attitudes is observation of the subject under somewhat more artificial but experimentally manipulatable conditions. For example, Abbott (1957) has reported overprotectiveness by mothers of stutterers from direct observation of experimental and control mother-child pairs ($N = 30$ in each group) in a free-play situation. Goldman and Shames (1964a, b) have examined the manner in which parents of stuttering and nonstuttering children establish goals both for themselves and for their children. Goal-setting behavior was assessed by observing the subjects' estimates of their own performance on a motor task ($N = 30$ in each group) and of their children's performance on the same task and in telling a story ($N = 48$ in each group). Estimates were given after each of a number of predetermined "successes" and "failures" were experienced by the subjects. While parents of stutterers and nonstutterers did not differ significantly in setting goals for themselves, the parents of stutterers were found to set higher standards for their children. The results were highly task-specific and varied under the conditions of either "success" or "failure"; nevertheless it was concluded that stutterers' parents, especially the fathers, set more unrealistic goals for their children generally, and higher speech goals specifically, than parents of nonstutterers. Johnson (1942, 1955), using clinical interview data, also reported differences between the two parent groups centering primarily around the stutterer's parents' concern about the adequacy of the child's speech.

The majority of studies of parental adjustment report few or no differences between parents of stutterers and those of nonstutterers. Those differences that have been reported tend to center around subtle attitudes of parental aspirations and protectiveness, and there is evidence that these attitudes may be specifically related to the speech area. In addition, recent research suggests that parents of the stutterer may disagree in their evaluations of the child, with the father expressing somewhat more deviant and unrealistic attitudes. In summary, the studies reviewed present no evidence to support the contention that the parents of stuttering children are severely maladjusted or have a particularly aberrant personality pattern. Generalizing such attitudes among parents of all speech-defective populations, and relating parental personality—that of the father as well as the mother—to therapy with the stuttering child require empirical investigation.

Personality and Adjustment of the Child Who Stutters. Considerable research has been reported on the personality and adjustment of the stuttering child. Clinical interview data and projective techniques have been used in the majority of studies, and investigators have reported divergent results.

Robbins (1962 [see Footnote 2], 1964), examining case histories, found that

[2] Personal communication.

hypersensitivity and shyness were outstanding traits shared by children who stutter ($N = 566$); but when these children were compared with the non-stutterers previously studied by Johnson (1959), more similarities than differences in personality and adjustment were noted. On the other hand, Moncur's (1955) earlier clinical data revealed that stutterers ($N = 42$) showed more symptoms of nervousness and maladjustment than did a matched control group of nonstutterers.

The Blacky Pictures Test has been used by Eastman (1960) to test a psychoanalytic hypothesis that stutterers will show greater emotional disturbance related to the anal-sadistic phase of psychosexual development than to any other phase of development. The expectation that repressed hostility would be most characteristic of child stutterers ($N = 30$) was only partially confirmed. No control group of normal-speaking children was employed for purposes of comparison, and no reliability coefficients were reported for the scoring of this projective test.

Several investigators have employed a battery of projective tests to study the personalities of stuttering children in comparison to matched controls. Wyatt (1958), using a story-telling test battery, compared the mother-child relationship of 20 stuttering children in both initial and advanced stages of stuttering with 20 normal-speaking children. Of major interest was the finding that stutterers, more than nonstutterers, experience "distance anxiety," namely an intense fear of losing physical and emotional closeness to the mother. It was further reported that a strong fear of disaster was experienced more frequently by those children in the advanced stage of stuttering than by those in the initial stage; no significant differences on this variable, however, were found between advanced-stage stutterers and normal-speaking children. Moller (1960) has analyzed eight variables on both the Rorschach and the Wechsler Intelligence Scale for Children (WISC) in a comparison of children who stutter, "predelinquents," and adjusted boys ($N = 20$ in each group). Adjusted boys showed the most favorable scores on the Rorschach while, contrary to expectation, stutterers had many more indications of maladjustment than predelinquent boys, including less self-awareness and empathic ability, poorer interpersonal relationships, and greater anxiety. On the WISC, a more structured test, fewer such intergroup differences were reported. Both Wyatt and Moller have found more anxiety among stuttering children than among those who do not stutter. It it important to note that both studies required verbal responses from the stutterers; sensitivity to poor speech evaluation would be likely to lower the child's self-confidence, thus spuriously elevating his test anxiety. Further, in order to effectively distinguish between high-anxious stutterers and low-anxious controls, the latter must be shown to be "truly" low-anxious rather than exhibiting strong repression and denial (Zimbardo, Barnard, and Berkowitz, 1963).

Martin (1962), in the single study of perseverative behavior, compared mild, moderate, and severe stuttering cases ($N = 52$) with a group of normal-speaking children ($N = 109$) on four motor tasks. No significant differences in behavior rigidity were found either between stutterers and nonstutterers, or among mild, moderate, or severe stutterers.

In general, there continues to be little evidence that the stuttering child has a particular pattern of personality or is severely maladjusted. Greater anxiety in interpersonal relationships, with attendant symptoms of oversensitivity and shyness, has been noted in stutterers; but, considering the premium placed on early and effective verbal communication in our culture, it is unclear whether these findings result from etiological or from expected consequential factors in stuttering. Thus far, research on the stuttering child remains largely descriptive, with some investigators reporting a positive relationship between stuttering and adjustment. External criteria—for example, school achievement and social relationships—have not been correlated with these findings. In particular, the effect of stuttering upon the child's self-perceptions, his peer relationships, and his choice of activities and interests have not been closely examined as factors relevant to therapeutic planning.

Personality and Adjustment of the Adult Stutterer. A greater variety of personality assessment techniques and experimental procedures have been used in studying the adult stutterer. In spite of this diversity of approach to the problem, the findings in this area remain largely inconsistent and few trustworthy generalizations are possible. Nevertheless, the reader will note that several studies are quite carefully designed and raise a number of possibilities for future research.

Projective tests have been widely used in research dealing with the personality and adjustment of the adult stutterer. Emerick (1966), for example, reported no differences among tonic stutterers, clonic stutterers, and nonstutterers ($N = 20$ in each group) in responses to frustration measured by the Rosenzweig Picture-Frustration Test. He noted, however, that since all the stutterers had received therapy, their usual responses to frustration may have been altered, thus obscuring personality differences among the three groups. Tuper and Chambers (1962), using the Picture Identification Test, concluded that stutterers ($N = 48$), in contrast to a group of normal-speaking college students, were overly sensitive to blame and criticism and exhibited quite negative attitudes toward affiliation needs. In a pilot study (Rieber, 1962) of stutterers and clutterers ($N = 20$ in each group), the low scores of stutterers on a figure-drawing test were interpreted as indicating their greater dependency, introversion, and withdrawal. Since no control group of normal-speaking adults was utilized in this study, the results are somewhat difficult to interpret.

Several studies have utilized projective techniques to test psychoanalytic hypotheses related to stuttering. Carp (1962) and Eastman (1960) both reported that areas of psychosexual conflict significantly related to stuttering ($N = 20$ and 30, respectively) were revealed by the Blacky Pictures Test. There was no general agreement, however, as to the phase of psychosexual development—oral, anal, or phallic—most likely to be involved in the disorder. According to the psychoanalytic model, stutterers have difficulty expressing their aggressive impulses, tending to turn the aggression against themselves or to express it in subtle ways. Earlier studies (Madison and Norman, 1952; Quarrington, 1953), using the Rosenzweig Picture-Frustration Test, reported inconsistent findings of strong tendencies toward self-aggression among stutterers. In a more recent analysis of both written and oral responses to the TAT, Solomon (1963) concluded that while stutterers and nonstutterers ($N = 35$ in each group) did not differ in terms of broad categories of aggression (for example, "strong aggression"), stutterers expressed more themes involving a particular kind of aggression, namely more subtle and less physically violent aggression. This carefully designed study tested quite specific, theoretically derived hypotheses and, unlike previous studies, included a second speech-defective group (voice and articulation disorders) as an additional control measure. The findings, while sometimes difficult to interpret, are nevertheless interesting and point up the need for examining more specific variables in stuttering research. Projective studies designed to examine gross personality differences between stutterers and nonstutterers have thus far yielded such inconsistent results that no generalizations about the personality or adjustment of the adult stutterer are possible.

Only two investigators have used personality inventories to measure the emotional adjustment of adult stutterers. From an analysis of responses to the Guilford-Zimmerman Temperament Survey and the Gordon Personal Profile, Anderson (1967) concluded that his group of stutterers and a matched control group ($N = 50$ in each group) were highly similar in general emotional stability. The two groups, however, were found to differ on several less global personality traits. Stutterers were reported to be more shy and less self-assured than nonstutterers, but friendlier and more respectful toward others than the normal-speaking controls. On the other hand, Sergeant (1962) reported poorer social adjustment, less self-confidence, and greater emotional instability among stutterers ($N = 60$), as determined both by the Bell and Bernreuter inventories. It is to be noted, however, that while these characteristics were found significantly less often among normal speakers, they were shared to a large extent by several of the speech-defective groups studied.

The apparent trend away from the use of personality inventories is further reflected in the fact that only one recent investigator has employed the MMPI, the only one of the inventories used in research with speech-handicapped groups which was empirically derived and which has been shown to have more than face validity. Lanyon (1966) correlated the MMPI scores of 25 severe stutterers at the beginning of therapy with independent speech improvement ratings. The stutterers who improved as a result of speech therapy were reported to resemble those who improved as a result of psychotherapy, in terms of ego-strength and nondeviancy in personality and thinking patterns. Unlike the psychotherapy group, however, those who had stuttering therapy were found to be more energetic, less pessimistic, and less socially alienated.

The clinical interview as an assessment technique has been utilized by Robbins (1962, 1964), who reported some traits showing maladjustment among a large population of adult stutterers ($N = 490$). Martyn (1968) and Wingate (1964), in clinical studies of recovered stutterers ($N = 48$ and 50, respectively), reported high spontaneous recovery rates and a tendency for recovery to occur during adolescence, a period of development ordinarily considered one of increased psychological stress. Investigation of the hypothesis of a "critical" or optimum period of changes in stuttering behavior and a comparison of the personalities of recovered stutterers with those of improvers and nonimprovers in therapy would appear to be promising avenues of research with direct practical implications.

The association between stuttering and anxiety has been investigated with a number of quite different experimental and personality assessment techniques. Agnello (1962) found no differences between stutterers and nonstutterers ($N = 50$ and 450, respectively) in scores on the Taylor Manifest Anxiety Scale. Brutten (1957) and Gray and Karmen (1967) used a measure of palmar perspiration (PSI) as an anxiety index with a group of stutterers and a matched control group ($N = 33$ in each group), with quite contradictory results. Unlike Brutten, who reported intergroup differences in anxiety in a verbal situation, Gray and Karmen found no differences under either verbal or nonverbal conditions. Further, they were able to demonstrate a relationship between anxiety and severity of the disorder. Groups with high and low nonfluency exhibited less anxiety than did a moderately dysfluent group. Santostefano (1960), using both the Rorschach Content Test (RCT) and laboratory-induced stress, concluded that stutterers are more anxious and hostile than nonstutterers ($N = 26$ in each group). Santostefano's inference of stutterers' hostility from their poorer recall of a learning task after experienced stress, as well as the validity of the RCT and the validity of measuring anxiety in stutterers with a complex verbal task, all raise serious doubts about the credence to be placed in the offered conclusions.

Several investigators, rather than assessing the overall personality or relative adjustment of the stutterer, have sought to study what might be considered more basic personality variables such as level of aspiration (Emerick, 1966), perseverative tendencies or rigidity (Kapos and Standlee, 1958; King, 1961; Wingate, 1966), self-concept (Gildston, 1967; Wallen, 1959), and the social interaction characteristics of stutterers (Buscaglia, 1962; Sheehan, Hadley, and Gould, 1967). Earlier studies suggested that stutterers set a somewhat lower level of aspiration than nonstutterers, that stutterers are more perseverative than nonstutterers, and that stutterers do not have a different self-concept than nonstutterers (Goodstein, 1958a). Several studies in the past decade have reported quite different results. Emerick (1966) found that tonic and clonic stutterers did not differ significantly from normal-speaking controls ($N = 20$ in each group) in goal-setting behavior as measured by the Cassel Group Level of Aspiration Test. Wingate (1966), King (1961), and Kapos and Standlee (1958), each using different measures of behavioral rigidity, agreed that there was no evidence of a general perseverative factor among stutterers. With regard to self-concept, Gildston (1967) and Wallen (1959) have found that stutterers may indeed exhibit significantly less self-acceptance and a lower degree of personality integration than normal speakers.

Recent research on social-role perception and interpersonal interaction has suggested that stutterers experience some difficulty in accurately appraising the roles of others (Buscaglia, 1962), and that the frequency of stuttering behavior varies directly with the gap between perceived status of the self and that of the listener (Sheehan, Hadley, and Gould, 1967). In an investigation of the relative difficulty of speaking to authority figures and to peers, Sheehan, Hadley, and Gould reported no significant differences in the responses from severe and mild stutterers. The studies of basic personality variables, particularly the experimental work done by Sheehan, Hadley, and Gould, deserve close attention by researchers interested in therapeutic planning.

In summary, the most general conclusion to be drawn from the studies of adult stutterers is that while stutterers appear to exhibit some differences in personality from normal speakers, there is little evidence to support the contention that they are neurotic or severely maladjusted. Although there is evidence that adult stutters are somewhat more anxious, somewhat less self-confident, and somewhat more socially withdrawn than nonstutterers, there is additional evidence that efforts to differentiate stutterers from nonstutterers in terms of a particular syndrome of maladjustive traits have proved unfruitful.

The inconsistencies in reported results—present among studies using identical test instruments and among studies utilizing different personality measures—have been due in part to the preference of most researchers for examining gross personality differences between broadly defined subject groups which may in fact be quite heterogeneous. The necessity for studying more specific personality variables has already been noted. Additionally, it is important to recognize an implicit assumption in the majority of the studies reviewed, namely, that stuttering is a single entity and that, therefore, the stuttering population is a homogeneous one. In fact, at the present time there appears to be no general agreement on a standard definition of stuttering and its possible variants (St. Onge, 1963; St. Onge and Calvert, 1964; Wingate, 1962). Thus, the criteria for inclusion in a stuttering group have ranged from "any auditorially perceived failure in fluency" (Gray and Karmen, 1967), to the diagnosis of stuttering by a speech clinician or lay person (Wallen, 1959). The fact that few studies have carefully specified and operationally defined their criteria for subject selection obscures possible differences in dynamic patterns among the stutterers themselves, and among stutterers, normal-speaking adults, and other speech-defective individuals. A small number of studies have compared the personality characteristics of "subtypes" of stutterers with the personality characteristics of nonstutterers (Emerick, 1966; Martin, 1962; Sheehan, Hadley, and Gould, 1967; Wyatt, 1958), but a great deal more research is required before the implications of these studies can be applied to the prevention and treatment of stuttering problems.

Evaluation of the Studies of Stuttering. While a large number of investigators have studied the personality and adjustment of stutterers and their parents, areas of agreement in reported results have been quite limited. Because of such inconsistencies, and due to methodological limitations such as inadequate control measures, small numbers of subjects and the use of unvalidated instruments, few trustworthy generalizations are evident. There is some evidence to support the conclusion that stutterers' parents, while not maladjusted themselves, do tend to play a role in the development of stuttering, primarily through attitudes of criticalness and overprotection which may be implicitly conveyed to the child. There tends to be no consistent evidence that either the child or the adult who stutters has a consistent personality pattern different from that of the nonstutterer. Greater anxiety, hypersensitivity, and lack of self-confidence have been reported among stutterers, but there is little evidence of neuroticism or severe maladjustment within this population. One important problem—the relationship between personality and therapeutic progress—remains relatively unexamined by research workers.

SUMMARY AND EVALUATION

A survey of the literature since 1958 has yielded few conclusive findings regarding the role of psychological variables in the major functional disorders of speech. While some studies have used careful procedures and have reported provocative findings, their number has been small. The methodological and conceptual inadequacies of the greater proportion of studies were so important that generalizations about the personality and adjustment of speech-disordered individuals remain nearly as limited as those drawn a decade ago. Unfortunately, no new breakthroughs appear to have emerged in this area of research.

In spite of steady research efforts to differentiate speech-disordered and normal-speaking persons, the results have continued to be inconsistent and there is no evidence that either the parents or the speech-defective individuals themselves are severely maladjusted or have an identifiable personality pattern. The sources of some inconsistencies have been clarified through the use of within-groups variables, the simultaneous comparison of several speech-defective groups, and the use of several personality measures in a single study. The criteria for subject selection, however, remain unclear, the reliability and validity of the assessment techniques are questionable, and sample size remains small.

Perhaps the most serious criticism to be made of the majority of studies is the tendency to focus upon rather global differences between two groups, a speech-handicapped group and a normal-speaking group. Since these two groups are already known to be clearly distinguishable, the demonstration that these two groups can be differentiated on still another dimension, such as adjustment, is not a major contribution to our understanding of the phenomenon under study. Rather a focus upon within-group differences as they relate to differential etiological or severity considerations would seem far more likely to shed light on the problem as would data about the relationships between personality factors and various treatments for functional speech disorders. It also would seem worthwhile to concentrate research efforts on more specific, perhaps theoretically derived, personality variables, such as the nature and quality of aggression (Solomon, 1963), than upon such broad and general concepts as adjustment.

Our review of the research over the past decade is rather disappointing in that the problems and concerns discussed ten years ago (Goodstein, 1958a) are still very apparent and few, if any, new perspectives have emerged. The implications of the surveyed literature for the prevention and treatment of functional speech disorders are small, largely because the attempt to establish personality differences appears to have become an end in itself. The critical role of personality variables in preventive and therapeutic work, unfortunately, has been relatively ignored by research workers. To this point, most practitioners will find extremely limited clinical applications yielded by the current research literature on the relationship between personality variables and functional speech disorders.

REFERENCES

ABBOTT, T. B., A study of observable mother-child relationships in stuttering and non-stuttering groups. Doctoral thesis, Univ. Florida (1957).

AGNELLO, J., The effects of manifest anxiety and stuttering adaptation: Implications for treatment. *Asha*, **4**, 377 (1962).

ANASTASI, ANNE, *Psychological Testing*. (3rd ed.) New York: Macmillan (1968).

ANDERSLAND, PHYLLIS B., Maternal and environmental factors related to success in speech improvement training. *J. Speech Hearing Res.*, **4**, 79-90 (1961).

ANDERSON, E. G., A comparison of emotional stability in stutterers and non-stutterers. Doctoral thesis, Wayne State Univ. (1967).

ARONSON, A. E., PETERSON, H. W., and LITIN, E. M., Voice symptomatology in functional dysphonia and aphonia. *J. Speech Hearing Dis.*, **29**, 367-380 (1964).

ARONSON, A. E., PETERSON, H. W., and LITIN, E. M., Psychiatric symptomatology in functional dysphonia and aphonia. *J. Speech Hearing Dis.*, **31**, 115-127 (1966).

ARONSON, A. E., BROWN, J. R., LITIN, E. M., and PEARSON, J. S., Spastic dysphonia: I. Voice, neurologic, and psychiatric aspects. *J. Speech Hearing Dis.*, **33**, 203-218 (1968).

BECKEY, R. E., A study of certain factors related to retardation of speech. *J. Speech Dis.*, **7**, 223-249 (1942).

BERLIN, C. I., A study of attitudes towards the non-influences of childhood of parents of stutterers, parents of articulatory defectives, and parents of normal-speaking children. Doctoral thesis, Univ. Pittsburgh (1958).

BERLINSKY, S., Measurement of the intelligence and personality of the deaf: A review of the literature. *J. Speech Hearing Dis.*, **17**, 39-54 (1952).

BLUEMEL, C. S., Concepts of stammering: A century in review. *J. Speech Hearing Dis.*, **25**, 24-32 (1960).

BRUTTEN, E. J., A colorimetric anxiety measure of stuttering and expectancy adaptation. Doctoral thesis, Univ. Illinois (1957).

BUSCAGLIA, L. F., An experimental study of the Sarbin-Hardyck Test as indexes of role perception for adolescent stutterers. Doctoral thesis, Univ. Calif. (1962).

BUSS, A. H., *Psychopathology*. New York: Wiley (1966).

BUTLER, KATHERINE G., The Bender-Gestalt Visual Motor Test as a diagnostic instrument with children exhibiting articulation disorders. *Asha*, **7**, 380-381 (1965).

CARP, FRANCES M., Psychosexual development of stutterers. *J. projective Tech.*, **26**, 388-401 (1962).

CRONBACH, L. J., Response sets and test validity. *Educ. psychol. Meas.*, **6**, 475-494 (1946).

CRONBACH, L. J., *Essentials of Psychological Testing*. (3rd ed.) New York: Harper & Row (1970).

DICKSON, S., Differences between children who spontaneously outgrow and children who retain functional articulation errors. *J. Speech Hearing Res.*, **5**, 263-271 (1962).

EASTMAN, D. F., An exploratory investigation of the psychoanalytic theory of stuttering by means of the Blacky Pictures Test. Doctoral thesis, Univ. Nebraska (1960).

EMERICK, L. L., An evaluation of three psychological variables in tonic and clonic stutterers and in non-stutterers. Doctoral thesis, Michigan State Univ. (1966).

FERGUSON, L. W., *Personality Measurement*. New York: McGraw-Hill (1952).

FREEMAN, EDITH H., FEINGOLD, B. F., SCHLESINGER, K., and GORMAN, F. J., Psychological variables in allergic disorders: A review. In D. S. Holmes (Ed.), *Reviews of Research in Behavior Pathology*. New York: Wiley (1968).

FREUND, H., *Psychopathology and the Problems of Stuttering*. Springfield, Ill.: Charles C Thomas (1966).

GILDSTON, PHYLLIS, Stutterers' self-acceptance and perceived parental acceptance. *J. abnorm. Psychol.,* **72,** 59-64 (1967) .

GOLDMAN, R., and SHAMES, G. H., A study of the goal-setting behavior of parents of stutterers and parents of non-stutterers. *J. Speech Hearing Dis.,* **29,** 192-194 (1964a).

GOLDMAN, R., and SHAMES, G. H., Comparisons of the goals that parents of stutterers and parents of non-stutterers set for their children. *J. Speech Hearing Dis.,* **29,** 381-389 (1964b).

GOODSTEIN, L. D., Functional speech disorders and personality: A survey of the research. *J. Speech Hearing Dis.,* **1,** 359-376 (1958a).

GOODSTEIN, L. D., Functional speech disorders and personality: Methodological and theoretical considerations. *J. Speech Hearing Res.,* **1,** 377-382 (1958b).

GRAY, B. B., and KARMEN, JANE L., The relationship between nonverbal anxiety and stuttering adaptation. *J. commun. Dis.,* **1,** 141-151 (1967).

JOHNSON, W., A study of the onset and development of stuttering. *J. Speech Dis.,* **7,** 251-257 (1942).

JOHNSON, W., A study of the onset and development of stuttering. In W. Johnson (Ed.), *Stuttering in Children and Adults.* Minneapolis: Univ. Minnesota (1955).

JOHNSON, W. (Ed.), *The Onset of Stuttering.* Minneapolis: Univ. Minnesota (1959).

KAPOS, E., and STANDLEE, L. S., Behavioral rigidity in adult stutterers. *J. Speech Hearing Res.,* **1,** 294-296 (1958).

KING, P. T., Perseveration in stutterers and non-stutterers. *J. Speech Hearing Res.,* **4,** 346-357 (1961).

KINSTLER, D. B., Covert and overt maternal rejection in stuttering. *J. Speech Hearing Dis.,* **26,** 145-155 (1961).

LANYON, R. I., The MMPI and prognosis in stuttering therapy. *J. Speech Hearing Dis.,* **31,** 186-191 (1966).

LANYON, R. I., and GOODSTEIN, L. D., *Personality Assessment.* New York: Wiley (1971).

LEREA, L., and WARD, B., The social schema of normal and speech-defective children. *J. soc. Psychol.,* **69,** 87-94 (1966).

MADISON, L. R., and NORMAN, R. D., A comparison of the performance of stutterers and non-stutterers on the Rosenzweig Picture-Frustration Test. *J. clin. Psychol.,* **8,** 179-183 (1952).

MARTIN, R., Stuttering and perseveration in children. *J. Speech Hearing Res.,* **5,** 332-339 (1962).

MARTYN, MARGARET, Onset of stuttering and recovery. *Behav. Res. Ther.,* **6,** 295-207 (1968).

MOLL, K. L., and DARLEY, F. L., Attitudes of mothers of articulatory-impaired and speech-retarded children. *J. Speech Hearing Dis..* **25,** 377-384 (1960).

MOLLER, HELLA, Stuttering, predelinquent, and adjusted boys: A comparative analysis of personality characteristics as measured by the WISC and the Rorschach Test. Doctoral thesis, Boston Univ. (1960).

MONCUR, J. P., Symptoms of maladjustment differentiating young stutterers from non-stutterers. *Child Develpm.,* **26,** 91-96 (1955).

PECKARSKY, A. K., Maternal attitudes towards children with psychogenically delayed speech. Doctoral thesis, New York Univ. (1953).

PERRIN, E. H., The social position of the speech defective child. *J. Speech Hearing Dis.,* **19,** 250-252 (1954).

QUARRINGTON, B., The performance of stutterers on the Rosenzweig Picture-Frustration Test. *J. clin. Psychol.,* **9,** 189-195 (1953).

RIEBER, R. W., An investigation of dependent and independent characteristics of stutterers and clutterers. Paper presented at the International Convention of the Association of Logopedics and Phoniatrics, Vienna (1962).

ROBBINS, S. D., 1000 Stutterers: A personal report of clinical experience and research with recommendations for therapy. *J. Speech Hearing Dis.,* **29,** 178-186 (1964) .

ST. ONGE, K. R., The stuttering syndrome. *J. Speech Hearing Res.,* **6,** 195-197 (1963).

ST. ONGE, K. R., and CALVERT, J. J., Stuttering research. *Quart. J. Speech,* **50,** 159-165 (1964).

SANTOSTEFANO, S., Anxiety and hostility in stuttering. *J. Speech Hearing Res.,* **3,** 337-347 (1960).

SERGEANT, R. L., An investigation of responses of speech defective adults on personality inventories. Doctoral thesis, Ohio State Univ. (1962).

SHEEHAN, J., HADLEY, R., and GOULD, E., Impact of authority on stuttering. *J. abnorm. Psychol.,* **72,** 290-293 (1967) .

SHERRILL, D. D., Peer, teacher, and self-perceptions of children with severe functional articulation disorders. Doctoral thesis, Univ. Nebraska (1967).

SOLOMON, A. L., Personality and behavior patterns of children with functional defects of articulation. *Child Develpm.,* **32,** 731-737 (1961) .

SOLOMON, I. L., Aggression and stuttering: An experimental study of the psychoanalytic model of stuttering. Doctoral thesis, Yeshiva Univ. (1963).

THILE, E. L., An investigation of attitude differences in parents of stutterers and parents of non-stutterers. Doctoral thesis, Univ. S. Calif. (1967).

TRAPP, E. P., and EVANS, JANET, Functional articulatory defect and performance on a nonverbal task. *J. Speech Hearing Dis.,* **25,** 176-180 (1960).

TUPER, H. L., and CHAMBERS, J. L., An analysis of stutterers' responses to the Picture Identification Test. *Asha*, **4**, 377 (1962) .

WALLEN, A., A Q-technique study of the self-concepts of adolescent stutterers and non-stutterers. Doctoral thesis, Boston Univ. (1959).

WINGATE, M. E., Evaluation and stuttering: I. Speech characteristics of young children. *J. Speech Hearing Dis.*, **27**, 106-115 (1962).

WINGATE, M. E., Recovery from stuttering. *J. Speech Hearing Dis.*, **29**, 312-321 (1964).

WINGATE, M. E., Behavioral rigidity in stutterers. *J. Speech Hearing Res.*, **9**, 626-629 (1966).

WOOD, K. S., Parental maladjustment and functional articulatory defects in children. Doctoral thesis, Univ. S. Calif. (1946a).

WOOD, K. S., Parental maladjustment and functional articulatory defects in children. *J. Speech Dis.*, **11**, 255-275 (1946b).

WYATT, G. L., Mother-child relationship and stuttering in children. Doctoral thesis, Boston Univ. (1958).

WYLIE, H. L., FERANCHACK, Patricia, and McWILLIAMS, Betty J., Characteristics of children with speech disorders seen in a child guidance center. *Percept. mot. Skills*, **20**, 1101-1107 (1965).

ZIMBARDO, P. G., BARNARD, J. W., and BERKOWITZ, L., The role of anxiety and defensiveness in children's verbal behavior. *J. Personality*, **31**, 79-96 (1963).

CLINICAL FOLLOW-UP OF 192 NORMALLY HEARING CHILDREN WITH DELAYED SPEECH

H. A. Beagley
Margaret Wrenn

A group of normally hearing speech-delayed children attending an audiology clinic were followed up clinically in order to determine their ultimate level of speech development. The results show that at follow-up the majority had improved considerably and that spontaneous improvement was more evident in the average and highly intelligent group in contrast to the dull, although the latter showed a surprisingly good response to speech therapy. A small group (16 percent) showed no improvement and a still smaller group (4.2 per cent) actually showed regression of speech, the latter group consisting of children who were found to be severely subnormal.

A readier availability of speech therapy for the entire clinical category of normally hearing but speech delayed children seems desirable.

INTRODUCTION

It is generally understood among the general public that a child starts to use words during his second year of life and becomes reasonably fluent during his third year, to his parents' evident satisfaction. Many authorities, notably Sheridan in this country, have indicated the median ages corresponding with the various stages of speech development as related to general paediatric development.

Some children make even more gratifying progress

Reprinted with permission of the authors and publisher from *The Journal of Laryngology and Otology*, 1970, **84**(10), 1001–1011.

in their parents' eyes, using single words by the end of their first year and speaking quite freely in their second year. But a group of apparently normal children continues to alarm parents and others by a marked reluctance or inability to initiate expressive speech until their fourth year or even later, and with school age approaching the concern increases accordingly. However, most of these presumably normal children do in fact start to speak, quite abruptly in some cases, and the concern felt for them subsides.

Children with such manifest speech delays are often referred to audiological clinics for opinion due to the fact that speech delay is one of the cardinal signs of deafness. However, the group being considered now have normal hearing and the presumption has been that they are normal in most other respects too and are simply one end of a continuum of normality.

To check the subsequent speech development of such children a review of a group of 397 normally hearing but manifestly speech delayed children attending the Nuffield Hearing and Speech Centre since 1962 was undertaken.

METHOD

The parents of these 397 children were sent a questionnaire (see appendix) to complete and further letters and school reports were obtained in some cases. A pro-portion (34) were summoned to the clinic specially to elucidate certain points or to have a further audiogram or psychological assessment. When one allows for those that did not reply or could not be traced or whose questionnaire was discarded as incomplete or contradictory, or cases deliberately eliminated from the series, e.g. cases where actual hearing loss was later diagnosed or had developed subsequently for organic reasons, a total of 192 replies was left, representing a retrieval rate of just under 50 per cent. This indicates a perennial problem in all retrospective follow-up studies. Nevertheless, the 192 cases represent an appreciable bulk of clinical material which is examined in the following paragraphs. It must be stressed that only overt speech behaviour is considered in this study as it was felt that it was the only aspect of speech development on which the parents or other informants could be expected to report. What was assessed was the child's ability to speak as recorded by an adult listener. No report was requested on other aspects of language development.

The questionnaire was devised to elicit the progress of the child's speech development and the state of his speech behaviour at the time of follow-up. Information was also sought about specific treatment for speech problems and about attendance at nursery school and play group, since the latter two are often recommended as a measure for promoting speech development.

The second part of the questionnaire invited the parent to indicate the level of speech development reached at the time of follow-up. It was necessary that the judgements invited from the parents should be judgements they felt capable of making. The nine point scale on which speech behaviour was evaluated was derived from a study of norms given in the literature, McCarthy (1954), Metraux (1950), Morley (1957), Sheridan (1960), Whetnall and Fry (1964), and corresponds fairly closely to the various age milestones for speech given by these authorities.

The speech levels distinguished in this study are as follows:

1. Not using voice except for shouting or crying.
2. Making sounds but not babbling.
3. Babbling but has no words.
4. Babbling a great deal with one or two words.
5. Using a few single words (5 or 6).
6. Using a lot of single words (20 or more).
7. Putting two or three words together.
8. Speaking in short sentences of three or four words.
9. The accepted 5 year level; child speaking in more complex sentences than level 8.

From the responses to the questionnaire each subject was assigned a speech level corresponding to one of the above categories.

RESULTS

For the total sample of 192 the course of speech development as found on follow-up is shown below:

An analysis of the sample by sex shows that of the 192 speech delayed normally hearing subjects, 137 were male, 59 female. There was a high preponderance of male subjects and the difference between the sexes is statistically highly significant (p < 0.0002, binomial test).

The distribution of birth orders in the sample was significantly different from that of the general population. There were more second and third born children in the sample and fewer first and fourth born. (χ^2 = 16.94, d.f. = 3, p < 0.001.)

The ages of the children in the sample at the time of referral are shown in the histogram Fig. 1. The modal age is 4 years and the mean 3 years 3 months $\pm$ 1 year 6 months S.D. The age at follow-up is shown in Fig. 2. This histogram shows an approximately Gaussian distribution with a mean age of 6 years 0 months $\pm$ 2 years 2 months S.D. The probable reason for the different pattern of distribution between the two histograms is that the time intervals between referral and follow-up were not constant.

The speech levels at referral are shown in Fig. 3. The modal value is at levels 4 and 5. It will be seen that 5 subjects are classified as having attained a speech level of 9, which is taken as the normal level for a five year old, but these children were nevertheless regarded as being speech delayed as their speech showed minor

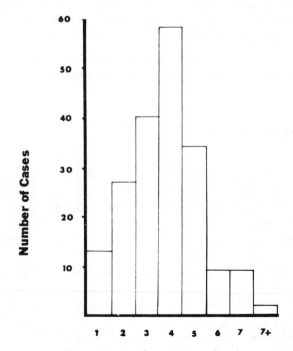

Figure 1.   Age in years at referral.

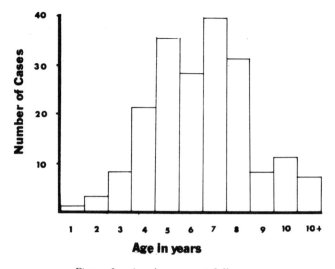

Figure 2. Age in years at follow-up.

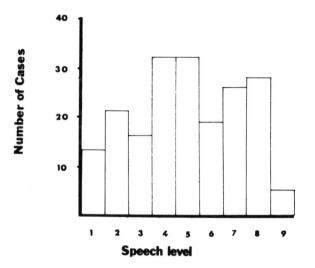

Figure 3. Speech level at referral.

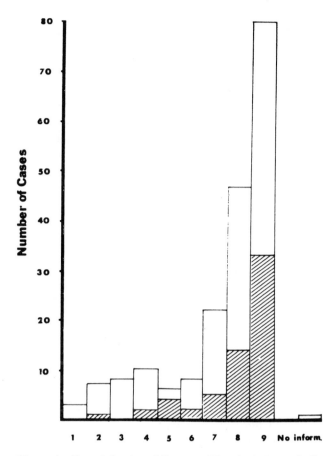

Figure 4. Speech level at follow-up. The shaded area indicates the number of patients who received speech therapy.

defects and in any case they had reached or passed the age of 5 years and there was indeed an element of infantilism in their speech. The speech level at follow-up is shown in Fig. 4. This histogram shows that a striking improvement in speech had occurred throughout the whole group between referral and follow-up. Within the group are a proportion whose speech level had remained static (31), as well as a small number (8) whose speech had actually regressed (See Table I).

Table II shows other possibly relevant conditions present in the 192 children followed up in this review.

Table I.

Improved	153	79.7%
Not improved	31	16.1%
Regressed	8	4.2%
	192	100 %

There were some cases whose speech actually regressed. Table III gives details of these cases and it is clear that they are of subnormal intelligence.

Of the 192 children studied 62 received specific treatment for speech delay; in almost every case this consisted of formal speech therapy given by a speech therapist. The following Table indicates the number of children receiving speech therapy, subdivided into categories according to their level of intelligence. The number of increments in speech level during treatment is indicated and the mean increment is shown for each category. It is interesting to see that the children with the lowest intelligence made relatively the greatest progress, while those at the upper end of the intellectual scale gave the least apparent response to treatment, in terms of increments of speech level.

If one considers the children as falling into two main groups, dull group (I.Q. 80 or below) and average and bright group (I.Q. 81–120+), and compares their respective performances, with and without treatment (speech therapy) certain points emerge.

(i) In those children of average and high I.Q. (n = III) the majority showed considerable spontaneous improvement with or without speech therapy; the dif-

Table II.

	I no.	II percentage
Psychiatric abnormality	36	18.7
Subnormal intelligence	34	17.7
Slow paediatric development	16	8.3
Perinatal or neonatal damage	14	7.2
Aphasia or autism (suggested but not confirmed)	9	4.6
Fostered or in institutional care	8	4.2
Cerebral damage and/or epilepsy	7	3.6
Spasticity and/or motor retardation	7	3.6
Disturbed family background	7	3.6
Prematurity	6	3.1
Adopted	4	2.1
Hypothyroidism	3	1.5
Visual defect	3	1.5
Bilingual home	3	1.5
Cross laterality, dyslexia	1	0.5
No indication of reason for speech delay	41	21.3
	199*	

* Some children have more than one condition and the total of column I exceeds 192.

ference between the treated (36) and the untreated (75) was not statistically significant. ($\chi^2 = 1.16$, d.f. = 1, n.s.)

(ii) Of those children with an I.Q. of 80 or less (n = 81), those receiving speech therapy (26) showed significantly improved speech following speech therapy compared with those who were not so treated (55). ($\chi^2 = 6.12$, d.f. = 1, p < 0.02.)

(iii) On the other hand, when all children receiving treatment (n = 62) are considered the number of cases showing any improvement, regardless of magnitude, is not significantly different in the low I.Q. group (26) as compared with the average and high I.Q. group (36). ($\chi^2 = 0.0002$, n.s.) Note that in this test we are comparing numbers of cases while in Table IV we are dealing with mean incremental speech levels within different I.Q. groups.

But of the children who received no speech therapy (130) the average and high group (75) showed significantly greater spontaneous improvement than did the low I.Q. group (55). ($\chi^2 = 12.09$, d.f. = I, p < 0.0001.)

These findings are interpreted to mean that while children of average and high I.Q. achieved considerable spontaneous improvement, the low I.Q. group did not; but on the other hand the latter group showed a gratifying response to speech therapy in many cases.

There were also 31 cases whose speech had not improved at the time of follow-up. These cases considered under their appropriate I.Q. ratings show a spread from extremely intelligent (I.Q. 138) to extremely retarded (I.Q. 32), as shown in Table V. What is immediately apparent from this Table is that the highly intelligent group show a predominance of emotional disturbance, while the retarded children appear to be speech delayed primarily as a result of their low intelligence. Other associated conditions are set out in the Table.

A critical age for the speech delayed child is his fifth year on account of the imminence of admission to school. In the follow-up 61 children aged 5 and over were still considered to be speech delayed, and this includes 16 of the 31 children classified as 'unimproved' in Table I and Table V. When the histories of these children were inspected it became immediately apparent that mental retardation was the principal feature in their speech delay, only 7 of the 61 having an I.Q.

Table III.

Speech level at referral	Speech level at follow-up	Intellectual status
5	4	I.Q. 68
4	3	ESN
4	3	S.Q. 47
5	1	ESN
5	1	SSN
2	1	I.Q. below 30
2	1	S.Q. 31
2	1	D.Q. 50

Note
I.Q.—Intelligence Quotient.
S.Q.—Social Quotient.
D.Q.—Development Quotient.
No formal testing possible:
  ESN—Educationally subnormal.
  SSN—Severely subnormal.

Table IV. Increments in speech level after speech therapy (n = 62).

I.Q.	n	Mean increment	Range
120	9	0.5	0 to 5
100–119	8	1.4	0 to 4
90–99	13	1.7	0 to 3
80–89	11	2.5	0 to 6
79 and below	21	2.8	−1 to 7

of 100 or more. The main details are set out in the Table below.

Finally, although 153 cases had made a demonstrable improvement in their speech development at the time of follow-up 102 cases were still actually below the expected level of speech development for their age.

DISCUSSION

There seems little doubt that the majority of normally hearing speech retarded children make considerable progress in their speech development either spontaneously or as a result of speech therapy or both. The finding that there is no statistically significant improvement in the normal and high I.Q. groups with or without speech therapy is simply a reflection of the steady on-going development of speech in these cases and not an argument against the employment of speech therapy, rather the reverse in fact. The grading scale which was employed in assessing speech development is rather

compressed at the lower end and this is reflected in a less dramatic rate of development between, say, levels 8 and 9, the 3 year and 5 year levels respectively, at the upper end of the scale. And as only overt speech is considered and such conditions as articulatory deficiencies disregarded in assessing improvement in speech development it seems clear that there is much to be achieved by speech therapy. An improvement from level 8 to level 9 can in itself be a very worthwhile achievement and is the sort of progress that can be anticipated in the case of many of the more intelligent children.

On the other hand, the duller children, who constitute an appreciable minority of this normally hearing speech delayed group start from a much lower level of speech development for their age and this gives rise to a more dramatic improvement in terms of speech levels than in the case of the brighter children. In addition the duller children show much less spontaneous improvement than do the brighter ones and this is reflected also in their relative response to treatment.

These two factors combine to favour the more widespread use of speech therapy for this entire group, with the exception possibly of the grossly subnormal. While admittedly an improvement from, say, level 3 (babbling but using no words) to level 7 (putting two or three words together) may not mean that a child has reached his full speech potential for his age, it is still a worthwhile result when one considers the lower rate of spontaneous improvement in this group.

In this study only just under one-third of the 192 children had systematic speech therapy. This was due

Table V. Clinical features of 31 speech retarded children whose speech was unimproved at follow-up.

I.Q.	Emotionally disturbed	Psychotic	ESN	SSN	Other conditions		No apparent cause	No. of cases
101–138	6	1	—	—	motor defect immature personality	1 1	—	9
80–100	2	—	3	—	—		2	7
60–79	—	—	1	2	—		—	3
59 and below	—	—	—	12	including encephalitis, ? aphasia,	1 1	—	12
Total	8	1	4	14	2		2	31

Table VI.

No. of cases	Mean age	Mean speech level	Mean I.Q.	Received speech therapy
61	7y 3m	6.5	71.6	39.4%

to a number of factors, the thought that an otherwise normally hearing child would improve without specific help, and the reluctance on some occasions of parents to agree to speech therapy are undoubtedly considerations, but probably a more important factor is the availability of trained personnel to give speech therapy, especially in the local authority areas where there are often unfilled vacancies for speech therapists. It would appear from this study that the majority of speech retarded children should have speech therapy starting at the nursery school stage and continuing as long as seems necessary during the early school years, and that children of low I.Q. should not be omitted from such a regime solely by reason of their lower intellectual ability.

The 31 children who showed no progress in speech development are spread right through the various I.Q. levels, but whereas the bright children showed a predominance of emotional and psychiatric disturbances the very dull apparently showed speech retardation as a function of general mental retardation. Appropriate management for the emotional and psychiatric conditions of the former group would seem to be called for, in addition to speech therapy.

Some results of this study do not seem to have any very ready explanation. It is difficult to see why there should be a predominance of male children, and a predominance of second-born children. Within Morley's group there was no difference in sex distribution but there was a predominance of first-born children. However, Morley's study, based as it was on the speech development of normal children is probably more representative of the general population, whereas the findings in this study refer to a selected group, those who are normally hearing but speech delayed.

This study, being primarily a clinical follow-up, is complicated by the fact that the interval between referral and follow-up is not constant. To eliminate irregularities due to this factor it would be necessary to carry out a prospective study of groups matched for age, degree of speech retardation and such other relevant factors as intellectual status. Such a close control is not feasible in a retrospective survey, but nevertheless some interesting trends are observed.

REFERENCES

McCarthy, D. A. (1954) *Language development in children.* In Carmichael, L. (Ed.) Manual of child psychology. 2nd edition. New York.

Metraux, R. W. (1950) *Journal of Speech and Hearing Disorders,* **15,** 37.

Morley, M. E. (1957) *The development and disorders of speech in childhood.* Edinburgh and London.

Registrar General's *Statistical Review of England and Wales for the year 1966,* part II. London.

Sheridan, M. D. (1960) *Developmental progress of infants and young children.* London.

Whetnall, E., and Fry, D. B. (1964) *The deaf child.* London.

APPENDIX

Name: No.   DoB

Follow up on Late Development of Speech

Any information you can give us from your own experience will enable us to help other parents and children (Strike out yes or no as necessary).

Is your child now speaking normally?   YES/NO
At what age did speech become normal?   years   months
At what age did you think that your child's speech was retarded?   years   months
Has your child attended a nursery school or play group?
Name of school your child attends now
Address of school

If your child's speech is still delayed, what level has it reached now?
(Pick one of the answers below.)
Is your child
- ☐ Speaking in short sentences like a younger child?
- ☐ Putting two or three words together, but not talking in longer sentences, e.g. Daddy car, all gone.
- ☐ Using a lot of single words?
- ☐ Using a few single words?
- ☐ Babbling a great deal with one or two words, e.g. Mummy, Daddy.
- ☐ Making sounds but not babbling?

☐ Not using voice except for shouting or crying?
Is your child's speech:
    1. Clear except for a few sounds that are difficult to understand,
e.g. s, sh, th, v, f, l, r, w.   YES/NO
    2. Understood only by the family?   YES/NO
    3. Understood by strangers?   YES/NO

Has your child had treatment for a speech problem?   YES/NO
    If so, where?   How long?
Do you have any further comments about your child's speech?
    (Continue overleaf if necessary)

A STUDY OF THE EFFECTIVENESS OF THE S-PACK PROGRAM IN THE ELIMINATION OF FRONTAL LISPING BEHAVIOR IN THIRD-GRADE CHILDREN

Bruce P. Ryan

This clinical study evaluated the effectiveness of the S-Pack Program in eliminating frontal lisping behavior. The subjects were 10 male and 8 female third-grade children with frontal lisps. Six clinicians put them through the three-part establishment program. This was followed by a 15-day transfer program carried out by their parents. An articulation screening test (UOST), the Predictive Screening Test of Articulation (PSTA), and the Arizona Articulation Proficiency Scale (AAPS) administered before and after the program indicated significant improvement in /s/ production. An analysis of a sample of conversational speech taken at the end of the program revealed that 50% of the children demonstrated 90% or better /s/ productions. The S-Pack is an effective, efficient procedure for correcting frontal lisps.

A number of authorities (Fairbanks, 1940; Van Riper and Irwin, 1958; Fletcher, Bradley, and Casteel, 1961; Templin, 1957; Mowrer, Baker, and Schutz, 1968; Pendergast et al., 1966; and Snow, 1963) have commented on the frequent occurrence of /s/ problems among school-age children. These studies suggest that 2-24% of all children demonstrate /s/ problems or lisping behavior. Fairbanks (1940) stated that 90% of all speakers with articulation difficulties demonstrate some form of lisping behavior.

Because there is such a high incidence of lisping behavior, especially frontal lisping, it is important to develop effective therapeutic methodology to deal with the problem. In recent years, improvements in teaching strategies, especially programmed learning, have appeared on the educational scene. Programmed learning based on operant conditioning principles apparently has much to offer the teaching-therapeutic fields (Skinner, 1953; Sloane and Mac-Aulay, 1968). Mowrer, Baker, and Schutz (1968) describe a program for the control of articulation behavior which focuses on the frontal lisp. This program is now available through commercial sources under the title of the S-Pack (1968).

The purpose of this clinical study was to evaluate (cross-validate) the efficiency of the S-Pack in eliminating frontal lisp behavior among third-grade children. If the S-Pack could be shown to be a rapid and effective method of eliminating frontal lisp problems, it would be of valuable aid to the speech

Reprinted with permission of the author and publisher from
Journal of Speech and Hearing Disorders, 1971, **36**(3), 390–396.

clinician, especially in the public-school setting where so many children with /s/ problems are found.

THE PROGRAM

Subjects. In a previous study, Ryan (1969) discovered 52 third-grade children in the Eugene Oregon School District #4 who had articulation problems, 30 of whom demonstrated frontal lisping behavior. However, only 18 of these 30 met the following criteria and were, therefore, included in this study: (1) no previous speech therapy for the /s/ sound, (2) normal dentition, defined as possession of two upper and two lower central incisors in a normal overjet-overbite position, and (3) an error score of 15/30 or fewer possible /s/ responses on the preprogram S-Pack test. Of the 18 subjects, there were ten boys and eight girls; the mean age was 105.44 months with a standard deviation of 4.36 months. The subjects were located in ten different elementary schools. Of these 18, ten demonstrated only a frontal lisp problem, while eight demonstrated a frontal lisp plus other sound errors.

Tests and Testers. All the subjects had received the University of Oregon Screening Test or UOST (Ryan 1966), the Arizona Articulation Proficiency Scale or AAPS (Barker, 1960; Barker, 1963), and the Predictive Screening Test of Articulation or PSTA (Van Riper and Erickson, 1968) as part of a previous study by Ryan (1969). An AAPS cut-off score of 96.0 or below had been used to define the original articulation problem population of 52 children. Three testers trained in the administration and scoring of these tests during the Ryan (1969) study were available to retest the children on these three tests within two weeks after the completion of the S-Pack home program.

There are five tests within the S-Pack itself: (1) a pretest of 30 items, (2) a Part I Criterion Test of 10 items, (3) a Part II Criterion Test of 10 items, (4) a Part III Criterion test of 10 items, and (5) a posttest of 30 items, which was administered after the home program. A correct response was defined as a closed teeth /s/—an /s/ sound uttered with the teeth in normal overjet-overbite position, approximating but not necessarily touching each other, with the tongue behind the teeth—regardless of its acoustical quality. After completion of the S-Pack posttest, a final test was administered consisting of a two-minute sample of conversational speech during which the number of correct and incorrect /s/ sounds, scored on the basis of closed teeth /s/ only, was computed.

Clinicians. Six clinicians administered the S-Pack program to the 18 children. The clinicians made no special preparations for administration of the program other than studying a copy of the S-Pack beforehand and discussing basic procedures and modifications. Because the S-Pack only requires the clinician to be able to differentiate between the closed teeth /s/ and the open teeth /s/ and to read and follow directions, an extensive training program was considered unnecessary as these behaviors were already part of the clinician's repertoire from past experience.

The S-Pack Program. The S-Pack program is individually administered in four parts: (1) Part I (64 items), which establishes a closed teeth /s/ in single words and phrases, (2) Part II (84 items), which establishes a closed teeth /s/ in sentences, (3) Part III (51 items), which establishes a closed teeth /s/ in storytelling (there is a criterion test for each part which the child must pass before he moves from one part to another), and (4) a home or transfer program of 15 daily lessons (350 items) which reviews the first three parts. Reinforcement is provided on a continuous schedule throughout the program in the form of tokens which can be exchanged for small trinkets. However, in the home program, parents and children decided on what reinforcers would be used. These varied. Explicit instruction manuals for both clinicians and transfer/home people and special stimulus materials for use in the home/transfer program are all provided in the S-Pack kit.

The first three parts of the program were administered in three consecutive daily sessions. No effort was made to shape the /s/ acoustically; the only explicit objective was the closed teeth /s/. Clinicians were instructed to follow the procedures outlined in the S-Pack program with only the modifications and clarifications discussed below:

1. Instruct and reward for teeth closure in /s/ word only. (Mowrer, Baker, and Schutz, 1968, reported that children sometimes finished the program with "clenched teeth talking.")
2. Reinforce or give a token for each /s/ word in a phrase or sentence. (There was often more than one /s/ word in a program item.)
3. Reinforce any extra /s/ word pronounced correctly by the child.
4. Use only token reinforcement during the first three parts. Social reinforcement may be employed before and after sessions.
5. Use a mirror no smaller than 4 × 6″ held no farther than 18″ from the mouth of the child.
6. Make the following written changes in the program:
   a. Part II, Item #74, p. 58, draw in a picture of a sailboat. Item #89, p. 74, should be corrected to read "The dog is *out of* the water."
   b. Part III, Items #25, 26, p. 20, are missing. Omit. For items #77, 78, 79, p. 49, insert picture of a boy sleeping.
7. The trinkets in the kit and/or additional ones secured by the clinicians may be used as reinforcers.

The home or transfer program procedure was also expanded. It was conducted by one of the following people: parents, teacher-aide, volunteer adult, older child in the school, another child in the classroom, or a sibling. Before the program was started, these people were contacted in the above preferential order to participate. The home or transfer person had to meet the criteria of (1) possession of an adequate /s/ sound, (2) ability to read, and (3) time to work with the child at least 10 minutes a day for a three-week period or 15 sessions.

The transfer person was trained the Monday after the week in which the first three parts were completed. The training session was conducted in the following manner: (1) the clinician administered the Day 1 session of the home program to the child while the transfer person observed, (2) the clinician then took the child's part in the Day 1 session of the home program and made four random errors while the transfer person administered the Day 1 program, and (3) the transfer person administered the Day 1 program to the child while the clinician observed. If the transfer person failed to detect errors or to administer the program properly, he was given a second training session. If he failed again, he was dismissed and another transfer person sought. All of this training took place in one session of less than an hour. In addition, the transfer person was instructed to work only on the /s/ and /z/ sounds. The time, place, and reinforcers (the transfer person selected these) to be used at the transfer site (usually the home) were also decided in this session.

Two rules regarding interruption in the home program were adopted: (1) if the child missed two consecutive days due to illness or extenuating circumstances, the week's program was begun again; (2) if the child missed five consecutive days due to causes other than illness, the transfer person was replaced; and (3) if the child missed more than five consecutive days due to illness, the entire first three parts and home/transfer program were begun again.

RESULTS

The results of the pre- and posttests of the University of Oregon Screening Test (UOST), Arizona Articulation Proficiency Scale (AAPS), Predictive Screening Test of Articulation (PSTA), and S-Pack tests are shown in Table 1.

TABLE 1. The number of children who passed the UOST, means and standard deviations and *t* scores of the AAPS, PSTA, and S-Pack tests before and after administration of the S-Pack program for 18 third-grade children with frontal lisps.

Tests	Pre-M	SD	Post-M	SD	Difference	t
UOST	(1 passed)		(12 passed)		11	
AAPS (100%)	93.30	1.93	98.30	2.05	5.00	7.32*
PSTA (47 items)	30.30	4.63	44.00	3.00	13.70	10.24*
S-Pack Test (30 items)	2.16	3.53	29.16	1.50	27.00	29.02*

*Significant at 0.01 level of confidence

The number of children who improved on the UOST was 11. One reason that more did not pass the post screening test is that they still demonstrated other sound errors. In addition, some of the children overgeneralized their new closed teeth /s/ to /θ/ words, for example, *sumb* for *thumb*. The postscores differ significantly from the prescores in the direction of improvement on both the AAPS and PSTA. An AAPS score of 94.0 commonly reflects the performance of a child who has a lisp. There are 15 /s/ items on the PSTA. Hence, it is not unexpected that both of these scores would improve greatly if the children had been taught an appropriate /s/ sound. The testers scored the /s/ sound as correct only if it was both acoustically accurate and with closed teeth.

Although it was not instructed for and reinforced, 17 out of 18 children demonstrated acoustically accurate closed teeth /s/s. This same phenomenon is reported by Mowrer, Baker, and Schutz (1968). Only one child demonstrated the clenched teeth behavior described by them. Other factors which may have influenced the scores somewhat were: maturation, over generalization of /s/ to /θ/ words, and intertest fluctuation. Examination of raw scores revealed that a number of children made posttest errors on the /θ/ sound, a behavior which they had not demonstrated during the pretests.

There was a total of 30 points on the S-Pack pre- and posttests. A mean change of 27.0 points occurred between the pre- and posttests. Individual criterion test mean scores ranged from 9.67 to 9.77, indicating that the children improved as the program progressed, even though the items became increasingly difficult. A child was required to score 8/10 for each criterion test before he could proceed to the next. Only one child had to repeat Part II. The remainder of the children passed all the criterion tests on the first trial.

Conversational Speech Sample. The two-minute conversational sample was scored as the number of closed teeth /s/s of the total /s/ sounds produced to yield the percentage of accurate /s/ sounds. The mean percentage of correct /s/ sounds in conversation was 77.11, with a standard deviation of 30.3. The range was 17 to 100 with a median score of 92. Assuming that their /s/ sounds were acoustically accurate, this means that 50% of the children scored 92% and above correct /s/ sounds in conversational speech. Eight children scored 100%. This carry-over information is important because the true test of the efficiency of any speech-sound production program is conversational usage, and because there is no special provision for /s/-sound production in normal conversation in the S-Pack program. The other 50% of the children scored 89% and below, suggesting that the S-Pack program may not be enough to aid these children in correct use of the /s/ sound in conversational speech. It is possible that some parents reinforced correct /s/ sounds in conversation during the home program while others did not. There were no apparent differences between males and females or between those children with only /s/ errors and those with multiple errors.

Error Scores. Another measure of the efficiency of any program is the error score generated throughout the program. Ideally, the error rate should be small, indicating that the steps in the program are not too difficult. There was a mean of 29.14 errors, with a standard deviation of 23.83 per child during the first three parts of the program, or a mean of 9.71 per part. This represents 10% error (there are approximately 300 /s/ responses in the program). The error rate reported for the 15-lesson home program was a mean of 8.86, with an *SD* of 9.18, or 3%. There are approximately 350 /s/ responses in the home program. Both error percentages are relatively low, indicating that the children went through the program with 90% accuracy or better.

Time of the Program. Still another measure of the efficiency of a program is the time required to complete it. The first three parts of the program, exclusive of the five tests, required a mean of 41.61 minutes, with an *SD* of 8.48 or a mean of 13.87 minutes per part. This is less than the 20 minutes per part suggested by Mowrer, Baker, and Schutz (1968). The home program required a mean of 159.54 minutes, with an *SD* of 50.41 for 15 lessons, or a mean of 10.62 minutes per home lesson. When 10 minutes for test administration and 30 minutes for parent training are added, the total time commitment of the clinician is approximately only 80 minutes per child. Based on a five-hour working day broken into 20-minute units, it is conceivable that the clinician could complete /s/ therapy with 15 children a week. At this rate it should not take long to clear up at least 50% of all frontal lisp problems in a clinician's case load. The other 50% would probably require further training time to achieve a conversational level of /s/ proficiency.

The Transfer Program. The transfer program was carried out by 14 mothers, one father, one grandmother, one sister, and one teacher-aide, commonly in the home. Only three of the mothers failed to report home data when phoned. Only one child had to be recycled by the parent for additional home lessons. No transfer person failed the training program. The most common reinforcer used in the home setting was money (used by eight). The next most common was candy (used by three). Three transfer people chose to use roller skating, staying up late, doll clothes, and a grab bag of toys. Three mothers used multiple reinforcers, commonly candy and money. The procedure of allowing parents and children to decide on reinforcers apparently was satisfactory. All of the transfer people reported completion of the home program, although three mothers did not turn in complete data to substantiate this. Their three children scored only 55, 24, and 17%, respectively, on the conversational sample. The transfer/home program was successful as measured by the S-Pack test. The transfer person training program and continuous contact with the transfer people during the transfer program undoubtedly played an important role. The question of how vital this extensive transfer procedure is will be answered only by future study.

Clinicians' Reactions. The clinicians' personal reaction to the S-Pack program was generally favorable; they found the program to be efficient and effective. Some suggested that subprofessionals could be trained to administer the first three parts. Mowrer, Baker, and Schutz (1968) offer data to support the efficacy of that procedure. All of the clinicians were concerned about the lack of a high level of carry-over into conversational speech by 50% of the children, and suggested that group therapy, role playing, and creative drama might aid in this respect. They also recommended that a Part IV be added to the first three, preceding the home training program and incorporated into it, to reinforce correct /s/ sounds in conversational speech. They also pointed out that there was no provision in the program for reading and recommended that a Part V on reading be added.

The results of this study suggest that the S-Pack or programmed articulation therapy for the common frontal lisp sound error is extremely effective.

REFERENCES

Barker, J., A numerical measure of articulation. *J. Speech Hearing Dis.*, **25,** 79-88 (1960)

Barker, J., *The Arizona Articulation Proficiency Scale.* Beverly Hills, Calif.: Western Psychological Services (1963).

Fairbanks, G., *Voice and Articulation Drillbook.* New York: Harper and Row (1940).

Fletcher, S., Bradley, D., and Casteel, R., Tongue-thrust swallow, speech articulation, and age. *J. Speech Hearing Dis.*, **26,** 201-208 (1961).

Mowrer, D., Baker, R., and Schutz, R., Operant procedures in the control of speech articulation. In H. Sloane and B. MacAulay (Eds.), *Operant Procedure in Remedial Speech and Language Training.* Boston: Houghton Mifflin (1968).

Pendergast, K., Soder, A., Barker, J., Dickey, S., Gow, J., and Selman, J., An articulation study of 15,255 Seattle first grade children with and without kindergarten. *Except. Child.*, **32,** 541-547 (1966).

Ryan, B., The prediction of articulation proficiency of first grade children. Final Report. Eugene, Ore.: Univ. Ore. Off. Scientific Scholarly Res. (1969) .

Ryan, B., The University of Oregon Screening Test—UOST. Eugene, Oregon: Univ. of Oregon Speech and Hearing Center (1966).

S-Pack. Palos Verdes Estates, Calif.: Educ. Psychol. Res. Assoc. (1968).

Skinner, B. F., *The Science of Human Behavior.* New York: Macmillan (1953).

Sloane, H., and MacAulay, B. (Eds.), *Operant Procedures in Remedial Speech and Language Training.* Boston: Houghton Mifflin (1968).

Snow, K., A detailed analysis of articulation responses of "normal" first grade children. *J. Speech Hearing Res.*, **6,** 277-290 (1963).

Templin, M., Certain language skills in children: Their development and interrelationships. *Child Welf. Monogr.*, No. 26, Minneapolis: Univ. Minnesota (1957).

Van Riper, C., and Erickson, R., *Predictive Screening Test of Articulation.* Kalamazoo, Michigan: Western Michigan Univ. Continuing Educ. Off. (1968).

Van Riper, C., and Irwin, J., *Voice and Articulation.* Englewood Cliffs, New York: Prentice-Hall (1958).

PERCEIVED PARENTAL BEHAVIOR AMONG STUTTERERS AND NONSTUTTERERS

Karen H. Bourdon
David E. Silber

In this study, the perceptions of parental behavior of 24 stuttering children in public school settings were compared to those of 24 of their classmates. It was hypothesized that the stutterers would perceive their mothers as more dominating, controlling, and overprotective than the nonstutterers, and would describe their fathers as more lax and retiring. Contrary to expectations, there were no discernible differences between the two groups, nor were there differences in perceptions between the 10 mildest and 10 most severe stutterers. The results were discussed in terms of the light they throw on previous descriptions of stutterers' parents; it was hypothesized that general personality functioning of the parents was probably of lesser importance than specific, albeit unwitting, reinforcing behaviors.

The disorder of stuttering has been described as perhaps the "most complex disorganization of function in the field of medicine and psychiatry [Bluemel, 1960, p. 30]." Numerous theories of stuttering have been advanced; psychologically oriented theories of etiology fall into two clusters: those positing that stuttering is the neurotic symptom of an unconscious conflict and those suggesting that stuttering is due to anticipatory tension (surrounding speaking) on the part of the stutterer (Bloodstein, 1959). All theories agree in viewing parental behavior and attitudes as the precipitating factor in this disorder, either by the parents teaching an avoidance-struggle type of speaking behavior or bringing about psychosexual fixations through their child-rearing practices (e.g., Murphy, 1960).

There have been some data corroborating the assumption that parents of stutterers are more critical, demanding, and perfectionistic than parents of nonstutterers. Using interview and observation techniques, Glauber (1958) reported that mothers of stutterers are narcissistic, possessive, and perfectionistic, while at the same time encouraging of overdependence. Despert (1943, 1946) described the mother of the stuttering child as overanxious, oversolicitous, overprotective, and overperfectionistic, and, again, as behaving in a way that fosters prolonged overdependence. Moncour (1952) reported that parents of stutterers are more dominating than parents of nonstutterers and have excessively high standards for their children. Thus, the parents of stutterers appear to be more critical and restrictive in their attitudes toward their children than parents of nonstutterers.

It is assumed that these parental behaviors render the stutterer more susceptible to habitual stuttering, and that such parental characterics are more or less intimately connected with the unique difficulty of the stutterer. Such connections between deviant parental behavior and the perception of such behavior by their offspring have been shown among other psychopathological populations, for example, schizophrenic *S*s (e.g., Kohn & Clausen, 1956; Reichard & Tillman, 1950). However, it has never been shown that the stutterer perceives those characteristics in his parents that psychological investigation suggests are present. The purpose of this study was to determine whether such perceptions are reported by a stuttering child, and whether these perceptions are quantitatively different from those of a nonstuttering child of similar background.

It was predicted that stuttering children would report different patterns of parent behavior from nonstuttering children, and that these differences would mirror the personality portraits drawn by earlier investigators of sutterers' parents.

METHOD

Subjects. There were 24 experimental and 24 control *S*s for this experiment. All experimental *S*s were recruited from public schools in the Washington, D. C. area and were described by school personnel (teachers, speech therapists) as stuttering discernibly when speaking. None of the stutterers, however, had any neurological deficiency or involvement reported

From *Journal of Abnormal Psychology*, 1970, **75**, 93-97. Copyright 1970 by the American Psychological Association. Reprinted by permission.

in their records. Although it was hoped that all *S*s would be living with their biological parents, it was found that 3 experimental *S*s were not: 1 had been adopted, and 2 had had one parent remarry. Accordingly, 3 of the control *S*s were selected to mirror this family pattern. Characteristics for the two groups of experimentally naïve adolescents are summarized in Table 1.

Material and procedure. The Children's Report of Parent Behavior Inventory (CRPBI) was used to obtain ratings of parental behavior. This instrument, developed by Schaefer (1965), contains items that yield scale scores for 18 behavioral patterns: Acceptance, Acceptance of individuation, Child-centeredness, Control, Control through guilt, Extreme autonomy, Hostile control, Hostile detachment, Enforcement, Inconsistent discipline, Instilling persistent anxiety, Lax discipline, Non-enforcement (lack of knowledge of child's activities), Possessiveness, Positive involvement, Rejection, Withdrawal of relations, and Intrusiveness. These scales are made up of 8–16 individual questions which can be answered as "like" (my parent), "somewhat like," and "not like." The reliabilities range .38–.93 per scale, with an average reliability of .76. Schaefer (1965) reported that the scale elicits different perceptions of parents from groups of delinquents and nondelinquents, and from underachieving and overachieving children. There are separate forms for rating paternal and maternal behavior.

The CRPBI was administered to *S*s while they were in school, with no other explanation than that an experiment of some importance was being performed, and they were to answer the questions as honestly as possible. They were told that their names would not be placed on any question or answer sheets, and that strict confidentiality would be maintained. An explanatory letter was sent to all parents to obtain permission to test their children. Thus, some of the stutterers knew that speech problems were being investigated, although this was minimized in the actual testing period as much as possible.

RESULTS

The answers were converted to a 3-point scale, so that the lowest possible score ("not like" my parents) was 1, and the highest score ("like") was 3. These scores were then averaged across scale items and *S*s and plotted for experimental and control groups; the re-

sults for both the maternal and paternal ratings are plotted in Figures 1 and 2. It is apparent from Figures 1 and 2 that the patterns for stutterers and nonstutterers were remarkably similar. This was statistically confirmed by analyses of variance, using groups as one dimension and the 18 scales as the within-groups second dimension (Lindquist, 1953). Table 2 summarizes the results of

TABLE 2

ANALYSIS OF VARIANCE OF PERCEIVED MATERNAL TRAITS AND PATERNAL TRAITS AS REPORTED BY STUTTERERS AND NONSTUTTERERS

Source of variation	Sum of squares	df	Mean square	F
Between *S*s	1,563.8	47		
Groups (A)	5.4	1	5.4	0.15
Error	1,558.4	46	33.9	
Within *S*s	83,773.6	385		
Perceived maternal traits (B)	64,547.4	17	3,796.9	71.0*
A × B	450.2	17	26.5	
Error	18,775.9	351	53.5	
Between *S*s	2,873.4	47		
Groups (A)	0.8	1	0.8	—
Error	2,872.6	46	62.5	
Within *S*s	83,755.2	385		
Perceived paternal traits (B)	62,589.4	17	3,681.7	61.2*
A × B	47.7	17	2.8	—
Error	21,118.1	351	60.2	

* *p* < .01.

these analyses, showing there were no differences in results attributable to between-group variation. When *t* tests were performed on the groups' scores for each scale—recognizing that the possibility of a significant re-

TABLE 1

CHARACTERISTICS OF THE EXPERIMENTAL AND CONTROL GROUPS

Variable	Experimental group (stutterers)	Control group (nonstutterers)
Number	24	24
Sex		
males	17	17
females	7	7
Racial grouping Caucasian	20	20
Negro	4	4
Age (mean yr.)	15.83	15.67
Grade (mean yr.)	10.20	10.04
IQ score (mean)	111.8	114.2
IQ score (median)	115	116.5

TABLE 3

MEAN SCALE SCORES, MATERNAL AND PATERNAL PERCEPTIONS FOR THE MILD AND SEVERE STUTTERERS

Scale	Mean maternal score		Mean paternal score	
	Mild	Severe	Mild	Severe
Acceptance	2.11	2.30	2.24	2.19
Child-centeredness	1.83	1.98	1.79	1.80
Possessiveness	1.60	1.78	1.50	1.68
Rejection	1.65	1.51	1.56	1.60
Control	1.96	2.01	1.85	2.07
Enforcement	1.79	1.75	1.71	1.95
Positive involvement	2.03	2.18	1.98	2.05
Intrusiveness	1.61	1.78	1.36	1.65
Control through guilt	1.63	1.65	1.39	1.46
Hostile control	1.66	1.59	1.53	1.73
Inconsistent discipline	1.56	1.63	1.41	1.56
Nonenforcement	1.69	1.46	1.68	1.50
Acceptance of individuation	2.24	2.50	2.20	2.25
Lax discipline	1.65	1.68	1.50	1.46
Instilling persistent anxiety	1.59	1.46	1.41	1.49
Hostile detachment	1.63	1.38	1.63	1.59
Withdrawal of relations	1.49	1.69	1.46	1.74
Extreme autonomy	1.86	1.63	2.01	1.63

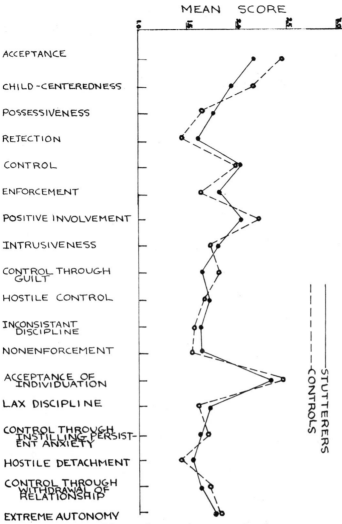

FIG. 1. Mean scale score for maternal ratings.

sult due to chance was thus heightened—no statistically significant results occurred.

It was suggested a posteriori that mild stutterers might perceive their parents differently than severely incapacitated stutterers; to assess this possibility, the 10 mildest and most severe stutterers were compared with each other in terms of their performance. Again, the average scale scores were quite similar, as shown in Table 3, and the differences, when analyzed using an analysis of variance, were attributable to chance factors.

DISCUSSION

Contrary to expectations, the stuttering children did not perceive their parents to be excessively controlling, possessive, or intrusive. They did not indicate that their parents resorted to the inculcation of guilt or anxiety as control devices, nor did they perceive their mothers as dominating or their fathers as lax and nonenforcing. Further, they ascribed to their parents almost identical patterns of behavior as the nonstutterers did: understanding, unresponsiveness, and adequate control methods.

Though contrary to the expected results, the findings of this study are provocative and suggest that excessive theoretical emphasis has been given to the role of parents in the stuttering problems of their children. Stutterers' parents may in fact be describable as dominating, posesssive, critical, etc., but this may reflect more the parental norm than the uniqueness of such parents among all parents. Further, such descriptions of adults by other adults may be inappropriate for characterizing the behavior of parents in interactions with their children.

Of course, an alternative possibility is that the experimental Ss were more defensive and may have felt the need to protect their parents by dissimulation in their answers. However,

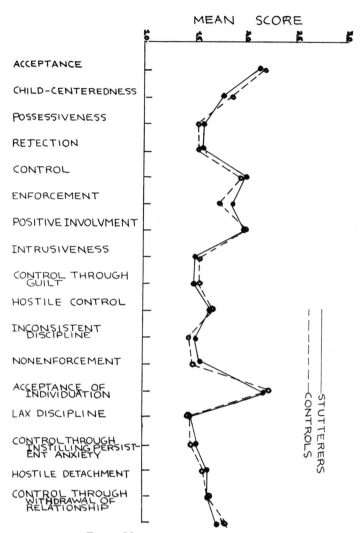

Fɪɢ. 2. Mean scale score for paternal ratings.

Sheehan (1958) reviewed the literature concerning the personality of stutterers and has concluded that they are no more problem ridden than children who do not stutter. Further, if stutterers were consciously or unconsciously motivated to paint an idealized home situation, this would have shown up in a composite profile different from that of the control Ss.

Parents may unwittingly contribute and support the stuttering behavior of their children even though they are not perceived as markedly dominating, controlling, or rejecting. They may, for example, reinforce such behavior by calling attention to it, by attempting to aid the stuttering child overcome his difficulty, by making him embarrassed and hence overconscious of it, etc. Thus, it might be profitable now to direct research attention to specific interactions between parents and their stuttering children which might have

a supporting or facilitating effect on the stuttering.

REFERENCES

Bʟᴏᴏᴅsᴛᴇɪɴ, O. *A handbook on stuttering for professional workers.* Chicago, Ill.: National Society for Crippled Children and Adults, 1959.

Bʟᴜᴇᴍᴇʟ, C. C. Concepts of stammering: A century in review. *Journal of Speech and Hearing Disorders,* 1960, **25,** 24–32.

Dᴇsᴘᴇʀᴛ, L. D. Psychopathology of stuttering. *American Journal of Psychiatry,* 1943, **99,** 881–885.

Dᴇsᴘᴇʀᴛ, L. D. Psychosomatic study of 50 stuttering children. *American Journal of Orthopsychiatry,* 1946, **16,** 100–113.

Gʟᴀᴜʙᴇʀ, I. P. The psychoanalysis of stuttering. In J. Eisenson (Ed.), *Stuttering—a symposium.* New York: Harper, 1958.

Kᴏʜɴ, M. L., & Cʟᴀᴜsᴇɴ, J. A. Parental authority behavior and schizophrenia. *American Journal of Psychiatry,* 1956, **26,** 297–313.

LINDQUIST, E. F. *Design and analysis of experiments in psychology and education.* Boston: Houghton Mifflin, 1953.

MONCOUR, J. P. Parental domination in stuttering. *Journal of Speech and Hearing Disorders,* 1952, **17,** 155–165.

MURPHY, A. T., & FITZSIMONS, R. *Stuttering and personality dynamics.* New York: Ronald Press, 1960.

REICHARD, S., & TILLMAN, C. Patterns of parent-child relationships in schizophrenia. *Psychiatry,* 1950, **13,** 247–257.

SCHAEFER, E. S. Children's reports of parental behavior: An inventory. *Child Development,* 1965, **6,** 413–424.

SHEEHAN, J. G. Projection studies of stuttering. *Journal of Speech and Hearing Disorders,* 1958, **23,** 18–25.

REFERENCES

Arasteh, J. D. Creativity and related processes in the young child: A review of the literature. *Journal of Genetic Psychology,* 1968, **112,** 77–118.

Barnes, F. P. *Research for the practitioner in education.* Arlington, Va.: National Association of Elementary School Principals, 1964.

Borg, W. R., & Gall, M. D. *Educational research: An introduction.* New York: David McKay, 1971.

Campbell, D. T., & Stanley, J. C. *Experimental and quasi-experimental designs for research.* Chicago: Rand McNally, 1963.

Circirelli, B. G. Educational models for the disadvantaged. In H. J. Walberg & A. T. Kopan (Eds.), *Rethinking urban education.* San Francisco: Jossey-Bass, 1972.

Cronbach, L. J. *Essentials of psychological testing.* (3rd ed.) New York: Harper & Row, 1970.

Cronbach, L. J., & Suppes, P. J. *Research for tomorrow's schools.* National Academy of Education, 1969.

Deutsch, M., & Whiteman, M. Social disadvantage as related to intellective and language development. In M. Deutsch, I. Katz, & A. R. Jensen (Eds.), *Social class, race and psychological development.* New York: Holt, Rinehart and Winston, 1968.

Downie, N. M., & Heath, R. W. *Basic statistical methods.* (3rd ed.) New York: Harper & Row, 1965.

Freeman, F. N. Controlling concepts in educational research. *Supplementary Educational Monographs,* 1942, **55,** 38–47.

Frierson, E. C. The gifted. *Review of Educational Research,* 1969, **39,** 25–37.

Guilford, J. P. *Fundamental statistics in psychology and education.* (4th ed.) New York: McGraw-Hill, 1965.

Haskett, G. J. Research and early education: Relations among classroom, laboratory, and society. *American Psychologist,* 1973, **28,** 248–256.

Haywood, H. C. Mental retardation as an extension of the developmental laboratory. *American Journal of Mental Deficiency,* 1970, **75,** 5–9.

Heal, L. W. Research strategies and research goals in the scientific study of the mentally subnormal. *American Journal of Mental Deficiency,* 1970, **75,** 10–15.

Hempel, C. G. *Philosophy of natural science.* Englewood Cliffs, N. J.: Prentice-Hall, 1966.

Karmel, L. J. *Measurement and evaluation in the schools.* New York: Macmillan, 1970.

Kerlinger, F. N. *Foundations of behavioral research: Educational and psychological inquiry.* New York: Holt, Rinehart and Winston, 1966.

McClelland, D. C. Testing for competence rather than for "intelligence." *American Psychologist,* 1973, **28,** 1–14.

McNemar, Q. *Psychological statistics.* (3rd ed.) New York: Wiley, 1962.

Mouly, G. J. *The science of educational research.* (2nd ed.) New York: Van Nostrand Reinhold, 1970.

Neale, J. M., & Liebert, R. M. *Science and behavior: An introduction to methods of research.* Englewood Cliffs, N.J.: Prentice-Hall, 1973.

Newland, T. E. Psychological assessment of exceptional children and youth. In W. M. Cruickshank (Ed.), *Psychology of exceptional children and youth.* (3rd ed.) Englewood Cliffs, N.J.: Prentice-Hall, 1971.

Newman, J. Psychological problems of children and youth with chronic medical problems. In W. M. Cruickshank (Ed.), *Psychology of exceptional children and youth.* (3rd ed.) Englewood Cliffs, N.J.: Prentice-Hall, 1971.

Nolan C. Y. A 1966 reappraisal of the relationship between visual acuity and mode of reading for blind children. *New Outlook for the Blind,* 1967, **61,** 255–261.

Nunnally, J. C. *Psychometric theory.* New York: McGraw-Hill, 1967.

Scott, W. A., & Wertheimer, M. *Introduction to psychological research.* New York: Wiley, 1962.

Telford, C. W., & Sawrey, J. M. *The exceptional individual.* (2nd ed.) Englewood Cliffs, N.J.: Prentice-Hall, 1972.

Travers, R. M. W. *An introduction to educational research.* (2nd ed.) New York: Macmillan, 1965.

Tuckman, B. W. *Conducting educational research.* New York: Harcourt Brace Jovanovich, 1972.

Turney, B. L., & Robb, G. P. *Research in education: An introduction.* Hinsdale, Ill.: Dryden Press, 1971.

Underwood, B. J. *Psychological research.* New York: Appleton-Century-Crofts, 1957.

Van Dalen, D. B., & Meyer, W. J. *Understanding educational research: An introduction.* New York: McGraw-Hill, 1966.

Warren, S. A. Editorial: Classification systems and AAMD. *Mental Retardation,* 1973, **11,** 2.

Woody, R. H. *Behavioral problem children in the schools.* New York: Appleton-Century-Crofts, 1969.

INDEX